Prentice-Hall's Explanation of the Tax Reform Act of 1986

Prepared by Prentice-Hall Information Services

Harold A. Grossman, J.D., Editor-in-Chief
Donald E. Mindrebo, J.D., Managing Editor

Coordinating Editor

Alan S. Robinson, J.D.

Contributing Editors

Norman Arkawy, J.D.
Julian Block, J.D., LL.M. (Taxation)
James Boylan, J.D.
Caroline C. Bristol, J.D.
Peter F. Daly, B.A.
Alan G. DeNee, J.D.
Stephen A. Friedman, J.D.,
  LL.M. (Taxation)
John Kent Graham, J.D.
Richard D. Grant, J.D.
Craig M. Heller, J.D.
Marvin Hillman, J.D.
Kurt D. Horning, J.D.
Susan C. Hughes, J.D.
Jessica Indig-Brown, J.D.
Gerald M. Levinson, J.D.
Lawrence H. MacKirdy, J.D.
Robert W. McGee, J.D., Ph.D., C.P.A.

Robert J. Murdich, J.D.
Richard Niles, J.D.
Lillian V. O'Brien, B.S.
Melvin Orenstein, J.D., LL.M. (Taxation)
Aaron I. Reichel, J.D.
Alan Rubin, J.D.
Emma H. Rubinsky, J.D.
Rosemary Saldan, J.D.
Gustav J. Schlaier, J.D.
Alfred Tamburro, J.D.
Robert Trinz, M.S. (Taxation)
Mary Jeanne Vellardito, J.D.
Anne Waldron, J.D.
Peter Wang, J.D.
Robert C. Wilkie, J.D.
Sylvia Woods, J.D.
Denis L. Yurkovic, J.D.

Editorial Assistants

Sherri L. Nickles   Angela Sweikart
Barbara A. Vetrano

Production Staff

Peter Benedict   Gregory B. Miller
Carl Giaimo   Ken Pawson
Gail Gneiding   Kerry Reardon
Arthur Sabatini

As passed by the House of Representatives (September 25, 1986)
and sent to the Senate.

This publication is designed to provide accurate and authoritative information in regard to the subject matter covered. It is sold with the understanding that the publisher is not engaged in rendering legal, accounting,
or other professional service. If legal advice or other expert assistance is
required, the services of a competent professional person should be sought.

—*From a Declaration of Principles jointly adopted by a Committee of the
American Bar Association and a Committee of Publishers and Associations.*

TABLE OF CONTENTS

2   **Table of Contents**

Table of Contents

3

Table of Contents

Paragraph [¶]

6   Table of Contents

[The page following this is 11.]

THE TAX REFORM ACT OF 1986

A Brief Overview

It's the most drastic overhaul of taxes in the last 40 years. The new law has something for every taxpayer. It's so all-encompassing, that from now on the tax law will be called, The Internal Revenue Code of 1986. This book will take you through and explain each provision of the new law—in detail. But first, here's a rundown of the key provisions of the new law to set the scene.

Individual Tax Rate Reductions. The centerpiece of the TRA is a cut in individual tax rates. The top tax bracket will be reduced from 50% to 28% over two years.

The TRA scraps the current fifteen brackets with a top rate of 50% and substitutes two brackets: 15% and 28%. There is a blended rate for 1987—a mix of the old and new rates with a five-bracket rate schedule featuring a 38.5% top rate. Beginning in 1988, the new rate system is fully in place (with annual adjustments to offset inflation). Starting 1-1-88, the first $29,750 of taxable income is subject to the 15% rate (first $17,850 for singles). Income in excess of $29,750 ($17,850 for singles) is taxed at the 28% rate. But there is a catch.

> **5% SURTAX:** Starting in 1988, the TRA imposes a 5% surtax on income between $71,900 and $149,250 ($43,150 and $89,560 for singles). This is designed to phase out the benefit high-income taxpayers get from the 15% bracket.

Net result: Each additional dollar you earn between the two income levels is taxed at an effective rate of 33%. If your taxable income exceeds the higher level, there is an additional phaseout for the personal exemption. [See ¶101.]

Personal Exemptions. The TRA increases the personal exemptions you claim for yourself, your spouse and your dependents. The current exemption figure of $1,080 goes to $1,900 in 1987, $1,950 in 1988 and $2,000 in 1989. The personal exemption amount will be adjusted for inflation starting in 1990. However, older taxpayers can no longer claim extra exemptions for being age 65 or over. Nor can blind taxpayers (but see below).

Another crackdown. Under the TRA, starting in 1987, a dependent who can be claimed on someone else's return can no longer take a personal exemption on his own return.

New requirement. You may have to get a Social Security number for your child next year. Starting with returns filed after 1987, a taxpayer claiming a dependent who is over four years old, must include the dependent's Social Security number on his return.

Standard Deduction. The TRA gives a big boost to the flat standard deduction for nonitemizers. The deduction is increased to $5,000 for joint filers and surviving spouses. ($3,000 for singles, $4,400 for heads of households, and $2,500 for marrieds filing separately). This takes effect in 1988 (for 1987, the amounts are $3,760 for joint filers and $2,540 for singles and heads of households, and $1,880 for marrieds filing separately). There is an extra standard deduction of $600 for each married person age 65 and over and each blind taxpayer, starting in 1987. The extra deduction is $750 if the blind or elderly person is single and not a surviving spouse. This is in addition to the full standard deduction. Another break: Taxpayers age 65 or over or blind may claim the higher 1988 standard deductions for 1987. The standard deductions are adjusted for inflation starting in 1989.

Children. In 1986, your child can use his $1,080 personal exemption to shelter his unearned income from tax. In 1987, if he can be claimed as a dependent on your return, your child has no personal exemption. The TRA, however, does provide some relief. Starting in 1987, unlike earlier years, your child can use $500 of his standard deduction to offset unearned income. That, of course, leaves only $2,070 to shelter his earned income ($2,570 full standard deduction less $500). [See ¶102.]

Itemized Deductions. You can still get deductions for charitable contributions, real estate taxes, and state and local income and property taxes.

The rules for deducting charitable contributions are relatively unchanged. For example, the charitable deduction for nonitemizers goes off the books at the end of 1986, as scheduled.

If you donate appreciated property (e.g., stock) in 1986 that would have produced long-term capital gain if sold, you will not only get a deduction for the property's full fair market value in 1986, you also pay no tax on the paper gain. Under the TRA, after 1986, the untaxed portion of a donation of appreciated property is considered a tax preference item for purposes of the alternative minimum tax. [See ¶712].

Moving expenses. Before 1987, the deduction for job-related moving expenses can be claimed by taxpayers whether or not they itemize. Starting in 1987, it can be taken only by employees and self-employed persons who itemize their deductions. [See ¶116.]

Sales tax. State and local sales taxes are no longer deductible, starting in 1987. So if you're buying a big ticket item (e.g., a car) in the near future, do it before the end of 1986.

Interest. Starting in 1987, interest paid on consumer debt (for instance, car loans and credit card charges) is not deductible regardless of when the debt is incurred. That includes interest on tax underpayments (except deferred estate taxes). Interest on debt incurred for investment reasons can be written off only up to the amount of your investment income. The cutback for both kinds of interest is phased in over five years.

> **KEY EXCEPTION:** You can continue to deduct mortgage interest on your principal residence and a second home. However, mortgage interest on the part of a loan that exceeds the cost of a home (plus any improvements) is subject to the interest deduction crackdown, unless the loan proceeds are used for medical or educational purposes. But even if the proceeds are used for medical or educational purposes, the loan can't exceed the fair market value of the home—less any other outstanding mortgage. *Special grandfather rule:* Interest on debt incurred before 8-16-86 will be deductible even though it exceeds the cost basis of the residence.

Medical expenses. Starting in 1987, the TRA increases the deduction floor for unreimbursed medical costs from 5% to 7½% of adjusted gross income.

Miscellaneous deductions. The TRA changes the rules for deducting miscellaneous expenses. This category includes investment-connected expenses (e.g., stock market publications), fees paid to tax return preparers and all business expenses (including business travel and entertainment) incurred by an employee and not reimbursed by an employer.

Starting in 1987, a taxpayer's total miscellaneous expenses, with a few minor exceptions (e.g., gambling losses to the extent of gambling winnings), are deductible only to the extent the total exceeds 2% of the taxpayer's adjusted gross income. [See ¶126.]

Withholding and Estimated Taxes. The TRA requires changes in the income tax withholding tables in 1987 and 1988. It also affects the estimated taxes of many individual taxpayers.

Key change. Before 1987, individuals could avoid underpayment penalties if their quarterly estimated tax payments equaled the lesser of 80% of their current year's tax bill or 100% of their prior year's liability. Amounts withheld from wages are considered estimated tax payments. The TRA lifts the 80% figure to 90%, starting in 1987. It leaves the 100% figure unchanged.

Capital Gains. One of the biggest changes introduced by the TRA is the elimination of the tax-favored treatment of net long-term capital gains. The TRA does away with the 60% net long-term capital gain exclusion. Individual taxpayers must treat net long-term gain (profit on property held more than six months) like ordinary income. Effective date: Tax years beginning after 12-31-86.

NOTE: Even though ordinary income is taxed in 1987 at blended rates higher than 15% and 28%, the top tax rate is 28% on net long-term capital gains in 1987. [See ¶302]

Short-term gains. In 1987, the top tax on net short-term capital gains is taxed at the blended rate applicable to ordinary income. Top rate: 38.5%. The maximum is 50% before 1987. The 15% and 28% brackets will take full effect starting in 1988.

The TRA does not do away with the distinction between capital gains and losses and ordinary income and deductions. For example, as under current law, you still net your capital gains and losses. Capital losses fully offset capital gains. However, to the extent your capital losses exceed your capital gains, the net loss can only be deducted against $3,000 of ordinary income in any one year. One difference from prior law: Starting in 1987, both long- and short-term capital losses offset ordinary income, dollar-for-dollar. Capital losses that cannot be deducted against the current year's ordinary income can still be carried forward to later years.

Selling publicly-traded securities. This is the last year you get a tax choice when you sell publicly-traded securities during the last five trading days of the year. Starting in 1987, you pay tax the year you make the sale. In 1986, however, you can treat the transaction as an installment sale and pay tax in 1987 (i.e., when the cash settlement is made). Or you can elect out of installment tax treatment and pay tax in 1986, the year you make the sale).

Capital Gain for Corporations. The TRA eliminates the preferential capital gains treatment for corporations. Corporate net long-term gain is taxed at the same rates as corporate ordinary income. Effective 1-1-87, despite a higher tax rate on ordinary income, the top rate on corporate capital gain is 34%.

IRA Contributions. The TRA makes major changes in the tax rules for Individual Retirement Accounts. Many taxpayers who belong to a company-funded retirement plan can no longer deduct their IRA contributions. That includes members of corporate pension and profit-sharing plans, Keogh plans, and those with 403(b) annuities. Effective date: Tax years starting after 1986.

• *Full deduction:* You can continue to make deductible IRA contributions of up to $2,000 annually ($2,250 for a spousal IRA) if (1) neither you nor your spouse belong to a company-funded retirement plan or (2) either you or your spouse do belong and your adjusted gross income is less than $40,000 ($25,000 if single). For this purpose, adjusted gross income does not take into account the IRA contribution.

• *Partial deduction:* Your deductible IRA contribution is reduced proportionately if you or your spouse belong to a company retirement plan and your adjusted gross income is between

$40,000 and $50,000 ($25,000 and $35,000 for single taxpayers). For example, a married plan member with an adjusted gross income of $45,000 can make a $1,000 deductible IRA contribution ($1,125 to a spousal IRA). *Reason:* His adjusted gross income is half-way between the $40,000 and $50,000 phaseout levels.

• *No deduction:* Plan members with adjusted gross incomes in excess of $50,000 ($35,000 for singles) cannot claim a deduction for an IRA contribution. [See ¶1101]

Cash or Deferred SEP. In tax years starting after 1986, employers can give employees a choice: continue to take all your compensation in cash or have up to $7,000 of it contributed to a simplified employee pension. To the extent the employee goes the SEP route, he owes no tax on the amount contributed.

Retirement Plan Rules. The changes in the retirement plan rules may be the most sweeping in the entire TRA. In general, they take effect in plan years starting after 1988.

More plan coverage. A qualified retirement plan cannot discriminate in favor of employees who are officers, shareholders or highly paid. Under prior law, a plan did not discriminate against the rank and file if it covered as few as 56% of all employees. The new TRA minimum percentage test is 80%.

Quicker vesting of benefits. A qualified retirement plan must provide for accrued benefits to vest within a certain period of time. The TRA shortens the vesting period, so employees are entitled to benefits sooner.

Minimum benefits for integrated plan members. Under prior law, it was possible for an employer to avoid making any retirement plan contributions for lower-paid employees, if the plan was integrated with Social Security. The TRA, however, ensures that all employees will receive at least some employer-provided retirement plan benefits in addition to Social Security benefits. [See ¶1110.]

Employee contributions. Starting after 1986, the TRA imposes special nondiscrimination rules for employee contributions. In general, the new rules are violated if highly-paid employees make disproportionately large contributions to the plan.

Loans to plan members. For plan years starting after 1986, the TRA reduces the $50,000 borrowing limit by the member's highest outstanding loan balance during the preceding 12 months. Also starting after 1986, the more-than-5-year repayment period applies only to the purchase of a principal residence by a plan member, his child or grandchild.

Pensions for early retirees. Starting in 1987, the TRA ties the normal retirement age for pensions to the Social Security retirement age (currently 65, but scheduled to increase from 65 to 67 between years 2000 and 2022.) Early pension benefits are also tied into the reduction in Social Security benefits for early retirement (e.g., at age 62, you get 80% of the benefit you would receive at age 65). Anyone retiring at age 62, for example, can receive 80% of the top-dollar pension benefit at age 65. The 80% dollar limit is reduced for early retirees before age 62. The $75,000 safe harbor for pension benefits starting on or after age 55 is repealed.

> **NOTE:** Pension benefits that accrued before 1987 will not be reduced to TRA levels.

New Plan Withdrawal Rules. The TRA completely revamps the rules on retirement plan withdrawals.

Early withdrawals. Under prior law, retirement plan withdrawals before age 59½, death, or disability were taxable. But there was no tax penalty if the ordinary employee wanted to tap his retirement plan for personal purposes (e.g., to buy a car or pay college tuition). Only early withdrawals from an IRA or from a retirement plan by 5% owners, were subject to a 10% penalty.

> **NEW LAW CHANGE:** The TRA imposes a 10% penalty on early withdrawals from all retirement plans by all taxpayers, starting in 1987. *Exceptions:* IRA and plan rollovers, life annuities, early retirement and certain hardships.

Another change. Before 1987, a withdrawal was considered to be first a withdrawal of nontaxable employee contributions. Only withdrawals in excess of employee contributions were taxable. Starting in 1987, the TRA treats a withdrawal on a pro rata basis—only part of the withdrawal is tax-free as a return of the employee's contribution. Exception: withdrawals from plans that permitted employee withdrawals on May 5, 1986.

Withdrawals at retirement. The special tax breaks for lump-sum payouts are curbed, starting with distributions after 1986. Ten-year averaging is replaced by five-year averaging. However, you are entitled to elect five-year averaging only once—and then only after you reach age 59½. The lump-sum capital gains break is phased out over six years.

> **SPECIAL RELIEF:** An employee who was at least age 50 on 1-1-86, is entitled to special treatment: He can choose between ten-year averaging using 1986 tax rates and five-year averaging using the new tax rates. He can also disregard the six-year phaseout for capital gain treatment and tax his capital gain at a flat 20%. If he elects this special relief, he cannot elect lump-sum treatment again after reaching 59½.

Mandatory withdrawals. In years starting after 1988, all members of a company retirement plan, Keogh plan, or tax-sheltered an-

nuity must start making plan withdrawals no later than April 1 of
the year after the year they become age 70½.

Three-year rule. Before the TRA, all retirement plan annuity
payouts were first treated as a tax-free recovery of the employee's
contributions if the payments in the first three years equaled or exceeded the employee contributions. This special rule is repealed for
annuities starting after July 1, 1986.

Cash or Deferred (Sec. 401k) Plans. The TRA limits the
amount that can be deferred. The maximum deferral drops from
$30,000 to $7,000, in years starting after 1986.

Also starting in 1987, the TRA applies new 401(k) rules to prohibit discrimination in favor of highly compensated employees.
These same rules also apply to employer matching contributions, in
years starting after 1986.

Tough New Rules for T&E Deductions. Starting in 1987:

• The deduction for business entertainment expenses (including
meals) is limited to 80% of cost.

• The deduction for business meals on overnight travel is also
reduced by 20%.

• The deductible portion of employee unreimbursed travel and
transportation expenses and entertainment expenses is lumped in
with other miscellaneous expenses. Most miscellaneous deductions
are deductible only to the extent the total exceeds 2% of the employee's annual adjusted gross income.

EMPLOYER REIMBURSEMENT: An employer reimbursement
for employee travel and entertainment is not subject to the 2% floor.
The reimbursement is tax-free to the employee and deductible by the
employer. Reimbursement deductions attributable to meals and business entertainment are reduced by 20%, however.

• The TRA completely eliminates the deduction for the so-
called quiet business meal. You get a business entertainment deduction for a meal only if business is discussed before, during, or
after the meal.

Investment Real Estate Hit Hard. The TRA is tough on real
estate investments.

Depreciation. For properties placed in service after 1986, the
TRA both lengthens the depreciation period and changes the rate at
which the properties can be written off. The TRA increases the depreciation period from 19 years to 27½ years for residential rental
property and 31½ years for commercial property. And both types
must be written off using straight-line depreciation. This produces
equal deductions over the whole writeoff period. [See ¶201 et seq.]

At-risk Rules. The TRA brings real estate under the restrictions of the so-called at-risk rules. The at-risk rules limit the loss writeoff on an investment to the cash invested plus borrowed amounts on which the investor is personally liable (i.e., recourse debt). Up to now, the at-risk rules have applied to all investments except real estate. The TRA extends the at-risk rules to real estate put in service after 1986.

> **BIG EXCEPTION:** Real estate bought with nonrecourse (i.e., no personal liability) debt is exempt from the at-risk rules if the financing comes from a bank, the Government, or is insured by the Government.

Tax shelters. Beginning in 1987, loss writeoffs from tax shelters can generally shelter only income from other properties or other tax-sheltered investments. But here again there is an exception for real estate. [See ¶501 et seq.]

Rehabilitation credit. The TRA reduces, but does not eliminate, the big tax credit for rehabilitating certain types of buildings. The credit is equal to a percentage of the cost of rehabilitating older commercial and industrial properties and certified historic structures (including residential properties). There are only two credits: a 20% credit for historic structures and a 10% credit for industrial and commercial properties originally placed in service before 1936. The new credits generally apply to property placed in service after 1986. [See ¶217.]

Low-income housing credit. Before the TRA, investors were allowed special fast writeoffs for the cost of rehabilitating low-income housing. This break will go off the books at the end of 1986, and the TRA does not extend it. The TRA does provide a new tax credit for owners of low-income housing put in service after 1986 and before 1990. There are three separate credits for: (1) new construction and rehabilitation of existing housing; (2) certain federally subsidized new construction and rehabilitation; and (3) acquisition cost of existing housing [see ¶218].

Investors in cooperative apartments. Owners of stock in cooperative apartments are entitled to a special pass-through income tax break. They can deduct their share of real estate taxes and mortgage interest paid by the cooperative. However, before the TRA, this break was available only to individual stockholders. Starting in 1987, the TRA allows corporations, trusts, estates and partnerships to become stockholders in a cooperative apartment. This change facilitates the investment in cooperative apartment stock. [See ¶623.]

Homeowner's breaks untouched. The TRA did not change four tax breaks for homeowners: (1) property taxes remain fully deductible; (2) interest remains fully deductible on a mortgage taken out to buy a principal or second home; (3) a homeowner can continue to avoid current tax on a sale by spending the proceeds on the purchase of a new home; (4) homeowners age 55 or over still have a one-time exclusion that allows them to escape tax on the first $125,000 of sale profit, whether they replace the home or not.

Municipal Bonds. The TRA continues favorable tax treatment for most municipal bonds. You can still buy municipal bonds that pay tax-free interest. And the bonds you now own continue to pay tax-free interest.

TRA change. The interest on some municipal bonds will not be tax exempt. (These are bonds that finance certain private activities) But even this crackdown generally applies only to bonds issued after 9-1-86. [See ¶1301 et seq.]

> **NOTE:** Tax-free interest on private activity bonds issued on or after 8-8-86 is subject to the toughened alternative minimum tax. [See ¶711.]

Tax Shelter Crackdown. The TRA rules prevent you from using a loss from a "passive activity" to shelter your "active income" (e.g., salary) or "portfolio income" (e.g., dividends, interest, and capital gains). You are allowed to write off tax shelter loss only against other tax shelter income. If you have no other current tax shelter income, your loss is carried over to offset tax shelter income in future years. If you haven't used up the loss by the time you sell the investment, it is offset against your otherwise taxable gain on the sale.

The crackdown takes effect gradually over a five-year period. In 1987, investors can write off 65% of tax shelter losses against non-tax shelter income. In 1988, only 40% can be written off. In 1989 and 1990, writeoffs are limited to 20% and 10% respectively. The crackdown is fully in place starting in 1991. The phase-in applies only to tax shelter investments made prior to the date of enactment of the '86 Act. In 1987, losses from investments made after the enactment date are fully subject to the passive loss rule. There are exceptions for the first $25,000 loss or credit from rental realty, low-income housing credits, and working interests in oil and gas drilling. [See ¶503.]

Some Corporations Helped, Others Hurt. The TRA slashes some corporate tax bills dramatically. Other corporations face tax hikes. Why the difference? It's mainly because of the repeal of the investment tax credit. [See ¶208.] Corporations that invest heavily in equipment and machinery may pay bigger post-TRA tax bills. All corporations, however, benefit from new lower tax rates. [See ¶601.]

New Tax Rate Cut. The new tax rates become fully effective for tax years starting on or after 7-1-87.

Taxable income	*New rates*
Less than $50,000	15% of taxable income
Over $50,000 but not over $75,000	$7,500 plus 25% of the excess over $50,000
Over $75,000 but not over $100,000	$13,750 plus 34% of the excess over $75,000
Over $100,000 to $335,000	$22,250 plus 39% of the excess over $100,000
Above $335,000	Flat 34% on all income

A corporation benefits from the rate reduction in the tax year that includes 7-1-87. Income received at any time during that year is taxed under blended rates, combining the old and the new. The rates that apply to your corporation depend on how much of its tax year falls after 7-1-87.

Installment Sales. Taxpayers selling under a revolving credit plan may no longer use the installment method for sales made after 12-31-86. They must report their profits in the year the sale is made. And the use of the installment method is limited if the taxpayer has outstanding debt—the smaller the debt, the more profit qualifies for installment reporting. This change is effective 1-1-87 for sales made on or after 3-1-86. [See ¶803.]

Bad debts. Effective for tax years starting after 12-31-86, all taxpayers will use the specific charge-off method to deduct bad debts; the reserve method will no longer be available (except for certain commercial banks). [See ¶807.]

Equipment Purchases. The TRA repeals the investment tax credit for property placed in service after 1985. Nevertheless, it retains much of the simplicity and fast writeoffs of the accelerated cost recovery system (ACRS). You can continue to write off some equipment purchases over five years. There are special rules on business cars. Most other equipment is now written off over seven years. [See ¶201 et seq.]

Starting with equipment placed in service in 1987, you may be in line for bigger deductions in the early years after purchase, because of two TRA changes: (1) depreciation deductions are computed using a faster rate, and (2) you can expense (i.e., deduct currently) a larger amount the year you purchase equipment and place it in service.

For property placed in service before 1987, ACRS is computed using the 150% declining balance method. That means your first year deduction is one-and-a-half times as large as it would be using straight-line depreciation. In general, depreciation on most personal property placed in service after 1986 is figured on the 200% declining balance method. So for property with the same writeoff period, you get first year deductions that are twice as large as straight-line depreciation—or one-third more than under pre-1987 law.

Even if the property must now be written off over seven years, instead of five, your total deductions for the first two years are still larger than those figured under pre-1987 law—despite the new, longer writeoff period.

What's more, you can elect to use the new depreciation rules on property placed in service after 7-31-86. For example, suppose you purchase a $5,000 piece of business equipment that qualifies for five-year writeoffs under both the old and new systems. You place the equipment in service on 8-1-86. Under the old rules, you get a $750 depreciation deduction for 1986. But if you elect to use the new double declining balance system, your 1986 deduction is $1,000.

Larger expensing deduction. Before 1987, you can elect to expense each year up to $5,000 of the cost of property used in your business. The TRA raises to $10,000 the amount of equipment that you can expense in a year, starting with 1987.

The expensing deduction cannot, however, be used by large purchasers. If a company buys more than $200,000 of eligible property during a year, the expensing deduction ceiling is reduced on a dollar-for-dollar basis for purchases in excess of $200,000. [See ¶206.]

> **NOTE:** You cannot claim depreciation deductions on the portion of equipment purchases that you expense. And since the investment tax credit is eliminated as of 1-1-86, you no longer forfeit a tax credit when you elect to expense equipment purchases.

Timing purchases. One TRA provision cuts back on the first year depreciation deductions that you would otherwise be entitled to take. Before 1987, you get the same first-year depreciation deduction on property, regardless of when during the year it is actually placed in service. So equipment placed in service in January is treated the same as equipment placed in service in December. In general, this remains true under the TRA. Equipment placed in service after 1986 is treated as if you started using it on July 1, no matter when during the year you actually start using it. (This also means that it will take six years to write off five-year property.) However, there is an exception for year-end purchases.

Business Car Writeoffs. The TRA changes the writeoffs for cars placed in service after 1986. Cars are now five-year writeoff property. And it actually takes six years to write off the cost of a car. Reason: Under the TRA, your depreciation deductions start on July 1 of the year you place the car in service. So the five-year writeoff period runs over into a sixth calendar year.

> **TAX SURPRISE:** Despite the longer depreciation periods, there will only be a small cut in your annual writeoffs—at least in the early years. Reason: The TRA accelerates the rate at which you writeoff

your cost. For example, under the old rules you can deduct 63% of your cost in the first two years; under the TRA, it's 52%.

Under prior law, you could use the accelerated method of computing deductions only if you used your car more than 50% for business. Otherwise, the car had to be written off through straight-line depreciation. There was also a cap on depreciation deductions for cars costing over $12,800. Your depreciation deductions for a business car could not exceed $3,200 for the first year and $4,800 for subsequent years. (These figures were reduced proportionately for cars used only partially for business.) The TRA leaves the 50% business use rule intact. And depreciation deductions for cars costing more than $12,800 continue to be subject to deduction caps. However, the yearly amount of the caps is reduced to reflect the new, slightly less favorable depreciation schedule. [See ¶202.]

Fringe Benefits.   The TRA reinstates the tax-free treatment of several widely used fringe benefits. For instance, the tax-free status of educational assistance and group legal services plans expired at the end of 1985. The new law extends these tax breaks for two years, through 1987.

The exclusion from tax for educational assistance benefits had been subject to an annual cap of $5,000 per employee. Benefits in excess of this amount were treated as taxable compensation. The TRA increases the maximum exclusion for educational assistance payments to $5,250, starting in 1986.

Untouched Tax Breaks.   Under the TRA, employers can continue to provide their employees tax-free fringe benefits, such as:

- Up to $50,000 of group-term life insurance;
- $5,000 of death benefits;
- Dependent care assistance (but subject to an annual $5,000 ceiling starting in 1986).
- Health insurance (but see below).

Most fringe benefits that are tax-free must be provided to employees on a nondiscriminatory basis. That means the employer must provide the benefits to rank-and-file workers as well as to key employees. Starting in 1987, health plans funded through an insurance carrier are covered by nondiscrimination rules, the same rules that apply to self-insured health plans. So employers can no longer provide tax-free health plan benefits on a key employee-only basis. [See ¶1151 et seq.]

New Tax Deduction for Self-Employed Taxpayers.   Starting in 1987, a self-employed individual is allowed to deduct 25% of what he pays himself under a medical reimbursement plan. The plan can also cover his dependents if it covers his employees' dependents. The remaining 75% of the payments are deductible medical expenses. [See ¶1161.]

Stock Option Plans. There are two basic kinds of executive option plans—statutory (incentive stock options) and nonstatutory (nonqualified).

Sequence of exercise. Starting with options issued after 1986, an executive no longer must exercise incentive stock options in the order they are granted to him. This is the same rule that has applied to nonqualified options. What this means: If the price of the stock falls well below the option price, the executive can be issued a second incentive option with a lower exercise price.

No capital gain. Under prior law, with an incentive stock option, the bargain element (the spread between the option's exercise price and the price of the stock) was taxed as long-term capital gain when the stock was sold (as long as the stock was held for more than one year before sale). With the loss of the capital gain exclusion the bargain element in both options is taxed at the same rates as ordinary income.

Family Tax-Saving Strategies. Perhaps the simplest way for a parent to shift taxable income to a child is to give the child a gift of income-producing property. The TRA puts an end to this basic income-shifting technique for many families. Investment income received by a child under age 14 is generally taxed to the child at the parent's top rate. And, it makes no difference if the source of the income came from someone other than the parent—it's still taxed to the child at the parent's highest marginal rate. Effective date: Income received after 1986, even if cash or property was transferred to the child before 1987.

What's more, starting in 1987, your child cannot use his or her personal exemption to shelter income if the child can be claimed as a dependent on your return. However, a minor can use up to $500 of his or her standard deduction to offset unearned income from any source. [See ¶102.] The child is allowed to use his or her own tax rate on another $500 of investment income. Result: If the child is under age 14, only income in excess of $1,000 must be taxed at the parent's top tax rate. [See ¶1405.]

Clifford Trust Repealed. How the trust works: The parent transfers income-producing property to a trust that lasts more than ten years. The trust income is distributed and taxed to the low-bracket child. The property reverts to the parent when the trust terminates.

After the TRA, the trust income is taxed to the person who funds the trust if the property reverts to him (or to his spouse) — even if the reversion takes place more than ten years after the transfer to the trust. In other words, the income-splitting benefit of the short-term trust is eliminated, regardless of the age of the child. Effective date: Income from property transferred to a trust after March 1, 1986. [See ¶1402.]

> **IMPORTANT:** The income-splitting benefit of a Clifford trust set up on or before March 1, 1986 may also be undercut. Reason: After 1986, trust payouts to a child under age 14 can be taxed at the parent's top rate.

Minimum Tax. *Individuals.* The basic structure of the alternative minimum tax for individual taxpayers stays the same under the TRA. However, the rate goes to 21% (from 20%) starting in 1987. And the special exemptions that apply to the tax ($40,000 for joint filers, $30,000 for singles) are phased out for taxpayers with alternative minimum taxable income in excess of $150,000, if married or $112,500, if single. The exemptions are cut by 25% of the amount of alternative minimum taxable income that exceeds these levels. Result: More taxpayers will be subject to the alternative minimum tax.

Two items are no longer subject to minimum tax because they are no longer tax-preferred under the regular tax: the dividend exclusion and the long-term capital gain exclusion. The bargain element of incentive stock options continues to be a tax preference subject to minimum tax. Individual taxpayers cannot use losses from passive investments to offset minimum taxable income. Unlike the phase-in rule for loss writeoffs of regular tax, this takes full effect in 1987. [See ¶701 et seq.]

Corporations. The TRA substantially changes the corporate minimum tax. Starting in 1987, the corporate minimum tax is like the individual minimum tax: it's paid only if it exceeds the regular income tax. (Before the TRA, it was an add-on to the regular corporate tax.) The tax rate is 20%. The exemption is the first $40,000 of minimum taxable income. The exemption amount is reduced by 25% of a corporation's minimum taxable income above $150,000. [See ¶701 et seq.]

> **SPECIAL CORPORATE PREFERENCES:** One half the difference between a corporation's book income and its regular taxable income is a taxable preference in 1987, 1988, and 1989. After 1989, earnings and profits will be used to determine the preference. Corporations also treat as a tax preference a portion of intangible drilling costs.

All taxpayers. The TRA also makes other changes in the minimum tax rules. Here are some key changes that affect both individuals and corporations:

• *Municipal bond interest.* Interest on some tax-exempt bonds issued after August 7, 1986 for a nongovernment purpose will be a preference item.

• *Charitable contribution of appreciated property.* To the extent that untaxed appreciation is allowed as a regular tax deduction, the appreciation on charitable contributions is a preference item, starting in 1987.

• *Net operating losses.* NOLs are deductible against minimum taxable income only to the extent of 90% of that income, *starting in 1987.*

• *Intangible drilling costs.* Intangible drilling costs are a preference item to the extent of the difference between (1) the IDC deduction and (2) the excess of what could have been deducted using 10-year amortization over 65% of net oil and gas income.

• *Depreciation.* Accelerated depreciation for both real and personal property placed in service after 1986 is still a tax preference. However, in later years, when straight-line depreciation exceeds accelerated, the excess can offset other tax preferences.

• *Installment sales.* Taxpayers in the business of selling goods or real estate cannot use the installment method to defer minimum taxable income for tax years beginning after 1986.

• *Completed contract.* Income for the minimum tax cannot be deferred by using the completed contract method of accounting in years starting after 1986.

Life Insurance. The basic tax-favored treatment of life insurance stays in place under the TRA. However, the TRA does add some changes that affect life insurance policyholders. [See ¶1001 et seq.]

Lump-sum payout to spouse-beneficiary. Previously, a spouse who chose to take an installment payout of life insurance proceeds got an income tax break. The spouse could receive up to $1,000 of tax-free interest annually on the unpaid amount. The TRA repeals the $1,000 interest exclusion.

Interest on policyholder loans. The TRA restates the rule that interest on debt incurred to buy or carry single-premium life insurance is not deductible (the IRS has already stated that this rule includes loans against the cash value of single-premium policies).

The new law also places a cap on the amount of interest an employer can deduct when borrowing against a life insurance policy purchased on the life of an employee. Interest may be deducted only on the first $50,000 of borrowing. Effective date: Insurance contracts purchased after June 20, 1986.

IRS enforcement procedures. At the same time it lowers rates and eliminates deductions, the TRA toughens tax penalties. It also provides for more information reporting and increases the IRS budget for agents, audits and the expansion of compliance systems.

Steeper penalties. The penalty for failure to pay taxes goes from 1/2% to 1% per month for amounts assessed after 1986, regardless of when the failure to pay occurred. The penalty for substantial underpayment of taxes is also doubled—from 10% to 20% for returns due after 1986. In addition, the negligence and fraud penalties are expanded after 1986.

More reporting. Taxpayers will have to provide the Government with more information on real estate transactions, Federal contracts, and royalty payments.

For example, the person responsible for closing a real estate transaction must report the transaction for contracts closing after 1986. The penalty for not filing information returns stays at $50 for each failure. However, the yearly limit increases from $50,000 to $100,000 for returns due after 1986. [See ¶1521.]

The TRA also adds a new penalty of up to $5 for each inaccurate or incomplete information return (up to an annual maximum of $20,000). Effective date: returns due after 1986. [See ¶1501.]

Estate and Gift Tax. The big news in estate and gift taxes is what didn't happen. The TRA made relatively few changes.

Generation skipping transfer tax. Under prior law, this special tax was imposed on transfers in trust set up to benefit two or more generations younger than the generation of the grantor. The tax was paid when the child died and was roughly equivalent to the estate tax that would have been owed if the property had been directly transferred from the grandparent to child and then again from parent to child. Any unused portion of the decedent's unified credit could be used to shelter generation-skipping transfers and an additional $250,000 exemption is available for transfers to grandchildren.

Under the TRA, the credit and exemption are replaced with a single $1 million dollar exemption per transferor ($2 million for joint transfers by married couples). However, for the first time, the TRA subjects direct transfers from grandparents to grandchildren to the generation-skipping tax, subject to a $2 million per grandchild exclusion for transfers made prior to 1-1-90. The tax itself is a flat rate equal to the maximum estate and gift tax rate (now 55% but scheduled to decline to 50% in 1988). Effective date: In general, transfers after the date of enactment. [See ¶1413.]

New Income Tax Rates for Trusts and Estates. Trusts and estates use a special tax rate schedule starting in 1988. (There's a special rate schedule for 1987). The first $5,000 of trust income is taxed at 15%; anything over that is taxed at 28%. The benefit of the 15% bracket is phased out where taxable trust income is between $13,000 and $26,000.

Neither trusts nor estates paid estimated income taxes under prior law. And estates could pay income tax in four equal installments starting with the due date of the return and every three months thereafter. In tax years starting after 1986, trusts and estates must follow the same estimated income tax rules as individuals. And the special installment payment rule for estates is repealed in tax years starting after 1986.

Miscellaneous TRA Changes.

• *Dividend exclusion.* The $100/$200 dividend exclusion for individuals is repealed after 1986. [See ¶604]

• *Two-earner married couples.* The deduction for working married couples is repealed for tax years after 1986. [See ¶106]

• *Income averaging.* After 1986, general income averaging is repealed. [See ¶107]

• *Earned income credit.* Starting in 1987, a tax credit for low-income working individuals with children is increased from 11% of the first $5,000 to 14% of the first $5,714 of earned income (maximum credit: $800). The credit is phased out at a rate of 10% for income levels over $6,500. Thus in 1987, there is no credit if adjusted gross income exceeds $14,500. The phaseout level and the maximum are between $9,000 and $17,000 respectively, after 1987. The maximum amount and the phaseout levels will be adjusted annually for inflation starting 1987. [See ¶108]

• *Office at home deductions.* Most miscellaneous itemized deductions, including those for the business use of an employee's home, are limited by a 2%-of-adjusted gross income-floor after 1986. Also starting in 1987, no home office deduction (other than deductions for mortgage interest and property taxes) are allowed because an employee leases his home office to his employer. Allowable home office deductions are limited to a taxpayer's gross income less his business expenses, other than expenses allocable to the home office itself. The amount of other home office deductions is limited to gross income from the business activity. [See ¶129]

• *Political contributions tax credit.* The TRA knocks out the credit for contributions made to political candidates and organizations after 1986. The maximum credit in 1986 is one-half the dollar amount of the contributions (up to $100 for joint filers, $50 for singles). [¶131.]

- *Casualty loss deduction.* Under the TRA, casualty losses to nonbusiness property cannot be deducted unless (1) an insurance claim is filed, and (2) the losses are not covered by insurance. Effective date: Losses sustained after 1986. [See ¶1005.]

- *Hobby expenses.* Before 1987, hobby expenses are deductible up to the amount of hobby income. Additionally, starting in 1987, your otherwise deductible hobby expenses are aggregated with your other miscellaneous itemized expenses. The total is deductible only to the extent it exceeds 2% of adjusted gross income. The test of whether an activity is considered a business or a hobby is based upon its profitability. Starting in 1987, in order to be presumed a business, the activity must be profitable in three out of five consecutive years. Before 1987, the presumption was two out of five years. A special exception continues to apply to horse breeding or racing. [See ¶130.]

- *Prizes and awards.* All prizes and awards made after 1986 are taxable to the recipient, with two exceptions: (1) Awards for charitable, scientific, artistic or similar achievements are tax-free if the recipient assigns the prize or award to a tax-exempt charity or a governmental unit. (2) Employee awards of personal property (e.g., a watch or crystal bowl) for length of service or safety achievements are tax-free to the extent they are deductible by the employer. The per-employee deduction limit is generally $400. However, it is possible to deduct $1,600 if the employer has a qualified award plan. [See ¶111]

- *Corporate dividend received deduction.* The 85% dividend received deduction for corporations is lowered to 80% for dividends received or accrued after 1986 in tax years ending after 1986. [See ¶602.]

- *Tax on liquidating distributions.* Generally speaking, starting with liquidations completed after 1986, property distributed in a complete liquidation is deemed to have been sold by the corporation at its fair market value. Thus, the corporation is taxed on any appreciation. This repeals the *General Utilities* rule. It permitted a corporation to escape paying income tax on appreciated property by undergoing a complete liquidation and distributing the property to its shareholders. [See ¶615 et seq.]

- *Research credit.* The tax credit for research expenses expired at the end of 1985. The TRA extends the credit beyond 1985 and applies it to expenses incurred before 1989. The amount is lowered to 20% (it was 25%) of the increase in current research expenses over the average in the three preceding years. The TRA targets the credit to technological research that leads to new business. [See ¶211 et seq.]

- *Targeted job credit.* The tax credit for hiring people from one or more of nine targeted groups (e.g., economically disadvantaged

Vietnam veterans) expired at the end of 1985. Although the TRA limits the credit in some respects, it extends the credit for three years—to wages paid by employers who start work before 1989. [See ¶1701.]

• *Tax Accounting.* Manufacturers cannot currently deduct their direct costs of production (e.g., wages and raw material costs). They must be inventoried and offset against proceeds from sales. Up to now, a variety of rules applied to a manufacturer's indirect costs of production: some had to be inventoried (e.g., rent); others were included in inventory for tax purposes only if they were inventoried on financial reports (e.g., retirement plan contributions); still others were currently deductible (e.g., advertising expenses).

Under prior law, both retailers and wholesalers had to include in inventory the direct costs of acquiring goods of resale. But none of their indirect costs had to be inventoried. The treatment of indirect expenses when constructing your own property was less certain.

Beginning in 1987, the TRA sets up uniform rules that apply to all costs incurred in manufacturing or constructing property or in purchasing and holding property for resale (producing farms are exempt from the new rules). Interest costs will generally be capitalized where the interest is allocable to real property construction or the construction of personal property but is long-lived and to be used by the taxpayer. Comprehensive capitalization rules will also apply to long-term contracts. [See ¶805 et seq.]

• *Tax years for S corporations and personal service corporations.* The TRA requires that all partnership, S corporations, and personal service corporations conform their tax years to the tax years of their owners, starting after 1986. Exception: The years can be different if you can establish a business purpose for the difference. [See ¶808.]

• *Unemployment compensation.* Unemployment benefits received after 1986 are fully taxable. The TRA repeals the limited exclusion for unemployment benefits. [See ¶109.]

• *Interest rate on tax overpayments and underpayments.* Starting in 1987, the interest rate paid to taxpayers on tax overpayments will be the Federal short-term rate plus 2%. Taxpayers will pay the Federal short-term rate plus 3% on underpayments. The rates will be adjusted quarterly based on the rate during the first month of the preceding calendar quarter. [See ¶1511.]

• *Foreign earned income exclusion.* Starting in 1987, the TRA puts a $70,000 cap on the income exclusion available to American taxpayers who have their tax home in a foreign country. [See ¶1201 et seq.]

Impact on State Taxes. Many states start their tax computations with federal adjusted gross income or, in the case of corporations, federal taxable income with certain adjustments. This means that, unless their legislators act fast, items which affect federal adjusted gross income or taxable income in the new tax law are going to affect state taxes. Remember to bear these points in mind when you are assessing how the new tax law's rules will affect your tax liability. And make sure you consult the *P-H State and Local Tax Service* to keep on top of changes in your area.

[The page following this is 101.]

INDIVIDUALS

[¶101] **Rate Reductions for Individuals.** The new law introduces new and deceptively simple tax rate schedules. Prior law taxed individuals in as many as 15 brackets at rates that began at 11% and went as high as 50%. This structure is replaced with what appears to be a two-bracket rate setup—15% and 28%. However, the top tax rate is actually 33%. Reason: Beginning with the 1988 tax year, there are two separate 5% surtaxes for high-income taxpayers.

• The first 5% surtax phases out the tax benefit a taxpayer gains from having part of his income taxed at the 15% rate. The surtax commences at prescribed income levels and ends at the point where the 13% differential between the 15% and 28% brackets is recouped.

Example: For marrieds filing jointly for 1988, the first $29,750 of income is taxed at 15%, and the excess above $29,750 is taxed at 28%. The 5% surtax begins at taxable income in excess of $71,900 and ends at $149,250. Thus, if taxable income is $149,250, the surtax reaches a maximum of $3,867.50. That figure represents an extra 13% tax on the first $29,750 of taxable income.

• The second 5% surtax phases out the tax benefit gained from personal and dependency exemptions. This surtax kicks in at the point where the first 5% surtax is levied in full—that is, at the point where the tax benefit from the 15% rate disappears.

Example: For marrieds filing jointly for 1988, the second surtax begins at taxable income in excess of $149,250.

The second surtax disappears once the tax benefit gained from exemptions is recouped. Each personal and dependency exemption is equal to $1,900 for 1987, $1,950 for 1988, and $2,000 for 1989. Thus, for 1988, the maximum personal exemption surtax for a high-bracket taxpayer is $546 per exemption claimed. That figure is 28% of $1,950.

Special rates for 1987. To reconcile the new schedules with prior law's schedules, Congress came up with "blended" rate schedules for 1987 only.

WATCH THIS: The special rate schedules for 1987 have five conventional tax brackets. That is, there are no surtaxes levied on high-income taxpayers.

Another fundamental change. Beginning with tax year 1987, tax brackets start at taxable income of zero. Taxable income is adjusted gross income less personal exemptions less (1) the standard deduction (which replaces the zero bracket amount) or (2) total itemized deductions, whichever is greater. Under prior law, the zero bracket amount was built into the tax rate schedules. Thus, the lowest bracket began at the point where taxable income exceeded the applicable zero bracket amount. The nonitemizer found taxable income by subtracting personal exemptions (and the special charitable deduction) from AGI. The itemizer arrived at taxable income by subtracting from AGI the total of personal exemptions and the excess of itemized deductions over the zero bracket amount.

Following are the new tax rates for 1987 and 1988. The tax rates for 1988 reflect the first 5% surtax. The second 5% surtax depends on the number of personal and dependency exemptions claimed by the taxpayer.

MARRIEDS FILING JOINTLY OR SURVIVING SPOUSES

Tax Year 1987		Tax Year 1988	
Taxable Income (TI)	Tax Payable	Taxable Income (TI)	Tax Payable
$0—$3,000	11% of TI	$0—$29,750	15% of TI
$3,000—$28,000	$330 + 15% of (TI − $3,000)	$29,750—$71,900	$4,462.50 + 28% of (TI − $29,750)
$28,000—$45,000	$4,080 + 28% of (TI − $28,000)	$71,900—$149,250	$16,264.50 + 33% of (TI − $71,900)*
$45,000—$90,000	$8,840 + 35% of (TI − $45,000)	$149,250 +	28% of TI**
$90,000 +	$24,590 + 38.5% of (TI − $90,000)		

*Reflects first 5% surtax.

**PLUS lesser of (1) 28% of the sum of personal and dependency exemptions or (2) 5% of (TI − $149,250).

HEADS OF HOUSEHOLD

Tax Year 1987		Tax Year 1988	
Taxable Income (TI)	Tax Payable	Taxable Income (TI)	Tax Payable
$0—$2,500	11% of TI	$0—$23,900	15% of TI
$2,500—$23,000	$275 + 15% of (TI − $2,500)	$23,900—$61,650	$3,585 + 28% of (TI − $23,900)
$23,000—$38,000	$3,350 + 28% of (TI − $23,000)	$61,650—$123,790	$14,155 + 33% of (TI − $61,650)*
$38,000—$80,000	$7,550 + 35% of (TI − $38,000)	$123,790 +	28% of TI**
$80,000 +	$22,250 + 38.5% of (TI − $80,000)		

*Reflects first 5% surtax.

**PLUS lesser of (1) 28% of the sum of personal and dependency exemptions or (2) 5% of (TI − $123,790).

SINGLE TAXPAYERS

Tax Year 1987		Tax Year 1988	
Taxable Income (TI)	Tax Payable	Taxable Income (TI)	Tax Payable
$0—$1,800	11% of TI	$0—$17,850	15% of TI
$1,800—$16,800	$198 + 15% of (TI − $1,800)	$17,850—$43,150	$2,677.50 + 28% of (TI − $17,850)
$16,800—$27,000	$2,448 + 28% of (TI − $16,800)	$43,150—$89,560	$9,761.50 + 33%* of (TI − $43,150)
$27,000—$54,000	$5,304 + 35% of (TI − $27,000)	$89,560 +	28% of TI**
$54,000 +	$14,754 + 38.5% of (TI − $54,000)		

*Reflects first 5% surtax.
**PLUS lesser of (1) 28% of the sum of personal and dependency exemptions or (2) 5% of (TI − $89,560).

MARRIEDS FILING SEPARATELY

Tax Year 1987		Tax Year 1988	
Taxable Income (TI)	Tax Payable	Taxable Income (TI)	Tax Payable
$0—$1,500	11% of TI	$0—$14,875	15% of TI
$1,500—$14,000	$165 + 15% of (TI − $1,500)	$14,875—$35,950	$2,231.25 + 28% of (TI − $14,875)
$14,000—$22,500	$2,040 + 28% of (TI − $14,000)	$35,950—$113,300	$8,132.25 + 33% of (TI − $35,950)*
$22,500—$45,000	$4,420 + 35% of (TI − $22,500)	$113,300 +	28% of TI**
$45,000 +	$12,295 + 38.5% of (TI − $45,000)		

*Reflects first 5% surtax. The maximum surtax, or rate adjustment, equals 13% of the maximum amount of taxable income within the 15% bracket applicable for marrieds filing jointly.
**PLUS lesser of (1) 28% of the sum of personal and dependency exemptions or (2) 5% of (TI − $113,300).

Following are three examples that illustrate the operation of the new rates.

Example (1): Joint return filers Mr. and Mrs. Anderson have $60,000 of taxable income in 1987 and 1988. Their tax bill for 1987 is $14,090. That's $8,840 plus 35% of ($60,000 − $45,000). Their tax bill for 1988 is $12,932.50. That's $4,462.50 plus 28% of ($60,000 − $29,750).

Example (2): Joint return filers Mr. and Mrs. Jones have taxable income of $85,000 in 1987 and 1988. Their tax bill in 1987 is $22,840. That's the sum of $8,840 plus 35% of ($85,000 − $45,000). Their tax bill in 1988 is $20,587.50. That's the sum of $16,264.50 plus 33% of ($85,000 − $71,900). The tax reflects a 5% surtax on the $13,100 of taxable income in excess of $71,900.

Example (3): For tax years 1987 and 1988, joint return filers Mr. and Mrs. Smith have three dependent children and $160,000 of taxable income. Their tax bill for 1987 is $51,540. That's the sum of $24,590 and 38.5% of ($160,000 − $90,000). Their tax bill for 1988 is the sum of two figures:

(1) Flat tax of 28% on all income [income exceeds point at which first 5% surtax is levied in full] ... $44,800.00

(2) Lesser of:
    (a) 28% of ($1,950 exemption × 5) $2,730.00
    (b) 5% of ($160,000 − $149,250) 537.50   537.50

Total $45,337.50

Estates and trusts. The tax rate schedules for estates and trusts are as follows:

Tax Year 1987		Tax Year 1988	
Taxable Income (TI)	Tax Payable	Taxable Income (TI)	Tax Payable
$0—$500	11% of TI	$0—$5,000	15% of TI
$500—$4,700	$55 + 15% of (TI − $500)	$5,000—$13,000	$750 + 28% of (TI − $5,000)
$4,700—$7,550	$685 + 28% of (TI − $4,700)	$13,000—$26,000	$2,990 + 33% of (TI − $13,000)
$7,550—$15,150	$1,483 + 35% of (TI − $7,550)	$26,000 +	28% of TI
$15,150 +	$4,143 + 38.5% of (TI − $15,150)		

NOTE: The taxable income amounts at which the 28% rate starts will be adjusted for inflation, beginning with the 1989 tax year. See ¶105.

Act Sec. 101(a) amends Sec. 1, relating to tax imposed on individuals, effective for tax years beginning after 12-31-86. Act. Sec. 101(b) amends Sec. 15(d), relating to inflation adjustments.

【¶102】 **Standard Deduction Reactivated and Increased.** Beginning with tax year 1987, the new law replaces the zero bracket amount with the standard deduction. The basic standard deduction amounts for taxpayers other than the elderly and the blind are as follows:

	1987	1988
Marrieds filing jointly and surviving spouses	$3,760	$5,000
Heads of household	$2,540	$4,400
Single taxpayers	$2,540	$3,000
Married filing separate returns	$1,880	$2,500

Boost for the elderly and the blind. For the 1987 tax year, taxpayers who are age 65 or over or are blind (defined as under prior law) may claim the higher standard deduction shown in the 1988 column. Also, beginning with the 1987 tax year, the standard deduction for an unmarried taxpayer who is not a surviving spouse and is age 65 or over or blind is increased by an additional standard deduction of $750. For a married taxpayer who is age 65 or over or blind, the additional standard deduction is $600. Thus, the additional standard deduction is $1,200 if both spouses are blind or 65 or over, or one is age 65 or over and the other is blind.

> **Example:** Ted and Andrea Smith are both age 66 and file jointly. They may claim a $6,200 standard deduction for tax year 1987 ($5,000 plus $1,200 for age 65 or over status).

> **Example:** Arthur Smith, a blind taxpayer, may claim a $3,750 standard deduction for tax year 1987 ($3,000 plus $750 increase). If Arthur were 65 or over, his standard deduction would be $4,500 ($3,000 plus $1,500 increase).

Dependent child's unearned income. Effective for the 1987 tax year, the standard deduction of a taxpayer (such as a child) who may be claimed as a dependent on another's return cannot exceed the greater of $500 or his earned income. Result: For 1987, if a child has no earned income, his or her unearned income in excess of $500 is subject to tax at a minimum rate of 11% (15% in 1988). The tax rate may be higher if the child is under age 14 and has "net unearned income" [see ¶1405 *et seq.*]. Another change: Effective for 1987, a taxpayer who may be claimed as a dependent by another taxpayer cannot claim a personal exemption [¶103].

By contrast, for tax year 1986, a dependent child with no earned income does not pay tax on the first $1,080 of unearned income (it's sheltered by the personal exemption).

Taxpayers ineligible for standard deduction. The standard deduction is zero for the following five categories:

- Married taxpayers filing separately if either spouse itemizes deductions.

- Individuals who are nonresident aliens.

- U.S. citizens with excludable income from U.S. possessions.

- Individuals who file returns for periods of less than 12 months because of accounting period changes.

- Estates or trusts, common trust funds, or partnerships.

Definition of taxable income. The new law simplifies the calculation of an individual's tax liability. Here's a comparison of the old and new definitions of taxable income for computing tax liability.

Under prior law, nonitemizers arrived at taxable income by subtracting the charitable deduction for a nonitemizer and all personal exemptions from AGI. The nonitemizer went directly to a tax table or tax rate schedule to figure tax liability. The zero bracket amount was incorporated in both the tax rate schedules and tax tables.

Thus, the tax tables and schedules indicated a zero tax liability if taxable income did not exceed the applicable ZBA.

Taxpayers who itemized reduced their itemized deductions by the applicable ZBA (to avoid getting twice the allowable ZBA) and subtracted the remaining (so-called excess) itemized deductions and personal exemptions from AGI to arrive at taxable income. Then, like a nonitemizer, the itemizer went to a tax table or tax rate schedules.

Under the new law, a nonitemizer offsets AGI with the standard deduction and personal exemptions to arrive at taxable income (the charitable deduction for nonitemizers is eliminated). An itemizer offsets AGI with personal exemptions and *all* itemized deductions to arrive at taxable income. Since the standard deduction has already been taken into account in arriving at taxable income, the new tax rate schedules and tax tables begin at the first dollar of taxable income.

Tax tables. The IRS is authorized to prepare tax tables reflecting the tax liability of itemizers and nonitemizers. Since the prior tables that incorporated the ZBA are replaced by tables that do not incorporate the standard deduction, the Committee Reports authorize the IRS to adjust the size of the intervals between taxable income amounts in the new tables to reflect meaningful differences in tax liability.

The standard deduction, the additional standard deduction, and the special $500 standard deduction for a taxpayer who can be claimed as a dependent by another, will be indexed for inflation beginning in 1989.

Act Sec. 102(a), relating to definition of taxable income, the basic standard deduction and additional standard deduction, amends Sec. 63. Act Sec. 102(b), relating to tax tables, amends Sec. 3(a). Act Secs. 102(a) and (b) are effective for tax years beginning after 12-31-86.

[¶103] **Personal Exemptions Increased.** The new law raises the personal exemption for an individual, the individual's spouse, and each dependent to $1,900 for 1987, $1,950 for 1988, and $2,000 for 1989. By contrast, each personal exemption was $1,080 for tax year 1986.

Personal exemptions will be indexed for inflation beginning with the 1990 tax year. See ¶105.

Phase-out of personal exemption for high-income taxpayers. Beginning with the 1988 tax year, the new law phases out the tax benefit that a high income taxpayer gains from personal exemptions. The phase-out affects *all* exemptions that may be claimed on a return including exemptions for a spouse and dependents. The purpose: to limit the windfall that wealthy taxpayers may reap from lower tax rates. The mechanism for the phase-out is a 5% surtax that begins at the point where the tax benefit from the 15% rate disappears [¶101], and ends where the tax benefit from personal exemptions is recouped in full.

The phase-out of personal exemptions by way of a surtax begins at the following levels of taxable income:

Filing Status	Taxable Income*
Marrieds filing jointly or surviving spouses	$149,250
Heads of household	$123,790
Single taxpayers	$ 89,560
Marrieds filing separately	$113,300

*Beginning with tax year 1989, these figures will be indexed for inflation.

For tax year 1988, the surtax is equal to the lesser of

• # of personal exemptions × $1,950 × 28% [nominal top tax bracket], or

• 5% of the excess of taxable income over the appropriate dollar figure from our table.

For 1988, the exemption is totally phased out at $10,920 of income per exemption above the figures shown in our table.

Example: Mr. and Mrs. Sample have four dependent children and file a joint return for tax year 1988. If they have $180,000 of taxable income, the surtax is equal to $1,537.50. That's 5% of $30,750 ($180,000 − $149,250). Put another way, the Sample family's personal exemptions are effectively reduced to $6,209, as follows:

Gross exemptions ($1,950 × 6 exemptions)	$11,700
Amount lost by way of surtax ($1,537.50 × 1/.28)	(5,491)
Net effective deduction for exemptions	$ 6,209

Example: John Cable is a single taxpayer with no dependents. His taxable income for 1988 is $120,000. Result: Cable's surtax is $546 ($1,950 × 28%). In other words, Cable's personal exemption is completely phased out.

Elderly and the blind. Under prior law, a taxpayer could claim an additional personal exemption if he was age 65 or over or blind. The new law repeals this additional personal exemption, beginning with the 1987 tax year. However, the loss of this extra exemption is recouped in part by way of an additional standard deduction for the elderly or blind ($750 extra for an unmarried taxpayer other than a surviving spouse, $600 for a married taxpayer). See ¶102.

Dependent child loses personal exemption. Under the new law, no exemption is allowed a taxpayer (such as a child) who can be claimed as a dependent by another taxpayer (e.g., a parent). This restriction eliminates the double benefit allowed under prior law when a dependent child was also allowed to claim a personal exemption on his or her own return.

> **NOTE:** It doesn't matter that the parent doesn't claim the dependency deduction. The key factor is that the parent *could have* done so.

Act Sec. 103(a), relating to increase in personal exemptions, amends Sec. 151(f). Act Sec. 103(b), relating to repeal of additional exemptions for taxpayers age 65 or over or blind, amends Sec. 151 by striking out (c) and (d) and redesignating (e) and (f) as (c) and (d), respectively. Act Sec. 103 is effective for tax years beginning after 12-31-86.

[¶104] **Tax Return Filing Levels.** The new law makes conforming changes to Sec. 6012 (which defines those taxpayers required to file a return) to accommodate the personal exemptions, new standard deductions, and additional standard deduction that may be claimed by the elderly. In general, a taxpayer must file a return only if his gross income equals or exceeds the following levels:

Taxpayer Class	*1987 Gross Income Level	*1988 Gross Income Level
Marrieds filing jointly, both under age 65	$ 7,560	$ 8,900
Marrieds filing jointly, one spouse age 65 or over	$ 9,400	$ 9,500
Marrieds filing jointly, both age 65 or over	$10,000	$10,100
Surviving spouse under age 65	$ 5,660	$ 6,950
Surviving spouse age 65 or over	$ 7,500	$ 7,550
Head of household under age 65	$ 4,440	$ 6,350
Head of household age 65 or over	$ 7,050	$ 7,100
Single person under age 65	$ 4,440	$ 4,950
Single person age 65 or over	$ 5,650	$ 5,700
Married filing separate return	$ 1,900	$ 1,950
Married whose spouse may be claimed as a dependent by another taxpayer	$ 1,900	$ 1,950

*The figures shown represent the sum of the personal exemption, the regular standard deduction, and the additional standard deduction for taxpayers age 65 or over.

Other rules. In general, a taxpayer must file an income tax return if his or her gross income equals or exceeds the exemption amount [see ¶103] if:

(1) The taxpayer may be claimed as a dependent by another taxpayer and has unearned income in excess of $500 or has total gross income in excess of the standard deduction.

(2) The taxpayer cannot claim any standard deduction [see ¶102].

The new law says that, for tax-filing purposes, an individual who may be claimed as a dependent by another has an exemption equal to zero [Sec. 6012(a)(1)(D)(ii), as amended by Act Sec. 104]. But the Conference Report is kindlier. It indicates that if a child has no earned income, he must file only if his unearned income exceeds $500. An estate of an individual under chapter 7 or 11 of the United States Code (relating to bankruptcy) must file a return if its gross income for tax year 1987 is not less than $3,780 ($4,450 for tax year 1988).

The new law makes other housekeeping changes to Sec. 6012 and numerous other Code Sections.

Act Sec. 104 amends the following Code Sections: Secs. 21, 32, 108, 129, 152, 172, 402, 441, 443, 541, 613A, 641, 667, 861, 862, 904, 1398, 2032A, 3402, 6012, 6013, 6014, 6212, and 6504. Act Sec. 104 is effective for tax years beginning after 12-31-86.

[¶105] Inflation Indexing of Rate Structures, Standard Deductions, and Exemptions. The new rate structures will be adjusted for inflation annually beginning with tax year 1989. Any inflation adjustments will apply to the breakpoint between the 15% and 28% brackets and to the income levels at which the two 5% surtaxes are applied. The standard deduction amounts also will be adjusted for inflation beginning with tax year 1989. The inflation adjustment for 1989 is equal to the percentage increase in the Consumer Price Index (CPI) for 1988 over the CPI for 1987. The personal exemption will be indexed beginning with tax year 1990. The adjustment for 1990 is equal to the percentage increase in the CPI for 1989 over the CPI for 1988. The 12-month period for measuring the CPI will end August 31 of each calendar year. In general, inflation adjustments that are not a multiple of $50 will be rounded down to the next lowest multiple of $50. For marrieds filing separately, inflation adjustments (to the rate structure and personal exemption) that are not a multiple of $25 will be rounded down to the next lowest multiple of $25.

Act Sec. 101(a), amends Sec. 1(f) (indexing of rate structure), Act Sec. 102(a) amends Sec. 63(c)(4) (indexing of standard deductions), and Act Sec. 103(a) amends Sec. 151(d)(3) (indexing of exemptions). Effective dates are shown above.

[¶106] Repeal of Two-Earner Deduction. Effective for tax years beginning on or after 1987, the new law repeals the special deduction granted to families when both spouses work. Under prior law, this deduction was equal to 10% of the lesser of (1) $30,000, or (2) the qualified earned income of the lower-earning spouse.

Act Sec. 131 repeals Sec. 222 (relating to two-earner deduction), effective for tax years beginning after 12-31-86.

[¶107] Repeal of Income Averaging. The new law repeals the general income averaging break for all taxpayers, effective for tax years beginning on or after 1-1-87.

Act Sec. 141 repeals Part I of Subchapter Q of the Internal Revenue Code, and makes technical amendments to Secs. 3, 5, and 6511, effective as shown above.

[¶108] Earned Income Credit Increased. The new law grants extra relief to taxpayers eligible for the earned income credit. Effective for the 1987 tax year, the earned income credit is equal to 14% of the first $5,714 of earned income for a maximum credit of $800. In addition, there's an increase in the income level at which the credit is phased down. For tax year 1987, the credit is phased down by 10% of AGI (or earned income, if greater) in excess of $6,500. There is no credit once AGI or earned income hits $14,500. For tax year 1988, the 10% phase-down begins when AGI or earned income exceeds $9,000 and ends when AGI or earned income equals $17,000.

Under prior law, the earned income credit was equal to 11% of the first $5,000 of earned income. The credit was reduced by 12 ⅔ % of AGI or earned income in excess of $6,500, and there was no credit once income exceeded $11,000.

Another change. The new law provides for automatic, CPI-based inflation adjustments to the earned-income dollar levels. For 1987, the basic $5,714 earned-income figure and the $6,500 phase-down level will be indexed for inflation between 8-31-84 and 8-31-86. The $9,000 phase-down level will be indexed beginning with the 1988 tax year. The adjustments will be rounded as follows: an adjustment that is not a multiple of $10 will be rounded to the nearest multiple of $10; or if the increase is a multiple of $5, it will be increased to the next highest multiple of $10.

Taxpayers eligible for the credit. As under prior law, the following taxpayers are eligible for the earned income credit:

• Marrieds filing jointly who are entitled to a dependency exemption for a child or stepchild.

• Surviving spouses or unmarried individuals who maintain a household for a dependent child or stepchild.

• A custodial parent, even if that parent agrees to let the non-custodial parent claim a dependency exemption for the child.

NOTE: Employers must notify employees whose wages are not subject to income tax withholding that they may be eligible for the refundable earned income credit. This rule does not apply if the employee is exempt from withholding under IRC Sec. 3402(h).

Act Sec. 111 amends Sec. 32(a), (b) and (f) and adds Sec. 32(i). It also makes technical and conforming changes to Sec. 3507, relating to advance payment of the earned income credit. Act Sec. 111 is effective for tax years beginning after 12-31-86.

[¶109] **Unemployment Compensation Fully Taxed.** The new law repeals the partial exclusion for unemployment benefits. All benefits received after 12-31-86 are included in taxable income.

Act Sec. 121 amends Sec. 85, relating to unemployment compensation, effective for amounts received after 12-31-86, in tax years ending after such date.

[¶110] **Limitations on Tax-Free Scholarships.** The new law overhauls the rules authorizing tax-free treatment for individuals who receive scholarships and fellowship grants from colleges, universities, and other educational institutions.

Scholarships and grants. Prior law excluded from taxable income scholarships and fellowship grants received by degree candidates from schools for their tuition, matriculation, and other fees and regular living expenses, like room and board. The exclusion also applied to allowances received to cover their expenses for travel, research, clerical help, or equipment.

Under the new law, the exclusion is limited to amounts used by degree candidates for "qualified tuition and related expenses" in accordance with the conditions of the grant or scholarship. Qualified expenses are limited to (1) tuition and fees for enrollment or attendance by a student enrolled in a school described in Sec. 170(b)(1)(A)-(ii), and (2) fees, books, supplies and equipment required for the course of study. There is no exclusion for grant or scholarship dollars used for room and board. The Committee Reports say that the exclusion applies only if the terms of the grant or scholarship do not earmark or designate its use for nonqualified expenses (e.g. room and board) and do not specify that the funds cannot be used for tuition or course-related expenses.

The Committee Reports clarify that the exclusion applies to individuals other than students attending a primary or secondary school or pursuing a degree at a university or college. These individuals are deemed "degree candidates," and thus are eligible for the exclusion, if they are granted a scholarship for full-or part-time study at an educational institution described in Sec. 170(b)(1)(a)(ii) that (1) provides an educational program acceptable for full credit toward a bachelor's or higher degree, or offers a training program leading to

¶110

gainful employment in a recognized occupation, (2) is authorized by Federal or State Law to provide such a program, and (3) is accredited by a nationally recognized accreditation agency.

Payments for teaching or research. As a general rule, compensation for teaching or research is fully taxable. But prior law excluded that part of scholarship or fellowship grants received as payment for teaching, research, or other part-time services, as long as all degree candidates were required to perform such duties.

The new law ends this special exclusion. Amounts received for teaching or research are taxable in full whether the compensation takes the form of a paycheck or a tuition reduction.

Special rule: The new law excludes from gross income amounts received as a "qualified tuition reduction." This is the amount of a tuition reduction received by an employee of an educational institution described in Sec. 170(b)(1)(A)(ii). The reduction in tuition must be for education (below the graduate level) at the employer's or other eligible institution. The tuition reduction can be for the employee or for a person treated as an employee under Sec. 132(f) (e.g., the employee's child). The exclusion applies to an employee who is an officer, owner, or highly compensated owner of the institution only if the tuition reduction is available to employees on a nondiscriminatory basis.

Other escape hatches remain open. The new rules for scholarships and fellowships do not affect the exclusion under Sec. 127 for employer-provided educational assistance to an employee [¶1162]. And taxpayers can continue to claim deductions for qualified work-related education expenses.

> **NOTE:** Under the new law, unreimbursed work-related educational expenses are deductible as miscellaneous itemized expenses subject to a new 2% floor. See ¶128.

Effective date and transition rule: The new law changes apply to tax years beginning after 12-31-86, but only for scholarships and fellowships granted after 8-16-86. The Committee Reports indicate that for scholarships and fellowships granted after 8-16-86 and before 1-1-87, prior law's Sec. 117 exclusion applies to amounts that are received prior to 1-1-87, and are attributable to expenses incurred prior to 1-1-87.

The Committee Reports also indicate that noncompensatory scholarships or grants newly includable in gross income are considered earned income for purposes of the special standard deduction rule that applies to a taxpayer who may be claimed as a dependent by another taxpayer [see ¶102].

Act Sec. 123(a) amends Sec. 117, relating to scholarships. Act Sec. 123(b) amends Sec. 74(a), relating to prizes and awards, Sec. 1441(b), relating to withholding of tax on nonresident aliens, Sec. 7871(a)(6), relating to Indian tribal governments treated as States for certain purposes, and the table of sections for part III of subchapter B of chapter 1. Act Sec. 123 is effective as shown above.

[¶111] Charitable and Employee Achievement Award Exclusions Cut Back. The new law modifies the exclusion for awards in recognition of charitable and like achievements. The exclusion applies only if the recipient designates that the prize is to be transferred by the payor to a governmental unit or to certain charitable, educational, religious, etc., organizations. Also, the new law authorizes an exclusion for "employee achievement awards." These are awards for length of service or safety achievement. There is an exclusion, subject to certain limitations, of up to $400 of cost ($1,600 if made under a qualified plan where the average cost does not exceed $400). Let's take a closer look at these provisions, which take effect starting with the 1987 tax year.

Limitation on exclusion for prizes and awards. The new law limits the exclusion from taxable income for prizes and awards made primarily in recognition of religious, charitable, scientific, educational, artistic, literary, or civic achievements. Prior law allowed the exclusion only if the winner satisfied two requirements. First, the recipient was selected without action on his part—that is, he did not apply for the prize or award by, say, entering a contest. Second, he is not required, as a condition of receipt, to render substantial future services.

The new law retains the two requirements and adds a third one that allows the exclusion only if the winner assigns the award to charity. Specifically, the recipient must "designate" that the prize or award is to be transferred by the payor to a governmental unit or tax-exempt charitable, educational, religious, etc., organization, contributions to which are deductible under Sec. 170(c)(1) or (2), respectively.

> **HOW TO DO IT:** The Committee Reports set an exclusion-qualification deadline that bars the winner's use of the award proceeds before they are assigned to charity. To pass muster, the winner's designation and the award-paying organization's fulfillment of that designation must occur before any impermissible use by the winner of the money or other property awarded. Otherwise, no exclusion and the award is taxable.

For a cash award, the designation/fulfillment has to occur before the winner spends, deposits, or otherwise invests the funds. Other impermissible uses include use of the property with the winner's permission or by someone associated with the winner, such as a family member.

Employee achievement awards. The new law provides an exclusion for employees who receive achievement awards that satisfy certain requirements. These employees can exclude such awards from their gross income, within separate limits of $400 and $1,600. Besides limits on amounts that employees can exclude, there are limits on amounts that employers can deduct.

Employee achievement award defined. It is an item of tangible personal property that an employer transfers to an employee for length-of-service achievement or for safety achievement. The property must be awarded as part of a meaningful presentation and under conditions and circumstances that do not create a significant likelihood of the payment of disguised compensation.

The Committee Reports provide examples of disguised compensation situations. They include employee awards made at the time of annual salary adjustments, as a substitute for a prior program of awarding cash bonuses or in a way that discriminates in favor of highly paid employees.

> **NOTE:** Only tangible personal property qualifies. There is no exclusion for awards of cash, gift certificates, or equivalent items.

Length-of-service awards. An employee may not exclude an award when it is received during his or her first five years of employment for the employer making the award or when he or she has previously received an award during that year or any of the preceeding four years, unless the previous award qualifies under the Sec. 132(e) exclusion for de minimis fringe benefits.

Safety-achievement awards. There is no exclusion for an award made to an employee not in the category of eligible employees or if, during the year, the employer previously made safety awards to more than 10% of the eligible employees.

Which employees are eligible and which ones ineligible? All are eligible, except for managers, administrators, clerical workers, and other professional employees.

Qualified plan award. It is defined as an employee achievement award provided under a qualified award plan—that is, an established written plan or program of the taxpayer that does not discriminate in favor of highly compensated employees, within the meaning of Sec. 414(q), as to eligibility or benefits.

Deduction limitations on employers. The new law bars a deduction for an employee-achievement award except to the extent its cost does not exceed the limitation imposed by Sec. 274(j). As a general rule, there is a $400 limit on the deduction by an employer for all safety and length-of-service awards (other than qualified plan awards) provided to the same employee during the tax year. There is, however, a ceiling of $1,600 on the deduction for all qualified plan awards, whether for safety or length of service, when an employer makes one or more QPAs to the same employee during the tax year.

NOTE: There is no parlaying of the separate $400/$1,600 limits. In addition to these separate limits, the $1,600 limit applies in the aggregate when an employee receives one or more QPAs during the year and also one or more awards that are not QPAs. That means no adding together of the $400 and $1,600 limits to allow deductions exceeding an aggregate of $1,600 for awards to the same employee in a tax year. For a partnership, the $400 and $1,600 limits apply to the partnership, as well as to each partner.

There is an average cost ceiling on awards. QPA treatment is unavailable if the average cost per recipient of all achievement awards made under all qualified award plans of the employer during the tax year exceeds $400. For purposes of the average cost calculation, QPAs of nominal value are not included.

When the cost of a QPA exceeds $1,600, its entire cost is added into the total of award costs under the plan. It is immaterial that the allowable deduction for the cost is only $1,600 or less.

Limitations on amounts excludable by employees. The fair market value of an achievement award is fully excludable from gross income by the employee when the cost of the award is fully deductible by the employer under the $400/$1,600 limits.

NOTE: The deduction limit amount for a tax-exempt employer is the amount that would be deductible if the employer were not tax exempt.

Example: International Widgets awards a crystal bowl as a length-of-service award (other than a QPA) to Jane Brown. For the year in question, International makes no other safety or length-of-service award to Jane; nor did it make a length-of-service award to her during the previous four years. The bowl cost International $375; its FMV is $415. The $415 is excludable from Brown's income.

Excess deduction awards. An employee cannot exclude the entire FMV of an achievement award when its cost exceeds the amount allowable as a deduction by an employer because of the $400/$1,600 limits. There is, however, a cap on how much an employee has to include in income.

The includable amount is the *greater* of (1) the portion of the cost to the employer that is not allowable as an employer deduction, but not an amount in excess of the award's FMV, *or* (2) the excess of the award's FMV over the maximum allowable employer deduction. An employee can exclude the remaining portion of the award's FMV.

Example: Consolidated Enterprises pays $500 for a watch (not a QPA) that goes as a safety award to John Green, an eligible employee. For the year in question, Consolidated made no achievement awards to Green and did not previously make safety awards to more than 10% of the eligible employees. Consolidated's deduction is limited to $400. Green must include as income the greater of (1) $100, which is the difference between the watch's cost ($500) and Consolidated's $400 deduction limit, or (2) the excess of the watch's FMV over Consolidated's $400 deduction. With an assumed FMV of $475, Green includes $100. With a FMV of $600, he includes $200.

An employee award's FMV, whether or not it comes under the definition of an achievement award, is includable in an employee's income under Sec. 61 and is not shielded from taxes by the exclusions under Sec. 74 for prizes and awards or under Sec. 102 for gifts, except to the extent the exclusions under Sec. 74(c) for achievement awards or under Sec. 132(e) for de minimis fringes apply. Consequently, the FMV of an employee award (or any part of it) not excludable from income must be included by an employer on the employee's W-2.

> **NOTE:** Any excludable award is excludable from wages for employment tax purposes and from the Social Security benefit base.

De minimis fringe benefits. The new law does not modify the Sec. 132(e) exclusion for de minimis fringes. Consequently, there is an income exclusion for an employee award when its FMV, after considering the frequency with which the employer provides similar benefits to its employees, is so small it is unreasonable or administratively impractical to require the employer to account for the award.

The Committee Reports explain when it is appropriate to disregard employee awards excludable under Sec. 132(e) in determining how frequently an employee receives a length-of-service award or how many employees receive safety awards in the same tax year. Ordinarily, they are disregarded. But they may need to be considered when an employer's practice of giving its employees length-of-service or safety awards that qualify under Secs. 74 and 274 affects the question whether other items given to these employees, particularly if given as length-of-service or safety awards, qualify as Sec. 132(e) de minimis fringes.

When is it unreasonable or administratively impractical to account for a particular item? An employer may have to account when a program exists under which it regularly accounts for other like items and complies with the statutory reporting requirements.

> **NOTE:** The IRS may refuse to treat fringes as de minimis when an employee receives items that have the maximum FMV, consistent with the exclusions for achievement awards and de minimis fringes. The Committee Reports say the IRS should question an exclusion when an employer provides several employee awards and other items, supposedly shielded by Sec. 132(e), to the same employees in the same year.

Traditional retirement gifts ordinarily treated as de minimis fringes. The Committee Reports clarify the applicability of the Sec. 132(e) exclusion for de minimis fringes to traditional retirement gifts received by an employee who retires after long service when the Sec. 74 exclusion for length-of-service award is inapplicable because the employee received such an award within the previous four years. In determining whether such a retirement gift passes muster as a de minimis fringe, the IRS should consider how long the employee worked for the employer.

> **Example:** Susan White receives a gold watch on retirement after 25 years of employment. Her watch can qualify as a de minimis fringe. It doesn't matter that other watches she previously received did not so qualify.

Act Sec. 122(a)(1) amends Sec. 74, relating to prizes and awards. Act Sec. 122(a)(2) makes conforming amendments to Secs. 4941 and 4945. Act. Sec. 122(b) adds new subsection (c) to Sec. 102, relating to gifts and inheritances. Act Sec. 122(d) amends Sec. 274, relating to certain entertainment, etc., expenses, and adds new Sec. 274(j). Act. Sec. 122(e), relating to treatment for purposes of employment taxes, amends Secs. 3121(a)(20), 3231(e)(5), 3306(b)(16), 3401(a)(20) and Sec. 209(s) of the Social Security Act. Act Sec. 122 is effective for prizes and awards granted after 12-31-86.

[¶112] State and Local Sales Taxes Aren't Deductible. Effective for tax years beginning on or after 1-1-87, the deduction for state and local sales taxes is repealed. Such taxes incurred in connection with the acquisition or disposition of business or investment property are added to basis or reduce the amount realized.

Act Sec. 134 amends Sec. 164, relating to deduction of taxes, effective as shown above.

[¶113] Nondeductible Medical Expense Floor Increased. The new law increases the nondeductible floor beneath medical expenses from 5% to 7.5% of adjusted gross income, starting with the 1987 tax year.

Accommodating personal residence in needs of handicapped. The Committee Reports say the full cost of certain home-related capital expenditures incurred by a physically handicapped individual qualifies as a medical expense (subject to the 7.5% floor). Qualifying costs include expenditures for: (1) constructing entrance or exit ramps to the residence; (2) widening doorways at entrances or exits to the residence; (3) widening or otherwise modifying hallways and interior doorways to accommodate wheelchairs; (4) railings, support bars, or other modifications to bathrooms to accommodate handicapped individuals; (5) lowering of or other modifications to kitchen cabinets and equipment to accommodate access by handicapped individuals; and (6) adjustment of electrical outlets and fixtures.

> **NOTE:** As a general rule, the cost of a medically related home improvement counts as a medical deduction only to the extent the cost

exceeds the increase in the home's value as a result of the improvement. Under the new law, the increase in the home's value as a result of qualifying improvements is deemed to be zero.

Act Sec. 133 amends Sec. 213(a), relating to medical expenses, effective for tax years beginning after 12-31-86.

[¶114] **Deduction for Adoption Expenses Repealed.** The new law repeals the itemized deduction of up to $1,500 for adoption expenses for children with special needs and replaces it with an expansion of the Adoption Assistance Program under Title IV-E of the Social Security Act [see ¶1711].

Act Sec. 135(a) repeals Sec. 222, relating to adoption expenses. Act Sec. 135(b) redesignates Sec. 223 as Sec. 220 and amends the table of sections for part VII of subchapter B of chapter 1. Act Sec. 135 is effective for tax years beginning on or after 1-1-87.

[¶115] **Housing Allowances for Ministers and Military Personnel.** The new law provides that the receipt of a tax-free parsonage housing allowance or an off-base military housing allowance does not cause the loss of deductions for home-mortgage interest and property taxes.

Act Sec. 144 adds new Sec. 265(6) effective for tax years before, on, or after 12-31-86.

[¶116] **Major Changes for Moving Expense Deduction.** Effective for the 1987 tax year, reimbursed and unreimbursed moving expenses migrate "below the line"—that is, they are deductible from AGI to arrive at taxable income. The changes apply to self-employeds as well as employees. Under current law, all eligible moving expenses—reimbursed and unreimbursed—are deducted above the line.

The new itemized deduction for moving expenses is *not* subject to a 2%-of-AGI floor [¶128]. A taxpayer who claims the standard deduction and does not itemize forfeits the deduction for moving expenses.

Act Sec. 132(c) amends Sec. 62 effective for tax years beginning after 12-31-86.

[¶117] **Major Crackdown on T&E Expenses.** The new law makes sweeping changes in the tax rules for business travel and entertainment expenses, effective for the 1987 tax year.

- A business meal is deductible only if it is "directly related" or "associated with" the active conduct of a taxpayer's trade or business. In other words, you must talk business at the table or have the meal before or after a substantial and bona fide business discussion. Under prior law, a "quiet business meal"—one held in an atmosphere conducive to business—was deductible even though business was not actually discussed [¶118].

• As a general rule, the deduction for business meals and business entertainment is limited to 80% of cost. The new rule also applies to meals consumed while away from home overnight on business [¶119].

• There are new limits on business-entertainment deductions for "skyboxes" at sports events [¶120].

• Deductions for tickets to entertainment events are generally limited to 80% of face value [¶121].

• Deductions for each day of business travel by luxury water transport are limited to twice the highest domestic federal per-diem reimbursement rate [¶122].

• Unreimbursed employee expenses for business travel, transportation, and entertainment become miscellaneous itemized deductions subject to a 2%-of-AGI "floor" [¶128].

Other travel crackdowns. Expenses for travel as a form of education [¶123] and certain types of charitable travel [¶124] are nondeductible. Finally, the new law eliminates deductions for attending investment-related seminars and conventions [¶125].

[¶118] **No More Deductions for Quiet Business Meals.** Under prior law, a taxpayer could deduct the cost of a meal with a business associate or client as long as the meal took place in an atmosphere conducive to business discussions. There was no requirement that business be discussed at the table. Effective for tax years beginning after 12-31-86, the new law eliminates the deduction for such "quiet business meals." Under the new law, a business meal, like business entertainment, is deductible (subject to the new 80% rule) only if it is "directly related to" or "associated with" the active conduct of a taxpayer's trade or business.

Directly related. In general, a business meal or business entertainment is "directly related" if four conditions are met:

• The taxpayer has more than a general expectation of deriving income, or a specific business benefit, from the meal or entertainment. However, the taxpayer is not required to show that income or a specific business benefit actually resulted.

• The taxpayer did in fact engage in business discussions during the meal or entertainment (or if he didn't, it was for reasons beyond his control).

• The principal nature of the expense was the active conduct of the taxpayer's trade or business.

- The meal or entertainment expense was for the taxpayer, his business guest or guests, and their spouses.

Example (1): Jack Arnold's company supplies computer products to Big Manufacturing Company. In 1987, Arnold has lunch with Big's head of purchasing as a way of keeping in touch with an important source of business. Result: The cost of the meal is not deductible (it would have been under the "quiet business meal" rule).

Example (2): Same facts as before, except that Arnold makes the lunch appointment to make a sales pitch about a new line of computer equipment. Result: The cost of the meal is deductible, subject to the new 80% rule [¶119].

Food and beverages consumed by a taxpayer while on travel status is considered a business meal that is directly related to the taxpayer's trade or business [see ¶119].

Associated with. A meal or entertainment is deductible if it directly precedes or follows a substantial and bona fide business (or practice) related discussion. The business discussion (or negotiation, transaction, conference, etc.) must be substantial in relation to the meal or entertainment. If the taxpayer's business guest is from out of town, the meal or entertainment can take place the day before or after the business discussion.

Additional requirements. The cost of a business meal, like the cost of business entertainment, is not deductible to the extent it is "lavish and extravagant" under the circumstances. And the cost of beverages and food is deductible as a business meal only if the taxpayer (or his representative) is present at the meal. The representative can be the taxpayer's employee, or an independent contractor acting on his behalf.

For example, the cost of food and beverages is not deductible as a business meal if one of the parties to a contract negotiation buys dinner for the other parties but doesn't attend the meal. It makes no difference that the other parties discuss business while they break bread.

The Committee Reports say the presence requirement is met if the taxpayer's independent contractor, such as an attorney or accountant, is present at the meal. The independent contractor must be someone who renders significant services on behalf of the taxpayer (other than attending meals on the taxpayer's behalf or providing services relating to the meal) and attends the meal to perform those services.

Example: Recreational Co. retains Attorney Adams to represent it in acquiring Accessories, Ltd. Adams and representatives of Accessories attend a dinner to discuss the acquisition and Recreational foots the bill. Result: Recreational can deduct the cost of the bill (subject to the 80% rule, see ¶119).

Suppose neither the taxpayer nor his representative attends the meal. Is the entire cost nondeductible? No. The taxpayer can claim the expense as a business gift. However, the deduction is limited to $25 per recipient per year. There's no requirement that a taxpayer be present at the time a business gift is made.

Act Sec. 142(a) amends Sec. 274(e), adds new Sec. 274(k), and makes other technical and conforming amendments to Sec. 274, effective for tax years beginning after 12-31-86.

[¶119] **New 80% Rule for Business Meals and Entertainment.** Effective for the 1987 tax year, the deduction for otherwise allowable business meals and business entertainment is limited to 80% of cost. The new rule applies also to (1) meals while away from home overnight on business, and (2) meals provided by employers to employees (but see exceptions, below). Meals consumed during a job-related move are affected as well.

Besides meals and entertainment, expenses subject to the 80% rule include taxes and tips related to the meal or entertainment and other related expenses (e.g., nightclub cover charges, room rental for cocktail party, and parking at the theater or sports arena). Transportation to and from the business meal or entertainment is not subject to the 80% rule.

Example: Tom Burke pays a $10 cab fare to meet his client for dinner at Sam's Place. The bill comes to $100 plus $6 tax and a $15 tip. Burke's deduction is $106.80. That's 80% of $121, plus the $10 cab fare.

Meals while on travel status. A taxpayer may deduct 80% of the cost of meals consumed while he is away from home overnight on business. Being on travel status automatically qualifies meals as being directly related to the taxpayer's trade or business, *but only if the taxpayer eats alone,* or eats with non-business-connected persons and claims a deduction for his meal only. Apparently, if a taxpayer on travel status has a meal with a business client or associate, he can deduct 80% of the cost only if the meal is directly related to or associated with his trade or business.

Example: Ted Smith, a Washington-based lawyer, flies to Los Angeles on business. If he eats lunch alone, 80% of the cost is deductible. But suppose he invites a client or business associate to lunch as a goodwill gesture and picks up the tab. Apparent result: A zero deduction for the cost of Smith's meal and his client's meal. Reason: The meal was not directly related to or associated with his trade or business.

OBSERVATION: From the tax viewpoint, it's preferable to eat alone while you're on travel status. This way, you don't have to cope with the new, tough deduction standards that apply to business meals.

Reimbursed expenses. If a taxpayer is reimbursed for the cost of business meals or entertainment (and makes an adequate accounting), the 80% rule applies to the one who makes the reimbursement, not the taxpayer.

> **Example:** During tax year 1987, Bill Pace, an executive with ABC Corp., spends $2,000 on business-related meals and entertainment. Bill makes a complete accounting of his expenses to ABC and is reimbursed in full. Result: ABC may deduct $1,600 of the reimbursement. Bill does not have to report the expense or the reimbursement on his tax return [see ¶128].

Per-diem arrangements. An employer may reimburse employees for away-from-home travel at a fixed per-diem rate. If the reimbursement does not exceed the government-approved maximum, the expenses are deemed accounted for if the employee (1) keeps a record of the time, place, and business purpose of his expenses, and (2) gives the same information to the employer. The employee is not required to keep track of actual expenses for travel, lodging, or meals. (Note: More than 10% owners must keep complete records, including the amount of each expense.)

In general, an employer may deduct only 80% of its reimbursement for away-from-home meals. But if the employee isn't required to keep track of meal expenses, how will the employer know what part of the per diem is subject to the 80% rule?

Probable result: As long as the per diem doesn't exceed the government maximum (currently $75), the employer will continue to deduct 100% of its reimbursement. An analogy can be made to the new rules for business travel by luxury water transport [¶122]. The 80% rule is not applied if the cost of on-board meals is not separately stated or clearly identifiable. The same rule should hold true for per-diem reimbursement arrangements.

Interplay of 80% rule and other limitations. In general, the 80% rule is imposed *after* application of limits imposed by Secs. 162 and 274 (e.g., disallowance of lavish and extravagant expenses), but *before* application of the new 2% floor for "second tier" miscellaneous itemized deductions [¶128].

> **Example:** During tax year 1987, Bob Smith, an employee, incurs $1,000 of business entertainment expenses for which he is not reimbursed. Of the total $1,000 expense, $200 is deemed lavish and extravagant. Smith's AGI is $50,000 and he has $500 of other "second tier" miscellaneous itemized deductions. Here's how he figures his deduction:
>
> Total business entertainment expense..................$1,000
> Less amount deemed lavish and extravagant..........(200)
>
>   800
> Less 20% reduction ....(160)
>
>   640

Plus other "second tier" miscellaneous
itemized deductions   500

                        1,140
Less 2% of adjusted gross income .... (1,000)
Deductible amount .... $ 140

A special rule applies for business travel by luxury water transport [see ¶122]. If the cost of meals and entertainment is separately stated, then the 80% rule is applied *before* computation of the new deduction limit on luxury water transport expenses.

Exceptions to 80% rule. Expenses that fall in the following categories are not subject to the 80% rule and are deductible in full:

- Amounts treated as compensation: The full value of the benefit must be treated as compensation to the recipients, whether or not they are employees.
- De minimis fringe benefits: These include items excludable under Sec. 132 as a subsidized eating facility or a de minimis fringe (e.g., holiday gifts of turkeys, hams, etc.).
- Employer-provided recreation: This consists of amounts paid for recreational, social, or similar activities or employee events (e.g., holiday parties or summer outings).
- Items made available to the public as samples or promotional material.
- Meals and entertainment sold to customers: The taxpayer must sell the item in a bona fide transaction for adequate and full consideration. For example, a restaurant can deduct the full cost of the meals it supplies to patrons.
- Sports tickets: Expenses to a sports event, to the extent otherwise allowable as a business deduction, are deductible in full if three conditions are met: (1) the event's primary purpose is to benefit a Sec. 501(c)(3) charity, (2) the entire net proceeds must go to the charity, and (3) the event uses volunteers to perform substantially all the event's work.

This exception covers the entire cost of a ticket package that includes seating at the event and related services, such as parking, use of entertainment areas, contestant positions, and meals furnished at and as part of the event. What's more, the special break applies to a charity golf outing even if the tournament offers prizes to participating golfers or uses paid concessionaires or security personnel.

SCHOOL GAMES HIT: Tickets to high school or college football or basketball games or other similar scholastic events are *not* covered by the exception. According to the Committee Reports, these games generally flunk the volunteers test—when the institutions (or parties acting on their behalf) pay individuals to perform such services as coaching or recruiting.

- Qualifying banquet meetings during 1987 and 1988. There is a full deduction during 1987 and 1988 for the cost of a meal that is provided as an integral part of a qualified banquet meeting, provided charges for the meal are not separately stated.

The two-year reprieve ends at the close of 1988. Starting 1-1-89, qualified banquet meeting meals are subject to the 20% disallowance rule in the same way as other meals.

A qualified banquet meeting is a convention, seminar, annual meeting, or similar business program that includes the meal. For the exception to apply, the banquet meeting must pass a three-step test: First, more than 50% of the participants at the meeting are away from home—that is, their travel expenses are deductible under the "overnight" rule; second, at least 40 persons attend the banquet meeting; and third, the meal is part of the banquet meeting and includes a speaker.

Act Sec. 142(b), relating to additional restrictions on expenses for meals, travel, and entertainment, adds new Sec. 274(n), effective for tax years beginning after 12-31-86.

[¶120] Skybox Rentals. A business may entertain its clients and customers by letting them use its leased skybox at a sports arena. Under prior law, the cost of the skybox was deductible if the entertainment was "directly related to" or "associated with" the taxpayer's business. Reason: Rented skyboxes were not considered to be nondeductible entertainment facilities.

The new law disallows part of the deduction for skyboxes that are rented for more than one event. The disallowance is phased in over a period of three years.

What is a skybox? A skybox is defined in the Committee Reports as a private luxury box or other facility at a sports arena that is separate from other seating and is available at a higher price (counting rental costs and charges for food and beverages) than other seating. The new rules come into play only if a skybox is rented at a sports arena for more than one event. For example, a skybox rental for two football games in the same stadium is covered by the new rules. Also covered: rentals by a taxpayer (or a related party) of different skyboxes in the same stadium, or reciprocal arrangements by two or more taxpayers to share skyboxes.

How the disallowance rule works. As under prior law, the taxpayer must use the skybox for "directly related" or "associated with" entertainment. If this condition is satisfied, the taxpayer's deduction is limited to the sum of the face value of the nonluxury box seat tickets for the seats in the leased skybox. All the seats in the skybox are counted, even though the box is not fully occupied during the event. However, the taxpayer may not deduct the excess cost of the skybox. The rule is phased in as follows: one-third of the excess cost is disallowed in 1987, and two-thirds is disallowed in 1988. The entire excess cost is disallowed for 1989 and later years.

The taxpayer may also deduct stated charges for food and beverages under the general rules for business entertainment.

> **REMINDER:** The deduction for skybox seats, food, and beverages is limited to 80% of cost [¶119].

> **Example:** In 1987, XYZ Corp. pays $6,000 to rent a 10-seat skybox at City Stadium for three football games. Nonluxury box seats at each event range in cost from $25 to $35 a seat. In March, an XYZ representative and five clients of XYZ use the skybox for the first game. The entertainment follows a bona-fide business discussion (e.g., merger talks), and XYZ incurs an $85 expense for food and beverages during the game. Although the method of allocation is yet to be determined, XYZ Corp. will likely compute its deduction for the first sports event as follows:

> (1) Food and beverages .... $ 85
> (2) Deduction for seats ($35 × 10 seats)   350
> (3) Excess cost of skybox
> $6,000/3 events $2,000
>   Cost of seats .... (350)
>
>   Excess cost 1,650
>   33.33% disallowance
>   for 1987 .... (550)
> $1,100   1,100
> $1,535
>   ×.80
> Deduction for first event $1,228

> **WATCH THIS:** The Committee Reports say that the face-value limitation can't be circumvented through an inflated price for nonluxury box seats.

Suppose City Stadium in our example tries to boost the deduction for box rentals by reserving and charging $50 a seat for a small group of seats not significantly better than the $35 seats. Since the $50 cost is inflated, it is disregarded.

Act Sec. 142(b) adds Sec. 274(l)(2), relating to skybox rentals, generally effective for tax years beginning after 12-31-86. There is a phase-in for tax years beginning in 1987 and 1988.

〖¶121〗 Ticket Deductions Limited to Face Value. The new law limits deductions for tickets to entertainment events to 80% of their face value, which includes tax.

The face-value limitation bars payments to

- a scalper for a ticket, even if not otherwise disallowed under Sec. 162(a)(2) as an illegal payment; and
- a legitimate ticket agency for the part of the cost in excess of the ticket's face value.

Charitable fund raisers' exception. The full deduction remains available for tickets for sporting events that are considered charitable fund raisers. A qualifying event must turn over the entire net proceeds to a charity and use volunteers for substantially all the work performed in carrying out the event. [See ¶119].

> **Example:** Delphic Information Systems pays a scalper $200 for two $40 tickets to a Broadway play. The tickets are used for entertainment "associated with" the active conduct of Delphic's business [¶118]. The deduction for the tickets is limited to $64. That's the $80 face value of the tickets times 80%.

> **COMMENT:** Local law allows legitimate ticket agencies to include their fees in the price they charge for tickets to plays, ball games, and other events. Mandating like-treatment for scalpers and agencies may adversely affect the ability of agencies to sell tickets to businesses.

Act Sec. 142(b) adds new Sec. 274(l)(1), relating to entertainment tickets, effective for tax years beginning after 12-31-86.

〖¶122〗 New Deduction Limit for Luxury Water Travel. The new law generally limits deductions for business travelers who use ocean liners, cruise ships, or other forms of "luxury water transportation." There is no exemption for someone who uses luxury water transportation because of an illness or disability that rules out travel on an airplane.

The deduction per day on the boat cannot exceed twice the highest per-diem amount paid by the U.S. government to traveling employees in the coterminous U.S., disregarding any limited special exception, such as a higher limit authorized only for high-ranking executive personnel.

> **Example:** Al Lang has to make a New York-to-London business trip. To ease the strain of travel across the Atlantic, he undertakes a six-day voyage on the S.S. Luxurious. The applicable per-diem amount is $75. Therefore, the per-diem-limitation allows Lang to deduct no more than $900 ($150 a day × 6 days).

The cost of on-board meals and entertainment is subject to the new 80% rule if these charges are separately stated. And the 80% rule is applied before the new per-diem limit. However, if the cost of on-board meals and entertainment is *not* separately stated and is not clearly identifiable, then the 80% rule does not apply. The taxpayer may claim a deduction equal to twice the applicable Federal per-diem limit.

Exceptions. The new law expressly bars application of the per-diem rules to expenses that are allocable to business-related conventions, seminars, or other meetings on cruise ships. Therefore, the new law leaves unchanged the Sec. 274(h)(2) rules that allow deductions of up to $2,000 for certain cruise-ship conventions, provided the ship is a U.S. flagship and all ports of call are in the U.S. or its possessions.

In addition, the exceptions from the water-travel per-diem-limitation are the same as the exceptions from the 20% disallowance rule [¶119].

Act Sec. 142(b) adds new Sec. 274(m)(1), relating to luxury water transportation, effective for tax years beginning after 12-31-86.

[¶123] **Travel as a Form of Education Is Nondeductible.** Beginning with the 1987 tax year, the new law bars any deductions for travel expenses by teachers and others when their travel is a form of education. But the law retains deductions for travel that is necessary to engage in activities that give rise to deductible education.

Example (1): Jack Peters is a French teacher who uses a sabbatical leave from his school for a journey to France to improve his understanding of its language and culture. His travel outlays are nondeductible.

Example (2): Alexander Verne, who is employed by a school to teach courses on French literature, goes to Paris to do library research that cannot be done elsewhere, or to take courses available only at the Sorbonne. Assuming his nontravel research or courses are deductible, his travel costs are also deductible.

NOTE: Just because Verne steers clear of the educational-travel prohibition does not mean he gets to fully deduct his travel. The travel deduction is trimmed by these new limitations:

- Meals must be reduced by 20% [see ¶119]; and
- Remaining unreimbursed away-from-home travel expenses are allowable only to the extent they exceed 2% of his adjusted gross income [see ¶128].

Act Sec. 142(b) adds new Sec. 274(m)(2), relating to travel as a form of education, effective for tax years beginning after 12-31-86.

[¶124] **Charitable Deduction Denied for Certain Travel.** The new law ends deductions for "charitable" trips that are disguised vacations. Charitable deductions will now be limited for travel expenses (including meals and lodging) incurred by volunteer workers who perform services away from their homes on behalf of charities. The deductions are allowable only if there is "no significant element of personal pleasure, recreation, or vacation" in the away-from-home travel.

The travel-expense disallowance rules apply to payments made directly by the taxpayer of his or her own expenses or of an associated person, such as a member of the taxpayer's family, as well as indirectly through reimbursement by the charity. A reimbursement includes any arrangement for the taxpayer to make a payment to the charity and its payment of the taxpayer's travel outlays. To stop an end run around the disallowance rules, the new law also bars reciprocal arrangements, where two unrelated taxpayers pay each other's expenses or members of a group contribute to a fund that pays for all of their expenses.

Exception. The Committee Reports say the deduction remains available for payment by the taxpayer of expenses for third parties who are participants in the charitable activity.

> **Example:** Virginia Hickey, a Girl Scout leader, takes her scouts on a camping trip. She gets a deduction for her payment of expenses for girls who belong to the group and are unrelated to her, but not for expenses for her own children.

You don't lose a deduction for your own expenses merely because you enjoy taking care of chores for a charity.

For example, what about Hickey's own expenses? They are deductible, provided she is on duty in a genuine and substantial sense throughout the trip, even if she enjoys the trip or supervising children. But her expenses are nondeductible if she (1) only has nominal duties relating to the performance of services for the group or (2) for significant portions of the trip is not required to perform services.

No effect on other deductions. The disallowance rules do not apply to deductions for travel (other than for charitable travel) on behalf of a charitable organization. These rules, for example, don't affect the deductibility of a Sec. 162 business expense incurred by an employee of a charity.

Act Sec. 142(d) adds new Sec. 170(k), relating to charitable contributions for certain travel expenses, and makes technical and conforming amendments to Sec. 170, effective for tax years beginning after 12-31-86.

[¶125] Investment Seminars Lose Tax Luster. The new law disallows deductions for costs of attending conventions, seminars, or similar meetings for investment purposes unrelated to carrying on a trade or business. The disallowance is aimed solely at expenses that serve a Sec. 212 purpose, such as production of income, not those that serve a Sec. 162 trade-or-business purpose.

Example: International Investors holds a convention at which stock market investors pay to discuss strategies with representatives of brokerage firms and listen to presentations from executives about their companies. Result: The Sec. 212 restriction bars deductions by the investors for their expenses, but doesn't affect the deductibility under Sec. 162 of expenses by stock brokers and others at the convention for business reasons. Among the expenses disallowed are travel to the convention site, attendance fees, and meals, lodging, and local travel while attending.

Act Sec. 142(c) adds new Sec. 274(h)(7), relating to deductions for seminars, and makes technical and conforming amendments to Sec. 274(h), effective for tax years beginning after 12-31-86.

[¶126] Major Changes for Miscellaneous Itemized Deductions and Employee Business Expenses. Effective for the 1987 tax year, the rules for miscellaneous itemized deductions and employee business expenses are changed in two fundamental ways:

- The new law creates two tiers of miscellaneous itemized deductions. Those deductions placed in the first tier are not subject to a percent-of-AGI floor. Deductions in the second tier are deductible only to the extent they cumulatively exceed 2% of adjusted gross income.

- Unreimbursed employee business expenses become "second tier" itemized deductions. In other words, they are subject to the new 2%-of-AGI "floor" and are not deductible at all if the taxpayer does not itemize deductions.

Under prior law, all miscellaneous expenses were treated alike and were not subject to a percent-of-AGI floor. And employee business expenses such as unreimbursed travel and transportation costs were deducted "above the line." In other words, they were adjustments to arrive at AGI and were available whether or not the taxpayer itemized other deductions.

[¶127] 'First Tier' Miscellaneous Itemized Deductions. The following expenses are deductible in full by taxpayers who itemize:

- Impairment-related work expenses of handicapped individuals [new Sec. 67(d)].

- Federal estate tax on income in respect of a decedent [Sec. 691(c)].

- Certain adjustments when a taxpayer restores amounts held under a claim of right [Sec. 1341].

- Amortizable bond premium [Sec. 171].

- Gambling losses to the extent of gambling winnings [Sec. 165(d)].

- Deductions allowable in connection with personal property used in a short sale.

Impairment-related work expenses are expenses of a handicapped individual [as defined in Sec. 190(b)(3)] for attendant care services at the individual's place of employment, or other expenses necessary for the individual to work, which are deductible under Sec. 162.

Other expenses that are deductible without regard to a percent-of-AGI floor include certain terminated annuity payments [new Sec. 72(b)(3)] and certain costs of cooperative housing corporations [Sec. 216].

[¶128] **'Second Tier' Miscellaneous Itemized Deductions.** Expenses in this category are deductible only to the extent they cumulatively exceed 2% of adjusted gross income. There are two groups of expenses subject to the new floor:

(1) *Miscellaneous expenses allowed under prior law.* This group consists of old-law miscellaneous expenses *other than* those expenses placed in the first-tier class of miscellaneous itemized deductions. Beginning with tax year 1987, all of the following expenses are affected by the new rule:

Employee Expenses

- Dues to professional societies
- Employment-related education
- Malpractice insurance premiums
- Expenses of looking for a job, including employment agency
fee
- Cost of having resume prepared
- Office-at-home expenses
- Subscriptions to professional journals and magazines
- Work clothes and uniforms
- Union dues and fees
- 80% of unreimbursed business-entertainment expenses

Expenses for Production of Income

- Legal and accounting fees
- Custodial fees related to income-producing property
- Fees paid to an IRA custodian
- Fees paid to collect interest or dividends
- Hobby expenses up to hobby income
- Investment counsel fees
- Rental cost of safe deposit box used to store non-tax-exempt securities

Other Expenses

- Fees paid for investment counsel

- Tax counsel and assistance

- Cost of tax services, periodicals, return preparation manuals, and similar expenses related to the determination, collection, or refund of a tax

- Appraisal fees establishing a casualty loss or charitable contribution

YEAR-END ACTION: Taxpayers should consider accelerating second-tier miscellaneous expenses. For example, if an individual is seeking investment counsel or tax-oriented estate planning advice, he or she would be wise to incur the expense in 1987 rather than 1988.

(2) *Employee business expenses.* Under prior law, employee travel and transportation expenses were "above the line" deductions *whether or not* the employee was reimbursed for the expenses by his employer. Since they were adjustments to arrive at AGI, the deduction was available even if the employee did not itemize deductions. An employee's expenses for business entertainment were claimed above the line to the extent of the employer's reimbursement. Excess entertainment expenses were deducted below the line (on Schedule A, as miscellaneous itemized deductions).

Under the new law, travel and transportation expenses up to the amount of the reimbursement continue to be claimed above the line. However, expenses in excess of any reimbursement become below-the-line miscellaneous deductions and are subject to the new 2% floor. The same holds true for an employee's business-entertainment expenses. Expenses up to the amount of any reimbursement are claimed above the line; excess expenses are claimed below the line and are subject to the 2% floor.

The following chart sorts things out. It shows how an employee handles his business-connected travel, transportation, and entertainment expenses under the old law and the new law:

EMPLOYEE BUSINESS EXPENSES

TYPE OF EXPENSE	PRIOR LAW	NEW LAW
Travel & Transportation		
*(1) Employee is fully reimbursed and makes an adequate accounting.	Neither expenses nor reimbursements are reported on the return.	Same as under prior law.
*(2) Employee is fully reimbursed but does not make an adequate accounting.	Reimbursement reported as income; expenses reported above the line.	Same as under prior law, but meal expenses while on travel status subject to new 80% rule [¶119].**

TYPE OF EXPENSE	PRIOR LAW	NEW LAW
(3) Expenses exceed reimbursements.	Reimbursement reported as income; all expenses claimed above the line.	Reimbursement reported as income. Expenses up to reimbursement claimed above the line; excess expenses claimed below the line, subject to 2% floor. 80% rule applies to unreimbursed meals.
(4) No employer reimbursement.	Expenses claimed above the line.	Expenses claimed below the line, subject to 2% floor. Meal expense subject to 80% rule.
Business Entertainment		
(5) Reimbursement equals expenses and employee accounts for expenses.	Same as Item (1), above.	Same as Item (1), above.
(6) Reimbursement equals expense, but no accounting by employee	Same as Item (2), above.	Same as Item (2), above. 80% rule applies to expenses.**
(7) Expenses exceed reimbursement.	Reimb. reported as income. Expenses up to reimb. reported above the line; expenses in excess of reimb. reported below the line.	Same as under prior law, except ded'n for unreimbursed expenses limited to 80% of cost [¶119]; and expenses reported below the line are subject to the 2% floor.
(8) No employer reimbursement.	Expenses claimed below the line.	Expenses claimed below the line, but subject to 80% rule and 2% floor.

*An adequate accounting to the employer generally consists of the time, date, place, business purpose and amount of expense (or mileage, in the case of car travel). For travel and transportation expenses, accounting is simplified if reimbursement does not exceed Government-approved per-diem or per-mile rate. Expenses for business travel, transportation, and entertainment are deductible by the employee only if he or she has kept the proper records.
**If the employee does not account for expenses, employer deducts 100% of reimbursement as compensation, and employee is subject to 80% rule.

What about outside salespersons? Under current law, an outside salesperson claims all business expenses above the line—entertainment as well as travel and transportation. Outside salespersons lose this preferential treatment under the new law. In other words, starting in 1987, they are in the same boat as regular employees.

Application of the 2% floor. The 2% floor comes into play after all other deduction limitations are taken into account.

Example: During tax year 1987, Ted Smith, an employee of XYZ Corp., incurs $2,000 of unreimbursed business-entertainment expenses. Smith's adjusted gross income for 1987 is $60,000. For simplicity, we'll assume Smith does not have other second-tier miscellaneous itemized deductions. *Result:* Smith's deduction for business entertainment is computed as follows:

Total entertainment expenses	$2,000
Less statutory 20% reduction	(400)
	$1,600
Less 2% of AGI	(1,200)
Net second-tier miscellaneous itemized deduction	$ 400

Entities subject to the 2% rule. The new law gives the Treasury authority to issue regs that will apply the 2% floor to pass-through entities, including mutual funds, grantor trusts, partnerships and S corporations. Estates, nongrantor trusts, cooperatives, and REITS will not be affected, however. The Treasury is also given authority to issue reporting requirements necessary to carry out this new provision.

Estates and trusts. In general, estates or trusts compute their AGI in the same way as individuals. However, expenses paid or incurred in connection with trust or estate administration that would not have been incurred had the property not been held in a trust or estate, are deductible in arriving at adjusted gross income.

Special break for performers. Effective for tax years beginning after 1986, qualifying performing artists can report their income and expenses as if they were independent contractors. Such artists will be entitled to a new above-the-line deduction for business expenses if they meet all of these conditions:

• they are employed as performing artists by two or more employers during the tax year;

• expenses relating to the profession of being a performing artist exceeded 10% of gross income attributable to services as a performing artist; and

• adjusted gross income (before deducting expenses relating to performing) does not exceed $16,000.

Act Sec. 132(a) adds new Sec. 67(a) and (b), relating to miscellaneous itemized deductions subject to 2% floor, new Sec. 67(c), relating to disallowance of indirect deduction through pass-through entity, new Sec. 67(d), relating to impairment-related work expenses of handicapped individuals, and new Sec. 67(e), relating to determination of adjusted gross income in the case of estates and trusts. Act. Sec. 132(b) amends Sec. 62(2), relating to trade or business deductions of employees and certain expenses of performing artists, and adds new subsection (b) to Sec. 67, relating to definition of qualified performing artists. Act. Sec. 132(d) makes a clerical amendment to the table of sections for part I of subchapter B of chapter 1. Act Sec. 132 is effective for tax years beginning after 12-31-86.

[¶129] Home-Office Deduction Rules Tightened. The new law overrides two Tax Court decisions that liberalized the rules for office-at-home deductions:

The Feldman decision. As a general rule, office-at-home expenses may be deducted only if the office is used regularly and exclusively as a principal place of business or as a place to meet or deal with customers and clients. An employee who uses an office-at-home in connection with his employment qualifies for deductions only if the use of the office is for the convenience of the employer. In *Feldman* (84 TC 1), the Tax Court held that the general rule for office-at-home expenses does not apply where the office was leased by the employee to the employer.

The new law denies home-office deductions where an employee leases a portion of his or her home to the employer. Independent contractors are treated as employees and the taxpayer for whom the services are performed is treated as the employer. The new rule does not apply to deductions that would be allowed in any event (i.e., home mortgage interest [¶509] or real property taxes).

The Scott decision. Otherwise allowable office-at-home expenses are limited to the gross income derived from the business activity conducted at the home office. In Prop. Reg. Sec. 1.280A-2(i)(2)(iii), the IRS defines gross income for this purpose as gross income from the business less expenses that are not related to use of the unit itself. Such expenses consists of office supplies, postage, payments made to others, etc. In *Scott* (84 TC 683), the Tax Court rejected the IRS definition of gross income. It held that gross income is not reduced by outside expenses required for the activity.

Result: The *Scott* decision meant a taxpayer could use net losses from his home-office-business to offset other income. If a taxpayer had $2,000 of gross income from his home-office business and $2,500 of expenses related to the business (postage, office supplies, business travel), he could deduct $2,000 of his home office costs even though he had zero net income from the activity.

In essence, the new law codifies the IRS approach. Home-office deductions (other than expenses deductible in any event, such as mortgage interest and property tax) are limited to gross income reduced by all deductible expenses that are not allocable to the use of the unit itself.

SILVER LINING: The new law allows taxpayers to carry forward any deductions disallowed by the gross-income limit, subject to the continuing application of the limit. Under prior law, such carryforwards were not allowed.

Act Secs. 143(b) and (c) amend Sec. 280A(c), relating to office-at-home deductions, effective for tax years beginning after 12-31-86.

[¶130] **Hobby Losses Rule Tightened.** The new law changes the hobby losses rule so that an activity is presumed to be operated for profit, rather than as a hobby, if it is profitable in *three* out of five consecutive years (was of two out of five under prior law). There's an exception for horse breeding, training, showing, or racing. These activities are presumed to be operated for profit, rather than a hobby, if profitable in two out of seven consecutive years.

Act Sec. 143(a) amends Sec. 183(d), relating to hobby losses, effective for tax years beginning after 12-31-86.

[¶131] **No Credit for Political Contributions.** The new law repeals the credit of up to $50 ($100 on a joint return) allowed individuals for half of their contributions to political candidates and certain political campaign organizations, starting with the 1987 tax year.

Act Sec. 112(a) repeals Sec. 24, relating to contributions to candidates for public office. Act Sec. 112(b)(1) amends Sec. 527(g), relating to treatment of newsletter funds. Act Sec. 112(b)(2) amends Sec. 642(a), relating to credits against tax estates and trusts. Act Sec. 112(b)(3) amends Sec. 901(i)(3), relating to cross references. Act Sec. 112(b)(4) amends Sec. 7871(a)(6), relating to Indian tribal governments treated as States for certain purposes. Act Sec. 112(b)(5) amends the table of sections for subpart A of part IV of subchapter A of chapter 1. Act Sec. 112 is effective for tax years beginning after 12-31-86.

[The page following this is 201.]

ACCELERATED COST RECOVERY SYSTEM AND INVESTMENT TAX CREDIT

[¶201] Overview. The new law revamps the ACRS system of depreciation that had been introduced as the key to economic expansion by the 1981 Tax Reform Act. In a word, the depreciation setup is being overhauled—and the investment tax credit is being repealed—to help pay for the dramatic reduction in personal income tax rates.

> **SOMETHING OLD, SOMETHING NEW:** The new system, which is generally effective for property placed in service after 12-31-86, retains many of the original ACRS rules. The 3, 5, 10, and 15-year classes are kept and two new classes are introduced (7 and 20-year property). There's no distinction made between new and used property and salvage value continues to be disregarded. Cars and light trucks are shifted from the 3-year to the 5-year class. Office equipment moves from the 5-year class to the 7-year class. Depreciation for property in the 3, 5, and 10-year classes is speeded up from 150% to 200% declining balance. The regular investment credit is repealed for property placed in service after 1985, but the expensing deduction is boosted from $5,000 to $10,000, effective for the 1987 tax year.

The big loser under the new ACRS setup is real estate. Both residential and nonresidential real property must be depreciated using the straight line method. The recovery period is extended to 27½ years for residential property and to 31½ years for nonresidential property.

The new law continues the old ACRS system's prohibition against component depreciation. The recovery period for an addition or improvement begins on the later of the date it is placed in service or the date the original property is placed in service. The recovery method for an addition or improvement is identical to the method used for the underlying property. For example, assume residential rental property is placed in service during 1987. In 1990, an improvement is made to the property. The cost of the improvement is recovered over a 27½-year period beginning in 1990.

There's a new alternative depreciation system that's used to compute corporate earnings and profits and the depreciation preference subject to the alternative minimum tax. The new system is also used to depreciate property used outside of the U.S., property financed with tax-exempts or leased to tax-exempt entities, and property imported from foreign countries that maintain discriminatory trade practices.

New complications. Many taxpayers will have three sets of depreciation rules to contend with: (1) the old "useful life" system of depreciation that applies to property placed in service before 1981 (and to property covered by antichurning transactions); (2) the original ACRS setup, which applies to assets placed in service after 1980 and before 1987 (and to property covered by transition rules and a new set of antichurning rules); and (3) the new ACRS setup.

Finally, businesses will have to watch the clock when they buy depreciable assets. Reason: If more than 40% of the year's depreciable acquisitions are placed in service in the final quarter, then all non-realty assets must be depreciated using a new "mid-quarter" convention instead of the normal mid-year convention.

The new ACRS rules apply to any new or used tangible depreciable property, other than (1) property depreciated with the unit-of-production method, or any other method not expressed in a term of years (other than the retirement replacement betterment method or similar method); (2) public utility property, if a normalization method of accounting is not used; (3) any motion picture or video tape; (4) a sound recording as described in Sec. 48(r)(5); or (5) any property subject to the original ACRS rules (e.g., because of a transition or antichurning rule).

[¶202] Asset Classes, Recovery Periods, and Depreciation Methods for Personal Property. The cost of property (other than residential rental property and nonresidential real property) is recovered over a 3, 5, 7, 10, 15, or 20-year period, depending on the type of property. The depreciation method for property in the 3, 5, 7, and 10-year classes is 200% declining balance, with a switch to straight line to maximize the deduction. The depreciation method for 15-and 20-year property is 150% declining balance, with a switch to straight line to maximize the deduction.

3-year property. This class includes property with a 4-year-or-less midpoint life under the ADR (Asset Depreciation Range) system, *other than* cars and light-duty trucks (they are shifted to the 5-year class).

Under the ADR system, property with a midpoint life of 4 years or less includes: special handling devices for the manufacture of food and beverages; special tools and devices for the manufacture of rubber products; special tools for the manufacture of finished plastic products, fabricated metal products, or motor vehicles; and breeding hogs. Racehorses more than 2-years old when placed in service, and other horses more than 12-years old when placed in service, are included in the 3-year class.

5-year property. This class consists of property with an ADR midpoint of more than 4 years and less than 10 years. This includes assets such as computers, typewriters, copiers, duplicating equipment, heavy general purpose trucks, trailers, cargo containers and trailer-mounted containers. The new law specifically includes the following items in the 5-year class: cars, light-duty trucks, computer-based telephone central office switching equipment (assigned a new ADR midpoint of 9.5 years), semiconductor manufacturing equipment (assigned a new ADR midpoint of 5 years), renewable energy and biomass properties that are small power plant production facilities, qualified technological equipment [¶205], and equipment used with research and experimentation.

7-year property. This new class includes (1) any property with an ADR midpoint of 10 years or more and less than 16 years, and (2) property with no ADR midpoint that is not assigned to another class. Included in this class: office furniture, fixtures and equipment (was in the 5-year class), railroad track (assigned a new 10-year midpoint) and single-purpose agricultural and horticultural structures (assigned a new 15-year midpoint).

10-year property. This class includes property with an ADR midpoint of 16 years or more and less than 20 years (e.g., assets used in petroleum refining, or in the manufacture of tobacco products and certain food products).

15-year property. This class consists of property with an ADR midpoint of 20 years or more and less than 25 years. Specifically included in this class are municipal sewage treatment plants, telephone distribution plants, and comparable equipment used by nontelephone companies for the two-way exchange of voice and data communications (assigned a new 24-year ADR midpoint). "Comparable equipment" does not include cable television equipment used primarily for one-way communication.

20-year property. This new class consists of property with an ADR midpoint of 25 years and more, other than Sec. 1250 real property with an ADR midpoint of 27.5 years and more. Municipal sewers, which are assigned a 50-year midpoint, are in this class.

In the case of a short tax year, the Conference Agreement says the ACRS deduction for property in the 3, 5, 7, 10, 15, and 20 year classes is computed as if the property had been in service for half the number of months in the short tax year.

Asset reclassification. The new law gives the Treasury authority to reclassify assets to reflect their anticipated useful life and anticipated decline in value over time. Initially, the Treasury is expected to focus on assets that have no ADR midpoint, clothing held for rental, and scientific equipment.

Five-year freeze: The new law prevents the Treasury from assigning certain assets a longer recovery period than the 1986 TRA specifies. The Treasury may, however, assign a shorter recovery period to these assets. The freeze applies to the following assets, as long as they are placed in service prior to 1-1-92: horses, cars, light general purpose trucks, semiconductor manufacturing equipment, computer-based telephone central office switching equipment, research and experimentation property, qualified technological equipment, renewable energy and biomass properties, railroad track, single-purpose agricultural and horticultural structures, telephone distribution plants and comparable equipment, municipal wastewater treatment plants, and municipal sewers.

The Committee Reports say that the Treasury may reclassify property affected by the freeze if the property is placed in service after 12-31-91 and before 7-1-92. However, the Treasury must notify the House Ways and Means Committee and the Senate Finance Committee of the proposed change at least six months before the change is to go into effect.

Averaging conventions and depreciation percentages. The half-year convention applies to all property assigned to the 3, 5, 7, 10, 15 or 20-year classes. All property is treated as placed in service (or disposed of) in the middle of the year. Thus, a taxpayer gets a half-year of depreciation when he places an asset in service and a half-year of depreciation when the property is disposed of or retired from service. Salvage value is ignored. The original ACRS system had statutory depreciation percentages. The new system prescribes the depreciation methods we've listed and does not provide recovery tables.

   SPECIAL HELP: The following table was prepared by the Prentice-Hall Editorial Staff. It lists recovery percentages for property in the 3, 5, 7, 10, 15, and 20-year classes. Percentages are based on the mathematical application of the prescribed depreciation methods. (There are no official recovery percentages at this time.)

Annual Recovery (Percent of Original Depreciable Basis)

Recovery Year	3-Year Class (200% d.b.)	5-Year Class (200% d.b.)	7-Year Class (200% d.b.)	10-Year Class (200% d.b.)	15-Year Class (150% d.b.)	20-Year Class (150% d.b.)
1	33.00	20.00	14.28	10.00	5.00	3.75
2	45.00	32.00	24.49	18.00	9.50	7.22
3	15.00*	19.20	17.49	14.40	8.55	6.68
4	7.00	11.52*	12.49	11.52	7.69	6.18
5		11.52	8.93*	9.22	6.93	5.71
6		5.76	8.93	7.37	6.23	5.28
7			8.93	6.55*	5.90*	4.89
8			4.46	6.55	5.90	4.52
9				6.55	5.90	4.46*
10				6.55	5.90	4.46
11				3.29	5.90	4.46
12					5.90	4.46
13					5.90	4.46
14					5.90	4.46
15					5.90	4.46
16					3.00	4.46
17						4.46

Recovery Year	3-Year Class (200% d.b.)	5-Year Class (200% d.b.)	7-Year Class (200% d.b.)	10-Year Class (200% d.b.)	15-Year Class (150% d.b.)	20-Year Class (150% d.b.)
18						4.46
19						4.46
20						4.46
21						2.25

*Year of switch to straight line to maximize depreciation deduction.

OBSERVATION: The original ACRS system gave the taxpayer a half-year of depreciation for the tax year he placed an asset in service, but allowed him to recover the balance of depreciable basis over the years remaining in the property's recovery period. There was no recovery allowance for the year of disposition or retirement. Thus, conceptually, the taxpayer was considered to have placed property in service at the beginning of the recovery period, but was allowed only a half-year's worth of depreciation for the placed-in-service year. By contrast, the new system views property as placed in service in the middle of the first year. For example, the statutory recovery period for 3-year property begins in the middle of the year an asset is placed in service and ends three years later.

In practical terms, the new rule means taxpayers must wait an extra year to recover the cost of depreciable assets—the actual writeoff periods are 4, 6, 8, 11, 16, and 21 years.

Another difference. Under the original ACRS system, there was no recovery deduction in the year of an asset's disposition or sale. The new system gives the taxpayer a half year of depreciation for the year of disposition or sale.

Special election. Taxpayers may elect to recover the cost of assets placed in service after 7-31-86 and before 1-1-87, using the modified ACRS rules. The election may not be used for property covered under the transition rules [¶209]. The Committee Reports indicate that the election may be made on an asset-by-asset basis. The election makes sense for assets that stay in the 3-, 5-, or 10-year recovery class under the modified ACRS setup. Reason: The modified ACRS rules produce a larger recovery deduction in the early years than the original ACRS rules did. However, the election shouldn't be used for assets that are shifted into a longer recovery class under the modified ACRS setup.

Example (1): In October 1986, Ace Corp. buys and places into service $300,000 of assets that qualify as 3-year property under the original and the modified ACRS rules. Without the special election, Ace's ACRS deductions are $75,000 for the first year (25%), $114,000 for the second (38%), and $111,000 for the third. With the special election (unless a transitional rule applies, see ¶209), depreciation deductions are $99,000 for the first year (33%), $135,000 for the second (45%), $45,000 for the third year (15%) and $21,000 for the fourth year (7%).

Example (2): Barry Stanford buys a car in November, 1986. Lori Mack buys a car in February, 1987. Both cars cost $10,000 and are used 100% for business.

Result: Under the original ACRS rules, Stanford's car is 3-year recovery property. His depreciation is figured from statutory tables. His writeoffs are $2,500, for 1986; $3,800, for 1987; and $3,700, for 1988.

Mack's depreciation is figured using a five-year recovery period and 200% declining-balance with a switch to straight-line. Her writeoffs are $2,000 for 1987; $3,200 for 1988; $1,920 for 1989; $1,152 for 1990; $1,152 for 1991; and $576 for 1992.

NOTE: If Stanford used the special election for post-7-31-86 assets, his ACRS deductions would be the same as Mack's.

Example (3): Widget Corp. buys a new machine in January 1986 and January 1987. Each costs $100,000 and each machine is 5-year property under the old and new law.

Result: Widget's depreciable basis is $100,000. Widget's depreciation deductions for the 1986 acquisition, figured from statutory tables, are $15,000, for 1986; $22,000, for 1987; and $21,000, for 1988, 1989, and 1990.

Widget's depreciation for the 1987 acquisition is figured using 200% declining-balance with a switch to straight-line. A half-year convention is used. Depreciation writeoffs are $20,000 for 1987; $32,000 for 1988; $19,200 for 1989; $11,520 for 1990; $11,520 for 1991; and $5,760 for 1992.

New dollar caps for 'luxury' autos. Sec. 280F places dollar limits on the amount of annual depreciation that may be claimed for "luxury" business autos. For autos placed in service after 4-2-85, 1985, first-year depreciation was capped at $3,200 and depreciation in each succeeding year was capped at $4,800. Under prior law's three-year ACRS setup, the caps came into play when a car's cost exceeded $12,800 [$3,200 + ($4,800 × 2)]. The new law adjusts the dollar caps on depreciation so that the price range of cars affected by the caps remains roughly the same. Thus, effective for autos placed in service after 12-31-86, the dollar caps are $2,560 for the first year, $4,100 for the second year, $2,450 for the third year, and $1,475 for each succeeding year. Result: Depreciation deductions that may be claimed on business autos are as follows (percentages are applied to original depreciable basis):

First year	Lesser of $2,560 or 20%
Second year	Lesser of $4,100 or 32%
Third year	Lesser of $2,450 or 19.20%
Fourth year	Lesser of $1,475 or 11.52%
Fifth year	Lesser of $1,475 or 11.52%

Sixth year .... Lesser of $1,475 or 5.76%

Any depreciable basis remaining after six years is recovered at a rate that cannot exceed $1,475 a year.

Example (1): In January 1987, ABC Corp. places in service a $12,900 car and a $15,000 car. The business/investment use percentage of each car is 100%. Results:

	Car (1) Depreciation	Car (2) Depreciation
1987	$2,560	$2,560
1988	4,100	4,100
1989	2,450	2,450
1990	1,475	1,475
1991	1,475	1,475
1992	743	864
1993	97	1,475
1994	-0-	601
Total	*$12,900*	*$15,000*

The dollar caps must be reduced if business/investment use is less than 100%.

Example (2): A self-employed taxpayer buys a $20,000 car in April 1987. He uses the car 70% for business, 30% for personal driving. Result: His depreciation deduction for 1987 is $1,792 (lesser of $2,560 × 70% business use, or 20% of $14,000).

If qualified business use in the placed-in-service year does not exceed 50%, then the car's basis must be recovered over five years using the straight-line method and the half-year convention. What's more, depreciation is limited to the dollar caps adjusted for business/investment use percentage). If qualified business use falls to 50% or less of total use during the recovery period, part of depreciation claimed in prior years is recaptured and the taxpayer must switch to straight line depreciation.

New rules for leased cars? Lessees of luxury business cars must cope with an annual income inclusion that, in effect, reduces the deduction for lease payments. This income inclusion is the leasing equivalent of the investment credit and depreciation caps that applied to buyers of luxury business cars and is figured with the aid of special tables in the Sec. 280F regulations. Since the investment credit is repealed for post-1985 buyers, the income inclusion tables may well be revised for cars leased after 12-31-85. The new depreciation dollar caps may result in yet another set of leasing tables for post-1986 leases. The Treasury may also revise the one-time-only income inclusion that applies for the year that a leased car (or other "listed property") is used 50% or less for business.

Special rule for final-quarter purchases. Under ACRS, there's a natural temptation to accelerate purchases of personal property planned, for say, the first quarter of the next tax year into the last months of this tax year. *Reason:* You get a half-year of recovery deductions in the first year regardless of when the asset is placed in service.

This strategy continues to work under the new ACRS setup, if you avoid a new snare. If the aggregate bases of property placed in service during the last three months of the tax year exceed 40% of the aggregate bases of all the property placed in service during the year, then the taxpayer cannot use the mid-year convention. Instead, he must use the mid-quarter convention for *all property* (other than nonresidential real property and residential rental property) placed in service during the year. For purposes of the 40% rule, residential rental property and nonresidential realty is ignored. The Committee Reports indicate that members of an affiliated group [within the meaning of Sec. 1504, without regard to Sec. 1504(b)] are treated as one taxpayer for purposes of the 40% determination.

Under the mid-quarter convention, the first-year depreciation allowance is based on the number of quarters that the asset was in service. Property placed in service at any time during a quarter is treated as having been placed in service in the middle of the quarter.

> **AVOID THE PITFALL:** Businesses must carefully time their equipment purchases and placed-in-service dates. The mid-quarter convention is avoided as long as the aggregate bases of property placed in service during the last three months of the tax year do not exceed 66% of the aggregate bases of property placed in service during the first nine months of the tax year.

> **Example:** During the first nine months of its tax year, XYZ Corp. places in service $124,000 of depreciable nonrealty assets. XYZ can place in service another $81,840 of non-realty assets during the last three months (66% of $124,000) without running afoul of the new rule.

For tax years in which some placed-in-service property is covered by prior law ACRS, and other placed-in-service property is covered by the new ACRS rules, the 40% determination is made with respect to all the property. However, the mid-quarter convention applies only to property depreciated under the new ACRS rules.

Optional recovery methods. A taxpayer may elect to recover the cost of assets using the straight-line method over the applicable ACRS recovery period. The taxpayer also may elect to use the alternative depreciation system [¶205]. In either case, the mid-year convention applies (unless the taxpayer fails the new year-end rule and must use the mid-quarter rule) and salvage value is ignored. An election to use an optional recovery method for a particular class of property is binding for all property in that class placed in service during the year. The election is irrevocable.

Recapture provisions. The recapture rules for tangible property (other than residential rental or nonresidential real property) remain the same: All gain on a disposition is treated as ordinary income to the extent of ACRS deductions claimed by the taxpayer. For purposes of recapture, deductions allowed under Sec. 179 (expensing), Sec. 190 (removal or architectural and transportation barriers) or Sec. 193 (tertiary injectant expenses) are treated as depreciation deductions.

Other rules. You may continue to set up mass asset accounts for any property in the same ACRS class and placed in service in the same year. As under prior law (unless otherwise provided by regulations), the full amount of proceeds realized on a disposition of property from a mass asset account is treated as ordinary income (with no reduction for basis). But no reduction is made in the depreciable basis remaining in the account. For technical reasons, the repeal of the investment tax credit [¶208] will result in an expanded definition of assets eligible for inclusion in mass asset accounts.

The new law continues to condition eligibility of public utility property for ACRS recovery on the normalization of ACRS tax benefits in setting rates charged to customers and in reflecting results in regulated books of account. The new law also provides for the normalization of excess deferred tax reserves resulting from a reduction in corporate income tax rates. If such reserves are not normalized, the taxpayer must use the depreciation method, useful life determination, averaging convention, and salvage value limits used to set rates and reflecting operating results in regulated books of account.

[¶203] Real Estate Depreciation. Taxpayers have been on a rollercoaster ride when it comes to depreciating real estate. Property placed in service before 1981 was depreciable over its useful life (e.g., 35 to 40 years for new property). The recovery period dropped all the way down to 15 years for property placed in service after 1980, edged up to 18 years for property placed in service after 3-15-84, and went to 19 years if placed in service after 5-8-85.

Effective for property placed in service after 12-31-86, the new law boosts the recovery period to 27.5 years for residential rental property and to 31.5 years for nonresidential real property. What's more, the recovery method is slowed down to the straight-line rate using the mid-month convention. Residential rental property is defined the same way it was under prior law. A property qualifies if at least 80% of the gross rental income is rental income from dwelling units.

Residential rental property includes manufactured homes which are residential rental property. Residential rental property does not include hotels, motels, and other establishments rented to transients. Nonresidential real property is any Sec. 1250 property that is not residential rental property and that either has no ADR midpoint or has an ADR midpoint that's not less than 27½ years. Because the mid-month convention applies, there is no adjustment made for short tax years.

SPECIAL HELP: The following tables were prepared by the Prentice-Hall Editorial Staff. They list recovery percentages for residential rental and nonresidential real property. They are based on a mathematical application of the prescribed depreciation methods. (There are no official tables at this time.)

Recovery Percentages for Residential Rental Property

Recovery Year	Month Placed in Service											
	1	2	3	4	5	6	7	8	9	10	11	12
1	3.48	3.18	2.88	2.58	2.27	1.97	1.67	1.36	1.06	.76	.45	.15
2—27	3.64	3.64	3.64	3.64	3.64	3.64	3.64	3.64	3.64	3.64	3.64	3.64
28	1.88	2.18	2.48	2.78	3.09	3.39	3.64	3.64	3.64	3.64	3.64	3.64
29	-0-	-0-	-0-	-0-	-0-	-0-	.05	.36	.66	.96	1.27	1.57

Recovery Percentages for Nonresidential Real Property

Recovery Year	Month Placed in Service											
	1	2	3	4	5	6	7	8	9	10	11	12
1	3.04	2.78	2.51	2.25	1.98	1.72	1.46	1.19	.93	.66	.40	.13
2—31	3.17	3.17	3.17	3.17	3.17	3.17	3.17	3.17	3.17	3.17	3.17	3.17
32	1.86	2.12	2.39	2.65	2.92	3.17	3.17	3.17	3.17	3.17	3.17	3.17
33	-0-	-0-	-0-	-0-	-0-	.01	.27	.54	.80	1.07	1.33	1.60

Example: Realty Corp. bought an apartment building in January 1986. It buys an apartment building and a department store building in January 1987. Each costs $300,000.

The 1986 apartment building has a 19-year ACRS recovery period. Realty's depreciation is figured from statutory tables. Its writeoff is $26,400 for 1986, and $25,200 for 1987.

The 1987 apartment building is assigned a 27½ -year useful life, and the department store building is given a 31½ -year life. Realty's depreciation for the apartment building is $10,440, for 1987, and $10,920, for 1988. Its writeoffs for the department store building are $9,120 for 1987, and $9,510 for 1988.

A taxpayer may elect to recover the cost of residential property and nonresidential realty using the straight-line method (and the mid-month convention) over a 40-year period. A table for 40-year recovery is shown at ¶205.

New rule for leasehold improvements. If a building is erected on leased property, its cost must be recovered over the 27½ or 31½ year period, regardless of the term of the lease. The cost of other improvements to leased property is recovered using the applicable ACRS recovery period. When the lease is terminated, the lessee figures gain or loss by reference to the improvement's basis at that time. As a result of the new rule, Sec. 178 is amended to cover only the amortization of lease-acquisition costs. Such costs may be amortized over the lease term. However, under the new law, any lease renewals (including renewal options and any other period for which the parties reasonably expect the lease to be renewed) must be included in figuring the amortization period, but only if less than 75% of the lease-acquisition cost is for the lease's remaining term (excluding any renewal period remaining on the lease acquisition date).

Depreciation recapture. Gain on a disposition of residential rental or nonresidential realty is not recaptured as ordinary income to the extent of depreciation deductions claimed by the taxpayer.

Act Sec. 201(a) amends Sec. 168(a) and (b), relating to applicable depreciation methods under ACRS, Sec. 168(c), relating to recovery periods, Sec. 168(d), relating to applicable conventions and special mid-quarter convention, Sec. 168(e), relating to classification of property, Sec. 168(f), relating to property not covered by ACRS, 168(g)(7), relating to election to use alternative depreciation method, Sec. 168(i)(1), relating to authority of the Treasury Secretary to reclassify assets, Sec. 168(i)(3), relating to lease term, Sec. 168(i)(4) relating to general asset accounts, Sec. 168(i)(5), relating to changes in use. Sec. 168(i)(6), relating to additions or improvements to property, Sec. 168(i)(8), relating to treatment of leasehold improvements, and Sec. 168(i)(9), relating to normalization rules. Act. Sec. 201(d)(4) makes technical and conforming amendments to Sec. 280F, relating to luxury automobiles and other listed property. Act. Sec. 201(d)(5) makes technical and conforming changes to Secs. 291(a)(1), 291(c)(1), and 291(e)(2). Act Sec. 201(d)(6) makes technical and conforming changes to Secs. 312(k)(4). Act Sec. 201(d)(7) makes technical and conforming changes to Sec. 465(b)(3)(C), Sec. 46(c)(8)(D)(v), and Sec. 4162(c)(3). Act Sec. 201(d)(8) amends Sec. 467, relating to certain payments for the use of property. Act. Sec. 201(d)(9) through (d)(14) makes technical and conforming changes to Secs. 514(c)(9)(B)(vi)(II), 751(c), 1245(a)(1), 1245(a)(2), 1245(a)(3), 1245(a)(5), 1245(a)(6), 4162(c)(3) 6111(c)(3)(B), 7701(e)(4)(A), and 7701(e)(5). The above provisions generally apply to property placed in service after 12-31-86 in tax years ending after that date. Transition rules are covered at ¶209. Act Sec. 203(a)(1)(B) allows taxpayers to elect the new ACRS system for assets placed in service after 7-31-86 and before 1-1-87.

[¶204] **Antichurning Provisions and Nonrecognition Transactions.** There's a new set of antichurning provisions for personal property. The modified ACRS setup does not apply if (1) the property was owned or used at any time during 1986 by the taxpayer or a related person; (2) the property is acquired from a person who owned it at any time during 1986 and, as part of the transaction, the user of the property did not change; or (3) the taxpayer leased the property to a person (or someone related to the person) who owned or used the property during 1986. (A special rule prevents multiple churning transactions.) In such churning transactions, the taxpayer must use the original ACRS system. Note: The modified ACRS may be elected for assets placed in service after 7-31-86. [See ¶203.]

A special rule applies to property used for personal purposes before 1987 and converted to business use after 1986. In this case, the property is treated as having been placed in service when it is first used for business. In other words, the antichurning rules don't apply to converted property.

> **IMPORTANT:** The antichurning rules do not apply if their application would result in a more generous writeoff for the placed-in-service year than the new ACRS system allows.

> **Example:** A business auto used by John Smith during 1986 is transferred to Donald Smith, a related taxpayer, in 1987. The transaction is *not* covered by the antichurning rules. Reason: If the antichurning rules applied, then Donald Smith would be able to depreciate the car over three years (prior law's ACRS recovery) instead of over five years using the half-year convention (new law's recovery rule).

Real estate. There are no 1986/1987 antichurning rules for real estate. *Reason:* The new ACRS setup results in a much slower writeoff than under the original ACRS system. If there were antichurning provisions, taxpayers would deliberately disqualify transactions in order to use the more liberal old law provisions.

> **COMMENT:** The original antichurning provisions remain in place. These provisions prevent taxpayers from converting pre-ACRS property (e.g., placed in service prior to 1981) into ACRS property. Thus, a taxpayer who owned real estate before 1981 could not qualify for the modified ACRS rules by engaging in a 1987 churning transaction.

Nonrecognition transactions. A special rule applies to transactions covered by Secs. 332, 351, 361, 371(a), 374(a), 721 or 731 [other than termination of a partnership under Sec. 708(b)(1)(B)]. Here, the transferee is treated as the transferor for purposes of computing the depreciation deduction. This treatment is limited to that part of the transferee's basis that does not exceed the adjusted basis in the hands of the transferor. If the transferee's basis is more than the transferor's basis, then the excess is depreciated under the new law's ACRS rules.

Another special rule applies if a taxpayer disposes of property and then reacquires it. In such cases, the depreciation deduction is computed as if the property had not been disposed of.

NOTE: The special rules for nonrecognition transactions and for dispositions and reacquisitions do not apply to any transaction covered by the antichurning rules.

Act Sec. 201(a) amends Sec. 168(f)(5), relating to property placed in service in churning transactions, and Sec. 168(i)(7), relating to treatment of certain transferees and property reacquired by the taxpayer. Act. Sec. 201(a) is generally effective for assets placed in service after 12-31-86 in tax years ending after that date.

[¶205] Alternative Depreciation System. Effective for property placed in service after 12-31-86, the new law creates an alternative depreciation system that must be used to:

(1) Compute the portion of depreciation treated as a tax preference for purposes of the corporate and individual alternative minimum tax [¶701 *et seq.*].

(2) Figure the earnings and profits of a domestic corporation or an "80/20" company.

(3) Compute depreciation allowances for property that is:

- Tangible property used predominantly outside the U.S.

- Leased or otherwise used by a tax-exempt entity.

- Financed with the proceeds of tax-exempt bonds.

- Imported from foreign countries that maintain discriminatory trade practices or otherwise engage in discriminatory acts.

How the new system works. In general, depreciation is computed using straight-line recovery without regard to salvage value. Exception: For purposes of the minimum tax, depreciation of personal property is computed using the 150% declining-balance method. In general, the mid-year convention applies, but the taxpayer must use the mid-month convention for residential rental property and nonresidential real property. *Note:* The mid-quarter convention must be used for all personal property placed in service during the year if the new year-end 40% rule is failed [¶203].

The recovery periods under the alternative depreciation system are:

- 5 years for cars, light general purpose trucks, qualified technological equipment, and semiconductor manufacturing equipment.

- 9.5 years for computer-based telephone central office switching equipment.

- 10 years for railroad track.

- 12 years for personal property with no class life.

- 15 years for single-purpose agricultural or horticultural structures.

- 24 years for municipal waste water treatment plants and telephone distribution plans and comparable equipment used for 2-way exchange of voice and data communications.

- 27.5 years for low-income housing financed by tax-exempts.

- 40 years for nonresidential real and residential rental property, and 1245 property which is real property with no useful life.

- 50 years for municipal sewers.

Other property has a recovery period equal to its class life.

PLANNING AID: The tables below show straight-line depreciation percentages under the alternative recovery system for property in the 5, 9.5, 12, and 40-year classes.

Important. These tables are not official material, but were prepared by the Prentice-Hall Editorial Staff. However, the table for the 5, 9.5, and 12-year classes is identical to the IRS table used under prior law to compute optional recovery allowances for property used outside the United States. These optional recovery allowances are computed using the straight-line method and the mid-year convention [IRC Sec. 168(b)(3)(A) and (B)(iii), prior to amendment by the new law]. Straight-line recovery tables for other class lives may be found at Prop. Reg. Sec. 1.168-2(g)(3) [¶15,602.66 P-H Federal Taxes].

The table for property in the 40-year class is identical to the 40-year table prescribed by the IRS for property subject to prior law's tax-exempt entity leasing provisions [Temp. Reg. 1.168(j)-1T ¶15,602.95 P-H Federal Taxes] and for real property not used predominantly for business under Sec. 280F [IRS Pub. 534]. The IRS 40-year table uses straight-line and the mid-month convention.

Recovery Percentages Under
Alternative Depreciation System

Recovery Year	5-Year Class	9.5-Year Class	12-Year Class
1	10	5	4
2	20	11	9
3	20	11	9
4	20	11	9
5	20	11	9
6	10	11	8
7		10	8
8		10	8
9		10	8
10		10	8
11			8
12			8
13			4

Recovery Percentages for 40-Year Class

Recovery Year	Month Placed in Service											
	1	2	3	4	5	6	7	8	9	10	11	12
1	2.4	2.2	2.0	1.8	1.6	1.4	1.1	0.9	0.7	0.5	0.3	0.1
2—40	2.5	2.5	2.5	2.5	2.5	2.5	2.5	2.5	2.5	2.5	2.5	2.5
41	0.1	0.3	0.5	0.7	0.9	1.1	1.4	1.6	1.8	2.0	2.2	2.4

Qualified technological equipment: This is any computer or related peripheral equipment, any high technology telephone station equipment installed on the customer's premises, and any high technology medical equipment. A computer is any programmable electronic device that accepts information, processes it, and supplies the results with or without human intervention and consists of a central processing unit (CPU) containing extensive storage, logic, arithmetic, and control capabilities. Related peripheral equipment is an off- or on-line device designed to be controlled by a computer's CPU. Computer or related peripheral equipment does not include: any equipment that is an integral part of other property that is not a computer; typewriters, or calculators; adding or accounting machines; copiers, duplicating, or similar equipment; and any equipment used primarily for entertainment or amusement.

High technology medical equipment is any electronic, electromechanical, or computer-based high-technology equipment used in the screening, monitoring, observation, diagnosis, or treatment of patients in a laboratory, medical, or hospital environment.

Property used predominantly outside the United States. As under prior law, property falls in this classification if it is used outside the United States for more than half of a tax year. There's a special exception for a satellite or other spacecraft (or any interest therein) launched within the United States and held by a U.S. person.

Property leased or otherwise used by a tax-exempt entity. In general, the new law retains prior law's definition of tax-exempt use property, including the special rule that defines the recovery period as the greater of (1) 125% of the lease term or (2) the depreciation period that otherwise applies to the property. However, qualified technological equipment (as defined above) leased to a tax-exempt entity for five years or less is not treated as tax-exempt use property. A corporation that is 50% or more owned by one or more tax-

¶205

exempt entities (other than foreign persons or entities) is treated as a tax-exempt entity. The holdings of tax-exempt entities owning less than 5% of the stock are disregarded if the corporation is publicly traded.

Property financed with the proceeds of tax-exempt bonds. The new law modifies the definition of tax-exempt bond financed property to include any property that is financed directly or indirectly by an obligation that pays out tax-exempt interest under Sec. 103(a). The proceeds of an obligation are treated as being used to finance property acquired in connection with the obligation's issuance in the order in which the property was acquired. Tax-exempt bond financed property does not include qualified residential rental projects [as defined by Sec. 142(a)(7)].

Certain imported property. The President may by Executive Order mandate use of the alternative depreciation system for property imported from foreign countries that maintain trade restrictions or engage in discriminatory action or policies that unjustifiably restrict U.S. commerce. Property is imported if it was completed outside of the United States or less than 50% of its basis is attributable to value added in the United States. For this purpose, the United States includes its possessions and Puerto Rico.

Act Sec. 201(a) amends Sec. 168(g)(1)-(70, relating to alternative depreciation system for certain property, Sec. 168(h)(1)-(8), relating to tax-exempt use property, and Sec. 168(i)(2), relating to qualified technological equipment. Act. Sec. 201(b) amends Sec. 312(k)(3), relating to depreciation used for purposes of earnings and profits. Act. Sec. 201 is generally effective for property placed in service after 12-31-86 in tax years ending after that date.

[¶206] Increased Expensing Deduction. Instead of depreciating qualifying property under the modified ACRS system, a taxpayer may elect under Sec. 179 to treat all or part of its cost as a currently deductible expense in the placed-in-service year. Effective for qualifying property placed in service after 1986, the expensing deduction is equal to $10,000. The expensing deduction had been limited to $5,000 for tax years 1982-87. Qualifying property is recovery property that is bought for use in the active conduct of a trade or business.

The new law modifies prior law's expensing rules in four other ways:

 • If the aggregate cost of qualifying property placed in service during the tax year exceeds $200,000, then the credit is reduced dollar-for-dollar by the cost of qualifying property in excess of $200,000.

 • Marrieds filing separate returns are treated as one taxpayer for purposes of the $10,000 expensing limit (and the reduction that applies if qualifying property placed in service exceeds $200,000). Unless the taxpayers elect otherwise, 50% of the cost of qualifying property is allocated to each spouse.

• The amount expensed cannot exceed the taxable income derived from the trade or business in which the property is used. Taxable income of each trade or business is computed separately and without regard to the amount expensed. Any expensed amount in excess of taxable income is carried forward to future tax years and added to other amounts eligible for expensing.

• Conversion of the expensed property to personal use *at any time* before the end of the property's recovery period results in recapture income (excess of expensed amount over ACRS deduction that would have been allowed). A property is converted to personal use if it is not used predominantly for trade or business use. Under prior law, there was no recapture if the property was converted to personal use after the end of the second tax year following the tax year in which the property was placed in service.

NOTE: For purposes of computing a corporation's earnings and profits, any amount expensed under Sec. 179 is treated as a deduction ratably over five tax years, beginning with the tax year in which the expensing deduction is claimed.

Act Sec. 201(b) amends Sec. 312(k)(3)(B), relating to treatment for E&P purposes of amounts expensed under Sec. 179. Act. Sec. 202 amends Sec. 179(b), Sec. 179(d)(1) and Sec. 179(d)(10), relating to expensing of depreciable assets. Act. Secs. 201 and 202 are generally effective for property placed in service after 12-31-86 in tax years ending after that date.

[¶207] **Repeal of Finance Leases.** The new law repeals the finance lease provisions, effective for agreements entered into after 12-31-86.

Act Sec. 201 repeals Sec. 168(f)(8), relating to finance leases, generally effective for property placed in service after 12-31-86.

[¶208] **Investment Tax Credit Repeal.** The regular investment tax credit is repealed for property placed in service after 12-31-85. However, the investment tax credit continues to be available for (1) property covered by transition rules [¶209]; (2) certain qualified progress expenditures for periods before 1-1-86; and (3) the portion of adjusted basis of qualified timber property treated as Sec. 38 property under Sec. 48(a)(1)(F). A tax credit is available for qualified rehabilitation expenses [¶217]. In addition, effective for tax years beginning on or after 7-1-87, regular investment credits (other than the ITC available for timber property) carried forward or claimed under a transitional rule are reduced by 35%. In the case of a tax year beginning before and ending after 7-1-87, the 35% reduction is prorated based on the ratio that post-6-30-87 months in the tax year bears to total months in the tax year. For example, in the case of a tax year that is based on the calendar year, the reduction for 1987 is 17.5%. The reduction in the ITC compensates for the new, lower tax rates. The amount by which the credit is reduced can't be claimed as a credit in a future tax year.

Another change: The depreciable basis of transition property placed in service after 12-31-85 and eligible for the ITC under the transition rules must be reduced by the full amount of the ITC. The full basis reduction can't be escaped by claiming a reduced ITC percentage under Sec. 48(q)(4). However, the full-basis reduction is computed after taking into account the 35% reduction.

Special relief for possible estimated tax problems. The repeal of the ITC for assets placed in service after 12-31-85 may cause estimated tax problems (e.g., an estimated tax payment may have been based on the availability of the ITC). According to the Committee Reports, the conferees intend that no estimated tax penalties be imposed in such situations. However, relief is available only to the extent that (1) an underpayment results from taking into account the ITC on property placed in service after 12-31-85 and before the Reform Act's enactment date, and (2) the taxpayer pays the underpayment within 30 days after the enactment date.

> **NOTE:**   A taxpayer may be entitled to much broader estimated-tax relief under Act Sec. 1543 [see ¶1544].

Carrybacks. Qualifying farmers are allowed a 15-year carryback of existing ITC carryforwards. This carryback, which may be elected for the first tax year beginning after 12-31-86, is limited to the lesser of three amounts:

- 50% of existing carryforwards;
- The net tax liability for the carryback period; or
- $750.

Qualified farmers are those taxpayers who derived 50% or more of their gross income from farming in the three tax years before the tax year in which the carryback election is made.

Another special 15-year ITC carryback applies to domestic corporations engaged in the manufacture and production of steel. The new law also includes a new recapture penalty if the tax benefits of previously allowed ITCs on public utility property are not normalized, and special recapture rules for qualified progress expenditures.

Act Sec. 211(a) adds new Sec. 49(a), generally repealing the ITC for property placed in service after 12-31-85. Act Sec. 211(a) also adds new Secs. 48(b) through (e), relating to exceptions to the ITC repeal, 35% reduction in the ITC for tax years after 1986, the full basis adjustment requirement, and transition property [see ¶209]. Act. Sec. 211(b) provides special normalization rules, Act Sec. 211(c) makes conforming amendments to the table of sections for subpart E of part IV of subchapter A of chapter 1, and Act Sec. 211(d) provides a transition rule of limited application. Act Sec. 212 provides a 15-year carryback of existing carryforwards of steel companies, which may be elected by a qualifying corporation for its first tax year beginning after 12-31-86. Act Sec. 213 provides a 15-year carryback of existing carryforwards of qualifying farmers, elective as shown above.

[¶209] Effective Dates and Transition Rules. The new ACRS system, the new alternative depreciation system, and the increased expensing deduction are generally effective for property placed in service after 12-31-86, in tax years ending after that date. The investment tax credit is repealed for property placed in service after 12-31-85 in tax years ending after that date.

Transition rules for ACRS. Prior law's ACRS rules continue to apply for property constructed, reconstructed, or acquired under a written contract binding as of 3-1-86, and placed in service by the following dates:

Type of Property	Placed-in-Service Date
ADR midpoint of at least 7 years but less than 20 years	January 1, 1989
Property with no ADR midpoint	January 1, 1989
ADR midpoint of 20 years or more	January 1, 1991
Residential rental property and nonresidential realty	January 1, 1991

Real property covered by the rehabilitation tax credit transition rules [¶217] may be depreciated under prior law's ACRS rules.

There is no transitional relief for property with an ADR midpoint of less than seven years. For purposes of the transition rules, computer-based telephone switching equipment is considered to have an ADR midpoint of six years.

NOTE: Property covered by the antichurning rules [¶204] may be subject to prior law's ACRS system as well.

Transition rules for ITC. The investment tax credit is allowed for property constructed, reconstructed, or acquired under a written contract binding on 12-31-85, and placed in service by the following dates:

Type of Property	Placed in Service Date
ADR midpoint of less than 5 years	July 1, 1986
ADR midpoint of at least 5 years but less than 7 years	January 1, 1987
Computer-based telephone central office switching equipment	January 1, 1987

ADR midpoint of at least 7 but
less than 20 years
Property with no ADR midpoint   January 1, 1989
ADR midpoint of 20 years or more   January 1, 1989
                                                 January 1, 1991

Some taxpayers may have difficulty identifying the binding contract and placed in service dates of specific assets. Where the taxpayer's accounting system does not identify such dates, the Committee Reports indicate that the taxpayer is to assume that the first items placed in service after 12-31-86 (ACRS) or 12-31-85 (ITC) were those they had under a binding contract on that date. A similar rule is to apply to self-constructed property.

Corporate takeovers. A special rule applies if at least 80% of a target corporation's stock is acquired on or before 12-31-86 (ACRS) or 12-31-85 (ITC). Here, the acquiring corporation is treated as having purchased the assets before the general effective date, if it makes a Sec. 338 election to treat the stock purchase as an asset purchase after the binding contract dates.

Binding-contract rule. The transitional rules apply only to written contracts:

- In which the construction, reconstruction, erection, or acquisition is itself the subject matter of the contract.
- That are enforceable under state law against the taxpayer and do not limit damages to a specified amount (e.g., by use of liquidated damages provisions). A contract that limits damages to an amount equal to at least 5% of the total contract price is treated as not limiting damages.
- That are binding on the taxpayer. The grant of an unconditional put (i.e., an option to sell) to another taxpayer is a binding contract. However, an option to buy is not a binding contract.
- That are not substantially modified after 3-1-86 (ACRS) or 12-31-85 (ITC).

The binding-contract rule will not apply to supply agreements with manufacturers where the contract does not specify the amount or design specifications of the property to be purchased. Such agreements are not treated as binding contracts until purchase orders are actually placed. A purchase order for a specific number of items, based on the pricing provisions of the supply ageement, will be treated as a binding contract.

Special rules apply to films (TV or motion-picture) for purposes of the ITC transition dates: production on a film is treated as construction; written contemporary evidence of a binding contract in accordance with industry practice is treated as a written binding contract; and a license agreement between a TV network and a producer is treated as a binding contract. Finally, the ITC may be claimed on motion-picture films if financing was arranged by a public offering before 9-26-85, 40% of the funds was spent on films that began production before that date, and all the films financed by the public offering are required to be distributed under distribution agreements entered into before that date.

A taxpayer that enters into a binding contract for a component (e.g., an aircraft engine) is not considered to have entered into a binding contract for the entire property (e.g., the aircraft as a whole). If a taxpayer holds a binding contract and transfers his rights, the modified ACRS rules do not apply to the transferee, as long as the property wasn't placed in service before the transfer by the transferor. If a partnership that holds a binding contract undergoes a deemed termination and reconstitution under Sec. 708(b)(1)(B), then the old partnership is considered to have transferred its rights to the property under the contract to the new partnership.

There's special transition relief for written binding contracts that are not between the person who will own the property and the person who will build or supply the property. The relief applies to a written supply or service contract, or a lease agreement, that was binding on 3-1-86 (for ACRS recovery) or 12-31-85 (for ITC allowances). The exception applies only when the specifications and amount of the property are readily ascertainable from the terms of the contract or related documents.

Sale-leasebacks. Property that is sold and leased back is treated as having met the ACRS or ITC general or transitional effective dates if:

- The property qualified in the seller's hands under a transitional rule *or* was placed in service by the seller prior to 1-1-87 (for ACRS recovery) or 1-1-86 (for ITC allowances).

- The property was leased back by the buyer to the seller by the earlier of (1) the applicable placed-in-service date that applies under the transitional rules, or (2) three months after the property was originally placed in service.

Self-constructed property. The transitional rules apply to self-constructed property if a minimum amount was incurred or committed as of 3-1-86 (for ACRS recovery) or 12-31-85 (for ITC allowances) and construction or reconstruction began after the appropriate date. The minimum amount is the lesser of $1 million or 5% of the property's cost. The engineer or general contractor is treated as constructing the property. Construction is considered to have commenced when physical work of a significant nature starts. It does not include construction of minor parts or components, or preliminary work such as planning and designing, securing financing, etc.

¶209

Equipped buildings. A liberal transition rule applies to buildings, equipment and machinery to be used in the structure, and appurtenances (e.g., structures such as railroad sidings, and peripheral machinery and equipment). Prior law's ACRS rules, and prior law's investment credit allowances will continue to apply to the entire equipped building and its appurtenances if on or before 3-1-86 (for ACRS recovery) or 12-31-85 (for ITC allowances):

• A specific written plan existed for the work or acquisition (and the plan is not substantially modified after the appropriate date or dates),

• More than half the cost of the building and its equipment and machinery (but not appurtenances) was incurred or committed, and

• Construction or reconstruction of the property commenced.

If the more-than-50% rule is not met, then each item of machinery and equipment is treated separately for purposes of the transition rules.

IMPORTANT: The equipped building must be placed in service before the appropriate ACRS/ITC dates (shown in the chart) in order to qualify for the transitional rule.

A comparable transitional rule applies to plant facilities which are not housed in a building.

Property financed with tax-exempt bonds. In general, depreciable property placed in service after 12-31-86 must be recovered with the new alternative depreciation system to the extent it is financed with tax-exempt bonds issued after 3-1-86. However, this rule does not apply if

• The original use of the property commences with the taxpayer and the construction, reconstruction, or rehabilitation started before 3-2-86 and was completed after that date;

• A binding contract to incur significant expenses was entered into before 3-2-86 and some or all of the expenses were incurred after 3-1-86; or

• The property was acquired on or after 3-2-86 under a binding contract entered into before that date, and is described in an inducement resolution or other comparable preliminary approval adopted by the issuing authority (or voter referendum) before 3-2-86.

A post-3-1-86 refunding issue is treated as a new issue and the unrecovered cost of property financed with its proceeds must be depreciated using the alternative system. If significant costs (more than 10% of those reasonably anticipated) were made before 1-1-87, the alternative depreciation system does not apply to the extent the facilities are financed with an obligation issued solely to refinance a pre-3-2-86 issue.

Other transitional rules. The new law has special transitional rules for qualified urban renewal projects, projects licensed or certified by the Federal Energy Regulatory Commission, and qualified solid waste disposal facilities. There are other transition rules that benefit specific projects.

Act Sec. 203 provides effective dates and general transition rules for the revised ACRS system. Act Sec. 204 provides special transition rules for specific projects. Act Sec. 211(a) adds new Sec. 49(e), relating to transition rules for the ITC. Act Sec. 211(b) provides special normalization rules for public utility property. Act Sec. 211(c) makes a conforming amendment to the table of sections for subpart E of part IV of subchapter A of chapter 1. Act Sec. 211(d) provides a special ITC transition rule. Act Sec. 211(e) provides general effective date for ITC repeal (property placed in service after 12-31-85 in tax years ending after that date), and provides transition relief for certain films, effective date for normalization rules, and additional exceptions from the ITC repeal.

[¶210] **General Business Credit Offset Reduced.** The limitation on the income tax liability in excess of $25,000 of an individual or corporation that may be offset by the general business credit is reduced to 75% from 85%, effective for tax years beginning after 12-31-85.

Act Sec. 221, reducing the general business credit offset amount, amends Sec. 38(c)(1), effective for tax years beginning after 12-31-85.

Research and Development

[¶211] **Research Tax Credit Revived in Modified Form.** The new law grants a three-year lease on life to the research tax credit, which was scheduled to expire at the end of 1985. The credit will be available for eligible expenses paid or incurred through 12-31-88. Under prior law, the credit was 25% of the excess of qualified research expenses over average research expenses in the base period (generally, the three preceding tax years). Sixty-five percent of contract research expenses (for work done by others, including basic research by universities and tax exempt research organizations) counted as research expenses.

The new law reduces the R&E credit to 20% and keeps the base-period rule only for qualified research expenses, which are defined more narrowly than under prior law. The base period is the three-tax-year period ending with the tax year immediately preceding the first tax year of the taxpayer beginning after 12-31-83. Effective for tax years beginning after 1986, the new law introduces a new 20%

credit and a special set of operating rules for "basic research expenses," a new category that replaces prior law's contract research expenses.

Qualified research expenses. To be eligible for the regular credit, research expenses must qualify for expensing or amortization under Sec. 174, be conducted in the United States, and be paid by the taxpayer (e.g., not funded by government grant). In addition, the research must be research and development in the experimental or laboratory sense and must pass a new three-part test.

- It must be undertaken to discover information that is technological in nature. The research must fundamentally rely on the principles of the physical, biological, engineering, or computer sciences.

- Substantially all of the research activities must constitute elements of a process of experimentation relating to a new or improved function, performance, or reliability or quality. Research involves a process of experimentation only if the design of the item as a whole is uncertain at the outset. Examples: Developing and testing a new drug or designing a new computer system.

- The application of the research is intended to be useful in the development of a new or improved business component. This is a product, process, software, technique, formula or invention to be sold, leased or licensed or used by the taxpayer in a trade or business. Research is conducted for a qualified purpose if it relates to (1) a new or improved function; (2) performance; (3) reliability or quality; or (4) reduced cost.

The three requirements are first applied at the product level. If the product as a whole does not qualify for the credit, then subsets of the product are examined to see whether a portion of the total cost qualifies. For example, even if research on a new computer system as a whole does not satisfy all the tests, the development of a specific component (e.g., a new integrated chip or circuit) may qualify.

Special rules for internal use computer software. Software developed primarily for the taxpayer's internal use qualifies for the credit only if it is used in qualified research (other than the development of the software itself) or in a production process that involves a credit-eligible component. The development of internal use software for general or administrative functions (such as payroll or accounting) is ineligible for the credit.

Treasury regulations are to prescribe three more tests for internal use software. It must (1) be innovative; (2) involve significant economic risk; and (3) not be commercially available elsewhere.

Ineligible expenses. Research expenses related to the following items do not qualify for the credit:

- Style, taste, cosmetic, or seasonal design factors.
- The social sciences, arts, or humanities.
- Efficiency surveys, management studies, market research (including advertising and promotion), routine data collection, and routine quality-control testing or inspection.
- Expenses incurred after commercial production has begun.
- The costs of ascertaining the existence, location, extent, or quality of any ore or mineral deposit (including oil and gas). *Note:* Expenses of developing new or innovative methods of extracting minerals qualify.
- Development of any plant process, machinery, or technique for the commercial production of a business component, unless the process is technologically new or improved.
- Adaptation of a business component to suit a particular customer's needs.
- Partial or complete reproduction of an existing business component from plans, specifications, a physical examination, or publicly available information.

OBSERVATION: Although an expense is not eligible for the credit, it may qualify for expensing or 60-month amortization under Sec. 174.

Rental costs. Rental payments made for personal property are not eligible for the research credit. However, payments for computer time are eligible if made to further qualified research.

Basic research expenses. Effective for tax years beginning after 1986, there's a new tax credit equal to 20% of all basic research expenses in excess of a special base amount. The credit is available to any corporation other than an S corporation, a personal holding company, or a service organization as defined by Sec. 414(m)(3). Basic research consists of any original investigation for the advancement of scientific knowledge not having a specific commercial objective. The research does not have to be conducted in the same field as the taxpayer's trade or business. The expenses are not deductible until actually paid in cash under a written agreement between the taxpayer and the qualifying organization. The term qualified organizations includes most colleges, universities, tax-exempt scientific research organizations, and certain tax-exempt conduit or grant organizations (other than private foundations).

How to figure the 20% tax credit for basic research expenses. The credit is equal to 20% of the excess of qualifying basic research expenses over a special floor that consists of

- the minimum basic research amount, plus
- the maintenance-of-effort amount.

The minimum basic research amount is the greater of

- the average of contract research expenses during the base period [contract research expenses were the old-law equivalent of basic research expenses], or

- 1% of the average of in-house research expenses, contract research expenses, and credit-eligible basic research expenses during the base period.

In general, the base period is the three-tax-year period ending with the tax year immediately preceding the first tax year of the taxpayer beginning after 12-31-83.

The maintenance-of-effort amount is the average of all nondesignated university contributions made during the base period (as defined above), adjusted by the Sec. 1 cost-of-living factor for the calendar year in which the tax years begins, less the nondesignated university contributions made during the current tax year. Nondesignated university contributions are contributions to colleges, universities, tax-exempt research foundations, etc., for which a Sec. 170 charitable deduction was allowable and which weren't taken into account in computing the research credit.

Interplay of regular 20% credit and basic-research 20% credit. Basic-research expenses eligible for the new 20% credit are not eligible for and are not figured into the computation of the regular 20% credit (i.e., they are not included in base-period research expenses). However, basic-research expenses that are ineligible for the new 20% credit because of the special floor do count as expenses eligible for the regular 20% credit.

> **Example:** ABC Corp.'s qualified research expenses exceed base-period research expenses by $80,000. It has a total of $60,000 in basic research expenses. Assume the basic research floor amount is $20,000. Result: ABC may claim an $8,000 credit for basic research ($60,000 less $20,000 times 20%). It may also claim a $20,000 credit for qualified research expenses ($80,000 of qualified research expenses, plus $20,000 of basic research expenses for which the new credit was not claimed, times 20%). Total research credit: $28,000.

Other limitations. The research credit is now subject to the overall limitation that applies to general business tax credits (e.g., credits can offset only 75% of tax liability over $25,000) [¶210]. And a tough rule applies to sole proprietors, partners, beneficiaries of an estate or trust, and shareholders of S corporations: the research credit may offset only the tax attributable to the taxpayer's interest in the trade or business that generated the credit. That's the total tax bill less the tax that would be owed on income exclusive of the credit-producing trade or business.

> **OBSERVATION:** This credit limitation is much harsher than the general credit limit imposed by the new passive-loss rules [¶502]. The general limit restricts passive-source credits to tax owed on "passive activity" income only if the taxpayer does not materially participate in the activity. The limit on research credits applies whether or not the taxpayer materially participates in the trade or business that gives rise to the credits.

Act Sec. 231(a) adds new Sec. 30(h)(1), relating to termination of the research credit for amounts paid or incurred after 12-31-88, and new Sec. 30(h)(2), relating to computation of base-period expenses for tax years beginning before 1-1-89 and ending after 12-31-88. Act Sec. 231(b) amends Sec. 30(d), relating to definition of qualified research. Act Sec. 231(c)(1) amends Sec. 30(a), relating to reduction of research credit. Act Sec. 231(c)(2) amends Sec. 30(e), relating to expenses eligible for basic research expenses. Act Sec. 231(d) amends Sec. 38(b), relating to research credit treated as other business credits, redesignates Sec. 30 as Sec. 41, and makes technical and conforming amendments to Secs. 28, 41(g), 108(b)(2), 381(c), 936(h)(5)(C)(i)(I)(a), 6411, and 6511(d)(6). Act Sec. 231(d) also adds new Sec. 39(d) and makes technical and conforming amendments to the table of sections for part IV of subchapter A of chapter 1. Act Sec. 231(e) amends Sec. 41(b)(2)(A) [as redesignated], relating to denial of credit with respect to payments for certain leased personal property. The modifications to the research credit are generally effective for tax years ending after 12-31-85, except that the modifications to the basic research tax credit are effective for tax years beginning after 12-31-86.

[¶212] Augmented Deduction for Certain Contributions of Scientific Research Property. The general rule is that the charitable contribution deduction must be reduced by the amount of ordinary gain the taxpayer would have realized had the property been sold at fair market value instead of being donated. A special rule permits corporations to take an augmented charitable deduction for donations of newly manufactured scientific equipment or apparatus to a college or university for research use in the physical or biological sciences. The new law extends the category of eligible donees to include tax-exempt organizations that (1) are organized and operated primarily to conduct scientific research; (2) are described in Sec. 501(c)(3); and (3) are not private foundations.

Act Sec. 231(f), amends Code Sec. 170(e)(4), effective for tax years beginning after 12-31-85.

[¶213] Orphan Drug Credit Extended. The new law extends the 50% credit for clinical testing of orphan drugs for three years through 12-31-90.

Act Sec. 232, relating to the credit for clinical testing expenses for certain drugs, amends Code Sec. 28, effective upon enactment.

[¶214] Repeal of Rapid Writeoff of Trademark and Trade Name Expenditures and 50-year Amortization of Certain Railroad Property. The election to amortize over at least a 60-month period expenditures for acquiring, protecting, expanding, registering, or defending a trademark or trade name is repealed. Therefore, trademark and trade name expenditures will be capitalized and generally recovered on disposition of the asset. The repeal is effective for amounts paid or incurred after 12-31-86. However, prior law will continue to apply to expenditures incurred (1) pursuant to a written contract that was binding as of 3-1-86; or (2) as to developing, protecting, expanding, registering, or defending trademarks or trade names begun as of 3-1-86, if the lesser of $1 million or 5% of the cost has been incurred or committed by that date, provided in each case the trademark or trade name is placed in service before 1-1-88.

Repeal of 50-year amortization: Effective for expenses after 12-31-86, the new law repeals special 50-year amortization of railroad grading and tunnel-bore expenditures. Such expenses will be capitalized and recovered on disposition of the asset.

Act Sec. 241, repealing five-year amortization of trademark and trade name expenditures, repeals Sec. 177, effective generally for expenditures paid or incurred after 12-31-86. Act Sec. 242 repeals Sec. 185 (relating to 50-year amortization), effective for expenses paid or incurred after 12-31-86. Expenses covered by special transition rules may continue to be amortized over 50 years.

[¶215] Deduction for Loss in Value of Certain Bus Operating Authorities and Freight Forwarder Authority. An ordinary deduction is allowed ratably over a 60-month period for taxpayers who held one or more intercity bus operating authorities on 11-19-82. The deduction's amount is the aggregate adjusted bases of all bus operating authorities that were held by the taxpayer on 11-19-82, or acquired after that date under a contract binding on that date.

The 60-month period begins with the later of 11-1-82, or, at the taxpayer's election, the first month of the taxpayer's first tax year beginning after that date. Adjustments must be made to the bases of authorities to reflect amounts allowable as deductions.

Under regulations to be prescribed, corporate or noncorporate taxpayers holding an eligible bus operating authority can elect to allocate to the authority a portion of the cost to the taxpayer of stock in an acquired corporation (unless an election under IRC Sec. 338 is in effect). The election is available if the bus operating authority was held (directly or indirectly) by the taxpayer when its stock was acquired. Here, part of the stock basis is allocated to the authority only if the corporate or noncorporate taxpayer would have been able to make such an allocation had the authority been distributed in a liquidation to which prior law Sec. 334(b)(2) applied. The election is available only if the stock was acquired on or before 11-19-82 (or pursuant to a binding contract in effect on that date).

The provision is effective retroactively for tax years ending after 11-18-82. The period of limitations is extended for filing claims for refund or credit of any overpayment of tax resulting from this rule, if that claim is prevented on or before the date that is one year after date of enactment. In that case, a refund or credit claim may be made or allowed if filed on or before the date that is six months after that date. In addition, the new amortization provision also includes freight forwarders, contingent on deregulation.

Act Sec. 243, creating a deduction for loss in value of certain bus operating authorities, effective generally retroactively for tax years ending after 11-18-82, and for freight forwarder operating authority effective to tax years ending after the month preceding the deregulation month.

[¶216] Expensing of Costs for Removal of Architectural Barriers. The new law makes permanent the provision allowing expensing of up to $35,000 of costs incurred for removing architectural and transportation barriers to the handicapped and elderly. Under prior law, the expensing provision was not available for expenses incurred in tax years beginning after 12-31-85.

Act Sec. 244 extending the expensing deduction, amends Sec. 190(d)(2), effective for amounts incurred in taxable years beginning after 1985.

[¶217] Tax Credit for Rehabilitation Expenses. The new law replaces the three-tier rehabilitation credit with a two-tier credit for qualified rehabilitation expenses. The new credit percentage is 20% for the rehabilitation of certified historic structures and 10% for the rehabilitation of buildings, other than historic structures, originally placed in service before 1936.

Under prior law the rehabilitation tax credit was 15% for nonresidential buildings at least 30 years old, 20% for nonresidential buildings at least 40 years old, and 25% for certified historic structures.

As under prior law, the new credit for the rehabilitation of historic structures applies to both residential and nonresidential buildings, while the new credit for the rehabilitation of buildings (other than historic structures) only applies to nonresidential buildings.

Prior law provisions that determine whether rehabilitation expenditures qualify for the credit generally have been retained. An expenditure is not eligible for the credit unless the taxpayer elects to recover the rehabilitation costs using the straight-line method of depreciation. A lessee's expenditures don't qualify for the credit unless the remaining lease term, on the date the rehabilitation is completed, is at least as long as the applicable recovery period (31½ years for nonresidential property, 27½ years for residential property).

External-walls requirement. The new law significantly modifies the external walls requirement. The prior provision that required 75% of the existing external walls to be retained in place as external walls has been deleted, and replaced by the prior law alternate test. This test requires the retention in place of (1) at least 75% of the existing external walls, including at least 50% as external walls, as well as (2) at least 75% of the building's internal structural framework. So a completely gutted building cannot qualify for the rehabilitation credit. A building's internal structural framework generally includes all load-bearing internal walls and any other internal structural supports, including the columns, girders, beams, trusses, spandrels, and all other members that are essential to the building's stability. Although the external-walls requirement is waived for historic structures, the Secretary of the Interior is expected to continue generally to deny certification to rehabilitation where less than 75% of external walls are not retained in place.

Basis reduction. The new law deleted the prior law provision that required a basis reduction for only 50% of the credit for certified historic structures. So a full adjustment is required for both the 10% and 20% rehabilitation credits.

Effective date and transition rules: In general, the new rules are effective for property placed in service after 12-31-86. Special transition rules apply to:

- Property placed in service as rehabilitation property before 1-1-94, if the rehabilitation was completed under a written contract binding on 3-1-86.

- Rehabilitation of property (including any leasehold interest) acquired before 3-2-86 or acquired on or after that date, if (1) the rehabilitation was completed under a written contract binding on 3-1-86, and a historic certification application was submitted to the Department of the Interior (or its designee) before 3-2-86, or (2) the lesser of $1,000,000 or 5% of the rehabilitation cost was incurred before 3-2-86, or is required to be incurred under a written contract binding on 3-1-86.

There are additional transition rules for specific projects.

Property covered by the transition rules is eligible for a 20% credit (historic rehab), 13% credit (nonresidential buildings at least 40 years old), or 10% credit (for nonresidential buildings at least 30 years old). However, a full basis adjustment is required even if the project is covered by the transition rules. There are special credit rules for certain specific projects.

ACRS BREAK: A rehabilitation project covered by the transition rules is exempted from the new law's longer writeoff period for real estate [¶203]. Transition property can be depreciated (using straight line) over a 19-year recovery period even if placed in service after 12-31-86.

Act Sec. 2, relating to tax credit for rehabilitation expenditures, amends Code Secs. 46(b), 48(g), and 48(q)(3), effective as shown above.

[¶218] **Low-Income Housing Credits.** Owners of residential rental property providing low-income housing will be allowed new credits under the new reform law. These credits replace existing tax incentives for low-income housing such as preferential depreciation, five-year amortization of rehabilitation expenditures and special treatment of construction period interest and taxes.

Here's a rundown of the new credits:

New construction and rehabilitation. A new credit of up to 9% is allowed each year over a 10-year period. The credit is taken on expenses for new construction and rehabilitation of each qualifying low-income housing unit. To qualify for the credit, expenses must exceed $2,000 per low-income unit. The credit rate is equivalent to a credit with the present value of 70%.

New construction and rehabilitation financed with tax-exempt bonds or similar federal subsidies. A maximum credit of 4% each year for 10 years is allowed on the construction and rehabilitation financed with tax-exempt bonds or similar federal subsidies, such as FMHA loans. These expenses must also exceed $2,000 per low-income unit to qualify for the credit. The credit rate is equivalent to a credit with a present value of 30%.

ADJUSTMENTS TO CREDIT PERCENTAGES: For buildings placed in service after 1987, the 9% and 4% credit percentages, above, will be adjusted monthly by the Treasury to reflect the present values of 70% and 30% at the time the building is placed in service.

Cost of acquiring existing housing. There is also a credit for acquiring each low-income housing unit. The maximum credit is 4% each year over a 10-year period on the cost of acquiring each low-income housing unit. To qualify for the credit, the property must not have been placed in service within the previous 10 years. If the low-income housing project is financed at least in part by the federal government, the Treasury Secretary may under certain conditions waive the 10-year requirement. This credit will be granted even when there is no rehabilitation.

¶218

State volume limitation. Low-income rental housing tax credits can be issued by each state in an amount equal to $1.25 per state resident. Qualified housing expenditures that are not financed with tax-exempt bond proceeds must receive credit authority from the state. Expenditures from tax-exempt bond financing that qualify for the credit receive the credit without reducing a state's credit authority. No separate volume limitation is applied to low-income rental housing tax credits for these projects. The reason: tax-exempt bonds for multifamily rental housing are limited under state volume limitations.

States must reserve at least 10% of their credit authority for projects that are developed by certain nonprofit organizations that foster low-income housing.

Targeting requirement. To receive the credit:

• At least 20% of units in a project must be occupied by individuals having incomes of 50% or less of area median income, adjusted for family size; or

• At least 40% of units in project must be occupied by individuals having incomes of 60% or less of area median income, adjusted for family size.

Income limits may be adjusted for areas with unusually low family income or high housing costs relative to family income. The gross rent charged to tenants in units eligible for the credit may not be more than 30% of the qualifying income for a family of its size. Gross rent includes the cost of utilities, other than telephone. Once a project qualifies for the credit it must continue to satisfy the eligibility requirements for a 15-year period. If it doesn't, prior credits will be recaptured.

Qualifying units. All rental units must be suitable for occupancy. They will not qualify for the credit if they are used on a transient basis. Thus, hotels, dormitories, hospitals, nursing homes, lifecare facilities, and retirement homes will not qualify. Single room occupancy housing used on a nontransient basis will qualify even though such housing may provide eating, cooking, and sanitation facilities on a shared basis.

Basis adjustments. The basis of the housing project with respect to which the housing credits are allowed must be reduced by any rehabilitation credits. However, the project's basis for depreciation is not reduced by the housing credits claimed.

Act Sec. 252 relating to the granting of the low-income housing credit, adds new Sec. 42, effective for property placed in service after 1986 (other than property grandfathered under the depreciation rules) and before 1990. Property placed in service after 1989 may qualify for the credit if expenditures of 10% or more of the reasonably expected costs are incurred before

1-1-89, and the property is placed in service before 1-1-91. Special transitional rules apply under Sec. 252(f).

[¶219]   **Merchant Marine Capital Construction Funds.** The new law recodifies the tax provisions of the Merchant Marine Act of 1936, and adopts the same definitions of terms as those included in the Merchant Marine Act, as added.

Tax treatment of nonqualified withdrawals. Nonqualified withdrawals made after 12-31-85 are to be taxed at the maximum individual or corporate rate. Interest is payable from the date the withdrawn amount is reported. The rule is modified in cases where the taxpayer derived no tax benefit from depositing the funds.

Fund reports. The Transportation and Commerce Secretaries must certify to the Treasury Secretary that the monies in a fund are appropriate for vessel construction requirements. If fund balances exceed what is appropriate to meet vessel construction program objectives, the fundholder must develop appropriate program objectives within three years or treat the excess as a nonqualified withdrawal.

25-year deposit limitation. Monies must be withdrawn from the fund for a qualified purpose within 25 years. Monies that are not either withdrawn or committed by the end of the 25-year period are classified as nonqualified withdrawals, using a 5-year phase-in rule.

Act Sec. 261, relating to Merchant Marine Capital Construction Funds, adds new Code Sec. 7518, effective for tax years beginning after 12-31-86.

[The page following this is 301.]

CAPITAL GAINS AND LOSSES

[¶301] Long-Term Capital Gain Break Repealed. The new law repeals the capital gain deduction for individuals. Under prior law, individuals and other noncorporate taxpayers could deduct 60% of net capital gain from gross income. The $3,000 annual loss limitation for noncorporate taxpayers is retained, but long-term losses (like short-term losses) offset ordinary income on a one-for-one basis. Under prior law, long-term losses offset ordinary income on a two-for-one basis. Sec. 1231 gain will continue to be computed separately from long-term gain. Although individual and corporate capital gain will lose its special tax status, the Code's capital-gains statutory structure is retained to make it easier to reinstate a capital gains rate differential if there is a future increase in the tax rates.

Act Sec. 301 repeals the Sec. 1202 capital gains deduction, effective for tax years beginning after 12-31-86.

[¶302] Capital Gains Rate for 1987 and 1988. For tax year 1987, a noncorporate taxpayer's long-term capital gains and short-term capital gains will be taxed as ordinary income. However, long-term capital gains will be taxed at a maximum rate of 28%. But short-term gains will be taxed at ordinary rates. For tax year 1988, there will no longer be a distinction between short-and long-term capital gains. Gains will be taxed at a maximum rate of 28% (unless the taxpayer must pay a 5% surcharge, see ¶101).

Effective for the 1987 tax year, corporate long-term capital gains will be taxed as ordinary income but will be subject to a maximum tax rate of 34%. Prior law's special corporate capital gains rate of 28% is repealed.

The alternative tax rate for corporate net capital gains doesn't apply for gain included in income in tax years when the new corporate rates are fully effective (years starting on or after 7-1-87). For gain included in income in earlier tax years but after 12-31-86, the alternative tax rate is 34%.

Example (1): Bob and Jane are married and have taxable income, other than from capital transactions, of $50,000. They also sold stock they had held 15 months at a $10,000 gain. If these figures applied to 1986, their total tax liability would be $12,577, figured as follows:

Taxable ordinary income	$50,000
Taxable income from long-term capital gain (40% of $10,000)	4,000
Total taxable income	$54,000
Tax (38% marginal rate)	$12,577

If these figures applied to 1987, their total tax liability would be $13,390.

11% of first $3,000	$ 330
15% of next $25,000	3,750
28% of next $17,000	4,760
35% of next $5,000	1,750
28% of $10,000 (LTCG)	2,800
Total tax	$13,390

Starting in 1988, capital gains are added to ordinary income. For 1988, the tax would be $12,932.50.

15% of first $29,750	$ 4,462.50
28% on the excess	
($50,000 + $10,000 − $29,750)	8,470.00
Total Tax	$12,932.50

Example (2): Ted and Anne have $25,000 of taxable income for 1987, which includes $5,000 of long-term capital gains. Result: The long-term gain is taxed at a marginal rate of 15%.

Example (3): Al and Carol had long-term capital gains of $10,000 and long-term capital losses of $30,000 in 1986. Their long-term losses exceed their long-term gains by $20,000. In 1986, they can use $6,000 of this excess loss to offset $3,000 of ordinary income. Their capital loss carryforward as of 1-1-87 is $14,000 ($20,000 − $6,000). In 1987 and thereafter, they can deduct an additional $3,000 a year to offset $3,000 in ordinary income (assuming no additional capital gains) until the carryover is reduced to zero. Their carryover is $11,000 ($14,000 − $3,000) as of 1-1-88.

TIP: If you are planning to sell capital gain property in the next year or so, figure out whether it would be best to sell in 1986, 1987, or 1988, keeping in mind that tax is only one consideration. If the property is expected to appreciate substantially, it might be a good idea to hold onto it even though you might get hit with a higher tax.

Year-end strategies. Here are three strategies you can use before the end of 1986 to minimize the tax on your capital gain.

Strategy # 1: Before the end of 1986, consider selling property showing a long-term gain. Obvious reason: You avoid paying tax on the gain at the higher rates after 1986.

Strategy # 2: You may want to defer the tax on this year's short-term gains to next year. For example, suppose you bought stock three months ago. It is showing a paper gain. You want to sell the stock, but you do not want to pay tax on the short-term gain at the high 1986 rates.

Alternative moves: (1) You can defer the tax to 1987 by buying a put option for a long enough period to carry you into January 1987. A put option gives you the right to sell the stock to the put seller at an agreed-upon price (in this case, at or near the 1986 sale price). If the price of the stock goes up, you sell it in 1987. You don't exercise the put. If the price drops, you do exercise the put in 1987. Either way, you pay tax at the significantly lower 1987 rates.

(2) Set up a "short sale against the box" in 1986, but don't close the sale until 1987. A short sale happens when you have your broker borrow stock and sell it on your behalf. At this point, your profit is locked in. Gain from a short sale is automatically short term. However, you don't have to pay tax on the gain until the sale is closed at a later date. You close a short sale against the box by repaying the broker with the stock you own. Tax result: You nail down your 1986 profit, and you defer the tax on the short-term gain until 1987.

Strategy # 3: This is the last year you get a tax choice when you sell publicly traded securities during the last five trading days of the year. Starting in 1987, you pay tax the year you make the sale. In 1986, however, you can treat the transaction as an installment sale and pay tax in 1987 (i.e., when the cash settlement is made). Or you can elect out of installment tax treatment and pay tax in 1986 (i.e., the year you made the sale).

The tax flexibility you have by selling listed stocks or bonds during the last five trading days is especially important in 1986. You can have net short-term gain taxed in 1987 under the installment sale rules. And you can have net long-term gain taxed in 1986 by electing out of installment sale treatment.

> **NOTE:** Taxpayers who are at least 55 years' old can still exclude the first $125,000 of gain on the sale of a principal residence. The rule does not change under the new law.

Act Secs. 302 and 311, limiting the maximum tax rate on net capital gains to 28% and repealing the corporate alternative capital gain tax rate, amend Secs. 1 and 1211, effective for tax years beginning after 12-31-86.

[¶303] Changes for ISOs. Executive stock option plans may be either qualified (incentive stock options) or nonqualified. An advantage of an incentive stock option is that the taxpayer doesn't owe a tax until the stock acquired with the option is sold. Exercising a nonqualified option triggers a tax. However, the employer can deduct the nonqualified option when it is exercised, whereas there is no deduction when the incentive stock option is exercised.

These attributes do not change under tax reform. But the tax reform does create some new similarities.

Sequence of exercise. For options issued before 1987, executives had to use the first in first out method. They had to exercise options in the order they were granted, whether the options were qualified or nonqualified. The FIFO method won't be required for options exercised after 1986. So if the stock price falls below the option price, the company can issue the executive a second incentive option with a lower exercise price.

Capital gain. Since capital gains will be taxed at the same rate as ordinary income, there will no longer be a tax break when the stock is sold. Before the new law, the spread betweem the option's exercise price and the stock price (the bargain element) was taxed as long-term capital gain if the stock was held for more than a year before sale.

Special break for 1987. For 1987 only, the top capital gain rate will be 28%, compared to a top ordinary rate of 38½%. So incentive stock sold in 1987 will still get a tax break, provided it was held more than one year before sale.

Modified dollar caps. Starting in 1987, there is a $100,000 per employee limit on the value of stock covered by options that are exercisable in any one calendar year. Before 1987, the limit applied to the value of options granted in any one year.

Act Sec. 321 repeals the requirement that incentive stock options be exercisable in chronological order, and modifies the $100,000 limitation, amending Sec. 422A(b)(7) for options granted after 1986.

[¶304]   **Covered Call Options—Year-End Rule Expanded.** The qualified covered call exception to the loss deferral rule is denied to taxpayers who don't hold a covered call option for 30 days after the related stock is disposed of at a loss, when gain on the option is included in the next year.

Act Sec. 331 expands the year-end rule for straddles by amending Sec. 1092(c)(4)(E), effective for positions established after 1986.

[¶311]   **Capital Gains for Timber and Dairy Cattle.** The end of special treatment for long-term capital gains means that under the new law, taxpayers won't get that treatment for gain from timber dispositions treated as sales. However, the new law will let taxpayers revoke a past election (under Sec. 631(a)) to treat the cutting of timber as a sale or exchange.

Act Sec. 406 states that the capital gains amendments will not apply to any gain from the sale of dairy cattle under a valid contract with the U.S. Department of Agriculture under the milk production termination program for gains made after 1-1-87 and before 9-1-87.

Act Sec. 311, allowing the revocation of elections to treat the cutting of timber as a sale or exchange, amends Sec. 631(a), effective for elections made before 8-17-86.

[The page following this is 401.]

AGRICULTURE, ENERGY, AND NATURAL RESOURCES

Farming

[¶401] Limitation on Expensing of Soil and Water Conservation Expenditures. The new law limits the expensing deduction for soil and water conservation expenditures to amounts incurred that are consistent with a conservation plan approved by the Department of Agriculture's Soil Conservation Service. If no SCS plan exists for the location, improvement costs that are consistent with a state conservation agency plan will satisfy the federal standards. The following costs may not be expensed:

- Draining or filling of wetlands.
- Preparing land for installing and operating a center pivot irrigation system.

The Conference Report clarifies that while prior approval of the taxpayer's project by the SCS or comparable state agency isn't necessary to qualify the expenditures under this provision, there must be an overall plan for the taxpayer's area that has been approved by an agency in effect at any time during the tax year.

Act Sec. 401, relating to the limitation on expensing soil and water conservation expenditures, adds new Sec. 175(c)(3), effective for amounts paid or incurred after 12-31-86, in tax years ending after that date.

[¶402] Expenditures for Clearing Land. Land clearing costs to prepare for farming that were formerly deductible must now be added to the land's basis. The Committee Reports clarify, however, that routine brush clearing and other ordinary maintenance activities related to property already used in farming continue to be currently deductible. These expenditures must be ordinary and necessary business expenses under Section 162. According to the Committee Reports, the special election to expense fertilizer and soil conditioning expenditures is retained.

Act Sec. 402, relating to repeal of special expenditures for clearing land, repeals Sec. 182, and amends Secs. 263(a) and 1252(a)(1)(A), effective for amounts paid or incurred after 12-31-85, in tax years ending after that date.

[¶403] Dispositions of 'Converted Wetlands' or 'Highly Erodible Croplands.' A gain on the disposition of "converted wetland" or "highly erodible cropland" that's converted to agricultural use (other than livestock grazing) is treated as ordinary income. The Treasury is to apply rules similar to those under Sec. 1245. A loss is treated as a long-term capital loss.

"Converted wetland" means land that is

• converted wetland within the meaning of Section 1201(4) of the 1985 Food Security Act (16 U.S.C. 3801(4)); and

• held by the person who originally converted the wetland, by a person who at any time used the land for farming, or by a person whose adjusted basis in the property is determined by reference to the basis of the person in whose hands the property was converted. According to the House Committee Report, land that had been converted could become eligible for Section 1231 treatment in the hands of a later buyer or legatee, provided the buyer or legatee used the land only for nonfarming purposes.

Generally, the Food Security Act defines converted wetland as land that has been drained or filled to make possible the production of agricultural goods, if it wouldn't have been possible but for this action.

"Highly erodible cropland" means any land as defined in Section 1201(6) of the Food Security Act (16 U.S.C. 3801(6)) that the taxpayer uses for farming other than animal grazing.

According to the House Committee Report, generally highly erodible cropland is land that

• the Department of Agriculture classifies as class IV, VI, VII, or VIII land under its land capability classification system, or

• would have an excess average annual rate of erosion in relation to the soil loss tolerance level, as determined by the Department of Agriculture.

Act Sec. 403, treatment of dispositions of converted wetlands or highly erodible croplands, adds new Sec. 1257, effective for dispositions first used for farming after 3-1-86 in tax years ending after that date.

[¶404] **Prepayments of Farming Expenses.** Under the new law, cash-basis taxpayers who are in the trade or business of farming aren't allowed a deduction for specified amounts paid for feed, seed, fertilizer, and other similar farm supplies earlier than the time when these items are actually used or consumed (that is, until the tax year in which economic performance occurs). The limitation applies to prepaid expenses to the extent they exceed 50% of the deductible farming expenses for the tax year (other than prepaid farm supplies) for which economic performance has occurred.

Farming is defined in Sec. 464(c)—generally, the cultivation of land or the raising of any agricultural or horticultural commodity, including animals.

These provisions generally apply to any farmer to the extent that more than 50% of the person's farming expenses paid during the tax year (other than prepaid farm supplies) are prepaid expenses. The new law doesn't, however, treat the taxpayers as farm syndicates. Under the Committee Reports, for purposes of the 50% test, expenses include the farm operating expenses such as

- ordinary and necessary farming expenses under Sec. 162,
- interest and taxes paid,
- depreciation allowances on farm equipment, and
- other expenses generally reported on Schedule F of Form 1040.

The new law provides two exceptions to the 50% test. If either exception is met, prepaid expenses will continue to be deducted as under current law, even though the prepaid expenses are more than 50% of farming expenses for that year.

Exception (1): If a qualified farm-related taxpayer fails to satisfy the 50% test because of a change in business operations directly attributable to extraordinary circumstances. This includes government crop diversion programs and circumstances under Sec. 464(d).

Exception (2): If a qualified farm-related taxpayer satisfies the 50% test on the basis of the three preceding tax years. For this purpose, the farming expenses (other than prepaid farm supplies) for the three-year period are aggregated.

Farm-related taxpayer includes:

(1) any person whose principal residence is on the farm;

(2) any person with a principal occupation of farming; or

(3) any family member of persons described in (1) or (2).

The exception applies only to an eligible farmer's farming activities attributable to the farm on which the residence is located, or to farms included in the "principal occupation" of farming activities.

The House and Senate Committee Reports make clear that the new law doesn't amend the farming syndicate rules of Sec. 464, and that this provision will operate independently of that provision. Also, farmers won't have to generally take year-end inventories of prepaid items as a result of the new law.

For explanation of the treatment of preproductive period expenses of farmers, and of the treatment of expenses for replanting groves, orchards, or vineyards destroyed in natural disasters, see ¶805.

Act Sec. 404, on prepayments of farming expenses, adds Sec. 464(f), effective for amounts paid or incurred after 3-1-86, in tax years beginning after that date.

[¶405] Treatment of Discharge of Debt Income. The new law provides that discharge of debt income arising from an agreement between a solvent individual engaged in farming and an unrelated qualified person to discharge qualified farming debt is treated as income realized by an insolvent individual.

Generally, if an insolvent taxpayer has income from the discharge of trade or business debt, the taxpayer can exclude that income if the taxpayer's "tax attributes" are reduced by the amount of income. Tax attributes include otherwise unused net operating loss deductions, investment tax credits, foreign tax credits, capital loss carryovers, and basis of the taxpayer's depreciable property. If the amount of discharge of debt income exceeds the taxpayer's available tax attributes, tax on the excess income is forgiven to the extent of the taxpayer's insolvency.

According to the Senate Report, qualified farm debt is one incurred to finance producing agricultural products (including timber) or livestock in the United States, or farm business debt secured by farmland or farm machinery and equipment used in agricultural production.

Individuals are treated as engaged in farming if at least 50% of the average annual gross receipts during the three tax years preceding the year in which the discharge of debt occurs were derived from farming.

Further, the new law includes basis in farmland in the list of tax attributes that may be reduced by the discharge of debt income. However, all tax attributes other than basis in farmland, including property other than farmland, must be reduced before the discharge of debt income is applied against that attribute.

Act Sec. 405, on treatment of discharge of indebtedness income for farmers, adding Sec. 108(g), and amending Sec. 1017(b), effective for discharges of indebtedness occurring after 4-9-86, in tax years ending after that date.

【¶406】 Retaining Capital Gains Treatment for Sales of Dairy Cattle Under Milk Production Termination Programs. The amendments made by Title III (Capital Gains and Losses), Subtitle A (Individual Capital Gains) and Subtitle B (Corporate Capital Gains) don't apply to any gain from the sale of dairy cattle under a valid contract with the U.S. Department of Agriculture covering the milk production termination program to the extent the gain is properly taken into account under the taxpayer's accounting method after 1-1-87 and before 9-1-87.

Timber

【¶408】 Capital Gains for Timber. The end of special treatment for long-term capital gains means that under the new law, taxpayers won't get that treatment for gain from timber dispositions treated as sales. However, the new law will let taxpayers revoke a past election (under Sec. 631(a)) to treat the cutting of timber as a sale or exchange.

The option will allow elections made for tax years beginning before January 1, 1987, to be revoked without IRS consent. The revocation can cover any tax year ending after December 31, 1986. Such a revocation won't prevent a taxpayer from making another election in a later year, but any future revocations will require IRS consent. See also ¶311.

> **NOTE:** The new law keeps the existing breaks for reforestation, including the investment credit for qualified reforestation expenses. See also ¶208.

Act Sec. 311(d)(2) allows the revocation of elections to treat the cutting of timber as a sale or exchange, effective for tax years beginning after 12-31-86. Act. Sec. 211(a), allowing a credit for qualified reforestation expenses, adds Sec. 49(b)(3) effective for expenses incurred after 12-31-85 in tax years ending after that date.

Oil, Gas & Geothermal Properties

[¶409] **Intangible Drilling Costs.** The new law increases, from 20% to 30%, the amount of otherwise deductible intangible drilling costs [IDCs] that integrated producer corporations must capitalize and amortize. Moreover, the amortization period has been increased from 36 months to 60 months, beginning with the month in which the costs are paid or incurred. The new law continues the rule that amortization deductions of capitalized IDCs must be included in any recapture calculations under Section 1254.

The new law adds the provision that the portion of the property's adjusted basis that's attributable to intangible costs capitalized under these rules can't be included in the property's depletable basis.

Foreign IDCs. Under the new law, the option to deduct IDCs no longer applies to IDCs incurred outside of the United States. Such costs can now be recovered either (1) in equal installments over the 10-year period starting with the year in which the costs were paid or incurred, or (2) if the taxpayer elects, by adding them to the basis for cost depletion. Both the House and Senate committee reports stated that for these purposes, the United States includes the 50 states and the District of Columbia, plus those continental shelf areas that are adjacent to U.S. territorial waters and over which the United States has exclusive rights regarding exploring for and exploiting natural resources.

> **NOTE:** 60-month amortization for integrated producer corporations doesn't apply to these foreign costs.

Dry holes. The new law provides that the new foreign IDC rules don't apply to costs paid or incurred regarding a nonproductive well. The Conference Committee report states that the new general rule on IDC capitalization doesn't affect the option to expense dry hole costs in the year the dry hole is completed.

Act Sec. 411(a), increasing the required capitalization of IDCs for integrated producer corporations, amends Section 291(b), and Act Sec. 411(b)(1) requiring the amortization of foreign IDC, adds new Sec. 263(i) and makes a clerical amendment to Sec. 263(a), all effective for costs paid or incurred after 12-31-86, in tax years ending after that date. There is also a special transition rule for IDCs of U.S. companies with certain interests in North Sea development.

[¶410] Bonuses and Advance Royalties. The new law reverses *Commissioner v. Engle* [(1984), 464 U.S. 206, 53 AFTR2d 84-415], in which the Supreme Court held that taxpayers could treat lease bonuses and advance royalties as part of gross income from the property in computing percentage depletion under the post-1974 rules. The new law limits percentage depletion on oil, gas, and geothermal wells to amounts received for actual production, specifically excluding lease bonuses, advance royalties, and other amounts payable without regard to production.

Act Sec. 412(a)(1), which prohibits percentage depletion on oil and gas payments not related to production, adds Sec. 613A(d)(5), and Act Sec. 412(a)(2), which prohibits percentage depletion on geothermal payments not related to production, adds Section 613(e)(4), both effective for amounts received or accrued after 8-16-86, in tax years ending after that date.

[¶411] Gain From Disposition of Interest in Oil, Gas, or Geothermal Property. The new law has greatly expanded the scope of Sec. 1254, which previously required recapture only of IDCs. It now not only requires recapture of depletion on oil, gas, and geothermal property, but also depletion, mine exploration costs, and mine development costs on hard mineral property [See ¶414].

Thus, on disposition of Sec. 1254 property that involves only oil, gas, or geothermal production, the taxpayer must recapture the lesser of (1) IDCs that were expensed rather than added to basis, plus depletion deductions that reduced the basis of the property (that is, none after the adjusted basis of the property reaches zero), or (2) the amount realized (for a sale, exchange, or involuntary conversion) or fair market value (for anything else), minus the property's adjusted basis.

The new law keeps most of the other existing rules of Section 1254, dropping only the provision that allows the amount of recapturable IDCs to be reduced by the amount by which depletion would have increased if the expensed IDCs had been capitalized.

Act Sec. 413, relating to gain from disposition of an interest in Section 1254 property, amends Code Sec. 1254, effective for property placed in service after 12-31-86, except property acquired under a written contract entered into before 9-26-85 and binding at all times thereafter.

[¶412] **Mine Exploration and Development Costs.** The new law increases, from 20% to 30%, the amount of otherwise deductible mine exploration and development costs that corporations must capitalize. Moreover, those costs must now be amortized over 60 months, beginning with the month in which the costs are paid or incurred, instead of being written off under the schedule that was in the Code.

The new law requires that amortization deductions of mine exploration and development costs be included in any recapture calculations under the new rules of Sec. 1254 [see ¶414]. It also provides that the portion of the property's adjusted basis that's attributable to costs capitalized under these rules can't be included in the property's depletable basis.

Foreign costs. Under the new law, the option to deduct mine exploration and development costs no longer applies to costs incurred outside of the United States. Such costs can now be recovered either (1) in equal installments over the 10-year period starting with the year in which the costs were paid or incurred, or (2) if the taxpayer elects, by adding them to the basis for cost depletion. Both the House and Senate committee reports stated that for these purposes, the United States includes the 50 states and the District of Columbia, plus those continental shelf areas that are adjacent to U.S. territorial waters and over which the United States has exclusive rights regarding exploring for and exploiting natural resources.

> **NOTE:** Sixty-month amortization for corporations doesn't apply to these foreign costs.

Act Sec. 411(a), increasing the required capitalization of mine exploration and development costs for corporations, amends Section 291(b), Act Sec. 411(b)(2)(A), requiring the amortization of foreign mine development costs, renumbers Section 616(d) as Section 616(e) and adds new Sec. 616(d), Act Sec. 411(b)(2)(B), requiring the amortization of foreign mine exploration costs, amends Sec. 617(h), and Act Sec. 411(b)(2)(C) makes certain clerical amendments, all effective for costs paid or incurred after 12-31-86, in tax years ending after that date.

[¶413] **Percentage Depletion.** The new law raises, from 15% to 20%, the amount of "excess" percentage depletion on iron ore and coal (including lignite) that a corporation can't deduct. "Excess" percentage depletion is the amount by which the otherwise allowable percentage depletion deduction for the tax year exceeds the basis of the property, as adjusted through the end of the previous tax year.

Disposals. With the end of special treatment for long-term capital gains [See also ¶301], disposals of coal (including lignite) or domestic iron ore with a retained economic interest will no longer qualify for such treatment, although they'll still be considered as sales. The new law provides, however, that in a tax year for which the top rate on net capital gain is the same as the top rate on ordinary income, royalties on such disposals will nevertheless be eligible for percentage depletion.

Act Sec. 412(b), increasing the amount of percentage depletion on iron ore and coal disallowed for corporations, amends Sec. 291(a)(2), effective for tax years beginning after 12-31-86. Act Sec. 311(b)(3), allowing percentage depletion on certain coal and iron ore disposals treated as sales, amends Sec. 631(c), effective, except for a special transition rule, for tax years beginning after 12-31-86.

[¶414] Gain on Disposition of Mining Property. Under the new law, mine exploration and development costs and percentage depletion on hard mineral property are recaptured under the same set of rules—Sec. 1254—that apply to IDCs and, now, percentage depletion, on oil, gas, and geothermal property. These new rules take precedence over the old rules requiring recapture of mine exploration costs on disposition of the property (Sec. 617(d)), but leave in force the rules requiring recapture of mine exploration costs when a mine reaches the producing stage (Sec. 617(b)).

On a disposition of Sec. 1254 property that involves only solid mineral production, the taxpayer must recapture the lesser of (1) mine exploration and development costs that were expensed rather than added to basis, plus depletion deductions that reduced the basis of the property (that is, none after the adjusted basis reaches zero), or (2) the amount realized (for a sale, exchange, or involuntary conversion) or fair market value (for anything else) minus the property's adjusted basis.

The remaining rules are essentially those that already applied to IDC recapture. If the disposition is of part or all of an undivided interest, only a proportionate part of the deductions and expenditures have to be recaptured. However, if the taxpayer disposes of any other portion of the property (such as a full interest in part of the acreage) all of the deductions and expenditures have to be recaptured to the extent of the gain. The exception to the partial recapture rule is that if the taxpayer can establish—to the IRS's satisfaction—that the deductions and expenditures don't apply to the interest disposed of, there's no recapture on that disposition.

There's generally no recapture on any disposition, complete or partial, if the disposition is a gift, a transfer on death, or one of a group of certain tax-free transactions. Special rules apply to partnership property, and to sales or exchanges of S corporation stock if part of the gain is attributable to recapturable costs under Section 1254.

Act Sec. 413(a), relating to gain from disposition of an interest in mineral property, amends Sec. 1254, and Act Sec. 413(b), making a conforming amendment, adds Sec. 617(d)(5), both effective for property placed in service after 12-31-86, except property acquired under a written contract entered into before 9-26-85 and binding at all times thereafter.

Energy-Related Tax Credits and Other Incentives

[¶415] Business Energy Tax Credits. Although the regular investment credit has been repealed, the new law still allows businesses to take an investment credit on certain energy expenditures, as shown in the following table.

Property	Credit Percentage	From	To
Solar energy	15%	1-1-86	12-31-86
	12%	1-1-87	12-31-87
	10%	1-1-88	12-31-88
Geothermal	15%	1-1-86	12-31-86
	10%	1-1-87	12-31-88
Ocean Thermal	15%	1-1-86	12-31-88
Biomass	15%	1-1-86	12-31-86
	10%	1-1-87	12-31-87

Under prior Code rules, all of these credits were to have expired at the end of 1985. The prior law percentage was 10% for biomass property. The credits for wind energy property, intercity buses, alternative energy property, and small hydroelectric projects were allowed to expire as of the end of 1985, as was the residential energy credit.

The new law adds no new rules regarding dual-purpose solar or geothermal energy property. The Conference Committee, however, states that this is an area regarding which the Treasury should issue regs under existing law.

Long-term projects. A credit will still be available for certain long-term projects, involving alternative energy sources and small-scale hydroelectric facilities, if an "affirmative commitment" was made. Such a commitment exists only when engineering studies, permit applications, and binding contracts are made by the dates set out in Sec. 46(b)(2)(C) and (D). If a credit is otherwise available for projects that qualify under the affirmative commitment rules, the new law will allow it, but subject to some of the limitations that now apply to the investment credit on transition property [See also ¶209]. Thus, there will be a 17.5% reduction in the regular amount of such credits (10% on alternative energy projects, 11% for the hydroelectric facilities) for 1987, 35% in later years, and the adjusted basis of the property will have to be reduced by the full amount of the credit taken.

Act Sec. 421(a), which extends certain business energy investment credits, amends Sec. 46(b)(2)(A), and Act Sec. 421(b), regarding certain long-term projects, adds Sec. 46(b)(2)(E), both effective in periods after 12-31-85, under the standing investment credit transitional rules of Sec. 48(m).

【¶416】 Alcohol Import Duty. The new law adds new requirements to exemptions from tariff duties on ethyl alcohol for fuel use from certain areas. The exemptions apply to imports from U.S. insular possessions and countries of the Caribbean Basin Initiative (beneficiary countries). The new law generally requires that to come within the duty exemption, the alcohol must either be (1) dehydrated in and the product of a full-scale fermentation process in the insular possession or beneficiary country, or (2) must be dehydrated in an insular possession or beneficiary country from hydrous ethyl alcohol of a certain value (from 30% to 75% of the value of the final product, depending on the year involved) from another insular possession or beneficiary country.

Act Sec. 423, restricting certain exemptions from import duties on ethyl alcohol, amends Item 901.50 of the Appendix to the Tariff Schedules of the United States, implicitly amends general headnote 3(a) of the Tariff Schedules of the United States, Sec. 213 of the Caribbean Basin Economic Recovery Act, and Secs. 313(b) and (j)(2) of the Tariff Act of 1930, and makes conforming amendments to general headnote 3(a)(i) of the Tariff Schedules of the United States, the headnotes to part 1, subpart A, of the appendix to the Tariff Schedules of the United States, and Sec. 213(a)(1) of the Caribbean Basin Economic Recovery Act, all generally effective for articles entered after 12-31-86 and before the expiration date of item 901.50 of the Appendix to the Tariff Schedules of the United States. Special transition rules apply to articles from certain facilities.

【¶417】 Alcohol Fuels and Excise Taxes. Under the prior law, "neat" alcohol fuels (consisting of at least 85% alcohol not derived from petroleum or natural gas) were completely exempted from the 9-cents-a-gallon excise tax on special motor fuels. The new law repeals that exemption, and substitutes a reduction of 6 cents a gallon, for a special motor fuels excise tax of 3 cents a gallon on neat alcohol fuels.

The new law also extends the exemption for taxicabs from the excise taxes on motor fuels through 9-30-88.

Act Sec. 422(a), which repeals the special fuels excise tax exemption for neat alcohol fuels, amends Sec. 4041(b)(2)(A), effective for sales or use after 12-31-86. Act Sec. 417(b), extending the taxicab rules, amends Sec. 6427(e)(3), effective 10-1-85.

[The page following this is 501.]

TAX SHELTERS

〔¶501〕 Extension of At-Risk Rules to Real Estate. Under the at-risk rules, individuals and certain closely held corporations cannot deduct losses in excess of their actual economic investment in an activity. Under the new law, these at-risk rules have been extended to include the activity of holding real estate. Real estate was exempted under prior law.

Losses attributable to real property placed in service after 1986 will be deductible only up to the amount the taxpayer has placed at risk—that is, the amount the taxpayer could actually lose by engaging in the activity. This amount includes cash contributions to the activity, the adjusted basis of other property contributed to the activity, and borrowed amounts used in the activity for which the taxpayer is personally liable, or has pledged property not used in the activity as security for repayment of the borrowed amounts. A person is generally not considered at risk if he or she isn't personally liable for repayment of the debt (nonrecourse loans) or the lender has an interest other than as a creditor in the activity.

Exception for qualified nonrecourse financing. Taxpayers are not subject to the at-risk rules to the extent they use arm's-length third party commercial financing secured solely by real property. This exception will apply only if the third party lender is not (1) "related" to the taxpayer; (2) the seller of the property or someone "related" to the seller; or (3) a person who is paid a fee with respect to the taxpayer's investment in the property.

Certain qualified nonrecourse financing will be treated as an amount at risk when borrowing from a related person if the terms of the loan are commercially reasonable and on substantially the same terms as loans involving unrelated persons.

Commercially reasonable defined. A loan is commercially reasonable if there is a written unconditional promise to pay on demand, or at a specified time, a definite sum of money and the interest rate being charged is a reasonable market rate. If the interest rate is below the reasonable market rate a portion of the principal may be considered interest. In that case, the principal may exceed the fair market value of the property. An interest rate would not be commercially reasonable if it were significantly below the market rate of comparable loans made by qualified persons not related to the borrowers.

If the interest rate exceeds a reasonable market rate, or is contingent on profits or gross receipts, a portion of the principal amount may represent a disguised equity interest (and a portion of the interest in fact is a return on equity) with the result that the stated principal amount may exceed the fair market value of the financed property. Thus, generally, an interest rate would not be considered commercially reasonable if it significantly exceeds the market rate on comparable loans by unrelated qualified persons. Nor would an interest rate be considered commercially reasonable if it were contingent. However, interest rates that are not fixed may be commercially reasonable. Those rates, however, must be calculated with respect to a market interest index such as the prime rate charged by a major commercial bank, LIBOR, the rate on government securities (such as Treasury bills or notes), or the applicable Federal rate.

The terms of the financing would also not be considered commercially reasonable if, for example, the term of the loan exceeds the useful life of the property, or if the right to foreclosure or collection with respect to the debt is limited, except to the extent provided under state law.

Convertible debt is not treated as qualified nonrecourse financing. The conferees felt that it was not appropriate to treat investors as at risk with respect to nonrecourse debt that is convertible and that consequently represents a right to an equity interest, because taxpayers are not intended to be treated as at risk for amounts representing others' rights to equity investments.

Special rule for partnerships. The Senate Finance Committee Report stated that a partnership's nonrecourse financing may increase a partner's (including a limited partner's) amount at risk provided the financing is qualified nonrecourse for both the partner and the partnership. The amount the partners are treated at risk cannot be more than the total amount of the qualified nonrecourse financing at the partnership level. The special rule for partnerships is in Sec. 465(b)(6)(C).

Act Sec. 503, extending the at-risk rules to the holding of real property, amends Sec. 465. It applies to losses incurred after 12-31-86 with respect to property placed in service after 12-31-86. For an interest in an S corporation, a partnership, or other pass-through entity acquired after 12-31-86, the amendments apply to losses incurred after 12-31-86 that are attributable to property placed in service by the S corporation, partnership, or pass-through entity on, before, or after January 1, 1986. A special rule applies to an athletic stadium in Pennsylvania.

[¶502] **Losses and Credits From Passive Activities.** Congress seems determined to put tax shelters out of business. The crackdown started 10 years ago with the requirement that an investor's deductions not exceed his amount at risk. Almost every major tax law since 1976 has expanded the at-risk rule. And as we've seen, the new law isn't an exception. Having gone as far as it could with the at-risk rule, Congress decided to attack shelters with a new weapon called the passive-loss rule.

How it works. All income is placed into one of three baskets: (1) income from passive activities—such as limited partners' interests in a business; (2) active income (e.g., salary, bonuses, etc.); and (3) port-folio income (e.g., dividends and interest). Losses generated by "pas-sive activities" can offset only passive income. They cannot be ap-plied against income in the other two baskets—but they can be carried over to future years and applied against passive income. Similarly, tax credits from passive activities (other than foreign tax credits) can offset only the tax payable on passive income.

Practical result: A taxpayer's passive losses can still shelter every dollar of passive income. But if he doesn't have sufficient passive in-come, the deductions and credits generated by a passive activity don't do the taxpayer any good in the current year. He's got the tax equivalent of an umbrella on a sunny day.

> **Example:** Ellen Jones is an investor in two passive activities (she has an investment in two partnerships in whose businesses she do-esn't materially participate). One activity generates $3,000 of income; the other $10,000 of deductions (net loss). The $3,000 of passive income is sheltered by $3,000 of passive losses. Jones cannot use the remaining $7,000 of excess deductions to shelter her active in-come or portfolio income.

Annual passive losses in excess of annual passive income (e.g., the $7,000 of net loss in the example above), and excess credits, may be carried forward and used to offset future years' passive income or (for credits) the tax on that income. *Exception:* Losses are allowed in full when a taxpayer disposes of his entire interest in the passive activity.

Taxpayers affected. The passive-loss rule applies to individuals, estates, trusts, closely held C corporations (generally, if five or fewer individuals own directly or indirectly more than 50% of the stock), and personal service corporations (other than corporations where the owner-employees together own less than 10% of the stock). It's a wide-ranging measure that affects passive interests in any trade or business as well as tax shelters. There's a blanket exception for working interests in oil and gas properties and a limited exception for real estate investors.

The rules in general apply for tax years beginning after 1986, and are phased in during 1987—1991. Also, there is a transitional excep-tion for certain investors in low income housing. See ¶507.

Act Sec. 501 dealing with limitations on losses and credits from passive activities adds Sec. 469 generally effective for tax years beginning after 12-31-86, and as indicated in ¶507. Act Sec. 502 providing a transitional rule exception for investors in low income housing doesn't amend the Code.

[¶503] **Passive Activities.** There are two categories of passive activities:

- Any trade or business or, to the extent provided in regs any activity conducted for profit, in which the taxpayer does not materially participate; and

- Any rental activity, whether or not the taxpayer materially participates.

Passive trade-or-business activities. Any trade or business is a passive activity for a taxpayer who does not materially participate in the enterprise. Material participation is defined as a year-round active involvement in the operations of the activity on a regular, continuous, and substantial basis.

Example: Father supplies Son with capital to start a business and becomes a general partner in the venture. Although Father approves major capital outlays, he does not participate in the business on a regular basis. Result: Father cannot shelter portfolio or salary income with his share of start-up losses from the business.

NOTE: The term "trade or business" includes any activity involving research and experimentation under Sec. 174.

Signposts of material participation. According to the Committee Reports, there are three main factors to be considered, but none of them is conclusive of the presence or absence of material participation.

- Is the activity the taxpayer's principal trade or business? Examples: A person whose main business is farming is more likely to materially participate in a farm than an executive who invests in a farming operation. On the other hand, a taxpayer whose sideline business is producing documentaries is not engaged in a passive activity merely because his principal business is being a film executive.

- How close is the taxpayer to the activity? Although a taxpayer is more likely to be actively involved in a business that is located in his vicinity, proximity is not enough. He still must actively participate in the business. But distance from the enterprise is not always a bar. For example, a software developer who lives in New York may be actively involved in his company even if it's located in Silicon Valley.

- Does the taxpayer have knowledge and experience in the enterprise? For example, a doctor who knows little about cattle is unlikely to be materially involved in a cattle-feeding operation. However, even if the doctor had experience with cattle feeding, he still must be involved in day-to-day operations to avoid the passive-loss rule. In other words, rubber-stamping decisions made by others won't do.

Special exception: A farmer who materially participates in his farm holds on to that status after retirement; and so does the spouse of a deceased farmer.

The material-participation standard is applied to a taxpayer (or his or her spouse) who owns an interest in the business as a proprietor, general partner, or S corporation shareholder. A personal service corporation or closely held C corporation meets the standard if there is material participation by one or more shareholders owning more than 50% of the stock. A closely held C corporation may use an alternative test. The material participation standard is met if

- at least one full-time employee works full time and year-round in the active management of the activity,
- at least three nonowner employees work full time in the activity for the entire year, and
- business deductions of the activity exceed 15% of its gross income.

A taxpayer that directly or indirectly owns an interest in any activity as a limited partner automatically fails the material participation test. However, the Treasury is given authority to prescribe regulations that will prevent taxpayers from manipulating this rule to circumvent the passive-loss limitation. Example: A taxpayer would not be able to sop up large passive losses by converting his ownership of income-generating activities into limited partnership form. What's more, income from personal services to the passive activity isn't "passive activity income" that can sop up the losses from passive activities.

Rental activities. Rental activities, which are presumed to be passive, include all activities that generate income from payments for the use of tangible property, rather than for the performance of substantial services. Signposts of a rental activity: a lease term that is long in relation to the property's useful life; day-to-day expenses are insignificant in relation to rents or in relation to depreciation and carrying costs; and no significant services are supplied to each new lessee.

Examples of rental activities: long-term rentals of apartments, office equipment, and automobiles, or the rental of a vessel under a bare-boat charter or a plane under a dry lease (no pilot or captain and no fuel provided), and net-leased property. A property is net-leased if the lessor's deductions (other than rents and reimbursed amounts) are less than 15% of rental income, or when the lessor is guaranteed a specific return or is guaranteed against loss of income.

Examples of businesses that are not rental activities: short-term car rentals, and rentals of hotel rooms or similar space to transients.

In general, real estate rentals—short- or long-term—are presumed to be rental activities and thus are automatically passive in nature. There are three exceptions:

- Real estate dealers are generally not treated as engaging in a passive activity.

- Taxpayers may use up to $25,000 of real estate losses and credit equivalents to shelter nonpassive income if they are "active participants" [see ¶505].

- Mortgage interest on a principal residence or second residence is not subject to the passive-loss rule even if the taxpayer rents out the residence.

> **OBSERVATION:** Although residence interest is excluded, other residence-related deductions are subject to the passive rule if the taxpayer rents out the home and is not actively involved in his "rental business." This can happen if a management agent handles all aspects of the business, including approval of tenants (as is the case with some "rent-pooled" vacation homes).

[¶504]　How the Passive-Loss Rule Works. To begin with, a taxpayer must pass the expanded at-risk rule [¶501]. Deductions disallowed because the taxpayer's at-risk amount is insufficient are suspended by Sec. 465. Such deductions become subject to the passive-loss rule only if the taxpayer's at-risk amount increases in future years.

> **SALT IN THE WOUND:** A taxpayer's at-risk amount is reduced by losses allowed under Sec. 465 even if the losses are suspended by the passive-loss rule. Similarly, a taxpayer's basis is reduced by deductions (e.g., depreciation) even if the deductions are not usable currently because of the passive loss rule.

Losses from passive activities can offset only passive activity income and cannot shelter "active" income such as salary. "Portfolio income" generated by the activity or earned by the taxpayer is not passive income and can't be offset by passive losses. "Portfolio income" consists of (1) interest, dividends, and royalties (unless earned in the ordinary course of a trade or business); and (2) gain or loss on the sale of property that generates portfolio income or is held for investment. Income (e.g., interest) earned on working capital is treated as portfolio income.

Exceptions. A closely held C corporation (other than a personal-service corporation) may use passive losses and credits to offset its "net active income." This is taxable income of the company figured without regard to passive income or loss or portfolio income. And if a taxpayer becomes materially involved in what had been a passive activity, he may use suspended losses to offset the activity's income even though his interest is no longer passive.

Any tax credit generated by a passive activity (other than foreign tax credits) may offset only the tax attributable to passive income. That's the excess of the tax owed on all income less the tax that would be owed on non-passive-source income (passive-source credits are disregarded in both cases).

ALLOCATIONS REQUIRED: A taxpayer must allocate income, deductions, and credits among passive and active elements. And if he owns several passive activities, he must prorate suspended losses and credits among the activities.

Example: During 1987, AB General Partnership operates an investment counseling business out of one floor of a three-story building that it owns. The other two floors are net-leased to a commercial tenant. AB also has portfolio income (e.g., dividends and interest) and a passive interest in an income-producing farm.

Results: The partners can use two-thirds of the building's deductions to offset rental income and income from the farm. Any excess deductions from the rented portion of the building cannot be used to shelter portfolio income or income from the counseling business. Since the remaining one-third of the building's deductions are allocable to a business in which the partners materially participate, it is not subject to the passive-loss rule.

NOTE: If AB were organized as a closely held C corporation, it could use excess deductions from the rented portion of the building to shelter its net active income.

Example: John Smith is a passive investor in three ventures. He has $15,000 of deductions in excess of income from Venture A, and $10,000 of excess deductions from Venture B. Venture C produces $15,000 of passive income. *Result:* Smith can offset $15,000 of passive income with $15,000 of passive loss. His net passive loss of $10,000, suspended under new Sec. 469, is allocated as follows: Activity A, $6,000 ($10,000 net passive loss × $15,000/$25,000); Activity B, $4,000 ($10,000 net passive loss × $10,000/$25,000).

Suspended losses and credits may be carried forward (but not back) and used to offset future years' passive-source income. A suspended loss is allowed in full when the entire interest is sold to an unrelated third party in a taxable transaction. Suspended losses (and any loss on the sale) are deductible against income in the following order: any gain recognized on the transaction; net income or gain for the tax year from all passive activities; and any other income or gain. Losses from the sale or exchange of a capital asset are limited to the amount of gains from the sale or exchange of capital assets, plus $3,000 (in the case of individuals). The capital-loss limit is applied *before* the determination of the amount of losses upon a disposition. In an installment sale, passive losses become available as the buyer makes payments. Losses are freed up in the same ratio that gain recognized each year bears to the total gain on the sale.

   CREDITS VANISH: Since the passive-loss rule is designed to limit writeoffs to real economic losses, any unused suspended credits are not allowed when a passive activity is sold. In other words, the credits vanish into thin air.

A special rule applies if the taxpayer made a basis adjustment at purchase as a result of claiming a tax credit (e.g., a rehabilitation tax credit). When that property is disposed of, the taxpayer may elect to increase the property's basis by the amount of credit suspended by the passive-loss rules. However, the basis adjustment can't exceed the amount of the original basis adjustment.

Suspended losses are not freed up by

- a change in the form of ownership (e.g., transfer of proprietorship interest to an S corporation),
- a like-kind exchange (except to the extent of taxable "boot"), or
- a partial disposition of a passive activity.

Other transfers. Any suspended losses remaining at a taxpayer's death are allowed as deductions on his final return to the extent the basis of the property in the hands of the transferee exceeds the property's adjusted basis immediately prior to the decedent's death.

   Example: When John Smith dies, his basis in a limited partnership interest is $10,000 and its value is $20,000. If he holds $15,000 of suspended losses, $5,000 may be deducted on his final return (suspended losses minus the $10,000 excess of the transferee's basis over Smith's basis. If suspended losses are $10,000 or less, nothing is deductible.

Finally, if a taxpayer makes a gift of his entire interest in a passive activity, the donee's basis is increased by any suspended losses. If the interest is later sold at a loss, however, the donee's basis is limited to the fair market value on the date the gift was made.

[¶505] Limited Relief for Active Participants in Real Estate. The new law gives some relief to a natural person who actively participates in a rental real estate activity. He can offset nonpassive income with up to $25,000 of losses and credits (in deduction equivalents) from his "active" real estate interests. The limit is $12,500 for marrieds filing separate returns. The deduction equivalent of credits is the amount that, if allowed as a deduction, would reduce tax by an amount equal to the credit.

   IMPORTANT: The deduction equivalent of a low-income housing credit or rehabilitation credit counts toward the $25,000 allowance *whether or not* the taxpayer actively participates in the activity that gave rise to the credit. In the case of a low-income housing credit, this rule applies only to property placed in service before 1990, and only with respect to the original compliance period for the property, except if the property was placed in service before 1991, and 10% or more of total project costs are incurred before 1989.

Example: A taxpayer is an active participant in a real estate venture that produces $20,000 of credits in 1988, but no deductions or income. If he is a joint filer with taxable income of, say, $70,000 he may claim a $7,000 credit for 1988. Reason: In his 28% tax bracket, $25,000 of deductions would create a tax saving of $7,000. The $13,000 balance of his credit is suspended by the passive-loss rule.

Phase-out of $25,000 allowance. For deductions, the $25,000 allowance is reduced by one-half of the taxpayer's AGI in excess of $100,000 ($50,000 for marrieds filing separately). Thus, there is no allowance for deductions once AGI exceeds $150,000 ($75,000 for marrieds filing separately). For credits from qualifying rehabilitation projects [¶217] and low-income housing projects [¶218], the $25,000 allowance (in deduction equivalents) is reduced by one-half of the taxpayer's AGI in excess of $200,000 ($100,000 for marrieds filing separately). Thus there's no credit if AGI exceeds $250,000 ($125,000 for marrieds filing separately). For purposes of the credit phase-out, AGI is figured without regard to: (1) any net passive losses, (2) IRA contributions and (3) taxable social security benefits.

What if a taxpayer has both credits and losses from a real estate activity in which he actively participates? In this case, the Senate Finance Committee Report indicates that the credit that may be claimed (before application of the phase-out) equals (1) tax owed on income other than any net passive losses, but reduced by real estate deductions allowed under the relief measure, less (2) the tax he would owe if allowable real estate deductions equaled $25,000 (or a lesser limit, if his AGI exceeds the $100,000 or $200,000 limit). Credits are disregarded in both calculations.

Example: In January 1988, Warren Able becomes a general partner and active participant in a real estate venture that produces a rehabilitation tax credit. He is not involved in any passive activities. For tax year 1988, Able is allocated $10,000 of deductions and $10,000 of rehabilitation credits. The project does not throw off any income for the year. For 1988, Able's adjusted gross income without regard to the real estate deal is $90,000. His taxable income, counting $10,000 of real estate deductions, equals $70,000. The $25,000 allowance less $10,000 of deductions leaves a balance of $15,000.

Result: Able may claim $4,200 of rehabilitation tax credits for 1988. That's the equivalent of $15,000 of deductions in Able's 28% bracket. That $4,200 also represents the difference (disregarding credits) between (1) the tax Able would have paid counting $10,000 of real estate deductions, and (2) the tax payable counting $25,000 of real estate deductions. The $5,800 balance of his credit is suspended by the passive-loss rule.

The active-participation standard for rental real estate is more liberal than the material participation standard that applies to other activities. All that's required is that the taxpayer or his or her spouse participate in a bona fide sense. For example, making management decisions, such as approving tenants, lease terms, and repairs, is sufficient even if an agent handles the day-to-day affairs of the real estate rental activity. However, a taxpayer cannot be an active participant if he is a limited partner or holds a less than 10% interest in the real estate rental enterprise. The estate of a decedent who had actively participated in a real estate venture is deemed to actively participate in the venture for a two-year period following the decedent's death.

[¶506] Working Interests in Oil and Gas Properties Excepted From Passive-Loss Rule. A taxpayer who holds a working interest in an oil and gas property is exempted entirely from the passive loss rule, whether or not he materially participates in the activity. A working interest is one that is burdened with the cost of developing and operating the property. Typical characteristics: responsibility for authorizing expenses; receiving periodic reports about drilling, completion, and expected production; the possession of voting rights and rights to continue operations if the present operator steps out; a share in tort liability (e.g., uninsured losses from a fire); and some responsibility to share in additional costs.

A taxpayer whose liability is limited (e.g., he holds a limited partnership interest or S corporation shares) is not treated as owning a working interest. Also specifically excepted from the definition of a working interest: rights to overriding royalties or production payments; and contract rights to extract or share in oil and gas profits without liability for a share of production costs.

[¶507] Effective Date and Phase-In of Passive-Loss Rule. In general, the passive-loss rule applies to tax years beginning after 12-31-86. But there's a five-year phase-in for losses or credits from passive activities held on the new law's enactment date (these are called credits and losses from "pre-1987 interests"). The phase-in also applies if the taxpayer holds a contract to purchase a passive activity and the contract is binding on the date of enactment. For tax years beginning in 1987, 35% of passive losses and credits from pre-1987 interests is subject to the new rules. For tax years 1988, 1989, and 1990, the portion of the loss or credit from pre-1987 interests subject to the rules is 60%, 80%, and 90% respectively. For 1991 and later years, 100% of these passive losses and credits is subject to the passive loss rule.

Example: In June 1986, Dan Smith buys a limited partnership interest in a cattle deal. In January 1987, he buys a limited partnership interest in a farm. For tax year 1987, the ventures produce $70,000 of deductions but no income ($56,000 from the cattle deal and $14,000 from the farm). Here's how things work out for 1987:

Loss subject to phase-in [from activity held on enactment date]...		$56,000
Loss not subject to phase-in [from activity acquired after law's enactment date]............................		14,000
		$70,000
Amount subject to passive loss rule		
(1) $56,000 × .35	$19,600	
(2) $14,000 × 100%	14,000	
Total suspended losses	$33,600	(33,600)
Allowable losses		$36,400

NOTE: Any passive loss disallowed for a tax year during the phase-in period and carried forward may be allowed in a later year only to the extent there is net passive income in the later year (or the activity is disposed of).

Transitional exception for investors in low-income housing. Losses of certain investors of cash or property in specially defined "qualified low income housing projects" placed in service before 1989, which are sustained during a "relief period" aren't treated as losses from a passive activity for the passive activity loss rules. This applies to investors who are natural persons (and their estates for the first and second tax years ending after their death), who directly or through one or more entities hold an interest in the project on 12-31-86 (the date is 8-16-86 for initial investments after 12-31-83 in projects placed in service before 8-16-86), and who are required to make payments after 12-31-86 of 50% or more of the total original obligated investment. (An interest is treated as held on 8-16-86 or 12-31-86 if there's a binding contract to acquire it on such date). The "relief period" starts with the tax year of the investor's initial investment, and ends with the *earliest* of (1) the sixth tax year after the tax year of initial investment; or (2) the first tax year after the year the investor is obligated to make his last investment; or (3) the tax year that precedes the first year when the project ceases to qualify. The benefit of the above relief is obtained at the price of loss of any Sec. 42 low-income housing credit for the project.

[¶508] New Limits on Investment Interest Deductions. Taxpayers other than corporations have been limited by Sec. 163(d) in the amount they can deduct for interest on debt incurred to buy or carry property held for investment. The limit has been $10,000 a year, plus the taxpayer's net investment income. Beginning in 1987, investment interest will be deductible only to the extent of net investment income each year (with an indefinite carryforward of disallowed investment interest). Moreover, the scope of the investment interest limitation will be expanded. There's a five-year phase-in of the new rule.

Investment interest. Interest subject to the limitation includes all interest (except consumer interest and qualified residence interest) on debt not incurred in a person's active trade or business.

So if you borrow to purchase or carry investment property, the interest you pay is investment interest. Also, if you have a trade or business in which you do not materially participate, any interest expense allocable to the business activity is investment interest provided the activity is not a "passive activity" under the passive loss rule. If you borrow money to purchase or carry an interest in a passive activity, your interest expense will be investment interest to the extent the interest is attributable to portfolio income.

> **ALERT:** Any interest that is taken into account in determining your income or loss from a passive activity is not investment interest. In addition, it doesn't include interest allocable to a rental real estate activity in which the taxpayer actively participates.

Net investment income. This is defined as the excess of investment income over investment expenses.

Under the new law, investment income includes:

- Gross income from interest, dividends, rents, and royalties.
- Gain from the disposition of investment property.
- Portfolio income under the passive loss rules.
- Income from a trade or business in which the taxpayer does not materially participate if the activity is not a "passive activity" under the passive loss rule.

Investment expenses include deductions (other than interest) that are directly connected with the production of net investment income (including actual depreciation or depletion deductions allowable).

> **ALERT:** Interest income from activities subject to the passive-loss rules (explained at ¶502) is not treated as investment income. However, when calculating your net investment income, subtract from investment income the passive losses that are allowed under the passive loss phase-in provision.

2% floor on miscellaneous expenses. In determining deductible investment expenses, investment expenses are considered as those allowed after the application of the rule limiting deductions for miscellaneous expenses to those exceeding 2% of adjusted gross income. In computing the amount of expenses that exceed the 2% floor, expenses that are not investment expenses are intended to be disallowed before any investment expenses are disallowed.

Net lease property. Property subject to a net lease is not treated as investment property because it is treated as a passive activity under the passive loss rule. Income from rental real estate in which the taxpayer actively participates is not included in investment income.

Effective Date: The new investment interest rules are generally effective for tax years beginning after 12-31-86. There is a phase-in of the disallowance over a five-year period. During this phase-in period (1987 through 1990), the amount of investment interest disallowed is equal to:

(1) the excess of investment interest over prior law's $10,000 allowance ($5,000 for marrieds filing a separate return, and zero in the case of trusts), plus

(2) the applicable percentage of investment interest *up to* the $10,000 (or $5,000) allowance.

The applicable percentage is 35% for 1987, 60% for 1988, 80% for 1989, and 90% for 1990.

Example: For tax year 1987, Arnold Smith, an individual taxpayer, has $20,000 of investment interest in excess of investment income. Mr. Smith has no investments covered by the passive loss rule. The amount of investment interest expense disallowed for 1987 is computed as follows:

(1) Excess of $20,000 investment interest over prior
law's $10,000 allowance........................... $10,000
(2) 35% of the investment interest that does
not exceed $10,000 3,500

Total disallowed interest $13,500

Mr. Smith may deduct the $6,500 balance of his investment interest expense in excess of investment income.

For the investment interest limitation, for taxable years beginning on or after 1-1-87 and before 1-1-91, the amount of net investment income is reduced by the amount of losses from passive activities that is allowed as a deduction by virtue of the phase-in of the passive loss rule (other than net losses from rental real estate in which the taxpayer actively participates). For example, if a taxpayer has a passive loss which would be disallowed were the passive loss rule fully phased in (as in taxable years beginning after 12-31-90), but a percentage of which is allowed under the passive loss phase-in rule, the amount of loss so allowed reduces the amount of the taxpayer's net investment income under the investment interest limitation for that year.

Interest that is disallowed for a year during the phase-in period and carried forward may be allowed in a later year only to the extent the investment income in the later year exceeds the net investment interest paid or incurred in the later year.

Act Sec. 511, expanding the scope of the interest limitation deduction, amends Sec. 163(d), effective for interest paid or incurred in tax years beginning on or after 1-1-87 with a phase-in over a 5-year period. [See phase-in rules above.]

〔¶509〕 Qualified Residence Interest. Under the new law, qualified residence interest is deductible in full. It is neither investment interest nor consumer interest [¶510]. It is interest on debt secured by a security interest perfected under local law on the taxpayer's principal residence or second residence. A principal residence is one that qualifies for nontaxable exchange treatment under Sec. 1034. To qualify as a second residence, the taxpayer must use the dwelling as his or her residence for part of the year if he or she rents the home to others.

The amount deductible as qualified residence interest consists of interest on debt that does not exceed

- the taxpayer's cost for the residence, plus
- the cost of any improvements.

ALERT: Taxpayers whose homes have declined in value must be careful. Interest on the portion of a loan that exceeds the fair market value of the home at the time the loan is made will not be deductible.

If the debt exceeds the taxpayer's cost plus improvements, the excess is deductible as qualified residence interest only to the extent the borrowed amounts incurred after 8-16-86 are used for educational or medical purposes. If the amount of any debt incurred on or before 8-16-86, and secured by the residence on 8-16-86 (reduced by any principal payments) is more than the cost basis of the residence, then such amount is treated as the taxpayer's basis. Any increase in the amount of the taxpayer's debt that takes place after 8-16-86, but which is secured by the residence on 8-16-86 is treated as incurred after 8-16-86.

Interest on outstanding debt secured by the taxpayer's principal or second residence is fully deductible to the extent the debt does not exceed the fair market value of the residence.

Suppose the loan exceeds the sum of cost basis plus improvements, and the loan proceeds are used for personal purposes (e.g. purchase of a car). Unless the taxpayer qualifies for the 8-16-86 exception (see above), interest on the excess loan amount is treated as nondeductible consumer interest. There is a phase-in of the consumer interest rule [See ¶510].

Consider these examples:

Example (1): Mr. and Mrs. Smith bought a home for $80,000 ten years ago. In September 1986 the balance on their first mortgage is $50,000 and the market value of their home is $150,000.

Result: The Smiths can continue to deduct the interest on their first mortgage. They can also borrow another $30,000 using their home as collateral (e.g., refinance the first mortgage, obtain a second mortgage, or a "home equity credit line") and deduct the interest, regardless of how they use the $30,000.

Example (2): Same facts, except the Smiths refinanced their first mortgage in September 1986 and got a new mortgage for $90,000.

Result: The mortgage interest on $80,000 of the mortgage principal is deductible regardless of how the funds are used. The interest on $10,000 of the mortgage principal is deductible only if the $10,000 is used for educational purposes (e.g., to finance child's education) or medical purposes (e.g., to pay a large hospital bill).

If taxpayers borrow against the equity in their home to make an investment, the interest that's not deductible as qualified residence interest may be deducted as investment interest, subject to the new investment interest rules (and the phase-in of these rules).

Example (3): Mr. and Mrs. Jones bought a home for $125,000 ten years ago and have a balance on their first mortgage of $50,000. The fair market value of their home has increased to $200,000. In September 1986 they borrow another $100,000 against increased equity in their home and use the money to buy rental property.

Result: The interest on their original mortgage and $75,000 of the $100,000 loan is deductible as qualified residence interest. The interest on the remaining $25,000 of the $100,000 loan is deductible as investment interest [¶508] to the extent of the investment income.

NOTE: If the proceeds of the $100,000 loan are used to finance a business, then interest on $25,000 of the loan could be deducted as a trade or business expense.

Taxpayer's "cost" of the residence. In determining the cost basis of your residence, do not take into account any of the adjustments made under Sec. 1034(e), relating to the postponing of gain on the sale and purchase of a residence, or Sec. 1033(b), relating to involuntary conversions. Although you add the cost of improvements to your basis, do not make any adjustments for depreciation. If the residence is acquired from a decedent, the basis of the residence is determined under Sec. 1014, which would generally require the basis to be the fair market value of the residence at the date of the decedent's death or at an alternative valuation date. Generally, under this rule, the amount of debt on which the taxpayer may deduct interest will not be less then the purchase price of the residence.

Medical and educational expenses defined. Medical payments do not include amounts paid for insurance. Educational expenses includes tuition at a primary or secondary school, college or graduate school. It also includes amounts paid for living expenses while at those schools. The educational expenses must be for the taxpayer, his or her spouse, or dependent as defined in Sec. 152. And the qualified educational or medical expenses must be incurred within a reasonable period of time before or after the debt is incurred.

Special rules. The Senate Finance Committee reported that if a taxpayer owns more than two residences, he may designate each year which residence (other than his principal residence) he wants to have treated as his second residence. If a joint return is filed, a second residence includes a residence owned by the taxpayer or his spouse and which is owned by either or both spouses. For marrieds filing separate returns, each spouse can deduct qualified residence interest secured by one residence. In the alternative, one spouse can consent in writing to allow the other spouse to claim qualified residence interest on two residences (as long as one is a principal residence).

Use of second home. A taxpayer need not use the second residence if he or she does not rent it to others. If the residence is rented to others the taxpayer need not satisfy the requirement that the residence be used for personal purposes for the greater of 14 days or 10% of the number of days it is rented.

Housing cooperatives, state homestead laws. Interest on debt secured by the taxpayer's stock in a housing cooperative unit that is the taxpayer's residence won't be treated as nondeductible consumer interest to the extent the debt doesn't exceed the fair market value of the cooperative unit. The taxpayer's share of interest expense of the housing cooperative which is allocable to his unit and his share of the co-op's common residential areas also will not be treated as nondeductible consumer interest.

The taxpayer's debt secured by the stock in the cooperative is treated as debt secured by the residence of the taxpayer. However, there are situations where the taxpayer can not use the stock as security. For example, there may be state or local restrictions or the cooperative agreement may prevent it. In such cases the stock may be treated as securing such debt, if the taxpayer can establish to the satisfaction of the IRS that the debt was incurred to acquire the stock. The fact that state homestead laws may restrict the rights of secured parties with regard to certain residential mortgages will not necessarily make the interest nondeductible. The taxpayer's payment of interest will be qualified residence interest if the lenders security interest is perfected and the debt otherwise qualifies.

Act Sec. 511, adds Sec. 163(h), effective for tax years beginning after 12-31-86.

[¶510] **Personal Interest Is Nondeductible.** Starting with tax years beginning after 12-31-86, personal interest is no longer deductible. Personal interest is defined as interest on any debt, *other than* (1) interest on debt incurred or carried in connection with the taxpayer's trade or business or a Sec. 212-type investment activity, (2) qualified residence interest [explained at ¶509], (3) interest taken into account in computing the taxpayer's income or loss from passive activities for the year, or (4) interest payable on certain estate tax deficiencies. Interest on debt incurred in connection with a taxpayer's trade or business of performing services as an employee is *not* trade or business interest. For example, an employee who must supply his own car for work cannot deduct interest on a loan obtained to buy his business car. Interest on a tax deficiency is personal interest.

The disallowance of deductions for personal interest is phased in over a five-year period: 35% of personal interest is nondeductible in 1987, 60% in 1988, 80% in 1989, 90% in 1990, and 100% in 1991 and later.

Act Sec. 511 adds Sec. 163(h), effective as shown above.

[The page following this is 601]

CORPORATE TAX

[¶601] Corporate Tax Rate Lowered. Corporate tax rates are generally reduced. A three-step graduated rate structure is substituted for the five-step rate structure. The top corporate tax rate is reduced from 46% to 34%.

Income tax rate schedule. The corporate tax rates are as follows:

Taxable Income	Tax Rate (%)
Not over $50,000	15
Over $50,000 but not over $75,000	25
Over $75,000	34

For corporate taxable income in excess of $100,000, there's an additional 5% tax but that tax can't be greater than $11,750.

> **IMPACT:** The benefit of graduated rates for corporations with taxable income between $100,000 and $335,000 is phased out. Corporations with income in excess of $335,000, in effect, pay a flat tax at a 34% rate.

Effective Dates: The revised income tax rates are effective for tax years beginning on or after 7-1-87. For tax years that include 7-1-87, the old rates and the new rates will be blended.

Act Sec. 601, relating to corporate rate reductions, amends Sec. 11(b), applying to tax years starting on or after 7-1-87.

[¶602] Dividends-Received Deduction Decreased. The corporate dividends-received deduction is lowered to 80% from 85% for regular dividends received by corporations, dividends received on certain preferred stock, and dividends on debt-financed portfolio stock. The limit on the aggregate amount of the deduction is also lowered to 80% from 85% for corporations and insurance companies.

The decrease was necessary to prevent the reduction in corporate rates from resulting in a significant reduction in the tax rate on dividends eligible for this deduction.

Act Sec. 611, reducing the dividends received deduction, amends Secs. 243, 244, 246-246A, 805(a)(4)(B), applicable to dividends received or accrued after 12-31-86, in tax years ending after such date. The changes to Sec. 246(b) as to limitation on aggregate amount of deductions applies for tax years starting after 12-31-86.

[¶603] Extraordinary Dividends—Holding Period Lengthened for Basis Reduction. A corporation that disposes of a share of stock must reduce its basis (but not below zero) by the nontaxable portion of any extraordinary dividend paid on the share if the stock has not been held for more than two years before the date of announcement or declaration about the dividend. If there is no formal or informal agreement to pay the particular dividend before the declaration date, the date of this agreement is treated as the dividend announcement date for applying the two-year holding period requirement. A distribution that would otherwise be an extraordinary dividend under the two-year rule will not be considered extraordinary if the distributee has held the stock for the entire period the distributing corporation (and any predecessor corporation) has been in existence. The basis reduction is required only to figure gain or loss on the share's disposition. If the aggregate nontaxed portions of extraordinary dividends exceed the shareholder's basis, the excess is treated as gain from a sale or exchange at the time of disposition. Under prior law, this basis reduction was required only if the stock was sold or disposed of before it had been held for one year.

Different treatment of dividends on certain qualifying preferred stock applies. Absent the special rule under the basic definition of an extraordinary dividend (below), a preferred stock that pays a greater-than-5% dividend within any period of 85 days or less is paying an extraordinary dividend. This exception is intended to provide relief for certain transactions to the extent there is no potential for effectively purchasing a dividend that accrued prior to the date of purchase (dividend-stripping). Preferred stock is treated as qualifying if it meets certain dividend requirements. Also, dividends on qualifying preferred stock are treated as extraordinary dividends only to the extent the dividends received by the taxpayer during the period it owned the stock exceed the dividends it earned.

Taxpayers have the option of determining the distribution's status as an extraordinary dividend by reference to the share's fair market value on the day before the ex-dividend date, in lieu of its adjusted basis. The alternative fair market value test applies for Sec. 1059(c)(3)(B) (which treats certain dividends having ex-dividend dates within a 365-day period as extraordinary).

> **COMMENT:** Taxpayers may want to do this if the stock has significantly appreciated since its original purchase.

Fair market value must be established to the IRS. No part of a distribution may reduce basis twice, as for members of an affiliated group filing consolidated returns.

Extraordinary dividends are those that exceed 10% (5% for shares of stock preferred as to dividends) of the shareholder's basis in the share.

Also, the term "extraordinary dividend" is expanded to include any distribution (without regard to the holding period for the stock or the distribution's relative magnitude to a corporate shareholder in partial liquidation of the distributing corporation. A distribution here is treated as in partial liquidation if it satisfies the proper requirements. Also, the term extraordinary dividend includes any stock redemption that is non-pro rata (again, irrespective of holding period or the distribution's relative size).

The rules don't apply to distributions between an affiliated group's members filing consolidated returns, except as provided in regs.

Act Sec. 614, amending the holding period for basis reduction by the non-taxable portion of extraordinary dividends, amends Sec. 1059, applicable to dividends declared after 7-18-86, in tax years ending after that date. For purposes of Sec. 1059(c)(3), dividends declared after 7-18-86 are not aggregated with dividends declared on or before 7-18-86. Sec. 1059(e)(1) concerning redemptions, applies to dividends declared after the date of enactment, in tax years ending after such date.

〖¶604〗 Dividend Exclusion for Individuals Repealed. There is no longer a dividend exclusion for individuals. The limited exclusion of the first $100 of qualified dividends received by an individual shareholder and $200 by a married couple filing a joint return is repealed.

Act Sec. 612, relating to the repeal of the partial exclusion of dividends received by individuals repeals Sec. 116, and makes clerical changes affecting Secs. 301(g)(4), 584(c), 642(j), 643(a)(7), 702(a)(5), 854(a), (b), 857(c), applicable to tax years beginning after 12-31-86.

〖¶605〗 Stock Redemption Expenses. A corporation gets no deduction for any amount it pays or incurs in connection with its stock's redemption.

NOTE: This rule isn't limited to hostile takeovers but applies to any corporate redemption.

Expenses in hostile takeovers. This provision is intended to clarify the rule that all expenses a corporation incurs in buying back its own stock are nonamortizable capital expenses. The new rule is designed to emphasize this point. To prevent the corporation's hostile takeover, some corporate taxpayers, under prior law, have considered so-called greenmail payments as deductible business expenses.

Amounts subject to rule. Amounts subject to this rule include (1) amounts paid to repurchase stock; (2) premiums paid for the stock; (3) legal, accounting, brokerage, transfer agent, appraisal, and similar fees incurred in the repurchase; (4) any other expense that's necessary or incident to the repurchase whether representing costs incurred by the purchasing corporation or by the selling shareholder (and paid or reimbursed by the purchasing corporation), or incurred by persons or entities related to either; and (5) amounts paid to a selling shareholder (or any related person) under an agreement entered into as part of or in connection with a repurchase of stock, in which the seller agrees not to buy, finance a purchase, acquire, or in any way be a party or agent to acquiring the corporation's stock for a specified or indefinite period of time.

Exceptions. This rule doesn't apply to the dividends-paid deduction (within the meaning of Sec. 561), relating to payments (or deemed payments) for accumulated earnings. (Note: These amounts continue to qualify for the dividends-paid deduction the same way as under prior law.)

The rule also does not apply to

- personal holding company, and foreign personal holding company taxes, and for the regular income tax for regulated investment companies and real estate investment trusts;
- deductible interest; and
- otherwise deductible expenses incurred by a regulated investment company that is an open-end mutual fund as to redeeming its stock on a shareholder's demand.

Example: Costs incurred by a regulated investment company in processing redemption applications and issuing checks to pay for redeemed shares are deductible the same way as under prior law.

COMMENT: In denying a deduction for payments as to stock redemptions, no inference is intended regarding these payments' deductibility under prior law. Also, no inference is intended as to the character of these payments in the payee's hands.

Act Sec. 613, relating to the treatment of stock redemption expenses adds new Sec. 162(k) and redesignates old Sec. 162(l) as Sec. 162(m), effective for amounts paid or incurred after 2-28-86 in tax years ending after that date.

Net Operating Loss Carryovers

[¶606] **Limitations on Net Operating Loss and Other Carryovers.** The new law significantly curtails trafficking in net operating losses. Under prior law, corporations were frequently acquired and disposed of for the net operating loss deductions the target corporation could provide the acquiring corporation.

A new cap on NOLs. Briefly, after an ownership change, the taxable income available for offset by prechange NOLs is limited annually to a prescribed rate times the loss corporation's value immediately before the change. This is the general approach. To see how the new rules work, you need to understand a host of never-before-defined statutory terms (e.g., "Sec. 382 limitation" and such) as well as certain special rules, as we'll explain later.

NOTE: After a substantial ownership change, rather than reducing the NOL carryforward itself, the earnings against which an NOL carryforward can be deducted are limited under the new law. This limitation-on-earnings approach is intended to allow NOL carryforwards to survive after an acquisition, and, at the same time, limit a corporation's ability to utilize the carryforwards against another taxpayer's income.

Is there an ownership change? Before applying the special limitations explained below, find out first if there is an ownership change. An ownership change occurs generally if the percentage of stock of the new loss corporation owned by any one or more 5% shareholders has increased by more than 50 percentage points relative to the lowest percentage of stock of the old loss corporation owned by those 5% shareholders at any time during the testing period. It can also happen after an equity structure shift. The testing period is normally the three-year period ending on the day of an owner shift involving a 5% shareholder or any equity structure shift. (But the period can be shortened, for example, if there was an earlier ownership change.) In any case, no testing period will start before 5-6-86.

Whether an ownership change has occurred is figured by aggregating the increases in percentage ownership for each 5% shareholder whose percentage ownership has increased during the testing period. For this rule, all stock owned by persons who own less than 5% of a loss corporation's stock is generally treated as stock owned by a single 5% shareholder or any equity structure shift. Generally, all "stock" is taken into account except stock that (1) is not entitled to vote; (2) is limited and preferred as to dividends and does not significantly participate in corporate growth; (3) has redemption and liquidation rights that do not generally exceed the stock's issue price on issuance; and (4) is not convertible to any other class of stock.

An owner shift involving a 5% shareholder is any change in the respective ownership of a corporation stock that affects the stock percentage held by a 5% shareholder (any person who holds 5% or more of the corporation stock during the testing period) before or after the change. For this rule, all less-than-5% shareholders are aggregated and treated as one 5% shareholder. Thus, an owner shift involving a 5% shareholder includes (but is not limited to) these transactions—

- A taxable purchase of loss corporation stock by a person who holds at least 5% of the stock before the purchase.

- A disposition of stock by a person who holds at least 5% of the loss corporation stock either before or after the disposition.

- A taxable purchase of loss corporation stock by a person who becomes a 5% shareholder as a result of the purchase.

- A Sec. 351 exchange (involving nonrecognition of gain or loss on transfers to controlled corporations) that affects the percentage of stock ownership of a loss corporation by one or more 5% share-holders.

• A decrease in the loss corporation outstanding stock (e.g., by virtue of a redemption) that affects the stock ownership percentage of the loss corporation by one or more 5% shareholders.

• A debt conversion (or pure preferred stock that is excluded from the definition of stock) to stock if the loss corporation's stock ownership percentage by one or more 5% shareholders is affected.

• A loss corporation's stock issuance that affects the percentage of stock ownership by one or more 5% shareholders.

Equity structure shift.   An equity structure shift is any tax-free reorganization (within the meaning of Sec. 368) other than a divisive reorganization or an "F" reorganization. To the extent provided in regs, this term may include other transactions, such as public offerings not involving a 5% shareholder or taxable reorganization-type transactions (e.g., mergers or other reorganization-type transactions that do not qualify for tax-free treatment due to the nature of the consideration or the failure to satisfy any of the other requirements for a tax-free transaction). For determining whether an ownership change has occurred following an equity structure shift, the less - than-5% shareholders of each corporation that was a party of a re-organization will be segregated and treated as a single, separate 5% shareholder.

Multiple transactions.   Whether there's an ownership change is figured by comparing the relevant shareholder's stock ownership immediately after either an owner shift involving a 5% shareholder or an equity structure shift with the lowest percentage of such shareholders' ownership at any time during the testing period preceding either the owner shift involving a 5% shareholder or the equity structure shift. Thus, changes in ownership that happen because of a series of transactions involving both owner shifts involving a 5% shareholder and equity structure shifts may be treated as an ownership change.

IMPORTANT: The percentage of stock held by any person is determined on the basis of value. Changes in the holdings of certain preferred stock are disregarded. So would be changes in proportionate ownership attributable solely to fluctuations in the relative values of different classes or amounts of stock, under regs to be prescribed.

[¶607] **Attribution of Stock Ownership.** You apply the constructive ownership rules of Sec. 318 to find out who owns what stock for determining whether an ownership change has occurred. However, the rules for attributing ownership from corporations to their shareholders are applied without regard to the extent of the shareholders' ownership in the corporation. Thus, any stock owned by a corporation is treated as being owned proportionately by its shareholders. Similarly, stock attributed from a partnership, estate, or trust is not treated as being held by the entity. The family attribution rules of Sec. 318(a)(1) and 318(a)(5)(B) do not apply. But an individual, his spouse, his parents, his children, and his grandparents are treated as a single shareholder. "Back" attribution to partnerships, trusts, estates, and corporations from partners, beneficiaries, and shareholders will not apply except as provided in regs. Except as provided in regs., an option's holder is treated as owning the underlying stock if that presumption results in an ownership change.

No ownership change in certain stock transfers. In determining whether an ownership change has taken place, do not count any stock received or acquired in the following transactions:

- Stock acquired by reason of death.
- Stock acquired by gift or transfers in trust.
- Stock received in satisfaction of a pecuniary bequest.
- Property transferred between spouses or incident to divorce.
- Stock acquired by reason of divorce or separation.
- Employer securities acquired by a tax credit employee stock ownership plan or an employee stock ownership plan (but only if the ESOP holds at least 50% of the stock immediately after the transfer and certain other requirements are met) or by a plan participant.

[¶608] Continuity-of-Business-Enterprise Test. This is the next crucial issue after an ownership change (and before applying the special limitations). Reason: Unless the continuity-of-business-enterprise test is met during the two-year period starting on the change date, a loss corporation's NOL carryforwards (including any recognized "built-in" losses explained later) are disallowed completely (except to the extent of any recognized built-in gains or Sec. 338 gain explained later). Generally, the doctrine of business continuity requires the loss corporation (or the surviving corporation) to continue the loss corporation's historic business or use a significant portion of the loss corporation's assets in a business. This is the same test applicable to a tax-free reorganization under Sec. 368. The test applies regardless of the type of transaction that results in the change of control.

> **TAX TIP:** Changes in the loss corporation's key employees or its business location won't flunk the continuity-of-business test. The test may be met, even if the loss corporation discontinues more than a minor portion of its historic business.

[¶609]   How to Figure the Annual Limitation. Assuming that the business-continuity test is met, for any tax year ending after the change date, the amount of a loss corporation's taxable income that can be offset by a prechange loss cannot exceed the "Sec. 382 limitation" for that year. The *Sec. 382 limitation* for any tax year is the key figure. It is an amount equal to the loss corporation's value immediately before the ownership change, multiplied by the federal long-term tax-exempt rate published by the IRS (more about the federal prescribed rate later).

If the limitation for a tax year exceeds the taxable income for the year, the amount of the limitation for the next tax year is increased by the amount of the excess. The limitation is also increased by certain built-in gains. A *prechange loss* includes (1) for the tax year in which a change occurs, the portion of the loss corporation's NOL that is allocable (figured, except as provided in regs, on a daily pro rata basis without regard to recognized built-in gains or losses) to the period in such year before the change date, (2) NOL carryforwards that arose in a tax year preceding the tax year of the change, and (3) certain recognized built-in losses and deductions (explained later).

The change date is the date on which an owner shift resulting in an ownership change occurs, or the date of the reorganization for an equity structure shift resulting in an ownership change.

> **NOTE:** For any tax year in which a corporation has income that may be offset by both a prechange loss (i.e., an NOL subject to limitation) and an NOL not subject to limitation, taxable income is treated as having been first offset by the prechange loss. This rule minimizes the NOLs that are subject to special limitations.

Loss corporation's value. Generally, a loss corporation's value is the fair market value of its stock, including preferred stock, immediately before the ownership change. If there is a redemption connected with an ownership change—either before or after the change—the loss corporation's value is calculated after taking the redemption into account. Future regulations may treat other corporate contractions the same as redemptions. Also, regs may treat warrants, options, contracts to acquire stock, convertible debt, and similar interests as stock for determining the loss corporation's value. Stock value is usually (though not conclusively) proven by the price at which stock changes hands in an arms-length transaction. A loss corporation's value may be reduced by capital contributions.

The long-term tax-exempt rate is the highest of the federal long-term rates found under Sec. 1274(d) (relating to the Applicable Federal Rate imputed for OID, etc.), as adjusted to reflect differences between rates on long-term taxable and tax-exempt obligations, in effect for the month in which the change date occurs or the two prior months. The long-term tax-exempt rate will be computed as the yield on diversified pool of prime, general obligation tax-exempt bonds with remaining periods to maturity of more than 9 years. The IRS will publish the long-term tax-exempt rate within 30 days after the new law is signed by the President and monthly after that.

> **COMMENT:** The prescribed rate has been chosen as the measure of a loss corporation's expected return on its assets. Using a rate lower than the long-term federal rate is necessary to ensure that the NOL carryover value to the buying corporation is not more than its value to the loss corporation. Otherwise, there would be a tax incentive for acquiring loss corporations. If the loss corporation were to sell its assets and invest in long-term Treasury obligations, it could absorb its NOL carryovers at a rate equal to the yield on long-term government obligations.

Special rule for postchange year that includes change date. Since taxable income *before* the ownership change isn't subject to special limitations, a different limitation applies for the postchange year that includes the change date. For the tax year in which a change occurs, the annual limit doesn't apply to the portion of a loss corporation's taxable income allocable to the period of the year before the change date, figured (except as provided in regs) on a daily pro rata basis. The limitation here is equal to an amount that bears the same ratio to the Sec. 382 limitation (figured without regard to this rule) as the number of days in the year on or after the change date bears to the total number of days in the year. A similar allocation rule applies for short tax years. A postchange year is any tax year ending after the change date. Taxable income, for this rule, is computed without regard to recognized built-in gains and losses.

Capital contributions that are received by a loss corporation, the principal purpose of which is to avoid or increase the special limitations, will reduce the loss corporation's value. Except as provided by regs, a capital contribution made during the two-year period ending on the change date is presumed to be part of a tax avoidance plan.

> **NOTE:** This part of the new law's antiabuse rules is designed to prevent taxpayers from circumventing the special limitations. Taxpayers are discouraged from making preacquisition infusions of assets to inflate artificially a loss corporation's value (thereby accelerating the use of NOL carryovers).

Cash and other 'nonbusiness assets.' If at least one-third of the value of a corporation's assets consists of "nonbusiness assets," then the loss corporation's value is reduced by the excess of the value of these assets over the portion of the corporation's debts attributable to these assets. Nonbusiness assets include cash, marketable stock or securities, and any asset held for investment. The amount of a corporation's debt attributable to nonbusiness assets is the amount that bears the same ratio to the debts as the nonbusiness asset value bears to the corporation's total asset value. Stock or securities in a subsidiary are not nonbusiness assets. Instead, the parent is deemed to own its ratable share of the subsidiary's assets. A corporation is treated as holding stock in a subsidiary if it owns 50% or more of the combined voting power of all classes of stock entitled to vote, and 50% or more of the total value of all classes of stock. Exceptions are provided for RICs, REITs, and real estate mortgage investment conduits.

> **NOTE:** Like the special rule on capital contributions, this anti-abuse rule is similarly designed to prevent taxpayers from trafficking in loss corporations by reducing a loss corporation's assets to cash or other passive assets and then selling off a corporate shell consisting primarily of NOLs and cash or other passive assets.

[¶610] **Built-In Gains and Losses.** Built-in losses are subject to special limitations because they are economically equivalent to preacquisition NOL carryovers. Built-in gains (e.g., accelerated depreciation or installment sales reporting) are often the product of special tax provisions that accelerate deductions or defer income. So relief is available for these gains.

If a loss corporation has a net unrealized built-in gain, the amount of the limitation for any tax year ending within the five-year recognition period is increased by the recognized built-in gain for the tax year. The recognition period starts on the change date and ends at the close of the fifth postchange year. If a loss corporation has a net unrealized built-in loss, the recognized built-in loss for any tax year ending within the five-year period ending at the end of the fifth postchange year (the recognition period) is treated as a prechange loss subject to limitation. A net unrealized built-in loss is the amount by which the aggregate adjusted bases of a corporation's assets exceed its asset value immediately before the ownership change. If the value exceeds the bases, there's a net unrealized built-in gain. If 80% or more in value of the stock of a corporation is acquired in one transaction (or in a series of related transactions in a 12-month period), for determining the net unrealized built-in loss, the asset value may not exceed the grossed up amount paid for the stock properly adjusted for indebtedness for the corporation and other relevant items.

De minimis exception. The special rule for built-in gains (or losses) doesn't apply if the amount of a net unrealized built-in gain (or loss) does not exceed 25% of the value of the corporation's assets. For this rule, the total basis or value is computed by excluding any cash, cash item or marketable security that has a value that does not substantially differ from adjusted basis.

Limits on recognized built-in gains and losses. The recognized built-in gain (or loss) for a tax year cannot exceed the net unrealized built-in gain (or loss), reduced by the recognized built-in gains (or losses) for prior years ending in the recognition period. Recognized built-in gain is any gain recognized on an asset's disposition during the recognition period, if the taxpayer establishes that (1) the asset was held by the loss corporation immediately before the change date, and (2) the gain does not exceed the excess of the asset value on the change date over its adjusted basis on that date. Recognized built-in loss is any loss that is recognized on an asset's disposition during the recognition period, except to the extent the taxpayer establishes that (1) the asset was not held by the loss corporation immediately before the change date, or (2) the loss (or a portion of the loss) is greater than the excess of the asset's adjusted basis on the change date over its value on that date.

The amount of any recognized built-in loss that exceeds the Sec. 382 limitation for any post-change year must be carried forward (not carried back) under rules similar to the rules that apply to NOL carryovers and will be subject to the special limitations in the same manner as a pre-change loss.

The Sec. 382 limitation for any tax year in which gain is recognized by reason of Sec. 338 election (treating stock purchases as asset purchase) is increased by the excess of the amount of the gain over the portion of the gain taken into account in computing recognized built-in gains for the tax year.

Accrued deductions. Future regs may treat as built-in losses amounts that accrue before the ownership change date but are allowable as a deduction on or after that date (e.g., deductions deferred by Sec. 267 in related-party transactions). But depreciation allowances can't be treated as accrued deductions or built-in losses.

NOTE: The Treasury Department is directed to study built-in deductions and report to the tax writing committees by 1-1-89.

[¶611] The Bankruptcy Exception. The special limitations do not apply after an ownership change if

• the loss corporation was under a bankruptcy court's jurisdiction immediately before the ownership change, and

• its shareholders and creditors (determined immediately before the change) own 50% of its stock immediately after the change.

For this rule, a creditor's stock that was converted from debt is taken into account only if the debt was held by the creditor for at least 18 months before the bankruptcy case was filed or arose in the ordinary course of the loss corporation's business.

If the bankruptcy exception applies, the loss corporation's pre-change NOL carryovers are reduced by 50% of the excess of the discharged debt over the value of the stock transferred to the creditors.

Second ownership change. After an ownership change that qualifies for the bankruptcy exception, a *second* ownership change during the following two-year period will result in the elimination of NOL carryovers that arose before the first ownership change.

> **NOTE:** This limitation reflects the view that any value created during the two-year period is likely attributable to capital contributions. As explained earlier [¶609], these contributions are presumptively removed from a loss corporation's value.

Special rule for thrifts. A modified version of the bankruptcy exception applies to certain ownership changes of a thrift institution involved in a G reorganization or similar transaction. The bankruptcy exception is applied to qualified thrift reorganizations by requiring shareholders and creditors (including depositors) to retain a 20% (rather than 50%) interest. For this rule, the troubled thrift's deposits that become deposits in the acquiring corporation are treated as stock. The general bankruptcy rule that eliminates from the NOL carryovers interest deductions on debt that was converted doesn't apply to interest paid on deposits by thrifts qualifying under this rule.

> **NOTE:** Transactions involving solvent thrifts, including a purchase of a thrift's stock, or merger of a thrift into another corporation, are subject to the general rules relating to ownership changes.

[¶612] New Guidelines for Other Carryovers. In addition to the NOLs discussed earlier [see ¶606 et seq.], the new law also revises special limitations on unused business credits and research credits, excess foreign tax credits, and capital loss carryovers. In general, the new limitations applying to these carryovers (under Sec. 383) are similar to the new rules on NOL carryovers (under Sec. 382). Capital loss carryforwards will (under future regs) be limited to an amount determined on the basis of the tax liability that is attributable to so much of the taxable income as does not exceed the Sec. 382 limitation for the tax year, with the same ordering rules that apply under present law.

> **NOTE:** The new law expands the scope of Sec. 383, on carryovers other than NOLs to include passive activity losses and credits and minimum tax credits.

[¶613] Tax-Motivated Transactions. Acquisitions made to evade or avoid taxes remain under the strict sanctions of Sec. 269, usually resulting in the disallowance of deductions and credits. Similarly, the regulations governing the filing of consolidated returns (referred to as SRLY and CRCO rules) continue to apply.

Future regs may be prescribed to prevent the avoidance of the special limitations through the use of related persons, pass-through entities, or other intermediaries.

[¶614] **Effective Dates; Repeal of Old Rules.** The new law generally applies to an owner shift involving a 5% shareholder occurring after 12-31-86. As for equity structure shifts, it takes effect for reorganizations under plans adopted after that date. A reorganization plan is considered adopted on the earlier of the date when (1) the boards of directors of all parties to the reorganization adopt the plan or recommend its adoption, or (2) the shareholders approve.

The new law generally repeals the 1976 Tax Reform Act amendments that would generally limit the use of NOL carryovers and focus on changes of ownership alone. The repeal is retroactively effective as of 1-1-86.

Under special transitional rules, preexisting laws still apply to ownership changes on or after 1-1-87 in special situations. A transition rule applies if a petition was filed in a bankruptcy court before 8-14-86. Also, new law changes do not apply to (1) stock-for-debt exchanges and stock sales made pursuant to a plan of reorganization as to a petition for reorganization filed under Chapter 11 on 8-26-82, and which filed with a U.S. district court a first amended and related plan of reorganization before 3-1-86, and (2) ownership change of a Delaware corporation incorporated in August 1983, which may result from the exercise of a put or call option under an agreement entered into on 9-14-83, but only as to tax years beginning after 1991 regardless of whether an ownership change takes place. Similar special rules have been provided in other special situations.

Act Sec. 621, relating to limitation on net operating loss and excess credit carryforwards, amends Secs. 382 and 383, is effective generally after 12-31-86 and as shown above. It also makes a conforming amendment to Sec. 318(b)(5), and repeals 1976 Tax Reform Act amendments retroactively that would have extensively revised Secs. 382 and 383, relating to special limitations on NOL and credit carryovers.

General Utilities Doctrine Repealed

[¶615] **Gain and Loss Recognized on Liquidating Distributions (General Utilities Doctrine).** As a general rule, corporate earnings from sales of appreciated property are taxed twice:

- First, to the corporation when the sale occurs, and then
- To the shareholders when the net proceeds are distributed as dividends.

What happened at the corporate level? The income was taxed at ordinary rates if it resulted from selling inventory or other ordinary income assets. Of course, if capital assets held long-term were involved, capital gain rates applied. With some exceptions, shareholders were taxed at ordinary income rates to the extent of their pro rata share of the distributing corporation's current and accumulated earnings and profits.

Under prior law, an important exception (commonly known as the General Utilities doctrine) would permit the corporation to escape tax at the corporate level by distributing appreciated property to its shareholders and on certain liquidating sales of property. At the same time, the shareholder or third-party buyer would get a stepped-up, fair market value basis, with associated additional depreciation, depletion or amortization deductions. *Result:* The "price" of a step up in the basis of property subject to the *General Utilities* rule was typically that the shareholder paid a single capital gains tax on a liquidating distribution from the corporation. Broadly speaking, the new law repeals the *General Utilities* doctrine.

> **COMMENT:** The repeal of the *General Utilities* doctrine is designed to require the corporate level recognition of gain on a corporation's sale or distribution of appreciated property, irrespective of whether it occurs in a liquidating or nonliquidating context. Future regs will ensure that the purpose of the new rules is not circumvented by using any other provision, including the consolidated return regulations or the tax-free reorganization provisions.

Distributions in liquidation.   What happens now? Gain or loss is generally recognized by a corporation on a liquidating sale of its assets. Gain or loss is also generally recognized to a corporation on a distribution of its property in complete liquidation. The distributing corporation is treated as if the corporation had sold the property to the distributee-shareholders at its fair market value. However, gain or loss is not recognized for any distribution of property by a corporation to the extent there is nonrecognition of gain or loss to the recipient under the tax-free reorganization of gain or loss to the recipient under the tax-free reorganization provisions.

If the distributed property is subject to a liability, or the shareholders assume a liability connected with the distribution, the property value is treated as not less than the amount of the liability. Thus, in this case, gain is generally recognized to the extent the liability exceeds the distributor's basis.

Converting from C corporation to S corporation.   A corporate-level tax is imposed on any gain that arose before the conversion (built-in gain) and is recognized by the S corporation in any tax year, through sale or distribution, within 10 years of the date the S election took effect. The total amount of gain to be recognized is limited to the corporation's aggregate net built-in gain when the S corporation was converted. Gains on sales or distributions of assets by the S corporation are presumed to be built-in gains, except to the extent the taxpayer can establish the appreciation accrued after conversion.

The amount of tax is computed by applying the highest rate on ordinary income (or, if applicable, the alternative rate on capital gain income) to the lesser of (1) the recognized built-in gains of the S corporation for the tax year; or (2) the amount which would be the taxable income of the corporation for this tax year, if it were not an S corporation.

Any NOL carryforward arising in a tax year for which the corporation was a C corporation is allowed as a deduction against the lesser of the amounts above. The general business credit carryforward is allowed, as are certain other credits.

The tax does not apply to corporations that have always been S corporations.

> **COMMENT:** The rules generally apply to elections made after 12-31-86. The rules don't apply to S elections made before 1-1-87. Thus, the prior-law version of IRS Sec. 1374 applies.

The amount of built-in gains taken into account for any tax year cannot exceed the excess, if any, of the net unrealized built-in gain over the recognized built-in gains for prior tax years beginning in the 10-year period.

[¶616] Nonrecognition on Distributions in Complete Liquidation of Subsidiaries. There is an exception to the recognition rule for property distributed in a 100% liquidation involving a subsidiary—that is, when a subsidiary is completely liquidated into its parent.

> **COMMENT:** Since this kind of intercorporate transfer within the group is a nonrecognition event, a carryover basis follows. *Result:* The corporate level tax is paid if the corporation receiving this distributed property disposes of it to an outsider.

What happens when there's a liquidation of a subsidiary and an 80% corporate shareholder receives property with a carryover basis? The nonrecognition rule applies as to any property actually distributed to the controlling corporate shareholder (rather than pro rata share of each gain or loss). What about a minority shareholder receiving the property in this kind of liquidation? The distribution is treated the same way as a distribution in a nonliquidating redemption.

> **COMMENT:** Gain (but not loss) is recognized to the distributing corporation.

Suppose an 80% shareholder is a tax-exempt organization. Nonrecognition doesn't apply under the exception for 80% corporate shareholders unless the property received in the distribution is used by the organization in an unrelated trade or business right after the distribution. However, if the property later stops being used in the acquiring organization's trade or business, the organization is then taxed (along with any other tax imposed, like Sec. 1245 depreciation recapture). The tax is the lesser of: (a) the built-in gain in the property when the distribution is made; or (b) the difference between the property's adjusted basis and its fair market value at the time of the cessation.

Nonrecognition is also denied in subsidiary's liquidation when the controlling shareholder is a foreign corporation. The regs might provide some exceptions to this.

> **COMMENT:** It's expected that nonrecognition may be allowed if the appreciation on the distributed property is not being removed from the U.S. before recognition.

[¶617] Limiting Recognition of Losses. Two rules are provided to prevent the recognition of losses at the corporate level.

Some background. There is a concern that taxpayers might try various means to avoid the repeal of the *General Utilities* doctrine, or otherwise take advantage of the new rules, to recognize losses in inappropriate situations or inflate the amount of losses actually sustained. How? Under the general rule allowing loss recognition on liquidating distributions, taxpayers might be able to create artificial losses at the corporate level or to duplicate shareholder losses by contributing built-in loss property to the corporation. The two rules are as follows:

1. Generally, no loss is recognized by a liquidating corporation as to any property distribution to a related person (within the meaning of Sec. 267), unless it's distributed to all shareholders on a pro rata basis *and* the property is not acquired by the liquidating corporation in a Sec. 351 transaction (transfer to corporation controlled by transferor) or as a capital contribution five years before the distribution.

> **OBSERVATION:** A liquidating corporation wouldn't be allowed to recognize loss on a distribution of recently acquired property to a shareholder who, directly or indirectly, owns more than 50% in value of the corporation's stock. Also, a liquidating corporation can't recognize loss on any property (regardless of when or how acquired) that's distributed to this shareholder on non-pro rata basis.

2. Suppose a property's contribution to a corporation in advance of its liquidation is primarily to recognize loss on the property's sale or distribution and thus eliminate or limit corporate level gain. What happens? The basis (for loss) of any property acquired by corporation in a Sec. 351 transaction or a capital contribution is re-

duced (not below zero) by the excess of the property's basis on the contribution date over its fair market value then.

> **COMMENT:** It's assumed (except when the regs indicate otherwise) that any Sec. 351 transaction or capital contribution within a two-year period before the complete liquidation plan's adoption has this main purpose. It's possible that a contribution more than two years before the adoption might have a prohibited purpose. However, this is considered unusual.

Recapture in lieu of disallowance. If a plan of complete liquidation is adopted in a tax year following the date on which the tax return, including the loss disallowed by the above rule is filed, in appropriate cases, the liquidating corporation may recapture the disallowed loss on the tax return for the tax year in which the plan of liquidation is adopted. Alternatively, the corporation could file an amended return for the tax year in which the loss was reported.

> **Example:** Blake owns a 10% interest in Acme Corp., a calendar year corporation. On 1-1-87, he contributes to Acme nondepreciable property with a $1,000 basis and a $100 fair market value in exchange for additional stock. On 9-30-87, Acme sells the property to Green, an unrelated third party, for $200. Acme includes the $800 loss on its 1987 tax return. Then, on 12-31-88, Acme adopts a liquidation plan. Acme has two choices: (1) It could file an amended return reflecting that the $800 loss was disallowed, because the property's basis would be reduced to $200. (2) It could recapture the loss on its 1988 return. The recapture here is limited to the lessor of the built-in loss of $900 ($1,000, transferred basis less $200, property's value), or loss recognized on the property's disposition, $800 ($1,000 less $200 amount realized. Thus, unless Acme files an amended return, it must recapture $800 on its return for its tax year ending 12-31-88.

> **NOTE:** Future regs might provide that the presumed prohibited purpose for contributions of property two years in advance of the liquidation plan's adoption will be disregarded *unless* there is no clear and substantial relationship between the contributed property and the conduct of the corporation's current or future business enterprises.

[¶618] Nonliquidating Distributions of Appreciated Property. Generally, a corporation's tax treatment of nonliquidating distributions of appreciated property has, in the past, been the same as liquidating distributions. However, recently, nonliquidating distributions have been made subject to stricter rules than liquidating distributions. Corporations have usually been required to recognize gains as a result of nonliquidating distributions of appreciated property.

Under the new rules, nonliquidating distributions are treated the same as liquidating distributions. This means that gain must generally be recognized to a distributing corporation if appreciated property (other than the corporation's obligation) is distributed to share-holders outside of complete liquidation.

Repeal of exceptions to recognition. The new law repeals exceptions to recognition that were provided for nonliquidating distributions to 10%, long-term noncorporate shareholders, and for certain distributions of property relating to the payment of estate taxes or certain redemptions of private foundation stock.

[¶619] Election to Treat Sales or Distributions of Subsidiary Stock as Asset Transfers. The treatment of liquidating sales and distributions of subsidiary stock is, under the new law, conformed to the present law treatment of nonliquidating sales or distributions of such stock; thus, such liquidating sales or distributions are generally taxable at the corporate level.

> **NOTE:** According to the Conference Committee Report, it's appropriate to conform the treatment of liquidating and nonliquidating sales or distributions and to require recognition when appreciated property, including stock of a subsidiary, is transferred to a corporate or an individual recipient outside the economic unit of the selling or distributing affiliated group.

In certain cases, a corporate buyer and a seller of an 80%-controlled subsidiary can elect to treat the sale of the subsidiary stock as if it had been the sale of the underlying assets [Sec. 338(h)(10)]. Among the election filing requirements are that the selling corporation and its target subsidiary are members of an affiliated group filing a consolidated return for the tax year that include the acquisition date. If an election is made, the underlying assets of the company that was sold receive a stepped-up, fair market value basis. The selling consolidated group recognizes the gain or loss attributable to the assets. There is no separate tax on the seller's gain attributable to the stock.

> **COMMENT:** This rule offers taxpayers relief from a potential multiple taxation at the corporate level of the same economic gain, which might result when a transfer of appreciated corporate stock is taxed without providing corresponding step-up in basis of the corporation's assets.

The new rule expands the so-called "Sec. 338(h)(10) concept," to the extent provided in the regs, to situations in which the selling corporation owns 80% of the value of the subsidiary's voting power, but doesn't file a consolidated return. Similar principles may also be applied to taxable sales or distributions of controlled corporation stock.

> **NOTE:** Regulations under this elective procedure should flesh out the principles that support the liquidation-reincorporation doctrine.

For example, to the extent that regs make available an election to treat a stock transfer of controlled corporation stock to persons related to the corporation, there may be special rules for that corporation's Sec. 381(c) tax attributes so that net operating losses may not be used to offset liquidation gains, earnings and profits may not be manipulated, or accounting methods may not be changed. This election is expected to affect the way in which a corporation's distribution to its shareholders will be characterized for figuring shareholder level income tax consequences.

Report on corporation income taxation. The Treasury will consider whether changes in subchapter C (relating to income taxation of corporations and their shareholders) and related provisions are desirable. Report of its study will be made to the tax-writing committees no later than 1-1-88.

Effective Dates: The new law applies generally to (1) any distribution in complete liquidation, and any sale or exchange, made by a corporation after 7-31-86, unless the corporation is completely liquidated before 1987; (2) any Sec. 338 transaction for which the acquisition date occurs after 1986; and (3) any distribution (not in complete liquidation) made after 1986. Under a transitional rule, the new law does not apply to distributions or sales made under a liquidation plan adopted before 11-20-85. Transactions are treated as made under a pre-11-20-85 liquidation plan, if before 11-20-85:

- The liquidating corporation's board of directors adopted a resolution to solicit shareholder approval for a Sec. 336 or 337 transaction, or the transaction was approved by the shareholders or directors; or
- There was an offer to buy a majority of the liquidating corporation's voting stock, or the board of directors adopted a resolution recommending or approving an acquisition; or
- A ruling request was submitted to the IRS with respect to a Sec. 336 or 337 transaction (including a Sec. 338 election).

IMPORTANT: In any of these cases, all of the sales or distributions must be completed before 1-1-88.

Other grandfathered transactions include:

- Liquidations completed before 1-1-87.
- Liquidations under a liquidation plan adopted before 8-1-86 and completed before 1-1-88.
- Deemed liquidations under Sec. 338 as to stock purchases constituting control before 1-1-87.
- A liquidation of a corporation if a majority of the voting stock is acquired on or after 8-1-86 under a written binding con-

tract in effect before 8-1-86, and if the liquidation is completed before 1988.

• Deemed liquidations under Sec. 338, or actual liquidations, of companies that are acquired under a binding contract entered into before 8-1-86, if the deemed or actual liquidation occurs before 1-1-88.

Also, complete relief (except for ordinary income and short-term gain property) is provided for small, closely held companies on liquidating sales or distributions occurring before 1-1-89, if the liquidation is completed by that date. Relief phases out for these companies with value between $5 and $10 million.

Act Secs. 631-634, relating to recognition of gain and loss on liquidating distributions of property in liquidation amend Secs. 311, 336, 337, 367(e), 453(h)(1)(A), (B), (E), 453B(d), 1363(c), 1367(f)(2), 1374, repealing Secs. 332(c), 333, 334(c), 338(h)(12), with conforming and clerical changes made to Secs. 26(b)(2), 312(n)(4), 334(a), 341(e), 346(b), 453(h), 467(c)(5), 897(d), 1056(a), 1255(b)(2), 1276(c)(3), 1375(b)(1)(B), effective as to (1) any distribution in complete liquidation, and any sale or exchange made by a corporation after 7-31-86, unless such corporation is completely liquidated before 1-1-87, (2) any transaction under Sec. 338 for which acquisition date occurs after 12-31-86, and (3) any distribution (not in complete liquidation) made after 12-31-86; for built-in gains of S corporations, the rules apply to tax years starting after 12-31-86, but only in cases where the first tax year for which the corporation is an S corporation is by an election made after 12-31-86. Special exceptions apply for certain plans of liquidation and as to binding contracts.

Other Corporate Rules

[¶620] **Allocating Purchase Price in Asset Sales.** The new law requires both the buyer and the seller in certain asset acquisitions to divide the purchase price among the transferred assets using a prescribed formula. Under prior law, without a special rule, a seller would generally prefer to assign a larger portion of the purchase price to capital assets such as goodwill. A buyer, on the other hand, would favor a higher basis for inventory or other ordinary-income assets.

Effect on sales of going concerns. The new law's allocation rules apply only to "applicable asset acquisitions." An applicable asset acquisition is any transfer of assets that amounts to a business in which the seller's basis is determined wholly by reference to the consideration paid for the assets. For this rule, a group of assets will be considered a business, if their character is such that goodwill or going concern value could under any circumstances attach to the assets. For example, a group of assets that would be treated as an active trade or business within the meaning of Sec. 355 (involving the distribution of a controlled corporation's stock) will in all events be considered a business. In addition, businesses that are not active businesses under Sec. 355 will also be subject to this rule. A transfer will not be treated as not meeting the applicable-asset-acquisition test merely because a portion of the assets transferred qualifies for nonrecognition of gain or loss for like-kind exchange of property held for productive use or investment.

IMPORTANT: The new law covers both direct and indirect transfers of a business. So you must apply the special allocation rules to a sale of a business by an individual or a partnership, or a sale of a partnership interest in which the basis of the purchasing partner's proportionate share of the partnership's assets is adjusted to reflect the purchase price.

Who must allocate and how. Both the buyer and the seller must use the residual method to allocate the consideration received for the assets among the assets acquired in the transaction. The purchase price is a key factor in figuring the buyer's basis in the assets and the seller's gain or loss on the sale. Briefly, under the residual method, the goodwill and going concern value is the excess of the business's purchase price over the aggregate fair market values of the tangible assets and the identifiable intangible assets other than goodwill and going concern value. The method used here is the same as the one prescribed in Temporary Reg. Sec. 1.338(b)-2T for allocating purchase price to assets following a stock purchase.

Under that reg, the price of the assets acquired must be reduced by cash and cash-like items, then the balance is allocated first to certain tangible assets, followed by certain intangibles (neither allocation can be more than the assets' FMV). The remaining cost must then be allocated to goodwill and going concern value. Under prior rules, the price could be spread across these assets in proportion to their FMVs even though the purchase price was in excess of FMV.

NOTE: The mandatory use of the residual method doesn't restrict the IRS's ability to challenge the taxpayer's determination of any asset's fair market value by any appropriate method. For example, in certain cases, the IRS may reasonably make an independent showing of the value of goodwill or going concern value as a means of questioning the validity of the taxpayer's valuation of other assets.

Information required. Future regulations may require the seller and buyer to file information returns disclosing amounts allocated to goodwill or going concern value, and to any other categories of assets or specific assets.

Effective Date: The new law applies to transactions after 5-6-86, unless a contract was binding on and after 5-6-86.

OBSERVATION: Buyers of assets still negotiating without a binding contract since 5-6-86 should take a second look at their after-tax purchase costs. Since the new law is retroactively effective to 5-6-86, any price premium paid above the physical asset values must be assigned to goodwill rather than depreciable assets.

Act Sec. 641, providing special allocation rules for certain asset acquisitions, adds a new Sec. 1060 and redesignates former Sec. 1060 as Sec. 1061, effective as shown above.

[¶621] Related Party Sales. The rules limiting installment sales and ordinary income treatment on certain sales between related parties are modified. The definition of related parties is expanded so that persons and entities with certain more than 50% relationships are covered (rather than the 80% relationships under prior law) and certain other cases are covered. In some cases, ratable basis recovery by seller and conformity between buyer and seller regarding recognition of income and basis are required, instead of denying deferred income treatment to the seller.

Act Sec. 642, related to definition of related party, amends paragraph (2) of Sec. 707(b), paragraph (1) of Sec. 1239(b), paragraph (c)(1) of Sec. 1239, paragraph (2) of Sec. 1239(c) and amending paragraph (1) of Sec. 453(f), and adds a subsection (8) to Sec. 453(f), and amends Sec. 453(g), effective for sales after date of enactment in tax years ending after that date, unless made under a binding contract in effect before 8-14-86.

[¶622] Amortizable Bond Premium. The amortizable bond premium deduction is treated as interest, except as otherwise provided by regulations. Thus, for example, bond premium is treated as interest for applying the investment interest limitations.

NOTE: Suppose, before the new law's enactment, a taxpayer made an election under IRC Sec. 171(c) (election as to taxable bonds). This election applies to obligations issued after enactment only if the taxpayer chooses to have that election apply (under regulations to be issued by the IRS).

Act Sec. 643, relating to amortizable bond premium, amends Sec. 171 by redesignating subsection (e) as (f) and inserting new subsection (e), effective for obligations acquired after date of enactment, in tax years ending after that date. Elections in effect on that date may apply at taxpayer's option.

[¶623] Allocation of Housing Co-op Taxes and Interest. A tenant-shareholder in a housing cooperative can deduct his or her proportionate share of amounts paid for (1) real estate taxes allowable as a deduction to the cooperative that are paid on the cooperative's land or building and (2) interest allowable as a deduction to the cooperative paid on debt incurred to acquire the cooperative's land (and or building). Under prior law, the tenant-shareholder's proportionate share of the deduction was based only on the percentage of cooperative stock that he or she owned.

The problem. Some cooperatives distribute equal shares to all tenant-shareholders, others allow prepayment of a tenant-shareholder's share of the cooperative's debt, and others operate in jurisdictions where the local government separately assesses taxes regardless of the percentage of stock owned. The proportionate-share definition doesn't work in all situations.

Cooperative housing corporations that charge tenant-shareholders with a portion of the cooperative's interest or taxes in a way that reasonably reflects the cost to the cooperative of the interest or taxes allocable to each tenant-shareholder's dwelling unit may elect to have these tenant-shareholders deduct the separately allocated amounts for income tax purposes (rather than amounts based on proportionate ownership of shares of the cooperative).

In addition, the tax treatment of persons owning stock in cooperative housing corporations is extended to corporations, trusts, and other entities that are shareholders. Also, maintenance and lease deductions by tenant-shareholders are disallowed in situations where the amount paid by such tenant-shareholders is properly chargeable to the capital account of the cooperative.

What about depreciation? Tenant-shareholders using depreciable property in a trade or business or for the production of income can take depreciation to the extent of that portion of their stock's adjusted basis that's allocable to the depreciable property. Deductions that exceed this basis can be carried over to the next tax years. No deduction is allowed to the tenant-shareholders for any amount paid or accrued to the cooperative (in excess of proportionate interest and real estate taxes) to the extent that these amounts are properly allocable to amount chargeable to the cooperative's capital account. Any deduction disallowed is applied to increase the adjusted basis of the tenant-shareholder's stock.

> **COMMENT:** This rule generally prevents tenant-shareholder's (including a corporation) from obtaining deductions for the co-op's capital costs more quickly than if they had owned the unit.

Act Sec. 644, changing cooperative ownership requirements, amends Sec. 216(b) and (c) and adds new subsection (d) effective for taxable years beginning after 12-31-86.

[¶624] Co-op Refinancing Rules. The new law provides special rules for two specified limited-profit housing cooperatives that refinanced their debt. The rules apply to income earned on the reserve funds in tax years beginning before 1986 and payments made from the respective reserve funds in tax years beginning after 1985.

Act Sec. 644, sets up special rules for two housing cooperatives, generally effective for tax years starting before 1-1-86. However, the treatment of certain amounts paid from a qualified refinancing-related reserve shall apply to amounts paid or incurred, and property acquired in tax years starting after 12-31-85.

Real Estate Investment Trusts (REITs)

〔¶625〕 Qualification Requirements. The new law eases some of the qualification requirements for REITs. REITs have been relieved of certain shareholder and income and asset requirements for the first year that an entity otherwise qualifies as a REIT. Relief is also granted from certain income and asset requirements for the first year after a REIT receives new equity capital and certain new debt capital. In addition to these breaks REITs will be permitted to hold assets in wholly owned subsidiaries.

The new law also made some important changes in the definition of rents from real property. By modifying the definition, the new law enables REITs to perform those services that would not result in the receipt of unrelated business income if performed by certain tax-exempt entities, without using an independent contractor. The new law also includes in the definition of rents from real property (and the definition of interest) rent or interest that is based on the net income of the tenant or debtor, but only if such net income is based on amounts that would be treated as rents from real property if received directly by the REIT.

The new law also permits income from certain shared appreciation mortgages to be treated as qualifying income for a REIT.

Distribution requirements. The new law grants some relief from the distribution requirement when the REIT has certain types of income that are not accompanied by the receipt of cash. However, in that case the REIT must pay tax on the amounts not distributed. Also under the new law the minimum distribution requirement of regulated investment companies will apply to REITs.

Other changes. There is an expansion of the safe harbor granted REITs under which sales by a REIT may not be treated as prohibited transactions. There is also a modification in the computation of the amount of capital gains dividends that a REIT must pay. And one of the penalties relating to the distribution of dividends has been eliminated.

Act Sec. 661, providing that an entity may elect REIT status even though it meets the stock ownership test under Sec. 542(a)(2) or has fewer than 100 shareholders, amends Sec. 856(a)(6) and Sec. 857 and adds 856(h), effective for tax years beginning after 12-31-86.

〔¶626〕 Asset and Income Requirements. If a REIT owns a "qualified REIT subsidiary," all the assets, liabilities, and items of income, deduction, and credit of the subsidiary are to be treated as if they were those of the REIT. To be a qualified REIT subsidiary, 100% of the stock must be owned by the REIT during the entire period the subsidiary is in existence.

To qualify as a real estate investment trust, 75% or more of the trust's income must come from real property. Under the new law, if a REIT receives equity capital and invests it in stock or bonds, any interest, dividends, or gains from the sale of the investments qualifies as income for purposes of the 75% test. *Limitations:* Only income received for the one-year period beginning on the date that the REIT received such capital will qualify. In addition, during that period, stock or bonds bought with the new equity capital will be treated as "real estate assets" for purposes of the "75% asset test," which requires that 75% or more of the value of the trust's total assets must be in real estate assets, cash, cash items, and government securities. The new law defines equity capital as any amount received by the REIT in exchange for the REIT's stock (other than pursuant to a dividend reinvestment plan), or in the public offerings of the debt obligations of such trust which have maturities of at least 5 years.

For the income requirements any income derived from a "shared appreciation provision" is treated as gain recognized on the sale of the "secured property." A shared appreciation provision is any provision that is in connection with an obligation that is held by the REIT and secured by an interest in real property, which provision entitles the REIT to receive a specified portion of any gain realized on the sale or exchange of such real property (or of any gain that would be realized if the property were sold on a specified date). Secured property for these purposes means the real property that secures the obligation that has the shared appreciation provision.

Also, for the income requirements, the REIT is treated as holding the secured property for the period during which it held the shared appreciation provision (or, if shorter, the period during which the secured property was held by the person holding such property), and the secured property is treated as property described in Sec. 1221(1) if it is such property in the hands of the obligor on the obligation to which the shared appreciation provision relates (or if it would be such property if held by the REIT).

Act Sec. 662, providing that all assets, liabilities, and items of income, deduction, and credit of a "qualified REIT subsidiary" are treated as those same items of the REIT and providing that any income from a "shared appreciation provision" shall be treated as gain on the sale of secured property, adds Sec. 856(i) and (j) and amends Sec. 856(c) for tax years beginning after 12-31-86.

[¶627] **Rents and Interest.** The new law modifies the definition of rents from real property. The new definition permits REITs to perform those services that would not result in the receipt of "unrelated business income" if performed by certain tax-exempt entities, without using an independent contractor.

Under the new law rents or interest that are based on the net income of a tenant or debtor are treated as rent from real property or as interest, respectively, if certain conditions are met. To qualify, the rent (or interest) must be received from a tenant (or debtor) that receives substantially all of its income from the leased property (or the property that secures the loan) from the subleasing (or leasing) of substantially all of such property, and the rent received by the tenant (or debtor) consists entirely of amounts that would be treated as rents from real property (or interest) if received directly by the REIT.

Act Sec. 663, providing that amounts received by a REIT in connection with rental property qualify as rents from real property even though the REIT performs services, amends Sec. 856(d), (f) effective for tax years beginning after 12-31-86.

[¶628] Distribution Requirements. REITs must distribute 95% of their taxable income. The new law provides certain relief from this requirement when a REIT has certain types of income that are not accompanied by a receipt of cash. However, the REIT must pay tax on the amounts not distributed.

Act Sec. 664, providing relief from the requirement of having to distribute 95% of the REIT's taxable income, amends Sec. 857(a) and adds (e), effective for tax years beginning after 12-31-86.

[¶629] Treatment of Capital Gains. Under the new law, a REIT in determining the maximum amount of capital gain dividends that it may pay for a tax year cannot offset its net capital gain with the amount of any net operating loss, whether current or carried over from a previous tax year. If the REIT elects to pay capital gains dividends in excess of its net taxable income, the REIT would increase the amount of its net operating loss carryover by such amount.

Act Sec. 665, providing that a REIT's net operating loss would not be offset against its net capital gain for purposes of determining the maximum amount of capital gains dividends, amends Sec. 857(b) effective for tax years beginning after 12-31-86.

[¶630] Prohibited Transactions. A REIT may be hit with a 100% tax on net income from "prohibited transactions," excluding foreclosures. However, there are a number of safe harbors that permit the REIT to avoid the tax. Under the new law, the number of property sales that a REIT may make within the safe harbor is increased from five to seven or the adjusted bases of all sales is not more than 10% of the adjusted bases of all of the REITS assets as of the beginning of the year.

Under the new law, losses from prohibited transactions may not be taken into account in determining the amount of net income from prohibited transactions. However, any net loss from prohibited transactions may be taken into account in computing REIT taxable income.

Act Sec. 666, modifies the rules relating to prohibited transactions of REITs, amends Sec. 857(b)(6), effective for tax years beginning after 12-31-86.

[¶631] **No Penalty on Deficiency Dividends.** The penalty tax under Sec. 6697 relating to deficiency dividends is repealed by the new law. The penalty is now limited to regulated investment companies.

Act Sec. 667, repealing the penalty tax on deficiency dividends of REITs, amends Sec. 6697, effective for tax years beginning after 12-31-86.

[¶632] **Excise Tax on Undistributed Income.** The excise tax on undistributed income has been increased to 4% of the amount by which the required distribution exceeds the amount distributed in the taxable year. The required distribution is the sum of 85% of ordinary income, plus 95% of capital gain net income, increased by any prior shortfall in meeting the required distribution.

Act Sec. 668, amends Sec. 4981 increasing the excise tax on undistributed income, effective for calendar years beginning after 12-31-86.

REAL ESTATE MORTGAGE INVESTMENT CONDUITS (REMICs)

[¶633] **REMICs—A Brand New Tax Entity.** The new law creates a special tax vehicle for entities which issue multiple classes of investor interests backed by a pool of mortgages. The new vehicle is called the Real Estate Mortgage Investment Conduit (REMIC), which, as its name implies, is generally a conduit entity for tax purposes. There are complex rules covering qualification as a REMIC, and transfers to and liquidations of the entity. There are two tiers of ownership interests in REMICs and each is taxed differently.

The REMIC is intended to be the exclusive vehicle for issuing multiple-class mortgage-backed securities. Result: If the qualification requirements are met, any corporate, partnership, trust, or similar entity is granted pass-through REMIC status. For example, a REMIC organized as a partnership would be governed by the new REMIC Code Sections (860A through G) covering its transactions and the holders of its interests, not by the partnership provisions of Subchapter K.

Qualifying as a REMIC. The entity must be a calendar year taxpayer that elects REMIC status for the tax year, and, if applicable, for all prior tax years. The entity qualifies as a REMIC only if it meets two tests:

(1) Asset test. Substantially all assets at the close of the fourth month ending after the "startup day" and each quarter ending thereafter must consist of qualified mortgages and permitted investments. The "startup day" is any day selected by the REMIC that is on or before the first day on which REMIC interests are issued. A qualified mortgage is any obligation (including any participation or certificate of beneficial ownership interest) that is (1) principally secured by an interest in real property; (2) transferred to the REMIC on or before the startup day or is purchased by the REMIC within the three-month period beginning on the startup day. Stripped coupons and stripped bonds are treated as qualifying mortgages if the bonds from which the coupons or bonds were stripped would have been qualified mortgages. Regular interests in other REMICs transferred to the REMIC on or before the startup day and qualified replacement mortgages are treated as qualified mortgages. A qualified replacement mortgage is one that would have been treated as a qualified mortgage and is received either (1) in exchange for a defective mortgage within two years of the startup day; or (2) in exchange for another qualified mortgage within a three-month period beginning on the startup day.

Permitted investments are cash flow investments, qualified reserve assets, and foreclosure property. Cash flow investments are investments of amounts received under qualified mortgages for a temporary period before distribution to holders of REMIC interests. Such cash flow investments are limited to those that pay out passive income in the nature of interest. Qualified reserve assets are any intangible property held for investment as part of a qualified reserve fund. This is a fund maintained by the REMIC to provide for payment of expenses and to provide for additional security for payments due to holders of regular interests. Amounts in the reserve fund must be reduced as regular REMIC interests are retired. Foreclosure property is property that would be treated as foreclosure property under Sec. 856(e) if acquired by a REIT and is acquired by the REMIC in connection with the default or imminent default of a qualified mortgage. Foreclosure property ceases to be a permitted investment if it is held by the REMIC for more than one year after acquisition.

(2) Investors' interests. All interests in the REMIC must consist of one or more classes of regular interests and a single class of residual interests.

A regular interest is one with terms that are fixed on the startup day and unconditionally entitles the holder to receive a specified principal amount and provides that interest payments (or similar payments) are payable based on a fixed rate. Payments may be based on a variable rate, to the extent provided in regs. The payments on a regular interest can be contingent on the extent of prepayments from qualifying mortgages and the amount of income from qualifying investments. However, the regular interest cannot carry interest payments that are disproportionate to the specified principal amount. A residual interest is any REMIC interest which is not a regular interest and which is designated as a residual interest by the REMIC. There can be only class of residual interests, and distributions (if any) must be made pro rata to all holders.

The Treasury is to issue regulations that offer relief in the event of an inadvertent REMIC termination. But the relief is to be accompanied by appropriate sanctions (e.g., imposition of corporate tax for period of time in which qualification requirements are not met).

Although the REMIC is a conduit entity, it is subject to a penalty tax equal to 100% of its net income from prohibited transactions (computed without taking into account losses from or deductions connected with the prohibited transactions). Prohibited transactions include dispositions of qualified mortgages other than dispositions related to: a substitution of a qualified replacement mortgage for a defective mortgage; REMIC bankruptcy or insolvency; foreclosure, default or imminent default of a mortgage; or a qualified liquidation. Other prohibited transactions: income from assets a REMIC is not permitted to hold, income receive as compensation for services, and the disposition of a cash flow investment other than a disposition related to a qualified liquidation.

Other REMIC rules. The basis of any property received by a REMIC in exchange for regular or residual interests is generally equal to the fair market value of the property at the time of the transfer. Gain or loss is not recognized when a REMIC liquidates and sells its assets. However, all assets must be sold and the proceeds (other than amounts retained to meet claims) distributed to holders of REMIC interests within a 90-day period beginning on the day the liquidation plan is adopted.

Taxation of regular interests. Holders of regular interests are taxed as if they held a debt instrument and must report REMIC income on the accrual basis. The taxable original issue discount (OID) for an accrual period is based on the increase in the present value of the remaining payments on the instrument, taking into account payments includible in the stated redemption price but received on the regular interest during the period. The present value calculation is made at the beginning of each accrual period, using the yield to maturity of the instrument at the time of its issuance (compounded at the end of each quarter, adjusted for the length of the accrual period, and calculated based on certain prepayment assumptions to be specified in regs). The present value calculation takes into account any prepayments that have occurred before the close of the accrual period.

Gain on the disposition of a regular interest is treated as ordinary income to the extent of any unaccrued OID. This is the excess of:

(1) the amount that would have been includible in gross income if the regular interest yielded a return equal to 110% of the applicable federal rate [as defined in Sec. 1274(d), without regard to Sec. 1274(d)(2)], determined as of the time the taxpayer acquired his interest, over

(2) the total amount of ordinary income derived from the regular interest and included in the taxpayer's income prior to disposition.

Taxation of residual interests. At the end of each calendar quarter, the holder of a residual interest has ordinary income or loss equal to his daily portion of the REMIC's taxable income or loss. Distributions up to the holder's adjusted basis are taxed as ordinary income and excess distributions are treated as gain from the sale or exchange of the interest. The holder's adjusted basis is increased by the amount of REMIC taxable income that he takes into account and is decreased (but not below zero) by (1) distributions actually received; and (2) any net loss of the REMIC that the holder takes into account.

The amount of REMIC net loss that the holder may take into account is limited to the adjusted basis of his interest as of the close of the quarter (or time of disposition, if earlier), determined without regard to the net loss for the quarter. Any loss that is disallowed may be carried over indefinitely and may be used only to offset income generated by the same REMIC.

For determining the tax implications of holding a residual REMIC interest, REMIC taxable income or net loss is figured as if the entity were a calendar year individual using the accrual method of accounting, with four modifications. First, a deduction is allowed for those amounts that would be deductible as interest if regular interests were treated as debt of the REMIC. Second, market discount on any market discount bond held by the REMIC is includable for the year in which the discount accrues. Third, income, gain, loss or deductions from prohibited transactions are not taken into account. Fourth, deductions under Sec. 703(a)(2), other than deductions allowable under Sec. 212, are not allowed.

Special rules: A portion of net REMIC income taken into account by a holder may not be offset by any net operating losses (a special exception applies to thrift institutions). This same portion of income is treated as unrelated business income under Sec. 511, and is ineligible for a reduction in the rate of withholding tax in the case of a holder who is a nonresident alien.

The portion of income subject to the special rule is any excess of net REMIC income taken into account by the residual interest holder for any calendar quarter, over the sum of the daily accruals for the residual interest. The daily accrual is found by allocating to each day in the calendar quarter a ratable portion of the product of the adjusted issue price of the interest at the beginning of the accrual period, and 120% of the long-term federal rate. The initial issue price is the price paid for the interest at issuance. The adjusted issue price is the initial issue price plus the amount of daily accruals for the prior calendar quarters, less the amount of any distributions prior to the end of the calendar quarter.

Dispositions of residual interests. In general, the wash sale provisions of Sec. 1091 apply if the seller of a residual interest buys (or enters into another transaction that triggers Sec. 1091) any REMIC or comparable interest in a "taxable mortgage pool" (see below) within a prohibited period of time. The prohibited period commences six months before the disposition of the regular interest and ends six months after the date of the disposition.

Exchange of property for REMIC interests. The contribution of qualified mortgages or other property to a REMIC in exchange for regular or residual interests results in neither gain nor loss to the transferor. The adjusted bases of the interests received are equal to the adjusted bases of the property contributed.

If the issue price of a regular interest exceeds its adjusted basis (as determined above), the excess is included in gross income under rules similar to the accrual of market discount required by Sec. 1276(b). If the issue price of a residual interest exceeds its adjusted basis (as determined above), then the excess is amortized and included in the holder's income on a straight line basis over the expected life of the REMIC.

If the adjusted basis of a regular interest exceeds its issue price, the excess is treated as if it were amortizable bond premium (Sec. 171). If the adjusted basis of a residual interest exceeds its issue price, the excess is deductible ratably over the expected life of the REMIC.

Taxable mortgage pools. REMICs are intended to be the exclusive vehicle for issuing multiple class mortgage backed securities without the imposition of a double tax. To accomplish this goal, the new law treats any taxable mortgage pool (TMP) as a taxable corporation that is not an includible corporation for purposes of filing consolidated returns. This rule is generally effective beginning in 1992. A TMP is any non-REMIC entity (other than a domestic building and loan association) if (1) substantially all its assets consist of debt obligations and more than 50% of the obligations consist of real estate mortgages; (2) it is the obligor under debt obligations with two or more maturities; and (3) payments on the debt obligations bear a relationship to the payments on the debt obligations held by the entity (e.g., the underlying mortgages).

Other rules: The new REMIC provisions carry special rules that relate to REITs, certain financial institutions, and foreign holders.

Regulatory authority and Treasury study. The Treasury is granted broad authority to issue regs clarifying the application of the new REMIC rules. The conferees also request the Treasury to conduct a study of the REMIC provisions' effectiveness and their impact on thrift institutions.

Information reporting. Amounts includible in the income of a regular holder are subject to the information reporting requirements of Sec. 6049. What's more, the REMIC must report interest (and OID accrual) to a broad group of holders, including corporations, dealers in securities or commodities, REITs, common trusts funds, and certain other trusts. The REMIC also is required to report sufficient information to allow holders to figure the accrual of any market discount or amortization of any premium.

Act Sec. 671, providing new rules for real estate mortgage investment conduits, adds Secs. 860A through 860F. Act. Sec. 672 amends Sec. 1272(a), relating to OID accruals. Act Sec. 673 adds Sec. 7701(i), relating to taxable mortgage pools. Act Sec. 674, adds Sec. 6049(d)(7), relating to compliance provisions. Act Secs. 671-674 are generally effective for tax years beginning after 12-31-86. The amendments made by Act Sec. 672, relating to OID, apply to debt instruments issued after 12-31-86 in tax years ending after that date. The amendments made by Act Sec. 673, relating to taxable mortgage pools take effect on 1-1-92, and do not apply to any entity in existence on 12-31-91. The exception for entities in existence on 12-31-91 will cease to apply as of the first day after 12-31-91 on which there is a substantial transfer of cash or other property to the entity. The wash-sale rules contained in Act Sec. 673 apply to tax years beginning after 12-31-86.

Miscellaneous Provisions

[¶634] Regulated Investment Companies—Excise Tax Imposed. For any calendar year, a nondeductible excise tax applies on every RIC, equal to 4% of the excess, if any, of the required distribution for the calendar year, over the distributed amount for the calendar year. The excise tax is to be paid not later than March 15 of the succeeding calendar year. "Required distribution" for any calendar year means the sum of 97% of the RIC's ordinary income for the calendar year, plus 90% of the RIC's capital gain net income for the 1-year period ending on Oct. 31 of the calendar year; increased by the excess, if any, of the grossed up required distribution for the preceding calendar year, over the distributed amount for the preceding calendar year.

Special rules apply for RICs with tax years ending on Nov. 30 or Dec. 31, for dividends declared in December, earnings and profits, and treatment of certain capital losses.

Business development companies. A business development company registered under the Investment Company Act of 1940, as amended (15 U.S.C. 80a-1 to 80b-2) may qualify as a RIC.

Hedging exception. The computation of gross income of a RIC for the Sec. 851(b)(3) requirement that less than 30% of the gross income of the RIC be derived from the sale or exchange of stock or securities held for less than three months is modified. For applying this test, any increase in value on a position that is part of a designated hedge is offset by any decrease in value (whether or not realized) or any other position that is part of such hedge. This rule applies for calculating both gains from the sale or other disposition of stock or securities held for less than three months, and also the gross income of the RIC for Sec. 851(b)(3) purposes.

Treatment of series funds as separate corporations. For RICs having more than one fund, each fund is treated as a separate corporation, under Sec. 851. "Fund" means a segregated portfolio of assets, the beneficial interests in which are owned by the holders of a class or series of stock of the RIC that is preferred over all other classes or series in respect of such portfolio of assets.

Extension of period for mailing notices to shareholders. Generally, the notice requirements for shareholders are lengthened to 60 days from 45 days.

Act Secs. 651-657, imposing an excise tax on RICs and other technical requirements, enacts Sec. 4982, effective for calendar years beginning after 12-31-86; amends paragraph (1) of Sec. 851(a) (business development companies), effective for tax years beginning after 12-31-86; adds new subsection (g) to Sec. 851 (hedging transactions), effective for tax years beginning after date of enactment; adds new subsection (q) to Sec. 851 (series funds as separate corporations), effective for tax years beginning after date of enactment (with special rule for existing series funds); and amends Secs. 852(b)(3), 852(b)(5)(A), 853(c), 854(b)(2) and 855(c) (notice period), effective for tax years beginning after the date of enactment.

[¶635] Personal Holding Company Income Exception for Certain Computer Software Royalties and Securities Brokers. An exception to the definition and inclusion in personal holding company income is provided for computer software royalties received by certain corporations that: (1) are actively engaged in the business of developing computer software; (2) derive at least 50% of their gross income from such computer software; (3) incur substantial trade or business expenses; and (4) distribute most of their passive income other than computer software royalties. The exception is also extended to foreign PHCs.

AFFILIATED GROUPS: If the royalty recipient is a member of an affiliated group and another group member meets the first three requirements, then the recipient is treated as meeting the requirements.

Interest income received from specified sources by a particular broker-dealer in securities is not included in PHC income, for interest received after the enactment date.

In addition, excluded from the definition of passive investment income for subchapter S, is computer software royalties derived by a specified taxpayer, which royalties would not be treated as PHC income, effective for tax years beginning after 12-31-84. An exception from the definiton of PHC income also applies for certain royalties derived by a toy manufacturer from the licensing of toys, under rules similar to those provided for computer software royalties, effective for royalties received or accrued in tax years beginning after 12-31-81.

Act Sec. 645, amending the definition of PHC income, amends Secs. 543, 553, effective for royalties received before, on, and after 12-31-86.

[¶636] **Certain Entity Not Taxed as Corporation.** A special rule under which a certain trust will not be taxed as a corporation if, among other things, it makes an election and agrees not to exercise business powers contained in its trust instrument.

Act Sec. 646, relating to the treatment of certain entities as trusts for tax purposes. Election shall be in effect during the period (1) starting on the first day of the first tax year starting after the enactment date and following the tax year in which the election is made, and (2) ending as of the end of the tax year before the tax year in which the entity ceases to satisfy all conditions provided.

[¶637] **Special Rule for Disposing of a Subsidiary's Stock.** If for a tax year of an affiliated group filing a consolidated return ending on or before 12-31-87, there is a disposition of a subsidiary's stock, the amount that must be included in income will be included ratably over a 15-year period starting with the tax year in which the disposition occurs. This special rule applies only if the sub was incorporated on 12-24-69, and participates in a mineral joint venture with a corporation organized under the laws of the foreign country in which the venture is located.

Act Sec. 645, relating to the special rule for disposition of stock of subsidiary is effective as shown above.

[The page after this is Page 701.]

ALTERNATIVE MINIMUM TAX

[¶701] **Overview.** The new law repeals the corporate add-on minimum tax after 1986 and replaces it with an alternative minimum tax (AMT). It also expands the alternative minimum tax for individuals. The intent: to insure that no taxpayer with substantial economic income can avoid significant tax liability by using tax exclusions, deductions, and credits. The new law requires corporations to make estimated tax payments to cover their minimum tax.

Corporations. The alternative minimum tax base is equal to (1) regular taxable income, plus (2) tax preferences, less (3) certain deductions. Corporate preferences and adjustments include accelerated depreciation, capital gains, mining exploration and development costs, amortization of certified pollution control facilities, circulation expenditures, research and experimentation costs, tax-exempt interest, use of the completed contract method, percentage depletion, intangible drilling costs, charitable contributions of appreciated property, installment sales of dealer property, reserves for losses on financial institution bad debts, shipping company capital construction funds, and business untaxed reported profits. The resulting amount, called alternative minimum taxable income, is reduced by an exemption amount, then multiplied by 20%, the alternative minimum tax rate. This tax may then be offset by the minimum foreign tax credit to figure a tentative minimum tax. The new rules ensure that corporate taxpayers pay tax equal to at least 20% of their economic income above the exemption amount. Individual taxpayers must pay at least 21% of income above the exemption amount. The corporate exemption amount is $40,000, less 25% of the excess of alternative minimum taxable income over $150,000.

The amount of minimum tax owed is the amount by which the tentative minimum tax exceeds the regular tax.

Individuals. The new law retains much of the prior law's treatment of the AMT but increases the rate to 21%. It now, however, permits adjustments to deferral preferences. Reason: The minimum tax deduction may sometimes exceed the regular tax deduction, especially in the last few years of an asset's life. The amount of minimum tax liability relating to deferral preferences is allowed as a carryforward credit against regular tax liability.

In addition to some of the preferences that apply to corporations, individual tax preferences also include a limitation on itemized deductions, incentive stock options, passive farm losses, and passive activity losses. The exemption amount is reduced by 25% of the alternative minimum taxable income in excess of (1) $150,000 for joint returns; (2) $75,000 for trusts and married filing separately; and $112,500 for single taxpayers. Under prior law, dividends that were excludable from gross income (up to $100 per person, $200 for a joint return) were treated as a minimum tax preference. Since this exclusion has been repealed, there is no longer a preference for dividends.

The only itemized deductions allowed for minimum tax purposes are those for casualty and theft losses, gambling losses to the extent of gambling gains, charitable deductions, medical deductions (to the extent in excess of 10% of adjusted gross income), interest expenses (restricted to housing interest plus net investment income), and certain estate taxes. Disallowed investment deductions may be carried over. Miscellaneous itemized deductions and itemized deductions for state and local taxes aren't allowed, and the investment interest rule is not phased in. For minimum tax, for a loan refinancing that gives rise to qualified housing interest, interest paid on the new loan is treated as qualified housing interest to the extent that it is so qualified under the prior loan, and the loan amount wasn't increased. A residence isn't a qualified residence for minimum tax unless it meets the requirements for a qualified residence applying for regular tax. A refund of state and local taxes paid, for which no minimum tax deduction was allowed, isn't included in alternative minimum taxable income.

The AMT paid is allowed as a credit against the regular tax liability in later years. But the minimum tax credit can't reduce taxes below the later year tentative minimum tax. The minimum tax credit applies only to minimum tax liability incurred because of deferral preferences, such as depreciation, where the tax preference results from the timing rather than the amount of the deduction.

Taxpayers may elect to have minimum tax treatment apply for regular tax purposes. If an election is made, no preference is added or treated as an adjustment for minimum tax purposes. Nonrefundable regular tax credits (e.g., the general business credit) whose benefit is lost because of the minimum tax can be carried over for regular tax under the general carryover rules.

Incentive tax credits aren't allowed against the minimum tax. Credits that can't be used for regular tax because of the minimum tax can be used as credit carryovers against the regular tax.

Act Sec. 701, relating to the alternative minimum tax, amends Secs. 55-58 and adds new Secs. 53 and 59, effective generally for tax years beginning after 12-31-86.

Minimum Tax Adjustments and Preferences

	Corporate	Noncorporate
Depreciation	X	X
Pollution control facilities	X	X
Completed contract method	X	X
Percentage depletion	X	X
Intangible drilling costs	X	X
Installment sales of dealer property	X	X

	Corporate	Noncorporate
Mining exploration & development costs	X	X
Circulation expenditures	X	X
Research and experimentation expenditures	X	X
Tax exempt interest on nonessential function bonds	X	X
Charitable contributions of appreciated property	X	X
Incentive stock options		X
Passive farm losses		X
Passive activity losses		X
Bad debt reserves of financial institutions	X	
Shipping company capital construction funds	X	
Business untaxed reported profits	X	

Adjustments and Preferences for All Taxpayers

[¶702] Depreciation. For property placed in service after 1986, the excess of ACRS depreciation over alternative depreciation (Sec. 168(g)) is a preference for the year. Alternative depreciation is the straight-line allowance over the ADR midpoint life (40 years for realty other than low-income housing). This is an adjustment made similarly to the depreciation adjustment for computing earnings and profits. It's made by using a *total* alternative depreciation allowance *for all items*, instead of the year's total ACRS allowance in regular taxable income, to arrive at AMT income. It results in a reduction of the preference, since "negative adjustments" in the year's allowances for older assets (total deduction increased by alternative less lower ACRS allowance) offset "positive adjustments" (total deduction decreases) because of higher ACRS depreciation of newer items. Accelerated depreciation on personal property is computed using the 150% declining balance method with a switch to straight-line at the optimum point.

> **Example:** Baker Corp. fully deducts for regular tax the cost of a $6,000 asset the year it's placed in service, but writes it off evenly over three years for minimum tax. Result: Regular taxable income becomes $4,000 less than minimum taxable income in the first year, and $2,000 more than minimum taxable income in the second and third years. Suppose a $3,000 item is placed in service in year two. Then the $2,000 difference between the regular and minimum tax deduction for that item would offset the $2,000 minimum tax positive adjustment for the older asset.

For property placed in service before 1987, the old rules continue to apply. So the preference, composed of the excess of ACRS depreciation over straight-line is computed on an item-by-item basis.

No minimum tax adjustment is made for property depreciated under the income forecast or alternative recovery methods (Sec.

168(f)(1)-(4)). The general minimum tax rules (using a 15-year life) apply to rehabilitation expenditures of low-income housing (Sec. 167(k)) that is placed in service after 1986.

Adjusted basis. For computing the minimum tax, the adjusted basis of depreciable property subject to the adjustment is equal to the asset's cost less accumulated minimum tax depreciation. *Result:* Since allowances for regular tax purposes and for minimum tax differ, the adjusted basis of each asset, e.g., for gain or loss on disposition may also be different. Thus, a sale could result in gain for regular tax and in a loss for minimum tax.

Act Sec. 701, relating to depreciation, amends Secs. 56(a)(1) and 57(a)(7), generally effective for tangible property placed in service after 12-31-86.

[¶703] Pollution Control Facilities. Rapid amortization of a certified pollution control facility is a tax preference (as under prior law). Taxpayers must use the alternative recovery system for minimum tax purposes for facilities placed in service after 1986. The preference applies without regard to the applicability of Sec. 291 for regular tax purposes.

Act Sec. 701, relating to amortization of certified pollution control facilities, adds Sec. 56(a)(5), effective for tax years ending after 12-31-86.

[¶704] Completed Contract Method. Taxpayers using the completed contract or certain other methods of accounting for long-term contracts entered into after 2-28-86 for regular tax must use the percentage of completion method (as modified by Sec. 460(b)) on these contracts for minimum tax purposes. The tax preference is calculated by substituting the minimum tax for the regular tax treatment as an adjustment toward alternative minimum taxable income.

Act Sec. 701, relating to long-term contracts, amends Sec. 56(a)(3), effective for any long-term contract entered into after 2-28-86.

[¶705] Percentage Depletion. As under prior law, this tax preference is measured by the excess of the regular tax percentage depletion allowance over the property's adjusted basis at year-end (before the current year's deduction).

> **Example:** Oilman takes percentage depletion of $40,000 on a mineral property with a prededuction adjusted basis of $10,000. The tax preference is $30,000 ($40,000 − $10,000).

Act Sec. 701, redesignates old Sec. 57(a)(8) relating to depletion as new Sec. 57(a)(1), effective for tax years beginning after 1986.

[¶706] Intangible Drilling Costs. The new law on IDC tax preference items is basically the same as the prior law for individuals. But under the new law, the amount of intangible drilling costs treated as a tax preference is composed of the excess of the "excess intangible drilling costs" over 65% (rather than 100% as under prior law) of net income from oil, gas, and geothermal properties. Net oil and gas income is determined for this formula without subtracting excess intangible drilling costs.

Example: Taxpayer has $10,000 net oil and gas income (before subtracting excess intangible drilling costs) and $8,200 of excess intangible drilling costs. The tax preference is $1,700 or $8,200 minus 65% of $6,500).

Excess IDC is the regular IDC deduction minus the normative deduction (i.e, the amount that would have been deducted under 120-month straight-line amortization, or (at taxpayer's election) under a cost depletion method). There's no preference for costs of nonproductive wells. The IDC preference is computed separately for (1) geothermal deposit properties defined under Sec. 613(e)(3), and (2) other properties for which IDCs are incurred.

Example: Driller has oil wells with net oil and gas income of $10,000 and excess IDCs of $8,200, and geothermal deposit properties with net income of $10,000 and excess IDCs of $4,200. There's a $1,700 preference for the oil wells, and none for the geothermal properties.

Taxpayers can elect to amortize the year's IDCs ratably over a 10-year period for all tax purposes.

Act Sec. 701, relating to intangible drilling costs, amend Secs. 57(a)(2), and (b), and 59(e), generally effective for tax years beginning after 12-31-86.

[¶707] **Installment Sales of Dealer Property.** The installment method does not apply to the disposition of dealer property after 3-1-86 for minimum tax purposes. So taxpayers must recognize all gains on disposition in the year of disposition. The rule applies to inventory.

NOTE: For calendar year taxpayers electing the installment method for regular tax purposes, gain on dispositions made between 3-1-86 and 12-31-86 is treated as recognized in 1986 for minimum tax purposes. The effect is that amounts included in regular taxable income after 1986 under the installment method aren't included in alternative minimum taxable income for those years. The preference applies to the same transactions subject to proportionate disallowance of the installment method (i.e., dealer sales and sales of trade, business or rental property when the purchase price is more than $150,000).

Act Sec. 701 relating to installment sales of dealer property adds new Sec. 56(a)(6), effective for tax years beginning after 12-31-86.

[¶708] **Mining Exploration and Development Costs.** Costs paid or incurred after 1986 that are expensed (or amortized under

Sec. 291) for regular tax purposes are written off through straight-line amortization over 10 years for the alternative minimum tax. For personal holding companies, only the excess over 10-year amortization is a preference. The 10-year amortization rule applies for minimum tax without regard to the applicability of Sec. 291 for regular tax. Their minimum tax treatment is similar to that of depreciation.

> **Example:** Miner, who incurs a one-time expense of $1,000 for mining exploration and development, deducts $1,000 the year the expense was incurred in computing regular tax, but gets only a $100 deduction in each of 10 years for minimum tax purposes. Since these deductions differ, the basis of the property for gain or loss will also differ for regular and minimum tax purposes.

On a loss to the mining property (e.g., if a mine is abandoned), any remaining mining exploration and development costs that weren't amortized under the above rules are written off for minimum tax purposes.

Election. The new law allows an election to write off all or part of Sec. 616(a) mining exploration and development expenditures over 10 years from the year made for both regular and minimum tax purposes, to even out the regular and minimum annual deduction from them.

Act Sec. 701 relating to mining exploration and development costs amends Secs. 56(a)(2) and 59(e), effective for costs paid or incurred after 12-31-86.

[¶709] Circulation and Research & Experimental Expenditures. For individuals and personal holding companies, the excess of expensing circulation expenditures over three-year amortization (10-year amortization for R&E expenditures) is a preference. Amounts paid or incurred by noncorporate taxpayers after 1986 that are deductible against regular tax under Secs. 173 or 174(a) must be capitalized and ratably deducted over 3 years (circulation expenditures) or over 10 years (R&E expenditures) in computing alternative minimum taxable income. However, if the taxpayer's property generating the circulation expenditure or a specific project generating an R&E expenditure incurs a loss, then all hitherto unamortized expenditures relating to it, which could be taken as a Sec. 165(a) loss, are taken as a minimum tax deduction for the loss year. The rules also apply to Sec. 173 circulation expenditures of a personal holding company.

> **Example:** In 1987, John Smith incurs $30,000 of deductible circulation expenditures and $10,000 R&E expenditures, and deducts $40,000 in computing regular tax. He claims a minimum tax deduction for them of $10,000 (⅓ of $30,000) and $1,000 (1/10 of $10,000) respectively in 1987 and also in 1988. If in 1989 the newspaper that generated the circulation expenditure folds and the project giving rise to the R&E expenditures is abandoned, the remaining $10,000 circu-

lation expenditures and $8,000 of R&E expenditures are a minimum tax deduction for 1989.

Election. All or part of circulation or R&E expenditures can at the taxpayer's election be written off over a 3-year period (circulation expenditures) or a 10-year period (R&E expenditures) for all tax purposes to even out annual regular and minimum tax.

Act Sec. 701 relating to circulation and R&E expenditures amends Secs. 56(b)(2) and 59(e), effective for amounts paid or incurred after 12-31-86.

[¶710] Capital Gains. For individuals, the capital gains deduction has been repealed for regular tax purposes. Thus, for regular tax computation, the full amount of gain is taxed (but not more than 28% for 1987). Apparently, the difference between the 28% maximum capital gains rate and a higher regular rate is not considered a preference item. For individuals and corporations, capital gains are fully included in minimum taxable income.

[¶711] Tax-Exempt Interest on Private Activity Bonds. Interest on private activity bonds defined in new Sec. 142 [See 1301 et seq.] that are issued after 8-7-86 (except for bonds covered under the joint statement on effective dates of 3-14-86, bonds issued after 9-1-86) is a tax preference item. Examples include bonds financing mass commuting facilities, facilities to furnish water (other than irrigation), sewage disposal facilities, solid waste disposal facilities, and qualified multifamily residential rental projects. But interest on bonds refunding pre-1986 issues and interest on qualified Sec. 501(c)(3) bonds aren't preferences. The exception for certain refundings of bonds issued before 8-8-86 (or 9-1-86) also applies to a series of current refundings of an issue originally issued before those dates. This exception doesn't apply to refundings of pre-8-8-86 (or 9-1-86) bonds.

The Ways & Means Committee Report indicates that interest on the following types of bonds issued after 8-7-86 isn't intended to be a tax preference:

- Bonds exempt from the new, unified volume limitation because of transitional exceptions in the new law.
- Bonds subject to the limitation as advance refundings that are allowed under a transitional exception.
- Bonds only partly subject to the new volume limit (e.g., the over-$1 million part of nonessential function bonds).
- Bonds issued on behalf of Section 501(c)(3) organizations.

SILVER LINING: Expenses and interest incurred on tax-exempt bonds whose income is a preference reduce the preference for minimum tax, even though they're not deductible against the regular tax because of Sec. 265.

Act Sec. 701 relating to tax-exempt interest on private activity bonds amends Sec. 57(a)(5), effective for bonds issued after 8-7-86 and as shown above.

[¶712] **Charitable Contributions of Appreciated Property.**
A part of the contribution of appreciated long-term capital gain property (including Sec. 1231 trade or business property) is an item of tax preference. In general, the preference is composed of the amount of reduction in the regular tax charitable deduction that would result if all contributed long-term capital gain property were accounted for at its adjusted basis. In its computation: (1) Unrealized losses on contributed loss property reduce unrealized gains on contributed appreciated items. (2) Carryforwards of the charitable deduction because of the 30% limit are ignored—amounts carried forward are a preference only when deducted against regular tax. The preference doesn't apply to deduction carryovers on charitable contributions made before 8-16-86.

Act Sec. 701 relating to charitable contributions of appreciated property amends Sec. 57(a)(6), generally effective for tax years beginning after 12-31-86.

Additional Individual Preferences

[¶713] **Incentive Stock Options.** The new law retains as a preference item the excess of fair market value of the stock over the exercise price. However, for minimum tax purposes, the basis of stock acquired through the exercise of an incentive stock option after 1986 equals the fair market value taken into account in determining the preference amount.

> **Example:** Frank Canavan pays an exercise price of $10 to purchase stock having a fair market value of $15. The preference in the year of exercise is $5, and the stock has a $10 basis for regular tax purposes and $15 for minimum tax purposes. If, in a subsequent year, he sells the stock for $20, the gain recognized is $10 for regular tax purposes and $5 for minimum tax purposes.

[¶714] **Passive Farm Losses.** A passive farm loss is the loss incurred from a tax shelter farming activity. Individual passive farm losses are generally preferences. A taxpayer's insolvency reduces the preference amount. (Insolvency is the excess of liabilities over the fair market value of the assets—Sec. 108(d)(3)).

A tax shelter farm activity may be a farming syndicate (Secs. 464(c) and 461(i)(4)(A)) or any other farming activity where the taxpayer does not participate materially. A taxpayer materially participates if: (1) he meets the terms of the material participation standard for regular tax purposes (Sec. 469); (2) a family member (Sec.

2032A(e)(2)) participates; or (3) he meets the Sec. 2032A(b)(4) or (5) retired, disabled, or surviving spouse requirement.

Deductions in excess of the gross income allocable to the passive farm loss activity are disallowed for minimum tax purposes. Each farm is generally treated as a separate activity. The preference applies to personal service corporations.

> **NOTE:** Income from one passive farming activity cannot be netted against other passive farming activity losses. A disallowed farming loss must be carried forward and netted against future income from the same activity, or until there is a disposition.

Act Sec. 701 relating to passive farm losses amends Sec. 58(a), effective for tax years beginning after 12-31-86.

[¶715] **Passive Activity Losses.** The passive activity loss limitation for minimum tax purposes is identical to that for regular tax purposes, with the following exceptions:

- The minimum tax rule is effective in 1987, whereas the regular tax rule is phased in over five years;

- For minimum tax purposes, the disallowed loss amount is reduced by the excess of the taxpayer's liabilities over the market value of assets (applies only to insolvent taxpayers); and

- The minimum tax rules, including the passive farm loss rule, apply to the measurement and allowability of all relevant income, deduction, and credit items for limitation purposes. The passive loss disallowance is determined after all preferences and adjustments have been computed. So the suspended loss amount may be different for minimum and regular tax purposes.

Act Sec. 701 relating to passive activity losses amends Sec. 58(b), effective for tax years beginning after 12-31-86.

[¶716] **Dividends Excluded From Gross Income.** Prior law treated dividends excluded from gross income ($100 a person, $200 for joint returns) as a tax preference. The new law repeals the dividend exclusion, so it is no longer a tax preference.

Additional Corporation Preferences

[¶717] **Bad Debt Reserves of Financial Institutions.** As under prior law, bad debt reserve addition allowances above those based on an actual experience reserve are a tax preference for commercial banks and thrift institutions.

Act Sec. 701, relating to financial institution's bad debt reserves, in effect redesignates old Sec. 57(a)(7) as new Sec. 57(a)(4).

[¶718] Shipping Company Capital Construction Funds.
Shipping company capital construction funds, established under Sec. 607 of the Merchant Marine Act of 1936, are minimum tax preferences. Deposits to the fund after 1986 aren't deductible, and fund earnings after 1986 aren't excludable in computing minimum taxable income. Pre-1987 fund deposits or earnings are treated as withdrawn before post-1986 deposits or earnings.

Act Sec. 701 relating to shipping company capital construction funds amends Sec. 56(c)(2), effective for tax years beginning after 12-31-86.

[¶719] Effect of Section 291. Corporate minimum tax preferences are determined after applying Sec. 291 (which reduces the benefit of specified corporate preference items). So, for example, if Sec. 291 reduces a corporation's bad debt reserve for regular tax purposes, the amount of the reduction isn't double-counted by also being treated as a tax preference.

Act Sec. 701 relating to the effect of Sec. 291, adds new Sec. 59(f), effective for tax years beginning after 12-31-86.

[¶720] Business Untaxed Reported Profits. This rule states that a corporation's minimum taxable income (for 1987, 1988, and 1989) includes one-half of the excess of adjusted book net income over alternative minimum taxable income (before additions arising from the preference). Corporate book income is the net income or loss reflected in the taxpayer's applicable financial statement. Conforming adjustments are made to net income to reflect consolidated tax returns, to remove federal and foreign income taxes, and for other purposes. Alaska native corporations can adjust for cost recovery and depletion in their adjusted gross income computations.

Applicable financial statement. Book income is taken from the applicable financial statement. For corporations having more than one financial statement, the "applicable" statement for determining net book income is chosen based on a priority system.

• If financial statements are filed with the Securities and Exchange Commission, those statements are used.

• If statements are filed with the SEC, then certified audited statements used for credit purposes, reporting to shareholders, or for any other substantial nontax purpose are used.

• Next are financial statements that must be filed with the federal government or with a federal agency other than the SEC, or a state or local government or agency.

• If none of these statements exists, a financial statement or report used for credit purposes, for reporting to owners or for any other substantial nontax purpose becomes the applicable financial statement. Within this last category, a financial statement used for credit purposes has priority over one provided to owners. A financial statement used for any other substantial nontax purpose has the lowest priority.

If no financial statements exist, the financial net income or loss is equal to earnings and profits for the year. Taxpayers that don't file a financial statement with the SEC or other governmental agency and don't have a certified audited financial statement may elect to use earnings and profits. If the earnings and profits election is made, earnings and profits must be used as long as the taxpayer is eligible for the election.

Adjustments to income made after the financial statements have been issued won't be considered unless the financial statements are restated. If there are both unadjusted high priority and adjusted low priority financial statements, the high priority statements are to be used.

> **Example:** Acme Corporation provides its shareholders with certified audited financial statements. After issuance, the company determines that the results of operations would be better reflected if other generally accepted accounting principles were applied to certain items. So it prepares a second, unaudited set of financial statements for credit purposes, and does not recall the earlier statements.

The earlier certified statements will have priority over the later uncertified statements. But if the earlier statements weren't certified, the later statements would apply because statements used for credit purposes have priority over statements issued to shareholders if both or neither are certified. If both statements had equal priority, the later statement would be the applicable financial statement.

If supplementary documents are issued instead of restating previously issued financial statements, issuing the supplementary documents is considered the same as issuing restated financial statements.

Adjustments. The companies included in the consolidated tax return may not be the same as those included in the financial statements (i.e., foreign companies and Sec. 936 corporations cannot be consolidated for tax purposes). So the financial statements must be adjusted to include only those companies that are included in the consolidated tax return. Book income is adjusted to include actual or deemed distributions (as measured for tax purposes) from corporations not in the tax consolidated group. If an ownership interest in the other corporation is accounted for by the equity or consolidation method, an adjustment to reverse inclusion is required. Book income must be adjusted to eliminate dividends from corporations that are included in the consolidated tax return but included in the measure of financial statement net income only when dividends are paid.

Companies that have different year-ends for financial and tax purposes must take the prorata share of financial income from each applicable financial statement that falls within the tax year. Companies with a 52-53 week year will have a year-end that coincides with the same week as the 52-53 week year-end.

If the prorata share of financial statement income cannot be determined because the statement is not available by the time the tax return is filed, an estimate can be made. The tax return can be amended when the income figures become available. The Treasury may prescribe rules that will allow taxpayers to use adjusted net book income for the accounting year that ends within the taxpayer's tax year instead of amending the return.

Extraordinary items stated net of tax must be adjusted to remove any federal or foreign tax expense or benefits before the item is included in adjusted net book income.

Computation. A corporation's alternative minimum taxable income equals half of the excess of adjusted net book income over the alternative minimum taxable income figured before the preference is added.

Example (1): Able's adjusted net book income and alternative minimum taxable income (before including the preference amount) are $1,000 and $200, respectively. Half the excess of adjusted net book income over alternative minimum taxable income ($400) is added to alternative minimum taxable income ($200), which makes alternative minimum taxable income $600 [$200 + ½ ($1,000 − $200)].

Example (2): Baker has adjusted net book income of $200 and alternative minimum taxable income (before adjustment) of negative $100. Since adjusted net book income exceeds alternative minimum taxable income, half the $300 difference is added to alternative minimum taxable income, making alternative minimum taxable income $50 [− $100 + ½ ($300)].

Example (3): Charlie's adjusted net book loss is $300. The alternative minimum tax loss (before adjustment) is $700. Alternative tax loss, after adjustment, is $500 [− $700 + ½ ($400)].

NOTE: This provision has been criticized because it is viewed as giving the Financial Accounting Standards Board (the standard-setting organization for financial statement reporting) influence over tax policy, which is beyond the scope of its authority. Another criticism is that some companies might change their financial accounting policies to reduce their tax liability, thereby making their financial statements less meaningful.

Book income will be used to determine minimum income only for 1987, 1988, and 1989. After 1989, earnings and profits will be used instead. The earnings and profits definition is modified for pre-effective date transactions so as to more closely achieve the goals of the use of book income. A Treasury study is mandated.

Act Secs. 701 and 702 relating to business untaxed reported profits amends Sec. 56(f) and (g) effective for tax years beginning after 12-31-86.

[¶721] Alternative Minimum Tax Itemized Deductions. Most individual alternative minimum tax itemized deductions are unchanged. Thus, the only itemized deductions allowable are those for (1) casualty, theft, and gambling losses; (2) charitable contributions; (3) medical expenses; (4) qualified interest; (5) the Sec. 691(c) estate tax deduction; and (6) certain estate and trust distributions to beneficiaries. The law on qualified interest is changed as follows: limited business interests are included in the calculation to limit investment interest deductions under the regular tax, and consumer interest may not be deducted as a minimum tax itemized deduction, even if it would be deductible if treated as investment interest. There is an investment interest carryover.

Act Sec. 701, relating to alternative minimum tax itemized deductions amend Sec. 56(b)(1), effective for tax years beginning after 12-31-86.

[¶722] Minimum Tax Credit. Taxpayers can now use the amount of the minimum tax they pay as a credit that reduces the following year's regular tax, net of other nonrefundable credits (or the excess of this regular tax over the tentative minimum tax, if that's less). Unused credits can be carried over indefinitely, but can't be carried back. They can be carried over as tax attributes in corporate acquisitions covered by Sec. 381(a).

The year's minimum tax credit is in general composed of the aggregate post-1986 liability for alternative minimum tax reduced by regular tax, to the extent it wasn't previously used as a credit. However, taxpayers take into account in the alternative minimum tax computation only those liabilities that result from deferral preferences—but not from preferences that result from permanent exclusions for regular tax purposes. So the minimum tax for this credit is reduced by the amount of minimum tax liability that would have been incurred if the only preferences were the exclusion preferences, which are percentage depletion and regular tax itemized deductions that are denied for minimum tax purposes.

Example: Al and Carol Smith file a joint return with zero regular taxable income, $400,000 in deferral preferences, and $100,000 in exclusion preferences (including itemized deductions disallowed for minimum tax). With the 21% alternative minimum tax rate and the phase-out of the exemption, the minimum tax would be $105,000 [21% ($400,000 + $100,000 − $0)]. But if they had only exclusion preferences, the minimum tax liability would have been $12,600 [21% ($100,000 − $40,000 exemption)]. So the minimum tax credit that can be used next year is $92,400 ($105,000 − $12,600).

Act Sec. 701, relating to the minimum tax credit, adds new Sec. 53, effective for tax years beginning after 12-31-86.

[¶723]   Foreign Tax Credit. Under the new law, the foreign tax credit is generally allowable for purposes of the alternative minimum tax under rules similar to those for individuals under prior law. In the alternative minimum tax formula, the credit against the "tentative" minimum tax is generally figured on the tax base against which the minimum 20% or 21% rate is applied, while the regular tax reducing it is figured by using the regular foreign tax credit. The Sec. 904 limitation on the amount of the credit must be applied separately for minimum tax and regular tax purposes, because of the differences between regular taxable income and alternative minimum taxable income, in foreign tax applicable to them, and in the ratios of foreign taxable income to worldwide income. Taxpayers must also keep track of the foreign tax credit carryforwards allowable for both regular and minimum tax purposes.

When Sec. 904(credit limitation) is applied to the minimum tax rules and alternative minimum taxable income is increased by a percentage of the excess of book income over alternative minimum taxable income, the percentage of that income from sources within the United States will be treated the same as other U.S. source alternative minimum taxable income. So the book income preferences won't change the percentage that applies to the alternative minimum tax Sec. 904 limitation.

Up to 90% of tentative minimum tax liability, before foreign tax credits, can be offset by foreign tax credits, even if, under Sec. 904, more than 90% of the liability could be offset by the foreign tax credit. Foreign tax credits disallowed under this rule are treated, for carryover purposes, like credits disallowed under Sec. 904. This rule is applied before comparing the minimum and regular tax liability amounts.

Example. In 1987, a taxpayer has alternative taxable income of $10 million. In the absence of NOLs or foreign tax credits, tentative minimum tax liability (liability determined without regard to the amount of regular tax liability) would be $2.1 million. Foreign tax credits can't be used to reduce liability to less than $210,000, whether or not the taxpayer has any minimum tax net operating losses.

Act Sec. 701, relating to the foreign tax credit adds new Sec. 59(a), effective for tax years beginning after 12-31-86.

[¶724]   Incentive Tax Credits. Under prior law, taxpayers claimed nonrefundable credits against the regular tax even if they provided no benefit (that is, they reduced tax liability to less than the minimum tax liability). The portion of the credit that didn't provide a benefit because of the minimum tax was allowed as a carryover to other tax years.

The new law doesn't generally allow taxpayers to claim such credits for the current year to the extent they reduce the regular tax liability to less than the tentative minimum tax liability, but unused credits are allowed as carryovers to other tax years. Corporate taxpayers may use incentive tax credits to offset 25% of the tentative minimum tax liability. Income eligible for the Sec. 936 credit is not included in minimum taxable income of the Sec. 936 corporation.

Incentive tax credits aren't allowed against the minimum tax. Credits that can't be used for regular tax due to the minimum tax can be used as credit carryovers against the regular tax.

NOTE: Taxpayers don't have to file a form showing the minimum tax computation on account of this rule, if they don't owe a minimum tax and if the minimum tax doesn't limit the use of incentive credits.

Example: Al King has a $100 regular tax liability (disregarding incentive credits), and a $10 targeted jobs tax credit. If his tentative minimum tax was less than $90, he wouldn't have to file a minimum tax form.

Act Sec. 701, relating to incentive tax credits, amends Sec. 26(a)-(c), 28(d)(2), 29(b)(5), and 38(c), effective for tax years beginning after 12-31-86.

[¶725] Special Rules Apply for Net Operating Losses. Generally, they are the same as the prior law rules for the individual alternative minimum tax. The alternative minimum tax net operating loss and carryovers are computed separately. The computation takes the differences between the regular tax base and the alternative minimum tax base into account.

The net operating loss for alternative minimum tax purposes is computed the same way as the net operating loss for regular purposes, with the following two exceptions:

• Current year tax preference items are added back to taxable income; and

• Individuals may use only those itemized deductions (as modified under Sec. 172(d)) allowable in computing alternative minimum taxable income.

For computing the loss in years other than the loss year, the recomputed loss is deducted from the alternative minimum taxable income, as modified by Sec. 172(b)(2)(A), in the carryover year, whether or not the taxpayer is subject to the minimum tax in that year.

Example (1): In year one, Sherry Penn has income of $20,000. Her losses are $35,000, of which $10,000 are preference items. The alternative minimum tax net operating loss for the year is $5,000 [$20,000 − ($35,000 − $10,000)]. She can carry the $5,000 loss forward or back to reduce income that is subject to the alternative minimum tax.

¶725

Example (2): The following year, Penn has alternative minimum taxable income, without regard to the net operating loss deduction, of $20,000. She reduces her alternative minimum taxable income to $15,000 because of last year's $5,000 carryforward. Her net operating loss deduction for the regular tax isn't affected by this computation. She has a $15,000 loss carryover from last year, which she can use with the regular tax.

Transition rule. A transition rule for corporations allows, for alternative minimum tax purposes, all preeffective date regular tax net operating losses to be carried forward as minimum tax net operating losses. They can be carried forward to the first tax year for which the tax, as amended under the new law, applies. They can also be carried forward until used up. Prior law is retained for individuals with respect to the calculation of alternative minimum tax net operating losses.

Corporations that had a deferral of add-on minimum tax liability before 1987 because of certain net operating losses have to make an adjustment. For these corporations, the add-on minimum tax won't be imposed after 1986. But the alternative minimum tax net operating loss carried to the first year beginning after 1986 must be reduced by the amount of the preferences that gave rise to the liability. Net operating losses cannot offset more than 90% of minimum taxable income. Amounts disallowed because of the 90% limitation may be carried over to other taxable years.

Example: A taxpayer has $10 million of alternative minimum taxable income in 1987, and minimum tax NOLs of $11 million. The NOLs reduce alternative minimum taxable income to $1 million. So tentative minimum tax liability is $210,000. The taxpayer can carry forward $2 million of minimum tax NOLs to 1988. Since the allowability of net operating losses is determined before the allowability of foreign tax credits, this taxpayer wouldn't be allowed to use any minimum tax foreign tax credits before 1987.

An election under Sec. 172(b)(3)(C) to relinquish the carryback applies both for regular tax and minimum tax purposes.

Act Sec. 701, relating to net operating losses, amends Sec. 56(d), effective for tax years beginning after 12-31-86.

[¶726] Regular Tax Elections. For certain expenditures that would result in a tax preference if treated under the regular tax rules, taxpayers can elect to have the minimum tax rule for deducting the expenditure apply for regular tax purposes (a normative election). This rule applies to the following expenditures:

- Circulation expenditures.
- Research and experimental expenditures.
- Intangible drilling costs.
- Mining development and exploration expenditures.

Taxpayers can make these elections on a dollar-for-dollar basis. So a taxpayer who incurs intangible drilling costs of $100,000 on a well may elect normative treatment for any portion of the $100,000. To the extent the election applies, no deduction is allowed either for regular or minimum tax purposes. And the election may be revoked only with the Treasury Secretary's consent. Partners of S corporation shareholders can make the election separately for their allocable share of the expenditure.

Act Sec. 701, relating to regular tax elections, adds new Sec. 53, effective for tax years beginning after 12-31-86.

[¶727] Other Rules. The new law has several miscellaneous rules that affect the application of the alternative minimum tax. Corporations must make estimated tax payments for both minimum tax and regular tax purposes. Estates and trusts are allowed to take certain alternative minimum tax itemized deductions. The Treasury will issue regulations that prescribe how items treated for regular and minimum tax purposes are to be apportioned between the estate or trust and the beneficiaries.

The new law prescribes rules for allocating items that are treated differently for regular and minimum tax purposes for common trust funds, regulated investment companies, and real estate investment trusts. There are also rules on certain technical issues such as short tax years and exemption amounts for consolidated returns. As under prior law, the Treasury has been instructed to prescribe regulations for the application of the tax benefit rule to items that are treated differently for regular and minimum tax purposes.

Code sections suspending losses, such as Secs. 465, 704(d), 1366(d), and other sections specified in regulations are recomputed for minimum tax purposes to apply to amounts otherwise deductible for minimum tax purposes. The amount of the deductions suspended or recaptured may differ for regular and minimum tax purposes, respectively. This rule applies to all taxpayers subject to the at-risk rules.

For an estate or trust, instead of allocating tax preference items between the estate or trust and its beneficiaries (as under prior law), minimum tax will apply by determining distributable net income on a minimum tax basis (except to the extent inconsistent with the modifications under Sec. 643(a) with the minimum tax exemption amount being treated the same way as the deduction for personal exemptions under Sec. 643(a)(2).

[The page following this is 801.]

ACCOUNTING PROVISIONS

[¶801] Limits on Use of Cash Method and Easing of Accrual Method. Starting in 1987, the new law forbids C corporations, partnerships with any C corporation partners, tax shelters, and Sec. 511(b) tax-exempt trusts with unrelated business taxable income to use the cash method or a hybrid method reporting partly on a cash basis. *Exceptions:* Business (but not tax shelters) with average annual gross receipts (less returns and allowances) of $5 million or less for the preceding three tax years or the shorter period they conducted business, employee-owned service businesses in the field of health, law, accounting, engineering, architecture, actuarial science, performing arts or consulting (qualified personal service corporations), and farming and timber businesses can continue on the cash method.

Starting in 1987, the new law: (1) allows accrual taxpayers to report income from personal services (other than those typical of public utilities, banks, or financial institutions) no earlier than they are billed; (2) treats economic performance of services provided by nonemployees as occurring when they are performed or when they are billed, whichever is later (for employees it's when they're performed) for the "economic performance" deduction test; and (3) allows nonaccrual of billings for services that on the basis of experience the taxpayer won't collect, unless interest or a late penalty is charged.

Businesses that can continue using the cash method. Eligibility to use the cash method remains controlled by prior law rules, but is now in general limited to S corporations, sole proprietorships, and partnerships that have no C corporation partners. Qualified personal service corporations that can use it under the exception to the limitation must be substantially involved in performing services in fields listed above (function test). Also, all of their stock must be substantially owned (95% in value) by employees or former employees performing services in these fields, their estates, or anyone acquiring an ownership interest because of that person's death within the prior 24 months.

Employees may also own the stock indirectly through a holding company with subsidiaries in the same field of service. Stock owned by an ESOP or pension plan is considered owned by the plan beneficiaries. This ownership test operates without regard to community property laws, and stock owned by a partnership, S corporation or personal service corporation is considered owned by its partners or shareholders. Farming businesses (defined in new Sec. 263(d)(4)) that can use the cash method are generally those engaged in growing, raising, managing, or training crops or livestock; or raising or harvesting trees that bear fruit, nuts, or other crops, or Christmas or other ornamental trees. The $5 million or below three-year average gross receipts of other businesses that can use it is computed using the gross receipts (less returns or allowances) for the preceding three years (or shorter period when business was conducted). Gross receipts for short tax years are annualized. Affiliates or entities under common control treated as a "single employer" (Sec. 52(a), (b) or 414(m), (o)) are a single entity for the exceptions from the cash method prohibition.

> **NOTE:** The new law doesn't specifically state that gross receipts for the three-year test can be reduced by sales discounts.

Uncollectible billings. Accrual taxpayers now won't accrue income for personal services they don't expect to collect, if they don't charge interest or penalties for untimely payment. Those offering discounts for early payment accrue the gross amount billed, and reduce income by the discount when they're actually paid. According to the Ways and Means Committee Report, estimated uncollectible billings are computed as follows:

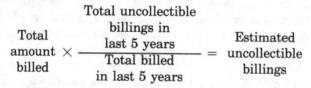

$$\text{Total amount billed} \times \frac{\text{Total uncollectible billings in last 5 years}}{\text{Total billed in last 5 years}} = \text{Estimated uncollectible billings}$$

According to the Committee Reports, the year's expected uncollectibles are computed by multiplying year-end outstanding receivables by the percentage of receivables created in the last five years that were determined to be uncollectible.

Taxpayers that have not been in existence for five years will use the shorter period of their existence in the formula. Partial or total worthlessness of unreported billings doesn't create a deduction; and their actual collection gives rise to reportable income. A change from the cash method required by the new law rules is considered a change in accounting method initiated by the taxpayer with IRS consent. To prevent duplication or omission of income and expense items, a Sec. 481 adjustment (spread generally over four years or less) must be made. It's expected that the concepts of Rev. Proc. 84-74, 1984-2 CB 736, will generally determine the actual timing of the adjustment items. For operating hospitals defined in new Sec. 144(b)(3)—in general JCAH-or-comparably-accredited hospital institutions, but not rest or nursing homes, day care centers, research labs, or ambulatory care facilities—the adjustments can be spread over up to 10 (rather than 4) years.

Transitional rule election. Taxpayers can elect to retain the cash method for any loan, lease, or a related party transaction entered into before 9-25-85.

Act Sec. 801, amends Sec. 461(i) and adds Sec. 448, effective for tax years beginning after 12-31-86, and as shown above.

[¶802] Simplified Dollar-Value LIFO for Small Business.
Starting in 1987, the new law replaces the prior law LIFO election to use a single inventory pool by businesses with average gross receipts of $2 million or less, with a simplified dollar-value LIFO election for businesses with average gross receipts of $5 million or less. This new simplified LIFO method calls for inventory pools grouped by Bureau of Labor Statistics Producer and Consumer general price index categories, for indexing annual cost changes by use of BLS monthly published indexes, and use of cumulative indexes developed by the link-chain method. It's designed to allow small businesses to use LIFO without undue complexities or excessive compliance costs. Businesses that elected the single pool method can continue using it under prior law rules. But they can't use the new simplified method at the same time, and can revoke the old election without IRS consent.

Electing simplified dollar-value LIFO. The new method can be used only by businesses that had average annual gross receipts (less returns and allowances) of $5 million or less for the preceding three tax years or the shorter period they were in business, determined under rules similar to those of new Sec. 448(c)(3)—See ¶801. All members of a controlled group (determined under Sec. 52(b) regs used for determining a "single employer") are considered a single taxpayer for measuring the gross receipts ceiling. The election (initially made for a tax year without IRS consent under regs to come) applies also to later years and covers all of the taxpayer's LIFO inventories. The taxpayer must change from the simplified dollar-value LIFO method to another method the first year it fails to meet the $5 million average annual gross receipts test. It may change to another method at any time, and needs to get the IRS's permission only if permission to change would have been required before adoption of simplified dollar-value LIFO. *Reason:* not to place taxpayers under any more of a burden than they would have been had they not adopted simplified dollar-value LIFO.

Operation of method. Inventory values using simplified dollar-value LIFO are generally computed under Reg. Sec. 1.472-8 but with these main differences:

• More than one inventory pool is used to avoid construction of an index specific to the taxpayer. Retailers using the retail method group their pools by the 11 general categories in the BLS consumer price index for all urban consumers (currently Table 3 for food expenditure categories and Table 5 for nonfood expenditure categories, monthly CPI detailed reports) noted in Reg. Sec. 1.472-8(e)(3)(iv). *Examples:* Food and beverages; apparel commodities.) All other taxpayers use the 15 general two-digit categories in the monthly BLS producers prices and price indexes for commodity groupings and individual items (currently Table 6). *Examples:* Farm products; furniture and household durables. The annual change in costs for each general category pool as a whole is measured by the percentage change for the year in the published index for the category.

• Present dollar inventory values are discounted back to equivalent values in the base year through the link-chain approach (a current cumulative index is constructed from year-by-year index components), rather than by comparing the dollar amount of inventory items measured in present year prices against the dollar amount of the same inventory items in base year prices (double-extension method).

The taxpayer selects a month of the year whose index he will use to measure annual changes in his pool; he must use the same month in later years unless the IRS consents to a change. Originally released BLS index figures are used, unless corrected figures are published *before* the taxpayer files his return—the index figure that's *actually* used for the year must be adhered to next year (any over or undervaluation will adjust itself automatically at the end of next year).

The first year when the simplified dollar-value LIFO method is used is the base year. Converting to the method may involve adjustments. On a change from FIFO, the taxpayer assigns inventory items to the new pools, combines their values, and the total is his base year layer. A change from a method that allows inventories to be stated at less than cost (e.g., FIFO) requires restoration of any previous writedowns from cost to income. (The base year dollar values will include these amounts.) Conversion from another LIFO method is done similarly, but preexisting LIFO layers must be preserved and prior year layers restated in base year dollars by comparing the prices paid to the item's present value.

> **Example:** ABC changes from FIFO to simplified dollar-value LIFO. Inventories consist of a chemical in the BLS "Chemicals and Allied Products" general category, and a high school chemistry text book in the BLS "Pulp, Paper, and Allied Products" general category. Published index numbers for the "Chemicals and Allied Products" general category are 200 for the prior year and 220 for the current year (the "first LIFO year"). The prior year's index number for "Pulp, Paper, and Allied Products" is 142 and for the current year it's 150. In the prior year, the present dollar value of the ending inventory was $30,000 for the chemical and $30,000 for the textbooks. In the current year, the present dollar value of the taxpayer's ending inventory is $35,000 for the chemical and $30,000 for the textbooks. Items in the two general categories are included in separate dollar-value LIFO pools. The

annual index for each pool is equal to one plus the percentage change in the index for the general category, as follows:

Pool	Current year index	Prior year index	Change	Percent change	Index
#1 220	200	20	0.1000	1.1000
#2 150	142	8	.0563	1.0563

In later years, the annual index would be multiplied by the cumulative index for the preceding year to compute the current cumulative index (in the first year the annual and cumulative index are the same). The present dollar value of the ending inventory for the current year is divided by the cumulative index to restate it in its equivalent value in base year dollars. This amount is assigned to the LIFO layers and multiplied by the cumulative index for the year to which the layer relates to find an indexed dollar value for that layer. The sum of the indexed dollar values for the layers is the ending LIFO inventory value for the pool. Here are the figures for the first year:

Pool #1

Current year dollar value of inventory	$35,000
Divided by index	1.100
Inventory in base-year dollars	$31,818

LIFO layers	Base-year dollar value	Dollar index	Indexed dollar value
Base-year	$30,000	1.0000	$30,000
First LIFO year	1,818	1.1000	2,000
Ending inventory	$31,818		$32,000

Pool #2

Current year dollar value of inventory	$30,000
Divided by index	1.0563
Inventory in base-year dollars	$28,401

	Base-year dollar value	Index	Indexed dollar value
Base year	$28,401	1.0000	$28,401
First LIFO year	0	0	0
Ending inventory	$28,401		$28,401

Total ending inventory:

Pool #1	$32,000
Pool #2	28,401
	$60,401

Act Sec. 802, relating to simplified dollar-value LIFO, amends Sec. 474, effective for tax years beginning after 12-31-86 and as shown above.

[¶803] Installment Sales—Allocating Debt. Under the old law, a taxpayer who sells property on the installment basis is taxed as payments are received, the rationale being that it would be unfair to require a tax on the entire gain in the year of sale when only a small portion of total sale proceeds may have been received in the year of sale. But a taxpayer that pledges the installment obligation is in a much better cash flow position than one that doesn't, so it was felt that there is often no need to defer taxing the gain when the installment receivables are turned into cash by pledging them.

The new law limits use of the installment method in three cases. The installment method is not available for:

- Certain installment receivables, based on the taxpayer's outstanding debt. Taxpayers who sell timeshares and residential lots may elect to pay interest on the deferred tax liability instead of being subject to the general installment sales rules. There's an exception for certain sales by a manufacturer to a dealer when the term of the installment obligation is based on the time the property is resold by the dealer;
- Revolving credit plan sales; and
- Sales of certain publicly traded property.

Proportionate disallowance rule in general. Use of the installment method is limited for sales of (real or personal) inventory, business, or rental property. The limit depends on the taxpayer's "allocable installment indebtedness." (AII). When applying the proportionate disallowance rule, installment debt from the sale of personal-use property by an individual, and property produced or used in farming aren't treated as applicable installment obligations. So installment debt from the sale of crops or livestock held for slaughter aren't AII. The calculation is annual rather than quarterly for taxpayers that don't have applicable installment debt that arose from an installment sale of either personal property by a person that regularly sells property of the same type on the installment method, or real property that was held for sale to customers in the ordinary course of trade or business. Otherwise, the calculation is quarterly. The Treasury is authorized to issue regs to prevent avoiding the proportionate disallowance rule when the calculation is made annually.

Allocable installment indebtedness. The allocable installment indebtedness is computed using this formula:

$$AII = \frac{a}{b + c} \ (d) - AII \ (p)$$

a = the face amount of "applicable installment obligations" outstanding at year-end

b = the face amount of all installment obligations (applicable and nonapplicable)

c = the adjusted basis of all other taxpayer assets (straight-line depreciation may be elected for determining adjusted basis)

d = average quarterly debt

AII(p) = AII from prior years' applicable installment obligations

Individuals exclude certain farm or personal use property, related secured debt, or related installment obligations from the computation.

"Applicable installment obligations" arise from the post-February 1986 installment sale of

- personal inventory property;

- real property held for sale in the ordinary course of trade or business; or

- real property (other than certain farm property) used in the trade or business or held for the production of rental income, provided (1) the selling price is more than $150,000, and (2) the seller or other affiliated group member holds the obligation.

In later years, taxpayers don't have to recognize gain from prior year applicable installment obligations for payments that aren't higher than the amount of AII attributable to the obligations. AII is reduced as payments are received. Payments on an applicable installment obligation that are in excess of the AII allocable to the obligation are accounted for under the ordinary installment method rules. Adjustments to individual allocable installment obligations generally aren't made except to reflect payments that don't result in gain recognition. But additional AII may be allocated to installment obligations that arose in prior years if the AII for a particular year is more than the applicable installment obligation amount arising in that year and outstanding at year-end. Any excess is first allocated to outstanding applicable installment obligations from the previous year (to the extent the face value exceeds the AII), and then allocated to each preceding tax year until the entire excess is allocated.

Indebtedness calculation. Average indebtedness is computed quarterly (annually for the two exceptions explained above). All debt included in the provision that is outstanding at the end of the quarter is included in the quarterly computation. Accounts payable, accrued debt, bank loans, bond debt, and other payables should be included in the computation. Debt payments made to avoid the limitation are to be ignored.

> **COMMENT:** This rule opens up a potential Pandora's box because of the "intent" requirement.

Affiliated groups. All persons treated as a single taxpayer under Sec. 52(a) or (b) are treated as one taxpayer for the proportionate disallowance rule. In applying the rule to the controlled group, the installment percentage is computed by combining the controlled group's assets and multiplying it by the aggregate average quarterly (or annual) controlled group's debt to find the total AII. The total AII is then allocated pro rata to the applicable installment obligations held by individual members of the group, regardless of the amount of debt held by any particular member. The regular provisions of the proportionate disallowance rule are then applied. The Treasury may issue regs that forbid using the installment method in whole or in part for transactions if the effect of the proportionate disallowance rule would be avoided by using related parties, pass-through entities, or intermediaries. So a corporation, partnership, or trust may be treated as related to its shareholders, partners, or beneficiaries if the proportionate disallowance rule otherwise might be avoided.

The regs may aggregate related party assets when applying the proportionate disallowance rule. For example, the assets and debt of a partnership and each partner may be combined to calculate the extent to which each partner may report gain from an installment sale of partnership assets.

> **Example:** Acme Company, a calendar year dealer in real property, started business in 1987. In that year, it sold one property, at a profit, for $250,000, but did not receive any payments in 1987. Acme's assets, excluding the installment obligation, had an aggregate adjusted basis of $1 million at the end of 1987. Acme's debt amounted to $200,000 on March 31, $250,000 on June 30, $400,000 on September 30, and $350,000 on December 31, for an average quarterly debt of $300,000. Acme's AII for 1987 is $60,000, computed as follows:

$$\text{AII} = \frac{a}{b + c} \ (d) - \text{AII} \ (p)$$

$$\frac{\$250,000}{\$250,000 + \$1,000,000} \ (\$300,000) - 0 = \$60,000$$

Acme is considered to have received $60,000 as of the end of 1987, even though nothing was actually received.

In 1988, Acme sold another property at a profit, for $400,000. No payments on either sale were received in 1988. The aggregate adjusted asset basis at the end of 1988 was $1,300,000, and average quarterly debt was $420,000. AII for 1988 is $80,000, computed as follows:

$$\frac{\$650,000}{\$650,000 + \$1,300,000} (\$420,000) - \$60,000 = \$80,000$$

So Acme is deemed to have received $80,000 in 1988, even though nothing is actually received.

In 1989, Acme sold a third property at a profit for $500,000, and the 1987 installment obligation was paid in full. No other payments were received. At year-end, aggregate adjusted asset bases, other than installment obligations, totaled $1,100,000, and average quarterly debt was $600,000. The first $60,000 of the $250,000 payment from the 1987 installment obligation won't result in gain recognition, and reduces the amount of AII that is treated as allocated to that obligation. The next $190,000 is treated as an additional payment on the obligation that results in the recognition of additional gain under the installment method.

The AII allocated to taxable income before 1989, for purposes of computing 1989 AII, is $80,000 ($60,000 from 1987 plus $80,000 from 1988, minus $60,000 from 1987). Acme's 1989 AII is $190,000, computed as follows:

$$\frac{\$900,000}{\$900,000 + \$1,100,000} (\$600,000) - \$80,000 = \$190,000$$

The entire $190,000 AII is allocated to the 1989 installment obligation. If the 1989 AII had been more than the amount of applicable installment obligations arising in 1989 and outstanding at year-end ($500,000), the first $500,000 is allocated to the 1989 installment obligation, and the remainder to the 1988 obligation.

Timeshares and residential lots. There is a special election for timeshares and residential lots. Under the election, the proportionate disallowance rule doesn't apply to installment obligations that arise when a dealer sells certain types of property to an individual. The election applies only if the individual's obligation isn't guaranteed or insured by any third person other than an individual. The obligation must arise from the sale of a timeshare or of unimproved land, the development of which will not be done by the land's seller, or any seller's affiliate.

For election purposes, a timeshare is a right to use a specified parcel of residential real property (including campground sites) for up to six weeks a year. All individual and related party timeshares are combined for determining whether the six-week test is met.

Sellers meeting these conditions can elect not to have the general installment sales rules apply, if the seller pays interest on the deferred tax liability attributable to use of the installment method. To make the election, the interest rate must be 100% of the applicable federal rate applicable to the maturity of the note, without regard to the three-month lookback rule of Sec. 1274(d)(2).

Exception for manufacturer/dealer sales. There is an exception for installment sales of tangible personal property by the manufacturer (or manufacturer's affiliate) to a dealer. The exception applies only if (1) the dealer must make principal payments only when the dealer resells or rents the property, (2) the manufacturer has the right to repurchase the property at a fixed or ascertainable price within nine months of the sale to the dealer, and (3) certain other conditions are met.

50% test. To meet the other conditions, the aggregate face amount of the installment obligations that otherwise qualify for the exception must equal at least 50% of total credit sales to dealers. This test must be met both in the current and preceding tax year. But if the taxpayer met all exception requirements in the previous year, then the taxpayer wouldn't fail to meet the 50% test before the second consecutive year in which the test was not actually met. The 50% test computes the receivables' aggregate face amount using the monthly receivable weighted average. The requirement must be met in the first tax year after enactment. Obligations issued before enactment meet the requirement if they are conformed to the law's requirement within 60 days of enactment. Receivables qualifying for the exception aren't subject to the law's installment method limitation provision.

Revolving credit plans. Taxpayers who sell property on a revolving credit plan aren't allowed to account for the sales using the installment method. Payments are treated as received entirely in the year of sale. The Treasury has regulatory authority to disallow use of the installment method when the tax rules would otherwise be avoided through related parties, pass-through entities, or intermediaries. Revolving credit plans are discussed in Reg. Sec. 1.453-2(d).

Phase-in. Taxpayers who sell property under revolving credit plans and who may no longer use the installment method may include income from the adjustment over four years or less. While the proportionate disallowance rule is generally effective for tax years ending after 1986 (for sales of property after February 1986), any property sales after February 1986 but before the taxpayer's first tax year ending after 1986 (i.e., if the taxpayer has a calendar tax year, or has a short tax period ending between 2-28-86 and 12-31-86) are treated as arising in the taxpayer's first tax year ending after 1986.

For installment debt arising from the sale of real property in the ordinary course of business, any gain attributable to allocable installment debt allocated to any of those installment obligations that arise (or are deemed to arise) in the first tax year ending after 1986, is taken into account ratably over the three tax years beginning with the first tax year. For installment debt arising in the second tax year ending after 1986, any gain is taken into account ratably over two tax years beginning with the second tax year.

For installment debt from the sale of personal property in the normal course of business, any increase in the taxpayer's tax liability for the first tax year ending after 1986 caused by applying the proportionate disallowance rule is treated as imposed ratably over three tax years, beginning with the first tax year. Any increase in tax liability in the taxpayer's second tax year ending after 1986 because of the proportionate disallowance rule (disregarding the ratable share of the prior year tax increase) is treated as imposed ratably over the two tax years beginning with the second tax year.

For applicable installment obligations other than those from the sale of real or personal property in the normal course of business, the proportionate disallowance rule is effective for tax years ending after 1986, for sales after 8-16-86. Sales after 8-16-86 and before the taxpayer's first tax year ending after 1986 are to be treated as arising in the first tax year ending after 1986.

The revolving credit plan sales rules are effective for tax years beginning after 1986. Adjustments resulting from a change in accounting method are taken into account over four years or less. Where four years are used, 15% is taken into account the first year, 25% the second year, and 30% in each of the next two years.

The rules for sales of publicly traded property take effect for sales after 1986.

Act Sec. 811, relating to allocation of indebtedness as payment on installments, adds Sec. 453C. The elimination of the installment method for sales on a revolving credit plan is effective for sales of property after 12-31-86. The proportionate disallowance rule is effective as of 1-1-87 for sales made on or after 3-1-86.

[¶804] No Installment Method for Publicly Traded Property. Sales of publicly traded property, including stocks and bonds, don't qualify for the installment method. The fair market value of an installment obligation received in exchange for property is equal to the fair market value of the property at time of sale. Gains or losses from sales made on an established market are recognized the day the trade is executed, not the settlement date, which may be a few days later. This rule applies both to accrual and cash basis taxpayers. Payments are treated as being received entirely in the year of sale. The Treasury has regulatory authority to disallow use of the installment method when the tax rules would otherwise be avoided through related parties, pass-through entities, or intermediaries.

Example: John Jones sells his interest in a wholly owned corporation. The corporation's only assets are stock or securities that are traded on an established securities market. The Treasury may deny use of the installment method to record gain because the transaction involves related parties.

Example: Jane Smith, a retiring partner in a large investment partnership, makes an installment sale of her interest. A substantial portion of the interest's value is attributable to stocks and securities held by the partnership. If she could not have sold or caused the sale of the partnership's assets directly, the gain on sale may be reported on the installment method.

Act Sec. 812, relating to publicly traded property, amends Secs. 453 and 453A, effective for sales after 12-31-86.

[¶805] Capitalization of Inventory Costs. Prior law required all direct material and labor costs to be included in inventory cost and deducted as cost of goods sold as the inventory is sold. Prior law also required certain indirect manufacturing costs to be included in inventory cost (thereby treating them as product costs rather than period costs). The new law requires that certain other indirect costs, previously classified as period costs and deducted at the end of the accounting period, be treated as product costs, included in the cost of the product, and deducted as the product is sold. Similar indirect costs, incurred for noninventory items, must also be capitalized.

NOTE: The new inventory accounting rules will result in major changes in the way companies account for inventory. The changes will defer deductions, increase taxable income, and may create an administrative nightmare for the accounting department.

Summary of changes. Certain (period) costs that are now deducted at the end of the accounting period will have to be capitalized, built into product cost, and deducted as part of cost of goods sold as each product is sold.

Example: Acme Publishing Company incurs costs of $900,000 in 1987 that would have been expensed under the old rules, but must now be built into inventory cost. If the inventory item is sold 20% in 1987, 50% in 1988, and 30% in 1989, the amounts that can be deducted as cost of goods sold will be $180,000, $450,000, and $270,000 in 1987, 1988, and 1989, respectively. Under the old rule, all $900,000 could have been deducted in 1987. The new rule permits a deduction of only $180,000 in 1987, which will increase 1987 taxes by $244,800 for a company in the 34% bracket [34% ($900,000 − $180,000)]. However, taxes in 1988 and 1989 will be reduced by a total of $244,800 because portions of the deferred costs can be deducted in those years. *Result:* Total deductions will be identical over three years, but cash flow will be pinched in the first year.

Items affected. Several items now being expensed will have to be capitalized and built into cost of goods sold. Among these are:

- costs incident to purchasing inventory (e.g., wages or salaries of employees responsible for purchasing);

- repackaging, assembly, and other costs incurred in processing goods while in the taxpayer's possession;

- storage costs (e.g., rent or depreciation, insurance premiums, and taxes attributable to a warehouse and wages of warehouse personnel);

- a portion of general and administrative costs allocable to these functions;

- a portion of pension and profit-sharing costs; and

- certain interest costs, including imputed interest.

The uniform capitalization rules only affect inventories valued at cost. So the rules won't affect inventories valued at market by a taxpayer using the lower of cost or market method, or by a dealer in securities using the market method. But the rules will apply to inventories valued at cost by a taxpayer using the lower of cost or market method.

> **NOTE:** The new law does not address the case where a taxpayer using the lower of cost or market method uses cost one year and market the next. When cost is used, the uniform capitalization rules apply. When market is used, the rules don't apply.

Other adverse effects. Implementing the change may be an administrative nightmare. Items to include or exclude will be difficult to determine in many cases. Allocation of general and administrative expenses must be arbitrary, and subject to challenge on audit.

If the Financial Accounting Standards Board rules on inventory accounting and imputed interest differ from the tax rules (which they do), it will necessitate establishing two new deferred tax accounts, which the accounting department will have to track.

Change in accounting method. The inventory change is regarded as a change in accounting method. The Sec. 481 adjustment resulting from the change is to be included in income over four years or less, using the provisions of Rev. Proc. 84-74, 1984-2 C.B. 736. Net operating loss and tax credit carryforwards may offset a positive Sec. 481 adjustment. For purposes of determining estimated tax payments, the Sec. 481 adjustment will be recognized ratably throughout the tax year of adjustment.

In computing the Sec. 481 adjustment, taxpayers using the simplified method for property acquired for resale must apply this method in restating beginning inventory. Taxpayers using LIFO that lack sufficient data to compute the adjustment precisely may use the methods of approximation available to manufacturers (based on the data for the three prior years for which there were increments in the inventory).

The new rules apply to all real or personal property produced by the taxpayer as well as property acquired for resale. But inventory acquired for resale that is personal (not real) property is excluded from the new rule for taxpayers having average annual gross receipts of $10 million or less for the three prior tax years. Gross receipts include those generated from all trades or businesses under common control, including partnerships, and corporations. A controlled group of corporations includes those corporations owned, directly or indirectly, more than 50% by the taxpayer.

Exceptions. The new capitalization rules don't apply to (1) property produced by taxpayers for their personal (not business) use; (2) deductible Sec. 174 research and experimental expenditures; (3) Sec. 616(a) deductible mine development costs and Sec. 263(c) deductible oil and gas or geothermal well intangible drilling costs; (4) property produced under contracts required to be reported under a long-term contract method; and (5) plants or animals produced in a farming business, (see below). The uniform capitalization rules apply to all depreciation deductions for federal income tax purposes. The Senate provision, which was not adopted, would have exempted existing assets from the capitalization of all tax depreciation. The Statement of Managers will provide that cushion gas (and emergency reserve gas to the extent provided by regulations) is not inventory under the capitalization rules. Taxpayers aren't required to allocate to this gas any portion of their overhead or other indirect costs under the new uniform capitalization rules. The Treasury will be directed to provide simplified methods of applying rules to retailers and wholesalers in appropriate circumstances, with examples to be provided in the Statement of Managers.

Self-constructed property and noninventory property produced for sale. The uniform capitalization rules for production activities is limited to tangible property. The rule for property acquired for resale includes both tangible and intangible property. For this purpose, tangible property includes films, sound recordings, video tapes, books, and other similar property embodying words, ideas, concepts, images, or sounds by the creator thereof. So the uniform capitalization rules apply to the costs of producing a motion picture or researching and writing a book.

Interest capitalization. Interest is capitalized and allocated only to real or personal property produced by the taxpayer that has (1) a long useful life; (2) an estimated production period of more than two years; or (3) an estimated production period of more than one year and a cost of more than $1 million. A property has a long useful life if it is real property that has a class life of at least 20 years. The production period begins when production begins and ends when the property is ready to be placed in service or sold.

Amount allocated. Interest on debt that is directly attributable to production expenditures is allocated to the asset's cost. Interest that could have been avoided had the production costs not been incurred is also allocated to the asset's cost. In other words, interest incurred on money borrowed to finance production of the item is capitalized, and interest that could have been avoided had the taxpayer used funds to pay off existing debt instead of to produce the item in question is also capitalized.

The avoided cost method of determining interest allocable to production applies irrespective of whether application of the method, or a similar method, is required, authorized or considered appropriate under financial or regulatory accounting principles. So a regulated utility must apply the avoided cost method even though a different method is authorized or required by FASB Statement No. 34 or the regulatory authority having jurisdiction over the utility.

Qualified residence interest is not capitalized. For flow-through entities, such as partnerships and S corporations, the interest capitalization rule is applied first at the entity level, then at the beneficiary level. Interest on debt incurred or continued for property used to produce capitalizable property shall also be capitalized.

Simplified method for taxpayers acquiring property for resale. The Treasury plans to provide a simplified method for applying the uniform capitalization rules for taxpayers who acquire property for resale. Those not electing the simplified method must apply the procedures and rules used by manufacturers. Once a method is chosen, it must be used consistently. IRS permission is needed to change.

Taxpayers using the simplified method will initially compute their inventory balances without regard to the new uniform capitalization rules. Costs to be capitalized under the new rules are then added, along with other costs, to determine the ending balance. So taxpayers using the LIFO method, for example, will calculate the particular year's LIFO index without regard to the new capitalization rules. Costs capitalized under the new rules will be added to the LIFO layers applicable to the various years for which the costs were accumulated. For taxpayers using the FIFO method who do not sell their entire beginning inventory during the year, a proportionate part of the additional costs capitalized in the beginning inventory will be included in the ending inventory.

The simplified method will be applied separately to each trade or business.

Four categories of indirect cost are allocable to inventory under the simplified method:

- Off-site storage and warehousing costs, including, but not limited to warehouse rent or depreciation, property taxes, insurance premiums, security costs, and other costs directly identifiable with the storage facility;
- Purchasing costs such as buyers' wages or salaries;
- Handling, processing, assembly, repackaging, and similar costs, including labor costs attributable to unloading goods, but not including labor costs attributable to loading of goods for final shipment, or labor at a retail facility, and
- The portion of general and administrative costs allocable to these functions.

Storage costs. Storage costs are included based on the ratio of total annual storage costs to the sum of the beginning inventory balance and gross purchases during the year.

> **Example:** Gannon, who uses FIFO, had $1 million in annual storage costs, beginning inventory (without simplified method adjustments) of $2 million, gross purchases of $8 million, and an ending inventory (without adjustment) of $3 million. The ratio of storage costs to beginning inventory and purchases is 10% ($1 million divided by $2 million + $8 million). So for each inventory dollar, 10 cents of storage costs must be capitalized. The ending inventory will be increased by $300,000. The $700,000 storage cost balance would be included in cost of goods sold.

For LIFO taxpayers, where ending inventory exceeds beginning inventory, the additional capitalized storage costs are calculated by multiplying the inventory increase for the year by the applicable ratio. If the taxpayer in the above example used LIFO instead of FIFO, an additional $100,000 (10% of $1 million) of storage costs would be included in ending inventory. But unlike FIFO, storage costs included in a LIFO beginning inventory remain in inventory until the LIFO layer is depleted (which only happens when the ending inventory is less than the beginning inventory), and aren't deducted as cost of goods sold.

Purchasing costs. Purchasing costs are allocated between inventory and cost of goods sold based on the ratio of purchasing costs to gross purchases during the year. So if the taxpayer in the above example had purchase costs of $500,000 during the year, the ratio of purchasing costs to gross purchases would be 6.25% ($500,000 divided by $8 million). So 6.25 cents of purchasing costs would be capitalized for each dollar's worth of items in ending inventory that were purchased during the year. If the FIFO method were used, $187,500 (6.25% of $3 million) of purchasing costs would be capitalized.

For taxpayers using LIFO, ending inventory consists of newly acquired items only to the extent that ending inventory exceeds beginning inventory. Capitalized purchasing costs would be computed by multiplying the increase in inventory that took place during the year (ending inventory less beginning inventory) by the applicable ratio. The taxpayer in the above example would capitalize $62,500 (6.25% of $1 million) of purchasing costs. In contrast to a FIFO taxpayer, the purchasing costs attributable to a LIFO taxpayer's beginning inventory would be retained in ending inventory.

Processing and repackaging costs. Processing, repackaging and similar costs are allocated based on the ratio of total processing, repackaging and similar costs to the sum of the beginning inventory balance and gross purchases during the year.

General and administrative expenses. General and administrative expenses that are allocable in part to storage, purchasing, and processing activities and in part to activities for which capitalization isn't required are allocated based on the ratio of direct labor costs incurred in a particular function to gross payroll costs.

Example: Baumgarth Company's accounting department has operating costs of $75,000 for the year. Its direct labor purchasing costs were $500,000 and gross payroll was $1.5 million. The portion of the accounting department cost subject to capitalization allocated to the purchase function would be $25,000 ($500,000 divided by $1.5 million × $75,000). If direct labor warehousing costs were $250,000, the accounting department cost allocated to the capitalizable storage and warehousing functions would be $12,500 ($250,000 divided by $1.5 million × $75,000).

Preproductive period expenses of farmers. The new law provides general, uniform rules for determining costs that must be capitalized by all producers of real or tangible personal property, including inventory, property held for sale, and assets constructed by the taxpayer for business use. Special rules apply to the capitalization of interest and farm costs. "Production" means construction, manufacture, development, improvement, and raising or growing, and also covers costs paid or incurred by the taxpayer on property produced for him under a contract. Prior law special rules dealing with capital expenditures of citrus and almond growers and certain farming syndicate expenditures (Sec. 278) and of amortization of real property construction period interest and taxes (Sec. 189) are repealed. Generally, the new rules cover costs and interest that are paid or incurred after 1986.

Production costs in general. Producers will generally capitalize direct production costs and an allocable portion of indirect production costs including taxes. Indirect production costs will be allocated among items produced, or between inventory and current expense costs, under rules similar to those of Reg. Sec. 1.471-11(d) and 1.451-3(d)(9). The new capitalization rules don't cover (1) property produced by taxpayers for their personal (not business) use; (2) Sec. 616(a) deductible mine development costs and Sec. 263(c) deductible oil and gas or geothermal well intangible drilling costs, (3) property produced under contracts required to be reported under a long-term contract method, (4) deductible Sec. 174 research and experimental costs, and (5) timber and certain ornamental trees such as evergreens that are more than six years old when severed from their roots. Deductible contributions to qualified retirement plans must be allocated (under regs to come) between production (for example, inventory) and other costs. This allocation is independent of (that is, made after) any allocation required by Sec. 412 minimum standard funding rules.

Timber. The rules for capitalizing and expensing timber costs haven't changed. So costs that would be capitalized under prior law will continue to be capitalized, and costs that were deductible before will continue to be deductible. The definition of timber under the new law is intended to be coextensive with the definition of timber, including ornamental trees, under prior law. Nothing in the definition of timber shall be construed to narrow the types of activities that constitute the growing of timber for purposes of the exclusion of timber from the uniform capitalization rules.

Special rules for interest. Interest costs allocable to production must be capitalized only if they're allocable to producing property that has (1) a production period of more than two years, or (2) a production period of more than one year and a cost over $1 million, or (3) a long useful life (this generally includes real property, including buildings and other real property classified as 15-year, 18-or 19-year property under prior law, and certain other long-lived assets).

The production period for this rule begins when construction or production begins and ends when the property is ready to be placed in service or held for sale. For plants or animals, the "production period" means the preproductive period. Planning and design activities generally don't cause the production period to begin. Interest on debt that can be directly traced to production or construction costs is first allocated to production or construction. These costs include the cumulative production costs, including previously capitalized interest that must be capitalized. If production or construction expenditures exceed debt directly traceable to them, interest on other debt will be allocated to this excess to the extent that interest costs would have been reduced if production costs hadn't been incurred, using the average of interest rates on the taxpayer's outstanding debt (other than debt that is directly traceable to production or construction).

Regulations are expected to prevent avoidance of these rules through use of related parties. If the production or construction is for a customer who makes progress or advance payments, the customer is treated as constructing the property to the extent of the payments. Thus, interest costs attributable to the payments are capitalizable by the customer, and the contractor capitalizes only interest attributable to the excess of accumulated contract costs over accumulated payments he receives during the year.

NOTE: The new rule may make it necessary for companies to set up a deferred tax account. A deferred tax account is necessary if a company uses different accounting methods for financial reporting and tax reporting, provvided the difference in revenue or expense that results from using different methods is of a temporary rather than permanent nature.

Capitalization by farmers and ranchers. For taxpayers in the business of farming, the new capitalization rules generally apply to plants and animals only if they have a preproductive period of over two years, and livestock held for slaughter is completely excluded from them. "Farming" includes operating nurseries or sod farms, and raising trees bearing fruits or nuts or other crops. It doesn't include the raising, harvesting, or growing of timber or ornamental evergreen trees that are more than six years old at the time they are severed from their roots. *Special rules:* Corporations and partnerships with corporate partners that must use the accrual method under Sec. 447 must capitalize costs and taxes regardless of the length of the preproductive period and must also capitalize preproductive period interest to the extent the period exceeds two years. Taxpayers using the Sec. 447(g) accrual period should be able to continue using it.

The "preproductive period" for plants begins when the plant or seed is first planted or acquired by taxpayer. It ends when the plant becomes productive or is sold. Using supplies produced on a farm is treated as their disposition. If there's more than one crop or yield, the first marketable crop or yield controls the end of the period. The "preproductive period" of a plant commercially grown in the United States is the average nationwide preproductive period for the particular crop. The Treasury is expected to publish periodically a list of various plant preproductive periods. The animal "preproductive period" begins at the time of acquisition, breeding, or embryo implantation, and ends when the animal is ready to perform its intended function. For example, the preproductive period for a cow used for breeding ends when the first calf is dropped. It's expected that capitalizable costs may be determined under regs using a reasonable valuation method (for example, a simplified method such as farm-price or unit-livestock-price).

Election to expense farmers' preproductive period costs. Farmers (including producers of livestock, nursery stock, Christmas, and other ornamental trees and agricultural crops) can elect to deduct all preproductive costs of tangible personal property produced in the farm business (for example, plant and animal costs) that were deductible under prior law. But if they make the election, any gain on disposition of the product is recaptured (in general treated as Section 1245 depreciation) and taxed as ordinary income to the extent of expensed deductions that otherwise would have been capitalized. Also, they have to use the alternative cost recovery system for all farm assets used predominantly in farming and placed in service in any tax years covered by the election. The election can't be made by (1) tax shelters as defined in Sec. 6161(b)(2)(C)(ii), (2) taxpayers required to use the accrual method under Sec. 447, and (3) farming syndicates, as defined in Sec. 464(c). And it can't cover pistachio nut planting, maintenance, or development costs.

The election also doesn't apply to the cost of planting, cultivating, maintaining, or developing any citrus or almond grove, incurred before the end of the fourth tax year after the trees were planted. If a grove is planted over more than one tax year, the part of the grove planted in each tax year is treated as a separate grove for determining the year of planting.

Partnerships and S corporations make the election at the partner or shareholder level. The election must be made in the first tax year that begins after 1986 during which the taxpayer is a farmer. Taxpayers making the election may (according to the House Committee Report) estimate the amount of preproductive period expenses that are subject to recapture using methods similar to one of the simplified inventory methods permitted to accrual method taxpayers under current law. The election can be revoked or changed only with IRS consent. It's binding on the taxpayer's spouse and minor children ("family members"), and on any corporations and their controlled groups and partnerships in which the taxpayer or his "family members" own at least a 50% direct or indirect (Sec. 318) interest by value. Minor children are defined as those who haven't attained age 18 before the close of the tax year.

The new uniform capitalization rules are generally effective for costs and interest paid or incurred after 12-31-86 in tax years ending after 1986. Assets constructed by the taxpayer for his or her own use that had substantial construction before 1987 are exempt from the new rules. There are special rules for urban renovation projects.

The new rules apply to inventories for the taxpayer's first tax year beginning after 1986. Adjustments resulting from the change in inventory accounting (under Sec. 481) must be spread over a period of no more than four years under rules for changes initiated by taxpayer and approved by the IRS (Rev.Proc. 84-74, 1984-2 C.B. 736). The law contemplates that (1) all changes in the rules for absorption of costs into inventory will be treated as accounting method changes; (2) inventory on hand as of the effective date be revalued to reflect the new, greater absorption of costs and; (3) Regs and rulings will allow taxpayers who can't revalue a part of the inventory because necessary information isn't available to revalue by estimates using available date (for example, FIFO inventories, and particularly the LIFO dollar value method). The House Ways & Means Report contains suggested rules for LIFO layer revaluations.

Expenses for Replanting Groves, Orchards, or Vineyards Destroyed in Natural Disasters. The new law provides that if a farmer experiences loss or damage because of freezing temperatures, disease, drought, pests, or casualty, the capitalization requirements of Secs. 278(a) and (b) don't apply to otherwise deductible costs. Deductible costs include replanting, cultivating, maintaining, or developing the grove, orchard or vineyard even though the costs aren't incurred solely by the farmer suffering the loss and even though replanting doesn't take place on the same property. However two conditions must be met:

- The taxpayer who owned the property at the time of the loss or damage must have an equity interest of more than 50% in the property.

- The additional persons incurring the loss must hold part of the remaining equity interest in the property and must materially participate in the planting, cultivation, maintenance, or development. Whether an individual materially participates in an activity is determined similarly to the method under Sec. 2032A (current use valuation of farm property).

Also, replanting costs can qualify even though the grove is replanted in a different location, provided the costs don't relate to acreage exceeding the acreage of the property on which the loss or damage occurred.

The special rule for preproductive period expenses following loss or damage due to freezing temperatures, and so forth, applies only to crops that are normally eaten or drunk by humans. So jojoba bean production, for example, doesn't qualify under this special exception.

Act Sec. 803(a), relating to capitalization of inventory costs, adds new Sec. 263A, generally effective for costs incurred after 12-31-86. The new rules for inventory take effect for tax years beginning after 12-31-86. If a change in accounting method is involved, an adjustment is required over four years or less. The new rules do not apply for internally used self-constructed property where substantial construction occurred before 3-1-86. Act Sec. 803, relating to capitalization where taxpayer produces property, adds new Sec. 471(b), amends Secs. 447(a) and (b) and 471(a), and repeals Secs. 189 and 278. Act Sec. 803, on deductions for expenses incurred in replanting citrus and almond groves, amends Sec. 278(c), effective for amounts expended or incurred after the enactment date in tax years ending after that date.

[¶806] **Accounting For Long-Term Contracts.** All direct costs, including research and experimental costs, that are incurred in a long-term contract, are allocated to that contract in a way similar to that outlined in Sec. 451. Certain other period (general and administrative) costs are also allocated in the case of cost-plus and federal long-term contracts. Interest costs are also allocated to the contract, using the same approach as that of Financial Accounting Standards Board Statement No. 34 (which includes avoided interest).

Interest accrues during the production period. The production period starts at the later of (1) the contract commencement date, or (2) for accrual method taxpayers, as soon as at least 5% of total estimated costs, including design and planning costs, have been incurred. The contract commencement date is the first date any costs (other than bidding or negotiation expenses) are incurred on the contract. The production period ends on the contract completion date.

The following costs are expensed as incurred, and are not capitalized as long-term contract costs: (1) expenses for unsuccessful bids and proposals; (2) research and development expenses that are not related to a particular contract; and (3) marketing, selling, and advertising expenses. Taxpayers using the completed contract method must capitalize an additional amount of costs equal to the fully reimbursed portion of independent research and development costs and unsuccessful bid and proposal costs attributable to federal government contracts that require certification of such costs.

The direct allocation, cost-plus, and federal contract rules do not apply for real property construction contracts that are initially estimated to be completed within two years of the commencement date, for taxpayers having average annual gross receipts of $10 million or less for the three years before the year the contract is entered into. Gross receipts include those generated from all trades or businesses under common control, including partnerships, joint ventures, and corporations. A controlled group of corporations includes those corporations owned, directly or indirectly, more than 50% by the taxpayer.

Construction contracts include any contract to build, rehabilitate, construct, reconstruct, or install an integral component to, or improvements to, real property.

A long-term contract is a contract for the production, manufacture, building, installation, or construction of property that is not started and completed in the same tax year. Manufacturing contracts are not treated as long-term contracts unless the manufactured item (1) is not included in the taxpayer's finished goods inventory, and (2) the item normally takes more than 12 months to complete (regardless of the completion period stated in the contract).

Aggregation. Two or more interdependent contracts may be treated as a single contract.

Accounting methods. The completed contract method can no longer be used, except by taxpayers that expect to complete the construction contract within two years, and have average annual gross receipts of $10 million or less. For taxpayers that cannot use the completed contract method, two other methods are available. The percentage of completion method may still be used, although the capitalization rules have changed, as explained at ¶805.

The other method, called the percentage of completion—capitalized cost method, is new. This method requires 40% of the contract to be accounted for using the percentage of completion method and 60% accounted for using the taxpayer's regular method. If the taxpayer's normal method is the completed contract method, 60% of the costs and revenues would be recognized upon contract completion. If an accrual method such as an accrual shipment method is used, the items in question would be accounted for at shipment date. The look-back method must be applied to the 40% portion of the contract that uses the percentage of completion method. So interest is paid to or by the taxpayer on the difference between the amount actually taken into account each year and the amount that would have been taken into account recomputing the 40% portion under the look-back method.

> **NOTE:** Taxpayers that use one accounting method on the tax return and another method on the financial statements must set up a deferred tax account to keep track of timing differences. So anyone that uses the percentage of completion—capitalized cost method must set up a deferred tax account, since the method is unacceptable for financial statement reporting.

Act Sec. 804, relating to long-term contracts, adds new Code Sec. 460, effective for contracts entered into after 2-28-86.

[¶807] Bad Debt Reserves. For tax years beginning after 1986, the new law eliminates the bad debt reserve method of deducting bad debts for taxpayers other than financial institutions. Taxpayers need not charge off wholly worthless debts on their books to deduct them. The reserve method is also repealed for dealers that guarantee, endorse, or provide indemnity agreements for debt arising out of the sale by a dealer of real or tangible personal property in the ordinary course of business.

> **NOTE:** The Committee Reports note that a delay in the charge-off of a debt on the books isn't intended to shift the deduction from the year when it's clear that the taxpayer actually became aware that the debt was wholly worthless.

ANOTHER POINT: The direct chargeoff method varies from generally accepted financial accounting principles, so companies that used the reserve method for both financial accounting and tax purposes and that must now change methods for tax purposes must set up a deferred tax account where none was required previously.

Transition rule. The change from the reserve method to the specific chargeoff method is a change in accounting method initiated by the taxpayer with IRS consent. To prevent duplication of deductions, the balance in any reserve account on the effective date must be taken into income ratably over four years. For guarantee bad debt reserves, the reserve balance is first reduced by the suspense account balance. The remaining balance is taken into income ratably over four years. (Sec. 481 adjustment).

Act Sec. 805, relating to bad debt reserves, repeals Code Sec. 166(c) and redesignates subsection (g) as subsection (f), effective for tax years beginning after 12-31-86.

[¶808] Conforming Tax Years for Partnerships, S Corporations, and Personal Service Corporations. The new law requires all partnerships, S corporations, and personal service corporations to conform their tax years to that of the owners. A partnership must have the same tax year as that of its majority interest partners, unless it establishes, to the Treasury's satisfaction, a good business reason for having a different tax year. If the majority owners don't have the same tax year, the partnership must adopt the same tax year as its principal partners. If the principal partners don't have the same tax year, and no majority of partners have the same tax year, the partnership must adopt a calendar year as its tax year.

> **Example:** Alpha Partnership's principal partner is Beta, Inc., a fiscal year corporation. Beta owns a 10% interest in Alpha's partnership profits and capital. The other partners are individual calendar year taxpayers who each have partnership interests of less than 5%. Prior law would require Alpha to adopt Beta's tax year, since Beta is Alpha's principal partner. The new law requires Alpha to adopt a calendar tax year, since that is the tax year of the majority of Alpha's partners.

An S corporation must adopt a permitted year, regardless of when the corporation elected to be taxed as an S corporation. A personal service corporation must adopt a calendar year.

Exception. When the Treasury is satisfied there is a business purpose for having a different tax year, that year will be permitted provided deferral is three months or less. So a partnership that can establish a good business purpose can have a September 30, October 31, or November 30 year-end, even if all the partners are calendar year taxpayers. But taxpayers will not receive an automatic three-month deferral. A business purpose must exist, and wanting to defer the tax is not considered a business purpose. Taxpayers that have already obtained the Treasury's permission for a different year-end don't have to request permission again because of the law change.

A partnership doesn't have to adopt the tax year of its majority interest partners unless partners having the same tax year have owned a majority interest in partnership profits and capital for the partnership's preceding three tax years. Tax years beginning before the new law's effective date are taken into account for determining whether the three-year test has been met.

> **Example:** John and Jane each have owned 50% of Delta Partnership since its inception in July 1984. Delta's fiscal year ends June 30. John and Jane are both calendar year taxpayers. Delta must conform its tax year to that of its principal partners for the tax year beginning July 1, 1987. So Delta will have two tax years ending in 1987. The first one spans July 1, 1986 to June 30, 1987. The second is from July 1 to December 31, 1987. So John and Jane will have 18 months' worth of partnership income dumped into their 1987 calendar year.

A partnership, S corporation, or personal service corporation that is required to change its tax year is treated as doing so with the IRS's consent. For a partnership or S corporation, each partner or owner may elect to take any resulting excess of income over expense into income ratably over the first four tax years (including the owner's year that would otherwise include the income or loss of the entity's short tax year) beginning after 12-31-86. Without an election, net income or loss for the short year is included currently in its entirety. The short tax year of a personal service corporation is annualized.

A partnership or S corporation that received permission to use a fiscal year-end under the provisions of Rev. Proc. 74-33, 1974-2 C.B. 489 (other than a year-end that resulted in a deferral of three months or less) can continue to use such taxable year. A partnership, S corporation, or personal service corporation may adopt, retain, or change to a tax year established by IRS if the use of such tax year meets the requirements of the 25% test as described in Rev. Proc. 83-25, 1983-1, C.B. 689 (25% or more of gross receipts for the 12-month period in question are recognized in the last two months of the period and the requirement has been met for the specified three consecutive 12-month periods).

To be classified as a personal service corporation for tax year determination purposes,

- the corporation cannot be an S corporation,
- the principal activity must be performance of personal services, if the services are substantially performed by employee-owners, and

- employee-owners are employees who own outstanding stock at least one day during the tax year.

NOTE: Personal service corporations may not deduct payments to owner-employees before the year paid.

The Sec. 318 attribution rules apply to determine constructive ownership, except that the attribution of stock owned by a corporation to the employee is applied without regard to any requirement that the employee own a certain percentage of corporation stock.

The new law ends (or at least curtails) a popular tax deferral strategy.

Example: Dr. Jones reports income on a calendar year basis and is the employee-owner of a professional corporation with a January 31 year-end. He earns $200,000 a year but receives a monthly salary of $10,000, or $120,000 for the year. Then, in January of the next year, the remaining $80,000 goes to him as a bonus. *Result:* the entire $200,000 is deductible by the fiscal year corporation in one tax year. But Jones reports the $200,000 over two tax years, $120,000 the first year and $80,000 the following year.

Under the new law, there would be no deferral because the corporation would have to change it's year-end to December 31. However, the corporation could have a September 30, October 31, or November 30 year-end if it could establish a business purpose to the satisfaction of the IRS. But tax deferral is not a business purpose.

Act Sec. 806, relating to tax years, amends Code Secs. 267, 441, 706, and 1378, effective for tax years beginning after 12-31-86.

[¶809] Qualified Discount Coupons. The new law repeals the provision that allows taxpayers to deduct the cost of redeeming qualified discount coupons in the current year, even though some coupons may actually be redeemed the following year. Only redemption costs actually incurred currently may be deducted currently.

Transition rule. Any change in accounting method required by the law change is regarded as a taxpayer-initiated change, with the IRS's consent. Any adjustment must first reduce any suspense account balance. The net amount is then taken into income ratably over four years or less. Net operating loss and tax credit carryforwards will be allowed to offset any positive Sec. 481 adjustment. For computing estimated tax payments, the Sec. 481 adjustment will be recognized in taxable income ratably throughout the year in question.

Act Sec. 823, relating to qualified discount coupons, repeals Sec. 466, and amends Sec 481(h), effective for tax years beginning after 12-31-86.

[¶810] Utilities Using Accrual Accounting. The cycle meter reading accounting method used by utilities does not recognize income as earned. Accrual method utility companies must now recognize utility service income the year it is earned. The time earned is the time the customer uses the service, not the time the meter is read or the time the invoice is mailed.

> **Example:** Apple and Stoneland Utility Company, a calendar year company, reads Smith's meter the 12th of each month. The reading for January 12, 1987 indicates that $310 of utility services have been rendered since the December 12 reading. On its 1986 tax return, A&S will include income of $190, or $10 a day for the last 19 days of December. Its 1987 tax return will include the $120 earned the first 12 days of January, 1987.

The following utility services are subject to this pro rata allocation formula: electrical energy, water or sewage disposal, gas or steam furnished through a local distribution system, telephone and other communications services, and the pipeline transportation of gas or steam. Similar rules should apply to other utility services that come into existence in the future. This allocation method applies to regulated and nonregulated utilities.

An accounting change resulting from this rule change is considered to be a taxpayer initiated change in accounting method with the IRS's consent. A Sec. 481 adjustment is required. The difference between the old and new accounting methods must be taken into income or expense ratably over no more than four years. Net operating loss and tax credit carryforwards will be allowed to offset any positive Sec. 481 adjustment. Taxpayers required to accrue income at the time utility services are furnished may accrue any deductions for related costs if economic performance has occurred. Any change in accounting method includes any related change in accounting method for the related items of expense or deduction. The Sec. 481 adjustment is to be computed on the net amount of the two changes and taken into income ratably over a four-year period.

Act Sec. 821, relating to utility accrual accounting, adds Code Sec. 451(f), effective for tax years beginning after 12-31-86.

[¶811] Contributions to Corporation's Capital as a Customer or in Aid of Construction. For tax years beginning after 1986, the new law repeals the special rule that treats contributions to regulated public utilities in aid of construction as excludable contributions to a corporation's capital. Instead, it expressly bars contributions to a corporation's capital in aid of construction or as a customer or a potential customer, from treatment as contributions to capital that are excludable from the corporation's income under Sec. 118.

The law change is intended to have a utility report as gross income the value of property or money that it receives to provide or encourage the provision of services to or for the benefit of the contributor (e.g., if the contribution results in the utility's providing services earlier or favoring the contributor in any way, regardless of whether it's the utility's general policy to require or encourage types of potential customers such as developers of multiple tracts to transfer property or money to the utility). It's intended that if all members of a particular group transfer property to a utility the value be included in the utility's income unless it's clearly shown that the benefit of the public as a whole was the primary motivating factor.

> **SILVER LINING:** The prior law's rules disallowing deductions and credits for expenditures made with contributions in aid of construction, and making the basis of property acquired with them zero, are gone too.

Act Sec. 824, amends Secs. 118 and 362(c), effective for contributions received after 12-31-86.

[¶812] Discharge of Debt. Prior law allowed deferral of gain recognition on the discharge of certain business debt. The new law requires taxpayers to recognize debt charges in income immediately, unless the taxpayer is insolvent or unless the discharge is under Title 11 (Bankruptcy).

Act Sec. 822, relating to discharge of debt, amends Code Sec. 108(a), effective for debt discharges occurring after 12-31-86.

[The page following this is 901.]

FINANCIAL INSTITUTIONS

[¶900] Overview. Generally, commercial banks and thrift institutions have the same income and deductions as ordinary business corporations and are subject to the same income taxes as ordinary business corporations. There are special rules, however, that only apply to these institutions. They include the deduction for bad debts, the deduction on interest used to purchase or carry tax-exempt bonds, gain or loss from the sale of securities, carrying net operating losses backward or forward, tax-free reorganizations, and immunity from taxation to protect financial institution depositors.

Bank. The term "bank" includes commercial banks, trust companies, and thrift institutions that are subject to federal or state bank supervisory authorities and a substantial part of whose business consists of receiving deposits and making loans and discounts or of exercising fiduciary powers similar to those permitted national banks.

Thrift institutions. For purposes of the Internal Revenue Code, thrift institutions are domestic building and loan associations, savings and loan associations, mutual savings banks, or cooperative nonprofit mutual banks. The Code further defines "domestic building and loan association" as building and loan or savings and loan institutions which are federally insured or subject to federal or state regulation, the business of which consists principally of acquiring public savings and investing in loans. Also, at least 60% of these institutions' assets must consist of certain "qualifying assets" (Sec. 7701(a)(19)(C); Reg. §301.7701-13A).

> **WARNING:** Although thrift institutions are included in the definition of bank, there are special Code provisions that apply only to commercial banks or thrift institutions (e.g., reserve for bad debt deduction). Therefore, in some instances, grouping all financial institutions under the heading "bank" would be misleading and incorrect.

[¶901] Reserve for Bad Debts. The new law eliminates some of the special rules that applied to commercial banks and thrift institutions in computing their deduction for bad debts.

Large banks. Large commercial banks must now use a method to figure their bad debt reserve deduction that is different from all other commercial banks. Banks that aren't large commercial banks can continue to use prior law. The provision was added because Congress felt that some banks, especially the larger ones, were using the reserve method for figuring losses from bad debts to substantially lower their income tax liabilities. Because an across-the-board elimination of the bad debt reserve deduction could result in some potential adverse effects on smaller banks, prior law was retained to balance these concerns.

A commercial bank is considered a "large bank" if for any tax year after 12-31-86, the sum of the averaged adjusted basis of all assets of that bank exceeds $500 million, or, if the bank is part of a bank holding company (i.e., parent-subsidiary controlled group), the sum of the adjusted bases of all the assets of that group exceeds $500 million.

Commercial banks different from thrifts.   For purposes of the bad debt reserve deduction, a commercial bank is defined as a domestic or foreign corporation whose business substantially consists of receiving deposits or making loans and discounts, or of exercising fiduciary powers like those permitted national banks, and who are subject to federal or state bank regulatory authorities. It doesn't include thrift institutions—domestic building and loan associations, savings and loan associations, mutual savings banks, or cooperative nonprofit mutual banks.

There are two methods to figure bad debts. For large banks, the new law provides for bad debt deductions only when the loans become wholly or partially worthless for tax years after 1986. This eliminates concern that the prior reserve methods of accounting resulted in deductions being taken for tax purposes for losses that substantially occurred in the future and were inconsistent with the treatment of other deductions under the all-events test.

Under the prior law, all banks could deduct bad debts by using a specific charge-off method or by using a reserve method. The charge-off method allows banks to deduct bad debts that have become worthless during the tax year. The reserve method allows banks to take a deduction equal to the amount necessary to increase the year-end bad debt reserve allowance to an amount computed under the experience method or the percentage of eligible loans method.

The experience method for banks generally is based on the average loan loss over the most recent six-year period. Under the percentage of eligible loans method, banks are allowed a deduction for additions to reserves sufficient to maintain a tax reserve up to 0.6% of eligible loans outstanding. After the 1987 tax year, the percentage method will be unavailable, leaving commercial banks with only the experience method of accounting to compute the bad debt deduction.

Computing bad debt deduction of large banks.   Unless large banks elect the cut-off method, they will have to recapture the amount of their bad debt reserves into income.

Four-year adjustment spread.   Under the adjustment spread method, a bank is treated as having initiated a change in its accounting method for its calculation of losses on bad debts in its disqualification year—the first year the bank can no longer use the reserve method, but no earlier than 12-31-86. The new law prevents large banks from getting a double deduction for bad debts. This accounting method change is treated as having been made with IRS consent.

By changing its method of accounting, a large bank must take into income the balance of any bad debt reserve accounts that exist on the last day of the year before the disqualification year—the first taxable year beginning after 12-31-86. Income for 1987 will be 10% of the reserves on the last day of the year before the disqualification year.

The income amount to be recaptured over the next four tax years after the disqualification year will be 20% in 1988, 30% in 1989, and 40% in 1990.

Banks may also elect to include more than 10% of their reserve balance in income in the first taxable year. If that election is made, $2/9$ of the remainder of the reserve balance (after reduction for the amount included in income in the first taxable year) must be included in income in the second taxable year, $1/3$ of the remainder in the third taxable year, and $4/9$ of the remainder in the fourth taxable year.

Financially troubled bank. Under the new law, if a bank's average of its nonperforming loans exceeds 75% of the average of its equity capital for the year, it's a financially troubled bank, and it doesn't elect the cut-off method, the bank doesn't have to recapture existing bad debt reserves. For each year that the bank is financially troubled, the recapture of the bad debt reserve is suspended.

If the bank is part of a bank holding company, then the determination of whether the bank is financially troubled is made with respect to all the banks in the holding company.

Nonperforming loans include loans that are "past due 90 days or more and still accruing," nonaccrual loans, and "renegotiated 'troubled debt'" under the Federal Financial Institutions Examination Council. Equity capital is assets less liabilities, but doesn't include the balance in any reserve for bad debts. Nonperforming loan and equity capital averages are based on the average of those amounts at each time during the taxable year that the bank is required to report for regulatory purposes.

> **IMPORTANT:** Allowing financially troubled banks to suspend the inclusion of their bad debt reserve in income doesn't affect the requirements that a large bank account for its bad debts using the specific charge-off method.

Cut-off election. Large banks may elect to account for existing loans using a cut-off method. For large banks electing the cut-off method, no change in the accounting method is presumed, and the bank continues to use the reserve method to account for bad debts on loans outstanding on the last day of the tax year before the disqualification year. By electing the cut-off method, all charge-offs and recoveries of the bank's loan are adjustments to the reserve accounts and not separate income and expense items.

No additional deductions in the disqualification year or thereafter are permitted for additions to the reserve for bad debts under the cut-off method.

Reductions in bad debt reserve for thrift institutions. Under the new law, thrift institutions that use the percentage of taxable income method may deduct 8% from taxable income as an addition to the reserve for bad debts. The prior law allowed thrift institutions using this method to deduct 40% as an addition to reserve for bad debts if 82% of the thrifts assets were qualified (72% for mutual savings banks without stock). That deduction phased down to zero when less than 60% of the thrifts assets were qualified.

Methods of treating bad debt. Thrift institutions can elect to treat bad debts by deducting for specific debts as they become wholly or partially worthless or by deducting an addition to the reserve for bad debts. For thrift institutions, the reasonable addition to the reserve for bad debts is equal to the reserve for losses computed under the "experience" method, the "percentage of eligible loans" method, or the "percentage of taxable income" method. While commercial banks and thrift institutions can elect to use either the experience or percentage of eligible loans methods, only thrift institutions can compute their bad debt reserve deduction using the percentage of taxable income method.

For thrift institutions electing the percentage of taxable income method, an annual deduction is allowed for a statutory percentage of taxable income. The addition to the reserve for bad debts under this method is an amount equal to the applicable percentage of taxable income for the taxable year involved, subject to special rules which are dependent on the percentage of qualifying assets held by the thrift institution.

Although these methods shouldn't be mixed, thrift institutions may switch between them from year to year. At a minimum, 60% of a thrift institution's assets must be "qualified" to be eligible for deductions under the percentage of taxable income method. For mutual banks without stock, however, 50% of their assets must be "qualified" to be eligible for the deduction under that method.

Qualified assets include cash, U.S. bonds, taxable bonds of states or municipalities, CDs in corporations issuing deposit accounts, residential real property loans, church loans, urban renewal loans, institutional loans, foreclosed property, and educational loans.

Calculating the bad debt deduction. The new law eliminates the rules reducing the amount of the percentage of taxable income deduction available to thrifts that hold 60% of their assets in qualifying assets, but fail to hold a sufficient percentage of qualifying assets to use the maximum percentage of taxable income deduction. It doesn't stop thrift institutions from continuing to use the experience method to calculate the addition to the reserve for bad debts.

The percentage of eligible loans method is unavailable to thrift institutions under the new law.

THRIFT 60% TEST: Only thrift institutions that hold at least 60% of their assets as qualifying assets are eligible for the full 8%-of-taxable-income deduction. And the 60% test applies to all thrift institutions.

No Sec. 291 tax preference. Thrifts that claim the 8% taxable income deduction won't have a tax preference for purposes of the 20% reduction of Sec. 291 under the new law. The excess of the percentage of taxable income deduction over the deduction that would have been allowable on the basis of actual experience will be treated as a tax preference item for computing the corporate minimum tax under Sec. 57.

Special recognition provision. The new law also provides for a special recognition provision that applies to reserve balances in excess of the balance computed under the experience method. Deductions claimed using the 8% taxable income method in excess of deductions computed under the experience method are still subject to recognition as income if distributed to shareholders.

Reserves for losses on loans of SBICs. The new law eliminates the special rules for computing the amount of bad debt reserves and bad debt reserve additions for losses on loans of small business investment companies (operating under the Small Business Investment Act of 1958) and state-created business development corporations.

Act Sec. 901, changes the method for determining reserves for bad debts for commercial banks, amends Sec. 585(a) and 585(b)(1), and adds Sec. 585(c), effective for tax years beginning after 12-31-86, and as shown. Act Sec. 901, changes the method for determining reserves for bad debts for thrifts, amends Sec. 291(e)(1)(A) and Sec. 291(e)(1)(B), amends Sec. 582(c)(1), adds Sec. 582(c)(5), amends Sec. 593(a), 593(b)(1), Sec. 593(b)(1)(B), Sec. 593(b)(2), removes Sec. 593(b)(3) and Sec. 593(b)(5), redesignates Sec. 593(b)(4) as Sec. 593(b)(3), and amends 593(e)(1)(B) effective for tax years beginning after 12-31-86. Act Sec. 901, eliminates reserves for losses on loans of SBICs and business development corporations, repeals Sec. 586, effective for tax years beginning after 12-31-86. Clerical amendments to Act Sec. 901.

[¶902] **Interest Incurred to Carry Tax-Exempt Bonds.** The new law denies banks, thrift institutions, and other financial institutions a deduction for 100% of their interest expense allocable to buying or carrying of tax-exempt obligations acquired after 8-7-86 for interest incurred after 12-31-86. It attempts to place financial institutions on an equal plane with all other taxpayers.

Bonds that are acquired after 8-7-86, in taxable years ending in 1986, are subject to the prior law's 20% disallowance rule for the taxable year ending in 1986. The bonds, however, are subject to the new law's 100% disallowance rule for subsequent taxable years.

Individuals and other corporations can't deduct interest payments on debt incurred or continued to buy or carry tax-exempt obligations. Legislative, judicial, and IRS interpretations, however, have generally permitted banks, thrifts, and other financial institutions to invest their depository funds in tax-exempt obligations without losing their deduction for interest paid on their deposits or their short-term obligations. And under the corporate tax-preference rules, financial institutions have had to reduce by 20% their interest deduction allocable to tax-exempt obligations acquired after 1982.

Tax-exempt obligations are defined as any obligations whose interest is wholly tax exempt and includes shares in regulated investment companies that distribute exempt-interest dividends during the recipient's tax year.

Computing pro-rata allocation of interest expense. The amount of interest allocable to tax-exempt obligations under the new law is figured in the same way as the 20% reduction in financial institution preference items that exist under the prior law (after taking into account any interest disallowed to all taxpayers under the general rules of Sec. 265). And this allocation rule is mandatory. Therefore, there is no deduction for that portion of a financial institution's otherwise allowable interest expense that is equivalent to the ratio of the average adjusted basis of tax-exempt obligations held by the financial institution and acquired after 8-7-86 to the average adjusted basis of the financial institution's total assets.

The term "interest expense" under the new law means the aggregate amount allowable to the financial institution as a deduction for interest for the tax year. The term "interest" includes amounts paid in respect of deposits, investment certificates, or withdrawable or repurchaseable shares, whether or not designated as interest.

20% disallowance rule continued. The 20% disallowance rule under prior law continues to apply to tax-exempt obligations acquired by financial institutions from 1-1-83 to 8-7-86. Financial institutions that have acquired tax-exempt obligations after 8-7-86 will reduce their otherwise allowable interest expense by the sum of 100% of interest allocable to tax-exempt obligations acquired after 8-7-86 and 20% of interest allocable to tax-exempt obligations acquired on or before 8-7-86.

Example: 25% of First State Bank's assets consist of tax-exempt obligations acquired after 8-7-86 and an additional 25% consists of tax-exempt obligations acquired between 1-1-83 and 8-7-86. First State Bank would be denied 30% of its otherwise allowable interest deduction—25% is attributable to obligations acquired after 8-7-86 and 5% (.20 × 25%) is attributable to obligations acquired between 1-1-83 and 8-7-86.

Under the disallowance rule of the new law, the acquisition date of an obligation is the date on which the holding period begins with respect to the obligations belonging to the acquiring financial institution. As such, bond acquisitions that are part of a tax-free reorganization aren't treated as a new acquisition under the new law.

Coordination with new Sec. 263A. Under the new law, the interest-disallowance rule must be applied to that portion of the financial institution's interest expense before new law provision Sec. 263A [¶805], relating to capitalization of certain preproductive expenses, can be applied.

Special face-amount certificate-company rule repealed. The new law subjects face-amount certificate companies that have registered under the Investment Company Act of 1940 and subject to state banking laws, to the same disallowance rules as other financial institutions. Previously, deductions on the interest paid or accrued on the certificates and on amounts received for the purchase of the certificates to be issued weren't disallowed.

Financial institutions defined. Financial institutions subject to the new disallowance rule include entities that accept deposits from the public in the ordinary course of their trade or business and that are subject to federal or state bank supervisory authorities. This includes commercial banks, thrift institutions, and foreign banks doing business in the U.S.

Exception for qualified tax-exempt obligations. The new law provides for an exception for qualified tax-exempt obligations acquired by financial institutions which applies whether the obligation is acquired at the original issuance or by a secondary purchaser. Qualified tax-exempt obligations are treated as acquired by the financial institution before 8-8-86 and interest allocable to these obligations remain subject to the prior law's 20% disallowance rule.

Qualified tax-exempt obligations include obligations that aren't private activity bonds and that are issued by an issuer which reasonably anticipates to issue, together with subordinate governmental entities, no more than $10 million of tax-exempt obligations—other than private activity bonds—during the calendar year. The bonds must be designated as qualified tax-exempt obligations by the issuer, and the issuer (including subordinate governmental entities) cannot designate more than $10 million of obligations for any calendar year. Also, refundings of outstanding bonds may qualify for this exception and count toward the $10 million limitation under the same terms as new issuers.

Qualified Sec. 501(c)(3) organization bonds [see ¶1301 et seq.] are not treated as private activity bonds for purposes of this exception. Also, for purposes of this exception, qualified Sec. 501(c)(3) bonds that are issued before 8-15-86 are treated as private activity bonds if they are IDB's, mortgage subsidiary bonds, student loan bonds, or other private loan bonds for which tax exemption is allowed under the prior law.

The new law defines subordinate governmental entities as entities deriving their issuing authority from another entity or as entities subject to substantial control by another entity. Entities shouldn't be considered subordinate solely because of geographical inclusion in a larger entity.

Transitional exceptions. There are transitional exceptions under the new law.

- *Tax exempt obligations acquired:* All tax-exempt obligations acquired under written commitments to purchase or repurchase the obligation before 9-25-85 are treated as obligations acquired before 8-8-86, and are subject to the 20% disallowance rule.

- *Specified identified projects:* Specified identified projects are treated as tax-exempt obligations acquired before 8-8-86 belonging to the first and all subsequent financial institutions acquiring the obligations.

There is an additional transitional rule that treats obligations issued under an allocation of a particular state's volume limitations for private activity bonds as acquired on or before 8-7-86 in the hands of the first and all subsequent financial institutions acquiring the obligations.

Act Sec. 902, denying financial institutions 100% of interest deduction allocable to tax-exempt obligations, amends Sec. 265 by striking out the second sentence from Sec. 265(2), by designating Sec. 265(1)-(4) as Sec. 265(a), and by adding Sec. 265(b), amends 291(e)(1)(B), Sec. 291(e)(1)(B)(i), and Sec. 291(e)(1)(B)(ii), and is effective for obligations acquired after 8-7-86 for interest incurred after 12-31-86 and as shown above according to the transitional exceptions. Clerical amendments to Act Sec. 902.

[¶903]   Net Operating Losses for Financial Institutions. The new law repeals the special rules for commercial banks and thrift institutions which allow them to carry net operating losses back to the preceding 10 tax years and forward to the succeeding 5 tax years. Now these financial institutions are subject to the same general rule as all other taxpayers, who are allowed to carry back net operating losses 3 tax years and forward 15 tax years.

Effective Date: Generally the new law is effective for bank and thrift NOLs incurred in tax years after 12-31-86; however, it has special carryover rules for banks and thrift institutions.

Special commercial bank rule retained. The new law retains the special 10-year carryback for commercial banks (not including thrift institutions) for that portion of NOLs attributable to bad debts for losses incurred in tax years beginning before 1994. Under this special rule, the portion of a commercial bank's NOLs attributable to deductions for losses on bad debts is the excess of the NOL for the taxable year over the net operating loss for that taxable year computed without regard to any deduction for losses or bad debts.

Special thrift rule. The new law allows thrift institutions that have incurred losses in tax years after 12-31-81 and before 1-1-86 to carry forward net operating losses to eight years. Under the prior law, they could only carry them forward five years. Also, for losses incurred by thrift institutions after 12-31-81 and before 1-1-86, the new law retains the prior law's special 10-year carryback rule.

The 18-year total carryover period is equal to the total carryover period available to taxpayers generally (3-year carryback and 15-year carryforward).

Act Sec. 903, repealing the special rules for net operating losses of financial institutions generally, amends Sec. 172(b)(1)(F), 172(b)(1)(G), and 172(b)(1)(H), effective for NOLs incurred after 12-31-86, and as shown above; special commercial bank rule on carryover period of NOLs incurred after 12-31-86 and before 1-1-94, amending Sec. 172(b)(1)(A), Sec. 172(b)(1)(B), redesignating Sec. 172(l) as 172(m) and adding new Sec. 172(l), adding new Sec. 172(b)(1)(L); adding special thrift rule on carryover period of NOLs incurred after 12-31-81 and before 1-1-86, adding Sec. 172(b)(1)(M).

[¶904] **Special Rules for Financially Troubled Thrifts.** The new law repeals the special rules relating to tax-free reorganizations, net operating loss carryovers, and FSLIC contributions which provide tax relief to financially troubled thrift institutions. Thrifts no longer will receive preferential tax treatment in these areas to the detriment of other taxpayers.

> **IMPORTANT:** New acquisitions and reorganizations involving financially troubled thrifts are subject to the same rules as any other reorganized corporation.

Tax-free reorganization status. The new law repeals the special provisions that provide a tax-free reorganization for the merger of a financially troubled thrift into another corporation. Under prior law, as long as certain conditions were met, a merger of a financially troubled thrift into another corporation qualified as a tax-free reorganization without complying with the continuity of interest requirement of Sec. 368.

Net operating loss carryovers. Under the new law, the special treatment of net operating losses in a financially troubled thrift are repealed. Prior law provided that when a financially troubled thrift was involved in a tax-free reorganization, the requirements to avoid limitations on net operating loss carryovers under Sec. 382 were considered met.

IMPORTANT: The new law substantially changes the special limitations on the use of NOL carryforwards under Sec. 382 and Sec. 383 [see ¶606 et seq.].

Special exception. The conversion of a mutual savings and loan association holding a federal charter dated 3-22-85, to a stock savings and loan association under the rules and regulations of the Federal Home Loan Bank Board, is specially excepted from the application of Sec. 383 under the new law.

FSLIC contributions. Under the new law, payments by the Federal Savings and Loan Insurance Corporation to financially troubled thrifts in connection with a merger are no longer excluded from the recipient thrift's income and no longer exempt from the general requirement that a taxpayer's basis in its assets be reduced by nonshareholder contributions to capital.

Expenses allocable to tax-exempt income. The new law provides that the FSLIC payments to financially troubled thrifts that were exempt under the prior law exclusion aren't subject to the provision disallowing a deduction for expenses attributable to such payments.

Effective Date: The repeal of the special rules are effective for acquisitions or mergers occurring after 12-31-88. The repeal of the special treatment for FSLIC payments is effective for payments made after 12-31-88, unless the payments are made under an acquisition or merger occurring on or before 12-31-88.

Act Sec. 904, repealing special rules for financially troubled thrifts involving tax-free reorganizations, net operating loss carryovers, and FSLIC contributions, repeals Sec. 597 and amends Sec. 265(a)(1) and Sec. 368(a)(3)(D), and is effective for acquisitions after 12-31-88 and for FSLIC contributions after 12-31-88, except as shown above.

[¶905] **Losses on Deposits in Insolvent Financial Institutions.** Because circumstances surrounding deposits in financial institutions are different from debts owed to taxpayers, the new law allows qualified individuals to elect to deduct losses on deposits arising from the insolvency or bankruptcy of a qualified financial institution as a casualty loss in the year in which the amount of the loss is reasonably estimated. The election must be made on the tax return for the taxable year and once made, cannot be changed without the IRS's consent.

Under prior law, a loss realized by a taxpayer from a deposit or account in a financial institution was deductible in the year it was determined that there was no prospect of recovery in the same manner as any other type of bad debt loss. Also, unless the deposit was created or acquired in connection with the taxpayer's trade or business, the loss on the deposit was treated as a short-term capital loss (the deduction of which is limited under the IRC).

Definitions. A qualified individual is any individual other than a 1% stock owner in the institution in which the loss was sustained, an officer of that institution, or certain relatives or "related persons" (as defined in Sec. 267(b)) of those owners or officers.

A qualified financial institution is a commercial bank (as defined in Sec. 581), a thrift institution (as defined in Sec. 591), a federally insured or state-insured or guaranteed credit union, or any other similar institution supervised or chartered under federal or state law.

Deposit means any deposit, withdrawable certificate, or withdrawable or repurchasable share of or in a qualified financial institution under the new law.

Under the new law, qualified individuals that elect to treat the loss on a deposit in a qualified financial institution as a casualty loss can't deduct the loss as a bad debt under Sec. 166.

IMPORTANT: The election applies only when the loss is caused by the insolvency or bankruptcy of the financial institution.

Qualified individuals don't have to claim the loss in the year in which the loss is first reasonably estimated. They can claim the loss in a later year either as a casualty loss deduction or as a bad debt deduction.

Method of accounting. Once the election is made, it's an election of an accounting method for the taxpayer with regard to all deposits in that qualified financial institution and requires that all the taxpayer's other losses on other deposits in the institution be treated in the same manner.

Amount of loss recognized. The amount of loss recognized under the election is the difference between the taxpayer's basis in the deposit and the amount which is a reasonable estimate of the deposit amount that will eventually be received.

Recovery of loss. If a loss that has been claimed as a casualty deduction is later recovered, then the lesser of the recovery amount or the tax benefit received from the election is included in income in the year of the recovery.

Interest treatment on frozen deposits. The new law specially provides for the treatment of interest on frozen deposits in certain financial institutions. Frozen deposits are deposits which, as of the close of the calendar year, may not be withdrawn because the qualified financial institution is threatened with bankruptcy or insolvency or is actually bankrupt or insolvent.

Under the new law, accrued, but unpaid interest on a deposit in a qualified financial institution for taxable years beginning after 12-31-82 and before 1-1-87, isn't includible in the depositor's taxable income for the taxable year when such interest isn't subject to withdrawal at the end of the taxable year. The interest income is includible in gross income in the taxable year in which the interest is withdrawable. Interest not included in gross income is treated as credited in the next calendar year.

Qualified individuals making this election must have it apply to the taxable year period beginning after 12-31-82 and before 1-1-87.

Qualified financial institutions can't take deductions for interest not includible in gross income until the interest is includible in gross income. For interest attributable to the period beginning 1-1-83 and ending on 12-31-87, the interest deduction of financial institutions is determined without regard to the qualified institution's interest deduction deferral.

Act Sec. 905, treatment of losses on deposits in insolvent financial institutions, adding new Sec. 165(l); prior Sec. 165(l) redesignated as Sec. 165(m), adding new sec. 451(f), effective for all tax years beginning after 12-31-82, and as shown above.

[The page following this is 1001.]

INSURANCE PRODUCTS AND COMPANIES

Life Insurance Products

[¶1001] Survivor-Spouse's $1,000 Annual Exclusion. Under the new law, all amounts paid to any beneficiary of a life insurance policy at a date later than the death of the insured (i.e., paid in installments or as an annuity) are included in gross income to the extent the amount paid exceeds the amount payable as a death benefit. The exclusion of the first $1,000 in excess of the pro rata portion of the death benefit from the annual gross income of the surviving spouse is repealed.

If an insurer pays insurance death proceeds to a beneficiary in installments or as an annuity, old law treated a prorated amount of each installment as a nontaxable payment of the death benefit, with the remainder generally includible in gross income. However, the first $1,000 received by a surviving spouse in any year in excess of the amount treated as a payment of the death benefit was excludable from gross income.

The new law requires insurers to compute the nontaxable annuity income based on sex-neutral mortality tables.

Act Sec. 1001 repeals Sec. 101(d), $1,000 interest exclusion from income of survivor-spouse.

[¶1002] Structured Settlements. Old law excluded from income any amount received because of personal injury or sickness, whether as a lump-sum or periodically and whether by suit or agreement. The person liable to pay periodic amounts may assign the liability to a life insurance company. The amount paid to the insurer for agreeing to fund the liability isn't included in the insurer's income.

The new law repeals the insurer's tax break for all structured settlements except "qualified assignments"; i.e., settlements resulting from personal injury or sickness. Damages awarded for any other torts don't qualify. So the full amount paid to the insurance company in these latter cases is included in its gross income.

However, the *annuitant's* structured settlement tax break is unaffected by the new law.

Rev. Rul. 79-220 [CB 1979-2 p. 74] shows how to structure tax-free annuity payments under Sec. 104(a)(2) in settlement of a suit for personal injuries.

Example: Brown sues Aker for personal injury damages. Before the trial, Brown accepts Aker's casualty insurance company's offer to settle for (1) a lump-sum payment of $80,000 and (2) $30,000 a year in monthly payments of $2,500 for the longer of Brown's lifetime or

20 years. To provide the $2,500 monthly payments, the casualty company buys a single-premium 20-years-certain immediate annuity from a life insurance company. Payments are made directly to Brown, but the casualty company owns the annuity contract.

Rev. Rul. 79-220 says the full amount of the monthly payments is excludable from Brown's income under Sec. 104(a)(2). Purchase of the annuity from the life insurance company was merely an investment by the casualty company to guarantee the funds to satisfy its continuing obligation to Brown.

Act Sec. 1002 amends Sec. 130 and adds new Sec. 197 to include the full amount paid to an insurer to assume the obligation to make periodic payments under the assignment and deduct the cost of the asset used to fund the payouts.

[¶1003] **Policyholder Loans.** The new law retains the present rule that amounts paid or accrued on debt to buy or maintain a single premium life insurance policy, including a contract in which an amount is deposited to pay a substantial number of premiums, are not deductible. Moreover, the deduction for interest on a policyholder loan is denied for loans to officers, employees, or owners of an interest in a trade or business of the taxpayer if such loans are, in the aggregate, more than $50,000 per officer, employee, or owner.

Act Sec. 1003 amends Code Sec. 264(a)(1) effective for interest on loans under policies purchased after 6-20-86.

[¶1004] **Personal Casualty Losses.** Under the new law, to the extent that a personal casualty loss of an individual is covered by insurance, it will be taken into account in figuring the personal casualty loss deduction only if the individual files a timely insurance claim for that loss.

Act Sec. 1004 adds new Sec. 165(h)(4)(E), effective for losses sustained in tax years beginning after 12-31-86.

[¶1005] **Funeral Expense Policies.** The new law provides that small burial policies may qualify as life insurance policies even though the policy provides for future increases in death benefits. To qualify, the initial death benefit under the policy must be $5,000 or less, and the contract must provide for fixed annual increases in the death benefit of no more than 10% of the initial death benefit, or 8% of the death benefit at the end of the immediately preceding year, provided the aggregate amount doesn't exceed $25,000.

Ed. note: The first printing of the conference bill contained no statutory language on this provision. This may be subject to a technical correction. As passed by the Conference Committee, the provision is effective for contracts issued after 12-31-84.

Life Insurance Companies

[¶1011] **Special Life Insurance Company Deduction Repealed.** The 20% special life insurance company deduction was enacted as part of the 1984 Tax Reform Act to ease the sudden, substantial increase in life insurance company tax liability. With the new law's overall reduction of corporate tax rates, this special relief is no longer necessary. Thus, the new law repeals the 20% special life insurance company deduction for tax years beginning after 12-31-86.

Certain debt-financed stock acquisitions. The new law also amends the special rule that applies when a life insurance company owns the stock of another corporation through a partnership, and acquired that stock through debt financing on 1-14-81. In determining the small life insurance company deduction under amended Sec. 806(a), tentative life insurance company taxable income is computed without taking into account any income, gain, loss, or deduction that's attributable to the ownership of that stock. Further, $^{46}/_{36.8}$ of any income, gain, loss, or deduction that's attributable to the ownership of that stock is taken into account in determining the company's taxable income.

Special rate on certain bonds. Despite the new law's repeal of corporate capital gains treatment, any gain recognized by any of 15 specified life insurance companies on redemption at maturity of any bond issued before 7-19-84 and acquired by the company before 9-25-85 is subject to tax at a 28% rate.

Act Sec. 1011(a) repeals Sec. 806(a) and redesignates Secs. 806(b), (c), and (d) as Secs. 806(a), (b), and (c), respectively. Act Sec. 1011(b) makes technical and conforming amendments to Secs. 453B(e)(2)(B), 465(c)(7)(D)(v), 801(a)(2)(C), 804, 805, 806, 813(a)(4)(A), 815(c)(2)(A)(ii), and the table of sections for subpart C of part I of subchapter L. Act Sec. 1011(c)(2) amends Sec. 217(k) of the 1984 TRA, relating to the special rule for certain debt-financed stock acquisitions. Act Sec. 1011(d), relating to the special rate on certain bonds, doesn't amend the Code. The provisions of Act Sec. 1011 are generally effective for tax years beginning after 12-31-86.

[¶1012] **Operations Loss Deduction of Insolvent Life Insurance Companies.** Before 1984, stock life insurance companies were allowed certain special deductions and had to add the amount of those deductions to a deferred tax account known as the policyholders surplus account (PSA). The tax deferral on these amounts ended when they were distributed to shareholders and in certain other situations. Amounts included in the company's income as a result of the ending of deferral couldn't be offset by the company's loss from operations or operations loss carryovers.

The 1984 Tax Reform Act repealed the deductions that gave rise to additions to the PSA. But while a stock life insurance company can no longer add amounts to its PSA, it must maintain its existing account and include in income amounts distributed directly or indirectly to shareholders from that account.

The new law creates an exception to the rule that includable income from PSA distributions can't be offset by current operations losses or unused loss carryovers. Under the new law, a stock life insurance company can apply such losses and loss carryovers against taxable income attributable to PSA distributions if

- the company was insolvent (its liabilities exceeded the fair market value of its assets) on 11-15-85;
- the company is liquidated under court order in a title 11 or similar case; and
- PSA distributions resulting from the liquidation would increase the company's tax liability for the liquidation year.

No carryover of any operations loss of the company that arises during or before the liquidation year can be used in any tax year following the liquidation year.

Act Sec. 1013, which does not amend the Code, is effective for liquidations on or after 11-15-85, in tax years ending after that date.

[¶1013] **Tax Exempts Engaged in Insurance Activities.** Under the new law, a charity or social welfare organization is tax exempt only if no substantial part of its activities consists of providing commercial-type insurance. "No substantial part" has the same meaning as under prior law applying to these organizations.

UBI. If the organization is tax exempt, the providing of commercial-type insurance is treated as unrelated business income. However, the insurance activities are taxed under the rules relating to insurance companies (Subchapter L of the Code) and not taxed under the UBI rules.

Commercial-type insurance generally is any insurance of a type provided by insurance companies. The issuance of annuity contracts is treated as providing insurance. Providing insurance or annuities under a qualified pension plan isn't considered providing commercial-type insurance.

Exceptions. Commercial-type insurance doesn't include

- insurance provided at substantially below cost to a class of charitable recipients;
- health insurance provided by a health maintenance organization of a kind customarily provided by these organizations and is incidental to the organization's principal activity of providing

health care. Organizations providing supplemental HMO-type services (such as dental services) also aren't affected by the new law if they operate in the same way as an HMO;

• property and casualty insurance provided directly or through a wholly owned corporation by a church or convention or association of churches for the organization. Property or casualty insurance doesn't include life, accident, and health insurance (whether or not cancelable). This exception doesn't apply if the insurance is provided not only to the church, but also to other persons;

• retirement and welfare benefits provided by a church, etc., directly or indirectly for the organization's employees and their beneficiaries. This exception doesn't apply if the insurance is provided to others.

Blue Cross/Blue Shield organizations. The new law provides special treatment for existing Blue Cross/Blue Shield organizations and other organizations that meet certain requirements and substantially all of whose activities are providing health insurance. Health insurance includes insurance that provides coverage of medical expenses.

Special treatment. The special treatment applies to Blue Cross/Blue Shield organizations that

• were in existence on 8-16-86;

• are determined at that time to be tax exempt and the exemption hasn't been revoked; and

• were tax exempt for the last tax year beginning before 1-1-87, provided that no material change occurs in the structure or operations of the organization after 8-16-86, and before the close of 1986 or any later tax year.

Material change in operations. According to the Conference Report, the Treasury must apply the following principles in determining whether a material change in operations or structure occurred.

• The merger or split up of one or more existing Blue Cross/Blue Shield organizations won't be a material change in operation or structure.

• If an existing Blue Cross/Blue Shield organization acquires a new line of business or is acquired by another business (other than a health business), the acquisition isn't a material change in operations or structure of the organization if (1) the assets of the other business are a de minimis percentage (that is, less than 10%) of the assets of the existing Blue Cross/Blue Shield organization at the time of the acquisition, or (2) the taxpayer can demonstrate to the Treasury that, based on all the facts and circumstances, the acquisition isn't a material change in operations or structure of the existing Blue Cross/Blue Shield organization.

• A material change in operations occurs if an existing Blue Cross/Blue Shield organization drops its high-risk coverage or substantially changes the terms and conditions under which high-risk coverage is offered by the organization from the terms and conditions in effect as of 8-16-86. A change in high-risk coverage is considered substantial if the effect of the change is to defeat the purpose of high-risk coverage. High-risk coverage for this purpose generally means the coverage of individuals and small groups to the extent the organization (1) provides coverage under specified terms and conditions as of 8-16-86, or (2) meets the statutory minimum definition of high-risk coverage for new organizations. A material change in operations doesn't occur if an existing organization alters its operations to provide high-risk coverage that meets the minimum standards under the new law for new Blue Cross/Blue Shield organizations.

The Conference Report states that, to the extent such determinations of tax exemption for any tax year beginning before 1987 weren't under audit or in litigation before 8-16-86, the IRS won't seek to revoke the determinations.

Existing organizations. Existing Blue Cross/Blue Shield organizations and other organizations eligible for this treatment are subject to tax as stock property and casualty insurance companies.

A special deduction is provided to these organizations as to their health business equal to 25% of the claims and expenses incurred during the tax year less the adjusted surplus at the beginning of the tax year. This deduction is calculated by computing surplus, taxable income, claims incurred, expenses incurred, tax-exempt income, and NOL carryovers, attributable to health business. Thus, the deduction isn't allowable as to items attributable to life insurance business. The expenses attributable to health business are those incurred during the tax year in connection with the administration, adjustment, or settlement of claims under health business. The deduction can't exceed taxable income attributable to health business for the year (calculated without regard to this deduction).

For organizations eligible for this deduction in the first tax year beginning after 12-31-86, the amount of the adjusted surplus to be applied in the first year for which the deduction is allowable is the surplus reported on the organization's annual statement (that is the annual statement approved by the National Association of Insurance Commissioners) at the close of the preceding year, adjusted by not taking into account distributions (such as distributions to shareholders, or contributions or loans to affiliates that reduce surplus, but not including ordinary and necessary expenses or deductible policyholder dividends) after 8-16-86. For orgniazations that first become eligible for the provision in a later tax year, the amount of the adjusted surplus for the first year of the deduction is the surplus reported on the annual statement at the close of the preceding year.

The initial surplus amount is adjusted under the provision at the close of each tax year by adding the taxable income or loss of the organization for the year (determined without regard to NOL carryovers and without regard to the deduction under this provision), plus net tax-exempt income for the year. Net tax-exempt income means dividends for which the dividends received deduction was allowed, and interest that is tax exempt, less the expenses of earning the tax-exempt interest that were disallowed under Sec. 265, and less the adjustment that was made for proration of tax-exempt income under Sec. 805(a) or 832(b)(5). If an organization eligible for the deduction doesn't take the deduction in any year, adjusted surplus must be calculated for the intervening years between the last year the organization took the deduction and the next year in which it takes the deduction, so as to take account properly of the calculation of the deduction in the later year.

The deduction applies only for regular tax purposes. Thus, the deduction is treated as a preference item for purposes of the corporate minimum tax.

In addition to this special deduction, these organizations are given a fresh start as to changes in accounting methods resulting from the change from tax exempt to taxable status. No adjustment is made under Section 481 on account of an accounting method change.

These organizations aren't subject to the treatment of unearned premium reserves generally applicable to property and casualty insurance companies. To ease the transition from tax exempt to taxable status, Blue Cross/Blue Shield organizations were given relief from the requirement that 20% of the increase in unearned premium reserves be included in income.

Finally, the basis of assets of these organizations is equal, for purposes of determining gain or loss, to the amount of the assets' FMV on the first day of the organizations's tax year beginning after 12-31-86. Thus, for formerly tax-exempt organizations using a calendar year and whose first tax year begins 1-1-87, the basis of each asset of the organization is equal to the amount of its FMV value on 1-1-87. The basis step-up is provided solely for purposes of determining gain or loss on sale or exchange of the assets, not for purposes of determining amounts of depreciation or for other purposes.

New organizations. The above special provisions apply to existing tax-exempt Blue Cross/Blue Shield organizations and to those other organizations that satisfy the additional criteria described below.

¶1013

Other organizations, to receive the special treatment described above, must meet these requirements.

- At least 10% of the health insurance (determined as a percentage of the total number of individuals covered annually) provided by the organization must be provided to individuals and small groups (disregarding Medicare supplemental coverage). A "small group" is the lesser of 15 individuals or the number of individuals required for a small group under the state law where the covered groups are located.

- The organization must provide continuous full-year open enrollment for individuals and small groups. Open enrollment includes conversions from group to individual coverage, without a lapse in coverage, provided the individual seeking to convert from group to individual coverage notifies the organization providing group coverage of his conversion request by the date of his separation from service. Conversion includes any change in the type of coverage.

- Any individual seeking health insurance must be offered coverage that includes coverage of pre-existing conditions of high-risk individuals without a price differential and the coverage becomes effective within a reasonable waiting period after the time coverage is sought. According to the Conference Report a reasonable waiting period is intended to be not more than three months. Further, health insurance coverage must be provided regardless of age, income, or employment status of persons under 65.

- At least 35% of the organization's health insurance premiums are determined on a community-rated basis. This is determined as a percentage of the total number of persons covered on an annual basis. Community rating means that premiums are determined on the basis of the average annual cost of health insurance over the population in the community.

- The organization must be organized and operated in a manner so that no part of the net earnings inures to any private shareholder's or individual's benefit.

- Substantially all of the organizations activities involve providing health insurance.

Fraternal societies. As to tax-exempt fraternal beneficiary societies that are engaged in insurance activities, the new law reemphasizes the requirement of prior law that they must keep an active lodge system. Also, the Treasury must audit and study tax-exempt fraternal beneficiary organizations that received gross annual insurance premiums exceeding $25 million in tax year 1984. The organization's use of revenue from insurance activities will also be studied. The results of the study and recommendations must be submitted to the House Ways and Means Committee, the Senate Finance Committee, and the Joint Committee on Taxation by 1-1-88.

Special rules. The provision is effective for tax years beginning after 12-31-86. A special rule for Mutual of America provides that this provision won't apply as to that portion of its business attributable to pension business. Another special rule for Teachers Insurance Annuity Association-College Retirement Equities Fund (TIAA-CREF) provides that this provision won't apply for that portion of its business attributable to pension business. For that purpose, pension business means administering qualified pension plans, tax-deferred annuities, unfunded deferred compensation plans of state and local governments, and individual retirement arrangements. Exceptions from the general provision are also provided for the YMCA (retirement fund), for administrative services performed by municipal leagues, for the Missouri Hospital Association, and for the dental benefit coverage by Delta Dental Plans Association through contracts with independent service providers so long as the provision of coverage is the principal activity of the Association. The Conference Committee doesn't intend any inference as to whether performing administrative service by tax-exempt municipal leagues, without more, is commercial-type insurance activities. Generally, however, performing administrative services as to insurance contracts by tax-exempt organizations may be subject to UBI.

Act Sec. 1012 redesignates Sec. 501(m) as Sec. 501(n) and adds new Sec. 501(m), relating to tax exemption of organizations engaged in insurance activities, and adds new Sec. 833, relating to treatment of Blue Cross/Blue Shield organizations effective as shown above.

[¶1014] Discounting Unpaid Losses. Under the new law, unpaid losses of life insurance companies—other than losses on life insurance contracts, which are discounted under life insurance rules—are subject to the new discounting rules applicable to unpaid losses of property and casualty companies. But unlike property and casualty companies, loss adjustment expenses of life insurance companies aren't subject to discounting. *Reason:* They're not deductible. This new rule applies for purposes of Secs. 805(a)(1) and 807(c)(2). For an explanation of the discounting rule, see ¶1022.

Act Sec. 1023 amends Secs. 807(c), 832(b)(5)(A)(ii) (as amended by Act Sec. 1022), and 832(b)(6), and adds new Sec. 846, effective for tax years beginning after 12-31-86.

Property and Casualty Insurance Companies

[¶1021] Unearned Premiums of P&C Companies. Under the new law, property and casualty companies (stock and mutual) can generally deduct only 80% of any *increase* in unearned premiums—or, conversely, must generally include only 80% of any *decrease* in unearned premiums —in figuring "premiums earned." Premiums earned, less losses incurred and expenses incurred, make up a P&C company's underwriting income.

> **Example:** At the end of 1986, PC Insurance Company, a calendar-year taxpayer, had $1,000 of unearned premiums on outstanding business. At the end of 1987, PC's unearned premiums totalled $1,100. In figuring premiums earned for 1987, PC's net deduction for the $100 increase in unearned premiums is $80 ($100 × 80%). (Under prior law, 100% of the increase would have been deductible.) At the end of 1988, PC's unearned premiums declined to $900. PC must include $160 ($200 × 80%) of the $200 decrease in figuring premiums earned for 1988.

Life insurance reserves that are included in unearned premiums aren't subject to this reduced 80% deduction/inclusion rule. Thus, increases and decreases in these reserves are still taken into account 100% in figuring premiums earned.

Also, the new law provides a special rule for insurance against default in payment of principal or interest on certain securities (including bonds, debentures, and notes) that have a maturity of more than five years. For such insurance, P&C companies can deduct 90% of the increase in unearned premiums and must include in income 90% of any decrease. Insurance on securities with a maturity of five years or less is subject to the general 80% rule.

Treatment of outstanding balances. The new law also provides that P&C companies must include in income 20% of the amount of unearned premiums outstanding at the end of the most recent tax year beginning before 1-1-87. This 20% is includable ratably over a six-year period, starting with the first tax year beginning after 12-31-86. Thus, 3⅓% of the amount outstanding is includable in each year of the period. This amount is included in income by adding it into the computation of premiums earned. Amounts attributable to life insurance reserves aren't taken into account in applying this ratable inclusion rule.

> **Example:** At the end of 1986, PC Insurance Company, a calendar-year taxpayer, had $1,000 of unearned premiums (no part of which is attributable to life insurance reserves) on outstanding business. PC must include in income $33.33 a year ($1,000 × 3⅓%) for 1987 through 1992. Thus, over the six tax years beginning after 1986, PC will have included in income 20% (6 × 3⅓%) of its 1986 year-end unearned premiums.

For unearned premiums that are attributable to insurance against default on securities with a maturity of more than five years, 10% of the amount outstanding at the end of the most recent tax year beginning before 1-1-87 must be included in income. This 10% is includable ratably over a six-year period, starting with the first tax year beginning after 12-31-86. Thus, 1⅔% of the amount outstanding is includable in each of the six years of the period.

If a company ceases to be taxable as a P&C company during the ratable-inclusion period, the inclusion schedule is accelerated. Thus, the remaining amount that's subject to the ratable-inclusion rule is included in the company's income for the tax year *preceding* the year in which the company ceases to be taxed as a P&C company. This rule applies only if a company ceases to be a P&C company for a tax year beginning before 1-1-93.

> **Example:** At the end of 1986, PC Insurance Company, a calendar-year taxpayer, had $1,000 of unearned premiums on outstanding business. No part of that $1,000 is attributable to life insurance reserves or insurance against default on securities. Thus, $200 (20% of $1,000) is subject to the ratable-inclusion rule. For 1987, PC includes $33.33 (3⅓% of $1,000) in income. For 1988, it includes the same amount. If PC ceases to be a property and casualty insurance company for tax year 1990, the amount it must include in income for 1989 is $133.34—that is, $200 minus the total amount it included in 1987 and 1988 ($66.66).

This acceleration of the inclusion schedule doesn't apply to the extent that a successor insurance company is subject to the requirements of Sec. 381(c)(22) (relating to carryovers of a transferor's corporate attributes in certain corporate readjustments).

Title insurers exempt. Title insurers are exempt from the reduced 80% deduction/inclusion rule. Instead, the new law applies discounting to title insurance state law unearned premium reserves. In applying the discounting rule, "undiscounted unearned premiums" at the end of the tax year is the amount of unearned premiums shown on the yearly statement filed for the year ending with or within that tax year. The discounting period is the period over which the unearned premium reserves are deferred under state law. Premiums received during any calendar year are treated as received in the middle of that year. The discount rate is the rate generally applicable to property and casualty insurance companies (see ¶1022). Title insurance case reserves are subject to discounting under the same method as property and casualty insurance loss reserves (see ¶1022).

Under a transitional rule for the first tax year beginning after 12-31-86, the amount of title insurance unearned premiums at the end of the preceding tax year (as defined in Sec. 832(b)(4)) is determined as if the discounting provisions had applied to the unearned premiums in that preceding tax year. In applying the discounting methodology for that preceding tax year, the interest rate and premium recognition pattern applicable to years ending in 1987 are used.

Under a fresh-start rule, any difference between the undiscounted and discounted unearned premiums for that preceding tax year generally isn't taken into account in determining a company's taxable income—but it will increase the company's E&P for its first tax year beginning after 12-31-86.

Act Sec. 1021 amends Sec. 832(b)(4)(B) (relating to the computation of premiums earned) and adds new Secs. 832(b)(4)(C) and 832(b)(7) effective generally for tax years beginning after 12-31-86. New Secs. 832(b)(4)(C) and 832(b)(7)(B)(ii) (relating to the inclusion in income of a percentage of unearned premiums outstanding at the end of the most recent tax year beginning before 1-1-87) are effective ratably over the six tax years beginning after 12-31-86 and before 1-1-93.

【¶1022】 Discounting Unpaid Losses. To take into account the time value of money, the new law imposes a pretax discounting rule on a P&C company's unpaid losses (reported losses that haven't been paid, estimates of losses incurred but not reported, resisted claims, and unpaid loss adjustment expenses).

A P&C company's underwriting income equals its premiums earned during the tax year, less expenses incurred and losses incurred. Under the new law, losses incurred in the tax year equals (1) losses paid, increased by (2) salvage and reinsurance recoverable outstanding at the end of the preceding tax year, and decreased by (3) salvage and reinsurance recoverable outstanding at the end of the current tax year; and the result of steps (1) through (3) is further increased by (4) unpaid losses on life insurance contracts plus *discounted* unpaid losses outstanding at the end of the current tax year, and then decreased by (5) unpaid losses on life insurance contracts, and *discounted* unpaid losses outstanding at the end of the preceding tax year. (Losses incurred may be further reduced by the new law's proration provision for certain dividends and tax-exempt income. See ¶1032.)

Discounted unpaid losses at the end of a particular tax year is the sum of the discounted unpaid losses (as of the end of that tax year) attributable to—and separately computed for—each accident year for each line of business. The amount of discounted unpaid losses attributable to a particular accident year is the present value of those losses as of the end of the tax year, figured by using (1) the undiscounted unpaid losses as of the end of the tax year, (2) the applicable interest rate, and (3) the applicable loss payment pattern for each line of business.

> **LIMIT:** The amount of *discounted* unpaid losses attributable to any accident year for any line of business can't exceed the aggregate amount of unpaid losses for that accident year and line of business as reported on the company's annual statement for the year ending with or within the tax year.

Definitions. "Accident year" means the calendar year in which the incident occurs that gives rise to the related unpaid loss.

"Line of business" means a category for the reporting of claims and claim payments on the NAIC-approved annual statement (Schedules O and P) for fire and casualty companies. Multiple peril lines, however, are treated as a single line of business.

"Undiscounted unpaid losses" are generally equal to the unpaid losses shown on the P&C company's annual statement for the fiscal year ending with or within the company's tax year, and include unpaid loss adjustment expenses shown on the statement. (Unpaid loss adjustment expenses won't be included in "expenses unpaid" in computing expenses incurred.) If any unpaid losses are discounted on the annual statement, they can be grossed up to their undiscounted amount, provided that the extent of the discounting can be determined from information disclosed on or with the annual statement.

The "applicable interest rate" is the rate for the calendar year with which the accident year ends. The rate will be determined by the Treasury, and will be phased in to 100% of a 60-month rolling average of applicable federal midterm rates (based on annual compounding). No month beginning before 8-1-86 will be included in the 60-month period.

The "applicable loss payment pattern" is the pattern for the calendar year with which the accident year ends. The loss payment pattern will be determined by the Treasury for each line of business once every five years starting with 1987. Thus, the loss payment pattern determined for 1987 will be the pattern for calendar years 1987 through 1991. The Treasury will determine the pattern based on the historical loss payment pattern for each line of business. The Treasury's determination must be made (1) by using the aggregate experience reported on relevant insurance company annual statements, (2) on the basis of the most recent published aggregate loss payment pattern data available on the first day of the determination year, (3) by assuming that all losses paid during a year are paid in the middle of that year, and (4) by applying a series of computational rules and assumptions provided under the new law.

The computational rules assume that losses on Schedule O lines are paid over a 4-year period, and that losses on Schedule P lines are paid over an 11-year period, starting with the accident year. For Schedule O lines, losses unpaid at the end of year 2 are treated as paid equally in years 3 and 4. For Schedule P lines, losses paid after the end of the 11-year period are generally treated as paid in year 11. But under a special limitation rule, the amount treated as paid in year 11 can't exceed the amount treated as paid in year 10. If the amount treated as paid in year 10 is zero or a negative amount, then the limitation rule is applied by using the average of the amounts treated as paid in years 8, 9, and 10, instead of the amount treated as paid in year 10. The Conference Report indicates that if the three-year average results in a negative amount, additional preceding years should be averaged in successively until the average is positive. The 11-year period can be extended by up to 5 years to take into account any excess. However, the amount that can be treated as paid in each year of the extension period is subject to the same limitation that applies to year 11—that is, it can't exceed the amount treated as paid in year 10. Any balance that remains at the end of the fifth year of the extension period is treated as paid in that fifth year.

A company can elect to apply the discounting rules for all its lines of business by using its *own* loss payment pattern for the most recent calendar year for which it filed an annual statement before the beginning of the accident year. The company must use the same series of computational rules and assumptions as the Treasury must use, including the assumption that all losses paid during a year are paid in the middle of that year. The election is available for each determination year, which is calendar year 1987 and every fifth year thereafter. Once the taxpayer makes a determination, it can't later redetermine its loss payment pattern to adjust for more recent information. The election isn't available for international or reinsurance lines. The Treasury is authorized to issue whatever regulations are necessary to carry out the purposes of this provision.

International and reinsurance lines. Under the new law, the discounting of unpaid losses for international and reinsurance lines of business is generally to be implemented by using a loss payment pattern determined by the Treasury based on a composite of all Schedule P lines (auto liability, other liability, medical malpractice, workers' compensation, and multiple peril). However, the Treasury is authorized to issue regulations requiring a company to follow a different loss payment pattern for international and reinsurance lines.

The Conference Report indicates that international and reinsurance business that is allocated to a particular line of business is discounted under the rules applicable to that line, and not under the general rule for international and reinsurance business.

Certain accident and health lines. Active life reserves for life insurance and noncancellable accident and health benefits that are subject to the life company reserve rules aren't subject to the new discounted unpaid loss rules. Also, unpaid losses relating to disability insurance (other than credit disability insurance) are to be determined under the general rules applicable to noncancellable accident and health contracts of life companies (Sec. 807(d)), with several adjustments.

For both life and P&C companies, accident and health coverage (other than disability) that isn't subject to the life company reserve requirements (for example, cancellable accident and health coverage) is subject to the discounting rules. However, instead of using a loss payment pattern, the rules will be applied on the assumption that unpaid losses are paid in the year following the accident year. (See also ¶1014.)

Title insurance. For title insurance companies, discounting applies to title insurance state law unearned premium reserves (see ¶1021). The discounting period is the period over which the reserves are deferred under state law. The discount rate is the rate generally applicable to P&C companies. Title insurance case reserves are discounted under the same method as P&C insurance loss reserves.

Effective Date: The new provisions for unpaid losses are effective for tax years beginning after 12-31-86. Under a transitional rule for the first tax year beginning after 12-31-86, the unpaid losses and expenses (as defined in Sec. 832(b)(5)(B), (6)) at the end of the preceding tax year as well as the unpaid losses (as defined in Secs. 807(c)(2) and 805(a)(1)) at the end of the preceding tax year are determined *as if* the discounting provisions had applied to the unpaid losses in that preceding tax year. In applying the discounting methodology for that preceding tax year, the interest rate and loss payment patterns for accident years ending with calendar year 1987 are used.

Under a fresh-start rule, any difference between the undiscounted and discounted unpaid losses for that preceding tax year generally aren't taken into account in determining a company's taxable income—but it will increase the company's E&P for its first tax year beginning after 12-31-86.

Further, the fresh-start rule won't apply to any reserve strengthening in a tax year beginning in 1986. Any such reserve strengthening will be treated as made in the company's first tax year beginning after 12-31-86.

Act Sec. 1023 amends Secs. 832(b)(5)(A)(ii) (as amended by Act Sec. 1022), 832(b)(6), and 807(c), and adds new Sec. 846, effective for tax years beginning after 12-31-86. It also makes a clerical amendment to the table of sections for part III of subchapter L (as redesignated by Act Sec. 1024).

[¶1023] **Deduction for PAL Contributions Repealed.** The new law repeals the mutual property and casualty company deduction for contributions to a protection against loss account for tax years beginning after 12-31-86. Also, mutual P&C companies must include in income the balance in their existing PAL accounts.

The amount of the PAL account balance that a mutual P&C company must include in income for any tax year beginning after 12-31-86 is the amount the company would have had to include if the PAL provision hadn't been repealed. For this purpose, no additions to the PAL account can be made for any tax year beginning after 12-31-86.

Act Sec. 1024(a) repeals part II of subchapter L (other than Secs. 822 and 826); redesignates parts III and IV as parts II and III, respectively; redesignates Secs. 822 and 826 as Secs. 834 and 835, respectively, and transfers them to the end of part II (as redesignated); and amends Sec. 831, relating to tax on nonlife insurance companies. Act Sec. 1024(b) amends Sec. 501(c)(15), relating to insurance companies as exempt organizations. Act Sec. 1024(c) makes conforming amendments to Secs. 832, 834(a) and (d) (as redesignated by Act Sec. 1024(a)), 835 (as redesignated by Act Sec. 1024(a)), 841, 842, 844, 891, 1201(a), 1504(b), 1563(b)(2), and the table of sections for part II of subchapter L (as redesignated by Act Sec. 1024(a)). Act Sec. 1024(d), which contains transitional rules for PAL account balances and unused loss carryovers under former Sec. 825, does not amend the Code. All provision of Act Sec. 1024 are effective for tax years beginning after 12-31-86.

[¶1024] **Revised Treatment for Small Mutual P&C Companies.** The new law changes the requirements for a property and casualty company to qualify for tax-exempt status. Under the new law, a mutual *or stock* P&C company or association qualifies as a tax-exempt organization if its net written premiums or its direct written premiums (whichever are greater) for the tax year don't exceed $350,000. Under prior law, only mutual companies could qualify for tax exemption, and then only if certain gross receipts didn't exceed $150,000. Life companies still can't qualify under the new law.

If a company is a member of a controlled group, the net or direct written premiums of *all* members of the group are treated as received by that company in applying the $350,000 limit. "Controlled group" for this purpose has the same meaning as in Sec. 1563(a), except that Sec. 1563(a)(4) (relating to life company controlled groups) and Sec. 1563(b)(2)(D) (relating to life companies as excluded members) don't apply, and a 50% (rather than an 80%) ownership test applies.

Special rates, deductions, and exemptions repealed. The new law repeals the special rates, deductions, and exemptions for small mutual P&C companies—namely, the cap on tax when income is less than $12,000, the alternative tax for small companies, and the special deduction for small companies having gross amount of less than $1,100,000. It also consolidates parts II and III of Subchapter L into part II.

New alternative tax. The new law replaces these provisions with a new alternative tax that, at the taxpayer's election, will apply instead of any tax imposed on P&C companies under new Sec. 831(a). Thus, both mutual and stock P&C companies can elect the new alternative tax. The alternative tax is computed by applying the regular corporate rates to the company's taxable investment income.

To be eligible for the alternative tax, the P&C company's net written premiums or direct written premiums (whichever are greater) for the tax year must exceed $350,000 and must not exceed $1,200,000. If a company is a member of a controlled group, the net or direct written premiums of all members of the group are treated as received by that company in applying the dollar limitations. "Controlled group" for this purpose has the same meaning as in Sec. 1563(a), except that Sec. 1563(a)(4) (relating to life company controlled groups) and Sec. 1563(b)(2)(D) (relating to life companies as excluded members) don't apply, and a 50% (rather than 80%) ownership test applies.

Transitional rule. Under a transitional rule, any unused loss carryover under Sec. 825 (as in effect before the 1986 TRA) that is from a tax year beginning before 1-1-87, and that could have been used in a tax year beginning after 12-31-86 but for that section's repeal, will be included in the NOL deduction under Sec. 832(c)(10) of the 1954 Code without regard to the limitations of Sec. 844(b) of the 1954 Code.

Act Sec. 1024(a) repeals part II of subchapter L (other than Secs. 822 and 826); redesignates parts III and IV as parts II and III, respectively; redesignates Secs. 822 and 826 as Secs. 834 and 835, respectively, and transfers them to the end of part II (as redesignated); and amends Sec. 831, relating to tax on nonlife insurance companies. Act Sec. 1024(b) amends Sec. 501(c)(15), relating to insurance companies as exempt organizations. Act Sec. 1024(c) makes conforming amendments to Secs. 832, 834(a) and (d) (as redesignated by Act Sec. 1024(a)), 835 (as redesignated by Act Sec. 1024(a)), 841, 842, 844, 891, 1201(a), 1504(b), 1563(b)(2), and the table of sections for part II of subchapter L (as redesignated by Act Sec. 1024(a)). Act Sec. 1024(d), which contains transitional rules for PAL account balances and unused loss carryovers under former Sec. 825, does not amend the Code. All provision of Act Sec. 1024 are effective for tax years beginning after 12-31-86.

[¶1031]   Self-Insured Medical Malpractice Insurance Pools. The new law adds a provision designed to encourage membership in self-insured medical malpractice insurance pools.

Exclusion for association. Under the new provision, an "eligible physicians' and surgeons' mutual protection and interindemnity arrangement or association" generally can exclude from income any initial payment it receives during the tax year from a new member—provided the payment (1) doesn't release the new member from current or future dues, assessments, or premiums, and (2) is required before membership benefits can be received. However, this exclusion won't apply to the initial payment if it's reasonable to expect that the payment will be deductible by any member under the rule described below.

If an association refunds to a member any amount that it previously excluded from income, the amount refunded isn't treated as a policyholder dividend; nor is it deductible by the association. Except for the termination of a member's membership, any amount distributed to a member is treated as paid out of surplus in excess of amounts excluded.

An "eligible physicians' and surgeons' mutual protection and interindemnity arrangement or association" is one that provides (1) only medical malpractice liability protection for its members, or (2) medical malpractice liability protection in conjunction with other liability coverage against claims related to a physician's or surgeon's professional practice. In addition, the association must

- have been providing medical malpractice protection (or have received a permit to offer and sell memberships) under the laws of any state before 1-1-84;
- not be subject to regulation by any state insurance department;
- be able to make unlimited assessments against all members to cover current claims and losses; and
- not be a member of, nor protected by, any state insurance guarantee plan or association.

Deduction for members. To the extent not otherwise allowable, the new provision allows a new member to treat his or her initial payment to an eligible association as a deductible Sec. 162 business expense for the tax year in which the payment is made. The deduction is limited, however, to the amount the member would have had to pay to an independent insurance company for similar annual coverage. That amount is further reduced by any annual dues, assessments, or premiums paid during the tax year. Excess payments not allowed as a deduction in the year paid can be carried forward for five years, subject to the same limitation. The deduction isn't available for any initial payment made by a person who is a member of more than one eligible association on or after the effective date of the new law.

If a member receives a refund of all or part of his or her initial payment, the member must include the refund in income to the extent he or she took a deduction for the initial payment. Amounts refunded in excess of the initial payment are also included in the member's income unless they're excludable under another provision of the Code.

Act Sec. 1031 does not amend the Code. It is effective for payments made to and receipts of eligible associations, and refunds of payments by eligible associations, after the date of enactment in tax years ending after that date.

[¶1032] **Proration for Tax-Exempt Interest and Dividends Received.** Under prior law, property and casualty insurance companies calculated underwriting income by deducting losses incurred (as well as expenses incurred) from premiums earned. "Losses incurred" generally consisted of losses paid during the year and increases in reserves for losses incurred but not paid.

The new law takes into account that all or part of an addition to loss reserves may come out of income that isn't taxable, giving rise to a double tax benefit. Thus, the new law introduces a proration provision that reduces a P&C company's deduction for losses incurred by 15% of (1) its tax-exempt interest and (2) the deductible portion of, dividends received (with special rules for dividends from affiliates).

Dividends from affiliates. For dividends from affiliates that are 100% deductible under Sec. 243, 244, or 245(b) (100% dividends), the amount that is subject to the percentage reduction by the recipient P&C company is that portion that is attributable to "prorated amounts"—that is, the portion attributable to tax-exempt interest and non-100% dividends received by the affiliate paying the dividend.

> **Example:** In 1987, PC Insurance Company, a property and casualty insurer, has tax-exempt interest of $1,000 and receives a $100 dividend from a nonaffiliate (80% deductible). PC also receives a $400 dividend from Affiliate Corp. (100% deductible by PC). Of that $400, $200 is attributable to tax-exempt interest and nonaffiliate dividends (prorated amounts) received by Affiliate Corp. Under the new law, PC's deduction for losses incurred must be reduced by $192 ([$1,000 × 15%]+ [$80 × 15%]+ [$200 × 15%]).

Special rules apply when a P&C company receives a 100% dividend from any *insurance* affiliate (including a life company). The decrease in the deductions of the recipient P&C company resulting from a portion of the dividend being attributable to prorated amounts is reduced (but not below zero) by the amount of any increase in the affiliate's taxable income or decrease in its deductions resulting from applying the new law's proration provisions (Sec. 832(b)(5)(B) for P&C companies, and Sec. 805(a)(4)(A) for life companies) to those amounts on the affiliate's level.

In figuring what portion of a 100% dividend is attributable to prorated amounts when the recipient is a P&C company and the paying corporation is an insurance affiliate, the dividend is treated as paid first out of earnings and profits attributable to prorated amounts. The portion of E&P attributable to prorated amounts is figured without any reduction for federal income taxes.

Exception. Generally, the proration provisions for P&C companies don't apply to interest or dividends received or accrued on obligations or stock acquired on or before 8-7-86. For 100% dividends from affiliates, the P&C company will be treated as having acquired the affiliate's stock on the later of (1) the date the affiliate acquired the obligation giving rise to tax-exempt interest or the stock on which the affiliate received a nonaffiliate dividend; or (2) the first day on which the P&C company and the affiliate were members of the same affiliated group. For example, a recipient P&C company will be subject to the proration provisions on the portion of a 100% dividend that is attributable to tax-exempt interest of the affiliate if the affiliate acquired the tax-exempt obligation after August 7, 1986—even though the P&C company acquired the affiliate's stock before 8-8-86.

Act Sec. 1022, relating to the reduction of deductions for losses incurred, amends Sec. 832(b)(5), effective for tax years beginning after 12-31-86.

[¶1033]   Study of P&C Companies.—The Treasury must conduct a study of the tax treatment of policyholder dividends by mutual property and casualty insurance companies, the treatment of property and casualty insurance companies under the minimum tax, and the effect of the 1986 TRA on revenue targets for the property and casualty insurance industry. The results of the study, together with recommendations, must be submitted to the House Ways and Means Committee, the Senate Finance Committee, and the Joint Committee on Taxation by 1-1-89.

Act Sec. 1025.

[The page following this is 1101.]

EMPLOYEE BENEFITS

Individual Retirement Arrangements

[¶1101] **IRA Deduction Restricted.** The new law restricts the deduction for contributions to individual retirement arrangements. Reason: The new law's lower tax rates are expected to stimulate additional savings and reduce the need for IRA deductions for those who participate in other tax-favored retirement plans. The new law continues to permit deductions for contributions, but the deduction is reduced proportionately for adjusted gross income between $40,000 and $50,000 (between $25,000 and $35,000 for unmarried taxpayers) if the taxpayer and his or her spouse file a joint return and either is an active participant in an employer-maintained retirement plan for any part of the plan year ending with or within the taxable year. Employer-maintained retirement plan means, for this purpose, a plan that is qualified under Sec. 401(a), an annuity plan qualified under Sec. 403(a), a simplified employee pension plan, a plan established for employees of the United States, a State, or a political subdivision, or by a government agency or instrumentality, a Sec. 501(c)(18) plan funded only by contributions of employees, or a tax-sheltered 403(b) annuity. For married taxpayers who file separate returns, deductible contributions for each spouse are phased out between $0 and $10,000 if the spouse participates in an employer-sponsored plan. The phase-out is based on adjusted gross income, determined *before* the reduction for deductible IRA contributions.

The new law provides for a minimum contribution of $200 for any taxpayer whose AGI is not above the phase out range even if the phase out rules would provide for a lesser contribution.

Active participation. The determination whether an individual is an active participant depends on the type of plan in which the individual participates or is eligible to participate in. Generally, an individual is an active participant in a defined contribution plan if any employer contribution or forfeiture is added to such individual's account during the tax year. In a defined benefit plan, an individual is an active participant if not excluded under the plan's eligibility requirements during any part of the plan year ending with or within the individual's tax year. Thus, individuals may be active participants in defined benefit plans for a year even though they accrue *no* benefits during the year. For example, an individual may meet the plan's eligibility requirements, but decline to make mandatory contributions to the plan. An individual is also treated as an active participant in a plan for any tax year during which that individual makes a voluntary or mandatory employee contribution, whether the employer contributes or not. The determination of whether an individual is an active participant is made without regard to whether the individual's rights under a plan are vested.

Certain members of reserve components of the Armed Forces and volunteer fire-fighters are not treated as active participants solely because of such service.

Qualified voluntary deductible contributions repealed. The new law repeals the deduction for "qualified voluntary employee contributions." Therefore, for taxable years beginning after December 31, 1986, individuals will not be permitted to make deductible voluntary employee contributions to qualified plans.

Act Sec. 1101, amends Sec. 219 to restrict deduction for certain contributions to IRAs, and repeals deduction for certain employee contributions to qualified plans, effective for tax years beginning after 12-31-86.

[¶1102]   Nondeductible IRA Contributions OK. The new law permits active participants in employer-sponsored plans to make *nondeductible* contributions to IRAs if they are not eligible to make deductible contributions, thus providing a limited tax incentive for discretionary retirement savings. Although these contributions may not be deducted, taxes on their earnings are deferred. An individual making a nondeductible contribution to an IRA must designate the contribution as such. The designation is made on the individual's tax return. Nondeductible contributions may be made up to the due date (without extensions) for filing the tax return for the year to which the designation relates. The new law permits an individual to treat contributions as nondeductible even though he or she is eligible to make deductible contributions.

Limits on nondeductible contributions. The maximum amount that may be contributed as a nondeductible contribution is the same as is permitted as a deductible contribution by an individual who is not an active participant in an employer-sponsored plan. Thus, the maximum permissible nondeductible contribution is $2,000 ($2,250 for a spousal IRA). These limits are reduced by the amount of any deductible contributions made by the taxpayer.

Contributions that exceed either the deductible limit or the nondeductible limit, whichever applies, are subject to an annual 6% excise tax on "excess contributions" under Sec. 4973. However, excess contributions made in one year may be applied against the contribution limits in a later year if the contributions in the later year are less than the limit. So if an employee who was an active participant in an employer-sponsored plan in a prior year made excess nondeductible contributions for the prior year, the excess may be recharacterized as a deductible contribution in the current year if the individual is no longer an active participant. Similarly, an excess deductible contribution could be recharacterized as a nondeductible contribution in a later year.

Distributions of nondeductible contributions. Distributions from IRAs are taxed under Sec. 72. Under special rules for IRAs, under Sec. 72 (1) all IRAs of an individual are treated as one IRA; (2) all distributions during the same taxable year are treated as one distribution; and (3) the value of the contract (determined after adding back any distributions during the year), income on the contract and investment in the contract is determined as of the close of the calendar year with or within which the individual's tax year ends. An individual who makes a nondeductible contribution to an IRA, or receives a distribution from an IRA during a taxable year, must provide information on the individual's tax return for the year which will enable the IRS to determine the proportion of the IRA balance, as of the end of the calendar year with or within which the taxable year ends, which represents nondeductible contributions. If the required information is provided, the portion of the amount withdrawn which bears the same ratio to the total amount withdrawn as the individual's aggregate nondeductible contributions bear to the aggregate balance of all of the individual's IRAs (including rollover IRAs and SEPs) is excludible from income for the taxable year of withdrawal. If the required information is *not* provided, distributions from an IRA to which both deductible and nondeductible contributions have been made are presumed to be distributed out of deductible contributions and earnings. This presumption may be rebutted by satisfactory evidence that all or part of the contributions were nondeductible.

Distributions that are treated as a return of nondeductible contributions are a nontaxable return of basis. The Committee Report accompanying the Senate's version of the Act, from which the provisions are derived, indicates that if an individual rolls over all or any part of the amount paid or distributed, the portion of the amount rolled over that represents nondeductible contributions retains its character as such in computing the tax on a later distribution.

If an individual overstates the amount of nondeductible contributions for any year, the new law imposes a $100 penalty.

The trustee of an IRA must report certain information to the Secretary of the Treasury and to the individuals for whom an IRA is maintained for each calendar year. This information includes (1) contributions to the IRA during the calendar year; (2) distributions from the IRA during the calendar year; and (3) the aggregate account balance as of the end of the calendar year. This information must be reported by the January 31 following the end of the calendar year. The penalty for failure to report the required information is $25 per day, to the maximum of $15,000.

Act Sec. 1102 amends Sec. 408 of the Code to add subsection (o) permitting nondeductible contributions to IRAs, amends Sec. 4973(b)(1) to include non-

deductible contributions in the definition of excess contribution, amends Sec.
408(d) to apply the Sec. 72 rules to distributions from IRAs, and amends Sec.
6693 to provide for penalty for overstating nondeductible contributions, effec-
tive for tax years beginning after 12-31-86.

**[¶1103] Spousal Deduction Allowed When Spouse Has
Small Amount of Earned Income.** Prior law conditioned the full
$2,250 spousal IRA deduction on one of the spouses having no
earned income or earned income of at least $250. This requirement
created an anomalous result when a spouse had minimal earned income. For example, a taxpayer earning $20,000 a year whose spouse
had no earned income for the same period could deduct the full
$2,250 spousal IRA contribution. On the other hand, a taxpayer
earning $20,000 whose spouse earned, say, $50 for the year could deduct only $2,050.

The new law eliminates the "no-compensation" requirement for
spousal IRAs. The spousal IRA is now available either if (1) a spouse
has no compensation for the tax year or (2) elects to be treated as
having no compensation for the year. And if a spousal IRA deduction is claimed on a joint return for a tax year, the spouse is deemed
to have elected to be treated as having no compensation.

Whether a spousal IRA contribution is deductible or nondeductible
depends on whether either spouse is an active participant in an employer-sponsored plan for the year, and whether the AGI of the couple is above the phase-out level [¶1101]. For example, if the AGI on
a joint return is above $50,000 and *either* spouse is an active partici-
pant in an employer-sponsored plan, the entire IRA contribution is
nondeductible. If AGI is less than $40,000, *or* if neither spouse par-
ticipates in an employer-sponsored plan, the IRA contribution is deductible. If either spouse participates in an employer-sponsored plan,
and AGI is between $40,000 and $50,000, a portion of the IRA contribution will be deductible. [¶1101].

Act Sec. 1103, amends Sec. 219(c)(1)(B) to permit full deduction for spousal
IRA where spouse has minimal income, effective for tax years beginning after
12-31-85.

[¶1104] Limits on Elective Deferrals to 403(b) Annuities.
Under prior law, contributions on behalf of employees under tax-
sheltered annuities, were subject to a special "exclusion allowance,"
which was the excess of (1) 20% of the participant's includable compensation, multiplied by the number of his years of service, over (2)
amounts previously contributed to such annuity contracts in his behalf. Alternatively, the employee could elect to have the same overall limitations as were applied to annual additions to defined contribution plans under Sec. 415(c)—the lesser of $30,000 or 25% of a
participant's compensation—apply. However, employees who worked

for a tax-exempt organization that didn't offer a salary reduction agreement were limited to a $2,000 IRA contribution.

To alleviate this disparity, the new law clamps a lid on the amount that an employee can elect to defer for a tax year under all 403(b) annuities. For tax years beginning after 12-31-86, the maximum amount of such deferrals cannot exceed the greater of $9,500 or the maximum permissible elective deferral for CODAs (as indexed). This limit is determined without regard to any community property laws and is coordinated with elective deferrals under a CODA and the IRA deduction limit.

Limitation on aggregate deferrals. Unlike the limit on annual additions to defined contribution plans under Sec. 415(c), the limit on elective deferrals to 403(b) annuities applies to total deferrals made on an employee's behalf under *all* qualified CODAs and 403(b) annuities which the employee participates in during his or her *tax year* (rather than a plan's limitation year). This limit, however, applies only to elective *employee* deferrals to a CODA or 403(b) annuity, and does not apply to employer contributions. As a result, total 403(b) and CODA contributions are subject to the Sec. 403(b)(2) exclusion allowance or, if the employee so elects, the new law's overall Sec. 415(c) limitations [¶1106].

Excess deferrals. Amounts of elective employee deferrals that exceed the limit for a tax year are included in the employee's income for the year and must be allocated among the CODA or 403(b) annuities the employee participates in by the following March 1. The plan or plans must distribute the excess allocations (plus earnings) to the employee by the following April 15. Such distributions (and earnings) are includable in an employee's income for the year to which the excess deferral relates, but are not subject to the additional 10% tax on early distributions under Sec. 72(t). Such excess deferrals will be taken into account in applying special nondiscrimination tests [¶1112] even though they are distributed, except to the extent that regulations to be issued by the Secretary of the Treasury provide otherwise. On the other hand, if an excess deferral is *not* distributed by April 15 following the year of deferral, the excess remains in the CODA (or 403(b) annuity) and will (1) be hit by the Sec. 72(t) penalty; (2) again be taxed when actually distributed notwithstanding that the excess was included in income for the year of deferral, and (3) be taken into account in applying the special nondiscrimination tests.

Example: For 1987, Taxpayer elects to defer $5,000 under a 403(b) annuity, and $5,000 under a CODA maintained by employer Y. Under the new law, however, Taxpayer may exclude only $9,500 from the $10,000 of elective deferrals. Consequently, the $500 excess, plus a proportionate share of earnings, must be withdrawn from the 403(b) annuity by April 15, 1988. Taxpayer must include the excess in his income for 1987 only, and is not subject to the additional 10% tax under Sec. 72(t) for early withdrawals. The excess deferral is taken into account when testing the annuities under the special nondiscrimination test [¶1112] for the year of deferral (subject to regulations to be issued). However, if the excess deferral were not made by 4-15-88, it would remain in the 403(b) annuity and be subject to the withdrawal restrictions. Moreover, Taxpayer would have no basis in the excess despite the inclusion of it in his 1987 income, and the full amount of the excess would again be included in his income when actually distributed. Finally, the undistributed excess deferral would be taken into account in applying the special nondiscrimination tests for the year of deferral.

Catch-up election for certain 'qualified' employees. The new law provides an exception to the annual limit on contributions (including elective deferrals) to tax-sheltered 403(b) annuities. Any "qualified" employee who has completed 15 years of service with an educational organization, hospital, home health service or agency, health or welfare service agency, or church, convention, or association of churches (so-called qualified organizations) can make additional salary reduction contributions. However, the additional contribution in any one year cannot exceed $3,000, and an aggregate limit of $15,000 applies to total additional contributions. In addition, the exception to the deferral limit is unavailable if a taxpayer's lifetime elective deferrals top his or her lifetime limit ($5,000 × years of service performed by the individual with the employer).

Effective Date: The annual deferral limit applies to deferrals that relate to employees' tax years beginning after 12-31-86. However, for a qualified CODA or 403(b) annuity maintained under one or more collective bargaining agreements ratified before 3-1-86, the deferral limit does not apply to contributions for years beginning before the earlier of the termination date of the last CBA (without regard to the extension of such CBA), or 1-1-89.

Act Sec. 1105, relating to the annual limit on elective deferrals to 403(b) plans, amends Sec. 402, effective as shown above.

Cash or Deferred Arrangements

[¶1105] **$7,000 Limitation on Elective Deferrals to CODAs.** Under prior law, amounts employees could elect to defer to a qualified cash or deferred arrangement or to receive in cash were subject to the same overall limitations as were contributions to defined contribution plans under Sec. 415(c)—the lesser of $30,000 or 25% of a participant's compensation. However, employees whose employer did not maintain a qualified CODA, were limited to a $2,000 IRA contribution.

The new law reduces the aggregate amount that an employee can elect to defer for a tax year under all qualified CODAs. Generally, for tax years beginning after 12-31-86, such deferrals cannot exceed $7,000 in any tax year of the individual. This limit is determined without regard to any community property laws and is reduced by elective deferrals under Sec. 403(b) tax deferred annuities. The $7,000 cap is indexed for inflation at the same time and in the same way as the dollar limitation on benefits from defined benefit plans under Sec. 415.

Limit on elective deferrals. Like the limitations on elective deferrals under 403(b) annuities, the $7,000 limit applies to all elective deferrals by an individual, under all cash or deferred arrangements in the individual's tax year (rather than the plan's limitation year). Moreover, the limits are coordinated with the benefits under a Sec. 457 unfunded deferred compensation plan of a state or local government, a Sec. 501(c)(18) plan, or a SEP.

The limit on elective deferrals to a CODA is reduced by the amount of the individual's contributions to a 403(b) annuity contract to the extent that the contributions are made through a salary reduction agreement. However, the $7,000 limit is *increased* (but not to more than $9500) by the amount of employer contributions to a 403(b) annuity made through salary reduction. Thus, if an individual maintains a 403(b) annuity in addition to a CODA, total elective deferrals may be as high as $9500.

The limit on elective deferrals applies only to elective *employee* deferrals to a CODA and not to employer contributions (other than employer contributions through salary reduction agreements). As a result, total employee and employer CODA contributions are subject to the new law's overall Sec. 415(c) limitations of the lesser of (1) $30,000 (or 25% of the defined benefit plan dollar limit, if greater); or (2) 25% of compensation.

Treatment of excess deferrals. Elective employee deferrals that, together with contributions to SEPs in which the employee participates and any contributions to a Sec. 501(c)(18) plan on the employee's behalf, exceed the $7,000 limit for a tax year are included in the employee's income for the year. The excess may be allocated among the CODAs the employee participates in by the following March 1. The plan or plans to which the excess deferrals are allocated may then distribute the excess allocations (plus earnings) to the employee by the following April 15.

Such distributions (and earnings) are includable in an employee's income for the year to which the excess deferral relates, but are not subject to the additional tax on early distributions. Earnings of the plan are allocated to excess contributions on a pro-rata basis. Excess deferrals are taken into account in applying special nondiscrimination tests if not distributed during the taxable year of deferral. Moreover, if an excess deferral is not distributed by April 15 following the year of deferral, the excess remains in the CODA and (1) may be subject to a penalty for early withdrawals if distributed later; (2) will again be taxed when actually distributed notwithstanding that the excess was included in income for the year of deferral; and (3) will be taken into account in applying the special nondiscrimination tests. Moreover, the undistributed excess deferral will *not* be treated as an investment in the contract by the employee.

> **Example:** For 1987, Taxpayer defers $5,000 under employer X's qualified CODA and $3,000 under employer Y's CODA. Under the new law, Taxpayer may only exclude $7,000 of the $8,000 of elective deferrals. Consequently, the $1,000 excess may be withdrawn from X's plan or Y's plan, or partially from both plans. If Taxpayer documents the $1,000 excess by 3-1-88, he can request that $750 (plus earnings) be distributed from X's plan, and that $250 (plus earnings) be distributed from Y's plan. If the $1,000 excess (plus earnings) is distributed from the CODAs by 4-15-88, Taxpayer is required to include the excess (plus income) in his income for 1987 only, and will not be subject to the 10% additional tax for pre-age 59½ withdrawals under Sec. 72(t). Employers X and Y will be required, except as may be otherwise provided by regulations, to take the excess deferrals into account when testing their CODAs under the special nondiscrimination tests for the year of deferral. However, if either CODA fails to distribute the excess by 4-15-88, the excess will remain in the plan and will be subject to the withdrawal restrictions. Moreover, Taxpayers will have no basis in the excess despite the inclusion of it in his 1987 income, and the full amount of the excess will again be included in his income when actually distributed. Finally, the undistributed excess deferral will be taken into account as elective deferrals in applying the special nondiscrimination tests for the year of deferral.

Effective dates. The new law's limitation on elective deferrals is generally effective for tax years beginning after 12-31-86. For partnerships having fiscal years ending in 1987, the $7,000 limit applies on a pro-rata basis. However, for plans maintained under collective bargaining agreements ratified before 3-1-86, the new law will not apply to contributions made for tax years beginning before the earlier of (1) the date the last such collective bargaining agreement ends (without regard for any extension of the agreement after 2-28-86) or (2) 1-1-89. Such contributions *will be* taken into account in applying the new limits to other plans in which an individual participates. The provisions of the new law do not apply to elective deferrals of an employer which are attributable to services performed before 1-1-87 even if the deferral is actually made during 1987, provided (1) the employee makes the deferral election before 1-1-87 and (2) the employer identifies the amount of the deferral before that date.

Act Sec. 1105, amending Code Sec. 402 and imposing new limits on maximum elective deferrals under cash or deferred arrangements, effective for plan years beginning after 12-31-86, and effective for plan years beginning after 12-31-88 for plans maintained by state or local governments. Effective as indicated for collectively bargained plans.

[¶1106] **Limits on Contributions and Benefits.** The early and deferred retirement adjustments to the $90,000 maximum limit for benefits under a defined benefit plan are now tied to the Social Security retirement age. Under prior law, the maximum was reduced for benefits beginning before age 62 and increased for benefits beginning after age 65. Now, the maximum permissible benefit will be reduced if payments begin before the Social Security retirement age, and will be increased if they begin after that age. (The Social Security retirement age, as defined in new Code Sec. 415(b)(8), is the retirement age in Sec. 216(l) of the Social Security Act, determined without regard to the age increase factor, and assuming early retirement age to be 62.) There is no longer a $75,000 maximum for benefits beginning at or after age 55—the dollar limit will be determined by regulations that are consistent with the reduction for benefits under the Social Security Act. However, if benefits begin before the Social Security early retirement age, the maximum dollar limit will be actuarially reduced. (In 1986, the Social Security retirement age is 65.)

Exceptions. Tax-exempt and governmental employers and organizations are exempt from the actuarial reduction provision and the change in normal retirement age. In addition, new provisions have been added to Sec. 415(b)(2) that allow a qualified plan for police or firefighters to continue to apply the under-age-62 and over-age-65 adjustments (and the $75,000 limit for benefits beginning at or after age 55), and to pay a cost-of-living indexed equivalent of a $50,000-a-year pension after 20 years of service even if the actuarial equivalent of the $90,000 or $75,000 limit would be less than the cost-of-living adjusted $50,000.

New Sec. 415(b)(9) provides that for commercial airline pilots, the normal retirement dollar limit applies at age 60 instead of the Social Security retirement age. *Reason:* the FAA requires airline pilots to retire at age 60.

The 100%-of-compensation limit of Sec. 415(b)(1)(B) has not been changed. Similarly, the 25%-of-compensation limit for annual additions to a defined contribution plan has not been changed, with one exception: contributions made by retired nonkey employees for retiree medical coverage are not subject to the 25% limit. However, the dollar limit for annual additions has been linked to the defined benefit plan dollar limit. It is now the greater of $30,000 or one-quarter of the dollar limit for defined benefit plans. Thus, the defined contribution dollar limit will exceed $30,000 when cost-of-living increases raise the defined benefit limit beyond $120,000.

Cost-of-living adjustments. The $90,000 limit for defined benefit plans will be adjusted for increases in the cost of living beginning in 1988. There will be no cost-of-living adjustment to the defined contribution limit until the defined benefit limit reaches $120,000. So for the immediate future (even after 1988), the dollar limit on annual additions will remain $30,000. If inflation causes the defined benefit limit to exceed $120,000, the defined contribution dollar limit will be one-quarter of the defined benefit limit each year.

Cost-of-living arrangements. The law now permits a defined benefit plan to maintain a "qualified cost-of-living arrangement" under which employer and employee contributions may be applied to provide cost-of-living increases to the primary benefit (Sec. 415(k)(2)). To qualify, the arrangement must not discriminate in favor of highly paid employees and must comply with all applicable qualification requirements of Sec. 401(a). For example, the right to the employer-provided portion of a cost-of-living benefit will accrue and vest along with the normal retirement benefit. However, a plan may provide that a participant will not be entitled to receive cost-of-living adjustments derived from employer contributions if the participant doesn't contribute the amount required under the plan or if the participant receives a lump-sum distribution of his or her accrued benefit derived from employer contributions. (Note, also, that a plan is *permitted* to include a qualified cost-of-living arrangement; it is *not* required.)

Participation in the arrangement must be voluntary. An employee may make an election in the year he or she attains the earliest retirement age under the plan or separates from service (or in both years). Adjustments must be limited to increases in the cost-of-living after the annuity starting date. The increases must be based on cost-of-living indexes prescribed by the Treasury, but a qualified arrangement may provide that an increase for any year will not be less than 3% of the primary retirement benefit.

Key employees generally may not participate in a qualified cost-of-living arrangement. However, if a plan is not top heavy, officers may participate if they are key employees solely because they are officers (i.e., they are not 5% owners or in one of the other categories included in Sec. 416(i)(1) except Sec. 416(i)(1)(A)(i)).

Employee contributions to a qualified cost-of-living arrangement won't be treated as annual additions to the employer's defined contribution plan under Sec. 415(c), but will be treated as additions in applying the limit for a combination of plans under Sec. 415(e). Transfers from a defined contribution plan will be treated as employee contributions to the cost-of-living arrangement (Sec. 415(k)(2)(A)(ii)) and will not be treated as distributions from the defined contribution plan (Sec. 402(e)(4)(N)). Moreover, the "balance to the credit of the employee" in the defined contribution plan will not include any amount transferred to a qualified cost of living arrangement.

Limit on compensation taken into account. Under prior law, a top-heavy plan could take only $200,000 of an employee's annual compensation into account in determining benefits. There was no limit on plans that were not top-heavy. New Sec. 401(a)(17) limits the amount for *all* qualified plans to $200,000 for plan years beginning after 12-31-88. The limit, which applies for all purposes in testing for discrimination, will be increased at the same time and in the same way as the dollar limit for defined benefit plans.

Annual additions. Instead of including only half of an employee's contributions or the amount in excess of 6% of compensation in annual additions, as under prior law, Sec. 415(c)(2) now defines the annual addition to include *all* employee contributions along with employer contributions and forfeitures.

For purposes of calculating the defined contribution plan fraction in applying the combined plan limit of Sec. 415(e), the prior law will still apply in calculating the fraction for years beginning before 1-1-87. Thus, recomputation is not necessary.

Reduction of benefit limit. Under prior law, the defined benefit plan limit for an employee with less than 10 years of *service with the sponsoring employer* was reduced by 10% for each year less than 10. Under present law, the 10% per year reduction in the dollar limit applies to years of *participation in the plan* rather than years of service with the employer; years of service will still be used in computing the reduction in the percentage of compensation limit.

> **Example:** Jack Wilks, whose salary was $70,000, retires after 8 years of service with 6 years of participation. His maximum benefit would be the lesser of 80% of $70,000 or 60% of $90,000 = $54,000. Bob Keyes, whose salary was $70,000, retires after 8 years of service with 7 years of participation. His maximum benefit would be $56,000 (70% of $90,000 = $63,000).

Effective Dates: The new provisions generally apply to years beginning after 12-31-86. However, a plan will not be disqualified for any year beginning before 1-1-89 if it complies with the new law in operation and is amended no later than the end of the first plan year beginning after that date, and the amendment is retroactive to the first plan year beginning after 1986. [See ¶1141.]

For collectively bargained plans under agreements ratified before 3-1-86, the new provisions won't apply until the agreement ends or 1-1-89, whichever is earlier.

Compensation limit. As noted, the $200,000 limit on compensation to be taken into account in determining benefits will apply to benefits accruing years beginning after 12-31-88. However, for collectively bargained plans, the limit will not apply until the later of the date described in the preceding paragraph or 1-1-91.

Tax on excess distributions. In addition to the Sec. 415 limits on benefits from defined benefit plans, new Sec. 4981 imposes a 15% excise tax on any "excess distributions" an individual receives in any calendar year from any combination of qualified retirement plans, tax-sheltered annuities, and IRAs. With certain exceptions, an "excess distribution" is the aggregate amount of retirement distributions an individual gets in a calendar year from all tax-favored retirement arrangements that exceeds $112,500 or 125% of the defined benefit plan dollar limit under Sec. 415(b)(1)(A), whichever is greater.

> **Example:** Retiree receives, in 1986, $77,000 from her defined benefit plan, $16,000 from a profit-sharing plan, and $27,000 from an IRA. Her total distributions ($120,000) exceed the Sec. 4981 limit ($112,500) by $7,500. She will have to pay an excise tax of $1,125 (15% of $7,500) in addition to her income tax.

The limiting amount will remain $112,500 until the Sec. 415(b)(1)(A) limit exceeds $90,000 (125% of $90,000 is $112,500).

Exceptions. The tax on excess distributions will be reduced by the amount, if any, of the tax imposed on early distributions attributable to the excess distribution (see ¶1123). Excess distributions do not include retirement distributions made after a retiree's death (these may be subject to an additional estate tax). Nor do they include retirement distributions paid to another person under a qualified domestic relations order if includable in the income of the recipient (these payments are treated as distributions to the person who receives them and will be subject to an excess distribution tax imposed on that person if the aggregate of distributions that person receives exceeds $112,500). Also excepted from the excise tax are amounts attributable to after-tax employee contributions and distributions which are not includible in income because of a rollover contribution.

Lump-sum distributions. If retirement distributions include a lump-sum distribution that is eligible for favorable tax treatment under Sec. 402(e)(4)(B), the limitation will be applied separately to the lump-sum distribution, and will be increased to 5 times the normal limit. In 1986, this will be $562,500 (5 × $112,500).

Postdeath distributions. Instead of an annual excess distribution tax, there is an additional estate tax equal to 15% of the individual's excess retirement *accumulation* when benefits are payable to an individual's beneficiaries after the individual dies.

Excess retirement accumulation is the excess of the value of the decedent's interests in all tax favored plans over the present value of annual payments of $112,500 (as indexed) for a period equal to the life expectancy of the decedent immediately before death. This tax may not be offset by any credits against the estate tax.

Effective Date: Distributions made after 12-31-86 except that for distributions made on account of a plan termination prior to 1-1-87, the provisions will not apply to distributions made before 1-1-88.

Accrued benefits. A transitional rule insures that a participant's previously accrued benefit under a defined benefit plan won't be reduced by the new limits or affected by the actuarial reduction for benefits beginning before the Social Security retirement age. The rule applies to a participant who was a participant as of 1-1-87 in a plan in existence on 5-6-86. If such an individual's accrued benefit as of the end of the last plan year beginning before 1-1-87 is greater than the new dollar limit, the accrued benefit is the dollar limit for that individual, provided that any change in the terms of the plan or any cost-of-living adjustment after 5-5-86 will not be taken into account. Moreover, an individual who is subject to the excise tax on excess may be able to elect instead to be covered by (1) a "grandfather" rule, which exempts from the tax benefits accrued as of 8-1-86; or (2) an alternate rule which increases the $112,500 limit. Under the grandfather rule, the part of the benefit accrued before 8-1-86 will be taken into account in determining whether there is an excess distribution, but the excise tax will be imposed only on the benefits accrued after 8-1-86. The grandfather rule is only available if accrued benefits as of 8-1-86 are equal to at least $562,500, and must be elected on a return for a year ending before 1-1-89.

If an individual does not elect the grandfather rule, then the amount of the distribution subject to the tax under the general rule will be applied to benefits accrued as of 8-1-86 by substituting for $112,500 the greater of $150,000, or $112,500, as indexed.

Reduction of accrued benefits. If a plan is amended to comply with the new defined benefit limits by the close of the first plan year beginning after 12-31-86, it may reduce accrued benefits to reflect the new limits. Such reduction will not be treated as a violation of Code Sec. 411(d)(6).

Act Sec. 1106 adds Secs. 401(a)(17); 402(e)(4)(N); 411(a)(3); 411(d); 415(b)(2)(F), (G), and (H); 415(b)(8); 415(b)(9); 415 and 415(k)(2); amends Secs. 415(b)(2) and (5); 415(c)(1) and (4); 415(d); and 416(a); (c); and repeals Sec. 416(d); and Act Sec. 1133 adds Sec. 4981, effective for distributions made after 12-31-86, except for distributions made on account of plan terminations before 1-1-87.

[¶1107] Unfunded Deferred Compensation Arrangements of State and Local Governments and Tax-Exempt Employers. Under Sec. 457, state and local governments may establish unfunded deferred compensation plans, under which employees may elect to defer receipt of current compensation. Provided the plan meets certain requirements, deferred amounts are not included in the employee's gross income until they are paid or made available. The new law extends the Sec. 457 rules applicable to unfunded deferred compensation plans maintained by state and local governments to such plans maintained by private tax-exempt organizations, and modifies pre- and post-death distribution rules for all such plans.

The maximum amount that can be deferred annually is the lesser of $7,500 or 33⅓ % of the employee's compensation (net of the deferred amount). However, the maximum deferral may increase to as much as $15,000 a year for the three years before the tax year in which the participant reaches the normal retirement age under the plan. The deferral limit is reduced by amounts contributed to a tax-deferred Sec. 403(b) annuity on behalf of the employee.

Offset for deferrals under qualified cash or deferred arrangements. The new law provides that the amount a participant may defer under an eligible deferred compensation plan must be reduced, dollar for dollar, by elective deferrals under a qualified cash or deferred arrangement (except a qualified cash or deferred arrangement maintained by a rural electric cooperative). An employee's elective deferrals under a SEP [¶1108], or deductible employee contributions to a 501(c)(18) [¶1109] plan, also reduce the amount the employee may defer under an eligible deferred compensation plan. As under prior law, amounts contributed to a tax-deferred 403(b) annuity are taken into account in figuring whether the employee's deferrals under an eligible deferred compensation plan exceed the limits on such deferrals.

Minimum distribution requirements. Under prior law, payments from an eligible deferred compensation plan that began before the employee's death were required to satisfy a payout schedule under which the benefits projected to be paid to the employee would be greater than 50% of the total benefits payable with respect to the employee. If the employee died before the entire amount deferred was paid out, any unpaid amount had to be paid to the employee's beneficiary over a period not greater than 15 years, unless the beneficiary was the employee's spouse, in which case payments could be made over the life of the spouse.

The prior law's distribution provisions for Sec. 457 plans permitted deferrals to accumulate on a tax-favored basis for a longer period than is permitted under a qualified plan. The new law modifies the distribution requirements for such plans to resolve this perceived anomaly. Under the new law, payments starting before the employee's death must be under a payout schedule providing for projected payments to the employee that are equal to at least 66⅔ % of the total benefits payable. Payments must begin no later than the "required beginning date," as defined in Sec. 401(a)(9).

If the employee dies after beginning to receive payments, but before the total deferred amount has been distributed, the remaining amount must be distributed at least as rapidly as under the original payout schedule. If the employee dies before beginning to receive benefits, the entire deferred amount must be distributed to the employee's beneficiary over a period not greater than 15 years, except that if the beneficiary is the employee's spouse, benefits may be paid over the life expectancy of the spouse.

If distributions (pre-or post-death) are to be made over a period greater than one year, the distribution must be made in substantially nonincreasing periodic payments, paid not less frequently than annually.

Constructive receipt. Amounts deferred under an eligible deferred compensation plan of a state or local government are generally includable in the employee's taxable income in the year paid or *made available.* The new law provides that benefits under such a plan won't be considered as made available merely because the employee is permitted to elect to receive a lump-sum payable within 60 days of the election. This rule applies, however, only if the total amount payable to the employee is not greater than $3,500, and no additional amounts may be deferred under the plan with respect to the employee. Thus, if the total benefits payable to an employee exceed $3,500, and the employee has the option to elect to receive a lump-sum benefit, the entire amount of the benefit would be immediately includable in the employee's taxable income even though the employee declined to exercise the option.

Transfers between eligible plans. Under the new law, a participant in an eligible governmental deferred compensation plan may elect to have any portion of the amount payable to the participant transferred to another eligible deferred compensation plan of a state or local government or tax-exempt organization. The amount transferred will not be included in the participant's income solely as a result of the transfer.

State judicial plans. Qualified state judicial plans and certain other plans of tax-exempt organizations are exempted from the new requirements for eligible deferred compensation plans.

Certain existing deferrals and arrangements. Under a grandfather rule, Sec. 457 does not apply to amounts deferred under a plan of a tax-exempt organization which (1) were deferred from tax years beginning before 1-1-87, or (2) are deferred later pursuant to an agreement which was in writing on 8-16-86, and which provided for annual deferrals of a fixed amount or amounts determined under a fixed formula on that date.

Act Sec. 1107, amends Code Sec. 457, permitting tax-exempt employers to maintain eligible deferred compensation plans and permitting certain cash-outs and transfers, effective for tax years after 12-31-86; coordinating deferrals under eligible deferred compensation plans of state and local governments with deferrals under other plans, and modifying the distribution requirements for eligible governmental deferred compensation plans, effective for tax years beginning after 12-31-88.

Simplified Employee Pensions

[¶1108]   Special Rules for SEPs. Under prior law the administrative costs and burdens of qualified pension plans provided a disincentive for small employers to establish such plans, in spite of the generous tax breaks accorded qualified plans. The new law changes the rules for simplified employee pensions (SEPs) to encourage the use of this low-cost retirement savings option. The changes further simplify the administration of SEPs, and add a special elective deferral feature for small employers.

Deferral elections under SEPs. Under the new law, employees who participate in a SEP (other than a SEP maintained by a state or local goverment) may elect to have contributions made to the SEP or paid to the employee in cash. Contributions to the SEP pursuant to such election are not currently taxable to the employee, and are not treated as employee contributions. Elective deferrals under a SEP are treated like elective deferrals under a qualified CODA, and are therefore subject to the same $7,000 cap on elective deferrals. Also, like elective deferrals under a CODA, elective deferrals under a SEP are exclusions from income, but are includable in the definition of wages for employment tax (FICA and FUTA) purposes.

The elective deferral option is available under a SEP only if certain conditions are met. First, at least 50% of the employees of the employer must elect to have amounts contributed to the SEP. Second, the employer must have no more than 25 employees at any time during the year preceding the year for which elective deferrals may be made. In addition, the amount deferred each year by *each* highly compensated employee, as a percentage of pay (the "deferral percentage") can be no more than 125% of the *average* deferral percentage of all other employees. Integration with Social Security contributions is not permitted for this test, nor can any nonelective SEP contributions be combined with the elective deferrals. Employer matching contributions conditioned on elective SEP deferrals are not allowed.

The definition of a highly compensated employee is the same as is applied for the special nondiscrimination test applicable to qualified cash or deferred arrangements under Sec. 401(k) [¶1116].

If the 125% test is not satisfied for a given year, rules similar to the rules regarding excess contributions to a qualified CODA apply.

When contributions deemed made. Under the new law, SEPs may be maintained on a calendar year basis, or on the basis of the employer's tax year. If the SEP is maintained on the basis of the calendar year, contributions made in a calendar year are deductible by the employer in the tax year with or within which the calendar year ends, and contributions are treated as made on the last day of the calendar year if made by the due date (plus extensions) for filing the employer's tax return. If the SEP is maintained on a tax-year basis, contributions are deductible for the tax year in which they are made. They are deemed made on the last day of a tax year if they are made on or before the due date (with extensions) for filing the employer's tax return for the tax year.

Participation requirements. Prior law participation requirements mandated that an employer maintaining a SEP make contributions to the SEP on behalf of each employee who had attained age 25, and performed services for the employer during at least three of the immediately preceding five years. The new law continues the service requirement, but reduces the age requirement to age 21 and adds a *de minimis* exception which permits the employer to decline to contribute on behalf of employees who do not receive at least $300 in compensation from the employer during the year.

Under the new law, the 100% participation requirement applies separately to elective deferral arrangements, and for the purposes of such arrangements all employees who are eligible to elect to have contributions made on their behalf instead of receiving cash are treated as receiving an employer contribution. Thus, an employer can establish a SEP funded entirely by elective deferrals and get 100% participation at no cost to itself (other than the nominal cost of administering to plan). Of course, at least 50% of the employer's employees must actually elect a deferral, and deferrals by highly compensated employees are limited by the actual deferrals of other employees.

Integration rules. Prior law permitted an employer to combine nonelective SEP contributions with employer OASDI contributions in testing the SEP for discrimination, provided the employer did not maintain another integrated plan. This permitted small employers to maintain plans which provided little or no benefit to rank-and-file employees, while contributing greater amounts on behalf of highly compensated employees than such employees could contribute to a personal IRA. The new law eliminates the prior integration rules, and requires nonelective SEP contributions to be tested for nondiscrimination under the new rules for qualified defined contribution plans [¶1110]. These rules permit a limited disparity between the contribution percentages applicable to compensation below and above the Social Security taxable wage base.

¶1108

Indexing of compensation limitation and de minimis threshold. The $200,000 limit on compensation taken into account in determining SEP contributions, and the $300 threshold for participation is indexed for inflation at the same time and in the same manner as the dollar limitation for defined benefit plans.

Act Sec. 1108, amends Code Secs. 219, 402, 404(h) and 408(k) to permit elective deferrals under SEPs, and makes conforming amendments to Secs. 3121(a)(5) and 3306(b)(5), effective for years beginning after 12-31-86.

501(c)18 Plans

[¶1109]   Contributions to Sec. 501(c)(18) Plans are Deductible. Sec. 501(c)(18) exempts from federal taxation any trust which is part of a pension plan funded only by the contributions of employees, provided the plan meets certain nondiscrimination requirements. Under prior law, employee contributions to such plans were deductible, through a fiction created by the IRS in *Rev. Rul. 54-190,* that the contributions were union dues. In 1982 the IRS declared *Rev. Rul. 54-190* obsolete, thus disrupting the historical treatment of contributions to Sec. 501(c)(18) plans. The new law provides a mechanism to allow deductions for such contributions, but subjects the deductible contributions to requirements similar to the rules for qualified cash or deferred arrangements, including the limits on annual elective deferrals and the special nondiscrimination rules. Thus, if an employee elects to make contributions to such a plan, the contribution is deductible up to the lesser of $7,000 or 25% of the compensation of the employee includible in income for the tax year. The amounts contributed to the plan reduce the $7,000 annual cap on elective deferrals under qualified cash or deferred arrangements and SEPs.

The election to make deductible contributions to a Sec. 501(c)(18) plan is available only if the plan satisfies a special nondiscrimination test similar to the test applicable to a qualified cash or deferred arrangement. If the test is not satisfied, rules similar to the rules applicable to excess contributions under a qualified cash or deferred arrangement apply.

Act Sec. 1109 amends Sec. 501(c)(18), providing for deductible contributions by employees under Sec. 501(c)(18) plans, effective for tax years beginning after 12-31-86.

Nondiscrimination Rules

[¶1110]   Nondiscrimination Rules for Integrated Plans. Prior law rules against discrimination in favor of highly compensated employees were intended to prevent management groups from using pension plans as a tax-avoidance device to shelter their own income, without providing for coverage of rank-and-file employees under such plans. The requirements of nondiscriminatory coverage were intended to assure that such employees were not omitted from the plans, while nondiscriminatory benefit requirements were meant to assure that the lower-paid employees received meaningful benefits under the plans. Because it was felt that a plan designed in good faith to supplement Social Security should be permitted to qualify for favorable tax treatment, the prior law's nondiscrimination rules permitted plans which provided benefits which, when aggregated with Social Security, were nondiscriminatory to qualify even though plan benefits by themselves did not meet the nondiscrimination standards.

However, it has been found that Social Security benefits don't adequately replace the preretirement earnings of low or middle-income workers. Because these individuals are frequently financially unable to save sufficiently for retirement, tax incentives are provided to encourage employers to provide workers with additional retirement benefits under qualified plans. The prior law's rules on integrating qualified plan benefits with Social Security benefits permitted employers to eliminate plan benefits for lower-paid employees, thus undermining the original policy—to provide tax incentives for the establishment of qualified plans. The new law revises and simplifies the rules governing the integration of qualified plans and ensures that *all* employees covered by these plans receive some minimum benefit.

Permitted disparity in defined contribution plans. Defined contribution plans are plans under which no specified *benefit* is provided, but rather contributions are allocated to individual accounts established for each plan participant. Under prior law, employer contributions could be allocated first to the accounts of participants having compensation in excess of a specified amount (generally the Social Security taxable wage base) until a percentage of excess compensation equal to the OASDI tax rate was allocated. Only if any employer contributions were left after this allocation was completed would employees who had no excess compensation receive a share. Thus, for example, in 1986 a profit-sharing plan could provide contributions of 5.7% of 1986 compensation in excess of $42,000 (the 1986 taxable wage base) and no contributions with respect to compensation up to $42,000. Therefore, employees earning less than $42,000 would receive no contribution for the year.

The integration rules for defined contribution plans are changed under the new law. Now these plans are qualified only if the excess contribution percentage—the percentage of compensation contributed with respect to excess compensation—does not exceed the lesser of 200% of the base contribution percentage, or the sum of (1) the base contribution percentage and (2) the greater of the rate of tax imposed on employers under FICA (5.7% for 1986) as of the beginning of the year, or 5.7%. The base contribution percentage is the percentage of compensation contributed to the plan with respect to that portion of compensation which is not excess compensation. The amount specified in the plan as the integration break point is called the "integration level."

For example, if a profit-sharing plan provides for contributions for each employee equal to 10% of the employee's compensation which is in excess of the Social Security taxable wage base, the plan need provide only a 5% contribution on compensation up to the taxable wage base. On the other hand, if the plan provides for a contribution of 12% of excess compensation in 1986, it must provide a base contribution of at least 6.3%. Why? Because the permitted disparity cannot exceed the OASDI tax rate of 5.7%.

A defined contribution plan may specify an integration break point which is less than the taxable wage base, but not one which is greater. Moreover, such a lower compensation level will not be permitted if it results in discrimination in favor of highly compensated employees.

Permitted disparity in defined benefit plans. To satisfy the new law's requirements for integrated defined benefit plans, a plan must be within the disparity limits prescribed for excess plans or offset plans.

Excess plans. An excess plan is one that is designed to provide benefits (or additional benefits) based on the portion of an employee's earnings in excess of the earnings on which Social Security benefits are based (covered compensation). A defined benefit pension plan meets the disparity limits for excess plans if (1) the excess benefit percentage does not exceed a "maximum excess allowance", (2) any optional form of benefit, preretirement benefit, actuarial factor, or other benefit or feature provided by the plan with respect to compensation in excess of an amount specified in the plan for the year (the integration level) is provided with respect to compensation below the integration level, and (3) benefits are based on average annual compensation.

The excess and base benefit percentages are computed in the same manner as the excess and base contribution percentages are computed for defined contribution plans, except that the computation is based on benefits rather than contributions. Thus, the term "excess benefit percentage" refers to the benefits provided under the plan (expressed as a percentage of compensation) with respect to that portion of compensation in excess of the integration level specified in the plan. The base benefit percentage refers to the benefits provided under the plan (expressed as a percentage of compensation) with respect to compensation not in excess of the integration level. The maximum excess allowance is, for benefits attributable to any year of service with the employer taken into account under the plan, ¾ of one percentage point. For total benefits under the plan, the maximum excess allowance is ¾ of one percentage point multiplied by all the participant's years of service with the employer (to a maximum of 35 years) taken into account under the plan. The maximum excess allowance will in no event exceed the basic benefit percentage.

Average annual compensation is the average of a participant's compensation over the three consecutive years of his service with the employer which produces the highest such average.

Offset plans. Offset plans are defined benefit plans under which each employee is provided with a benefit which, as a percentage of pay, is nondiscriminatory. This benefit is then reduced, or offset, for each employee by the employer-provided portion of the employee's Social Security benefit. A defined plan is within the disparity limits for integrated offset plans if it provides that a participant's accrued benefit derived from employer contributions (Sec. 411(c)(1)) may not be reduced by more than the "maximum offset allowance". For benefits attributable to any year of service with the employer taken into account under the plan, the maximum offset allowance is equal to ¾ of 1% of the participant's final average compensation. The maximum offset allowance for total benefits is ¾ of 1% of the participant's final average compensation multiplied by the participant's years of service with the employer (to a maximum of 35 years) taken into account under the plan. The maximum offset allowance may not be, however, greater than 50% of the benefit that would have accrued without regard to the offset.

Final average compensation is the participant's average annual compensation for the three consecutive years ending with the current year or, if the participant does not have three years of service, the full period of the participant's service. Final average compensation is determined without taking into account compensation in any year which is in excess of the Social Security taxable wage base.

The new law directs the Secretary of the Treasury to prescribe regulations under which a defined benefit plan may use two or more integration levels. According to the Conference Committee Report accompanying the new law, the regulations will require that the permitted disparity with respect to each such integration level be based on the percentage of compensation up to each level replaced by the employer-provided Social Security PIA.

Reduction of maximum excess or offset allowance. If an excess plan has an integration level in excess of covered compensation, the ¾ of one percentage point factor in the maximum excess allowance will be reduced under rules to be prescribed by the Secretary of the Treasury. The factor will also be reduced with respect to any participant in an offset plan who has final average compensation in excess of covered compensation. These reductions will be based on percentages of compensation replaced by the portion of Social Security primary insurance amounts attributable to employer contributions.

The maximum excess or offset allowance will also be reduced, under regulations to be prescribed by the Secretary of the Treasury, for defined benefit plans which provide for unreduced benefits commencing before the Social Security retirement age.

Covered compensation. Covered compensation means, as under prior law, the average of the Social Security taxable wage base for each year in the 35-year period ending with the year in which the employee attains age 65. In calculating covered compensation for any year, it must be assumed that no increases in the taxable wage base will occur after the year of determination and before the year in which the employee attains age 65.

Railroad plans. The new law provides a special rule for plans which include employees of a railroad who are entitled to benefits under Railroad Retirement Act of 1974. These plans may be integrated, under rules similar to the integration rules for Social Security benefits, with the employer-derived tier 2 railroad retirement benefits and any supplemental annuity under the Railroad Retirement Act of 1974.

Multiple plans. Regulations are to be prescribed by the Secretary of the Treasury to prevent the multiple use of the permitted disparities with respect to any employee covered by two or more plans.

Benefits based on final pay. A defined benefit pension plan (including an offset or excess plan) is not considered discriminatory merely because it provides that the employer-provided benefit for any participant is limited to the excess (if any) of (1) the participant's final pay with the employer, over (2) the employer-provided social security benefit attributable to the participant's service with the employer. The Secretary of the Treasury is directed to prescribe rules for "normalizing" accrued benefits for purposes of this rule. This limit may not, however, be applied to reduce minimum benefits under the top-heavy rules (Sec. 416).

For purposes of determining the final-pay limit that may be imposed by an integrated defined benefit plan, a participant's final pay is the total compensation paid to the participant by the employer during the participant's highest year of compensation ending with or within the five-year period ending with the year in which the participant separated from service with the employer.

Act Sec. 1111, amends Sec. 401(l) of the Code to provide new rules for the nondiscriminatory coordination of qualified plans with OASDI and makes conforming amendments to Sec. 401(a) effective generally for benefits attributable to plan years beginning after 12-31-88. For plans maintained pursuant to collective bargaining agreements ratified before 3-1-86, the effective date is the first day of the first plan year beginning after the earlier of the termination of the CBA (or 1-1-89, if later) or 1-1-91.

[¶1111] Minimum Coverage Requirements. Prior law required that qualified plans be for the benefit of employees generally, rather than for the benefit of only officers, shareholders, and highly compensated employees. To assure that plans did not disproportionately benefit members of the prohibited group, minimum coverage requirements were imposed. To meet these requirements, plans had to either cover at least 56% of all the sponsoring employer's employees, or to cover a classification of employees the Secretary of Treasury found to be nondiscriminatory. The determination of whether a classification was nondiscriminatory was made on the basis of all the facts and circumstances surrounding each case.

New percentage test. Under the new law, at least 70% of the sponsoring employer's nonhighly compensated employees must be covered by the plan, or the percentage of covered nonhighly compensated employees must be at least 70% of the percentage of highly compensated employees who are covered. However, for a cash or deferred arrangement or the portion of a defined contribution plan consisting of employee and matching employer contributions, an employee will be deemed to be covered under the plan as long as the employee is *eligible* to contribute under the plan. Thus, for example, if all nonhighly compensated employees of an employer are eligible to make elective deferrals under a CODA, but only 65% do, the plan may still satisfy the percentage test.

Average benefit percentage test. Plans which do not satisfy either of the new percentage tests will still be deemed to be in compliance with the test if they satisfy an "average benefit percentage test." A plan will, in turn, pass this alternative test if it satisfies the prior Sec. 410(b)(1)(B) classification test, and the average benefit percentage for nonhighly compensated employees (as a percentage of compensation) is at least 70% of the average benefit percentage for highly compensated employees.

The term "average benefit percentage" means, as to a group of employees, the average of each employee's "benefit percentage." The "benefit percentage" is the employer-provided contributions (including forfeitures) or benefits of an employee under a plan, expressed as a percentage of that employee's compensation (as defined under Sec. 414(s)).

Example: Assume that an employer has 100 employees, 40 of whom are covered by a plan which satisfies the prior law's classification test. Of the 40, 10 are highly compensated. The average benefit percentage of the highly compensated employees is 75%; the average benefit percentage of the remaining 30 employees is 55%. Because the average benefit percentage of the nonhighly compensated

¶1111

employees (55%) is greater than 70% of the average benefit percentage of the highly compensated employees (75%) the plan meets the new fair cross-section test.

In determining the average benefit percentage of a group of employees, elective deferrals under a cash or deferred arrangement are considered to be employer-provided contributions.

Excludable employees. Under the new law, as under prior law, certain employees can be excluded for purposes of the coverage tests. Generally, excludable employees are those who are included in a unit covered by a collective bargaining agreement, and nonresident aliens with no income from sources within the U.S. If a plan is maintained under a collective bargaining agreement between air pilots and one or more employers, persons not covered by the CBA may be excludable.

Minimum age and service requirements. If a plan has minimum age and service requirements for participation, as permitted under Sec. 410(a)(1), and all such employees are excluded from participation in the plan, such employees may be excluded from consideration in testing whether the plan meets the new percentage tests and, for the purposes of the average benefit percentage test, whether the plan covers a nondiscriminatory classification of employees. For the purpose of determining the average benefit percentages, the plan can exclude only those employees who fail to meet the *lowest* age and service requirements of *any* plan maintained by the employer.

If a group of employees who do not meet a plan's age 21 and one year of service requirement is covered by a separate plan, the employer may elect to test that group separately. If the separate plan meets either of the new percentage tests with respect to that group, the group can be excluded from consideration in determining whether any plan of the employer meets the new percentage tests, even though other employees not meeting the age and service requirements are not excluded. The Conference Committee Report accompanying the new law indicates that a group of employees not meeting the age 21 and one year of service requirement may be tested separately even if *not* covered by a separate plan, provided the group is defined in a nondiscriminatory manner, solely by reference to the age and service requirements.

Aggregation of plans. As under prior law, an employer may designate more than one plan as a unit to satisfy the coverage tests, provided the designated plans provide benefits which do not discriminate in favor of the prohibited group. For purposes of applying the average benefit percentage test, two or more comparable plans may be aggregated to determine whether the classification test under the prior law is satisfied. The general principles set out in Rev. Rul. 81-202 to determine comparability are still used, but must be modified to reflect the new integration rules [¶1110].

Separate lines of business. Generally, the rule under prior law, that all employees of a controlled group of corporations, members of an affiliated service group, or trades or businesses under common control, are aggregated and treated as employees of a single employer for purposes of the qualification requirements is preserved. However, if an employer establishes to the satisfaction of the Secretary of the Treasury that the employer operates separate lines of business or operating units for valid business reasons, a plan maintained for employees in one line of business or operating unit may satisfy the coverage requirements separately with respect to those employees, provided certain requirements are met [¶1115].

Dispositions and acquisitions. Under special transition rules for certain dispositions or acquisitions of businesses, if an employer becomes or ceases to be a member of a controlled group or affiliated service group, the coverage rules will be deemed satisfied with respect to any plan covering employees of such employer during the transition period (as defined in the bill), provided that (1) the coverage rules were satisfied immediately before the acquisition or disposition; and (2) the coverage under the plan does not change significantly during the transition period (other than by reason of the acquisition or disposition). The transition period is defined under the bill as the period beginning on the date of the acquisition or disposition and ending on the last day of the first plan year beginning after the acquisition or disposition.

Sanctions. The new law changes the penalty for a plan's failure to meet the new qualification requirements. Such plans will remain qualified with respect to nonhighly-compensated employees, but highly-compensated employees will be taxed on the present value of their employer-derived vested accrued benefits and income on any contributions to the extent such amounts have not been previously taxed.

Minimum participation rule. The general rule permitting several comparable plans to be designated as a single unit for the purpose of the nondiscrimination and coverage tests might in some cases permit arrangements which discriminate in favor of the prohibited group. The new law resolves this perceived problem by modifying the general rule. Now a plan will in no event be qualified unless it benefits the lesser of 50 employees or 40% of all the employer's employees. Comparable plans *may not* be designated as a single unit for the purpose of satisfying this requirement, nor can the test be applied on a line of business or operating unit basis. However, for a cash or deferred arrangement, or for the portion of a defined contribution plan calling for employee and matching employer contributions, all employees who are eligible to contribute are considered to benefit under the plan whether they actually contribute or not.

Employees who may be excluded under the general coverage rules (i.e., employees who have not satisfied age and service requirements, collective bargaining employees, etc.) may be excluded for the purposes of this requirement. However, if any highly compensated employee who is excludable is covered for more than one year, *all* employees must be counted.

The new law provides a transition rule, under which plans which do not satisfy this minimum participation rule may be merged or terminated. If a plan which fails to meet the minimum participation rule was in existence on 8-16-86, and there is no transfer of assets, merger or spinoff involving the plan after 8-16-86, the plan may be merged or terminated before the end of the first plan year for which the rule is applicable, and the excise tax on asset reversions will not apply. The present values of accrued benefits under the plans must be determined using the highest interest rate which may be used for calculating present values under Sec. 411(a)(11)(B). The minimum participation rule does not apply to multiemployer plans, unless they are plans established by unions for professionals (e.g., doctors or lawyers).

Act Sec. 1112 amends Secs. 401 and 410 of the Code to change coverage requirements for qualified plans. The changes are generally effective, for plan years beginning after 12-31-88; however, for plans maintained under collective bargaining agreements that were ratified before 3-1-86, the new law will not apply to plan years beginning before the earlier of (1) the date the last such collective bargaining agreement terminates (determined without regard for extensions of the agreement after 2-28-86) or (2) 1-1-91.

[¶1112] Tax-Sheltered Annuities Subject to Coverage and Nondiscrimination Rules. Under prior law, tax-sheltered Sec. 403(b) annuities—purchased for employees by tax-exempt charitable, educational or religious organizations, public schools, or state or local educational institutions—generally received significant tax advantages even though they were exempt from all of the coverage and nondiscrimination rules that applied to qualified plans. Because of this exemption, tax-exempt organizations could provide 403(b) annuities for any employees they chose, and thus could provide disproportionately large benefits to highly paid workers. To end this type of *carte blanche* for TEOs with respect to 403(b) annuities, the new law extends certain nondiscrimination rules to 403(b) annuity programs (other than those maintained by churches).

Nondiscriminatory coverage of nonelective 403(b) annuities. The new law provides that the Sec. 401(a)(4) nondiscrimination rules and Sec. 410(b) coverage rules for qualified plans also apply to any tax-sheltered annuity that an employer contributes to (so-called "nonelective contributions"). Thus, such 403(b) annuity programs must cover employees in general, rather than merely the employer's highly paid workers, and must satisfy either a percentage or fair cross-section test under Sec. 410. A tax-sheltered annuity meets the percentage test if either 70% of all nonhighly compensated employees benefit under the plan, or the percentage of nonhighly compensated employees who benefit under the plan is at least 70% of the percentage of highly compensated employees who benefit. On the other hand, a 403(b) plan that doesn't satisfy either of the preceding percentage tests still satisfies Sec. 410 if it benefits employees on the basis of a classification deemed by the IRS not to discriminate in favor of officers, shareholders, and highly paid workers, and the average benefit percentage for nonhighly compensated employees is at least 70% of the average benefit percentage for highly compensated employees.

The average benefit percentage for a group of employees is, for applying the fair cross-section test, the average of the employer-provided benefit of each employee within the group. For the classification test, the prior-law rule that the IRS must consider all of the facts and circumstances still holds true.

In addition to the percentage and classification coverage tests, 403(b) annuities (other than those maintained for church employees) must provide contributions or benefits that do not discriminate in favor of highly paid workers under Sec. 401(a)(4). An annuity program satisfies this requirement if either benefits or contributions for highly paid workers, when expressed as a percentage of their compensation, doesn't exceed a similar percentage for other employees. And contributions or benefits under 403(b) annuities may be integrated with the employer-provided portion of Social Security benefits as could qualified plan benefits and contributions under prior law. The rules governing Social Security integration are the same as the new rules for qualified plans [¶1110].

Qualified plans and 403(b) aggregation. A tax-sheltered annuity that, by itself, doesn't satisfy the preceding coverage and nondiscrimination tests, may be aggregated with a qualified plan maintained by the same employer to satisfy the tests provided both the plan and annuity provide comparable benefits and don't discriminate in favor of the highly paid. In applying the average benefit percentage component of the average benefit percentage test to a tax sheltered annuity, an employer may include all qualified plans in determining the average benefit percentages. Note, however, that this aggregation rule applies only for purposes of determining whether a *tax-sheltered annuity* satisfies the Sec. 401(a)(4) and 410(b) coverage and nondiscrimination tests; it is not applicable in determining whether the qualified plan satisfies these requirements. The categories of employees which may be excluded in applying the cov-

¶1112

erage rules to qualified plans may also be excluded in the case of tax-sheltered annuities. In addition, student employees of an educational institution who normally work less than 20 hours per week can be excluded.

Special rule for 403(b) annuities permitting elective deferrals. The new law provides special coverage and nondiscrimination rules for annuities permitting only elective (i.e., employee) deferrals, and for elective deferrals under 403(b) programs to which an employer also makes nonelective contributions. The general nondiscrimination rules continue to apply to nonelective contributions under the latter programs. Under the new law, a tax-sheltered annuity allowing elective deferrals will be discriminatory as to those deferrals unless *all* employees of the annuity sponsor have the option to make deferrals to the program. To insure all employees have the option of making elective deferrals, employers can't require minimum dollar or percentage contributions as a condition of participation other than reasonable *de minimis* contribution thresholds (i.e., a minimum yearly contribution of $300, 1% of compensation, or $25 monthly would be OK). Elective 403(b) deferrals include employer contributions under a salary reduction agreement (whether or not in writing) that are excludable from a worker's income.

> **NOTE:** Generally, for the special coverage and nondiscrimination rules that apply to elective deferrals, all employees (other than nonresident aliens with no U.S.-source income) must be included. This includes employees who haven't satisfied a program's minimum age or service requirements, or who are covered under collective bargaining agreements; such employees must be considered for purposes of the special elective deferral test. However, employees who participate in "eligible deferred compensation plans" (as defined in Sec. 457) may be excluded, and in applying the nondiscrimination tests to educational institutions, students who customarily work less than 20 hours per week may be excluded.

In addition, the Sec. 414(n) leased employee rules continue to apply for the special coverage and nondiscrimination tests. But the elective deferral rules apply only to the entity of the employer sponsoring the 403(b) annuity. For example, when determining whether all employees of an employer have a chance to make elective deferrals, the relevant workforce of a state university offering an annuity includes only university employees, not all employees of the state.

Exclusions. Tax-sheltered annuities for church employees are exempt from the new law's nondiscrimination rules. This includes a convention or association of churches, an elementary or secondary school controlled by such a convention or association, and certain "qualified church-controlled organizations." However, the Committee Reports that accompany the new law specifically provide that the new coverage and nondiscrimination rules apply to church-run universities and hospitals that sell goods or services to the public for profit and receive more than 25% of their support from certain specific sources.

Act Sec. 1120, relating to nondiscrimination requirements for tax-sheltered annuities, amends Sec. 403, effective for years beginning after 12-31-88.

[¶1113] **Minimum Vesting Standards.** Under the various alternative vesting schedules provided for in the prior law (i.e., 10-year cliff, 5-15 year graded, Rule of 45), the more mobile, shorter service employees were likely to terminate employment before vesting in any accrued benefits. Thus, the prior law did not meet the needs of women, minorities, and lower-paid employees. Accordingly, the new law provides for more rapid vesting than was required under prior law.

Vesting schedules. The three standard vesting schedules under prior law are replaced by two new schedules. A plan satisfies the first schedule if participants have a nonforfeitable right to 100% of their accrued benefits derived from employer contributions on completion of five years of service. The second schedule requires that participants be vested in 20% of their employer derived after three years of service, with an additional 20% vesting each year thereafter until the participant is 100% vested in the employer-derived accrued benefit after seven years of service.

Top-heavy plans. The prior law's vesting requirements for top-heavy plans are not changed under the new law. Thus, a top-heavy plan must still meet one of the two special vesting schedules applicable to top-heavy plans.

Class year plans. Class year plans, under prior law, were profit sharing, stock bonus, or money purchase plans which provided for separate vesting on a year-to-year basis. The new law repeals the class year vesting provisions.

Changes in vesting schedule. Under the new law, if a plan's vesting schedule is modified by plan amendment, the plan will not be qualified unless each participant with at least three years of service is permitted to elect, within a reasonable period after the adoption of the amendment, to have the nonforfeitable percentage of the participant's accrued benefit computed without regard to the amendment.

Multiple employer plans. The new law makes an exception for participants in multiemployer plans (within the meaning of Sec. 414(f)) who are covered by collective bargaining agreements. Under such plans a participant's benefit derived from employer contributions must be 100% vested no later than on the participant's completion of 10 years of service.

The new law also provides that a plan may require two years of service (down from three years) as a condition of eligibility to participate if the plan provides for 100% vesting on participation. The vesting provisions of the new law are also applicable to ESOPs [¶1172, et. seq.].

Act Sec. 1113 amends Secs. 410(a) and 411(a) of the Code, and Sec. 1012 of ERISA, to require more rapid vesting in accrued benefits, effective for plan years beginning after 12-31-88. However, for plans maintained pursuant to collective bargaining agreements which were ratified before 3-1-86, the new provision will not be effective for years beginning before the earlier of (1) the later of 1-1-89 or the termination of the collective bargaining agreement, or (2) 1-1-91.

[¶1114] Highly-Compensated Employee. Generally, qualified plans are prohibited from discriminating in favor of highly-compensated employees. Under prior law, it was not clear which employees were considered to be highly-compensated (except for the purpose of the special nondiscrimination rules for CODAs [¶1116]).

The new law redefines the group of highly compensated employees. Now, an employee is treated as highly compensated for a year if, at any time during the year or the preceding year, the employee (1) was a 5% owner of the employer; (2) received more than $75,000 in annual compensation from the employer; (3) received more than $50,000 in annual compensation from the employer and was a member of the top-paid group of the employer during the same year (i.e., one of the top 20% of employees by pay during the year); or (4) was an officer of the employer and earned more than 150% of the dollar limit on annual additions. If for any year no officer receives compensation in excess of this amount, the highest paid officer is treated as a highly compensated employee. The $50,000 and $75,000 thresholds are indexed at the same time and in the same manner as the adjustments to the dollar limits on benefits for defined benefit pension plans.

To identify which employees are highly compensated, all members of a controlled group of employers are treated as one employer.

The top-paid group of employees includes all employees whose compensation paid during the year is in the top 20% of the employer's workforce. Under a special rule, an employer may exclude certain employees in computing the size of the employer's workforce for purposes of calculating the number of employees who are in the top-paid group.

The following employees may be excluded in determining the size of the top-paid group (but not for identifying the particular employees in the top-paid group): (1) employees who have not completed 6 months of service; (2) employees who work less than 37½ hours per week; (3) employees who normally work fewer than six months a year; (4) except to the extent provided in regulations, employees who are included in a unit of employees covered by a bona fide collective bargaining agreement; (5) employees who have not attained age 21; and (6) employees who are nonresident aliens and who receive no U.S. source earned income.

Under this special rule, an employer may elect to apply numbers (1), (2), (3), and (5) above by substituting any shorter period of service or lower age than is specified in (1), (2), (3), or (5), as long as the employer applies the test uniformly for determining its top-paid group with respect to all its qualified plans and employee benefit plans.

> **Example:** An employer's total workforce is 100 employees, 20 of whom have not completed 6 months of service. None of the 100 employees is within any of the other excluded categories under this rule. Under the above rules for determining the top-paid group, 16 employees may be treated as included in the top-paid group. This is because the 20 employees who have not completed the minimum requirements for eligibility may be disregarded in determining the size of the top-paid group. The top-paid group cannot be larger than 20% of 80 employees (the number of employees who are not disregarded). Thus, the 16 employees of the employer that earn the highest compensation (including any employees who have not completed 180 days but who are among the 16 highest paid employees of the employer) are to be treated as in the top-paid group. Each of the employees in the top-paid group who earns more than $50,000 a year is treated as a highly compensated employee. Other employees (and any of the 16 employees earning less than $50,000) may also be a highly compensated employee under one of the other tests (e.g., officer or 5% owner).

The new law provides a special rule for determining which employees are highly compensated in any given year. Under this special rule, an employee who in the preceding year did not receive compensation in excess of $75,000, or was not a member of the top-paid group and receiving compensation in excess of $50,000, or was not an officer of the employer, is not treated as a highly compensated employee for the current year unless the employee is a 5% owner of the employer. This special rule doesn't apply to any employee who is among the highest-paid 100 employees in the current year.

An individual who was a highly compensated employee for the preceding year (without regard to one-year lookback or to the application of this special rule) remains highly compensated for the current year. The 100-employee rule is intended as a rule of convenience to employers with respect to new employees hired during the current year, increases in compensation, and certain other factors. If any employee is not within the top-100 employees by pay for the current year (and was not a highly compensated employee in the preceding year), then that employee is not treated as highly compensated for the year, but will be treated as highly compensated for the following year if the employee otherwise falls within the definition of highly compensated employee.

Example: A calendar year employer has 12,000 total employees in 1990 and in 1991, and for each year 4,000 employees may be disregarded in determining the number of employees to be treated as the number in the top-paid group. Thus, 1,600 (20% of 8,000) employees are in the top-paid group. The employer's highly compensated employees for 1991 will include the following:

(1) Any employee who at any time during 1990 or 1991 owned more than 5% of the employer;

(2) Any employee who, in 1990, (i) earned more than $75,000 in annual compensation, (ii) was an officer and earned more than 150% of the dollar limit on annual additions to a defined contribution plan; or (iii) earned more than $50,000 in annual compensation and was among the 1,600 most highly compensated employees; and

(3) Any employee who, in 1991, (i) was an officer and earned more than 150% of the dollar limit on annual additions to a defined contribution plan; or earned more than $50,000 in annual compensation, and (ii) was among the 100 most highly compensated employees.

Thus, an employee who is not a highly compensated employee in 1990 (without regard to this special 100-employee rule) will not be treated as highly compensated for 1991 unless such employee either (i) acquires ownership of more than 5% of the employer in 1991 or (ii) both becomes an officer earning more than 150% of the defined contribution dollar limit or earns more than $50,000 in 1991 and becomes one of the 100 most highly compensated employees in 1991.

NOTE: To figure who are highly compensated employees, "officer" and "5% owner" have the meaning set forth in Sec. 416(i) (relating to top-heavy plans).

The new law provides a special rule for determining the highly compensated employees in the case of employers who were incorporated on 12-15-24. Under this special rule, if more than one half of the employees in the top 20% of employees by pay earn less than $25,000 (indexed), then members of the top-paid group are determined without regard to whether they earn more than $50,000.

Under the new law, any family member (i.e., an employee's spouse, parent, and lineal descendants) of either a 5% owner or one of an employer's top-ten paid workers is treated with the employee as a single highly compensated employee in applying the special CODA nondiscrimination tests if the family member benefits under the CODA. For example, if the most highly compensated employee and his or her spouse both participate in an employer's CODA, then the deferrals made, and compensation earned, by each are aggregated for purposes of applying the special nondiscrimination test to the highly compensated employee's elective deferrals.

An employee who has separated from service continues to be treated as a highly compensated employee if the individual was a highly compensated employee when the separation from service occurred, or at any time after the employee attained age 55. Under this rule, an employee is treated as highly compensated if the employee was highly compensated at any time during the current or the preceding year. In addition, the Secretary is to prescribe rules to treat other former employees as highly compensated employees, if appropriate.

The Senate Finance Committee Report indicates that the Secretary of the Treasury will prescribe rules to treat an individual as separated from service if the employee performs only de minimis services for the employer during the year. Thus, an individual will not be able to avoid the rules regarding former employees by continuing to perform minimal services, and arguing that a separation from service has not occurred.

Act Sec. 1114, adds Code Sec. 414(q), defining highly compensated employee, and makes conforming amendments to Secs. 106(b), 117(d), 120(c), 120(d), 127(b), 129(d), 132(h), 274(e), 401(a), 404A, 406(b), 407(b), 411(d), 414(m), 415(c), 423(b), 501(c), 505(b), and 4975(d) and to ERISA Sec. 408(b) effective for plan years beginning after 12-31-86, except that certain of the conforming amendments are effective for plan years beginning after 12-31-87.

[¶1115] **Separate Lines of Business: Compensation.** Generally, the rule under prior law, that all employees of a controlled group of corporations, members of an affiliated service group, or trades or businesses under common control, are aggregated and treated as employees of a single employer for purposes of plan qualification requirements is preserved. However, the new law provides an important exception to this rule. If an employer establishes to the satisfaction of the Secretary of the Treasury that the employer operates separate lines of business for valid business reasons, a plan maintained for employees in one line of business may satisfy the nondiscrimination requirements if such plan satisfies the requirements as to those employees. This exception is not available, however, unless the plan also satisfies the prior law's classification test, taking into account all those employees who must be considered under the general rule.

Safe harbor for separate line of business. A line of business will be treated as a separate line of business if it is a separate, self-sustaining unit, and (1) the line of business has at least 50 employees who do not perform services for any other line of business; (2) the employer notifies the Secretary of the Treasury that the line of business is to be treated as a separate line of business; and (3) the employer receives a determination that the line of business may be treated as a separate line of business. However, (3) is not required if the "highly-compensated employee percentage" of the line of business or operating unit is not less than one-half, nor more than twice the percentage of all employees of the employer who are highly compensated. The "highly compensated employee percentage" is the percentage of all employees performing services for a line of business who are highly-compensated employees [¶1114]. The highly compensated employee percentage of a line of business will be treated as not less than one-half of the percentage of all employees of the employer who are highly compensated if at least 10% of all highly-compensated employees of the employer are employed by the line of business or operating unit. An operating unit in a separate geographic area operated separately for a bona fide business reason will be considered to be a separate line of business.

The net effect of these requirements is to require that any separate line of business or operating unit include a meaningful proportion of highly-compensated employees and other employees. Thus, an employer may not circumvent the nondiscrimination rules by attempting to claim, for example, that substantially all highly-compensated employees are in a separate line of business or operating units from other employees, and then providing discriminatory benefits to the highly compensated employees. The separate line of business exception will, however, permit separate businesses, which are under common control (or even separate divisions of a single corporation) but whose operations are essentially unrelated, to plan retirement benefit programs on the basis of the needs of the employees involved in their operations without being required to coordinate with other businesses whose employees have different needs and expectations.

The separate line of business exception will not apply in the case of an affiliated service group.

Compensation. The new law adopts a uniform definition of compensation for purposes of the new nondiscrimination requirements. Generally, compensation is compensation for service performed for an employer which is currently includible in income. An employer may elect to include salary reduction contributions to CODAs, tax sheltered annuities, or SEPs as compensation, provided that these contributions are treated as compensation on a consistent basis. The Secretary of the Treasury is directed to prescribe regulations providing for alternate definitions of compensation. However, such alternate definitions will only be available to employers if they do not discriminate in favor of highly-compensated employees.

Act Sec. 1115 adds Secs. 414(r) and 414(s), to the Code to provide exception to general coverage rules for separate lines of business, and to provide a uniform definition of compensation effective for plan years beginning after 12-31-86.

[¶1116] Cash or Deferred Arrangements. Under the nondiscrimination rules and contribution levels of the prior law, significant contributions by highly compensated employees were permitted without comparable participation by rank-and-file employees. Because a basic purpose of extending tax incentives to establish qualified plans is to provide for benefits to rank-and-file employees who might not otherwise save for retirement, the new law revises the nondiscrimination rules to better achieve this goal. At the same time, the new law tightens up the withdrawal provisions under the prior law to increase the likelihood that savings which receive favorable tax treatment are in fact used to provide retirement income.

Nondiscrimination requirements. The new law modifies the existing special nondiscrimination tests applicable to cash or deferred arrangements (CODAs) in several ways. First, the new law provides that the actual deferral percentage (ADP—the percentage of compensation deferred under a CODA) for an employer's highly compensated employees cannot exceed 125% of the ADP of the employer's eligible nonhighly compensated workers. Alternatively, the ADP of highly compensated employees cannot top 200% of the ADP of nonhighly paid workers, or the ADP of all nonhighly paid workers plus two percentage points, whichever is less. If a highly compensated employee participates in more than one CODA maintained by the employer, his or her elective deferrals under all the CODAs must be aggregated for purposes of the ADP computation. And the Treasury is authorized under the new law to prescribe regulations for the aggregation of elective CODA deferrals with employer matching contributions and qualified nonelective contributions. Qualified nonelective contributions are, for this purpose, employer contributions (other than matching contributions) which are not elective, and which are subject the same vesting and distribution restrictions as are applicable to elective contributions.

Aggregation for highly compensated. Under prior law, if any employee participated in more than one cash or deferred arrangement of the employer, elective deferrals under all the plans were required to be aggregated for purposes of the special nondiscrimination tests. The new law amends this requirement, and provides that only the elective deferrals of highly compensated employees must be aggregated. The Committee Report accompanying the new law indicates, however, that employers can elect to aggregate all employees under all CODAs and treat all such plans as one plan for purposes of applying the nondiscrimination test.

Highly compensated employees. The special nondiscrimination test for CODAs compares the average deferral, as a percentage of compensation, of the highly compensated employees with the average deferral of all other employees. Under prior law, highly compensated employees were simply the highest paid one-third of all employees. The new law redefines the group of highly compensated employees [¶1114].

¶1116

Excess contributions. The new law allows CODAs which don't satisfy the special nondiscrimination tests to distribute excess contributions, plus earnings thereon. If the excess contributions (plus earnings) are distributed within two-and-one-half months after the year of deferral, the plan can avoid the ten-percent excise tax which is otherwise payable. A CODA will not be disqualified because of a failure to satisfy the special nondiscrimination rules, provided the excess contributions, plus any earnings allocable thereto, are distributed by the end of the plan year following the year for which the contributions are made. Such excess contributions may be distributed without regard to the provisions of the plan until the date the plan is required to be amended to comply with the new limits (Sec. 1141), and may be made without the consent of the participant or the participant and spouse. These excess contributions may be distributed notwithstanding any other provision of law, and will not be subject to the penalty tax on early distributions [¶1123].

"Excess contributions" means, for any plan year, the aggregate of elective deferrals by highly compensated employees over the maximum elective deferrals that would be made by such employees without violating the special nondiscrimination rules applicable to cash or deferred arrangements. To figure the amount of excess contributions and the employees to whom the excess contributions are to be distributed, the elective deferrals of highly compensated employees are reduced in the order of their actual deferral percentages beginning with those highly compensated employees with the highest actual deferral percentages. The excess contributions must be distributed to those highly compensated employees for whom the reduction is made in order to satisfy the special nondiscrimination tests.

> **Example:** Elective deferrals by the three highly compensated employees—Adams, Brown, and Carter—are 10%, 8%, and 6% of compensation, respectively. Assume that the actual deferral percentage limit on elective deferrals for the highly compensated employees under the qualified cash or deferred arrangement for the 1987 plan year is 7%. To reduce the actual deferral percentage for Adams, Brown, and Carter to 7%, it is necessary first to reduce the elective deferrals of Adam's percentage, which is the highest, to 8% (the same as Brown, who has the next highest percentage). Since the actual deferral percentage for highly compensated employees still exceeds 7%, it is necessary to next reduce Adam's and Brown's deferrals to 7.5%. This reduces this actual deferral percentage for the group to 7%. Thus, excess contributions of 2.5% of compensation (plus income) must be distributed to Adams; while .5% of compensation (plus income) must be distributed to Brown.

Other restrictions. Restrictions on withdrawals from CODAs are substantially modified. First, the new law provides that distributions may be made to a participant in a qualified cash or deferred arrangement on account of the sale of a subsidiary or the assets used in a trade or business of the employer, or termination of the plan of which the arrangement is a part. Distributions on the sale of a subsidiary may be made to a participant even though the participant has not separated from service with the subsidiary. However, distributions on account of a plan termination, or because of a sale of a subsidiary or assets, must be a distribution of the participant's entire interest in the plan. Moreover, distribution on account of a sale of assets may be made only if substantially all of the assets used in a trade or business of the employer are sold.

The Committee Report accompanying the new law indicates that hardship withdrawals under a qualified cash or deferred arrangement are limited to the amount of an employee's elective deferrals. Hardship withdrawals are not permitted from income on any contributions or from employer matching or nonelective employer contributions taken into account for purposes of the special nondiscrimination test and, as under prior law, are not permitted from a pre-ERISA money purchase pension plan. Prior law standards relating to the definition of a hardship continue to apply. In addition, the new law imposes further restrictions to prohibit discrimination. Under Sec. 401(k)(4), as amended, a qualified cash or deferred arrangement cannot require, as a condition of participation in the arrangement, that an employee complete a period of service with the employer (or employers) maintaining the plan in excess of one year of service.

Also, an employer generally may not condition, either directly or indirectly, contributions and benefits (other than matching contributions) on an employee's election to defer compensation under a cash or deferred arrangement.

Effective Dates: The CODA nondiscrimination rules are generally effective for plan years beginning after 12-31-86. The provisions permitting withdrawals on plan termination or sale of assets apply to distributions after 12-31-84. (The new rules relating to aggregation of deferrals under multiple plans and distributions of excess contributions are effective for plan years beginning after 12-31-86.)

For a plan maintained under a collective bargaining agreement between employee representatives and one or more employers ratified before 3-1-86, the amendments are not effective for plan years beginning the earlier of (1) the later of (i) 1-1-89, or (ii) the date on which the last of the collective bargaining agreements terminates, or (2) 1-1-91. Extensions or renegotiations of the collective bargaining agreement, if ratified after 2-28-86, are disregarded.

Generally, under the new law tax-exempt organizations and state and local governments are not permitted to maintain CODAs. However, under a transitional rule, the provision is not immediately applicable to any cash or deferred arrangement maintained by a tax-exempt organization adopted before 7-1-86, or a CODA maintained

¶1116

by a state or local government that was adopted by the employer before 5-6-86. The provision is effective for years beginning after 12-31-88 for such plans.

The prohibition against conditioning receipt of other benefits on an employee's election to defer compensation under a CODA is also subject to a special transition rule, under which a CODA will not be considered to be nonqualified because it is part of a "qualified offset arrangement" with a defined benefit plan if the arrangement was maintained by the employer on 4-16-86 and at all times thereafter certain conditions are met. For this purpose, a federally funded research center engaged in cancer research is deemed to be an employer. For such an arrangement, benefit accruals under the defined benefit plan are treated as matching employer contributions.

Act Sec. 1116, amending Code Sec. 401(k) effective as shown above.

[¶1117] Matching Contributions and Employee Contributions. To assure that employers do not shift too much of the retirement savings burden to employees, and that plans providing tax-favored savings benefits to highly paid employees provide comparable benefits to rank-and-file employees, the new law applies special nondiscrimination rules to employer matching contributions and employee contributions under qualified defined contribution plans, and to qualified defined benefit plans to the extent contributions are allocated to separate accounts on behalf of individual employees. These new rules apply in lieu of the usual nondiscrimination tests.

Special nondiscrimination tests. Two alternative tests are applied to matching employer and employee contributions to a qualified plan, one of which must be met for the plan to remain qualified. Under the first test, the contribution percentage for highly compensated employees must be no greater than 125% of the contribution percentage for all other eligible employees. Alternatively, the plan may satisfy the nondiscrimination test if the contribution percentage for highly compensated employees does not exceed the lesser of 200% of the contribution percentage for all other eligible employees, or such percentage plus two percentage points.

Example: Corporation M maintains a money purchase pension plan which provides for mandatory employee contributions of up to 10% of pay. Employee contributions are "matched" by the employer, on a dollar for dollar basis. No other contributions by employees or the employer are permitted. It is determined that for the 1987 plan year, the average contribution by rank-and-file employees was 3% of pay. Thus, the average total contribution for such employees (i.e., the contribution percentage) was 6%. During the same year, the contribution percentage for highly compensated emloyees was 8% (four percent employee contributions plus four percent matching employer contributions). Because the contribution percentage for the highly-compensated employees (8%) exceeds 125% of the contribution percentage of all other employees, (6%) the first nondiscrimination test is not satisfied. However, the second test is satisfied. 8% is less than 200% of 6%, and does not exceed 6% plus two percentage points.

Contribution percentages. The contribution percentage for a specified group of employees is the average of the ratios (calculated separately for each employee) of the sum of matching contributions and employee contributions to the employees' compensation for the plan year. Under regulations to be issued, an employer may also include elective contributions to a CODA in determining the contribution percentage. Nonelective contributions may also be included, provided they are nonforfeitable when made, and are subject to the same withdrawal restrictions as elective contributions under a CODA. However, if when these CODA contributions and nonelective contributions are disregarded, other employer contributions favor highly compensated employees in a way that violates the general nondiscrimination rules, the nonelective contributions cannot be used in calculating the contribution percentage. Thus, contributions used to satisfy one nondiscrimination test cannot again be used to satisfy the special nondiscrimination test. The new law requires the Secretary of the Treasury to prescribe regulations to prevent the multiple use of the alternative nondiscrimination test for any highly compensated employee.

Highly compensated employees are defined the same as for purposes of the general nondiscrimination rules [¶1114]. In plans which require employee contributions as a condition of participation, otherwise eligible employees who do not make contributions are treated as participants on whose behalf no contributions are made for purposes of the special nondiscrimination tests.

Aggregation rules. If a highly compensated employee participates in more than one plan maintained by the employer, all employer matching contributions, employee contributions, elective contributions, and if the employer so elects, qualified nonelective contributions made by or on behalf of such employee are aggregated for the purpose of determining the contribution percentage for such employee. Of course, the employer could decide to aggregate plans with respect to *all* participating employees, rather than just the highly-compensated employee, to test whether the special nondiscrimination test is satisfied.

If a plan subject to the special nondiscrimination rules is combined with another plan, also subject to the special test, for the purposes of satisfying the coverage requirements of Sec. 410(b), or the general nondiscrimination requirements of Sec. 401(a)(4), such plans must be treated as one plan for the purposes of applying the nondiscrimination test for employer matching and employee contributions.

Excess contributions. Excess contributions are contributions by or on behalf of highly compensated employees which are in excess of the contributions which could be made for such individuals without violating the special nondiscrimination rules. If it is determined that the special nondiscrimination rules for employer matching contributions and employee contributions are not satisfied, the plan will be disqualified unless the excess contributions are distributed (or if forfeitable, forfeited) before the close of the following plan year. The rules for such distributions are generally the same as those applied to excess contributions to CODAs [¶1116]. Contributions which are forfeited may be used to reduce employer contributions or may be reallocated among other participants. However, no highly compensated employee who has been determined to have excess contributions may share in such reallocation.

The new law provides that excess contributions (other than those which are forfeited) may be distributed notwithstanding any other provision of law, and will not be subject to the additional tax on early withdrawals from qualified plans [¶1123].

Excise tax. The new law imposes an excise tax on the employer equal to 10% of the excess contributions (including excess contributions to a SEP or a 501(c)(18) plan). However, for this purpose excess contributions do not include excess contributions which are distributed or forfeited within two and one-half months after the close of the plan year in which the excess contributions arose.

Effective Dates: The provisions of the new law relating to matching employer and employee contributions are generally effective for plan years beginning after 12-31-86 or, in the case of tax-sheltered annuities, 12-31-88. However, a special effective date applies to plans maintained pursuant to a collective bargaining agreement. Under this special rule, for a plan maintained pursuant to a collective bargaining agreement between employee representatives and one or more employers ratified before 3-1-86, the amendments are not effective for plan years beginning before the earlier of (1) the later of (i) 1-1-89, or (ii) the date on which the last of the collective bargaining agreements terminates; or (2) 1-1-91. Extensions or renegotiations of the collective bargaining agreement, if ratified after 2-28-86, are disregarded.

Act Sec. 1117, amends Sec. 401 and Sec. 4979 of the Code to provide special nondiscrimination rules for employee contributions and matching employer contributions, and to provide for an excise tax on excess contributions, and makes technical amendments to Secs. 414 and 415, effective as stated above.

[¶1118] **Uniform Benefit Accrual Rule for Top-Heavy Determinations.** Plans which primarily benefit an employer's key employees, and which are top-heavy under Sec. 416, must satisfy additional, tough qualification requirements. To prevent employers from avoiding the Sec. 416 rules by artificially accelerating benefit accruals for non-key employees, so that plan benefits for key employees never exceed 60% of all benefits and the plan never becomes top-heavy, the new law sets a uniform accrual rule for all plans for top-heavy (or super top-heavy) determination purposes. Solely for the purpose of testing whether the present value of cumulative accrued benefits for key employees exceeds 60% of similar benefits for all employees (90% in the case of determining whether a plan is super top-heavy), cumulative accrued benefits are measured by applying the "fractional rule" method of testing minimum benefit accruals.

Fractional rule accrual method. The fractional rule method of testing minimum benefit accruals is satisfied if the benefit accrued under a defined benefit plan is no less than the normal retirement benefit (with compensation projected to normal retirement age at present levels) multiplied by a fraction, the numerator of which is actual years of participation and the denominator of which is years of participation if the participant separated from service at a plan's normal retirement age. In essence, a normal retirement benefit is projected using current compensation; then, the minimum benefit accrual is the portion that represents years of participation to the total number of years from plan entry date to normal retirement age (ignoring service breaks). For example, if the projected normal retirement benefit is $1,000 and an employee has ten years of participation against a maximum 40 years to normal retirement age, his or her benefit accrual is $2,500 [$1,000 × (10 years/40 years)].

> **Example:** A defined benefit plan provides a normal retirement benefit at age 65 of 30% of average compensation for the high three consecutive years. Participant, age 40, with average compensation for the high three consecutive years of $20,000, has completed 15 years of participation by the close of the current plan year. A minimum benefit accrual of $2,250 [30% × $20,000 × 15/40] will satisfy the fractional rule test. (The fraction numerator is years of participation; the denominator is the difference between 65 and entry age 25.)

Note that use of the fractional rule for purposes of testing benefit accruals applies *only* for purposes of determining whether a plan is top-heavy or super top-heavy. The new law does not require the use of the fractional rule for purposes of accruing plan benefits. Under an exception to this general rule, cumulative accrued benefits may be determined under any of the accrual methods described in Sec. 411(a) if the employer-sponsor uses that method for *all* plans which it maintains.

Act Sec. 1118, requiring that plan benefits be treated as accruing ratably for purposes of determining whether it is top-heavy, amends Sec. 416, effective for plan years beginning after 12-31-86.

[¶1119] Money Purchase Plans Can Now Allocate Forfeitures to Participants' Accounts. Even though money purchase pension plans are defined contribution plans providing individual accounts for participants, they must provide definitely determinable benefits as must defined benefit plans and thus must contain a definite contribution formula. Prior law also treated money purchase plans as defined benefit plans for forfeiture purposes, and so required that forfeitures under money purchase plans could not be used to increase participants' benefits, but instead had to be applied to reduce future employer contributions or to pay administrative costs under Sec. 401(a)(8). The new law limits the requirement that forfeitures not be used to increase benefits to defined benefit plans, and thus allows money purchase pension plans to reallocate forfeitures to other participants under a nondiscriminatory formula. These plans, however, are not *required* to allocate forfeitures and can still opt to use forfeitures to reduce future employer contributions or administrative costs.

Act Sec. 1119, creating uniform rules for forfeitures under all defined contribution plans, amends Sec. 401(a)(8), effective for years beginning after 12-31-85.

Treatment of Distributions.

[¶1121] Uniform Minimum Distribution Rules. Distributions from a qualified retirement plan, an IRA or a tax-sheltered annuity must begin no later than April 1 following the calendar year in which the employee reaches age 70½. The distinction, under prior law, between a participant who is a 5% owner and an "ordinary" employee has been removed from IRC Sec. 401(a)(9). Under prior law, a participant who was not a 5% owner could postpone the beginning of his distribution until he retired after age 70½. Now, distribution to any participant generally must begin at age 70½.

Exception. The prior law applies to an individual who reaches age 70½ before 1-1-88 if the individual is not a 5% owner in the plan year ending in the year the individual attains age 66½ or any succeeding plan year. Moreover, an employee will not be subject to the excise tax for failure to satisfy the minimum distribution requirement because distributions are made in accordance with an election made before January 1, 1984 in accordance with Sec. 242(b)(2) of TEFRA.

Penalty. The 50% excise tax formerly imposed on underpayments of benefits from an IRA is now imposed on distributions from any qualified retirement plan. As under prior law, the IRS may waive the penalty if the underpayment was due to a reasonable error and steps are being taken to correct the underpayment.

Act Sec. 1121, setting uniform minimum distribution requirements, amends Secs. 401(a)(9), 402(a)(5), 408(d)(3), and 4974, effective for distributions made after 12-31-88, except as noted above.

[¶1122] Taxation of Distributions. The tax treatment of lump-sum distributions has been changed drastically. Capital gains treatment is phased out, except for certain distributions made to individuals who were at least 50 years old on 1-1-86 under a "grandfather rule." Capital gains treatment will not be available at all (except under the grandfather rule) for distributions after 1992. For distributions made during 1987-1991, treatment of amounts attributable to pre-1974 participation as long-term capital gain will be phased out. In 1987, they will all be treated as capital gain taxable at a 20% rate. In the following years, decreasing percentages will qualify for the 20% capital gain tax:

1988	95%
1989	75%
1990	50%
1991	25%

The 10-year forward averaging provision for LSDs has been changed to a 5-year averaging provision, with one exception: An individual who was 50 years old before 1-1-86, may use 10-year averaging, computing his tax using the tax rate in effect in 1986.

Check this out. An individual who gets a large LSD may owe less tax using the 5-year averaging computation rather than 10-year averaging. For example, on $400,000 taxable as an LSD, the tax would be $97,440 with 5-year averaging; $102,602 with 10-year averaging. Averaging is no longer available for a distribution received before age 59½, except for an individual who was at least 50 years old on 12-31-85.

Annuities. Benefits under qualified (Sec. 403(a)) annuity plans and (Sec. 403(b)) annuities will be taxable only when they are actually distributed. Under prior law, a beneficiary was taxable on amounts actually paid *or made available.*

The basis recovery rules for distributions from plans to which employees contributed have been changed.

- *Amounts not received as annuities:* Amounts received prior to the annuity starting date are now treated partially as taxable employer contributions and income, and partially as nontaxable employee contributions. Under prior law, the amounts received were not taxable as income until they exceeded the employee's total contributions. Generally, the nontaxable portion of a distribution under the new provision (IRC Sec. 72(e)(8)) is the same percentage as the percentage of the employee's nonforfeitable account balance that represents employee contributions. So, for example, under prior law if an individual had contributed $20,000 to his plan, he could withdraw up to $20,000 without tax liability. Now, such withdrawal would be taxable. If the employee's nonforfeitable account balance were $50,000 at the time of the distribution, $8,000 of the $20,000 distribution (⅖) would be treated as nontaxable return of investment and $12,000 would be treated as taxable income. Employee contributions to a defined contribution plan or to a separate account of a defined benefit plan are treated as a separate contract, and a withdrawal is not treated as partially attributable to employer contributions. However, it may be partially taxable as earnings on the contributions.

• *Three-year rule:* Under prior law, if a retiree receiving annuity payments would recover his entire contribution within 3 years, there was no tax liability until the full recovery was received. This provision has been repealed, except for employees whose annuity starting date is before 7-1-86.

• *Exclusion ratio:* In computing the exclusion ratio for annuity payments, the expected total return is determined as of the date of the payment. An employee's total exclusion is limited to the amount the employee contributed. If an annuitant dies before his entire basis is recovered, the unrecovered amount may be claimed as a deduction in the annuitant's final taxable year. Under prior law, if an employee outlived his life expectancy, determined at the annuity starting date, he could exclude from taxation an amount greater than he had actually contributed.

Effective Date: In general, the new pre-annuity starting date rules apply to distributions after 12-31-86 in tax years ending after that date. But this provision applies only to the extent that amounts received before the annuity starting date, when increased by amounts previously received under the contract after 12-31-86, exceed the investment in the contract as of 12-31-86 for a plan which on 5-5-86 permitted the withdrawal of employee contributions before separation from service. The post-annuity starting date basis recovery rules are generally effective with respect to individuals whose annuity starting date is after 7-1-86. The change in the constructive receipt rule for annuity payments is effective for taxable years beginning after 12-31-85.

Act Sec. 1122, relating to the taxation of distributions, amended Secs. 72(b) and (e); 402(e); 403(a), (b), and (c); and repealed Secs. 72(d); 402(a)(2) and 403(a)(2), effective for distributions after 12-31-86, except as indicated above.

[¶1123] **Additional Tax on Early Distributions.** The new law establishes an additional tax on early distributions from any qualified retirement plan, qualified annuity, IRA, or tax-sheltered annuity before the recipient reaches age 59½. The tax is 10% of the taxable portion of the distribution that is attributable to employer contributions and the amount allocable to after-tax employee contributions and "matching" contributions.

Exceptions. The additional tax doesn't apply to any distributions prior to 3-15-87 and taxable in 1986 to individuals whose employment terminated in 1986, or to payments to an alternate payee pursuant to a qualified domestic relations order. Also excepted are distributions (1) that are part of a scheduled series of substantially equal periodic payments for the life of the participant (or the joint lives of the participant and the participant's beneficiary) or the life expectancy of the participant (or the joint life expectancies of the participant and the participant's beneficiary); (2) a distribution to an employee who has attained age 55, separated from service, and met the requirements for early retirement under the plan; (3) a distribution which is used to pay medical expenses to the extent the expenses are deductible under Sec. 213 (determined without regard to whether the taxpayer itemizes deductions); (4) distributions after the death of the employee; (5) certain distributions of excess contributions to and excess deferrals under a qualified cash or deferred arrangement; (6) dividend distributions under Sec. 404(k); and (7) distributions from ESOPs if received before 1-1-90.

Change in periodic payments penalized. If life annuity payments are changed before age 59½, the 10% tax will be imposed on the payments, plus interest for the period of tax deferral.

Conforming change. The 10% penalty for premature distribution from an annuity contract will now apply to 60-month payments (only life annuities will be excluded). And a change in annuity payments before age 59½, will subject the payments to the penalty tax that would have been imposed if the contract had not been exempt, plus interest for the deferral period.

Effective Date: Generally tax years beginning after 12-31-86; for Sec. 403(b) annuities, tax years beginning after 12-31-88.

Act Secs. 1123 and 1124, creating additional tax on early distributions, amends Sec. 72(m) and (q), changes Sec. 72(t) to 72(u), adds new Secs. 72(t) and 403(b) and repeals Sec. 408(f). The new rules will not apply with respect to benefits under a designation made by an employee before 1-1-84 under Sec. 242(b)(2) of TEFRA.

[¶1131] **New Limits on Employer Deductions.** The carryforward provision of Sec. 404(a)(3)(A) has been repealed. In the past, if an employer's contribution to a profit-sharing or stock bonus plan was less than the allowable 15% of compensation limit, the unused deductible amount could be carried over to the following year, allowing a deduction of up to 25% in that year. No more. The maximum amount that an employer may deduct in any one year is 15% of compensation. The only exception is for limitation carryforwards accumulated for tax years beginning before 1-1-87.

Combination of plans. Two or more profit-sharing or stock-bonus plans are treated as one plan for purposes of limiting employer deductions (Sec. 404(a)(3)(A)(iv)). The prior limitation on deduction for contributions to a pension and a profit-sharing plan has been extended to any combination of defined benefit and defined contribution plans if any employee is covered under both plans (Sec. 404(a)(7)). Thus, the limitation—the greater of 25% of compensation or the amount contributed to the defined benefit plans up to the funding standard of Sec. 412—applies to combinations of defined benefit pension plans and money purchase pension plans. A money purchase plan that limits employer contributions to amounts deductible under Sec. 404(a)(7) will not be treated as failing to provide definitely determinable benefits. A Sec. 412(i) plan funded exclusively with individual insurance contracts will be treated as a defined benefit plan.

Excess contributions taxed. New Code section 4972 imposes a 10% excise tax on "nondeductible contributions" by an employer to a qualified plan. The tax, which is on the employer, is determined as of the close of the employer's tax year.

Nondeductible contributions are defined as the sum of (1) the amount of the employer's contribution that exceeds the amount deductible under Section 404; and (2) any excess amount contributed in the preceding tax year that has not been returned to the employer or applied as a deductible contribution in the current year.

Example: Employer made an excess contribution of $100,000 in 1986. Employer pays nondeductible tax of $10,000. In 1987, employer makes the maximum deductible contribution. Employer pays a tax of $10,000 on the unreturned excess of 1986. In 1988, employer's contribution is reduced so that the $100,000 is deductible as a carryover. There is no tax for 1988.

Effective Date: Tax years of the employer beginning after 12-31-86, with the exception that unusued pre-1987 limitation carryforwards will be allowed.

Note: The tax on excess distributions is explained at ¶1106.

Act Sec. 1131, relating to adjustments to IRC Sec. 404 limitations, amends Secs. 404(a)(3)(A) and 404(a)(7) for taxable years beginning after 12-31-86.

[¶1132] Excise Tax on Reversions. Although assets of a qualified plan may not be diverted to uses other than for the exclusive benefit of employees and their beneficiaries, amounts remaining after the plan is terminated and all benefits have been distributed, as a result of actuarial error, may revert to the employer. A new provision of the law (Sec. 4980) imposes a 10% excise tax on any such reversions (except from a plan maintained by a tax-exempt Sec. 501(a) employer).

Who pays the tax. The tax is imposed on the employer.

ESOP exception. There is no taxable reversion if assets of a plan are transferred to an employee stock ownership plan and invested in employer securities within 90 days of the transfer, and at least half of the participants in the terminated plan are participants in the ESOP. This exception expires for terminations after 12-31-88.

Act Sec. 1132, relating to an excise tax on reversions of qualified plan assets, adds IRC Sec. 4980, effective for reversions occurring after 12-31-85, unless plan termination date is before 1-1-86.

[¶1133] Treatment of Loans. The new law makes it impossible for a plan participant to maintain a constant outstanding loan balance of $50,000 without income tax liability. In the past, a loan that bore reasonable interest and was repayable within five years would not be treated as a taxable distribution if the amount loaned and the balance of all outstanding loans to the participant from the plan did not exceed one-half of the present value of the participant's nonforfeitable accrued benefit or $50,000, whichever was less.

Present law. The $50,000 limit has been changed to "$50,000 reduced by the highest outstanding balance of loans from the plan during the one-year period ending on the day before the date on which such loan was made. . ."

Amortization. The law now requires level amortization over the period of the loan, with payments made not less frequently than four times a year. Under prior law, a loan could be repayable in a single balloon payment at the end of five years.

The difference. Under prior law, a participant could borrow $50,000 (assuming his vested accrued benefit was large enough), pay periodic interest but make no payment of principal for five years.

Then, after repaying the loan, he could immediately borrow another $50,000. The outstanding balance would always be $50,000. Now, the participant would have to repay his original loan at the rate of $10,000 a year (for a 5-year loan). And since the limit at any time is reduced by the highest outstanding balance during the immediately preceding one-year period, he would not be able to borrow more until at least one-half of the first loan was paid off.

> **Example:** Employee Adams borrows $50,000 from his profit sharing plan on 1-1-87. Under the terms of the loan agreement, Adams must pay $2,500 back to the plan every 4-1, 7-1, 9-1, and 1-1, beginning 4-1-87. As of 9-1-89, Adams has made 11 payments, totalling $27,500, leaving him with a balance of $22,500. Adams still cannot borrow more from the plan. Why? Adams' limit is $50,000 reduced by the highest outstanding balance during the one-year period ending on 9-1-89. His highest balance during this period, on 9-1-88, was $32,500. Thus, the maximum limit is $17,500. Since his outstanding balance on the existing loan is in excess of this limit, he cannot make another loan. In fact, he will not be able to make another loan until 4-1-90 when his outstanding balance is reduced to $17,500. How is this figured? His highest outstanding balance in the one-year period ending 3-31-90 (on 4-1-89) was $27,500; therefore his limit on 1-1-91 is $22,500 ($50,000 − $27,500). Since his outstanding balance is $10,000, he can borrow an additional $12,500.

Residence loan. The repayment period may be longer than five years only if the loan is used to acquire a principal residence *of the participant.* Prior law allowed an extended period loan for acquisition, construction, or rehabilitation of a principal residence for the participant or a member of the participant's family.

Nondeductible interest. Certain participants cannot claim tax deductions for interest they pay on loans from qualified plans. Interest paid by a key employee (as defined in Code Section 416) or any loan or interest paid by any employee if the loan is secured by elective deferral amounts in a cash-or-deferred plan or a Section 403(b) plan will be treated as nondeductible employee contributions to the plan.

Act Sec. 1133, changing the treatment of loans, amends Sec. 72(p), effective for loans made, extended, or revised after 12-31-86.

Other Pension Rules

[¶1134] **Deferred Annuity Contracts and Qualified Plans Put on More Equal Footing.** Prior law placed fewer restrictions on deferred annuity contracts than on qualified employee benefit plans, and gave employers the chance to fund substantial amounts of deferred compensation for employees while enjoying many of the same types of tax breaks available to qualified plans. In addition, because deferred annuities could be provided to a limited class of employees (e.g., the highly paid) rather than employees generally, prior law could be used to skirt the nondiscrimination rules that apply to qualified plans. The new law eliminates the bias in favor of deferred annuities and against qualified plans by providing that nonindividual owners of deferred annuity contracts (e.g., a corporation or trust) will be currently taxed on any increase in the cash surrender value of the deferred annuity over the contract's basis during the tax year. For these purposes, the "basis" of a deferred annuity equals the investment in the deferred annuity contract, i.e., the total amount of contract premiums paid minus policyholder dividends or other amounts that haven't been included in income. The owner of a deferred variable annuity contract—an annuity which battles the effects of inflation by combining the appreciation prospect (and depreciation risk) of a portfolio of common stocks with the guarantee against loss from longevity available through an annuity—is treated under the new law as owning a pro rate share of the assets and income of any separate account underlying the variable contract. Thus, the owner is now taxed on the unrealized appreciation of assets underlying a variable contract.

When an annuity is not an annuity. The new law achieves these results by providing that any annuity contract held by a person who is not a natural person (i.e., a corporation) will not be treated as an annuity contract under Sec. 72. However, a deferred annuity contract nominally owned by a nonindividual, but beneficially owned by a natural person, will be treated as being held by the natural person. Consequently, if a corporation holds a group annuity contract as agent for a group of persons who are the beneficial owners of the contract, the contract is treated as an annuity contract under Sec. 72. To prevent the IRS from running into problems in monitoring compliance with the rule that a deferred annuity cannot be used to fund nonqualified deferred compensation on a tax-favored basis, an employer will be treated as the holder of a contract that it nominally owns for the beneficial interest of employees.

Increase in annuity's cash surrender value over basis. The increase the cash surrender value of a deferred annuity contract over its basis equals the "income on the contract." This means a deferred annuity's net surrender value at the end of the tax year plus aggregate distributions under the contract for all years, over the investment in the contract (total contract premiums less dividends). The IRS is authorized to substitute fair market value for net surrender value if necessary to accurately reflect the income on a particular deferred annuity contract.

Exempt annuities. The new rules do not apply to deferred annuities acquired for purposes of estate administration, held as qualified funding assets by a structured settlement company, held by an employer with respect to a terminated pension plan, held by a qualified pension plan, an IRA or a 403(b) annuity, or immediate annuities.

¶1134

An immediate annuity is an annuity purchased with a single premium, which has a starting date no later than one year after the date of purchase.

Early withdrawal tax. The new law modifies the rules relating to the additional income tax on early withdrawals from deferred annuity contracts. Now, if a withdrawal is made from a deferred annuity contract before the owner dies, becomes disabled, or attains age 59½ a 10% additional income tax [see ¶1123] applies unless the withdrawal is part of a series of substantially equal periodic payments over the life of the owner, or the lives of the owner and a beneficiary.

If an individual commences receiving distributions before attaining age 59½ in a form that is exempt from the additional income tax, and the payment of the individual's benefits is later changed (before the individual attains age 59½) to a form that does not satisfy the conditions for the exemption, the Secretary of the Treasury is authorized to impose the 10% excise tax on all distributions under the contract received by the individual before age 59½, including amounts previously received in the exempt form. Moreover, the recapture tax will apply if the individual does not receive benefits in the exempt form for at least five years even if the individual is over age 59½ when the form is changed. The recapture will only apply to benefits received before age 59½.

If an annuity contract is owned by a nonnatural person (other than a qualified plan), there will be no additional tax imposed on an early withdrawal because there has been no tax benefit attributable to deferral of tax on the income on the contract.

As under present law, distributions under an annuity contract that constitutes a tax-sheltered annuity are not subject to a tax on premature withdrawals. Distributions under an annuity contract that is held by a qualified plan are subject to the additional income tax on premature withdrawals from a qualified plan.

Act Sec. 1135, relating to the tax treatment of deferred annuities owned by nonindividuals, amends Sec. 72, effective for contributions to annuity contracts made after 2-28-86, and applies to the early withdrawal tax effective for taxable years beginning after 12-31-86.

[¶1135] **Profits Not Required for Profit Sharing Plans.** In a major break with past law, the new law changes the rule requiring that employer contributions to a profit sharing plan be made out of profits. Now such contributions are not limited to the employer's current or accumulated profits. The new law applies without regard to whether the employer is tax-exempt.

Act Sec. 1136 adds Sec. 401(a)(27), effective for years beginning after 12-31-85.

[¶1136] Collective Bargaining Must Be Bona Fide. To prevent arrangements between employers and promoters of certain tax avoidance arrangements, whereby employers and their employees are superficially represented by agents in collective bargaining, but under which there's no good faith bargaining on retirement benefits, the new law clarifies that no agreement will be treated as a collective bargaining agreement unless it is a bona fide agreement between bona fide employee representatives and one or more employers.

Act Sec. 1137 amends Sec. 7701(a)(46), effective on enactment.

[¶1137] Penalty for Overstatement of Pension Liabilities. The law provides a new penalty for overstating income tax deductions for pension liabilities. Under prior law, if the IRS determined that pension liabilities had been overstated, the limit on employer deductions was recalculated using reasonable actuarial assumptions and the excess deduction was disallowed. Under the new provision (IRC Section 6659A), in addition to losing the deduction, the employer will be hit with a tax penalty.

If the amount of the deduction for pension liabilities claimed on an employer's tax return is 150% or more of the amount determined to be the correct deduction, a penalty is added to the employer's tax liability. The amount of the penalty is a percentage of the underpayment of tax, determined as follows:

10% if the claimed deduction is between 150 and 200% of the correct amount.

20% if between 201 and 250% of the correct amount.

30% if more than 250% of the correct amount.

> **Example:** Corporation (46% tax rate) claims $160,000 pension liability; correct valuation is $100,000. The $60,000 overvaluation results in an underpayment of $27,600 (46% of $60,000). The penalty of $2,760 (10% of the underpayment) is added to Corporation's tax in addition to the $27,600 it must pay to cure the underpayment.

De minimis exception. There is no penalty if the underpayment of tax is less than $1,000.

Waiver. The IRS may waive the penalty if the taxpayer shows that there was a reasonable basis for the deduction claimed and that the claim was made in good faith.

Act Sec. 1138, providing a penalty for overstating pension liabilities, adds IRC Sec. 6659A, effective for overstatements made after the date of enactment.

[¶1138] Treatment of Certain Fisherman as Self-Employed. Under prior law, certain fisherman were treated as self-employed individuals for employment tax purposes, but as common law employees for the purposes of determining whether a pension, profit sharing, or stock bonus plan maintained by the owner or operator of the boats on which they work was a qualified plan. Thus, such individuals were prevented from establishing Keogh plans. The new law provides that fisherman who are treated as self-employeds for employment tax purposes are treated as such for the rules on qualified pension profit sharing or stock bonus plans.

Act Sec. 1143, amends Sec. 401(c) effective for tax years beginning after 12-31-86.

[¶1139] **Interest Rate Assumptions for Mandatory Cash-Outs.** Prior law required that the interest rate assumption used to determine the present value of accrued benefits be no greater than the interest rate that would be used (as of the date of distribution) by the PBGC to determine the present value of a lump sum distribution on plan termination. This favorable interest rate requirement provided an inducement for employees to elect lump sum distributions rather than periodic payments of retirement benefits. Thus, the pre-retirement savings policy underlying tax incentives for qualified plans was subverted. Accordingly, the new law increases the interest rate assumption to be used in calculating lump sum payouts (and thus decreases the amount of such payouts). Under the new law, the PBGC rate must be used to determine whether the participant can be cashed-out involuntarily, and whether the value of the vested accrued benefit is less than $25,000. If the value of the benefit is less than $25,000, the amount to be distributed is calculated using PBGC rates. If the value is greater than $25,000, the amount to be distributed is required to be determined using an interest rate no greater than 120% of the interest rate (deferred or immediate, whichever is appropriate) that would be used by the PBGC (as of the date of distribution) on the plan's termination. In no event, will the amount to be distributed be reduced to *less* than $25,000 when 120% of the PBGC interest rate is used. As under prior law, for determining the PBGC interest rate as of the date of distribution, the PBGC rate in effect at the beginning of plan year can be used throughout the plan year if the plan so provides.

NOTE: The new law clarifies that a plan amendment adopting the new provisions will *not* be deemed to be a reduction in accrued benefits.

Act Sec. 1139 amends Secs. 411(a)(11) and 417 of the Code, and Sec. 203(e) of ERISA, changing the maximum interest rate assumptions to determine the amount of lump sum payouts. The amendment is applicable to distributions made after 12-31-84, and distributions required under Sec. 303 of ERISA but does not apply to distributions made between 12-31-84 and 12-31-85 if made in accordance with regulations issued under REA.

〔¶1140〕 Time Limit for 401(k) Opinion Letters. No later than 5-1-87, the Secretary of the Treasury is required to begin issuing opinion letters with respect to Sec. 401(k) master and prototype plans.

Act Sec. 1142, effective on enactment date.

〔¶1141〕 Required Plan Amendments. A plan must be amended to comply with all applicable provisions of the new law, but there is a long remedial amendment period—plan amendments must be made no later than the last day of the first plan year beginning on or after 1-1-89. To remain qualified, a plan must comply in operation with the new provisions as of the effective date of each provision (generally, years beginning after 12-31-86), and the amendments must apply retroactively to the effective date.

Treasury is directed to prescribe a model amendment which will allow plans to meet the requirements of the new law.

Collectively bargained plans. For a plan maintained pursuant to an agreement ratified before 3-1-86, the date for compliance with the new law provisions is the first plan year beginning after 1-1-91 or, if earlier, the first plan year beginning after the later of (1) 1-1-89 or (2) the termination of the bargaining agreement.

Act Sec. 1140, relating to plan amendments is effective on enactment.

〔¶1142〕 Regulations to be Issued. Under the new law the Secretary of the Treasury is required to issue, not later than 2-1-88, regulations regarding:

- the application of nondiscrimination rules to integrated plans (Act Sec. 1111),
- coverage requirements for qualified plans (Act Sec. 1112),
- minimum vesting rules (Act Sec. 1113),
- definition of highly compensation employee (Act Sec. 1114),
- separate lines of business and definition of compensation (Act Sec. 1115),
- 401(k) plans (Act Sec. 1116),
- nondiscrimination requirements for employer matching and employee contributions (Act Sec. 1117),
- nondiscrimination requirements for tax-sheltered annuities (Act Sec. 1120), and
- tax on excess distributions (Act Sec. 1133).

Act Sec. 1141 Requiring Secretary of the Treasury to issue regulations before 2-1-88, effective on enactment date.

[¶1143] Investment in Collectibles. Sec. 408(m) of the Code generally prohibits investment of IRAs in collectibles, because it is considered too difficult to verify the existence of collectibles. The new law creates a limited exception to this rule and permits IRA investment in legal tender gold and silver coins minted by the United States. Such coins must, of course, be held by a disinterested third party, and cannot be held by the individual investor. The exception applies to acquisitions after 12-31-86.

Act Sec. 1144, amends Code Sec. 408 to permit IRA investment in certain gold and silver coins, effective for acquisitions after 12-31-86.

[¶1144] Exemption from REA Survivor Benefit Requirements. The new law amends the joint and survivor annuity requirements of the Retirement Equity Act of 1984 [¶1898]. These requirements are not applicable to plans:

- Established before 1-1-54, by agreement between employee representatives and the federal government during a period in which the government operated a major part of the productive facilities of the industry under its seizure powers; and
- Which substantially limit participation to individuals who ceased to be employed in employment covered by the plan before 1-1-76.

Act Sec. 1145, amending survivor benefit requirements of REA effective on date of enactment.

[¶1145] Leased Employee. Generally, a leased employee must be treated, for pension coverage, as an employee of the recipient of his or her services unless he or she is covered by a "safe harbor" plan maintained by the leasing organization. The new law changes the requirements of a safe harbor plan in two ways. The required contribution rate has been raised from 7½% to 10%. And the plan must cover all employees of the leasing organization other than those who are not leased to recipients and those whose compensation from the leasing organization is less then $1,000 a year during the plan year and each of the 3 prior plan years.

The provision determining when an individual becomes a leased employee protected by Sec. 414(n) has been modified. For purposes of the requirements, service is to include any period during which the employee would have been a leased employee but for the requirement that substantially full-time services be performed for at least one year.

If leased employees constitute more than 20% of the nonhighly-compensated workforce of a recipient, the law now requires that such employees be covered by the recipient's pension plan regardless of whether the leasing organization maintains a safe harbor plan.

"Recipient" includes, in addition to the employer or employers for which services are performed, other employers aggregated as affiliated or under common control.

The new law directs the Treasury to issue regulations that will minimize the recordkeeping requirements for an employer which has no top-heavy plans and which uses leased employees "for an insignificant percentage of the employer's total work load."

Effective Date: Services performed after 12-31-86. Modification of years of service applies to taxable years beginning after 12-31-83.

Act Sec. 1146, relating to treatment of leased employees, amends Sec. 414(n) and (0), effective as shown above.

[¶1146] Tax Treatment of Federal Thrift Savings Fund. Beginning in 1987, a government employee is allowed to contribute up to 10% of the employee's rate of basic pay to the Thrift Savings Plan maintained by the Federal government. These employee contributions to the Thrift Savings Plan are not includible in the employee's income for the year of deferral, but rather are includible in income when distributed from the Plan.

Act Sec. 1147, adding new Sec. 7701(j), effective on date of enactment.

Fringe Benefit Plans

[¶1151] Nondiscrimination Rules. Under prior law, virtually every type of fringe benefit plan was governed by its own set of nondiscrimination rules as to eligibility and benefits. The new law sets up a comprehensive set of nondiscrimination rules for certain statutory fringe benefit plans and cafeteria plans. These tests aren't exclusive. A plan must satisfy prior law concentration tests in addition to the new nondiscrimination tests.

Statutory fringe benefit plans. Plans specifically covered by the new rules include employer group-term life insurance plans (under Section 79) and accident and health plans (under Section 105(e)), whether insured or self insured. Employers can elect to apply the new rules to qualified group legal services plans (under Section 120(b)), educational assistance programs (under Section 127(b)), and dependent care assistance programs (under Section 129(d)). Once the election is made, the plan will be considered as meeting the nondiscrimination contained in that section, if the plan meets the new comprehensive rules. Note that the group legal services and educational assistance exclusions are scheduled to expire before the effective date of the new rules.

Income inclusion. Under the new law, except as provided in regs, all employees must include in income an amount equal to the employee's employer-provided benefit under a statutory fringe benefit plan unless the plan is in writing, the employees' rights under the plan are legally enforceable, employees are given reasonable notification of benefits available under the plan, the plan is maintained for the exclusive benefit of employees, and the plan was established with the intention of being maintained indefinitely. In addition to applying to the previously mentioned statutory fringe benefits, these requirements apply to qualified tuition reduction programs (under Section 117(d)), cafeteria plans (under Section 125), fringe benefit programs providing no additional cost services, employee discounts, or employer provided operating facilities (under Section 132), and welfare benefit plans (under Section 505). The employer-provided benefit, for these purposes, is the value of benefits provided to the employee. If the plan doesn't meet these requirements, the income inclusion precludes a separate inclusion under the nondiscrimination rules.

A highly compensated employee who participates in a discriminatory statutory fringe benefit plan which meets the requirements of the previous paragraph must include in gross income only the discriminatory portion of the coverage provided (if a group-term life insurance or accident and health plan), or the discriminatory portion of the benefits provided (if another type of plan), provided such value is timely reported. Otherwise, it's the entire benefit. A plan will be considered discriminatory unless it passes both the nondiscriminatory eligibility test and the nondiscriminatory benefits test.

> **AMOUNT INCLUDABLE:** The amount includable is the "excess benefit," which is the excess of the employer-provided benefit over the "highest permitted benefit." The highest permitted benefit is determined by reducing the nontaxable benefits of highly compensated employees (beginning with the employee with the greatest nontaxable benefits) until such plan would not be treated as a discriminatory benefit plan. For these purposes, plans of the same type are to be aggregated. In addition, for group-term life insurance, the value of the discriminatory excess is the greater of the cost of coverage (under Section 79(c)) or the actual cost of coverage for an employee age 40. The excess benefit amount is includable in the employee's tax year with or within which the plan year ends. Note that the employer-provided benefit generally includes salary reduction.

Highly compensated. A highly compensated employee, for purposes of all employee benefit nondiscrimination rules, is the same as under the new uniform rules (new Sec. 414(q)) [¶1114]. Generally, this includes employees who (1) are 5% owners (under Sec. 416(i)); (2) earn more than $75,000 in annual compensation, (3) earn more than $50,000 in annual compensation and whose compensation is in the top 20% of all of the employer's employees, and (4) are officers of the employer (under Sec. 416(i)) and receive more than 150% of the dollar limit on annual additions to a defined contribution plan. It also includes former employees who were highly compensated at the time of separation from service or after age 55. Employees who are excluded from coverage under the plan [see ¶1155] are also excluded from determining who is highly compensated. Unlike the general rules, a family member of a highly compensated employee covered by a separate accident or health plan isn't treated as the employee.

Effective Date: The new nondiscrimination provisions are effective for plan years beginning after 12-31-87. However, if regs aren't issued by that time, the rules are effective for the earlier of plan years beginning at least three months after the regs are issued or plan years beginning after 12-31-88. For collective bargaining agreements ratified before 3-1-86, the new rules won't apply before the earlier of the termination of such agreements (without regard to extensions after that date) or 1-1-91. For church plans (under Section 414(e)(3)) maintaining insured accident and health plans, the new rules apply to years beginning after 12-31-88.

Act Sec. 1151(a), establishing the new nondiscrimination rules, adds new Secs. 89(a)-(c), and (k) generally effective for plan years beginning after 12-31-87 and as shown above.

[¶1152] Group-Term Life Insurance and Accident and Health Plans. Group term life insurance plans and accident and health plans (whether or not self-insured) and, if the employer elects, dependent care assistants, educational, assistance, and group legal service plans, won't be considered discriminatory if both a non-discrimination eligibility test and a nondiscrimination benefits test are met.

Eligibility test. A statutory fringe benefit plan must meet a three-part eligibility test. First, at least 50% of all eligible employees must not be highly compensated. However, if the percentage of highly compensated employees who are eligible isn't greater than the percentage of nonhighly compensated employees who are eligible, the 50% requirement would be considered met.

Second, at least 90% of the nonhighly compensateds must be eligible and would receive a benefit that's at least 50% of the value of the largest benefit available under all such plans to any highly compensated employee. Special rules define when such plans are aggregated. In addition, coverage of employees may be tested separately from dependents.

Third, a plan can't contain any provision relating to eligibility which (by its terms or otherwise) discriminates in favor of highly compensated employees.

Benefits test. A statutory fringe benefit plan meets the benefit test if the average employer-provided benefit received by nonhighly compensated employees under all plans is at least 75% of the average such benefit received by highly compensated employees. The average employer-provided benefit for highly compensated is equal to the aggregate of employer-provided benefits received by such employees divided by the number of such employees. The figure for nonhighly compensated employees is determined in a similar way.

In applying the test to health plans, an employer may elect to disregard any employee if the employee and his or her spouse or dependents are covered by a health plan maintained by another employer that provides core benefits (defined in ¶1155). In addition, the employer can elect to apply the benefits test separately to employees and dependents not covered by plans of other employees as opposed to those that are covered by such plans.

If the employer makes either election, the employer must get a sworn statement attesting to the existence of a spouse and dependents, and core benefits under another plan. In the absence of a statement, a nonhighly compensated employee and his or her dependents will be treated as not covered by another plan while a highly compensated employee will be treated as not having dependents and as being covered by another employer's plan.

For purposes of the election to disregard employees, an employer can't elect to disregard a highly compensated employee who receives health plan benefits that are more than 133 1/3% of the average employer-provided benefit of nonhighly compensated employees.

> **NOTE:** The new law contains the prior law rule that group-term life insurance benefits won't be treated as discriminatory if the amount of coverage bears a uniform relationship to compensation. The nondiscrimination rules can be applied to the value of such coverage expressed as a percentage of compensation, with the same cap on includable compensation that's applicable to qualified plans.

Alternative test. A group-term life insurance or an accident or health plan will be considered to meet both the eligibility test and the benefits test if at least 80% of the nonhighly compensated employees are covered by the plan and the plan doesn't discriminate (by its terms or otherwise) in favor of the highly compensated employees.

Aggregation rules. For health plans, an employer may treat a group of comparable plans as a single plan for purposes of the eligibility and alternative tests. Such plans are comparable if the smallest benefit available is at least 95% of the largest benefit available to any participant under any plan.

For other plans, the employer can elect to aggregate different types of statutory employee benefit plans, as long as all plans of the same type are included in the aggregation.

Accident or health plans. For purposes of the 50% arm of the eligibility test and the 80% alternative test, if the employer's health plan provides family coverage, the employer can apply the tests separately to the coverage for employees and the coverage for spouses and dependents as if two different plans.

A health plan's benefits may be integrated with benefits provided under Medicare, or any other law, or under any other health plans covering the employee or the employee's family as long as it does so in a manner that doesn't discriminate in favor of the highly compensated.

An exception is provided to the equal coverage requirement for employees who normally work less than 30 hours a week. A plan won't be considered discriminatory merely because an employer provided benefit is proportionately reduced for employees who normally work less than 30 hours a week. The exception applies only if the average workweek of nonhighly compensated employees is 30 hours or more. The Conference Committee report provides safe harbors for adjustments to such benefits.

The Conference Committee authorizes Treasury to disregard certain state-mandated benefits when applying the nondiscrimination tests to accident and health plans.

Disability benefits. A disability benefit plan providing an excludable benefit won't fail the nondiscrimination rules merely because benefits bear a uniform relationship to total or regular compensation or benefits are integrated (but not so as to discriminate in favor of the highly compensated) with benefits provided under any law or any other accident plan covering the employee.

Act Sec. 1151(a) , relating to nondiscrimination benefits and eligibility tests adds Secs. 89(d)(g), effective generally for plan years beginning after 12-31-87, and as shown at ¶1151.

[¶1153] **Cafeteria Plans and Other Plans.** The new law makes a number of changes to the cafeteria plan rules. The new rules make it clear that any qualified benefit (as defined in the new law) provided to a highly compensated under a discriminatory plan (as to eligibility) is included in the gross income of such employee. The prior law nondiscrimination benefits test is gone. However, the prior law concentration tests of benefits for key employees is retained. The end result is that in addition to meeting the cafeteria plan rules, each benefit must meet any separate nondiscrimination or concentration tests applicable to it.

The new law also makes it clear that the rules apply to plans that don't offer cash or taxable benefits.

The new law also does the following:

- Permits full-time life insurance sales representatives to be treated as employees for certain cafeteria or plan purposes;

- Allows employees of educational organizations to elect post-retirement life insurance in cafeteria plans;

- Clarifies that salary reduction under cafeteria plans is excluded from FICA and FUTA wage basis; and

- Applies the new uniform definitions of highly compensated employee, excludable employee, and employer to cafeteria plans.

Other plans. A dependent care assistance program, for which the employer didn't elect statutory fringe benefit treatment, is subject to a special benefits test. A plan will meet the requirements if the average benefit provided to nonhighly compensated employees is at least 55% of the benefits provided to highly compensated employees. For purposes of providing benefits under a salary reduction agreement, employees with compensation (under Section 415(q)(7)) below $25,000 are disregarded. For these purposes, the average benefit for nonhighly compensated employees is equal to the value of benefits provided on their behalf divided by the number of nonhighly compensated. The average benefit for the highly compensated is computed separately.

In addition, dependent care assistance programs must meet the prior law Section 129(d)(4) concentration test limiting the benefits available to 5% owners.

Act Sec. 1151(d), relating to cafeteria plans, amends Sec. 125, generally effective for plan years beginning after 12-31-87 and as shown in ¶1151. Act Sec. 1166, relating to certain full-time insurance salespeople, amends Sec. 7701(a)(20), effective for years beginning after 12-31-85. Act Sec. 1151(d)(2), relating to FICA and FUTA rules amend Secs. 3121(a)(5), 3306(b)(5), and 209(e) of the Social Security Act, effective for taxable years beginning after 12-31-83. Act Sec. 1151(f), dealing with dependent care assistance programs amends Sec. 129, effective as shown in ¶1151.

[¶1154] Line of Business Exception. If an employer establishes to the Treasury's satisfaction that separate lines of business or operating units are operated for bona fide business reasons, the employer may apply the eligibility, benefit, and alternative tests separately to each line or unit. However, the plan must still satisfy a "reasonable classification test" requirements, on an employer-wide basis. The new law contains a rule (new Sec. 414(r)) under which a separate line of business will be treated as operated for bona fide business purposes.

A separate line of business or operating unit will be considered operated for bona fide business reasons if

- the line or unit has at least 50 employees,

- the employer notifies Treasury that such line is being treated as separate, and

- such line gets Treasury approval or meets Treasury guidelines.

A special safe harbor exempts a line of business from the last requirement if the percentage of highly compensated employees (compared to total employees) in the line of business is not less than 50% nor more than 200% of the percentage which highly compensated employees are of all employees. The 50% requirement will be met if at least 10% of all highly compensated employees of the employer perform services solely for such line of business.

Special rules apply to allocating headquarters personnel, affiliated service groups, and units in separate geographical areas.

Act Sec. 1151(a), dealing with nondiscrimination rules, adds new Sec. 89(g)(5), containing the line of business exception generally effective for plan years ending after 12-31-87 and as shown at ¶1151.

[¶1155] Excludable Employees. Under the new law, certain classes of employees may be disregarded in applying the nondiscrimination rules to any employee benefit plan if neither the plan, nor any other plan of the same type, provides eligibility for any employee in the class. If one employee is covered, then all such employees are included for purposes of the nondiscrimination rules. For purposes of cafeteria plans, all benefits under the plan will be treated as provided under plans of the same type. These classes are considered "excludable employees" for purposes of all employee benefit nondiscrimination rules. Those classes include:

- Employees who haven't completed one year of service (6 months of service for core benefits under health plans), or shorter if specified in the plan. An employee can be excluded until the first day of the first month beginning after the completion of the initial service requirement. Note that noncore benefits include dental, vision, psychological, and orthodontia expenses and elective cosmetic surgery.

- Employees working less than 17½ hours a week (or shorter if specified in the plan).

- Employees working not more than six months during any year (or shorter if specified in the plan).

- Employees who haven't attained age 21 (or lower, if specified in the plan).

- Employees covered by a collective bargaining agreement and the benefit in question was the subject of good faith bargaining, and

- Nonresident aliens with no U.S. earned income. For this class, the fact that some members may benefit won't make the plan discriminatory.

Line of business. If the employer elects to apply the rules on a line of business basis, the excluded employees are determined on such line of business basis.

Separate testing. Employees excludable on the basis of the age and service requirements may be tested separately even if some or all of the excludable employees are covered by a plan that also covers nonexcludable employees. Alternatively an employer may elect to test one group of excludable employees separately without testing all excludable employees separately if such group is defined in a nondiscriminatory manner solely by reference to the age and service requirements.

Aggregation. If an employer aggregates plans of different types for the benefits test, the excludable employee rules apply as if the same type. As a result, the lowest age and service requirement apply. The same is true for all other requirements.

Other plans. The definition of excludable employee also applies to tuition reduction plans, educational assistance programs, and *de minimis* fringe benefits.

Act Sec. 1151(a), relating to the nondiscrimination rules, adds new Sec. 89(h), defining excludable employees, generally effective for plan years beginning after 12-31-87 and as shown at ¶1151.

[¶1156] **Special Rules.** *Aggregation.* If an accident or health plan, alone, would fail the 50% arm of the benefit test or the alternative 80% test, the plan may be aggregated with one or more plans providing the same type of benefit, provided the average value of employer-provided coverage per employee in each such other plan is at least 95% of that in the failing plan.

Options. Each option or different benefit offered under an accident or health plan or group life insurance plan is treated as a separate plan. However, group-term life insurance that varies in proportion to salary isn't treated as a different option.

Former employees. Under regs to be issued, rules similar to the nondiscriminatory coverage rules are to apply separately to former employees. The Senate Committee Report sets forth reasonable restrictions (retirement, disability) on which to base such rules.

Self-employeds. For purposes of the rules governing group legal services plans, educational assistance programs, and dependent care assistance programs, a self-employed is treated as an employee. A self-employed's compensation is his or her earned income as defined in section 401(c)(2). Also for these purposes, a sole proprietor is treated as his own employer and a partnership is treated as the employer of its working partners.

Controlled groups. Employees treated as employed by a single employer under Sec. 414(b), (c), and (m) are treated likewise for purposes of Sections 79, 89, 106, 117(d), 120, 125, 127, 129, 132, 274(j), and 505 (with some exceptions the benefits subject to the "in writing" requirements). Special transitional rules apply when an organization becomes or ceases to be part of a controlled group as defined in Sec. 414(b), (c), (m) or (o). Also, leased employees are treated as employees of the organization for whom the employees perform services (that is, the lessee).

New definitions. Just as it does for cafeteria plans, the new law substitutes the new definitions of highly compensated employees [¶1114], employer, and excludable employees [¶1155] for welfare benefit plans.

Regulatory authority. Also the new law gives Treasury the authority to issue regs to carry out the new rules.

Effective Date: The new nondiscrimination provisions are effective for plan years beginning after 12-31-87. However, if regs aren't issued by that time, the rules are effective for the earlier of plan years beginning at least three months after the regs are issued or plan years beginning after 12-31-88. For collective bargaining agreements ratified before 3-1-86, the new rules won't apply before the earlier of the termination of such agreements (without regard to extensions after that date) or 1-1-91. For church plans (under Section 414(e)(3)) maintaining insured accident and health plans, the new rules apply to years beginning after 12-31-88.

Act Sec. 1151(a), relating to nondiscrimination rules, adds new Secs. 89(i)-(1); Act Secs. 1151(b)-(i), repealing and modifying the old rules, amend Secs. 79(d), 105(h), 117(d)(3), 120(b), 125(b)(1), 125(g), 127(b)(1), 129(d), 132(g), 414(n), 414(t), and 505(b)(2), generally effective for plan years beginning after 12-31-87 and as shown above.

[¶1157] Reporting and Penalty. If an employee is required to include any amount in income under the new requirements, the employer must report the amount to the employee and the IRS on Forms W-2 by the appropriate due date. Failure to provide the forms will result in an additional tax to the employer equal to the highest individual tax rate for the year in question multiplied by the amount of the total employer provided benefit of the affected employee for the same type of benefit. Only one such addition will be paid for any amount. Note that reasonable cause is a defense to the penalty.

In addition, employers who maintain group-term life insurance plans, accident and health plans, group legal services plans, educational assistance programs, dependent care assistance programs, or cafeteria plans must file informational returns showing, in addition to the previously required information, the number of highly compensated employees of the employer, the number eligible to participate and the number that participates. However, Treasury has the power to waive the requirement that all employers file, in favor of a filing by a representative group of employers.

Act Sec. 1151(a) and (b) relating to reporting and penalties adds new Secs. 89(l) and 6652(l), effective as shown in ¶1151. Act Sec. 1151(h), relating to information returns, amends Sec. 6039D, effective as shown in ¶1151.

Other Fringe Benefit Provisions

[¶1161] **Health Insurance Costs for Self-Employeds.**   The new law allows self-employeds (under Sec. 401(c)(1)) to deduct 25% of the amounts paid for health insurance for the self-employed and the individual's spouse and dependents. The amount is allowable as a deduction in calculating adjusted gross income. However, it isn't to be taken into account for purposes of determining the itemized medical expense deduction.

Limitations.   There are a number of limitations on the deduction. The taxpayer won't get the deduction to the extent the amount exceeds earned income (under section 401(c)(1)). The deduction is allowed only if the coverage is provided under one or more plans meeting the new fringe benefit nondiscrimination rules. As a result, other employees will have to be covered. In addition, there's no deduction if the self-employed is eligible to participate in a subsidized accident and health plan maintained by an employer of the self-employed or the self-employed's spouse.

Guidance.   The new law directs Treasury to provide guidance to self-employeds to help them comply with the new nondiscrimination rules.

> **NOTE:** Special rules apply for nondiscrimination purposes, if the year in question occurs before the effective date of the nondiscrimination rules.

Act Sec. 1161, adding the health insurance deduction for self-employeds, adds new Sec. 162(m), effective for tax years beginning after 12-31-86 and before 1-1-90.

[¶1162] **Educational Assistance and Legal Services Programs Extended.**   The new law extends the exclusions for educational assistance programs and group legal services plans for two more years. So the educational assistance exclusion will expire for tax years beginning after 12-31-87 and the group legal services exclusion will expire for tax years ending after 12-31-87. It also increases the cap on annual excludable educational assistance to $5,250 (from $5,000).

For cafeteria plans providing group legal services benefits, the new law is treated in the same manner as a change in family status. *Result:* Participants have 60 days after enactment (according to the

Senate Committee Report) to revoke the old election and make a new one that will apply to all legal services provided in 1986. However, if the plan provided that benefit on 8-16-86, the election can't be made.

Act Sec. 1162(a), relating to the educational assistance exclusion, amends Secs. 127(a)(2) and (d), effective for tax years beginning after 12-31-85; Act Sec. 1162(b), dealing with group legal services plans, amends Sec. 120(e), effective for years ending after 12-31-85.

[¶1163] **Qualified Campus Lodging.** The new law sets up rules for including in income qualified campus lodging provided by a school to an employee. Generally, gross income won't include the value of qualified campus lodging. However, it will be included to the extent the rent paid is less than the lesser of (1) 5% of the appraised value of the lodging or (2) the average of rentals paid (other than by employees or students) to the institution for comparable housing. So, if the rent is equal to or exceeds the lesser of those figures, no amount is includable in income.

Qualified campus lodging is lodging furnished to an employee (his or her spouse, or any dependents) of an educational institution (defined in Sec. 170(b)(1)(A)(ii). The lodging must be located on, or in proximity to, the campus of the institution and must be provided for use as a residence.

It's expected that regs will determine how an appraisal should be made for purposes of the exclusion.

Act Sec. 1164, relating to qualified campus lodging, adds new Sec. 119(d), effective for tax years beginning after 12-31-85.

[¶1164] **Vacation Pay Accrual Tightened.** For tax years beginning after 1986, the new law limits the deduction for additions to the earned vacation pay accrual account to amounts paid during the employer's current tax year or within 8½ months (rather than 12 months) after the close of the tax year in which the vacation pay was earned.

Act Sec. 1165, dealing with vacation pay accruals amends Sec. 463(a)(1), effective for tax years beginning after 12-31-86.

[¶1165] **New $5,000 Limit on Dependent Care Assistance Exclusion.** The new law limits the exclusion for employee-provided dependent care assistance to $5,000 a year ($2,500 for marrieds filing separately). Previously, the exclusion was limited to the amount of earned income—so, for most taxpayers, the new law represents a cut in the amount of the exclusion.

The new law also explains how to value child care when it's provided at a facility located on the employer's premises. Except to the extent provided in regs, the amount excludable is the value of services provided to employees who actually use the facility.

Act Secs. 1163(a) and (b), limiting the dependent care exclusion, amend Secs. 129(a) and (e) effective for tax years beginning after 12-31-86.

[¶1166] Welfare Benefit Study Due Date. The new law extends the due date of the study (mandated by the '84 TRA) on the possible means of providing minimum standards for welfare benefit plans for current and retired employees. The new due date is one year after the date of enactment of the new law.

Act Sec. 1167, relating to a welfare benefit study, amends '84 TRA Sec. 560(b).

[¶1167] Military Benefit Exclusion. The new law consolidates the tax treatment of military benefits. Generally, it excludes from income benefits that were authorized by law on 9-9-86 and that were excludable on that date. The Conference Committee report contains an exhaustive list, which the committee believes contains the only excludable benefits under non-Code provisions. Other benefits are excluded from income by the Code.

The Committee Report gives the Treasury the power to expand the list should it determine that any benefit was inadvertently omitted.

The new law prohibits any modification or adjustment to a benefit after 9-9-86 unless the adjustment is under a law or regulation in effect that day, and is determined by reference to a fluctuation in cost, price, currency or similar index.

Act Sec. 1168, relating to military benefits, adds new Sec. 134, effective for taxable years beginning after 12-31-86.

Employee Stock Ownership Plans

[¶1172] Termination of ESOP Credit. The new law moves up by one year the sunset of the payroll-based tax credit ESOP. As a result, the ESOP credit won't apply to compensation paid or accrued after 12-31-86. Unused credits can still be carried over under the rules of Section 404(i) and Section 6699. The new law also creates an exception to the repeal for one particular plan.

Act Sec. 1171, repealing the ESOP credit, repeals Secs. 41, 404(i), and 6699m and amends Secs. 38, 56, 108(b) and 401(a) for compensation paid or accrued after 12-31-86 in taxable years ending after that date. Act Sec. 1177(a) creates an exemption from the PAYSOP repeal.

[¶1173] Estate Tax Exclusion for Sales to ESOPs or EWOCs. To encourage the transfer of employer securities to ESOPs or eligible worker owned cooperatives (EWOCs), the new law establishes an estate tax exclusion of 50% of the qualified proceeds of a qualified sale of employer securities. A qualified sale of employer securities is a sale by the executor to an ESOP (under Sec. 4975(e)(7)) or an EWOC (under Sec. 1042(c)).

Qualified proceeds are the amounts received by the estate from the sale of employer securities before the due date (including extensions) for the estate tax return. Qualified proceeds don't include proceeds from the sale of employer securities if the securities were received from a qualified plan (under Sec. 401(a)) or a transfer pursuant to an option to acquire stock under Secs. 83, 422, 422A, 423, or 424.

Prohibited allocation rules. A statement must be filed by the executor with the IRS, in which the employer or the EWOC consents to the application of the new Sec. 4979A prohibited allocation penalty. These rules basically require the ESOP to inure to the exclusive benefit of the employees. Generally, the rules provide for an excise tax for violation of the prohibited allocation rules under new Sec. 409(n), equal to 50% of the prohibited allocation [see ¶1854]. Briefly, a prohibited allocation is one in which securities are allocated, within 10 years after the later of the sale or the allocation attributable to final payment of the acquisition loan, to the benefit of (1) a decedent whose estate makes the sale, (2) any person related to the decedent under Sec. 267(b), or (3) any other person who owns (under Sec. 318(a)) more than 25% of any class of outstanding stock of the corporation or 25% of the total value of any class of outstanding stock. In addition, the plan will be treated as having distributed to such person (or his or her estate), the amount so allocated.

Act Sec. 1172, relating to the new 50% exclusion, adds new Sec. 2057 and amends Sec. 409(n), effective for sales after the enactment date and before 1-1-92 by an estate required to file a return (including extensions of time) after the enactment date.

[¶1174] Securities Acquisitions Loans. The new law extends some of the breaks for loans used to acquire employer securities.

Dividends used to repay loans. The new law allows an employer to deduct dividends paid on employer securities, which are used to make payments on an employer securities acquisition loan (defined in Sec. 404(a)(9)). Such deduction would be allowable in the corporation's tax year during which the loan was repaid. Previously, the deduction was limited to dividends paid out to the employees or other beneficiaries.

Loans by regulated investment company. The new law provides that regulated investment companies (RICs) are eligible lenders for purposes of the 50% exclusion for interest paid on securities acquisition rules. Such treatment will flow through to the RIC's shareholders under rules similar to those in Sec. 103(a) for government obligations. One-half of the interest received on such loans will be treated as interest excludable under Sec. 103 for purposes of determining the amount of exempt-interest dividends the RIC may pay.

Loans to employer corporation. The 50% interest exclusion is also available to eligible lenders for interest received on a loan to a corporation to the extent that, within 30 days, employer securities are transferred to the plan in an amount equal to such proceeds and such contributions are allocated to participants' accounts within one year of the loan. In addition, the original commitment period of such loan isn't to exceed seven years. If the period is longer, the exclusion applies only to the first seven years.

The new law also provides that the exclusion is now available for interest on loans incurred after the date of enactment to an employer corporation to the extent the proceeds are used to refinance such loans. Previously, the exclusion was limited to loans to corporations or ESOPs, the proceeds of which were used to acquire such securities.

Effective Date: According to the Conference Committee report, the interest exclusion is extended to refinancing of loans used to acquire employer securities after May 23, 1984. According to the statute, that date only applies to the exclusion for RICs.

Act Sec. 1173(a), relating to the dividends paid deductions, amends Sec. 404(k), effective for tax years beginning after the date of enactment; Act Sec. 1173(b)(1), extending the interest exclusion to RICs amends Secs. 133(a) and 852(b)(5), effective for loans after the date of enactment including loans used to refinance loans used to acquire employer securities before the date of enactment if such loans were used to acquire the securities after 5-23-84; Act Sec. 1173(b)(2), extending the 50% interest exclusion for corporations, amends Sec. 133(b)(1), effective (1) for refinancing loans made after the date of enactment and (2) for securities transferred after the date of enactment for loans incurred after 7-18-84.

[¶1175] **Termination Distributions.** Under prior law, employer securities allocated to an employee's account under a tax credit ESOP couldn't be distributed within 84 months of allocation. There were a few exceptions. The new law adds plan terminations to the list of exceptions. Thus, the 84-month rule won't apply to distributions from terminated tax credit ESOPs [see ¶1172].

Act Sec. 1174(a), relating to termination distributions from certain ESOPs amends Sec. 409(d)(1), effective for termination distributions after 12-31-84.

[¶1176] **ESOP Distribution Rules.** The new law makes a number of changes to the ESOP distribution rules. An ESOP is to permit distributions to employees who separate from service before normal retirement age. Unless an employee elects otherwise, the distribution of the entire account balance will begin no later than one year after the later of the plan year (1) in which the participant ceases employment due to retirement, disability, or death or (2) which is the fifth plan year following separation from service (provided the participant doesn't return to the employer).

If any part of the employee's account balance includes securities attributable to a securities acquisition loan that hasn't been fully repaid, those securities subject to the loan won't be considered part of the account balance until the close of the plan year when the loan is repaid.

> **NOTE:** These rules are intended to accelerate the beginning of payment. If the general rules (Sec. 401(a)(14)) provide an earlier payment date, the participant should elect that schedule.

Distribution period. Unless the plan provides that a participant may elect a longer period, the plan is to provide distributions over a period not longer than five years. If the participant has an account balance greater than $500,000, the period may be five years plus one additional year (up to five additional years) for each $100,000 (or fraction thereof) of the excess. Those dollar figures are to be indexed under the rules of Section 415(d).

Act Sec. 1174(b), relating to the distribution requirements, adds new Sec. 409(o), and amends Sec. 409(a)(3), effective for distributions attributable to stock acquired after 12-31-86.

[¶1177] **Put Option Requirements.** The new law keeps the prior law requirement of the right to demand that benefits be distributed in the form of employer securities and the requirement that a participant receiving distributions of employer securities from a tax credit on leveraged ESOP be given a put option for securities that aren't readily tradable. However, the periods for payment of the option price are modified.

For put options exercised for stock that is part of a total distribution, the new law treats the distribution requirements as met if the amount is paid in substantially equal periodic payments (not less frequently than annually) over a period not greater than five years beginning not later than 30 days after the exercise of the options. In addition, there must be adequate security and reasonable interest paid on the unpaid amounts. Note that a total distribution is that distribution within one tax year to the receipient of his or her account balance.

For put options exercised as part of an installment distribution, the employer must pay the option price not later than 30 days after the options exercise.

Stock bonus plans. The new law extends the put option requirement for employer securities that aren't readily tradable to stock bonus plans. In so doing, stock bonus plans are also subject to the new ESOP distribution rules.

Act Sec. 1174(c)(1), relating to put option payouts, adds new Secs. 409(h)(5) and (6), effective for distributions attributable to stock acquired after December 31, 1986, but a plan may elect to have the amendment apply to all distributions after the date of enactment; Act Sec. 1174(c)(2), dealing with stock bonus plans, amends Sec. 401(a)(23), effective for distributions attributable to stock acquired after 12-31-86.

[¶1178]   **Limitation on Annual Additions.** Annual additions for participants in an ESOP are generally subject to the defined contribution limits under Sec. 415(c)(1), the lesser of 25% of compensation or $30,000. For ESOPs described in Sec. 4975(e)(7) or a tax credit ESOP, the amount is raised to the lesser of $60,000 or the amount of employer securities contributed to, or acquired by the plan. Under prior law, the increased limits applied only if no more than one-third of the employer contributions for the year were allocated to officers, 10% shareholders, and highly compensated employees (those making $60,000 or more).

The new law keeps the increased limits. However, it limits the prohibited group to highly compensated employees as defined in new Sec. 414(q) (explained at ¶1114).

Act Sec. 1174(d), relating to increased annual additions for ESOPs, amends Sec. 415(c)(6), effective for tax years beginning after 12-31-86.

[¶1179]   **Voting Rights Passthrough.** The new law allows certain closely held newspapers to establish ESOPs to be established with nonvoting stock, notwithstanding the voting rights passthrough requirements. However, those nonvoting shares would be treated as qualified employer securities only if the employer has that class of nonvoting stock outstanding *and* the specific shares acquired were outstanding for at least 24 months.

Act Sec. 1176(e), dealing voting rights, amends Sec. 401(a)(22), effective after 12-31-86. Act Sec. 1176(b), relating to qualified securities amends Sec. 409(l)(4), effective for securities acquisitions after 12-31-86. Act 1177(b) exempts a certain newspaper from all of the new ESOP rules.

[¶1180]   **Investment Diversification.** In an effort to avoid forcing employees near retirement age to have all their eggs in one basket, employees who have attained age 55 and completed at least 10 years of service must now be given an opportunity to diversify the investments in their own accounts.

The employee must be able to make the election within 90 days of the end of the plan year in the qualified election period. The qualified election period is the period consisting of the plan year in which the employer attains age 55 (or completes 10 years of service, if later) and ending with the fifth succeeding plan year.

The amount eligible for diversification must be at least 25% of the participant's account balance at the end of the year less amounts previously diversified. For the last year of the election period, the amount must be at least 50% of the account balance less amounts previously diversified.

To the extent that a participant elects to diversify, the new law requires an ESOP to offer at least three investment options that aren't inconsistent with the regs to be issued. Alternatively, the plan can meet the requirement by distributing to the participant, within 90 days after the close of the annual election period, the amount the employee elects to diversify.

ROLLOVER INTO IRA: According to the House Committee Report, a participant receiving a distribution in satisfaction of the election, can roll the distribution into an IRA.

Act Sec. 1175(a), allowing investment diversification, adds Sec. 401(a)(28) (A) and (B), effective for stock acquired after 12-31-86.

[¶1181] Independent Appraiser. Under the new law, the valuation of employer securities that aren't readily tradable on an established securities market, for all activities carried on by the ESOP, must be made by an independent appraiser (as defined in Section 170(a)(1)).

Act Sec. 1175(a), requiring an independent appraiser, adds Sec. 401(a)(28)(C), effective for stock acquired after 12-31-86, effective on enactment.

[The page following this one is page 1201.]

FOREIGN TAX

Foreign Tax Credit

[¶1201] **Separate Credit Limitations.** To restrict the taxpayer's ability to average high and low foreign taxes in calculating the foreign tax credit, the new law creates separate credit limitations for passive income, "high withholding tax interest," financial services income, shipping income, and dividends from noncontrolled Section 902 corporations. These separate limitations are generally in addition to those of prior Section 904(d), which prevented taxpayers from averaging foreign tax rates on other income classes that may be easily resourced or are generally subject to abnormally high or low foreign tax.

The separate passive income category replaces the category for passive interest income, and generally is any income that would be foreign personal holding company income under Subpart F. The new category includes foreign personal holding company inclusions and passive foreign investment company inclusions. It excludes high withholding tax interest, financial services income, shipping income, dividends from noncontrolled Section 902 corporations, export financing interest, high-taxed income, and foreign oil and gas extraction income. The term "export financing interest" means interest derived from financing the sale or other disposition for use or consumption outside the United States of property manufactured, produced, grown, or extracted in the United States by the taxpayer or a related person, when not more than 50% of the property's fair market value is attributable to products imported into the United States. The term "high-taxed income" means income that would be passive income if the sum of the foreign income taxes paid or accrued by the taxpayer as to the income and the foreign income taxes deemed paid by the taxpayer as to the income exceeds the highest U.S. tax rate multiplied by the amount of the income.

High withholding tax interest. This category covers interest subject to a foreign country's or U.S. possession's withholding or other gross-basis tax of at least 5%. It excludes export financing interest.

Financial services income. This category covers income derived in the active conduct of a banking, financing, or similar business, or derived from the investment by an insurance company of its unearned premiums or reserves ordinary and necessary for the proper conduct of its insurance business, and is of a kind that would be insurance income as defined in Section 953(a). It excludes export financing interest and high withholding tax interest.

Shipping income. This category covers income received or accrued by a person that is of a kind that would be foreign base company shipping income.

Dividends. This category covers dividends from a noncontrolled Section 902 corporation—that is, a foreign corporation in which the recipient owns between 10% and 50% of the voting power of its stock.

> **DE MINIMIS EXCEPTION:** A CFC has no separate category income in a tax year in which it has no Subpart F income due to the applicability of the Subpart F de minimis rule. The rule applies if the sum of foreign base company income and tax haven insurance income for the year is less than the lesser of 5% of gross income or $1 million. [See ¶1219.]

Transitional rules. Taxes paid or accrued in a tax year beginning before 1-1-87, as to interest income will be treated as taxes paid or accrued as to passive income. Taxes paid or accrued in a tax year beginning before 1-1-86, as to overall limitation income will be treated as such, except to the extent the taxpayer establishes the taxes were paid or accrued as to shipping income or financial services income. Taxes paid or accrued in a tax year beginning before 1-1-87, as to any other separate category of income described before that date will be treated as taxes paid or accrued as to a corresponding category of income described after the date.

Look-through rules. Interest, rents, and royalties received or accrued from a CFC in which the taxpayer is a U.S. shareholder will be treated as income in a separate category to the extent it is properly allocable. Dividends paid out of E&P of a CFC in which the taxpayer is a U.S. shareholder will be treated as income in a separate category in proportion to the ratio of the part of E&P attributable to income in that category to total E&P. Subpart F inclusions will be treated as income in a separate category to the extent the amount included is attributable.

Source rule. Except to the extent provided in regulations, interest paid or accrued by a CFC to a U.S. shareholder (or CFC related to the shareholder) will first be allocated to foreign personal holding company income in the passive income category.

Act Sec. 1201, relating to separate foreign tax credit limitations, adds new Secs. 904(d)(1)(A), (B), (C), (D), and (E) by striking out old (A) and redesignating old (B), (C), (D), and (E) as (F), (G), (H), and (I), and amends Secs. 864(d)(5)(A)(i), 904(d) subsection heading, 904(d)(1), 904(d)(2), 904(d)(3) and 954(b)(5), effective generally for tax years beginning after 12-31-86. A transitional rule, which applies for foreign taxes on interest paid by borrowers in 33 less developed countries, is phased out over the five-tax year period beginning with the taxpayer's first tax year beginning after 1989. A special rule applies to one U.S. corporation.

[¶1202] **Subsidies.** The new law codifies Reg. Sec. 1.901-2(e)(3), providing that income, war profits, and excess profits taxes won't be creditable to the extent that the foreign country uses the amount of tax to provide a subsidy to the taxpayer, a related person, or any party to the transaction or a related transaction, and the subsidy is determined by reference to the tax's amount or computation base.

Act Sec. 1204, relating to the treatment of certain subsidies, adds new Sec. 901(i) by redesignating old (i) as (j), effective for foreign taxes paid or accrued in tax years beginning after 12-31-86.

[¶1203] **Separate Limitation Losses.** The new law provides that losses for a tax year in a separate foreign tax credit limitation category offset U.S.-source income only to the extent that the aggregate of those losses exceeds the aggregate of foreign income earned in other categories. These losses will be allocated proportionately among the foreign income categories in which the taxpayer earns income in the loss year. U.S.-source losses are allocated proportionately among the foreign income categories, but only after the allocation of foreign-source losses.

Recharacterization rule. If foreign losses in one category are allocated to foreign income in a second category in this way and the first (loss) category has income in a later tax year, the income is recharacterized as income in the second category, previously offset by the loss, in proportion to the earlier loss allocation.

Act Sec. 1203, relating to separate limitation losses, adds new Sec. 904(f)(5), effective for losses incurred in tax years beginning after 12-31-86.

[¶1204] **Deemed-Paid Credit.** Under the new law, the deemed-paid foreign tax credit of a U.S. corporation owning at least 10% of the voting stock of a foreign corporation is computed with reference to the pool of the distributing corporation's post-1986 accumulated E&P and accumulated foreign taxes. The change is intended to prevent taxpayers from losing deemed-paid credits because the foreign corporation had a deficit in E&P in some years that the IRS considered to reduce accumulated profits (for prior years in which foreign taxes were paid), reducing the amount of creditable taxes. The new law is also intended to limit the taxpayer's ability to average high-tax and low-tax years, resulting in a deemed-paid credit that reflects a higher than average foreign tax rate over a period of years.

Pool of accumulated E&P. A U.S. corporation that owns at least 10% of the voting stock of a foreign corporation from which it receives dividends will be deemed to have paid the same proportion of the foreign corporation's post-1986 foreign income taxes as the amount of the dividends bears to its post-1986 undistributed earnings. Post-1986 undistributed earnings are the accumulated E&P for tax years beginning after 1986.

> **PROSPECTIVE ONLY:** The pooling will be prospective only— future dividends and Subpart F inclusions will be treated as made first out of the accumulated profits derived after the effective date, and then out of pre-effective date accumulated profits under the ordering principles of prior law.

Second-and third-tier corporations. Similar rules apply if the foreign corporation (first-tier corporation) owns at least 10% of a second foreign corporation (second-tier corporation), or if the first-tier corporation owns at least 10% of a second-tier corporation that owns at least 10% of a third corporation (third-tier corporation)—though there is a 5% stock ownership requirement calculated by multiplying the percentage owned by each corporation in the next lower-tier corporation.

Act Sec. 1202, relating to the deemed-paid credit, amends Sec. 902, 960(a)(1), 6038(a)(1)(B), 6038(c)(4)(C), and the table of sections for subpart A of part III of subchapter N of chapter 1, effective for distributions by foreign corporations out of, and inclusions under Sec. 951(a) attributable to, E&P for tax years beginning after 12-31-86.

[¶1205] Limitation on Carryback. Under the new law, taxes paid or accrued in a tax year beginning after 1986 may be treated as paid or accrued in a tax year beginning before 1987 only to the extent the post-1986 taxes could be carried back if the tax was determined by applying the tax rate in effect on the day before the Act enactment date. Such taxes will be treated as imposed on overall limitation income. No taxes paid or accrued in a tax year beginning after 1986 as to high withholding tax interest may be carried back.

Act Sec. 1205 does not amend the Code.

Source Rules

[¶1211] Personal Property. To more clearly reflect the situs of economic activity, the new law modifies rules for sourcing income from sales of tangible and intangible personal property. General rule: income from a sale of personal property by a U.S. resident is U.S.-source, and by a nonresident is foreign-source. Separate rules apply for inventory property, depreciable personal property, intangibles, sales through offices, and stock of affiliates.

Under prior law, income from the purchase and resale of tangible and intangible personal property generally was sourced at the place of the sale, which was deemed to be where title passes. Income from manufacture in one country and sale in another country was sourced half at the place of manufacture and half at the place of sale. Royalty income was sourced in the country of use.

U.S. resident. Under the new law, an individual is a U.S. resident if he or she has a tax home in the United States under Sec. 911(d)(3). A corporation, partnership, trust, or estate is a U.S. resident if it is a U.S. person under Sec. 7701(a)(30).

> **NOTE:** A U.S. citizen or resident alien won't be considered a resident of another country for a sale of personal property unless a 10% income tax on the gain is paid to the country.

Inventory property. Income from the sale of inventory property will be sourced by the old personal property rules under Secs. 861(a)(6), 862(a)(6), and 863(b).

Depreciable property. If depreciation deductions have been allocated against U.S. or foreign-source income, then gain from the sale of depreciable property must be similarly sourced. Gain in excess of these deductions will be sourced as if the property were inventory property. If certain depreciable property is used predominantly within or outside the United States in a tax year, the allowable depreciation deductions are allocated entirely against U.S. or foreign-source income, respectively.

Intangible property. Payments from the sale of intangibles will be sourced as if they were royalties only to the extent the payments are contingent on the intangible's productivity, use, or disposition. Payments from the sale of goodwill will be sourced where it was generated.

Sales through offices. If a U.S. resident maintains a foreign office or other fixed place of business, income from sales of personal property attributable to that office is foreign-sourced—provided a 10% income tax is paid to the foreign country. This rule doesn't apply for income sourced under the rules for inventory property, depreciable personal property, intangibles, or stock of affiliates.

If a nonresident has a U.S. office or other fixed place of business, income from the sale of personal property (including inventory property) attributable to the office is U.S. sourced, except for inventory sold for use, disposition, or consumption outside the United States if the taxpayer's office materially participated in the sale, and amounts included in gross income under Sec. 951(a)(1)(A).

Stock of affiliates. Income from the sale of stock in a foreign corporate affiliate by a U.S. resident is foreign-source income if the affiliate is engaged in the active conduct of a trade or business, and the sale takes place in the foreign country in which the affiliate derived more than 50% of its gross income during a three-year period.

The new law also repeals the Sec. 871(e) rule that, on a sale of intangible property in which more than 50% of the gain is from contingent payments, all the gain is considered so contingent.

Act Sec. 1211, relating to the source rules for personal property sales, adds new Sec. 865, repeals Sec. 871(e), and amends Secs. 861(a)(6), 862(a)(6), 863(b)(2), 863(b)(3), 864(c)(4)(B), 871(a)(1)(D), 881(a)(4), and 904(b)(3), effective generally for tax years beginning after 12-31-86. For a foreign person other than a CFC, the amendments are effective for transactions entered into after 3-18-86. The Treasury must conduct a study of the source rules for sales of inventory property and submit a report to the House Ways and Means Committee and Senate Finance Committee by 9-30-87.

[¶1212] **80-20 Corporations.** Previously, dividends and interest paid by a U.S. corporation deriving more than 80% of its income from foreign sources were treated as foreign-source income. Also, interest paid by a resident alien deriving more than 80% of his or her income from foreign sources was treated as foreign-source income.

Interest. Under the new law, interest received from a resident alien or U.S. corporation is treated as U.S.-source income, unless the resident alien or U.S. corporation meets an 80% foreign business requirement. The requirement is met and the interest is foreign source if at least 80% of the resident alien's or U.S. corporation's worldwide gross income is derived from foreign sources and is attributable to the active conduct of a trade or business in a foreign country or U.S. possession by the resident alien or U.S. corporation (or by a subsidiary or chain of subs) for a three-year period.

However, a related person that receives interest from a resident alien or U.S. corporation meeting the 80% foreign business requirement can only treat as foreign-source income the percentage of interest equal to the ratio of the resident alien's or U.S. corporation's foreign gross income to its worldwide gross income (for the three-year period).

Dividends. Under the new law, dividends received from a U.S. corporation other than a Sec. 936 possessions corporation are U.S.-source income.

However, nonresident aliens and foreign corporations receiving dividends from a U.S. corporation that meets the 80% foreign business requirement aren't subject to U.S. withholding tax on the percentage of the dividends paid that the U.S. corporation's foreign-source income bears to its worldwide gross income over the three-year period.

U.S. sourced but tax exempt. Under the new law, interest on deposits not effectively connected with the conduct of a U.S. trade or business and income derived by a foreign central bank of issue from bankers' acceptances are U.S. source income, but are exempt from U.S. withholding tax. Deposits are deposits with banks, deposits or withdrawable accounts with federal or state chartered savings institutions, and amounts held by an insurance company under an agreement to pay interest.

Act Sec. 1214, relating to the treatment of 80-20 corporations, adds new Secs. 871(i) by redesignating old (i) as (j), 881(d) by redesignating old (d) as (e), 1441(c)(10), and 6049(b)(5)(iv), and amends Secs. 861(a)(1), 861(a)(2)(A), 861(c), 861(d), and 6049(b)(5), (B), effective for payments after 12-31-86. A special rule applies for the treatment of certain interest. A transitional rule applies. A special rule applies for a particular U.S. corporation.

[¶1213] Transportation Income. The new law treats 50% of all income from transporation that begins or ends in the United States but not both as U.S.-source income. The rule doesn't apply to personal service income unless it is attributable to transportation between the United States and a U.S. possession. Previously, transportation income was allocated between U.S. and foreign sources in proportion to the expenses incurred.

The new law also repeals the special sourcing rules for the lease or disposition of vessels, aircraft, or spacecraft constructed in the United States, and the lease of aircraft to a regularly scheduled U.S. air carrier.

Tax on transportation income. The new law imposes a 4% tax on the U.S.-source gross transportation income of NRAs and foreign corporations. As under prior law, transportation income is gross income derived from, or in connection with, the use (or hiring or leasing for use) of a vessel or aircraft, or the performance of directly related services.

Exceptions. Transportation income received or accrued by an NRA or foreign corporation that is effectively connected with the foreign person's U.S. trade or business is instead taxed on a net basis. The income is effectively connected if the foreign person has a U.S. fixed place of business involved in earning transportation income, and substantially all the U.S.-source gross transportation income is attributable to regularly scheduled transportation.

Reciprocal exemption by residence. The new law provides that gross income derived by a foreign resident or a corporation organized in a foreign country from operating a ship or aircraft (including rental on a full or bareboat basis) is exempt from U.S. tax if the foreign country grants an equivalent exemption to U.S. citizens and U.S. corporations. Under prior law, the ship or aircraft had to be documented or registered under the law of a foreign country.

A foreign corporation may not claim the reciprocol exemption if 50% or more of the value of its stock is owned (or considered owned) by persons who aren't residents of a foreign country that grants U.S. persons an equivalent exemption. The 50% test won't apply to a foreign corporation if its stock is primarily and regularly traded on an established securities market in the foreign country in which it is organized, or if it is wholly owned by such a corporation.

Act Sec. 1212, relating to transportation income, adds new Secs. 872(b)(5), 872(b)(6), 883(a)(4), 883(c), and 887, repeals Sec. 861(e) by redesignating old (f) as (e), and amends Sec. 863(b)(1), 863(c)(2), 872(b)(1), 872(b)(2), 883(a)(1), 883(a)(2), and the table of subparts for part II of subchapter N, effective generally for tax years beginning after 12-31-86. A special rule applies for certain leased property. A special rule applies for four ships to be leased by the U.S. Navy.

[¶1214] Allocating Interest Expense. Under the new law, corporate members of an affiliated group must allocate and apportion interest expense against U.S. or foreign-source income on a consolidated group basis. Exception: Financial institutions may allocate interest expense separately, as one taxpayer, if their business is predominantly with unrelated persons and they are required by state or federal law to be operated separately from nonfinancial institutions.

Other expenses. Expenses other than interest not directly allocable to a class of income will be allocated and apportioned on a consolidated basis.

Asset method. Eliminating the use of the gross income method for allocating and apportioning interest expense, the new law provides that only the asset method can be used. Not taken into account under the asset method are tax-exempt assets and certain dividends (and stock on which the dividends are paid) for which a deduction is allowed. The adjusted basis of an asset that is stock in a foreign corporation in which affiliated group members own at least 10% of its voting stock will be increased by the foreign corporation's E&P attributable to the stock and accumulated while the taxpayer held it, and will be reduced by an E&P deficit.

The new law gives the Treasury the authority to prescribe regulations providing for

• resourcing income of any affiliated group member or modifying the consolidated return regulations,

• direct allocation of interest expense incurred to carry out an integrated financial transaction, and

• apportionment of the expense allocable to foreign source income subject to separate foreign tax credit limitations.

Act Sec. 1215, relating to rules for allocating interest, adds new Sec. 864(e) and amends the Sec. 864 section heading and the table of sections for part I of subchapter N of chapter 1, effective generally for tax years beginning after 12-31-86. Under transitional rules, for the first three years beginning after 12-31-86, the amendment generally will apply only to an applicable percentage (25%, 50%, 75%) of interest expenses paid or accrued by the taxpayer during the tax year as to an indebtedness not exceeding the outstanding indebtedness on 11-16-85. Special rules apply for two U.S. corporations.

[¶1215] **Research and Experimental Expenditures.** The new law modifies the rules for allocating research and experimental expenditures against U.S. and foreign-source income for one year while Congress analyzes the need for a permanent tax incentive. It doesn't renew the moratorium on the Reg. Sec. 1.861-8 rules.

The new law generally provides that 50% of all amounts allowable as a research and experimental expenditure deduction will be apportioned to U.S.-source income and deducted in determining U.S. taxable income. The remaining amount will be apportioned on the basis of gross sales or gross income. Exception: If research expenditures are incurred to meet legal requirements as to improvements or marketing of specific products or processes and the results aren't likely to generate much gross income outside a single source, they will be allocated entirely to that source.

Act Sec. 1216, relating to the modification of research expenditure allocation rules, does not amend the Code and applies to Secs. 861(b), 862(b), and 863(b) effective for tax years beginning after 8-1-86 and on or before 8-1-87.

[¶1216] **Space and Ocean Income.** Under the new law, except as provided in regulations, income derived from an activity conducted in space and from an activity conducted on or under water that isn't within the jurisdiction of the United States, a U.S. possession, or a foreign country (including Antarctica) by a U.S. person will be sourced in the United States, and by a non-U.S. person will be sourced outside the United States.

Exceptions. Space and ocean activities don't include those creating transportation income under Sec. 863(c), having to do with mines, oil and gas wells, or other deposits within the jurisdiction of a country, or creating "international communications income." International communications income is income derived from transmitting any communications or data between the United States and a foreign country, and is sourced 50% in the United States and 50% in the foreign country.

Bill Sec. 1213, relating to space and ocean income, adds new Secs. 863(d) and 863(e), effective for tax years beginning after 12-31-86.

Income Earned Through Foreign Corporations

[¶1217] **Subpart F Income.** Generally, the United States currently taxes a controlled foreign corporation's 10% or more U.S. shareholders on their pro rata share of the CFC's Subpart F income. The new law narrows exceptions to taxation under Subpart F and treats certain other types of easily manipulated income as Subpart F income.

Sale of nonincome producing property. Under the new law, the definition of foreign personal holding company income (FPHCI) for Subpart F purposes includes the excess of gain over losses from the sale or exchange of property that (1) gives rise to dividends and interest (other than those excluded under the active business exceptions for banks and insurance companies), royalties and rents (other than active business, unrelated party), and annuities, or (2) doesn't give rise to any income. The rule doesn't apply to gain from the sale or exchange of property that is inventory property in the hands of the seller or of property by a regular dealer in that property.

Commodities transactions. The new law provides that the definition of FPHCI includes the excess of gain over loss from any transaction (including a futures, forward, or similar transaction) in any commodity. As under prior law, the rule doesn't apply to gains from bona fide hedging transactions reasonably necessary to the conduct of a business by a producer, processor, merchant, or handler of a commodity in the way the business is customarily and usually conducted by others. A new exception covers active business gains if substantially all the CFC's business is as an active producer, processor, merchant, or handler of commodities.

Foreign currency gains. Under the new law, the definition of FPHCI includes the excess of foreign currency gains over foreign currency losses attributable to Sec. 988 transactions. Exception: This doesn't apply to transactions directly related to the business needs of the CFC.

Income equivalent to interest. The new law provides that the definition of FPHCI includes income equivalent to interest, including commitment fees for loans made.

Banking and insurance income. The new law repeals the rules excluding from FPHCI dividends, interest, and gains from the sale or exchange of stocks or securities received from unrelated persons in the active conduct of a banking, financing, or similar business, or from an insurance company's investment of unearned premiums, reserves, and certain other funds. The new law also repeals the rule excluding from FPHCI interest paid by a related person to a CFC if both are engaged in a banking, financing, or similar business. However, interest earned by U.S.-controlled foreign banks in connection with export financing for related U.S. persons would be eligible for deferral to the same extent that it was eligible under previous law.

Income from related persons. Excluded from FPHCI under the new law are (1) dividends and interest received from a related person that is created or organized under the laws of the same foreign country under whose laws the CFC is created or organized and has a substantial part of its assets used in its trade or business there, and (2) rents and royalties received from a related person for the use of, or the privilege of using, property within the country under whose laws the CFC is created or organized. The exclusion doesn't apply to the extent the interest, rent, or royalty reduces the payor's Subpart F income.

Definition of related person. Whether CFC income is foreign base company income may depend on whether it is received from a related person. Under the new law, the definition of "related person" includes an individual, corporation, partnership, trust, or estate that controls or is controlled by the CFC as well as a corporation, partnership, trust, or estate controlled by the same persons that control the CFC. For a corporation, control meant the direct or indirect ownership of 50% or more of the total combined voting power of all classes of voting stock or the total value of stock. For a partnership, trust, or estate, control is the direct or indirect ownership of 50% or more of the total value of beneficial interests in the entity.

Previously, a related person included an individual, partnership, trust, or estate that controlled the CFC, a corporation that controlled or was controlled by the CFC, or a corporation controlled by the same person or persons that controlled the CFC. For this purpose, control meant the direct or indirect ownership of stock possessing more than 50% of the total combined voting power of all classes of voting stock.

Shipping income. The new law repeals the rule excluding from foreign base company income the foreign base company shipping income reinvested in foreign base company shipping operations. The new law provides that foreign base company shipping income includes income derived from a space or ocean activity as defined in Section 863(d)(2).

Insurance income. The new law provides that the definition of insurance income subject to Subpart F taxation includes any income attributable to the issuing (or reinsuring) of any insurance or annuity contract in connection with risks in a country other than the CFC's country of incorporation, or in connection with same-country risks in an arrangement in which another CFC receives a substantially equal amount of premiums for insuring other-country risks, and would be taxed as if it were the income of a U.S. insurance company.

The new law subjects the related person insurance income of offshore captive insurance companies to current U.S. taxation. For the purpose of taking into account related person insurance income, the U.S. ownership threshold for CFC status is reduced to 25% or more. Related person insurance income means insurance income attributable to a policy of insurance or reinsurance as to which the primary insured is a U.S. shareholder in the foreign corporation receiving the income or a related person to the shareholder. The rule won't apply if:

- the corporation's gross related person insurance income for the tax year is less than 20% of its gross insurance income for the year,

- less than 20% of the total combined voting power of all classes of the corporation's voting stock and less than 20% of the total value of its stock and policies during the tax year are owned by persons who are the primary insured under any insurance or reinsurance policies issued by the corporation, or by persons related to those persons,

- the foreign corporation elects to treat the related person insurance income as income effectively connected with the conduct of a U.S. trade or business.

The new law repeals the 5% de minimis exception for income from insurance of U.S. risks and repeals the exceptions for investment income from unearned premiums and reserves.

Not used to reduce taxes. The new law provides that foreign base company income and insurance income doesn't include any income item received by a CFC if the taxpayer satisfies the Treasury that the income was subject to an effective rate of foreign income tax greater than 90% of the maximum rate of U.S. corporate tax. The rule doesn't apply to foreign base company oil-related income. Under prior law, a significant purpose test was used.

Deficits. The new law repeals the Sec. 952(d) chain deficit rule, and limits the Sec. 952(c) accumulated deficit rule allowing a CFC to reduce Subpart F income by the sum of its prior year E&P deficits.

To coordinate the Subpart F rules and the separate foreign tax credit limitation for passive income rules, the new law provides that prior year deficits in E&P and other companies' deficits in E&P don't reduce Subpart F income. Income recaptured as passive income under the foreign loss recharacterization rule is Subpart F income in accordance with the character of the original income requiring recapture.

Act Sec. 1221, relating to Subpart F income, adds new Sec. 953(c), repeals Secs. 954(b)(2) and 954(g) by redesignating old (h) as (g), and amends Secs. 864(d)(5)(A)(iii), 864(d)(5)(A)(iv), 952(a)(1), 952(c), 952(d), 953 section heading, 953(a), 954(a)(5), 954(b)(4), 954(c), 954(d)(3), 954(e), 954(f), 955(a)(1)(A), 955(a)(2)(A), 957(b), and table of sections for Subpart F of part III of subchapter N of chapter 1, effective generally for tax years of foreign corporations beginning after 12-31-86. A special rule applies for repeal of the exclusion for reinvestment shipping income. An exception applies for certain reinsurance contracts.

〔¶1218〕 Definition of CFC and FPHC. To prevent U.S. shareholders from avoiding tax on the earnings of U.S.-controlled foreign corporations, the new law amends the definitions of CFC and FPHC to consider stock value as well as voting power. Under the new law, the term "controlled foreign corporation" means a foreign corporation for which more than 50% of its total combined voting power of all classes of voting stock or the total value of its stock is owned by 10%-or-more U.S. shareholders on any day during its tax year. This rule applies in determining whether an insurance company is a CFC under the more than 25% U.S. ownership test. The stock requirement for FPHC status is met when more than 50% of its total combined voting power of all classes of voting stock or the total value of its stock is owned by or for no more than five U.S. citizens or residents.

Act Sec. 1222, relating to the definitions of CFC and FPHC, amends Secs. 552(a)(2), 957(a), and 957(b), effective generally for tax years of foreign corporations beginning after 12-31-86, except that for applying Secs. 951(a)(1)(B) and 956 the amendments will take effect on 8-16-86. A transitional rule applies for corporations treated as CFCs due to the amendments. A special rule applies to a particular individual beneficiary of a trust.

[¶1219] Supart F De Minimis and Full Inclusion Rules. Under the new law, none of a CFC's gross income for the tax year will be treated as foreign base company income (FBCI) or insurance income, if the sum of its FBCI and gross insurance income for the tax year is less than the lesser of 5% of gross income, or $1 million. All of a CFC's gross income for the tax year will be treated as FBCI or insurance income, if the sum of its FBCI and gross insurance income for the tax year exceeds 70% of gross income. Previously, the thresholds were 10% and 70% of FBCI.

Act Sec. 1223, relating to the Subpart F de minimus and full inclusion rules, amends Secs. 864(d)(5)(A)(ii), 881(c)(4)(A)(i), and 954(b)(3), effective for tax years beginning after 12-31-86.

[¶1220] CFC Status of Possessions Corporations. The new law repeals the exemption of corporations organized in U.S. possessions from CFC status. As a result, 10% or more U.S. shareholders will be currently taxed under Subpart F. Under prior law, a corporation created or organized in, or under the laws of, Puerto Rico or a U.S. possession wasn't a CFC if at least 80% of its gross income was from possession sources for the three-year period immediately preceding the end of the tax year and at least 50% of its gross income was from the active conduct of certain trades or businesses within a possession.

Act Sec. 1224, repealing the CFC exemption of possessions corporations, repeals Sec. 957 by redesignating (d) as new (c), effective generally for tax years of foreign corporations beginning after 12-31-86, except that for applying Secs. 951(a)(1)(B) and 956 the amendments will take effect on 8-16-86. A transitional rule applies to corporations treated as CFCs due to the amendment.

[¶1221] Passive Foreign Investment Companies. The new law provides that generally a U.S. person must pay U.S. tax and an interest charge based on the value of tax deferral when the shareholder disposes of his or her PFIC stock or receives an excess distribution. The rule doesn't apply to U.S. shareholders in PFICs that are qualified electing funds.

PFIC definition. A PFIC is a foreign corporation if 75% or more of its gross income for the tax year is passive income, or at least 50% of the average value of its assets during the tax year produce, or are held for producing, passive income. "Passive income" is income includible in the foreign tax credit limitation for passive income under Sec. 904(d)(2)(A). Passive income excludes income derived by bona fide banks and insurance companies. In determining whether the corporate shareholder is a PFIC under the asset test or income test, a proportionate part of the assets and income of a 25%-owned subsidiary is attributed to the corporate shareholder. A PFIC doesn't include a foreign investment company described in Sec. 1247 (one electing before 1963 to distribute income currently). It also doesn't include a corporation in a start-up phase of an active business or a corporation in transition from one active business to another active business.

Under the new law, the gain recognized on disposition of PFIC stock or on receipt of an excess distribution from a PFIC is considered as earned pro rata over the shareholder's holding period and is treated as ordinary income. The portion of distribution not characterized as excess distributions are taxable in the current year. An excess distribution is a current year distribution as to stock to the extent it represents a ratable portion of the total distributions as to the stock during the year that are in excess of 125% of the average amount of distributions as to the stock during the three preceding years.

A taxpayer who uses PFIC stock as security for a loan is treated as having disposed of the stock.

A U.S. person is considered to own his or her proportionate share of the stock of a PFIC owned by a (1) partnership, estate, or trust of which the U.S. person is a partner or beneficiary, or (2) foreign corporation for which the U.S. person owns 50% or more of the value of its stock.

Qualified electing funds. A U.S. person who owns (or is treated as owning) stock of a qualified electing fund must include in gross income his or her share of the PFIC's E&P, with basis adjustments for undistributed amounts and for distributions previously included in income. A qualified electing fund is a PFIC that properly elects qualified electing fund status and complies with Treasury requirements for determining E&P and ascertaining stock ownership. The election must be made before the 15th day of the third month of the tax year following the tax year for which the election is being made.

Subject to an interest charge, a U.S. shareholder in a qualified electing fund can elect to defer U.S. tax on amounts included in income for which no current distributions are received.

Act Sec. 1235, relating to passive foreign investment companies, adds new Secs. 542(c)(10), 551(g) by redesignating old (g) as (h), 904(g)(1)(A)(iii), 951(f), 1246(f), by redesignating old (f) as (g), 1291, 1293, 1294, 1295, 1296, 1297, and 6503(j) by redesignating old (j) as (k), and amends Secs. 532(b), 542(c), 851(b), 904(g)(1)(A), 904(g)(2) paragraph heading, and the table of parts for subchapter P of chapter 1, effective for tax years beginning after 12-31-86.

[¶1222] Accumulated Earnings and PHC. The new law provides that, for a foreign corporation, the accumulated earnings tax and personal holding company tax will be calculated by taking into account only capital gains and losses that are effectively connected with the conduct of a U.S. trade or business and aren't tax exempt under a treaty.

Act Sec. 1225, relating to a foreign corporation's accumulated earnings tax and PHC tax, adds new Secs. 535(b)(9) and 545(b)(7), effective for gains and losses realized on or after 3-1-86.

Special Provisions for U.S. Persons

[¶1223] Possession Tax Credit. The new law modifies the possession tax credit.

Active trade or business test. A U.S. corporation must meet an active trade or business test and a possession-source income test to qualify for the possession tax credit. Under the new law, the percentage of the corporation's gross income that must be derived from the active conduct of a trade or business in the possession increases from 65% or more to 75% or more for tax years beginning after 1986. As before, the corporation must derive 80% or more of its gross income from sources within a possession.

Received in U.S. The new law modifies the prior law rule that denied the possession tax credit for otherwise eligible income received by the U.S. corporation within the United States. The credit is available for active business income received from an unrelated person.

Qualified investment income. To allow the Puerto Rico government to implement its twin-plant program to encourage companies with Puerto Rico operations to develop or expand manufacturing in qualified Caribbean Basin countries, the new law modifies the definition of qualified possession-source investment income (QPSII). Prior law limited QPSII to income derived from investments within a possession in which the taxpayer conducted an active trade or business.

Under the new law, subject to conditions under regulations, an investment in a financial institution will be treated as for use in Puerto Rico—to the extent used by the financial institution (or the Government Development Bank for Puerto Rico or the Puerto Rico Economic Development Bank) for investment in active business assets or development projects in a qualified Caribbean Basin country consistent with Caribbean Basin Economic Recovery Act goals, and under a specific authorization granted by the GDBPR under Puerto Rico Treasury regulations. A similar rule applies for direct investment in the GDBPR or the PREDB. For this purpose, a qualified Caribbean Basin country is any beneficiary country (under Sec. 212(a)(1)(A) of the CBERA) that satisfies Sec. 274(h)(6)(A)(i) and (ii). The rule doesn't apply unless the person in whose trade or business the investment is made (or other recipient) and the financial institution (or the GDBPR or PREDB) certify to the Treasury and the Puerto Rico Treasury that the loan will be promptly used to acquire active business assets or to make other authorized expenditures, and the financial institution (or the GDBPR or PREDB) and the recipient agree to allow the Treasury and the Puerto Rico Treasury to examine their books and records to ensure that the requirements are met.

Treatment of intangibles. A possession corporation may derive some intangible income tax free if it elects either a cost-sharing rule or a ⁵⁰/₅₀ profit split method of computing taxable income. For companies that elect the cost-sharing rule, the new law sets the required cost-sharing payment at the greater of 110% of the payment required under present law, or the royalty payment that would be required (under Secs. 482 and 367 as amended by the law) if the possessions corporation were considered a foreign corporation as to manufacturing intangibles it is treated as owning. For companies that elect the ⁵⁰/₅₀ profit split, the new law increases the amount of product area research expenditures to 120% for computing combined taxable income.

Treatment of royalty payments. The new law requires that royalty payments relating to intangibles that a U.S. person transfers to a related foreign corporation or possessions corporation must be commensurate with the income attributable to the intangible. The standard applies in determining the amounts imputed under Sec. 367(d) and the appropriate Sec. 482 allocation in other situations.

Act Sec. 1231, relating to the possession tax credit, adds new Sec. 936(d)(4), repeals Sec. 936(a)(2)(C), and amends Secs. 367(d)(2)(A), 482, 936(a)(2)(B), 936(b), 936(h)(5)(C)(i)(I), and 936(h)(5)(C)(ii)(II), effective generally for tax years beginning after 12-31-86. A special rule applies for transfer of intangibles. Act Sec. 1231(f), also amends Sec. 936(h)(5)(C)(ii)(II), effective for tax years beginning after 12-31-82. A special transitional rule applies to a particular corporation.

[¶1224] Panama Canal Commission Employees. The new law clarifies that nothing in the Panama Canal Treaty or any implementing agreement is to be construed as exempting any U.S. citizen or resident from any U.S. tax under the 1954 or 1986 Code. The new law also provides that Panama Canal Commission employees and Defense Department civilian employees stationed in Panama may exclude from gross income allowances comparable to those excludable under Sec. 912(1) by the State Department employees stationed there.

Act Sec. 1232(a), relating to the treatment of individuals in Panama, is effective generally for all tax years, whether beginning before, on, or after the enactment date (or for a tax not imposed as to a tax year, to taxable events after the enactment date). Act Sec. 1232(b), relating to employees' allowances, is effective for tax years beginning after 12-31-86.

[¶1225] Foreign Earned Income Exclusion. The new law limits a qualifying individual's total foreign earned income exclusion for a tax year to $70,000. Previously, the maximum exclusion was $80,000, increasing to $85,000 in 1988, $90,000 in 1989, and $95,000 in 1990 and thereafter.

The new law also denies the Sec. 911 exclusion to individuals who violate federal travel restrictions. When an individual's activities in a foreign country violate regulations under the Trading With the Enemy Act or the International Emergency Economic Powers Act that include provisions generally prohibiting U.S. citizens and residents from engaging in travel-related transactions in that country

• the individual's foreign earned income won't include income attributable to services performed in that country during that period, and his or her housing expenses won't include expenses allocable to the period for housing there or for housing of his or her spouse or dependents in another country while present there, and

• the individual won't be treated as a bona fide resident of, or as present in, a foreign country for any day in which he or she was present in that country during that period.

> **NOTE:** Currently, Treasury regulations generally prohibit travel-related transactions of U.S. citizens and residents in Cuba, Kampuchea, Libya, North Korea, and Vietnam.

Act Sec. 1233, relating to the foreign earned income exclusion, adds new Sec. 911(d)(8) by redesignating old (8) as (9), and amends Sec. 911(b)(2)(A), effective for tax years beginning after 12-31-86.

Foreign Taxpayers

[¶1251] **Branch Profits Tax.** The new law imposes a 30% branch profits tax on the E&P of a U.S. branch of a foreign corporation attributable to its income effectively connected (or treated as such) with a U.S. trade or business. It retains the 30% second-level withholding taxes on dividends and interest paid by a foreign corporation to a foreign person, but reduces the U.S. business thresholds that trigger the taxes and modifies the determination of U.S. source interest subject to U.S. tax.

New branch profits tax. The base for the branch profits tax (the dividend equivalent amount) is the foreign corporation's effectively connected E&P for the tax year—reduced for an increase in U.S. net equity and increased for a decrease in U.S. net equity. "U.S. net equity" means U.S. assets (money and adjusted bases of assets) reduced by U.S. liabilities.

Treaty coordination. An income tax treaty between the United States and a foreign country will reduce or eliminate the branch profits tax only if the foreign corporation is a qualified resident of the foreign country, or the treaty allows a withholding tax on dividends paid by the foreign corporation. A "qualified resident" is a foreign corporation that is a resident of a foreign country unless more than 50% by value of its stock is owned by individuals who are neither residents of the foreign country nor U.S. citizens or resident aliens, or at least 50% of its income is used to meet liabilities to nonresidents of the foreign country or the United States. A foreign corporation will be treated as a qualified resident if its stock is primarily and regularly traded on an established securities market in the foreign country, or is wholly owned by another foreign corporation organized in that country and its stock is so traded. The Treasury may treat a foreign corporation as a qualified resident if it meets requirements that the Treasury establishes.

In general, if an income tax treaty between the United States and the country in which the corporation is a qualified resident specifically provides a branch profits tax, the treaty rate applies. If no branch profits rate is specified, the treaty rate on dividends paid by a U.S. corporation to its treaty country parent corporation applies. Any other treaty limitation on the branch profits tax applies.

If a foreign corporation is subject to the branch profits tax for a tax year, it is exempt from the second-level withholding taxes on dividends paid during that tax year. A foreign corporation that isn't a qualified resident cannot claim treaty benefits as to dividends paid by the foreign corporation that are subject to the second-level withholding tax, or received by the foreign corporation.

The Treasury may prescribe regulations to carry out the purposes of the provision.

Second-level withholding taxes. The new law provides that a portion of interest and dividends paid by a foreign corporation are U.S.-

source income if at least 25% of the corporation's worldwide gross income is effectively connected with the conduct of a U.S. trade or business for a three-year period. When the threshold is reached, the second-level withholding tax applies to a foreign corporation's payment of interest or dividends to a foreign person. Previously, the threshold was 50%.

Act Sec. 1241, relating to the branch profits tax, adds new Secs. 884 and 906(b)(6), and amends Secs. 861(a)(1), 861(a)(2)(B), and the table of sections for subpart B of part II of subchapter N of chapter 1, effective for tax years beginning after 12-31-86.

[¶1252] **Deferred Payments and Appreciation.** To prevent a foreign taxpayer from avoiding U.S. tax by receiving income after its U.S. trade or business has ceased to exist, the new law provides that an NRA or foreign corporation's income or gain for a tax year attributable to a transaction in another tax year will be treated as effectively connected with the conduct of a U.S. trade or business as long as it would have been so treated if it were taken into account in the other tax year.

If property is sold or exchanged within 10 years after being used or held for use in connection with a U.S. trade or business, income or gain attributable to the sale or exchange is treated as effectively connected.

Act Sec. 1242, relating to deferred payments and appreciation, adds new Secs. 864(c)(6) and (7), and amends Sec. 864(c)(1), effective for tax years beginning after 12-31-86.

[¶1253] **Tax-Free Exchanges by Expatriates.** Individuals who give up their U.S. citizenship for a principal purpose of avoiding U.S. tax may still make tax-free exchanges of U.S. property for foreign property. However, gain on the sale or exchange of property whose basis is determined in whole or in part by reference to the basis of property located in the United States, stock of a U.S. corporation, or a debt obligation of a U.S. person will be treated as gain from the sale of U.S. property. So a later recognized gain on the foreign property will be subject to U.S. tax.

Act Sec. 1243, relating to tax-free exchanges by expatriates, amends Sec. 877(c), effective for sales or exchanges of property received in exchanges after 9-25-85.

[¶1254] **Reinsurance Study.** The new law requires the Treasury to make a study of whether existing U.S. income tax treaties place U.S. reinsurance corporations at a significant disadvantage with their foreign competitors, and to report the results to the Senate Finance Committee and the House Ways and Means Committee before 1-1-88.

Act Sec. 1244, relating to foreign insurers, makes no changes in the Code.

Foreign Currency Transactions

[¶1261] **Foreign Currency Transactions.** There's a comprehensive new set of rules for the U.S. taxation of foreign exchange transactions.

Functional currency. Under the new law, all determinations must be made in the taxpayer's functional currency—that is, the U.S. dollar or the currency of the economic environment in which a significant part of the business activities of any qualified business unit of the taxpayer are conducted and that is used by the unit to keep its books and records. If the unit's activities are primarily conducted in U.S. dollars, its functional currency will be the U.S. dollar. "Qualified business unit" refers to any separate and clearly identified unit of a trade or business of a taxpayer that keeps separate books and records.

A taxpayer may elect to use the U.S. dollar as the functional currency for any qualified business unit that keeps its books and records in U.S. dollars or uses an accounting method approximating a separate transactions method, to the extent that regulations provide. The election will be effective for the tax year for which it is made and all later tax years unless revoked with Treasury consent.

A change in the functional currency is treated as a change in the taxpayer's accounting method for Sec. 481 purposes.

E&P and foreign taxes. For determining the tax of a shareholder of a foreign corporation, the corporation's E&P is determined in its functional currency. For a U.S. person, the E&P distributed (or deemed distributed or otherwise taken into account) must, if necessary, be translated into U.S. dollars at the appropriate exchange rate.

For computing the amount of foreign taxes deemed paid under Secs. 902 and 960, a foreign income tax paid by a foreign corporation is translated into U.S. dollars using the exchange rate as of the time of payment. An adjustment to the tax paid by a foreign corporation is translated into U.S. dollars using the exchange rate as of when the adjustment was made.

Foreign currency gain or loss on distributions of previously taxed E&P attributable to exchange rate movements between the times of deemed and actual distribution is treated as ordinary income or loss from the same source as the associated income inclusion. The Treasury may prescribe regulations for treating distributions of previously taxed E&P through tiers of foreign corporations.

Translation of branch income. The new law provides that taxpayers with branches whose functional currency isn't the U.S. dollar must use the profit and loss method to compute branch income. The taxpayer must compute the income or loss separately for each qualified business unit in the unit's functional currency, translating the amount to U.S. dollars using the weighed average exchange rate for the tax period over which the income or loss accrued. The taxpayer will recognize exchange gain or loss on remittances to the extent the currency's value at the time of the remittance differs from the value when earned. Remittances after 1986 are treated as paid on a pro rata basis out of post-1986 accumulated earnings. Exchange gain or loss on the remittances will be deemed ordinary income or loss, sourced by reference to the source of income.

Foreign currency transactions. Foreign currency gain or loss attributable to a Sec. 988 transaction must be computed separately and treated as ordinary income or loss. Forward contracts, futures contracts, and options that aren't marked to market are accorded capital gain or loss treatment if they are capital assets and certain identification requirements are met. To the extent that regulations provide, foreign currency gain or loss will be treated as interest income or expense.

Foreign currency gain or loss refers to gain or loss realized due to a change in the exchange rate on or after the booking date (the date that an asset or liability is taken into account for tax purposes) and before the date it is paid.

"Sec. 988 transaction" refers to transactions in which the amount that the taxpayer is entitled to receive or is required to pay is denominated in a nonfunctional currency, or is determined by reference to the value of one or more nonfunctional currencies. Sec. 988 transactions are: (1) the acquisition of, or becoming the obligor under, a debt instrument; (2) accruing or otherwise taking into account an item of expense or gross income or receipt to be paid or received on a later date; (3) entering into or acquiring a forward contract, futures contract, option, or similar financial instrument if it isn't marked to market at the end of the tax year; and (4) the disposition of a nonfunctional currency.

If a Sec. 988 transaction is part of a hedging transaction, all transactions that are part of the transaction will be integrated and treated as one transaction or otherwise treated consistently, to the extent that regulations provide. Neither the Sec. 1092 loss deferral rule nor the Sec. 1256 marked-to-market rules will apply.

Under the loss deferral rule, an obligor's interest in a foreign currency denominated obligation is a position, and a foreign currency for which there is an interbank market is presumed to be "actively traded" property. The new law repeals the special treatment that allowed banks to qualify for the hedging exception to the straddle provisions.

Generally the source of an amount treated as ordinary gain or loss is determined by reference to the residence of the taxpayer or the qualified business unit whose books properly reflect the asset, liability, or income or expense item. An individual's residence is the country of his or her tax base. A U.S. entity's residence is the United States, and a foreign entity's residence is a foreign country. A qualified business unit's residence is the country in which its principal place of business is located. A special rule governs certain related party loans.

The new law applies to Sec. 988 transactions entered into by an individual only to the extent that expenses allocable to the transaction would have been deductible under Sec. 162 or 212 (other than the part concerning tax-related expenses).

The new law authorizes the Treasury to prescribe regulations necessary to carry out the purpose of the new rules, including (1) procedures for taxpayers with qualified business units using a net worth accounting method before the new provisions were enacted, (2) the limitation of the recognition of foreign currency loss on certain remittances from qualified business units, (3) the recharacterization of interest and principal payments as to obligations denominated in certain hyperinflationary currencies, (4) alternative adjustments to the application of Sec. 905(c), and (5) the appropriate treatment of related party transactions (including transactions between the taxpayer's qualified business units).

Act Sec. 1261, relating to the treatment of foreign currency transactions, adds new Secs. 985, 986, 987, 988, 989, and 1092(d)(7), repeals Sec. 1256(e)(4) by redesignating old (5) as (4), and amends the table of subjects for part III of subchapter N of chapter 1, effective generally for tax years beginning after 12-31-86. For applying Sec. 902 and 960, the amendments are effective for E&P of the foreign corporation for tax years beginning after 12-31-86, and foreign taxes paid or accrued by the foreign corporation as to such E&P.

Tax Treatment of Possessions

[¶1271] **The U.S. Possessions.** The U.S. Virgin Islands, Guam, the Northern Mariana Islands, and American Samoa currently use the mirror system of taxation. Each possession transforms the 1954 Internal Revenue Code, as amended, into a local tax code by substituting its name for the name "United States" when appropriate. The new law eliminates the prior law requirement that Guam and the Northern Mariana Islands use a mirror system, coordinates these tax systems and that of American Samoa with the U.S. tax system, and reforms the mirror system in the Virgin Islands.

[¶1272] **The Virgin Islands.** The V.I. Revised Organic Act will be treated as if enacted before the Code, so that the Code will control in cases of conflict. The V.I. Act also will have no effect on any person's U.S. tax liability. The U.S. Treasury will have the authority to specify parts of the Code that won't be mirrored.

The Virgin Islands will be allowed to enact nondiscriminatory local taxes in addition to those of the mirror system, and to rebate or reduce the V.I. tax liabilities of

• non-U.S. individuals attributable to V.I. source income and income effectively connected with the conduct of a V.I. trade or business, and

• V.I. corporations with less than 10% U.S. stock ownership attributable to non-U.S. source income and income not effectively connected with the conduct of a U.S. trade or business.

Individuals. The United States will be treated as including the Virgin Islands for purposes of determining U.S. tax liability of U.S. or V.I. citizens or residents and, under the V.I. mirror Code, the Virgin Islands will be treated as including the United States for purposes of determining V.I. tax liability.

An individual qualifying as a bona fide V.I. resident on the last day of the tax year will pay tax to the Virgin Islands on worldwide income and have no U.S. tax liability.

For a U.S. citizen or resident (other than a bona fide V.I. resident) deriving V.I. income, V.I. tax liability will be a fraction of the individual's U.S. tax liability, based on the ratio of adjusted gross income derived from V.I. sources to worldwide adjusted gross income. That individual will file identical returns with the United States and the Virgin Islands and the individual's V.I. tax payment will be credited against his or her U.S. tax liability.

If spouses file a joint return and only one spouse is a V.I. resident, the resident status of the spouse with the greater adjusted gross income will control.

Corporations. The new law modifies the Sec. 881(b) rule for the exemption from 30% withholding to require that 65% of the corporation's income (formerly 20%) be effectively connected with a U.S. or U.S. possession trade or business and that no substantial part of the income can be used to satisfy obligations to persons other than U.S. or U.S. possession residents.

V.I. corporations qualify for the Sec. 936 credit.

[¶1273] **The Other Possessions.** *Taxing authority.* The new law grants Guam, American Samoa, and the Northern Mariana Islands full authority over their local tax systems for income from sources within, or effectively connected with a trade or business in, the possession and for income received or accrued by a resident of the possession. American Samoa already has this authority. However, each of these grants of authority is effective only if an implementing agreement is in effect between the possession and the United States, providing for elimination of double taxation, prevention of U.S. tax evasion or avoidance, exchange of information, and resolution of other problems.

The possession's tax law must not discriminate against U.S. persons or U.S. possession residents, and for the implementation year and the four following tax years, the possession's revenue must not decrease. The Northern Mariana Islands may retain the mirror system regardless of whether Guam enacts its own law.

Exclusion of possession income. For an individual resident of Guam, American Samoa, or the Northern Mariana Islands, gross income won't include income derived from sources within the possession, and income effectively connected with the individual's conduct of a trade or business within the possession. The individual won't be allowed any deductions (except the Sec. 151 deduction) or credits allocable or chargeable against excluded amounts. Amounts paid to a possession resident for services as a U.S. or U.S. agency employee are taxable. The new law gives the Treasury the authority to prescribe regulations for determining possession residency, source of income, and whether income is effectively connected.

The Sec. 876 exclusion from withholding for alien residents of Puerto Rico is extended to residents of Guam, American Samoa, and the Northern Mariana Islands.

Remuneration paid for services for the U.S. or a U.S. agency performed by a U.S. citizen within a possession is eliminated from the definition of wages subject to withholding to the extent the U.S. or U.S. agency withholds taxes under an agreement with the possession.

Corporations. The new law modifies the Sec. 881(b) rule for the exemption from 30% withholding to include American Samoa (as well as Guam, the Northern Mariana Islands, and the Virgin Islands), and to require that 65% of the corporation's income (instead of 20%) be effectively connected with a U.S. or U.S. possession trade or business for the three-year period ending at the end of its tax year. No substantial part of the income can be used to satisfy obligations to persons other than U.S. or U.S. possession residents. As under prior law, less than 25% in value of the corporations stock can be beneficially owned by foreign persons.

For Subpart F purposes, a corporation organized in Guam, the Northern Mariana Islands, or American Samoa won't be considered a U.S. person if at least 80% of the corporation's income for the three-year period ending at the end of its tax year was from sources in the possession or effectively connected with a trade or business there, and at least 50% of gross income for the period was from the active conduct of a trade or business in that possession.

[¶1274] Cover Over. Guam, American Samoa, the Northern Mariana Islands, and the Virgin Islands will receive the net collection of income tax as to individuals who are bona fide residents of the possession, the taxes withheld on compensation of U.S. government personnel stationed in the possession, and taxes paid to the United States by civilian employees resident in the possession.

[¶1275] Guamanian Banks. The new law repeals the rule that treated interest income on U.S. government obligations held by banks organized in Guam as effectively connected income.

Act Sec. 1236, relating to interest received by Guam banks, amends Sec. 882(e), effective for tax years beginning after 11-16-85.

Act Sec. 1271, relating to the authority of Guam, American Samoa, and the Northern Mariana Islands to enact revenue laws, makes no changes to the Code. Act Sec. 1272, relating to the exclusion of possession source income by individuals, adds new Sec. 3401(a)(8)(D), and 7655(b)(1) by redesignating old (1) and (2) as (2) and (3), repeals Secs. 153(4) by redesignating old (5) as (4), 932 and 935, and amends Secs. 32(c)(1)(C), 48(a)(2)(B)(vii), 63(c)(6), 876, 931, 933(1), 933(2), 1402(a)(8), 1402(a)(9), 6091(b)(1)(B)(iii), the table of sections for subpart A of part II of subchapter N of chapter 1, and the table of sections for subpart D of part III of subchapter N of chapter 1. Act Sec. 1273, relating to the treatment of corporations organized in Guam, American Samoa, or the Northern Mariana Islands, amends Secs. 881(b), 957(c), and 1442(c). Act Sec. 1274, relating to the coordination of U.S. and V.I. income taxes, adds new Sec. 932 and amends the table of sections for subpart D. Act Sec. 1275, relating to the eligibility of V.I. corporations to use the possession tax credit, adds new Sec. 934(b), repeals Sec. 934A, and amends Secs. 28(d)(3)(B), 48(a)(2)(B)(vii), 246(e), 338(h)(6)(B)(i), 864(d)(5)(B), 934, 936(d)(1), 7651(5)(B), and the table of sections for subpart D of part III of subchapter N of chapter 1. Act Sec. 1276, relating to the cover over of income taxes, amends Sec. 7654 and the table of sections for subchapter D of chapter 78. The amendments are generally effective for tax years beginning after 12-31-86. Under a special rule, the amendments apply as to Guam, American Samoa, or the Northern Mariana Islands (and residents and corporations) only if an implementing agreement is in effect between the United States and the possession. Special rules for the Virgin Islands provide that the Sec. 1275(c) amendments apply as to Virgin Islands (and residents and corporations) only if an implementing agreement is in effect between the United States and the Virgin Islands, and also cover the application of the Sec. 1275(b) amendment for pre-1987 open years. A rule provides that if an implementing agreement isn't executed within the first year of the Act, the Treasury must report to the Senate Finance Committee, the House Ways and Means Committee, and the House Interior and Insular Affairs Committee. A rule provides that if a U.S. person becomes a resident of Guam, American Samoa, or the Northern Mariana Islands, the Sec. 877(c) rules will apply during the 10-year period beginning when he or she became a resident, effective for dispositions after 12-31-86 in tax years ending after that date.

¶1275

[¶1281] **Transfer Prices for Imported Property.** Under the new law, if property is imported into the United States in a transaction between related persons within the meaning of Sec. 482, the costs taken into account in computing the buyer's basis or inventory cost of the property cannot be greater than the costs taken into account in computing the property's customs value.

"Customs value" is the value taken into account for determining the amount of any duties that may be imposed on importing property. "Import" means the entering, or withdrawal from warehouse, for consumption—unless regulations provide otherwise.

Act Sec. 1248, relating to the transfer prices for imported property, adds new Sec. 1059A, and amends the table of sections for part IV of subchapter O of chapter 1, effective for transactions entered into after 3-18-86.

[¶1282] **Income of Foreign Governments.** The new law codifies the rule under Reg. Sec. 1.892-1(a)(3) that the tax exemption for foreign governments is limited to investment income.

The exemption applies to a foreign government's income received from (1) U.S. investments in stocks, bonds, or other domestic securities owned by the government, or financial instruments held to execute its financial or monetary policy, or (2) interest on deposits in U.S. banks of moneys belonging to the government.

Commercial activities. The exemption won't apply to a foreign government's income derived from the conduct of U.S. or foreign commercial activity, or received from or by a controlled commercial entity. A "controlled commercial entity" is an entity engaged in commercial activities if the government (1) directly or indirectly holds a 50% or more value or voting interest in the entity, or directly or indirectly holds any other interest that provides the foreign government with effective control of the entity.

International organizations. Also exempt from U.S. taxation is the income of an international organization received from U.S. investments in stocks, bonds, or other domestic securities owned by it, or from interest on deposits in U.S. banks of moneys belonging to it, or from any other U.S. source.

Act Sec. 1247, relating to income of foreign governments and international organizations, amends Sec. 892, effective for amounts received on or after 7-1-86, except that no amount will be required to be deducted and withheld due to the amendment from any payment made before the enactment date.

[¶1283] **Dual Residence Companies.** The new law limits double dipping by dual resident companies—that is, the use of a deduction by a corporation that is a U.S. resident and a resident of another country to reduce the U.S. tax of commonly owned corporations in both countries.

Under the new law, a corporation's "dual consolidated loss" for a tax year cannot reduce the taxable income of another member of its affiliated group for that or any other tax year. A "dual consolidated loss" is the net operating loss of a U.S. corporation subject to a foreign income tax on worldwide income or on a residence basis. To the extent provided in regulations, a dual consolidated loss won't include a loss that doesn't offset the income of a foreign corporation under foreign income tax law.

Act Sec. 1249, relating to the treatment of dual residence corporations, adds new Sec. 1503(d), effective for net operating losses for tax years beginning after 12-31-86.

[¶1284] Withholding Tax on Foreign Partners. The new law generally provides that if a partnership has any income, gain, or loss effectively connected (or treated as such) with the conduct of a U.S. trade or business, the withholding agent must withhold a 20% tax on any amount distributed to a foreign partner.

Limitation. If the partnership's gross income effectively connected with a U.S. trade or business over a three-tax year period is less than 80% of the partnership's total gross income over that period, then withholding is required only on the proportion of current distributions that the partnership's gross income effectively connected with its U.S. trade or business bears to its total gross income over its previous three tax years.

Exceptions. Withholding isn't required

- on the portion of any distribution for which a 30% (or lower treaty rate) tax must be withheld under Sec. 1441 or 1442, or

- if substantially all the U.S.-source income and effectively connected income of a U.S. partnership is properly allocated to U.S. persons—unless regulations provide otherwise.

Act Sec. 1246, relating to the withholding tax on amounts paid by partnerships to foreign partners, adds new Sec. 1446, and amends Sec. 6401(b)(2) and the table of sections for subchapter A of chapter 3, effective for distributions after 12-31-87 (or, if earlier, the effective date of Sec. 1446 regulations, but no earlier than 1-1-87).

[¶1285] Compliance Provisions for U.S. Individuals and Foreign-Owned Corporations. The new law provides that a U.S. citizen applying for a passport and a resident alien applying for a permanent resident visa (green card) will have to file an IRS information return. The return must include the individual's taxpayer identification number, a passport applicant's foreign country of residence, information as to whether a green card applicant must file a tax return, and other information required. A new $500 penalty will apply for each failure to provide a statement through willful neglect. Any U.S. agency that collects the return must provide it to the Treasury.

Collection of tax. Under the new law, pensions and similar payments delivered outside the United States are subject to withholding, unless the recipient certifies to the payor that the recipient isn't a U.S. citizen who resides abroad or a tax-avoidance expatriate. Previously, the recipient could elect not to have withholding apply.

Foreign-owned corporations. Under the new law, a foreign-controlled U.S. corporation, and a foreign-controlled foreign corporation engaged in a U.S. trade or business must furnish certain information as to its transactions with any related party (under Secs. 482, 267(b), or 707(b)(1)).

Foreign-controlled corporations and U.S.-controlled foreign corporations must furnish information that Treasury requires for carrying out the installment sales rules.

Act Sec. 1234(a), relating to information returns for U.S. individuals, adds new Sec. 6039E, and amends the table of sections for subpart A of part III of subchapter A of chapter 61, effective for applications submitted after 12-31-87 (or, if earlier, the effective date of Sec. 6039E regulations, but no earlier than 1-1-87). Act Sec. 1234(b), relating to withholding on deferred payments abroad, adds new Sec. 3405(d)(13), effective for payments after 12-31-86.

Act Sec. 1245, relating to information as to foreign-owned corporations, adds new Secs. 6038(a)(1)(F) and 6038A(b)(4), and amends Secs. 6038(a)(1), 6038A(b)(1), 6038A(b)(2), 6038A(b)(3), and 6038A(c)(2), effective for tax years beginning after 12-31-86.

[¶1286] Dividends-Received Deduction. Under the new law, a deduction is allowed for dividends received by a U.S. corporation from a foreign corporation (other than an FPHC or a passive foreign investment company) if the taxpayer owns at least 10% of its stock by vote and value. The allowable deduction is based on the proportion of the foreign corporation's post-1986 earnings that have been subject to U.S. corporate income tax and that have not been distributed. Amounts of Subpart F income previously taxed that are distributed to U.S. shareholders reduce E&P in arriving at the proportion.

NOTE: The new law elsewhere reduces the 85% dividends-received deduction to 80% [See ¶602.].

Act Sec. 1226(a), relating to the dividends-received deduction, amends Sec. 245(a), effective generally for distributions out of E&P for tax years beginning after 12-31-86. Act Sec. 1226(b), relating to the reduction of E&P, amends Sec. 959(d), effective for distributions after the enactment date.

[¶1287] Special Transitional Rules. The new law provides special rules for one U.S. corporation concerning the application of Sec. 954 to certain dividends and for one U.S. corporation concerning the application of Sec. 897.

Act Sec. 1227, relating to Sec. 954, applies for Sec. 954(c)(3)(A), effective for dividends received after 12-31-86.

Act Sec. 1228, relating to Sec. 897, is effective on the enactment date.

[The page following this is 1301.]

TAX-EXEMPT BONDS

[¶1301] **Overview.** The tax exemption for interest on bonds issued by state and local governments (i.e., obligations of a state, the District of Columbia, U.S. possessions, or their political subdivisions) continues under the new law, with some significantly changed rules. The rules for tax-exempt "private activity" obligations, issued to provide conduit financing for activities other than general governmental operations or governmentally owned-and-operated facilities, have been significantly tightened and the "private activity" category is more broadly defined. Also, restrictions on all tax-exempts (i.e., both governmental issues and private activity issues) have been expanded or added. The Conference Report says that prior law principles continue to control the tax exemption except to the extent of amendments made.

> **NEW CODE SETUP:** The statutory rules for tax-exempt bonds (as changed by the new law) have been technically reordered. They are now included in Sec. 103 and new Secs. 141—150. Sec. 103A has been deleted, and the provision governing determination of marital status (old Sec. 143) has been redesignated as Sec. 7703. Sec. 103 grants the tax exemption to interest on state and local obligations. But it denies the exemption to (1) private activity bonds that aren't "qualified bonds" (the definition of private activity bonds and statutory rules for "qualified" bonds are in new Secs. 141—147); (2) arbitrage bonds (new Sec. 148 contains the arbitrage restrictions to be complied with for exemption); and (3) bonds that don't meet the requirement of Sec. 149. New Sec. 150 contains definitions and special rules.

Bonds now become "private activity bonds" (taxable unless they fit under a specifically exempt category—i.e., unless they are "qualified bonds") in either of these two cases: (1) more than 10% of the proceeds of the issue (or $15 million per facility, if that's less, for output facilities) is for direct or indirect use in a trade or business of anyone except a governmental unit, *and* direct or indirect payments of more than 10% of the debt service on the bonds (or $15 million per facility, if that's less, for output facilities) are made with respect to such trade or business; and (2) more than 5% of the proceeds of the issue, or $5 million if that's less, is used to make or finance loans to entities other than state or local governments. And for qualified private activity bonds, at least 95% of the proceeds must be spent for the exempt purpose of the borrowing [¶1302]. The new law repeals the prior-law tax exemption for several categories of exempt facility private activity bonds (formerly exempt activity IDBs) and adds a new exempt category for hazardous waste disposal facilities [¶1303]. It retains the general 12-31-86 sunset date for qualified small issue bonds (formerly small issue IDBs); but postpones the sunset date for small issue manufacturing facilities until 12-31-89 and treats small issue bonds for first time farmers same as manufacturing bonds. A new category of qualified redevelopment bonds is designed to finance redevelopment of blighted areas [¶1304].

Qualified nonhospital bonds for Sec. 501(c)(3) organizations will now have to fit under a $150 million limit, ¶1305. Qualified mortgage bonds and mortgage credit certificates (MCCs) can now be issued through 12-31-88 under changed rules, and the trade-in-value of MCCs issued for exchanged qualified mortgage authority has been upped to 25%. And limited equity housing cooperatives can elect multifamily residential rental project rules for bonds providing the housing [¶1306.]

A single volume cap now covers other private activity bonds and qualified mortgage bonds; qualified veterans' mortgage bonds remain subject to their prior law volume cap [¶1307]. And all private activity bonds have to meet public approval requirements and comply with prohibited facilities and change in use restrictions [¶1308].

Major rule changes for all tax-exempts involve arbitrage and advance refunding. Arbitrage restrictions that apply to all tax-exempt bonds prevent investment of their proceeds in materially higher yielding obligations. The minor portion of bond proceeds not covered by arbitrage rules has been whittled down to 5% of the bond proceeds. The arbitrage restrictions have been expanded to cover acquisitions of taxable investment property such as deferred payment contracts to fund pension plans. The new law eliminates the prior law election under regs to forgo the temporary period exception and be allowed to earn higher arbitrage. Restrictions on nonpurpose investments have been expanded. And the new law extends to all tax-exempts a requirement of rebating to the U.S. of arbitrage earned on the gross proceeds of an issue invested in nonpurpose obligations [¶1309]. Also, only qualified 501(c)(3) bonds and governmental bonds can now be advance refunded, and advance refundings, where permitted, are subject to severe restrictions [¶1310].

Among other rules: Information reporting has been extended to all tax-exempts. And rules for GSOCs (state-established corporations for the benefit of state citizens with power to borrow and invest in business enterprises) have been repealed as deadwood [¶1311; 1312].

Tax exempt interest on private activity bonds (but not qualified 501(c)(3) bonds) is now a tax preference for the individual and corporate minimum tax [see ¶711]. And depreciation on property financed with tax exempts is subject to an alternative depreciation system [see ¶205].

Effective Dates:　The rules generally apply to bonds issued after 8-15-86. However, provisions and bonds covered by the Joint Statements on Effective Dates of 3-14-86 and 7-17-86 apply to bonds issued on or after 9-1-86. The Joint Statements cover the amendments to the definition of a private activity bond, including refunding bonds, (i.e., they cover the 10% trade or business use test (10% or

$15 million for output facilities), the 5% unrelated use limitation, and the $5 million limitation contained in the amended private loan restriction). The Joint Statement's 9-1-86 effective date *doesn't* cover bonds that under prior law are (1) industrial development bonds; (2) bonds that would be IDBs, treating Sec. 501(c)(3) organizations as private persons engaged in trades and businesses; (3) student loan bonds; (4) mortgage revenue bonds; or (5) other private ("consumer") loan bonds for which tax exemption is permitted. Major exceptions to these dates are noted as part of the coverage of the law changes [or at ¶1313].

> **CAUTION:** The rules are subject to various effective date transitional rules and exceptions, often targeted to specific situations.

Act Sec. 1301(a) dealing with tax exempt bonds amends Sec. 103. Act Sec. 1301(b) dealing with tax exemption requirements adds Code Secs. 141—150. Act Sec. 1301(c) dealing with a direction to amend arbitrage regs. to eliminate the election to forgo the temporary period exception and Act Sec. 1301(d) dealing with modifications in the SLGS program, and Act Sec. 1301(e) dealing with IRS advance ruling policy on management contracts don't amend the Code. Act Sec. 1301(f) increasing the MCC trade-in rate amends Sec. 25(b)—(f). Act Sec. 1301(g) dealing with failures to report on compliance with residential rental project rules adds new Sec. 6652(j). Act Sec. 1302(h) dealing with deleting the report on mortgage revenue bonds repeals '84 TRA Sec. 611(d)(7). Act Sec. 1301(i) dealing with the direction to amend output regulations doesn't amend the Code. Act Sec. 1301(j) repeals Sec. 103A and redesignates old Sec. 143 as new Sec. 7703. Act Sec. 1302 providing that treatment of Sec. 501(c)(3) bonds as private activity bonds doesn't indicate their treatment in future legislation, doesn't amend the Code. Act Sec. 1303 deals with repeal of GSOC provisions (see ¶1312 for Sections amended). Subtitle B of Title XIII (Act Sec. 1311 et. seq.) deal with effective dates and transitional rules. These law changes are generally effective as indicated above and at ¶1302—1313.

[¶1302] General Restrictions on Tax-Exempts. The requirements of tax-exempt obligations issued to finance activities other than general governmental obligations or governmentally-owned-and-operated facilities (i.e., of private activity bonds) have been significantly tightened.

Prior law provided limited exemptions for private activity state and local bonds. These bonds have been in general treated as follows:

• If all or a major part (more than 25% according to regs) of the gross proceeds of a bond issue was for direct or indirect use in a trade or business of a nonexempt (i.e., private) person, and if the payment of a major part (as defined in the regs) of the issue's principal and interest was derived from or secured by the business, the bonds (known as industrial development bonds—IDBs) became taxable. However, IDBs that finance specified exempt activities, bonds issued for development of industrial parks, and exempt "small issues" of IDBs (up to $1 million issues, or issues whose amount when added to capital expenditures wasn't more than $10 million) remained tax-exempt.

• If a significant portion of a bond issue was to be used for mortgages on owner-occupied-residences, the bonds (known as Mortgage Subsidy bonds—MSBs) became taxable. However, qualified mortgage bonds financing the purchase or qualified rehabilitation or improvement of single-family owner-occupied homes, and qualified veterans' mortgage bonds financing mortgage loans to veterans remained tax-exempt.

• Sec. 501(c)(3) bonds financing activities of charitable, educational, etc., organizations (e.g., private nonprofit hospitals or colleges), and bonds issued by qualified governmental units to finance student loans were also tax exempt. IDBs and student loan bonds, qualified veterans' mortgage bonds, and qualified mortgage bonds had to meet separately designed state bond volume limits.

Use and security interests tests. Under the new law, bonds become private activity bonds (taxable unless they fit into a specifically exempt category) if (1) more than 10% of the gross proceeds of the issue (or $15 million per facility, if that's less, in case of financing for construction, rehabilitation or operation of output facilities) is for direct or indirect use in a trade or business of anyone except a governmental unit (*use test*); and (2) more than 10% of the principal of or interest on the bonds (or $15 million per facility, if that's less, in case of output facilities) is secured by or to be derived from property to be used in such a trade or business (*security interest test*). Bonds transitioned under Reg. Sec. 1.103-7(b)(iii) are under the new law treated consistent with the transition rule of the regs.

For a private activity bond to enjoy exemption, it must be a "qualified bond." Such a bond issue must fit in one of these exempt categories: (1) exempt facility bonds; (2) qualified mortgage bonds; (3) qualified veterans' mortgage bonds; (4) qualified small issue bonds; (5) qualified student loan bonds; (6) qualified redevelopment bonds; or (7) qualified 501(c)(3) bonds. It must also be within the applicable bond volume cap [¶1307], and meet certain other requirements (now in new Sec. 147). Law changes covering exempt categories of private activity bonds are explained later.

NOTE: The IRS is directed to modify the present rules for determining private use of output facilities (Reg. Sec. 1.103-7(b)(5)) to reflect the reduced limits on private use of governmental bonds and to delete the de minimis 3% rule. The Conference Report notes that the presence of a nongovernmental person acting solely as a conduit for the exchange of power output among governmentally-owned and operated facilities is to be disregarded in deciding whether the use and security interest tests are satisfied. And "swapping" of power between governmentally owned and operated utilities and investor-owned utilities under certain conditions does not give rise to trade or business use. It also notes that spot sales (under single agreement for 30 days or less) of excess power capacity other than under an output contract with specific buyers aren't treated as trade or business use.

The House Ways & Means Committee Report notes that for the percentage and dollar limit *use tests* that classify a bond issue as a "private activity bond" issue, nongovernmental use in a trade or business includes the use of the bond proceeds in all activities (1) of a nongovernmental person other than a natural person, (2) of the federal government, or (3) of Sec. 501(c)(3) charitable organizations. As under prior law, nongovernmental use can involve use of the bond proceeds; or use of bond-financed property through its ownership or its actual or beneficial use via a lease or a management, incentive payment or output contract. The use of bond proceeds or a facility as a member of the general public doesn't count—but such use must be on the same basis as is available to other members of the general public. What is nongovernmental use is determined by the facts and circumstances.

> **Example:** A school building can be incidentally available for scout meetings or community recreation on an equal basis; and municipal parks are generally available. But operation of bond-financed mass commuting facilities by private persons under a longer-term management contract, use of a ball park mostly for a team's at-home games, use of a government-owned-and-operated convention center by an organization under an extended contract, use of a typical airport by airlines, or use of bond proceeds to provide a nonexempt business with electricity (rather than merely offering volume discounts) are uses in a nongovernmental trade or business for the test.

The new law clarifies that both direct and indirect payments to a bond issuer by a private user of bond financed facilities are considered for the security interest test. The Senate Finance Committee Report notes that these payments can be either formally pledged as security or directly used to pay debt service, but that they don't include revenues from generally applicable taxes (as opposed to special charges imposed on those satisfying the "use test" rather than on the public generally). *Example:* If land is sold to private persons for redevelopment, lump-sum or installment payments for the land to the government whose tax revenues secure the bonds, or to an agency acting for it, are considered for the security interest test. The same applies if lease payments by a private lessor of a facility, or receipts from a special user tax (e.g., a ticket tax at a stadium) are the formally pledged bond security.

> **MANAGEMENT CONTRACTS:** Effective on the date of enactment, the new law directs the IRS to liberalize its current advance ruling guidelines (Rev Proc. 82-14, 1982-1 CB on private use under management contract as a trade or business use, and Rev Proc 82-15, 1982-1 CB 460 on qualified 501(c)(3) bonds) to allow up-to-5-year man-

agement contracts to provide for prescribed flat-amount or share-of-
gross-revenue fees under certain conditions. One such condition is that
at least 50% of the payments must be on a fixed-fee basis.

Private loan bonds. If at least 5% of the gross proceeds of the issue (or $5 million if that's less) is to be used to make or finance di-
rect or indirect loans to others than governmental units, the bond is
a private activity "private loan" bond (consumer loan bond under
prior law), taxable unless it's in a specifically exempt category (e.g.,
exempt facility bonds, mortgage revenue (formerly mortgage subsidy)
bonds or student loan bonds). Excluded from the private loan bond
category are (1) loans to anticipate government tax receipts of a general nature and for an essential government function (e.g., short-
term tax and revenue anticipation notes (TANs and RANs)), and (2)
bonds to finance schools, highways, and government buildings and
government owned and operated facilities. Also excluded are these
exempt private activity issues: bonds issued as part of the Texas
Veterans' Land Bond program (with their prior law sunset date of
March 15, 1987 deleted by the new law), bonds issued as part of the
Oregon Renewable Source Small Energy Conservation Program and
the Iowa Industrial New Jobs Training Programs—but they must
comply with the "related-use" requirement.

Related-use requirement. The new law generally requires an exempt private activity bond issue to devote at least 95% (90% under
prior law) of the bond proceeds for the exempt purpose of the borrowing. [For federally guaranteed student loan bonds, however, see
¶1305]. Costs of issuance (including attorney fees and underwriter's
spread) don't count towards the satisfaction of the 95% requirement.
Private trade or business use of govermental bond proceeds in excess
of 5% of the bond proceeds must be related to government facilities
also being financed with the bonds. Private use satisfies this requirement only if the financing provided for the private use is propor-
tional to the total financing provided by the issue for the related
governmental facility.

> **CAUTION:** Aggregate costs of the issuance of exempt private ac-
> tivity bonds that are paid from bond proceeds can't exceed 2% of the
> amount of the bonds.

Other rules. Current law is retained on the treatment of certain
volunteer fire departments as qualified issuers of tax-exempt bonds,
with a clarification that the 95% "related use" requirement, above,
must be adhered to.

The law framers intend that generally for bonds (including refunding bonds) issued after 8-15-86, the use of bond-financed property by a university to perform general (but not product development) research supported or sponsored by private persons under a
cooperative research agreement shouldn't be treated as private business use (and the research support shouldn't be treated as a repay-

ment of the bonds), if the resulting technology is available to sponsors and to unrelated nonsponsors on the same terms. For example, an agreement with a right of first refusal at a competitive price determined when the technology is available for use wouldn't be business use. [For qualified 501(c)(3) bonds generally, see ¶1305.]

Effective Dates: In general, these changes apply to bonds issued after 9-1-86. However, (1) the rule that indirect payments satisfy the security interest test, (2) the private loan bond rule and the exceptions from it, (3) the volunteer department bond rule, and (4) the rules on cooperative research agreements apply to bonds issued after 8-15-86.

[¶1303] **Exempt Facility Private Activity Bonds.** The new law repeals the prior law tax exemption for IDB financing of convention and trade show facilities, parking facilities, (but note that parking, such as airport parking, may be exempt as functionally related and subordinate to an exempt facility), sports facilities, air and water pollution control facilities, and industrial park IDBs, for bonds issued after 8-15-86 with transitional exceptions. A transitional exemption for certain hydroelectric generating facilities whose FERC approval was pending and whose application for license (and not just for a preliminary permit) was docketed when the exemption for such facilities expired (generally 12-31-85) is retained by the new law.

Categories of exempt facility private activity bonds, which remain exempt under the new law, and the new category for hazardous waste treatment facilities are enumerated below. As explained previously [¶1302], at least 95% of the proceeds of a bond issue must be devoted to provide the exempt facilities that qualify it. And while the bonds can continue to finance property functionally related and subordinate to the exempt facilities, office space financed with exempt-facility bonds is limited to office space located at the exempt facility and of a size necessary for the facility's day-to-day operations (as opposed to administrative office buildings). Exempt facility categories, (covered by new Sec. 142), generally for bonds issued after 8-15-86, include:

• *Multifamily qualified residential rental projects.* The new law removes the prior-law special rules for multifamily residential rental projects located in targeted areas that are financed by these IDBs. [For election by limited equity housing cooperatives of residential rental housing rules, see ¶1306. For "qualified redevelopment bonds" see ¶1304].

The new law allows the bond issuer to qualify for tax-exempt financing if the issue elects to meet either of the following: (1) at least 40% of the units must be occupied by tenants whose income is no more than 60% of the area median income, or (2) at least 20% of the units must be occupied by tenants whose income is no more than 50% of area median income. The election must be made on or before the date of issuance. The low-or-moderate income occupancy requirement and, under the new law a tenant's low or moderate income status, must be satisfied continuously during a qualified project period (generally redefined as starting when 10% of the project's residential units are first occupied (or at bond issuance, if later), and ending the earliest of (1) 15 years after 50% of the units are occupied, (2) when no tax exempts on the project remain outstanding, or (3) when Sec. 8 of the '37 U.S. Housing Act assistance terminates. However, if a tenant's income qualifies when he initially occupies a unit or on a later determination date, only an increase to above 140% of the qualifying income level (after adjustment for family size) will disqualify the tenant from being counted for the project's income occupancy requirement. The new law clarifies that family size adjustments (same as under Sec. 8 of the '37 U.S. Housing Act) are required for determining the area median incomes used to qualify tenants as having low or moderate income.

> **Example:** If a project qualifies under the test requiring 60% or less of area median income, *a family of four* with such income will count towards qualifying it, but a single person will count only if his income is 42% or less (i.e., there's a 10% reduction of the 60% benchmark for each family member under four).

Projects that (1) charge significantly lower-than-market rents to low-income tenants and (2) elect (when they make the occupancy percentage election) to have at least 15% of the low income units occupied by tenants with 40% or less of the area median income, can have tenants counted for the income occupancy requirement as long as the tenant's family income doesn't increase up to more than 170% of the otherwise applicable maximum.

Operators of exempt bond-financed projects must certify annually to the IRS that they have complied with the low-and-moderate-income occupancy requirements, and the IRS can request certification of other data to monitor compliance.

> **PENALTY:** Each failure to certify (unless due to reasonable cause and not wilfull disregard) is penalized $100 per failure, but doesn't in itself affect the tax-exempt status of the bonds.

As under prior law, noncompliance with the income occupancy rules must be corrected within a reasonable period after discovery. However, the violation of these rules in general occurs only on a (other than temporary) rental to a nonqualified person at a time when the income occupancy requirements rules aren't met. As under present law, interest on bonds financing the project becomes taxable retroactively to the date of their issuance if the occupancy requirements aren't complied with. Further, interest accrued on bond-financed loans from the first day of the tax year when the project ceases to qualify as "qualified residential rental property" until the project complies with the income occupancy requirements will now be nondeductible [¶1308]. The new law also calls for an at-least annual report by the IRS to Congressional Committees on the compliance with qualified residential rental project rules.

• *Airports* are generally defined as under prior law. They include related storage and training facilities. Tax exempt airport bonds can't now be used to finance hotels, retail shops (including food and beverage facilities) that are larger in size than needed to serve passengers and employees at the airport, retail facilities for passengers (e.g., rental car lots) located outside the terminal, office buildings for nongovernmental persons other than airport authorities, and industrial parks or manufacturing facilities.

• *Docks and wharves* are generally defined as under prior law. They include related storage and training facilities. Tax-exempt bonds financing them now can't be used to finance hotels, retail shops (including food and beverage facilities) that are larger in size than needed to serve passengers and employees at the port, office buildings for nongovernmental persons other than port authorities, and industrial parks or manufacturing facilities.

• *Mass commuting facilities* are in general defined as under prior law. But bonds financing them can't finance hotels, retail shops inside a terminal that are larger than needed to serve passengers and facility employees, retail facilities (other than public parking) outside the mass commuting terminal, office buildings for nongovernmental persons other than employees of the operating authority, or industrial parks or manufacturing facilities.

> NOTE: Airports, docks and wharves, and mass commuting facilities must be governmentally owned—this requirement is measured by a safe harbor rule.

• *Local furnishing of electricity and gas* (with a retained requirement for furnishing electricity and gas within two contiguous counties or a city and one contiguous county and retained exceptions provided by Secs. 644 and 645 of the '84 TRA).

• *Hazardous waste disposal facilities.* This new category of tax-exempts that can be issued after the date of enactment is limited to financing disposal facilities to incinerate and entomb hazardous waste as defined under Sec. 1004 of the Solid Waste Disposal Act. Facilities subject to permit requirements under the Resource Conservation and Recovery Act generally qualify. Eligible facilities must be owned and operated by persons not related to the producers of the hazardous waste, and must receive and dispose of hazardous waste from the general public rather than serve only a single or limited group of persons. There's an exception for facilities owned or operated by the waste producer that permits exempt bond financing only of the part of the facility used by the general public. The conferees intend that hazardous waste doesn't include radioactive waste, and that prior law rules regarding solid waste disposal IDBs also continue to apply here.

• *Sewage and solid waste disposal facilities,* in general are defined as under prior law, but with the exemption for certain alcohol producing and steam generating facilities repealed.

Other exempt categories include

• *Local district heating or cooling facilities,* and

• *Facilities for furnishing of water* (including irrigation systems).

[¶1304] Small Issue Private Activity Bonds and New Qualified Redevelopment Bonds. The new law retains the 12-31-86 sunset date for small issue IDBs (now qualified small issue bonds covered in new Sec. 144(a)) other than for manufacturing facilities, but postpones the prior law sunset date for small issue IDBs financing manufacturing facilities for another year (i.e., through 12-31-89). "Small issue" bond issues must now devote at least 95% of the bond proceeds to the exempt purpose of the borrowing. The new law also (1) treats small issue bonds for first-time farmers the same as manufacturing bonds for small-issue IDB sunset dates—i.e., they can be issued through 12-31-89; (2) expands the definition of "first-time farmer" to include previously insolvent farmers (by disregarding previous ownership of land disposed of in a Sec. 108 transaction); and (3) allows first-time farmers to use up to $62,500 to acquire used agricultural equipment. However, the new law also restricts the aggregate small-issue IDB financing for all depreciable property used in farming to a lifetime limit of $250,000 per principal user (including persons "related" to him). Bonds that were issued under prior law are counted towards the new $250,000 limit, as is depreciable property financed under the first-time farmer exceptions. The law changes are generally effective for bonds issued after 8-15-86.

Qualified redevelopment bonds. A new category of state-law authorized tax-exempt private activity bonds can be issued after 8-15-86 by qualified governmental units for preplanned redevelopment in a locally designated "blighted area." Qualified redevelopment bonds are covered in new Sec. 144(c). Real property tax revenue increases that result from the redevelopment must be first devoted to debt service on the bonds. But owners or users of the property in the "blighted areas" can't be subjected to higher charges or fees, or assessed under a rate or method higher than that of property outside this area. The bonds can be secured by pledges of generally applicable taxes if the taxes are the principal security for the bonds. At least 95% or more of the proceeds of the bonds must finance the exempt purposes. These purposes are (1) the acquisition under condemnation of real property to be transferred to nongovernmental persons; (2) clearing and preparing land for redevelopment and its transfer to nongovernmental persons for fair market value; (3) rehabilitating or redeveloping the real property; and (4) relocating occupants of the acquired real property.

A "blighted area," designated by the general purpose local government unit in which it's located (e.g., cities or counties) under state-established criteria before the bonds are issued, must generally subtend at least 100 contiguous acres. However, the area can be less, if (1) it's at least 10 contiguous acres and (2) generally no more than 25% of bond financed land is provided to one person (or a group of related persons) under a pre-approved plan. Criteria for designation should consider excessive, previously improved vacant land; vacant, old or substandard buildings; excessive vacancies and real property tax delinquencies. A finding of a substantial number of statutory factors is needed for the designation as "blighted."

Aggregate blighted areas designated, as such, by a government unit can contain only up-to-20% of the government unit's real property measured by assessed value. For areas designated in different years, the percentages determined at time of designation are aggregated for this test. Also, special rules apply if there are areas designated before 1-1-86 for which qualifying activities were in progress on that date.

Qualified redevelopment bonds must meet requirements that apply to private activity bonds generally. No more than 25% of the proceeds may be used for certain recreational and commercial activities. No proceeds can be used to finance private or commercial golf courses, country clubs, massage parlors, hot tub or suntan facilities, liquor stores, or race track or other primarily gambling facilities. However, the restriction on acquisition of land doesn't apply.

NOTE: Bonds financing governmental facilities such as street paving, sidewalks, street lighting, etc., don't have to meet the qualification requirements of qualified redevelopment bonds. Rules for financing of qualified redevelopment and the governmental facilities through a single issue are expected to be developed by the Treasury Department.

[¶1305] **Qualified 501(c)(3) Bonds and Student Loan Bonds.** Generally for bonds issued after 8-15-86, the proceed of which will be for the use of Sec. 501(c)(3) organizations, the new law continues the exemption if they're "qualifed 501(c)(3) bonds" (new Code Sec. 145). To qualify under this category, at least 95% of the net bond proceeds must be used for qualified activities. Rules similar to the 95% "related use" test covered at ¶1302 (the private business use and security interest tests using a 5% rather than 10% benchmark), apply. As under prior law, use of bond proceeds in an unrelated trade or business (determined under Sec. 513(a)) is a nonexempt use. Also, facilities financed with qualified 501(c)(3) bonds must be owned by a Sec. 501(c)(3) organization or by or on behalf of a governmental unit—ownership by others would presumably result in a violation of the above 95% use limitations.

The Senate Finance Committee intends that: (1) bonds for state and local government-owned universities or hospitals should be treated as governmental bonds rather than qualified 501(c)(3) bonds, to the extent that such entities are government agencies or instrumentalities (determined similarly as under prior law); and (2) the IRS should adopt rules for allocating costs of mixed-use facilities, (e.g., where eligible facilities of a Sec. 501(c)(3) organization are part of a larger facility, or where portions of a Sec. 501(c)(3) organization facility may be used by nonexempt persons), according to a reasonable method that reflects the proportionate benefit derived by their users. Only the parts of such facilities (including common elements) owned and used by Sec. 501(c)(3) organizations are eligible for 501(c)(3) bond financing. [For cooperative research agreements see ¶1302.]

Similarly to IDBs, the term of qualified 501(c)(3) bonds can't be longer than 120% of the economic life of property financed by them. Exceptions relate to pooled financings for two or more Sec. 501(c)(3) organizations, and to certain FHA insurance programs that require longer loan terms.

> **NOTE ON 501(c)(3) BONDS:** The new law (Act Sec. 1302) provides that the treatment of Sec. 501(c)(3) bonds as private activity bonds isn't an indication of their treatment in future legislation. Any future law change that applies to private activity bonds will apply to Sec. 501(c)(3) bonds only if the future legislation so expressly provides.

$150 million limit for non-hospital 501(c)(3) bonds. A qualified 501(c)(3) bond issue must either be a "qualified hospital bond" issue, or must fit within a $150 million limit on outstanding non-hospital qualified section 501(c)(3) bonds other than qualified hospital bonds). For qualified hospital bonds, at least 95% of the net proceeds must be used to finance an accredited hospital facility (rest or nursing homes, day care centers, medical school facilities, research laboratories or ambulatory care facilities aren't "hospitals"). The hospital must be either governmentally owned or owned by a Sec. 501(c)(3) organization, and operated by a Sec. 501(c)(3) organization.

Any non-hospital qualified Sec. 501(c)(3) bond issue qualifies under the dollar limit if its authorized face amount (when added to the face amount of outstanding tax-exempt qualified 501(c)(3) non-hospital bonds that benefit the organization during a 3-year "test period") makes the total face amount go over $150 million. The $150 million limit takes into account only qualified section 501(c)(3) bonds. The Conferees intend that if an issue is partly used for hospitals, only the portion actually used for hospitals is exempt from the $150 million limit as hospital bonds. They also permit Sec. 501(c)(3) organizations to elect not to treat bonds as qualified 501(c)(3) bonds (e.g., to participate in a multifamily residential rental project and benefit from bonds qualifying as qualified residential rental bonds). Bonds issued before 8-16-86 for Sec. 501(c)(3) organizations count toward the limit only if more than 25% of the proceeds were to be used directly or indirectly by such an organization or organizations and the new law security interest test is satisfied.

Student loan bonds. The new law continues the exemption of qualified student loan bonds (new Sec. 144(b)), defined as under prior law (including bonds issued by qualified government units or qualified scholarship funding corporations in connection with the GSL and PLUS programs of the U.S. Department of Education). It also expands this exempt category to cover certain state supplemental loan programs, including any state approved program of general application not covered by Part B of Title IV of the 1965 Higher Education Act (relating to guaranteed student loans), if loans under it are limited to the difference between (1) total cost of attendance and (2) other student assistance with certain exceptions. However, at least 90% of the proceeds (under rules similar to the "related use requirements" covered at ¶1302) of bonds connected with the GSL and PLUS programs must be used for the purpose of the borrowing; and that percentage rises to "at least" 95% in the case of supplemental student loan bonds. Also, student loan bonds can't be issued to finance loans to students who are enrolled in schools outside the issuing state unless they are legal residents of the issuing state. The law changes are effective generally for bonds issued after 8-15-86.

[¶1306] Mortgage Subsidy Bonds, MCCs, and Limited Equity Housing Bonds. Under the new law, mortgage subsidy bonds are renamed mortgage revenue bonds (new Sec 143). The prior law sunset dates have been postponed for a year—mortgage revenue bonds and mortgage credit certificates (MCCs) can be issued through 12-31-88 under changed rules. The alternative to issue mortgage credit certificates instead of qualified mortgage bonds has been retained. However, the maximum aggregate principal amount of MCCs that can be distributed by an electing issuer is increased to 25% (up from prior law's 20%) of qualified mortgage bond authority that is exchanged for authority to issue MCCs. Here are some other law changes.

At least 95% of bond proceeds other than issuance costs and amounts deposited in a reasonably required reserve fund must be used for loans to first-time home buyers. But as under prior law, there's no requirement that a minimum percentage of financing in targeted areas be provided to first-time homebuyers. Bond issuance costs paid from bond proceeds of mortgage revenue bonds generally can't exceed 2% of the amount of the bonds (3½% if the bond issue doesn't exceed $20 million). Except in targeted areas, all bond-financed loans must be made to persons having incomes of 115% or less of the median income in the state or in the area, whichever is higher. In targeted areas, a third of the financing can be made to borrowers without regard to the income limit, and the balance must be provided to mortgagors with income not exceeding 140% of the higher area or statewide median income. The purchase price of bond-financed residences can't be greater than 90% (110% in targeted areas) of the average area purchase price applicable to the residence. The new law repeals the prior law requirement that issuers of qualified mortgage bonds and MCCs annually publish and file with the Treasury Department statements on their policies for issuance of these bonds and MCCs.

> **CAUTION:** Qualified mortgage bonds must now fit within unified state volume limits for private activity bonds [see ¶1307]. Qualified veterans' mortgage bonds remain subject to their separate prior law volume cap.

Under the new law, at least 95% of the proceeds of *qualified veterans' mortgage bonds* must be used to finance veteran's mortgage loans. Bond issuance costs aren't counted towards this requirement, and generally can't exceed 2% of the amount of the bonds.

Limited equity housing cooperatives can elect multifamily residential rental project rules. Limited equity housing cooperatives can now irrevocably elect to treat any limited cooperative equity housing as residential rental property rather than as owner-occupied housing. Under the election, bonds issued to provide the housing will be governed by targeting and compliance rules that apply to multifamily residential rental projects. The cooperative's tenant shareholders won't get a Sec. 216 deduction for their ratable share of interest and taxes paid by the cooperative. And bonds issued to finance units in the cooperative will be counted towards the state's volume limitation for qualified mortgage bonds, but will be treated as IDBs for multifamily residential rental property for all other purposes. A failure to elect will make the financing subject to all limitations that cover qualified mortgage bonds, including first-time purchaser and purchase price limitations.

To make the election, (1) the cooperative must be a cooperative housing corporation (Sec. 216(b)(1)), (2) the cost of its stock can't exceed the amount paid by the original shareholders (as adjusted for cost of living increases) plus cost of improvements and certain other payments, (3) the cooperative's net asset value in excess of combined transfer values of outstanding stock must be used only for public or charitable purposes and not directly benefit any shareholder, and (4) the cooperative must continue to qualify as a limited equity cooperative during the period when the tax-exempts are outstanding. [For new rules affecting multifamily residential rental project bonds, see ¶1302—1303].

Effective Date: These rules generally apply to bonds issues after 8-15-86, and MCCs issued under bond authority exchanged after 8-15-86.

[¶1307] Single Volume Cap Now Covers Private Activity Bonds and Qualified Mortgage Bonds. Instead of the separate volume limits for most private activity bonds and for qualified mortgage bonds, a single annual volume cap, effective for bonds issued after 8-15-86, covers exempt facility bonds, small issue bonds, qualified redevelopment bonds, student loan bonds, qualified mortgage bonds, and private loan bonds for which an exemption is provided (new Sec. 146).

> **CAUTION:** Private use of proceeds of governmental bonds (which aren't classified as private activity bonds) in excess of 15 million dollars and up to the permitted 10% of private use is also subject to the new volume cap. Note that this rule only covers governmental bond issues in excess of $150 million.

Qualified veterans' mortgage bonds remain subject to their separate prior law volume cap. Bonds not covered by a volume cap include (1) qualified 501(c)(3) bonds; (2) exempt facility bonds for governmentally owned airports and docks and wharves; and (3) exempt facility bonds for solid waste disposal facilities if all property financed with the bonds is governmentally owned.

The new unified annual volume cap for each state until 12-31-87, is equal to the greater of $75 per resident of the state or $250 million. After 1987 the cap it reduced to the greater of $50 per resident or $150 million. The District of Columbia is treated as a state for the volume limit. U.S. possessions with populations more than the least populous state are limited to the $75/$50 per capita amounts. U.S. possessions with populations less than the least populous state have a volume limit equal to the per capita amount *actually received* by the least populous state (i.e., the $250/$150 million safe harbor divided by the least populous state's population). In general, the new volume limit is administered similarly to the prior law limits on IDBs, student loan bonds and qualified mortgage bonds. A federal allocation formula is provided, subject to an override by the Governor (during an interim period), or by state legislation.

> **NOTE:** There are no set-asides for particular types of bonds from the new volume cap.

Carryforward of volume cap. An issuer can irrevocably elect to carry forward for up to three succeeding years a part of the new volume cap, but only for specific carryforward projects that are irrevocably designated in advance. The election can't cover projects financed with small issue bonds, and carryforward authority to issue qualified mortgage bonds or MCCs is limited to those issued by their new sunset date. The name of the user of an exempt facility and the proposed address of the facility needn't be specified when a carryforward election is made as long as the facility can be otherwise identified with reasonable certainty.

[¶1308] **Prohibited Facilities, Public Approval, and Changes in Use.** Private activity bonds issued after 8-15-86 (with transitional exceptions) can't be used to provide airplanes, skyboxes or private luxury boxes, health club or gambling facilities, or alcohol stores. (Exception: A health club can be financed by qualified Sec. 501(c)(3) bonds if the health club is directly used for the organization's exempt purpose). And all private activity bonds issued after 12-31-86 must meet public approval requirements. This usually involves approval of the bond issue or the financing of a facility by a voter referendum, or by the legislature or elected executive officer of the issuing government unit (and government units where financed facilities are located) after a public hearing. Issues refunding previously approved bonds, whose maturity is no later than that of the original bonds, are excepted from the public approval rule.

Loss of deductions when qualified use or ownership of facilities changes. Effective for changes in use occuring after 8-15-86, in addition to any loss of tax exemption that may result under other rules, the new law generally denies for property financed with private activity and private loan bonds the tax deduction for interest (including the interest element of user fees) that accrues during the period that starts from the first day of the year in which property financed by these bonds is used in a way not qualifying for its exempt financing and ends when the property is again used for the bonds' qualified purpose (or until the bonds are redeemed, if that's earlier). In general, the nondeductible amount is equal to the interest (or its equivalent) paid on the bond-financed loans.

Special rules. First, in case of qualified mortgage and qualified veterans' mortgage bonds, interest on a bond-financed mortgage loan becomes nondeductible if the financed residence ceases to be a principal residence of a mortgagor for a continuous period of at least a year. IRS can waive the disallowance in case of hardship (e.g., if residence is occupied by minor children of deceased mortgagor). Second, for exempt facility bonds financing a qualified residential rental project, interest on the financed loan accruing from the first day of the tax year when the project ceases to qualify until the date it starts qualifying is nondeductible. Finally, if any part of a facility financed with proceeds of qualified 501(c)(3) bonds is no longer used by a qualifying organization, the Sec. 501(c)(3) organization that continues to own the part of the facility and benefits from the bonds has income from an unrelated trade or business. The amount of that income is at least equal to the fair rental value of that part of the facility for the period of unqualified use. According to the Senate Finance Committee Report, interest on the bond-financed loans isn't deductible against income from the business from the first day of the year when the change in use occurs.

In addition, if all or part of a facility financed by tax-exempt bonds is required to be owned as a condition of the exemption by (or on behalf of) a government unit or Sec. 501(c)(3) organization, and stops being so owned, then amounts paid or accrued for that part of the facility's use become nondeductible to the extent of interest accrued on the exempt financing from the date such ownership ceases. Regs can prescribe rules for allocating interest when only a part of a facility has a change in use or ownership.

[¶1309] **Arbitrage Restrictions Tightened.** Generally for bonds issued after 8-15-86, the arbitrage rules now cover 95% of the bond proceeds. Under prior law any tax exempt obligation became taxable if it was an arbitrage bond—in general if more than 15% of the proceeds of the issue were reasonably expected to be used (directly or indirectly) either to acquire taxable obligations that produce a materially higher yield or replace funds used for such arbitrage. The new law reduces the 15% (minor portion) leeway down to the lesser of: (a) 5% of the proceeds, or (b) $100,000. However, reasonably required reserve or replacement funds (limited by the new law to no more than 10% of bond proceeds unless the Treasury specifically approves a larger amount for an issue) are no longer treated as part of the "minor portion" amounts. *Note:* Amounts deposited in the reserve are subject to the rebate requirement (see below) up to the allowed 10% amount. The new law also spells out that deliberate or intentional acts to produce arbitrage render the bonds "arbitrage bonds" whose interest is taxable retroactively from the date the bonds are issued. These rules generally apply to bonds issued after 8-15-86 (but for bonds covered by the Joint Statements of Effective Dates of 3-14-86 and 7- 17-86, they apply to bonds issued on or after 9-1-86).

Determination of materially higher yield. The Senate Finance Committee Report notes that prior law reg determinations of what's a "materially higher yield" are in general retained under the new law. Generally, the maximum permitted spread between the acquired taxable obligations and the tax exempt issue has been 0.125 percentage points (plus costs, that varied depending on whether the acquired taxable investments were "purpose obligations" acquired to carry out the purpose of the issue or "nonpurpose obligations"). The maximum permitted spread for "acquired program obligations" (purpose obligations acquired under student loan and other programs that contemplated their acquisition) is the greater of (1) 1.5 percentage points plus reasonable administrative costs, or (2) reasonable and direct costs of the loan program.

The rule treating bond insurance premiums as interest on the bonds if the insurance reduces their interest rate is retained, and it's intended that similar treatment be extended under regs to costs of other credit enhancement devices (e.g., letters of credit obtained through arms'-length transactions such as competitive bidding). However, credit enhancement fees are to be treated as interest only to the extent they represent a reasonable charge for the transfer of credit risk (i.e., indirect payments of issuance costs through credit enhancers aren't interest expenses). The rules apply generally to bonds issued after 8-15-86 (but for bonds covered by the Joint Statements of 3-14-86 and 7-17-86 they apply to bonds issued on or after 9-1-86).

> **CAUTION:** The Senate Finance Committee Report states that the new law's requirement to determine yield consistently with original discount rules [Secs. 1273 and 1274] overrules the result in *State of Washington v. Comm.* (CA-DC, 1982) 50 AFTR2d 82-5914, 692 F2d 128. For bonds issued after 12-31-85, bond yield means the discount rate at which all anticipated payments of principal and interest on the bonds equals the net proceeds of the issue *after deducting the costs of issuance.* The deduction of issuance costs in effect allows payment of issuance costs out of arbitrage.

'Arbitrage investment' definition broadened and temporary period exception tightened. The arbitrage restrictions have been expanded to cover the acquisition of any taxable investment property with proceeds of tax-exempts. According to the Senate Finance Report, this can cover a materially higher yield investment regardless of its purpose (i.e., even if it's acquired as an acquired purpose or acquired program obligation). For instance, a purchase of a deferred payment contract, or of an annuity contract to fund a pension plan of a qualified government unit is subject to the same arbitrage restrictions as direct funding of the pension plan with bond proceeds (for bonds issued to fund deferred compensation arrangements the rules apply to bonds issued after 9-25-85). However, the arbitrage restrictions don't apply to real or tangible property acquired with bond proceeds for reasons other than investment. The rules apply generally to bonds issued after 8-15-86 (they apply to bonds issued on or after 9-1-86 for bonds covered by the Joint Statements of 3-14-86 and 7-17-86).

The new law eliminates the prior law election under the regs to forgo the temporary periods exception to the arbitrage rules and be allowed to earn arbitrage on purpose obligations of 0.5 percentage points over the yield of tax exempts. And a new statutory rule covering the initial temporary period applies to pooled financings (other than of mortgage revenue bonds). Initial temporary periods for pooled financings are limited to six months (other than for certain GSL and PLUS student loan bonds during a two-year transition period which doesn't apply to bonds issued after 12-31-88). And temporary periods for repayments that will be relent are limited to three months. The rules generally apply to bonds issued after 8-15-86 (or to bonds issued on or after 9-1-86 for bonds covered by the Joint Statements).

Restrictions on nonpurpose investments expanded. The new law extends to all tax exempts (including refunding issues), a prior law restriction on most IDBs and qualified mortgage bonds that limits the amount of bonds proceeds that can be invested in nonpurpose obligations. Under the new law, no more than the amount of 150% of the debt service on the issue for the bond year can be invested in nonpurpose obligations at any time during the year, and that investment must be reduced promptly when the outstanding issue is reduced or repaid. The Senate Finance Committee Report notes that this restriction doesn't apply to investments during temporary periods during which unlimited arbitrage can be earned (however, the rebate, see below, can apply to such amounts), and it doesn't require the sale of investments at a loss that would exceed the amount otherwise rebatable to the U.S. at that time or credited to mortgagors under qualified veterans' mortgage bond rules (see below).

Rebate. The new law extends to all tax exempts a requirement (previously applicable to most IDBs) of rebating to the United States, the arbitrage earned on the gross proceeds of an issue invested in nonpurpose obligations. The term "gross proceeds" is intended to be broadly interpreted, and include the original proceeds, the investment return and repayment of principal received from investing the original proceeds and amounts used or available to pay debt service. Nonpurpose obligations, for these purposes, include amounts invested in a debt service reserve fund or an escrow established with proceeds of a refunding issue.

Arbitrage profits to be rebated are equal to (1) the excess of (a) the total earned on the nonpurpose obligations (but not on the arbitrage itself) *over* (b) the amount that would have been earned if they were invested at yield equal to the yield of the tax exempts, *plus* (2) all income earned on the arbitrage itself.

The Senate Finance Committee Report notes that this requires a separate accounting of bond proceeds from tax and other revenues, but that the IRS can prescribe simplified accounting for limited bond issues.

For late payments of the arbitrage rebate, the Treasury can waive loss of tax exemption on the bonds where the error or late payment is not due to willful neglect, and to condition the relief on a payment of a penalty of up to 50% of the amount not properly paid. Interest accrues on the amount not properly paid in the same way as on late payments of tax. The Treasury can waive the penalty and interest.

The rebate rule doesn't apply to a bond issue all of whose gross proceeds are spent for their governmental purpose within six months from the issue date (only one six-month period is allowed even for an issue in series, or for more than one draw-down of proceeds).

Special rules and exceptions to the arbitrage and rebate rules relate to:

• *Bonds financing operations of small government units* with general taxing powers that reasonably expect to issue, at most, $5 million of tax-exempts in the calendar year.

• Governmental bonds (but not tax and revenue anticipation notes) and qualified 501(c)(3) bonds, if all but a minor portion of the gross proceeds of an issue are spent for the exempt purpose of the borrowing within six months. If the gross proceeds of an issue, other than the lesser of 5% or $100,000 of the proceeds are so spent, there's an additional six months to spend the remainder before rebate payments are required. And for this exception, redemption of the allowable de-minimis portion before the added six months expires is treated as an expenditure for the purpose of the borrowing.

• The new law retains a prior law alternative of either a credit on qualified mortgage revenue bonds to mortgagors or the rebate to the U.S., and extends such a choice to *qualified veterans' mortgage bonds.*

• *Arbitrage earned on GSL and PLUS student loan bonds* during an initial 18-month temporary period isn't subject to the rebate requirement to the extent that (1) the bond proceeds are used by the end of the 18-month period to finance student loans, (2) the arbitrage profits are used to pay the costs of issuance and reasonable administration costs financed with the proceeds of the issue, and (3) the costs are not reimbursed. The transition rule doesn't apply to bonds issued after 12-31-88.

• *Proceeds of tax and revenue anticipation notes.* Under a safe harbor rule, if at the end of six months (or a lesser period after issuance, the cumulative deficit of the governmental unit has exceeded 90% of the issue size, proceeds and earnings on them are treated as having been spent for purposes of the arbitrage rebate requirement. Cumulative cash flow deficit is here defined as the excess of the amount the governmental unit spends during the six months period (or the shorter term of the bonds) over the sum of all amounts (other than the bond proceeds) that are available for payment of expenses during the period. Redemption of bonds isn't treated as an expenditure for a governmental purpose under the rebate rules. This safe harbor rule doesn't affect the amounts of tax anticipation notes that may be issued or that qualify for temporary periods.

• *Student loan bonds.* The new law repeals the prior law's direction for special regs to the extent inconsistent with the new arbitrage restrictions.

• Effective on date of enactment, the Treasury is directed to modify the SLGS program to provide investments similar to those offered by money market funds paying yields that would eliminate arbitrage profits and operate the program at no net cost to the government. The new rules would permit demand deposits under the SLGS program by deleting advance notice requirements related to the purchase of SLGS and minimum maturity requirements.

The rebate rules and the special rules in general apply to bonds issued after 12-31-85, but for bonds and provisions covered by the Joint Statements of 3-14-86 and 7-17-86 they apply as to bonds issued on or after 9-1-86, and for arbitrage rebate requirements for certain pooled financing, they apply to bonds issued after 3:00 p.m. EDT, 7-17-86.

[¶1310] New Restrictions on Advance Refundings. Under prior law, bonds other than IDBs and mortgage subsidy bonds could be advance refunded. Mortgage subsidy bonds and IDBs couldn't be refunded more than 180 days before the refunded bonds were redeemed unless the refunded bonds had a maturity of less than three years.

Under the new law, advance refunding bonds are those issued more than 90 days before the refunded bonds are redeemed (e.g., called so no further interest accrues) and refundings before 1-1-86 are treated as advance refundings only if the refunded bonds weren't redeemed within 180 days of the issuance of the refunding bonds. And, *only qualified 501(c)(3) bonds and governmental bonds* can be advance refunded.

Restrictions that apply in instances where advance refundings are permitted (if they aren't met, the refunding bonds become taxable) are

• Bonds originally issued before 1-1-86 can be advance refunded 2 times, with a transitional rule permitting one additional advance refunding after 3-14-86 if the bonds were advance refunded 2 or more times before 3-15-86. Bonds originally issued after 12-31-85 can be advance refunded only once.

• In the case of advance refundings of bonds originally issued after 12-31-85, that produce debt service savings (determined without regard to issuance costs), the refunded bonds must be redeemed no later than the first date on which their call isn't prohibited.

• In the case of bonds originally issued before 1-1-86 and advance refundings that may produce debt service savings, the refunded bonds must be redeemed no later than the first date on which the issue may be called at a premium of 3% or less.

• The temporary period during which unlimited arbitrage profits may be earned on the refunding bonds expires 30 days after the date of their issuance, and for the refunded bonds no later than the date of issuance of the advance refunding bonds.

• The 150% of annual debt service limitation on nonpurpose investments [see ¶1309] doesn't apply to advance refunding proceeds invested in an escrow for the redemption of the refunded bonds.

• Advance refundings are generally prohibited if they involve a device to obtain a material financial advantage other than savings arising from lower interest rates (e.g., so called flip-flop devices, proceeds of prior issue invested in higher escrow to pay future debt service and advance refunding bonds used to pay project costs, advance refundings enabling the issuer to get a rebate of prior issue's insurance, etc.).

• Reserve funds and minor portions for advance refunding bonds [see ¶1309] can't exceed the lesser of the amount so dedicated for the refunded bonds, or the amounts permitted under the new law.

• In the case of advance refundings of governmental bonds, advance refunding bonds are subject to the new unified volume cap on private activity and qualified mortgage bonds to the extent of permitted private use of the refunded bonds in excess of $15 million [see ¶1307].

Effective Dates: The new advance refunding rules generally apply to advance refunding bonds issued after 8-15-86 in case of advance refundings of 501(c)(3) organization bonds, other private activity bonds for which advance refunding was permitted under prior law, and governmental bonds originally issued after 8-15-86. They generally apply to bonds issued on or after 9-1-86 for bonds and provisions covered by the Joint Statements of 3-14-86 and 7-17-86.

[¶1311] **Information Reporting Extended to All Tax-Exempts.** Information reporting rules, similar to those previously applicable to IDBs and certain other qualified bonds have been extended by the new law to cover *all* tax-exempts. In general, the information required is the same as under prior law, but the new law authorizes the IRS to vary the type of specific information required of facility and nonfacility bonds respectively. And it's intended that IRS allow issuers of small amounts of bonds to file a simplified consolidated report.

[¶1312] **General Stock Ownership Corporation (GSOC) Provisions and Determination of Marital Status.** Effective 1-1-84, (in the Committee Report—the date of enactment in the statute), the new law repeals as deadwood, provisions relating to General Stock Ownership Corporations, (state-established corporations for the benefit of state citizens with power to borrow and invest in business enterprises). No GSOC has been organized, and GSOCs could be organized only before 1984.

Redetermination of marital status. To make place for Code provisions dealing with tax-exempt bonds (new Secs. 141-147), the new law has redesignated the provision dealing with determination of marital status (old sec. 143) as Sec. 7703.

Act Sec. 1303 dealing with repeal of GSOC rules repeals Code Secs. 1391-1397, Sec. 172(b)(1)(j), 1016(a)(21), 3402(r) and 6039B, and amends Sec. 172(k)(2) and (4), and redesignates Sec. 172(b)(1)(k) as 172(b)(1)(j), and Secs. 1016(a)(23)-(27) as Secs. 1016(a)(21)-(26), effective as shown above. Act. Sec. 1301(j) redesignates old Sec. 143 (determination of marital status) as new Sec. 7703 effective on date of enactment.

[¶1313] **Other Rules and Effective Dates.** The new law permits one current refunding of certain FSLIC and FDIC guaranteed bonds that were used to finance multifamily rental housing, provided no additional volume of outstanding bonds results and certain other requirements rendering the refunding in substance a renegotiation of interest rates are satisfied. The refundings are subject to all the new arbitrage provisions of the new law. The rules apply to bonds issued after enactment.

The rules in the Exempt Bond Title of the new law are generally effective for obligations issued after 8-15-86. However, for provisions and bonds covered by the Joint Statements on Effective Dates of 3-14-86 and 7-17-86 the new rules generally apply to bonds issued on or after 9-1-86. Major exceptions to this rule are usually noted as part of the coverage of the law changes involved.

General transitional rules. (1) *Binding contract and started construction exceptions.* This rule in general excepts from the new law changes, bonds financing facilities covered by pre-9-26-85 approval in an inducement resolution or comparable approval, and either whose construction, reconstruction, or rehabilitation began before 9-26-85, or which are covered by a pre-9-26-85 binding contract to incur more than 10% of reasonably anticipated costs of construction, or which are acquired under a pre-9-26-85 binding contract. However, for bonds actually issued after the enactment date, specified new law rules are engrafted into Sec. 103 for purposes of this exception.

(2) Refunding issues. In case of non-advance refundings, the new law changes (other than those dealing with arbitrage and information reporting) don't apply to bonds whose proceeds are used exclusively to refund tax exempt bonds that were issued on or before 1-1-86, and whose amount isn't greater than the amount of refunded bonds, and which have a maturity no later than 17 years after issue or comply with the rule requiring maturity to be no more than 120% of economic life of financed facilities. In case of advance refundings, certain tax exempt governmental bonds and 501(c)(3) organization bonds are excepted from the new law rules subject to certain conditions. Another transitional rule permits one additional advance refunding of bonds issued on or before 1-1-86 which may be advance refunded under the new law.

(3) Additional transitional rules cover many situations or projects. Also, a transitional rule covers pre-1988 obligations that were covered by specified transitional rules of the '84 TRA.

[The page following this is 1401.]

TRUSTS AND ESTATES; MINOR CHILDREN

Trusts and Estates

[¶1401] Income Taxation of Trusts and Estates. The new law revises the tax rate schedules for nongrantor trusts and estates. Under the revised rates the first $5000 of taxable income of trusts is taxed at 15%. Any taxable trust income over $5000 is taxed at 28%. Additionally, the benefit of the 15% bracket is phased-out when the taxable income of the trust is between $13,000 and $26,000.

The tax rates for estates under the new law are the same as for nongrantor trusts. [For more details and a tax rate schedule, see ¶101.]

Act Sec. 101, revising rate schedules applicable to trusts and estates, amends Sec. 1, effective on 7-1-87 with blended rates for 1987 returns.

[¶1402] Revision of Grantor Trust Rules. The new law abolishes income-shifting breaks for Clifford Trusts. As a general rule, income from 10-year and other grantor trusts is taxed to the grantor, not the beneficiary, if the property put into the trust will revert to the grantor or the grantor's spouse. It is immaterial how long the trust lasts. These new rules will not apply when the trust may revert only after the death of the income beneficiary who is the grantor's lineal descendent.

The 10-year rule was replaced with a rule that treats a trust as a grantor trust when the grantor has a reversionary interest whose value, at the time of the transfer of the property into the trust, amounts to more than 5% of the value of the transferred property.

Also, if a grantor's spouse is living with the grantor at the time of the creation of any power or interest held by the spouse, the grantor is treated as holding that power or interest—a restriction that kills spousal remainder trusts.

What the old rules allowed. By way of background, the grantor trust rules treat the grantor of a trust as its owner when there is a transfer of property to a trust by a grantor who retains certain powers or interests over the trust. As a result, income attributable to the trust is taxed to its grantor—that is, the person who sets up the trust, rather than to its beneficiary.

But a prior-law exception to the grantor trust rules allowed a grantor-to-beneficiary shift of the taxes on trust income used to pay for, say, college costs. The exception became applicable when at least ten years had to elapse before certain powers and interests that were retained by the grantor could revert to the grantor.

Consequently, a long-favored way for many high-bracket individuals to shift income from themselves to children, grandchildren and other lower-taxed family members is to transfer money, stocks, real estate or other income-generating assets for a period of at least ten years into reversionary trust arrangements known as "Clifford" or "short-term" trusts. During the period that the trust is in existence, the income is taxed to the child or other person named to receive the trust income. At the end of the trust period, the grantor regains the assets used to fund the Clifford Trust.

A spousal remainder trust provides another way for a parent-to-child shift of the taxes on income earmarked for educational expenses. One parent funds the trust. It can be set up for less than ten years and the specified period can end upon the child's completion of college, with the trust asset then becoming the property of the grantor's spouse.

Effective Date: Generally, the revised rules apply to trust transfers made after 3-1-86. That translates into no income shifting for income from Clifford Trusts started after that date.

There is, however, an exception from the new rules for Clifford trusts that were created under a binding property settlement entered into on or before 3-1-86. These trusts are unaffected by the new rules and can continue to shift income to the beneficiary.

Remember, though, that the income shifted through pre-March-2 trusts is subject to the new rules for taxing unearned income received by children under the age of 14. [See ¶1405—1407.]

> **Example:** Assume that a parent set up and funded a pre-March-2 trust. The trust named an under-14 child as beneficiary. *Result* : The trust income is taxed at the parent's tax rate, not the child's.

Assume, instead, that the trust is set up by someone other than the parent or that the child is over 14. In that event, the trust income continues to be taxed at the child's rate.

Act Secs. 1401 and 1402, relating to the taxation of grantor trusts, amends Secs. 672, 673, 674, 676 and 677, effective as shown above.

[¶1403] Taxable Years of Trusts. Under the new law, all trusts, both existing and newly created, must use a calendar taxable year. However, tax exempt trusts under Sec. 501(a) and wholly charitable trusts under Sec. 4947(a)(1) may use a fiscal year.

If a trust has a taxable year different than the taxable year of its beneficiaries, prior law allowed the deferral of taxation by one month for each month that the taxable year of the trust ended sooner than the taxable year of its beneficiaries. So, for a trust with a taxable year ending on January 31, and with the trust beneficiary on a calendar year, the taxation of trust income distributed to the beneficiary was deferred 11 months.

Act Sec. 1403, relating to taxable years of trusts, adds new Sec. 645, effective for taxable years beginning after 12-31-86.

[¶1404] **Trusts and Estates To Make Estimated Income Tax Payments.** The new law requires that both new and existing trusts and estates pay estimated tax in the same manner as individuals. An estate, however, need not pay estimated tax in its first two years. The law also repeals the rules that allowed estates to pay their income tax over four equal installments after the year it is earned.

Under prior law trusts and estates were not required to make estimated tax payments and estates could elect to pay income tax in four equal installments beginning with the due date of the return and for each three-month period thereafter.

Trustees are allowed to assign any amounts of a trust's quarterly payments to the beneficiaries. The election is made on the tax return of the trust. Since the return is to be filed within 65 days after the end of the trust's taxable year, the amount of the credits assigned to the beneficiaries is considered a distribution under the 65-day rule of Sec. 663. Thus, the beneficiaries are deemed to have received the distribution on the last day of the trust's year. According to the Conference Committee's statutory language, the amount deemed distributed won't be treated as a payment of the trust's estimated tax, but will be treated as a payment of the beneficiary's estimated tax on the January 15 following the tax year. This election is available only to the extent the trust's total estimated tax payments for the year exceeds its own tax liability. However, the Committee Report indicates the beneficiaries will still treat the credit as received at the time the election is made for their estimated taxes.

Act Sec. 1404, requiring trusts and estates to make estimated income tax payments and repealing estate's election to pay income tax in four equal installments, amends Secs. 643 and 6654 and repeals Sec. 6152, effective for taxable years beginning after 12-31-86.

Minor's Income

[¶1405] **New Tax Rules for Child's Unearned Income.** The new law cracks down on family income splitting, a device used by higher-bracket parents to cut overall family taxes by shifting income-producing assets to lower-bracket children. The mechanism for the crackdown is new Sec. 1(j), which is effective for tax years beginning after the date of enactment.

The new law taxes "net unearned income" for a child under 14 at the parent's tax rate, even if the money or other property was given to the child before 1987.

If the child is age 14 or older, his or her net unearned income is taxed at the child's rates, not the parent's. [See ¶1406 for the calculation of the tax on net unearned income for a child under 14.]

¶1405

What the old rules allow. Under prior law, a family was able to reduce its aggregate tax liability by shifting income-producing property among family members. Consider, for example, parents who wanted to minimize taxes paid or income from funds set aside for the college education of their child. A common maneuver for these parents, whose dividend income would otherwise be taxed at their high tax bracket, was to transfer shares of stock into a custodian account for their child. By doing so, they deflected part of the family's income to a child taxed at a lower rate.

What the new rules allow. There are two sets of rules for taxing unearned income received by children. The first set is for children under 14 years of age, while the second is for children over 14 years of age and older.

Children under the age of 14. For an under-14 child, net unearned income, including income derived from gifts made *before* 1987, is taxed at the parent's rate—that is, as if the parent had received the income, rather than at the child's lower rate. The under-14 rules remain applicable until the child reaches age 14.

Exemption from the under-14 rules. Certain kinds of income are exempt from the new rules and continue to be taxed at the child's rate. The exemption is for all wages earned by the child, whether the wages come from babysitting, delivering newspapers, or even from a job with a business owned by a parent.

Child age 14 or over. The under-age-14 rules no longer apply when a child reaches the age of 14 before the close of the tax year in question. Instead, a more advantageous set of rules applies. In general, all unearned income is taxed at the child's rate (as is earned income).

Other changes. The new law does more than just put a crimp in income splitting by upper-bracket families. It also exposes more of a family's income to tax and will require many more parents to file income tax returns for their children. Reason: Beginning with the 1987 tax year, a taxpayer cannot claim a personal exemption if he or she is eligible to be claimed as a dependent by another taxpayer [see ¶103].

> **NOTE:** Starting in 1987, the parent must include the child's social security number on the parent's return and the child must include the parent's number on the child's return.

[¶1406] Computing Unearned Income of Child Under 14. The child's net unearned income is taxed to the child at the parent's top marginal rate—that is, the peak tax bracket of the parent. Thus, income received from bank accounts, CDs, money market funds, stocks, and the like regardless of who set up or bought the property that belonged to one or both parents is taxed to the child at the parent's top rate. The new provision applies if (1) the child has not attained age 14 before the close of the tax year, and (2) either parent of the child is alive at the close of the tax year.

How to calculate tax. The tax is imposed on a child's net unearned income and equals the *greater of*:

(1) The tax that would be imposed on the child's income without the special rules on the child's unearned income; or

(2) The sum of the tax that would be payable had the child not received unearned income, and the child's share of the parental-source tax.

The child will pay tax at the parent's rates on his or her *net unearned income.* The child's *net unearned income* is the child's unearned income less the sum of $500 and the greater of: (1) $500 of the standard deduction or $500 of itemized deductions, or (2) the deductions allowed the child that are directly connected with the production of the child's unearned income. The net unearned income cannot exceed the child's total taxable income for the year in question. These rules can best be explained with examples.

Example (1): Johnny Jones, age 13, has $300 of unearned income and no earned income. His standard deduction is $300 which is allocated against his unearned income. Johnny pays no tax.

Example (2): Tommy Green, age 13, has $1,400 of unearned income and no earned income. The $1,400 is first reduced by his standard deduction of $500. Of the remaining $900, $500 is taxed at Tommy's rates, and the remaining $400 is net unearned income and taxed at the top rate of his parents.

Example (3): Debbie Smith, age 12, has $700 of earned income and $300 of unearned income. Her standard deduction is $700. The standard deduction is first applied against Debbie's unearned income. The $400 balance of the standard deduction is allocated against the $400 of earned income. She does not have any net unearned income. The remaining $300 is taxed at Debbie's rates.

PARENT'S LOOKBACK: A parent must do an "as if" calculation of his own return before he completes his child's. He must figure the difference between (1) the tax he would have paid had his income included each under-age-14 child's unearned income, and (2) the tax he actually pays.

Net unearned income is taken into account in determining the parent's low-bracket phase-out and the phase-out of the personal exemptions the parent may be eligible to claim. However, net unearned income is *not* taken into account by a parent in computing any deduction or credit he or she might be entitled to claim.

More complications. A further calculation is required if there is more than one under-age-14 child with unearned income. Each child's share of the parent's tax is prorated based on the ratio of each child's unearned income to total unearned income of the parent's children.

What if the child's parents are divorced? In this situation, the custodial parent is the one whose tax income is taken into account when computing the tax on a child's unearned income. And if the parents are married but file separate returns, the income of the parent with the greater taxable income is taken into account.

[Ed note: The Conference Committee Report indicates that the provisions on a child's unearned income are effective for tax years beginning after the date of enactment. However, the Conference Bill states that the effective date is as shown below.]

Act Sec. 1411, relating to unearned income of minor children under age 14, amends Sec. 1, effective for taxable years beginning after 12-31-86.

[¶1407] Trust Income. Special rules apply to income received by children from property put into arrangements known as Clifford or ten-year trusts. These trusts are discussed at ¶1402. Presumably, income received by an under-14 child if from property put into a trust before 3-2-86, is subject to the new rules on net unearned income. This income continues to be taxed at the *child's* rate when the child is over 14. For trust transfers after 3-1-86, all of the trust income received by the child is taxed to the grantor.

[¶1408] Coping With the New Rules on Child's Income. Taxpayers can use these strategies to minimize or avoid the new rules on unearned income:

Gift of assets that defer income: The new rules for a child's unearned income do not apply once a child reaches age 14. So the idea is to give younger children assets that defer taxable income until a child reaches that age. Some examples:

• U.S. Government Savings (EE) bonds: income may be deferred until the bond is cashed in. Note that this won't work if a child already owns EE bonds and has elected to report each year's interest accrual as income (to take advantage of his personal exemption and low rates). Reason: The child can't change his mind—he must continue to report each year's Savings Bond accrual as income.

• Growth stock: Typically, growth stock pays little in the way of dividends. However, the profit on an astute investment may more than offset the lack of dividends. The child can hold the stock until he reaches age 14. If he sells it at a profit, he'll be taxed at his low rates.

• Deep discount municipal bonds: Such bonds produce tax-free income during ownership. If the bond matures on or after the date when the child reaches age 14, the discount (face value less cost basis) is taxed in the child's low tax bracket.

Employment of child: Taxpayers in a position to do so should employ their children in their business and pay them a reasonable wage for the work they actually perform (e.g., light office help, such as filing). Result: The child's earned income will be sheltered by the new standard deduction (and the parent's business gains a deduction for the wages). The new under-age-14 rules have no effect on earned income, even if derived from a parent's business.

Estate and Gift Taxes

[¶1421] **Information Necessary for Valid Current Use Valuation Election.** An executor may elect to value certain real property used in farming or other closely held business operations for estate tax purposes based on its current use rather than its full fair market value. There was concern that, in certain cases, the federal estate tax return (Form 706) did not sufficiently inform taxpayers of what information must be provided to elect current use valuation and that an agreement to the election by all persons with an interest in the property is required to be attached to Form 706. So the new law provides limited relief permitting additional time to supply information necessary for a valid election.

For decedents dying *before* January 1, 1986, if the estate made a timely current use valuation election and provided substantially all the information elicited by Form 706, the election is valid. However, if the estate fails to provide the Treasury with additional information with respect to the election within 90 days after the information is requested, the election will be disallowed as invalid.

This relief does not apply to the estate of any decedent if the statute of limitations for assessment of tax has expired before the date of enactment of the new law.

Act Sec. 1421, relating to information necessary for valid special use valuation election, is effective on the date of enactment with a special targeted transitional exception.

[¶1422] **Estate and Gift Tax Break for Qualified Conservation Contributions.** The new law liberalizes the estate and gift tax deduction rules for contributions of certain property interests to charitable organizations, the U.S., or state or local governments.

Until now, the estate, gift, *and income* tax deductions for a "qualified conservation contribution" of a partial interest in real property (including a gift in which the mineral interest was retained by the donor) were conditioned on the requirement that the gift be made for, and limited by its terms to, certain defined conservation purposes [Code Sec. 170(h)(4)(A)].

The new law keeps this requirement for the income tax deduction. Now, however, gifts that don't satisfy the conservation purpose requirement will still qualify for estate and gift tax deductions. There's also a targeted amendment for certain gifts to Acadia National Park in Maine.

Act Sec. 1422(a), liberalizing the estate tax rules for contributions of real property, redesignates Sec. 2055(f) as Sec. 2055(g) and adds new Sec. 2055(f), and Act Sec. 1422(b), liberalizing the gift tax rules for contributions of real property, redesignates Sec. 2522(d) as Sec. 2522(e) and adds new Sec. 2522(d), all effective for transfers and contributions made after 12-31-86.

【¶1423】 **Indirect Transfer to Qualified Organization.** The new law allows an estate tax charitable deduction to a particular estate that transferred property indirectly to charity, according to the decedent's wishes.

【¶1431】 **Generation-Skipping Transfer Tax.** As part of the Tax Reform Act of 1976, the generation-skipping transfer (GST) tax was imposed, naturally, to tax generation-skipping transfers. What is a generation-skipping transfer? It's one that allows a beneficiary in a generation below the transferor to enjoy benefits of ownership in the property without having the property included in his or her estate (or pay gift tax) when it is transferred to (or for the benefit of) beneficiaries in an even lower generation.

Example: A transfers property in trust in which his child, B receives the income for life and the remainder passes to A's grandchildren, C, on the child's death.

Since B, the grantor's child, had only a life estate in the trust corpus (other nontaxable ownership interests include the right to be trustee, a limited power of appointment, powers subject to ascertainable standards relating to health, education and support, and power to invade under "5 or 5" powers under Sec. 2014) it would not be included in the child's gross estate for estate tax purposes. So the GST tax was invented to impose an equivalent estate (or gift tax) on the transfer of the beneficial enjoyment of the trust corpus or income from A's child to A's grandchild in the above example. "Generation-skipping" is involved because the original transfer is taxed in A's generation and again in C's generation but it "skips" taxation in B's generation. In other words, the loophole was the use of long-term trusts that split the beneficial enjoyment of property between individuals in more than one generation without the imposition of an estate or gift tax on the shift of interest between the different generations. Under prior law, the estate or gift tax rate bracket of the skipped generation, B, above, formerly called the "deemed transferor"—was used as a measuring rod to tax the transfer as if the property was actually transferred outright to C from B.

Enter another taxable event—the direct skip. Under prior law and the new law, GST tax is imposed on a "taxable termination" and a "taxable distribution." The former is illustrated in the example above when B's death terminates B's life income interest in the trust and the trust property passes to C, the generation-skipping beneficiary. A "taxable distribution" results whenever there is a distribution of trust property to the generation-skipping beneficiary.

> **NOTE:** Prior law generation-skipping distributions of trust income were not subject to the GST tax. Under the new law, the distributions are subject to the tax whether from trust income or trust corpus but the recipient can take an income tax deduction for the GST tax imposed on the distribution.

The direct skip loophole closed: Since the GST tax replaced the estate tax in B's generation (see our example above) estate planners had to get around both the estate tax and the GST tax. The way to do it was to avoid G's generation altogether (if B could afford it) and have A make the transfer *directly* to the grandchild, C—the so-called "layering" technique. This loophole is now closed by the new law. Now a generation-skipping transfer includes *any* transfer of property to (or for the benefit of) persons two or more generations below that of the transferor without the payment of estate or gift tax in the "skipped" generation even when the "skipped" person in that generation (B above) had no ownership interest in the property. So the new GST definition now includes "direct" generation-skipping transfers, i.e., (A to C above. C is called the "skip person") as well as transfers in which a member of the skipped generation has an interest in or power over the property.

Generation assignment changes. The new classification are the same as under prior law except that lineal descendants of the transferor's spouse also are assigned to generations like those for similar descendants of the transferor. Also, there's a special rule on generation assignment for the grantor's grandchildren: When the grandchild's parent who is a lineal descendant of the grantor is deceased, the grandchild is "moved up" a generation, so transfers to that grandchild would not be GSTs.

Now for the good news. (1) For each grantor there is a special $2,000,000 GST exemption per grandchild for direct skips in trust or otherwise. This can be doubled to $4,000,000 for married individuals who elect to treat the transfers as made one-half by each. This exemption expires on January 1, 1990.

(2) Also, every person is permitted to make GSTs aggregating as much as $1,000,000 during his or her lifetime and at death, that will be completely exempt from the GST tax. By electing to treat the GSTs as made one-half by each, a married couple has as much as

$2,000,000 of GSTs they can make without GST tax. Transfers above that amount are subject to tax at a rate equal to the maximum gift and estate tax rate. The former $250,000 exclusion for GSTs to grandchildren was repealed.

> **WATCH THIS:** When a person allocates all or a part of the $1,000,000 exemption to a GST, all future appreciation on the designated exempt property is also exempt. So if a grantor transfers $1,000,000 in trust for his children and grandchildren and allocates the entire $1,000,000 exemption to the trust, none of the trust will ever be subject to GST tax even if the trust property increases to $10,000,000. But if only $500,000 of the exemption is allocated, one-half of the value of all distributions to the grandchildren will be subject to the GST tax and one-half the value of the trust property will be subject to that tax when the children's interest terminates.

QTIP property. Part of the $1,000,000 exemption can be allocated to offset a GST on the death of the transferor's surviving spouse when the property qualified as terminable interest property for estate and gift tax purposes under Secs. 2056(b)(7) and 2523(f).

Other exemptions. As under prior law, GST amounts subject to estate and gift taxes are exempt. Also, the GST doesn't apply to any amount exempt from gift tax because of the gift tax $10,000 exclusion (Sec. 2503(b)) or the exclusion for tuition and medical expense payments under Sec. 2503(e).

Flat rate. Under the new law, all GSTs not covered by the exemptions or exclusions are taxed at a flat 55% rate which is equal to the present maximum estate and gift tax rate scheduled to go down to 50% in 1988.

Tax base and liability for payment. Under the new law, generation-skipping transfers are taxed as follows:

(1) Taxation distributions. Distributions are subject to tax on the amount received by the transferee. The transferee pays the tax.

(2) Taxable terminations. The value of the property in which the interest terminates is the amount subject to tax. The trustee pays the tax.

(3) Direct skips. The value of the property received by the transferee is the amount subject to tax. The person making the transfer pays the tax.

Effective Date: The GST tax changes apply to transfers made after enactment with (1)-(3) below. The $2 million per grandchild exclusion sunsets January 1, 1990.

(1) Lifetime transfers made after September 25, 1985 are subject to the amended tax; (2) transfers from trusts that were irrevocable on September 25, 1985 are exempt to the extent the transfers were not made out of corpus added after that date; (3) if the decedent was incompetent on September 25, 1985 and at all times until his death, transfers by will in existence on that date are exempt.

WATCH REFUND TIMING: The former GST tax is repealed retroactive to June 11, 1976, its effective date. Any tax paid will be refunded. Taxpayers who would otherwise be barred by the statute of limitations have one year from the date of enactment to file for refunds.

Delayed effective dates. Election may be made to treat *inter vivos* and testamentary contingent transfers in trust for the benefit of a grandchild as direct skips if the transfers occur before the date of enactment, and the transfers would be direct skips except that the trust instrument provides that, if the grandchild dies before vesting of the interest transferred, the interest is transferred to the grandchild's heirs (rather than the grandchild's estate). Transfers treated as direct skips as a result of this election are subject to federal gift and estate tax on the grandchild's death in the same way as if the contingent gift over had been to the grandchild's estate.

There is an exemption from the revised generation-skipping transfer tax testamentary direct skips occurring under wills executed before the date of enactment if the testator dies before 1-1-87.

Act Secs. 1431-1433, relating to the generation-skipping transfer tax, repeals Secs. 2601—2603, 2611—2614, 2621—2622, retroactive to June 11, 1976 and adds Secs. 2601—2604, 2611—2613, 2621—2624, 2631—2632, 2641—2642, 2651—2654 and 2661—2663, effective as shown above.

[The page following this is 1501.]

COMPLIANCE AND TAX ADMINISTRATION

Penalties

[¶1501] **Information Reports.** The accuracy of information reporting is of vital importance to the federal taxation system. Under the new law, several penalties for inaccurate or incomplete returns have been increased.

Consolidated penalties for information reporting failures. To promote fairness in their application and to simplify their administration, the penalties for failure to file an information return with the IRS and for failure to supply a taxpayer with a copy of the information return have been consolidated. And the maximum penalty for each category of failure has been raised from $50,000 to $100,000. Also, a new $5 penalty (maximum $20,000 in a calendar year) has been added for a failure to include correct information on an information return which is due after December 31, 1986 (the penalty applies to both omissions of information and inclusions of incorrect information on both returns filed with the IRS and copies supplied to the taxpayer). But the maximum $20,000 cap doesn't apply when the rules have been intentionally disregarded. The new penalty doesn't apply at all if the penalty for failure to supply a correct taxpayer I.D. number has been imposed.

Interest and dividend returns. Special, stricter rules apply to interest and dividend returns or statements. While the information reporting penalties don't apply to failures that are due to reasonable cause and not willful neglect, interest and dividend reporting failures will be excused only if the taxpayer exercised due diligence. And the maximum amount limitations applicable to the other penalties don't apply.

Failure to supply TIN. The maximum penalty for failing to supply taxpayer identification numbers is increased from $50,000 to $100,000.

Effective Date: These changes apply to returns which have a due date (determined without regard to extensions) that is after December 31, 1986.

Act Sec. 1501, revising penalties for failure to file information returns and statements, adds new Sec. 6721 through 6724, and amends Secs. 6041(d), 6042(c), 6044(e), 6045(b), 6049(c), 6050A(b), 6050B(b), 6050E(b), 6050F(b), 6050G(b), 6050H(d), 6050I(e), 6050K(b), 6052(b), and 6676(a), effective for returns due (without regard to extensions) after 12-31-86. Secs. 6652(a) and 6678 are repealed.

Act Sec. 1501(c)(2) amends Sec. 6042(c), relating to information reports for payments of dividends and corporate earnings and profits. Act Sec. 1501(c)(3) amends Sec. 6044(e), relating to information reports for patronage dividends. Act Sec. 1501(c)(5) amends Sec. 6049(c), relating to information returns for payments of interest. Act Secs. 1501(c)(2), (3), and (5) are effective for information returns due (without regard to extensions) after enactment date.

[¶1502] Increased Penalty for Failure to Pay. The new law increases in specified situations the amount of delinquency penalty imposed for a failure to either pay the tax shown or required to be shown on a taxpayer's return from .5% to 1% per month. The increased rate applies on the earlier of the IRS's notice and demand for immediate payment where collection of the tax is in jeopardy, or 10 days after a notice before levy is given.

Relief for penalty overlap eliminated. The penalty imposed for a failure to pay the tax required to be shown on a taxpayer's return will also no longer be reduced by the penalty imposed for a failure to file a return.

Effective Date: The new provisions apply to amounts assessed after December 31, 1986, whether the failure to pay began before or after that date.

Act Sec. 1502, increasing the penalty for failure to pay tax, adds new Sec. 6651(d), and deletes Sec. 6651(c)(1)(B), effective for assessments after 12-31-86.

[¶1503] Penalties for Negligence and Fraud. Under the new law, the negligence penalty now applies to an underpayment of *any* tax in the Code. The new law continues the application of the penalty to the *entire* amount of the underpayment, not just the portion attributable to negligence.

> **WATCH THIS:** In redefining negligence under the new law, *any* failure to report on a return an amount that has been reported on an information return (not just for interest and dividend payments) will now automatically be treated as negligence for purpose of the penalty, unless there's clear and convincing evidence to the contrary.

Fraud penalty rate increased. The rate at which the penalty for fraud is imposed is increased from 50% to 75%. However, the fraud penalty now applies only to the part of an underpayment that is actually attributable to fraud. Before, if there was a million dollar underpayment and even a dollar of it was attributable to fraud, the *entire* underpayment was subject to the penalty. Under the new law, if any fraud is found, the taxpayer has the burden of showing what part of an underpayment isn't attributable to fraud. The limitation period rules aren't affected—if a return is fraudulent in some respects, the limitation period on the entire return never expires.

Act Sec. 1503, relating to the fraud and negligence penalty provisions, amends Sec. 6653, effective for returns due after 12-31-86.

[¶1504] Penalty for Substantial Understatement. The new law increases the penalty for substantial understatement of tax liability from 10% to 20% of the amount of the underpayment attributable to the understatement.

Act Sec. 1504, relating to penalties for substantial understatement, amends Sec. 6661(a), effective for returns due after 12-31-86.

Interest Provisions

[¶1511] Differential Interest Rate. Prior law required taxpayers to pay interest on tax underpayments and required Treasury to pay interest on overpayments. The underpayment and overpayment rates were identical —the prime rate.

The new law pegs the overpayment rate to the Federal short-term rate plus two percentage points, and the underpayment rate to the Federal short-term rate plus three percentage points, both rounded to the nearest full percentage. The rate is adjusted quarterly, is determined during the first month of each quarter, and takes effect the following quarter. For example, the January federal short-term rate is the rate used to determine the interest to be charged on underpayments and overpayments for April, May, and June. The Secretary determines the interest rate based on average market yield on outstanding U.S. marketable obligations with remaining maturity periods of three years or less.

Treasury may prescribe regulations for netting overpayments and underpayments covering the first three years after enactment.

Act Sec. 1511, relating to interest on tax underpayments and overpayments, amends Code Sec. 6621, effective for interest for periods after 12-31-86.

[¶1512] Interest on Accumulated Earnings Tax Underpayments. The new law imposes interest on accumulated earnings tax underpayments from the return due date. Prior law imposed interest from the date IRS demands payment of the tax.

Act Sec. 1512, relating to interest on the accumulated earnings tax, amends Code Sec. 6601(b), effective for returns due (without regard to extension) after 12-31-85.

Information Reporting Provisions

[¶1521] Reporting of Real Estate Transactions. The new law expands the obligation to report the gross proceeds of sales of stock, commodities, etc., to the IRS. Starting in 1987, one of the participants in a real estate transfer also must report the sale of that real estate, including single-family homes.

Who is responsible for reporting. The responsibility for reporting sales on Forms 1099 falls on a number of participants in a descending order of responsibility. This means that the first person responsible for reporting is the real estate broker. Under this rule, "broker" is defined as the person responsible for the closing (including an attorney or a title company). In the absence of that person, the responsibility then passes to the mortgage lender, then to the seller's broker, then to the buyer's broker, and finally, any other person designated in IRS regs to be prescribed.

Sales of single-family homes. In the past, if you sold your principal residence, the only "notice" to the IRS would be your new address on Form 1040, if you failed to submit Schedule D, used when there is a taxable gain, or Form 2119, used when a home seller: (1) postpones tax on all or part of the gain by buying a replacement residence, (2) elects the over-age-55 exclusion of up to $125,000, or (3) suffers a loss, which is nondeductible.

Co-op apartments. The expanded reporting requirements apply to "real estate transactions." An apparently yet-to-be-resolved question is whether a literal reading of the law exempts sales of co-op apartments. The reason for the uncertainty is that the usual interest in a co-op is personal property; ownership is evidenced by a stock certificate that entitles the owner to occupy a certain apartment within a building and to use the common grounds.

No uncertainty, though, for condo owners. They own real estate, in the same way as owners of single-family homes.

Backup withholding. Real estate transactions are subject to the backup withholding requirements under Sec. 3406 only to the extent required by IRS regs. The Finance Committee indicated that it expects Treasury to provide guidance on how the backup withholding will work.

Act Sec. 1521(a) amends Sec. 6045, relating to returns of brokers. Act Sec. 1521(b), amends Sec. 3406(h)(5), relating to backup withholding. Act Sec. 1521 is effective, without regard to whether the IRS has issued implementing regulations, for real estate transactions closing after 12-31-86.

[¶1522] Reporting of Persons Receiving Federal Contracts. The new law requires Federal executive agencies to file information returns with the IRS on persons who receive Federal contracts, subcontracts, and licenses. A return must state the name, address and identification number of each person and whatever other information Regs may prescribe.

Act Sec. 1522(a), dealing with information reporting on persons receiving Federal contracts, adds Sec. 6050M; Act Sec. 1522(b) amends the table of sections for subpart B of part III of subchapter A of chapter 61, effective for all contracts and subcontracts entered into (and licenses granted) before, on, or after 1-1-87.

〔¶1523〕 Reporting of Royalties. The new law requires payers of royalties to file Forms 1099 on payments aggregating $10 or more in a calendar year.

Royalties required to be reported. They include payments with respect to the right to exploit natural resources, such as oil, gas, coal, timber, sand, gravel, and other mineral interests, as well as payments for the right to exploit intangible property, such as copyrights, trade names, trademarks, books and other literary compositions, musical compositions, artistic works, secret processes or formulas, and patents.

Act Sec. 1523(a) adds Sec. 6050N, relating to returns regarding payment of royalties. Act Sec. 1523(b)(1) amends Sec. 3406(b), relating to backup withholding. Act Sec. 1523(b)(2), amends Sec. 6041(a), relating to information at source. Act Sec. 1523(b)(3), amends Sec. 6676(a) and (b), relating to failure to supply identifying numbers. Act Sec. 1523(c), amends the table of sections for subpart B of part III of subchapter A of chapter 61. Act Sec. 1523 is effective for payments made after 12-31-86.

〔¶1524〕 Reporting Dependent's Taxpayer I.D.s. Beginning with all returns due on or after January 1, 1988 (without regard to extensions), any individual who claims a dependency deduction for a dependent who is 5 years old or older, must report the dependent's taxpayer I.D. number (social security number) on the individual's tax return. The penalty for failure to do so is $5 a TIN per return.

RELIGIOUS EXEMPTION: There is a special rule for religious groups that are exempt from the social security laws.

Act Sec. 1524 adds Sec. 6109(e), relating to identifying numbers, and Sec. 6676(e), relating to failure to supply identifying numbers, effective for returns due (without regard to extensions) after 12-31-87.

〔¶1525〕 Reporting Tax Exempt Interest. Beginning with returns for tax years starting after 12-31-86, taxpayers who must file a return will have to report how much tax-exempt interest they have received or accrued during the tax year.

Act Sec. 1525 adds new Sec. 6012(d), effective for tax years starting after 12-31-86.

〔¶1526〕 Separate Mailing Requirement for Certain Information Reports Eased. The new law reduces mailing costs for payors of interest, dividends, and patronage dividends who must provide copies of information returns to the recipient of the payment. The payors can do so either in person (as under prior law) or in a statement mailing by first-class mail.

Other enclosures that can accompany statement mailing. Only three kinds of enclosures, says the Senate Committee Report, can be made with a statement mailing: (1) a check, (2) a letter explaining why no check is enclosed (such as, for example, because a dividend has not been declared payable), or (3) a statement of the taxpayer's specific account with the payor (such as a year-end summary of the taxpayer's transactions with the payor).

> **NOTE:** These three kinds are in addition to the other enclosures, such as other information reports or tax forms, that the IRS previously permitted to be enclosed.

Statements on envelopes and enclosures. The statement "Important Tax Return Document Enclosed" must appear on both the outside of the envelope and each enclosure (the check, letter, or account statement).

> **WARNING:** A mailing is not considered a statement mailing if the payor encloses any other material, such as advertising, promotional material, or a quarterly or annual report. Such enclosures are impermissible because they may make it less likely that some taxpayers will recognize the importance of the information report and use it in completing their returns.

Act Sec. 1501(c)(2) amends Sec. 6042(c), relating to information reports for payments of dividends and corporate earnings and profits. Act Sec. 1501(c)(3) amends Sec. 6044(e), relating to information reports for patronage dividends. Act Sec. 1501(c)(5) amends Sec. 6049(c), relating to information returns for payments of interest. Act Secs. 1501(c)(2), (3), and (5) are effective for information returns due (without regard to extensions) after enactment date.

Tax Shelter Fees and Penalties

[¶1531]　Tax Shelter Ratio Test Tightened for Shelter Registrations. Tax shelter organizers must register certain shelters with the IRS. Prior law required registration when, among other things, the shelter ratio (the ratio of deductions and 200% of the credits to cash actually invested) was greater than 2 to 1. The new law substitutes 350% for 200% in determining the above ratio.

Act Sec. 1531 amends Sec. 6111(c)(2), relating to tax shelter ratios, effective for tax shelters in which interests are first offered for sale after 12-31-86.

[¶1532]　Increased Penalty for Not Registering Shelter. As of the enactment date, the minimum penalty for failure to register is higher. The increased penalty is the greater of 1% of the aggregate amount invested in the shelter or $500 (up from the greater of $500 or 1% (up to $10,000) of the aggregate amount invested). The prior law $10,000 cap on the penalty has been eliminated.

Act Sec. 1532 amends Sec. 6707(a)(2), relating to penalty for failure to register tax shelters, effective for tax shelters in which interests are first offered for sale after enactment date.

[¶1533] **Higher Penalty for Not Reporting Tax Shelter Registration Number.** The new law increases the penalty for a tax shelter investor who fails to include the shelter registration number on a return, unless due to reasonable cause. The increased penalty is $250 (up from $50) in the case of returns filed after enactment date.

Act Sec. 1533 amends Sec. 6707(b)(2), relating to penalty for failure to furnish tax shelter identification number, effective for returns filed after enactment date.

[¶1534] **Bigger Penalty for Not Keeping Shelter Investor List.** As of the enactment date, there is a greater maximum penalty for a shelter organizer or seller who fails to maintain a list of investors in a potentially abusive tax shelter, unless the failure is due to reasonable cause. The penalty is still $50 for each name missing from the list, but the maximum is raised to $100,000 (from $50,000) in any calendar year.

Act Sec. 1534 amends Sec. 6708(a), relating to failure to maintain list of investors in potentially abusive tax shelters, effective for failures occurring or continuing after enactment date.

[¶1535] **Interest on Substantial Underpayments Attributable to Shelters.** Under the new law, the rate of interest imposed on underpayments of tax of more than $1,000 that are attributable to sham or fraudulent transactions (and tax-motivated transactions, as already provided by prior law) is 120% of the generally applicable interest rate.

Act Sec. 1535 amends Sec. 6621(c), relating to interest on substantial underpayments attributable to tax-motivated transactions, effective for interest accruing after 12-31-84 (but not on underpayments with respect to which there was a final court decision before enactment date).

Estimated Taxes

[¶1541] **Individual Estimated Tax Payments.** The new law increases from 80% to 90% the proportion of the current year's tax liability that an individual taxpayer must make as estimated tax payments to avoid the penalty for underpayment of estimated tax. Under this rule, quarterly estimated tax installments must be 22.5%, 45%, 67.5%, and 90% of the year's tax liability (up from 20%, 40%, 60%, and 80%). Under the new law, estimated tax payments based on 90% of actual tax liability for the current year, or on 100% of last year's tax, *whichever is less,* avoid the penalty for underpayment of estimated tax.

Act Sec. 1541, relating to estimated tax payments by individuals, amends Secs. 6654(d)(1)(B)(i), 6654(d)(2)(C)(ii), 6654(i)(1)(C); 6654(j)(3)(B), effective for taxable years beginning after 12-31-86.

[¶1542] Private Foundation's Investment Income Excise Tax. The new law requires private foundations to make quarterly estimated payments of the excise tax on investment income. These payments are to be made in the same manner as regular corporate estimated income taxes.

Act Sec. 1542 adds Sec. 6154(h), effective for taxable years beginning after 12-31-86.

[¶1543] Unrelated Business Income Tax. Tax-exempt organizations must make quarterly payments of estimated tax for the unrelated business income tax. Payments are to be made in the same manner as regular corporate estimated income taxes.

Act Sec. 1542 adds Sec. 6154(h), effective for taxable years beginning after 12-31-86.

[¶1544] Waiver of 1986 Estimated Tax Penalties. To cover the many changes that increase tax liabilities from the beginning of 1986, the new law allows individual taxpayers until 4-15-87, and corporations until 3-15-87 (the final filing dates for calendar year returns) to pay their full 1986 income tax liabilities without a penalty of underpayments of estimated tax to the extent that the underpayments are attributable to changes made by the new law.

Act Sec. 1543, relating to waiver of estimated tax penalties, effective as noted above.

Tax Court and Tax Cases

[¶1551] Attorney Fees. The new law extends permanently the provisions authorizing awards of reasonable attorney's fees in tax cases. Also, it eliminates the previous $25,000 cap on such awards, and substitutes a $75 an hour limitation, unless the court determines that a higher rate is justified and expert witnesses are to be compensated under prevailing market rates, but no higher than the highest rate of compensation for expert witnesses paid by the U.S. In addition, the new law authorizes funding of attorneys' fee awards from the same source as non-tax cases. The present-law burden of proof is unchanged.

Effective Date. The new law applies to amounts paid after September 30, 1986, in civil actions or proceedings commenced after December 31, 1985. The provision relating to funding of fees applies to actions begun after February 28, 1983.

Act Sec. 1551, relating to attorney fees, amends Sec. 7430, effective as shown above.

[¶1552] Exhaustion of Administrative Remedies. The new law provides that failure to exhaust administrative remedies is an additional basis for the imposition of the discretionary penalty by the Tax Court.

Act Sec. 1552, dealing with administrative remedies, amends Sec. 6673, effective for proceedings commenced after enactment date.

[¶1553] Tax Court Inventory. The Tax Court and the IRS are now required to report to Congress, every two years beginning with 1987, on Tax Court case inventory and measures taken to close cases more efficiently.

Act Sec. 1552(c), relating to the Tax Court inventory report, is effective for 1987 and each 2-calendar year period thereafter.

[¶1554] Tax Court Periodic Practice Fees. The new law authorizes the Tax Court to impose a periodic registration fee on practitioners admitted to practice before it. The Tax Court is to establish the amount of the fee and the frequency of its collection, but the fee may not exceed $30 per year.

Act Sec. 1553, relating to practice fees, adds Sec. 7475 and is effective 1-1-87.

[¶1555] Jurisdiction Over Late Payment Penalty. The new law provides that the Tax Court has jurisdiction over the penalty for failure to pay an amount shown on the return if the Tax Court already has jurisdiction to redetermine a deficiency on that return.

Effective Date. The new law is effective for any action or proceeding before the Tax Court which has not become final before the date of enactment.

Act Sec. 1554, relating to determinations by the Tax Court, amends Sec. 6214, effective as shown above.

[¶1556] Attendance by United States Marshals. The new law provides that the U.S. Marshal for any district in which the Tax Court sits must attend any session of the Tax Court when requested to do so by the Chief Judge.

Act Sec. 1555, relating to attendance by U.S. Marshals, amends Sec. 7456, and is effective on the date of enactment.

[¶1557] Provisions Relating to Special Trial Judges. The new law consolidates into new Sec. 7443A of the Code a number of provisions relating to Special Trial Judges. It specifies that Special

Trial Judges are to be paid 90% of the salary paid to Tax Court Judges, and that Special Trial Judges are to be reimbursed for travel and subsistence expenses to the same extent as are Tax Court Judges.

Effective Date: Generally the new law will be effective on the date of enactment. The provision relating to the salary of Special Trial Judges is effective on the first day of the first month beginning after the date of enactment.

Act Sec. 1556, relating to Special Trial Judges, adds new Sec. 7443A, and is effective as shown above.

[¶1558] Retirement Pay of Tax Court Judges. The new law permits Tax Court judges meeting specified age and tenure requirements to elect to retire, practice law after retirement, and receive retirement pay.

Act Sec. 1557, relating to retirement pay of Tax Court Judges, amends Secs. 7447 and 7448, generally effective on the date of enactment.

[¶1559] Interlocutory Appeals and Survivor's Annuities. Under the new law, an appeal from an interlocutory order of the Tax Court is authorized if a Tax Court judge includes in an interlocutory order a statement that a controlling question of law is involved, that there is substantial ground for difference of opinion regarding it, and that an immediate appeal from the order might materially advance the ultimate termination of the litigation.

The Court of Appeals is given discretion as to whether to permit the appeal. Neither the application for nor the granting of an appeal stays proceedings in the Tax Court, unless a stay is ordered by either the Tax Court or the Court of Appeals.

Also under the new law, the survivors annuity provisions covering Tax Court Judges are conformed to those applicable to other Federal judges. This provision is generally effective on November 1, 1986.

Act Sec. 1558, relating to appeals from interlocutory orders of the Tax Court, adds Sec. 7842(a)(2), effective for Tax Court orders entered after enactment date.

Act Sec. 1559, relating to annuities for surviving spouses and dependent children of Tax Court Judges, amends Sec. 7448, generally effective 11-1-86.

IRS Administrative Provisions

[¶1561] Third Party Recordkeeping Disputes—Limitations. For disputes between a third-party recordkeeper and the IRS that are not resolved within six months after the IRS issues an administrative summons, the statute of limitations on assessments and collection is suspended until the issue is resolved. The issue isn't resolved while an action to compel the production of documents is pending. The third party recordkeeper must notify a John Doe taxpayer (unidentified in the summons) whose records are the subject of the dispute that the statute of limitations has been suspended. The statute is suspended whether or not the third party gives notice.

As under prior law, the statute is suspended from the date a taxpayer intervenes in a dispute between the IRS and a third-party recordkeeper until the dispute is resolved.

Act Sec. 1561 amends Sec. 7609(e) and (i), relating to suspension of the statute of limitations for third-party recordkeepers, effective on enactment date.

[¶1562] Authority to Rescind Notice of Deficiency With Taxpayer's Consent. Under prior law, an IRS 90-day letter could not be withdrawn once this statutory notice of deficiency had been issued. Under the new law, it can be withdrawn if the IRS and taxpayer both agree to have it withdrawn.

Act Sec. 1562, relating to the authority to rescind a deficiency notice, adds new Sec. 6212(d), effective for deficiency notices issued on or after 1-1-86.

[¶1563] IRS Can Abate Interest Due to Its Own Errors or Delays. The new law gives the IRS the authority to abate interest that is generated because an IRS official either fails to perform a ministerial act in a timely fashion or errs in performing a ministerial act, provided the taxpayer is not at least significantly responsible for the delay. Although the IRS is authorized to abate interest, it is not required to do so, except in cases of erroneous refunds of up to $50,000.

This provision is not intended to be used routinely, but is to be used in cases where failure to abate would be perceived as grossly unfair. Interest is to be abated only for the time attributable to the failure to perform the ministerial act that occurs after the IRS contacts the taxpayer. Only those acts occurring after preliminary prerequisites, such as conferencing and supervisory review, would be considered ministerial acts for this purpose.

> **Example:** If there's an unreasonable delay in issuing a 90-day letter (deficiency notice) after the IRS and the taxpayer have completed efforts to resolve the matter, there would be grounds for interest abatement. The IRS can issue regulations that provide guidance as to what will be considered timely performance of ministerial acts, and define ministerial acts.

Generally, the IRS cannot charge interest on refunds made because of IRS error, until the date it demands repayment. For instance, a taxpayer who gets a $1,000 refund, rather than the $100 refund he rightfully claimed, because of an IRS error will not be charged interest on the excess $900 until the date repayment is claimed. But there are two exceptions to the no-interest-on-refund-rule. A taxpayer will be charged interest on an erroneous refund, if:

- the taxpayer (or a related party) has in any way caused the overstated refund to occur, or
- the erroneous refund exceeds $50,000.

Act Sec. 1563, relating to IRS abatement of interest, adds new Sec. 6404(e), effective for interest accruing in tax years beginning after 12-31-78.

[¶1564] **Interest and Compounding Halted on Suspended Deficiency.** The new law suspends both the interest on a tax (income, estate, gift, and certain excise taxes) deficiency and the compounding of interest on previously accrued interest. The suspension starts 31 days after the taxpayer has filed a waiver of restrictions on assessment of the underlying taxes and ends when a notice and demand is issued to the taxpayer.

Act Sec. 1564, relating to the suspension of compounding where interest on the deficiency is suspended, amends Code Sec. 6601(c), effective for interest accruing after 12-31-82.

[¶1565] **No Levy on Certain Military Disability Payments.** Under prior law, various payments, including unemployment benefits, workmen's compensation, a portion of ordinary wages, and certain pensions and annuities, are exempt from levy (the IRS cannot seize these assets in payment of delinquent taxes). The new law adds various military service-connected disability payments to this list of exempt items. Direct compensation payments are included, as well as other support payments for education and housing.

Act Sec. 1565, relating to certain service-connected disability payments exempt from levy, amends Code Sec. 6334(a), effective for payments made after 12-31-86.

[¶1566] **IRS Seizure and Administrative Sale Increased to $100,000.** Prior law allowed the IRS to seize property used in violating the tax law, and to sell personal property valued at $2,500 or less using administrative rather than judicial action, after having the property appraised and after giving notice to potential claimants. A claimant could post a $250 bond and require the government to proceed to sell the property by judicial action.

The new law allows the Treasury to administratively sell up to $100,000 of personal property. An appraisal would be necessary. Notice to potential claimants would have to be published in a newspaper. Potential claimants can require a judicial forfeiture action by posting a $2,500 bond.

Act Sec. 1566, relating to an increase in value of personal property subject to certain listing and notice procedures, amends Code Sec. 7325, effective on date of enactment.

[¶1567] IRS Special Agent's T&E Recordkeeping. Law enforcement officers generally are not subject to the Sec. 274(d) substantiation rules and the Sec. 132 income and wage inclusion rules for specified use of a law enforcement vehicle. Under prior law, IRS special agents were not classified as "law enforcement officers" for this purpose. Under the new law, they are considered law enforcement officers.

Act Sec. 1567, relating to automobile recordkeeping requirements for federal law enforcement officers, clarifies the applicability of Secs. 132 and 274, effective 1-1-85.

[¶1568] Disclosure of Returns and Return Information To Certain Cities. Cities having populations of over 2 million (determined on the basis of the most recent available decennial U.S. census data) that impose an income or wage tax may, at the Treasury Secretary's option, get returns and return information for the same purposes for which states get it. Cities must reimburse the IRS for this information. The disclosure and safeguard rules that apply to states also apply to cities, as do the state requirements for maintaining a system of standardized information requests, the reasons for the request, and the strict security against information release. The law permits disclosure only for the local jurisdiction's tax administration. Disclosure of returns or return information to an elected official or to the chief official of the local jurisdiction is forbidden. Unauthorized disclosure by an employee of an agency receiving this information will subject the employee to fine and imprisonment as provided by Sec. 7213 and to the civil action provided by Sec. 7431.

Act Sec. 1568, relating to disclosure of returns and return information to certain cities, amends Sec. 6103(b), effective on enactment date.

[¶1569] Priority of Local Law in Certain Forfeitures. The new law provides that a forfeiture under local law of property seized by a law enforcement agency of either a State or a political subdivision of a State relates back to the time of seizure. The provision does not apply to the extent that local law provides that someone other than the governmental unit has priority over the governmental unit in the property. For purposes of this provision, a State or local tax agency is not considered to be a law enforcement agency.

Act Sec. 1569, relating to the treatment of certain forfeitures, adds new Sec. 6323(i)(3), effective on enactment date.

[¶1570] Release of Certain Seized Property to Owner. Under the new law, before the sale of the seized property of a delinquent taxpayer, the IRS must determine (based upon criteria prescribed by the Treasury) whether the purchase of the property at the minimum price is in the best interests of the federal government. Property would continue to be sold to the highest bidder who meets or exceeds the minimum price.

If no bid meets or exceeds the minimum price, the government would buy the property at the minimum price only if in its best interests. If not in the best interests of the government, the property would be released back to the owner. The property would still be subject to a government lien. Also, any expense of the levy and sale would be added to the amount of delinquent taxes due.

Act Sec. 1570, relating to manner and conditions of sale of seized property, amends Sec. 6335(e)(1), effective for property seized after enactment date and for property seized on or before enactment date, if held by U.S. on such date.

[¶1571] Allocation of Employee Tips. Prior law required employers to provide an information report of an allocation of tips in large food or beverage establishments. The regs provide two ways to make this allocation. One is to allocate based on the portion of gross receipts of the establishment attributable to the employee during a payroll period. The second is to allocate based on the portion of the total number of hours worked in the establishment attributable to the employee during a payroll period.

Under the new law, the method of allocation based on the number of hours worked may be used only by an establishment that employs less than the equivalent of 25 full-time employees during a payroll period. Establishments employing the equivalent of 25 or more full-time employees would have to use the portion-of-gross-receipts-method to allocate tips during the payroll period (without an agreement between the employer and employees).

Act Sec. 1571, relating to modification of tips allocation method under Reg. §31.6053-3(f)(1)(iv), is effective for payroll periods beginning after 12-31-86.

[¶1572] Treatment of Forfeitures of Land Sales Contracts. Generally, before Federal tax liens can be extinguished, notice must be given to the Government. The new law provides that forfeitures of land sales contracts are subject to these notification requirements, effective for forfeitures after the thirtieth day after the day of enactment. The effect of this provision is to provide the Government with both notice and the opportunity to redeem the property, which it currently has with respect to most other transfers of real estate.

Act Sec. 1572, relating to treatment of forfeitures of land sales contracts, adds new Sec. 7425(c)(4), effective as noted above.

[¶1581] **Withholding Schedules To Mesh With Actual Liability.** The new law also requires the IRS to make changes in Form W-4 and the withholding tables used by employers. Reason for the changes: To have the amount withheld from an employee's wages more closely match the employee's actual tax liability under the amendments made by the new law.

All employees must file revised W-4 Forms by 9-30-87. If an employee fails to do so, an employer must withhold income taxes as if the employee claimed one allowance (if the employee checked the "Single" box on the most recent Form W-4 that the employee filed) or two allowances (if the employee checked the "Married" box).

The new law also repeals the prior authority of the IRS to issue regs that permit employees to request decreases in withholding.

Act Sec. 1572(a) [Ed. Note: This Act Section is misnumbered in Committee Bill and is subject to technical correction.]requires modification of withholding schedules, as stated above. Act Sec. 1572(b) amends Sec. 3402(i), relating to certain decreases in withholding not permitted, effective on enactment date. Act Sec. 1572(c), relating to employees filing new Forms W-4, effective for wages paid after 9-30-87.

[¶1582] **Report on Return-Free System.** The new law directs the IRS to report to Congress on the possibility of a return-free system for individuals. The IRS must report its findings within six months after the date of enactment of the new law.

Act Sec. 1572 [Ed. Note: This Act Section is misnumbered in Committee Bill and is subject to technical correction], effective as indicated above.

[The page following this is 1601.]

EXEMPT AND NONPROFIT ORGANIZATIONS

[¶1601] **Exchange of Membership Lists.** The new law adds another item to the list of activities that won't be considered an unrelated trade or business of an organization otherwise tax exempt under Section 501. Any trade or business of such an organization that consists of exchanging or renting lists of donors to or members of the organization won't be considered "unrelated." This overrules *Disabled American Veterans v. U.S.* [(Ct. Cl., 1981), 650 F. 2d 1128, 48 AFTR 2d 81-5047], which held otherwise.

Act Sec. 1601, adding a UBI exemption, adds new Sec. 513(h)(1), effective for exchanges and rental of membership lists after the date of enactment.

[¶1602] **Distribution of Low Cost Items.** The term "unrelated trade or business" of a tax-exempt organization won't include activities relating to the distribution of low cost items incidental to soliciting contributions. An article is considered low cost if all items distributed to a single taxpayer cost, in the aggregate, not more than $5. Note that the $5 will be indexed after 1987.

A distribution will be considered incidental to soliciting charitable contributions if (1) the recipient didn't request the distribution, (2) the distribution is made without the express consent of the recipient, and (3) the article is accompanied by a request for a donation and a statement that the recipient can keep the low cost item regardless of whether a donation is made.

Act Sec. 1601, adding a UBI exemption, adds new Secs. 513(h)(2) and (3), effective for distributions of low cost articles after the date of enactment.

[¶1603] **Trade Show UBI Exemption Expanded.** The new law excludes from the definition of an "unrelated trade or business," trade show activities of Section 501(c)(3) organizations (charitable organizations such as churches and schools) and Section 501(c)(4) organizations (civic leagues, social welfare organizations). Previously, the exclusion was limited to Section 501(c)(5) organizations (labor or agricultural organizations) and Section 501(c)(6) organizations (business leagues and chambers of commerce). The exclusion applies to trade shows or conventions at which suppliers of the organization educate attendees on new developments or products related to the organization's exempt activities.

Act Sec. 1602, relating to the UBI exemption, amends Sec. 513(d)(3), effective for activities in taxable years beginning after the enactment date.

[¶1604] **Tax Exemption for Certain Title Holding Companies.** The new law creates a new type of tax-exempt organization—a corporation or trust that is organized for the exclusive purpose of acquiring, holding title to, and collecting income from real property and remitting it to certain tax-exempt organizations that are shareholders or beneficiaries. The organization can have no more than 35 shareholders or beneficiaries and only one class of stock or beneficial interest.

The new law limits participation in the trust or corporation to certain qualified plans, government entities, and Section 501(c)(3) organizations. In addition, the shareholders or beneficiaries have certain powers to dismiss the investment adviser and to terminate their interests.

NOTE: The new law also allows the organization to use the exception to the tax on unrelated business income under the Section 514 debt-financing rules for real property.

Act Sec. 1603, relating to tax-exempt title holding companies, adds new Sec. 501(c)(25) and amends Sec. 514(c)(9), effective for taxable years beginning after 12-31-86.

[¶1605] Membership Organization Deduction Rules. The new law creates an exception to the general rule that a membership organization can deduct expenses for furnishing goods and services to members only from income derived from transactions with members. The exception applies to membership organizations engaged primarily in the gathering and distribution of news to their members for publication. According to the Senate report, the exception applies to the Associated Press.

Act Sec. 1604, relating to membership organizations, amends Sec. 277(b), effective on the date of enactment.

[¶1606] Technological Transfer Organization Tax Exemption. The new law creates a tax exemption for a certain organization that transfers technology from universities and scientific research organizations to the private sector. Among the requirements is that the organization was incorporated on July 20, 1981. The only organization this seems to apply to is the Washington Research Foundation. This provision overrules the Tax Court decision in *Washington Research Foundation* [P-H Memo TC ¶85,570].

Act Sec. 1605, creating a tax exemption is effective on the date of enactment.

[¶1607] Definition of Government Official. The new law raises the compensation limit for determining who is a government official in the definition "disqualified person" under the self-dealing rules. That term now includes officials in the executive, legislative, or judicial branch of a state, possession, local government, or District of Columbia with compensation of $20,000 or more. The limit had been $15,000.

Act Sec. 1606, defining government officials amends Sec. 4946(c), for compensation received after 12-31-85.

【¶1608】 Acquisition Debt Exception. Under the new law, the Section 514(c) acquisition indebtdness rule doesn't apply to certain debts incurred with bonds to acquire land for a community college in 1984 and which will be sold in 1986 or 1987.

Act Sec. 1607, relating to acquisition indebtedness, creates an exception for a sale by a certain community college.

【¶1609】 Amounts Paid for Special Seating. The new law allows taxpayers a charitable deduction for contributions incurred for renovating a certain college football stadium merely because the taxpayer receives the right to buy special seating in the stadium.

Act Sec. 1608 creates an exception for football fans of a certain university for amounts paid in taxable years beginning after 12-31-83.

[The page following this is 1701.]

OTHER PROVISIONS

[¶1701] Jobs Credit Modified and Extended. The new law extends the targeted jobs credit for three years so that it applies to wages paid individuals who begin work before January 1, 1989.

Now the bad news. The credit for first-year wages paid is reduced to 40% (from 50%) of the first $6,000 of qualified wages. The 25% credit for the first $6,000 of wages paid in an individuals second year of employment is repealed. Also, no wages paid to a targeted group member will be taken into account if the individual (1) is employed by the employer less than 90 days (14 days for economically disadvantaged summer youth employees) or (2) has completed less than 120 hours of work (20 hours for summer employees).

The new law also extends the authorization for appropriations through fiscal year 1988.

Act Sec. 1701, modifying the targeted jobs credit, amends Secs. 51(a), (b), (c), (d) and (i) and ERTA Sec. 261(f)(2), for individuals beginning work after 12-31-85 and before 1-1-89.

[¶1702] Collection of Diesel Fuel Excise Tax. The new law authorizes certain qualified retailers to elect imposition of the 15¢ a gallon excise tax on the sale of diesel fuel used in highway vehicles on the wholesaler (rather than the retailer) of the fuel. It will be imposed on the manufacturer when the sale is directly to the retailer.

The retailer is required to notify the seller in writing of the election. Failure to notify will result in the retailer being liable for the tax and will result in the imposition of a penalty of 5% of the tax involved.

Act Sec. 1702(a) amends Sec. 4041(n), relating to imposition of tax on special fuels; Act Sec. 1702(b) amends Sec. 6652, relating to failure to file certain information returns, registration statements, etc., effective for sales after the first calendar quarter beginning more than 60 days after the date of enactment.

[¶1703] Social Security Coverage for Clergy. The new law makes two changes for clergy with respect to Social Security coverage. First, the rules under which Treasury can grant an exemption from coverage have been clarified.

Second, the new law establishes a window under which a previous exemption can be revoked. The application for revocation must be filed no later than the due date of the first income tax return for the first taxable year beginning after the date of enactment but before the applicant becomes entitled to benefits. However, once revoked, the clergyman can't again seek an exemption.

Act Sec. 1704(a), granting exemptions, amends Sec. 1402(e), effective for applications filed 12-31-86. Act Sec. 1704(b), permitting revocations, is effective, generally, for service performed in taxable years ending on or after the enactment date.

[¶1704]   Indian Tribe FUTA Liability Cleared.   The new law relieves two Indian tribes of Federal Unemployment Tax owed by each for services performed before 1988 and during a period they weren't covered by a state unemployment compensation program, if they weren't covered by state unemployment coverage on June 11, 1986.

Act Sec. 1705 relieves two Indian tribes of FUTA liability for work performed before 1-1-88.

[¶1705]   Technical Service Personnel.   Under the new law, individuals retained to provide services as engineers, designers, drafters, computer programmers, systems analysts, and other similarly skilled personnel for a technical services firm to its clients are to be considered employees of the firm for purposes of withholding income and employment taxes. Such status can't be avoided if the employee later incorporates and claims to be an employee of the corporation.

Act Sec. 1705, relating to technical service employees, amends Sec. 530 of the '78 Revenue Act, effective for services rendered after 12-31-86.

[¶1706]   Gasoline Excise Tax.   The new law applies the 9¢ a gallon gasoline excise tax on the earlier of removal or sale of the gasoline by the refiner or importer, or the terminal operator (if a bulk transfer). The 9¢ a gallon tax will also apply to gasoline removed or sold by a blender or compounder, subject to a credit for tax paid and collected by the refiner or importer. The tax will be reduced to 3¢ a gallon for registered-gasohol producers who blend at the terminal (defining gasohol as gasoline that's at least 10% alcohol). Gasoline later separated from gasohol is taxable at 5⅔¢ a gallon.

> **NOTE:** Every person subject to the excise tax must register with the Treasury before incurring any liability.

Blenders can claim a credit for tax paid on purchases of gasoline to the extent the blended gasoline isn't used as fuel. The buyer may get a refund on establishing that the ultimate use isn't as a taxable fuel. A special accelerated refund procedure is provided for gasohol blenders who buy tax paids.

The new law also establishes a floor stock tax for gasoline subject to the tax held by a dealer for sale on 1-1-88, but which was not previously taxed, of 9¢ a gallon. Special rules apply for obtaining a refund of such taxes if the dealer is entitled to such refund under Section 6416.

Finally, Treasury is given fairly broad regulatory authority and is directed to study gasoline tax evasion (and report by 12-31-86).

Effective Date: The gasoline excise tax applies to gasoline removed after 12-31-87. The sales taxes on gasoline are scheduled to expire after 9-30-88; however, according to the statute, the 3¢ tax on gasohol producers will continue to apply to sales until 1-1-92.

Act Sec. 1703 relating to the gasoline excise tax amends Secs. 4081-4083, 4101, 6421 and 6427, effective 1-1-88 and as shown above.

[¶1707] **Exclusion for Certain Foster Care Payments.** Under prior law, a foster parent could exclude from income amounts paid as reimbursements from an appropriate governmental authority for the cost of caring for a qualified foster child in the taxpayer's home. To get the exclusion, the taxpayer had to account for the expenses. Any excess reimbursement would have to be included in income.

The new law makes two changes to the rules. First, the exclusion will apply to certain payments made for the cost of care for a qualifying foster adult. A qualifying individual is a person placed by appropriate state agencies. However, no exclusion can be claimed for more the five individuals over the age of 18 (as opposed to 10 children). Second, the new law gets rid of the accounting requirement by extending the exclusion to all amounts received by the foster parent, for care of the foster child, not just reimbursements.

Act Sec. 1707(a), extending the foster care exclusion, and Act Sec. 1707(b), dealing with payments, amend Sec. 131 effective for taxable years beginning after 12-31-85.

[¶1708] **Extension of Rules for Spouses of Vietnam MIAs.** The new law reinstates retroactively four tax relief provisions that apply to families of members of the U.S. Armed Forces missing in Vietnam. The provisions, which expired on December 31, 1982, will apply to all taxable years beginning after that date. The four provisions do the following:

(1) For defining a surviving spouse (for filing status purposes), the date of death of an MIA is the date on which the determination of death is made.

(2) The income of an MIA who died in MIA status is exempt from income tax for the year in which the determination of death is made and any prior year that ends after the first day the MIA served in a combat zone.

(3) The spouse of a person in MIA status can elect to file a joint return.

(4) The rules under Section 7508(a) postponing the performing if certain acts by reason of service in a combat zone, apply to spouses of MIAs. Those acts include filing returns and paying taxes.

Act Sec. 1708(a), extending the rules for MIAs, amends Secs. 2(a)(3)(B), 692(b), 6013(f)(1), and 7508(b), effective for taxable years beginning after 12-31-82.

[¶1709] **Native Alaskan Income from Reindeer Tax Exempt.** The new law exempts from tax, income from the sale of reindeer held in trust by the government for native Alaskans under the 1937 Reindeer Industry Act.

Act Sec. 1709, relating to the reindeer industry, amends Sec. 8 of the 1937 Reindeer Industry Act as if included in that law.

[¶1710] **AFDC/Medicaid Quality Control Study.** Under the new law, the study by Health and Human Services and the National Academy of Sciences on the federal quality control system, originally due within 18 months after the enactment of the 1985 Consolidated Omnibus Budget Reconciliation Acts is now due one year after a contract is entered into for the studies.

Act Sec. 1710, relating to quality control studies, amends Sec. 12301 of the '85 Consolidated Omnibus Budget Reconciliation Act.

[¶1711] **Adoption Assistance Program Expanded.** The new law repeals the itemized deduction for adoption expenses for children with special needs. In its place, is an expanded Adoption Assistance Program of Title IV-E of the Social Security Act.

The program will provide 50% federal matching funds to states to pay "nonrecurring adoption expenses" for the adoption of a special needs child. Such expenses include adoption fees, court costs, attorneys fees, and other expenses directly related to legal adoption of a special needs child which aren't incurred in violation of state or federal law.

Act Sec. 1711, relating to adoption assistance, amends Social Security Act Secs. 471(a), 473(a), and 475(3), effective for expenditures after 12-31-86.

[The page following this is 1801.]

TECHNICAL CORRECTIONS

[¶1800] Overview. The Technical Corrections Title (Title XVIII) of the new law mostly contains technical, clarifying, conforming, and clerical amendments to the rules enacted by the 1984 Tax Reform Act ('84 TRA), the 1984 Retirement Equity Act (REA), and other recent legislation. Many of these amendments have a far-reaching substantive effect, and are in the nature of significant new law changes. They are generally effective as if included in the original provisions of the legislation to which they relate, and are thus often retroactive. These law changes also include transitional and special rules that cover specific taxpayers.

The Technical Corrections provisions are treated as enacted immediately before the provisions of other Titles of the new law. They would be, therefore, normally treated as supplanted or varied by any conflicting or varying law changes made by the other Titles (as of the effective date of these law changes), under the general rules for interpreting legislation.

Amendments to the Tax Reform Act of 1984

[¶1801] Finance Lease Rules. In 1982, TEFRA liberalized the determination of whether a transaction is a lease for limited-use property and fixed price purchase options. The effective date of these "finance lease" rules (originally scheduled to generally cover agreements made after 1983) was postponed by the '84 TRA to cover agreements made after 1987. The new law allows an election, under regs to be issued, to have this postponement apply to pre-3-7-84 acquisitions, construction starts, or binding contracts, even though a transitional rule excepts such property from the postponement.

The new law also allows the postponement for specified farm finance lease agreements, which relate to property allocable to persons other than C corporations that became partners or beneficiaries of partnership-or-grantor-trust-lessors before 9-26-85.

Act Sec. 1801(a)(1) relating to the election to postpone finance lease rules amends Sec. 12(c)(1) of the '84 TRA effective as if included in that provision. Act Sec. 1801(a)(2) relating to farm finance leases doesn't amend the Code.

[¶1802] Telephone Excise Extension Clerical Omission Corrected. The 3% telephone excise tax now applies by statute to bills first rendered in 1983-87. The new law restores "1985" to the text of the law.

Act Sec. 1801(b) amends Sec. 4251(b)(2), effective as if included in the '84 Tax Reform Act.

[¶1803] **Alcohol and Tobacco Taxes, Electronic Fund Transfers.** The new law clarifies that all members of a controlled group of corporations (defined the same as in Sec. 1563 but with a 50% (rather than 80%) common ownership test) are treated as one person for the electronic transfer requirements. The Treasury can apply this to a common-controlled group, including its noncorporate members. It's understood that these rules will be administratively applied only to taxes due after 3-28-85.

Distilled spirits in foreign trade zone on 10-1-85. The new law clarifies that distilled spirits held in a foreign trade zone on 10-1-85 and entered into U.S. customs territory after that date are subject to the $2 per proof gallon floor stocks tax imposed under the '84 TRA, despite provisions of 19 USC Sec. 81a, et seq. or other laws.

Act Sec. 1801(c)(1) and (2) relating to electronic fund transfers adds Secs. 5061(e)(3) and 5703(b)(3), effective generally for taxes paid after 9-30-84. Act Sec. 1801(c)(3) relating to foreign trade zones adds Sec. 27(b)(7)(F) of the '84 Tax Reform Act.

[¶1804] **Tax-Exempt Entity Leasing Rules Clarified.** Generally for property placed in service after 5-23-83, the '84 TRA sharply curtailed the exploitation of the benefits of ACRS depreciation and the investment credit for "tax-exempt use property" by "tax-exempt entities." The new law clarifies and amends these rules, as well as the special rules connected with them that are engrafted into the investment credit rules, and the treatment of transactions structured as service contracts.

19-year realty used in an unrelated trade or business. For 19-year realty, only the part used under a "disqualifying lease" is tax-exempt use property, and only if over 35% of the property is so leased. The new law clarifies that the part of 19-year realty that's used under an over-20-year lease (treated as a disqualifying lease) in an unrelated trade or business of the tax exempt entity isn't considered as used under a disqualifying lease (including for the 35% threshold).

Scope of tax-exempt entity rules expanded. The term "tax-exempt entity" can include certain previously tax-exempt organizations (Sec. 168(j)(4)(E)). The new law clarifies that the rules for these organizations cover any property (other than property owned by the former tax-exempt or its successor), rather than only property leased to the organization. The organization must have been tax-exempt at any time during the five-year period ending when the property was first used by the former tax-exempt (i.e., when it was first placed in service under a lease to it, or is treated under the new law as used by it by virtue of membership in a pass-through entity that leases or owns it).

For property owned by partnerships and other pass-through entities (Sec. 168(j)(9)), the new law treats a "tax-exempt controlled entity" (generally defined as a taxable corporation "owned" at least 50% by value by tax exempt entities) as a tax-exempt entity or its successor. Alternatively, such a subsidiary organization can make an irrevocable election binding its tax-exempt entity owners to have them treat gain recognized on a disposition of an interest in it, and dividends allocable to its nontaxable income and interest that is received or accrued from it, as unrelated business taxable income. Unless earlier application is elected, these rules generally apply to property placed in service after 9-27-85 except for property acquired under a binding written contract in effect on 9-27-85. The new law also clarifies that the Federal Home Loan Mortgage Corporation isn't a tax-exempt entity.

Other tax-exempt lease rules. The new law repeals IRS authority to determine if high technology telephone station or medical equipment is subject to rapid obsolescence. And it clarifies that the determination whether a tax-exempt partner's share of partnership items is treated as derived from an unrelated trade or business is made without regard to the unrelated debt-financed income rules of Sec. 514.

Investment credit and tax-exempt leasing rules. The new law clarifies that any part of property that's treated as "tax-exempt use property" under rules governing property leased to or owned by partnerships (Sec. 168(j)(8) or (9)), is ineligible for the investment credit under rules governing property used by certain tax exempts or by government units or foreign persons or entities (Sec. 48(a)(4), (5)). It applies rules similar to the tax-exempt use property partnership rules to investment credits on property leased to thrift institutions (Sec. 46(e)(4)), and clarifies that the credit for rehabilitation expenditures on buildings leased to thrifts is to be governed by rules for buildings leased to tax exempt entities. And it clarifies that (1) the Sec. 47(a)(7) short-term lease exception from investment credit recapture rules for aircraft under specified pre-1990 leases of up to three years for use predominantly outside the U.S. doesn't cause the aircraft to cease being Sec. 38 property until total use under such a lease exceeds three years, and (2) such use extends the general recapture period.

Service contracts treated as leases of property. The tax-exempt leasing definition of "related entity" is added through a reference to the Sec. 7701(e) rules dealing with arrangements structured as service contracts.

Effective Dates: The new law makes the following clarifications to the tax exempt leasing rules of the 1984 law. The new law (1)

Clarifies that the exception for property acquired (or covered by a binding contract) before 10-22-83 relates only to treatment of property owned by partnerships (Sec. 168(j)(9)). (2) Clarifies that the exception for certain aircraft used by a foreign person or entity applies only to aircraft originally placed in service after 5-23-83 (and before 1-1-86). (3) Amends the exception relating to pre-5-23-84 government action by making a special rule for certain credit unions and for other specific situations. (4) Broadens the "substantial improvement" exception to the rule that improvements qualify for transitional relief, to clarify that it applies to real property, and to personal property not covered by pre-3-29-85 binding contracts or started construction. (5) Among provisions affecting specific situations, clarifies the exception relating to Clemson University, and Pennsylvania Railroad Station in Newark, New Jersey.

Act Sec. 1802(a)(1) relating to 19-year realty amends Sec. 168(j)(3)(D). Act Sec. 1802(a)(2) relating to the definition of tax exempt entity rules amends Sec. 168(j)(4)(E) and(j)(9). Act Sec. 1802(a)(3) relating to high technology items amends Sec. 168(j)(5)(C). Act Secs. 1802(a)(4)—(8) relating to tax-exempt partners' shares and investment credit rules amends Sec. 168(j)(8) and (9), Sec. 46(e)(4) and Sec. 48(a)(5), and adds Sec. 47(a)(9). Act Sec. 1802(a)(9) relating to service contracts amends Sec. 7701(e)(4). Act Sec. 1802(a)(10) relating to effective date rules amends 1984 Tax Reform Act Sec. 31(g)(3), (15)(D), (4), (17)(H), (20)(B). These changes and certain clerical amendments made are effective as if included in the 1984 Tax Reform Act and as noted above.

[¶1805] **Changes in Treatment of Debt Instruments.** The new law changes in this area involve original issue discount, market discount, imputed interest, and amortization of bond premium.

Short-term nongovernmental and government obligations. Based on longstanding judicial authority and regs, the new law expressly treats gain realized on post-1984 dispositions of short-term nongovernment obligations as ordinary income to the extent of the holder's ratable share of OID, based on the number of days he held it. The holder can irrevocably elect to compute the accrued OID under an economic accrual formula. The rules cover obligations (whether or not tax-exempt) with a fixed maturity of a year or less, other than those of the U.S., a U.S. Possession, a state or its political subdivision, or the District of Columbia. Generally for obligations acquired after 7-18-84, the new law also no longer defines short-term government taxable obligations for ordinary income treatment of acquisition discount on their disposition as those payable without interest and issued on a discount basis. And it allows an irrevocable election to compute the holder's acquisition discount under an economic accrual formula.

CLARIFICATION: OID on a short-term debt instrument is deductible only in the year of payment by cash method obligors. A new law provision stating this is designed to clarify that a similar proposed provision was deleted during enactment of the 1984 Act only because it was thought to be an unneeded declaration of preexisting law.

Accrual taxpayers, dealers, banks, mutual funds, and certain others must include in income on a current basis the OID or acquisition discount on short-term obligations. Effective for obligations acquired after 9-27-85, this mandatory accrual covers interest on the obligation, OID and acquisition discount, or any combination of them, that is allocable to the tax year.

Market discount rules. Generally for obligations issued after 7-18-84, under the new law, the transferor of a market discount bond in a Sec. 351 nontaxable corporate organization exchange is taxed on any accrued market discount whether or not he receives stock or securities in the exchange. The Committee Reports note that the corporate transferee of the bond gets a Sec. 362(a) carryover basis for it that reflects the transferor's gain, and has a market discount bond if the bond's stated redemption price exceeds this basis.

The new law also clarifies that a bond acquired by a taxpayer at original issue (or a bond with a transferred basis determined by reference to the basis of the person who acquired it at original issue) isn't a market discount bond. *Exceptions.* Bonds whose holder has a cost basis for them that's less than their issue price (e.g., bonds acquired by large investors at "wholesale" prices lower than those available to "retail" customers), and bonds issued under a Sec. 368(a)(1) reorganization plan in exchange for bonds having market discount, can be market discount bonds. For the rules treating accrued market discount as ordinary income on disposition (Sec. 1276), the above exception for bonds issued in a reorganization covers only bonds issued after 7-18-84 if they have the same term and interest rate as the bonds they're exchanged for.

The new law also provides rules for treatment of market discount on debt instruments whose principal is paid in more than one installment. These rules apply to debt instruments acquired after enactment date.

Until the Treasury issues regs for computing market discount, the conferees intend that the holder can elect to accrue market discount either at a constant interest rate; or in proportion to accrual of OID; or for non-OID obligations in proportion to stated interest paid during the accrual period.

Other imputed interest and OID rules. The new law:

• Clarifies that the discount rate for determining unstated interest, for pre-7-1-85 "related party" sales or exchanges covered by former Sec. 483(f) as in effect before enactment of the "Simplification of Imputed Interest Rules" (P.L. 99-121) is 6% compounded semiannually;

- Gives the Treasury authority to designate in regs other publicly traded property that's treated, for purposes of the OID rules, like property that's regularly traded on an established market;

- Requires the current inclusion in income of acquisition discount on stripped bonds and coupons by the "stripper" or anyone with a transferred basis from him, and provides that stripped bonds and coupons are subject to the general rules of Sec. 1286 with certain modifications;

- Makes a technical change in Sec. 483(d)(1) to clarify what OID debt instruments are excluded from the Sec. 483 rules;

- Clarifies that P.L. 98-612, effective 10-31-84, (the stop-gap legislation which extended pre-'84 TRA rules for debt instruments received for property with certain limitations and special rules), covers only sales *after 12-31-84* —but it didn't accelerate the 12-31-84 effective date of the 1984 Act; and

- Clarifies that interest on debt instruments issued in post-1984 transactions for property (whether or not with adequate stated interest) can't be computed under a method other than economic accrual (as described in Rev. Rul. 83-84, according to the Committee Reports). The new law also changes the date of the binding contract exception to this rule for transactions involving adequate stated interest—it will apply to contracts binding on 6-8-84 (rather than 3-1-84).

- The new law clarifies that current inclusion of OID covers capital asset obligations issued after 1984 (and not on 12-31-84 and later).

Amortizable bond premium. The new law extends amortization of bond premium (elective for taxable obligations) to obligations issued by individuals. It requires amortizable bond premium to be computed under a constant yield method, using the basis of the bond, and compounding at the end of each "accrual period" (defined in Sec. 1271(a)(5)). These rules cover obligations issued after 9-27-85. *Special rule.* A Sec. 171(c) election effective on the enactment date of the new law won't cover post-9-27-85 obligations unless the taxpayer elects otherwise under regs to come. And for determining the amortizable bond premium of bonds received in post-5-6-86 exchanges for property in which the bond acquires an exchanged (substituted) basis, the basis of the bond can't be more than its fair market value immediately after the exchange. This rule also applies to such bonds if they're later transferred and retain a substituted basis (e.g., if given as a gift). However, bonds received in a bond-for-bond reorganization exchange are generally not covered by this rule.

Act Sec. 1803(a)(1)—(4) and (8) relating to short-term obligations amends Sec. 1271(a)(3), 1281(a), 1282(a), 163(e)(2), and 1283(d)(3), and adds Sec. 1271(a)(4). Act Sec. 1803(a)(5)—(6) and (13) relating to market discount rules amends Sec. 1276(d)(1) and 1278(a)(1). Act Secs. 1803(a)(7) and (10) and 1803(b) relating to other OID and imputed interest rules amend Sec. 483(d)(1), 1273(b)(3) and 1281(b)(1), and 1984 Tax Reform Act Sec. 44(b)(3), and 44(b)(4) as added by Sec. 2 of P.L. 86-12 and 44(g). Act Sec. 1803(a)(9) dealing with "related party sales" doesn't amend the Code. Act Sec. 1803(a)(11) and (12) dealing with amortizable bond premium amends Sec. 171(b)(3) and (d) and adds Sec. 171(b)(4). These and certain changes are effective as if included in the 1984 Tax Reform Act and as indicated above.

[¶1806] **Law Changes for Corporations and Shareholders.** Law changes in this area include the dividends received and dividends-paid deductions, complete liquidations of subsidiaries and reorganization provisions, earnings and profits computations on distributions of appreciated property, and golden parachute payments.

Corporate dividends-received deduction for debt financed stock of foreign corporations. The new law clarifies how the limitation percentage for the dividends received deduction in case of debt-portfolio stock (Sec. 246A(a)) is applied to dividends from Sec. 245(a) foreign corporations. *Example:* Assume 60% of a Sec. 245(a) foreign corporation's gross income is effectively connected with the conduct of a U.S. trade or business. In addition, 70% of the foreign corporation's purchase price for portfolio stock of the foreign corporation is debt-financed. Under Sec. 246A, the domestic corporation generally deducts 15.3% (30% *times* 85% *times* 60%) of the dividend from the foreign corporation.

45 (or 90)-day holding period. The dividends-received deduction is denied if the dividend stock isn't held for 45 days (90 days for certain preference dividends), without counting more than 45 (or 90) days after the ex-dividend date or days when the corporation's risk of loss is diminished. The new law deletes a prior law condition for this denial. Dividend stock acquired after 3-1-86 doesn't have to be disposed of for this denial to occur. Denial, for example, occurs automatically if the stock hasn't been held for the required period by the 45th (or 90th) day after the ex-dividend date. Both Committee Reports also note that an out-of-the-money call option that doesn't protect against loss if the stock price falls doesn't cause a denial of the deduction (citing Rev.Rul. 80-238).

Interest incurred to buy or carry tax-exempts. The '84 TRA authorized regs that would prevent tax avoidance through linking of borrowings to investments, or diminishing risks through use of related persons, pass-through entities, or other intermediaries (Sec. 7701(f)). The new law provides that these rules (generally effective 7-18-84), will apply to law restrictions that disallow interest incurred by corporations and individuals to buy or carry tax-exempts (Sec. 265(2)) as to term loans made after 7-18-84, demand loans outstanding after 7-18-84 (other than those outstanding on 7-18-84 and repaid before

9-18-84) and it clarifies that post-7-18-84 loan renegotiations, extensions, or revisions will be considered post-7-18-84 loans. It also defines term and demand loans similarly to their definition in the rules for below-market-interest loans.

Loss on sale of mutual fund stock after exempt-interest dividend. A law change prevents the purchase of regulated investment company stock just before the ex-dividend date, the receipt of an exempt-interest dividend, and the stock's disposition at a recognized loss after waiting 31 days. If stock (whose holding period begins after 3-28-85) isn't held for more than six months, loss on its sale or exchange is denied to the extent of exempt-interest dividends received on it. Regs can make exceptions for periodic liquidation plans. They can also shorten the six-month period to no less than 31 days or to the interval between regular tax-exempt interest dividends, (whichever is longer), if the mutual fund regularly distributes at least 90% of its net tax-exempt interest.

Dividends-paid deduction of a holding or investment company. To prevent a holding or investment company that isn't a regulated investment company (RIC) from effecting a capital-gains taxed redemption and then being free of accumulated earnings tax under Sec. 562(b)(1), the new law denies (except to the extent permitted by regs) the dividends-paid deduction against the accumulated earnings tax in cases of liquidation and redemption distributions by such companies after 9-27-85.

Affiliated groups. Under the new law, for tax years beginning after 1984, the term "stock" for determining an affiliated group doesn't generally include preferred stock with redemption and liquidation rights that don't exceed the *issue price* of the stock (rather than "the paid-in capital or par value" represented by it, as under prior law). This redefinition makes irrelevant the stock's accounting treatment when it's issued. Also, under the new law, a DISC or a corporation with post-1984 accumulations of DISC income (rather than a DISC or "former DISC") won't be an includable corporation. The Committee Report notes that under current law there's less reason to keep a former DISC and its parent from filing consolidated returns, and this law change isn't intended to affect the status of certain S corporations with DISC subsidiaries "grandfathered" by the 1982 Subchapter S Revision Act.

Effective Dates: The new law:

• Sunsets the '84 TRA grandfather rule for 6-22-84 members of an affiliated group, which deals with the determination whether they continue to be such members for pre-1988 years. The grandfather rule stops applying as of the first day after 6-22-84 on which the corporation won't qualify as a group member under pre-'84 TRA law;

- Clarifies the exception to the grandfather rule that covers post-6-22-84 "selldowns", by making it inapplicable for transactions that don't reduce the percentage (by value) of the "solddown" corporation's stock that's held by the other group members;

- Applies the sell-down exception in certain cases when there's a pre-6-22-84 letter of intent between the corporation and a securities underwriter;

- Allows a common parent to irrevocably elect to have the '84 TRA amendments apply to tax years beginning after 1983; and

- Allows an Alaska Native corporation to offset the income of its profitable nonnative subsidiary with its own NOLs.

Complete liquidation of subsidiaries. Several law changes are designed to coordinate the rules for nontaxable complete liquidations of subsidiaries, with '84 TRA changes in the definition of affiliated groups.

First, Sec. 332 now won't apply unless the corporation receiving a liquidating distribution is the owner of the liquidating corporation's stock under the 80% voting and value tests of Sec. 1504(a)(2). According to both Committee Reports, other rules governing the definition of affiliated groups (except that disregarding intergroup stock transfers—(Sec. 1504(a)(5)(E)) also apply. And the new rule will apply even if the corporations involved in the liquidating distribution aren't "includible corporations" under Sec. 1504(b). These rules generally cover distributions under post-3-28-85 complete liquidation plans. They also generally cover distributions under *earlier* complete liquidation plans if: (1) any distribution is made in a tax year beginning after 1984 (or after 1983, if the common parent elects earlier application of 1984 Act rules), and (2) the liquidating corporation and any corporation receiving complete liquidation distributions are members of a group filing consolidated returns for the year that includes the distribution date. However, these rules don't apply if the liquidating corporation is an affiliated group member under affiliated group transitional rules of '84 TRA Sec. 60(b)(2), (5) (6) or (8).

Second, the Sec. 337(c)(3) definition of "distributee corporation" is amended to define it as any corporation that receives a Sec. 332 complete liquidation distribution from the selling corporation, as well as any corporation "up the line" that receives a Sec. 332 distribution in complete liquidation of a distributee that had received a Sec. 332 distribution. These rules apply to complete liquidation plans involving any distribution in tax years beginning after 1984 (or after 1983, if the common parent irrevocably elects earlier application of '84 TRA rules).

Third, the Sec. 338 definition of "qualified stock purchase" is conformed to the Sec. 1504(a)(2) definition for purchases begun after 12-31-85.

NOTE: These rules are designed to prevent certain occurrences. For a parent and a subsidiary that wouldn't have met Sec. 332 ownership but would have met those of Sec. 1504, the rules would prevent a complete liquidation by the subsidiary with a Sec. 337 nontaxable sale of assets (see Sec. 337(c)(2)), and the subsidiary's liquidation also being nontaxable to the parent under Reg. §1.1502-14(b) consolidated return rules. For a parent and a subsidiary that would have met Sec. 332 ownership rules but not those of Sec. 1504, the rules would prevent a nontaxable Sec. 332 liquidation of the subsidiary with the parent also liquidating tax free under Sec. 337.

E&P adjustment on appreciated property distributions. Under the new law, for distributions or redemptions in tax years beginning after 9-30-84, a corporation's distribution of appreciated property increases its earnings and profits by the excess of the property's fair market value (FMV) over the property's adjusted basis. The distribution then results in a decrease to earnings and profits under the rules of Sec. 312(a), using fair market value instead of adjusted basis to measure the decrease. This change isn't intended to affect earnings and profits determinations as to one-month (Sec. 333) liquidating distributions. Other E&P law changes: The current law rule covering redemptions (old law Sec. 312(n)(8) now redesignated as (n)(7)) applies to redemption distributions in tax years beginning after 9-30-84, and as a result of the special rule for certain foreign corporations (old law Sec. 312(n)(9) now redesignated (n)(8)) the rule covering installment sales (old (n)(6) redesignated as (n)(5)) now applies to tax years beginning after 12-31-87 (rather than 12-31-85).

Reorganizations. Under the new law, the transferor corporation doesn't recognize gain or loss on any exchange of property under the reorganization plan, regardless of whether properties received are distributed under the plan. The liquidation provisions of Secs. 336 and 337 don't apply to any liquidation of a transferor corporation under the reorganization plan. And the basis of property that it receives under the plan will be the same as it would be in the hands of the transferor of the property, adjusted by gain or loss recognized to such transferor on such transfer. No gain or loss is recognized by the acquired corporation on the disposition under the plan of stock or securities it receives in a party to the reorganization. Gain is recognized on distribution of boot. Special rules govern transfers to creditors of the acquired corporation. In "C" type (stock for assets) reorganizations, no gain or loss is recognized to the transferor on any disposition of stock or securities of another party to the reorganization, which it receives under the plan. But the transferor can have taxable gain (under Sec. 311(d)) on distributions of other property that it receives. And the new law clarifies that distributions to creditors satisfy the distribution requirements of Sec. 368(a)(2)(G). The new rules apply to reorganization plans adopted after the enactment date.

The new law provides that as to plans adopted after 7-18-84, for a "D" reorganization, the term "control" is defined by Sec. 304(c), if the transaction meets the requirements of Sec. 354(b)(1)(A) and (B)—i.e., if the transferee acquires substantially all the transferor's assets; and the stock, securities, and other properties received by the transferor, as well as its own properties, are distributed under the reorganization plan. It also clarifies that for plans adopted after 7-18-84, a C reorganization involving a drop-down of assets to a subsidiary will continue to qualify as a C reorganization despite the rules of Sec. 368(a)(2)(A).

Collapsible corporation income can relate to short-term period stock. For sales and exchanges after 9-27-85, gain from the sale or exchange of a collapsible corporation can be ordinary income even if the stock was held for 6 months or less.

Golden parachute provisions. For agreements after 6-14-84, the new law excludes from treatment as "parachute payments," those payments relating to small business corporations (defined similarly to S corporations) whose stock wasn't readily tradeable on an established securities market or otherwise, provided there was shareholder approval for the payment. It also excludes any part of a payment that the taxpayer establishes by clear and convincing evidence to be reasonable compensation for services to be rendered on or after the change of control, from treatment as "excess parachute payments". And it reduces "excess parachute payments" by amounts that the taxpayer proves to be reasonable compensation for services actually rendered before the change in control (for this rule, reasonable compensation for services before the change is first offset against the base amount). Further, it excludes from treatment as "parachute payments" payments to or from qualified retirement plan trusts or annuities or SEPs. Such payments aren't considered in determining if the threshold for excess parachute payments is exceeded.

In addition, it treats all members of an affiliated group (specially defined) as a single corporation for the golden parachute rules, and treats an officer or "highly compensated individual" of any member of the group as that of the single corporation. The new law also limits the number of persons treated as "highly compensated individuals," to employees (or former employees) who are among the *lesser* of (1) the highest-paid 1% performing personal services for the corporation, or (2) the highest-paid 250 individuals who perform services for the corporation or for each member of an affiliated group that's treated as a single corporation for the golden parachute rules. Finally, payments under agreements that violate securities laws or regulations can be parachute payments only if these laws or regs are generally enforced (the burden of proving such a violation is on the IRS).

NOTE: The Senate Committee Report notes that these changes are retroactive as if included at the inception of the golden parachute rules, and that shareholder approval for a payment could be obtained for earlier transactions after the enactment date of the new law. The Conference Report notes that the amendments intend no inference as to the definition of a change in control.

Corporate tax preferences. Among technical and clerical changes in this area is an amendment to Sec. 291(a)(4) as in effect before enactment of the '84 TRA, clarifying that the cutback of preferences relating to DISC income doesn't apply to S corporations for years beginning after 1982.

Other law changes. The new law also delays the effective date of '84 TRA amendments relating to distributions of appreciated property (Sec. 311(d)) for a specified parent-subsidiary group (extends a transitional exception to cover pre-1988 distributions).

Act Sec. 1804(a) and (b)(1) dealing with the dividends received deduction amends Secs. 246A(a) and 246(c). Act Secs. 1804(b)(2) and (3) dealing with related party rules and interest incurred to carry tax-exempts amends 1984 TRA Secs. 53(e)(3) and 54. Act Sec. 1804(c) dealing with mutual fund stock amends Sec. 852(b)(4). Act Sec. 1804(d) dealing with the dividends paid deduction amends Sec. 562(b)(1). Act Sec. 1804(e) dealing with affiliated groups amends Sec. 1504(a)(4) and 1984 TRA Sec. 60(b)(4). Act Sec. 1804(e)(6)—(8) dealing with complete liquidation of subsidiaries amends Secs. 332(b)(1), 337(c)(3)(B) and 338(d)(3). Act Sec. 1804(f) dealing with appreciated property distributions amends Sec. 312(b), repeals Secs. 312(c)(3) and (n)(4), redesignates Sec. 312(n)(5)—(9) as (n)(4)—(8). Act Secs. 1804(g) and (h) dealing with reorganizations amend Secs. 358(a), 361 and 368(a)(2) and (c). Act Sec. 1804(i) relating to collapsible corporations amends Sec. 341(a). Act Sec. 1804(j) dealing with golden parachute payments adds Secs. 280G(b)(2), (5), (6), (d)(5) and amends Secs. 280G(b)(2) and (4), (c) and (d). Act Sec. 1804(k) dealing with corporate tax preferences amends pre-1984 Act version of Sec. 291(a)(4), 1984 Act Secs. 68(e)(2) and (3) and (c)(2), and Sec. 57(b)(1) and (2). The law changes are effective as if included in the 1984 TRA and as shown above.

[¶1807] Partnership and Trust Rules. The new law clarifies that the partnership rules for allocating cash basis items to periods to which the items are attributable, under economic accrual principles, apply, for periods after 3-31-84, if the allocation is needed, even though no change in partnership interests occurs during the current tax year. It also makes clear, that the rules for treating as a disguised sale a partner's post-3-31-84 transfer of money or other property to a partnership, accompanied by a related transfer by the partnership to the transferor or another partner, can also apply to treat a transaction as an exchange of property. And it limits the application of the Sec. 761(e) rule that distributions not otherwise treated as exchanges are treated as exchanges for purposes of specified Code provisions to distributions of partnership interests (subject to regs exceptions to the rule).

Transfers of partnership or trust interest by corporations. The new law specifically limits the gain recognized by a corporation on post-3-31-84 distributions of partnership or trust interests to which Sec. 311 applies, to gain that would have been recognized if the distributed interest were sold (that is, a sale at its FMV). To prevent avoidance of the Sec. 311 nonrecognition of losses rule, Regs can provide that gain on a distributed partnership interest is computed independently of any loss on property contributed to the partnership for the principal purpose of recognizing that loss. Also, both Committee Reports note that treatment of "unrealized receivables" such as depreciation recapture under Sec. 751(a) remains applicable to the distribution of partnership interests.

Like-kind exchanges. Under the new law, to get like-kind exchange nonrecognition for post-3-31-84 transfers, property received by the taxpayer must be identified *on or before* the 45th day after his transfer of relinquished property (rather than "before" that day).

Estate or trust distributions in kind. The new law clarifies that an estate or trust's election to recognize gain or loss on post-6-1-84 distributions of property (formerly Sec. 643(d)(3) now redesignated as 643(e)(3)) applies to all distributions during the tax year that it covers, unless it's revoked with IRS consent.

Effective Date: The new law creates an exception from the '84 TRA rules that treat multiple trusts for tax years beginning after 3-1-84 as a single trust under some circumstances, for trusts that were irrevocable on 3-1-84 except for the parts of the trusts that are allocable to later transfers.

Act Sec. 1805(a) (b) and (c)(2) dealing with allocation of cash method items, disguised sales, and certain distributions amends Secs. 706(d)(2), 707(a)(2), and 761(e). Act Sec. 1805(c)(1) dealing with transfers of partnership or trust interests adds new Sec. 386(d). Act Sec. 1805(d) relating to like-kind exchanges amends Sec. 1031(a)(3). Act Sec. 1806 dealing with trusts amends Code Sec. 643(e) (formerly (d)), and 1984 Act Sec. 82(b). These and clerical changes are effective as if included in the 1984 TRA and as indicated above.

〔¶1808〕 Accounting Changes. In the area of the "economic performance" requirement for taking deductions, the new law requires cash basis tax shelters to satisfy the "economic performance" requirement for deducting a payment made, if economic performance occurs *before the close* of the 90th day after year-end (rather than *within* 90 days after year-end). This is intended to cover, for instance, deductions as to wells spudded just before year-end. Also, pre-11-23-85 nonrefundable payments to an insurer to insure against tort liability relating to asbestos are declared to satisfy the economic performance test for Sec. 461(h).

Designated tort settlement funds. Irrevocable "qualified payments" to a "designated settlement fund" established under a court order principally for satisfying present and future personal injury or property damage claims against the taxpayer (or related persons) can (at taxpayer's election revocable only with IRS consent) be treated as satisfying "economic performance" for purposes of Sec. 461(h). Among the requirements: (1) The fund can't receive payment other than "qualified payments" (court ordered payments in money or property that can't be retransferred to the taxpayer, and can't include stock or debt of the taxpayer or a related person). (2) A majority of those administering the fund must be parties independent to taxpayer. (3) The fund's terms can't allow the taxpayer to hold any beneficial interest in it (this can occur if taxpayer's future liability is contingent on the fund's income).

The rules don't apply to worker's compensation payments or Sec. 461(f) contested liability. Related persons are defined in Sec. 267(b). The fund is, under special rules, taxed as a separate entity at maximum trust rates on income from its investments, reduced only by administrative costs (including state and local taxes) and by incidental expenses (including legal, accounting, and actuarial expenses that would have been deductible by a corporation) but not on the qualified payments. For tax procedural purposes it's treated as a corporation. The taxpayer's property contributions to the fund are treated as sales of the property at fair market value—they can result in gain or loss, and his deduction is limited to fair market value. No deduction is allowed the taxpayer for a contribution of insurance settlements that are excluded by the taxpayer. The fund can't deduct its distributions. The new law makes clear that trust or escrow payments made to other types of funds to satisfy tort liability won't (except as permitted by regs.) satisfy "economic performance." Transitional rules relate to a corporation that filed a Chapter 11 reorganization petition on 8-26-82 and a restated plan of reorganization before 3-1-86.

The Conference Report notes that: (1) The settlement fund rules don't affect the treatment of Sec. 130 personal injury liability assignments, (2) Payments by a designated settlement fund to a claimant are treated as made by the taxpayer for determining the claimant's taxable income, (3) Taxpayers cannot both exclude an amount recovered and deduct an amount paid to the fund on the same liability. It also notes that, except as provided in Regs, escrow accounts, settlement funds, or similar funds are subject to current tax, and that if the contribution to it isn't deductible, the account or fund is taxable as a grantor trust (this reverses a finding in Rev.Rul. 71-119, 1971-1 CB 163).

Limitations on farming businesses. The new law clarifies that any tax shelter (as defined in Sec. 6661(b)) will be generally treated as a farming syndicate for the Sec. 464 deduction limits on farming syndicates, but interests of persons whose "holdings are attributable to active management" won't be subject to Sec. 464.

Mining and solid waste reclamation and closing costs. The new law clarifies that the reserve established under the elective uniform method for deducting these costs before economic performance must be increased annually by accrued deductions allocable to the reserve. It also clarifies that the '84 TRA rules become effective on 7-18-84, for tax years ending after that date.

Decommissioning nuclear power plants. The new law clarifies the operating rules for "qualified nuclear decommissioning reserve funds," which allow electing taxpayers to deduct contributions made to them. Among them: (1) A contribution is considered made during a tax year if made within 2½ months after year-end (this can be relaxed by regs for payments as to pre-1987 tax years); (2) the Sec. 486A tax on fund income is instead of any other federal income tax—this tax isn't deductible and procedurally it's treated like a corporate income tax; and (3) the fund can invest only in assets similar to those allowed to Black Lung Trust Funds. It also clarifies that the '84 TRA rules are effective for tax years ending after 7-18-84.

Deferred payments for services. The new law clarifies that contributions to qualified retirement plans or annuities and deferred compensation plans covered by Sec. 404 and 404A, won't be subject to Sec. 467(g) Regs on deferred payments for services. The new law also allows a specified taxpayer formerly providing architectural reserves to use the cash method.

Effective Dates: The new law also clarifies the effective date for 1984 Act rules on loss carrybacks for deferred statutory or tort liability deductions (they apply to losses for tax years beginning after 1983). And it allows an election under regs to come to have Sec. 461(h) apply to the taxpayer's entire tax year in which 7-19-84 occurs.

Act Sec. 1807(a) amends Secs. 461(i)(2), (4), 468(a)(1) and (2), 468A(a), (c), (d), (e) and (f), and 1984 TRA Sec. 91(g)(2)(A), and adds Sec. 468A(g), and 1984 TRA Sec. 91(g)(5)—(6). Act Sec. 1807(a)(7) dealing with designated tort settlement funds adds Code Sec. 468B. Act Sec. 1807(b) relating to deferred payments for services amends Sec. 467(g). These and clerical changes made are effective as if included in the 1984 Act (generally for tax years ending after 7-18-84, and as to tax shelter rules for deductions allowable after 3-31-84) and as indicated above.

[¶1809] **Tax Straddle Rules.** Generally as to positions established after 7-18-84, the new law (1) allows payments that compensate a lender of securities used in a short sale (e.g., for dividends and interest payments), to reduce interest and carrying charges incurred on personal property that's part of a straddle which is required to be capitalized; (2) clarifies that the tax straddle rules don't apply to direct positions in stock, but can apply to positions in "interests in stock" such as exchange-traded stock options (other than qualified covered calls that offset stock); and (3) allows regs to ensure that elections by S corporations connected with the introduction of the mark-to-market and other straddle rules by the '84 TRA are properly coordinated with S corporation tax year limitations.

The new law also clarifies the treatment of losses from pre-1982 straddles. It expressly treats losses that are incurred on any positions by a commodities dealer in commodities trading, as incurred in a trade or business, thus confining this profit-motive presumption to such dealers (e.g., investment bankers regularly trading in commodities). The new law defines dealers to whom it applies. The House Committee Report notes that the new law restates the general rule that losses from a position in a straddle are deductible only if the position is part of a transaction entered into for profit (c.f. *Miller v. Comm.*, 84 TC 55). The Conference Report notes that an individual who owns a seat on the Commodities Exchange is a "commodities dealer", and that losses indirectly incurred by a commodity dealer (i.e., as a partner, S corporation shareholder, or beneficiary of a trust on transactions by these entities) are also treated as commodity dealer losses for this provision.

Act Sec. 1808 amends Secs. 263(g)(2)(B), 1092(d)(3) and 1984 TRA Secs. 102 and 108.

[¶1810]   Depreciation and Investment Credit. Generally for property placed in service after 3-15-84, the new law:

• Clarifies that elective straight-line recovery of low income housing is over a 15- 35- or 45-year period (and not a 19-year or 18-year period).

• Requires the mid-month convention to be used for 19-year (or 18-year) real property when computing ACRS allowances, the accelerated cost recovery tax preference item, and earnings and profits adjustments for depreciation. It similarly requires the monthly convention to be used for low-income housing, and makes other technical clarifications.

• In effect, generally limits films, videotapes, and sound recordings placed in service after 3-28-85 to depreciation through the income forecast or similar methods by excluding them from accelerated methods. and

• For property placed in service after 4-11-84, reinstates an inadvertently omitted provision in the definition of new investment credit property, to include in it the basis attributable to taxpayer's reconstruction of Sec. 38 property; and clarifies that the three-month sale-lease back rule doesn't apply to such property. It clarifies that, for example, if an owner places property in service by leasing it to L, and within three months sells it to P and leases it back from P subject to L's lease, the property can be new Sec. 38 property in P's hands. The Senate Committee Report notes that this would be the result under prior statutory language. The new law also allows the lessee and lessor to elect out of the three-month rule.

Real property financed with tax-exempt bonds. The new law clarifies that IDB-financed 19-year (or 18-year real property (with exceptions that include low-income housing) is recoverable no faster than under the straight line (without salvage) using a 19-year (or 18-year) period. It also clarifies that the '84 TRA rules covering realty financed with tax exempts don't apply to property excepted from the bond rules added by TEFRA in 1982 (described in TEFRA Sec. 216(b)(3)).

Transferees of recovery property. Under the new law, for Sec. 168(f)(10)(B)(i) basis carryover transfers (involving certain nontaxable corporate liquidations, reorganization exchanges, and partnership contributions and distributions—but now excluding terminations of partnerships because of at least 50% sales or exchanges of capital or profit interests within 12 months), the transferee "steps into the transferor's shoes" as to cost recovery deductions to the extent the transferee's basis doesn't increase. However, for transfers described in Secs. 168(f)(10)(B)(ii) (i.e., transfers between related persons) and 168(f)(10)(B)(iii) (i.e., sale-leasebacks), the transferee generally depreciates the property as a new owner, but remains bound by the transferor's Sec. 168(b)(3) or (f)(2)(C) elections of the straight-line method recovery and period to the extent his basis didn't increase. The new rules apply to property placed in service by the transferee after 12-31-85. The House Committee Report notes that the law changes don't intend to affect intergroup transactions of consolidated return filers.

Installment sales. The new law clarifies that the rule that denied installment sales treatment to depreciation recapture generally after 6-6-84 applies to sales of partnership interests.

Act Sec. 1809 amends Secs. 168(b)(2), (3) and (4), (f)(2), (10) and (12), 167(c), 48(b), (q), 57(a)(12), 312(k)(3) and 453(i)(2). The law changes are effective as if included in the 1984 TRA and as indicated above.

[¶1811] Foreign Tax Credit. The new law generally tightens the '84 TRA rules recharacterizing foreign income as U.S. income for the credit, and those recharacterizing dividends as interest income for the separate interest limitation on the credit.

Recharacterizing foreign income as U.S. income. For the special source rules of Sec. 904(g) (generally effective 3-28-85), the new law treats an 80/20 company (a domestic corporation that earns less than 20% of its gross income from U.S. sources over a 3-year period) as a U.S.-owned foreign corporation as to its interest and dividend payments which are treated as foreign source income under Sec. 861(a)(1)(B) and (2)(A). The new rule is designed to prevent conversion by U.S. taxpayers of U.S. source to foreign source income for the credit, by routing it through an 80/20 company. It's generally effective on 3-28-85.

Special effective date rule. For an 80/20 company's tax year ending after 3-28-85, *only* its post-3-28-85 income generally falls under the special source rules; but its income for the entire tax year is considered in determining whether it qualifies for nonapplication of the special source rules under the 10% threshold of Sec. 904(g)(5).

The new law also clarifies that the special source rules (Sec. 904(g)) apply despite any U.S. Treaty obligation to the contrary. *Exception:* A treaty entered into after 7-18-84 (the enactment date of the '84 TRA) can specifically override these rules by referring to Sec. 904(g)). The Committee Report notes that the '84 TRA generally takes precedence over preexisting treaty provisions (e.g., the Act's accumulated earnings tax provisions override a conflicting U.S.-Jamaica Treaty provision). And, the transitional rule that covers "applicable CFCs" is clarified and modified by the new law as to interest paid on obligations of affiliated foreign corporations that were issued before 6-22-84.

Recharacterizing dividends as separate limitation interest. The new law changes the definition of "designated payor corporations" that can give rise to dividends recharacterized as separate limitation interest income (Sec. 904(d)(3)). First, generally as of 12-31-85, it expressly makes any corporation formed or availed of for avoiding the recharacterization (look-through) rules (e.g., a foreign banking subsidiary majority- owned by foreigners and without 10% U.S. shareholders) a "designated payor corporation". Second, it engrafts rules dealing with 80/20 companies to the "designated payor" definition, to subject such companies to the separate credit limit for interest income generally as of 3-28-85 (and subject to the special effective date rule noted earlier).

The new law also (1) removes the de-minimis separate limitation interest (10%) exception to the recharacterization (Sec. 904(d)(3)(C)) in case of foreign personal holding company and Subpart F inclusions of income; (2) clarifies that if a "designated payor corporation" receives dividends and interest from another member of the same affiliated group (specially defined), they can be treated as separate limitation interest only if they're directly or indirectly attributable to separate limitation interest of any other member of the group;

and (3) makes a law change designed to ensure that dividends and interest received from a regulated investment company by portfolio (less than 10% voting stock) shareholders aren't treated as separate limitation interest.

Act Sec. 1810(a) dealing with recharacterizing foreign income as U.S. income adds new Sec. 904(g)(9), and amends 1984 TRA Sec. 121(b)(2)(D)(ii) and (b)(2)(E). Act Sec. 1810(a)(4) dealing with Treaty obligations doesn't amend the Code. Act Sec. 1810(b) dealing with recharacterization as separate limitation interest amends Secs. 904(d)(2), (d)(3)(C) and (E) and adds new Sec. 904(d)(3)(I). The law changes are effective as if included in the 1984 TRA (generally for distributions after 7-18-84) and as indicated above.

[¶1812] **Withholding on Sales of U.S. Real Property by Foreigners.** The new law makes the following modifications in the withholding system set up by the '84 TRA that replaced the information reporting system initially required by the 1980 Foreign Investment in Real Property Tax Act.

Dispositions or distributions by U.S. partnerships, trusts, or estates. On dispositions of U.S. real property interests by a domestic partnership, trust or estate, the partnership, trustee or executor will now withhold 28% of the gain realized on the disposition, to the extent it's allocable to a foreign partner or beneficiary or to a foreign "owner" of the trust under grantor trust rules (under prior law it was 10% of the total amount received). The new law covers dispositions that occur following 31 days after its enactment. Both Committee Reports note that regs are intended to provide exceptions to the withholding when the disposition is currently taxable at the entity (e.g., trust or estate) level; and that a partnership, trustee, or executor without sufficient sale proceeds to satisfy withholding (e.g., in case of installment sales) can request a qualifying statement from the IRS that allows it to withhold a lesser amount.

The new law also clarifies that distributions of U.S. real property interests to foreign persons are subject to withholding when they're taxable under any of the substantive FIRPTA rules (i.e., Sec. 897), and not just for sales of partnership, trust, or estate interests by foreigners (Sec. 897(g)). And it clarifies that the IRS can issue regs to require withholding on gains realized through tiers of entities.

Corporations. A foreign corporation's election to be treated as a domestic corporation for purposes of FIRPTA substantive and reporting provisions (Secs. 897 and 6039C) has been extended to cover the withholding provisions (Sec. 1445) as well. The temporary regs which require the electing foreign corporation to attach to a "nonforeign affidavit" a copy of the acknowledgement of the election provided it by the IRS, offer to U.S. buyers a reasonable assurance of the validity of the affidavit.

The new law also (1) clarifies that no withholding is required on liquidating or redemption distributions by domestic current or former "U.S. real property holding corporations" (U.S. RPHCs) to foreign shareholders of interests that are excluded from treatment as "U.S. real property interests" under Sec. 897(c)(1)(B); and (2) for dispositions of interests in nonpublicly traded domestic corporations, the corporation's affidavits for withholding exemption will now have to state both that the corporation isn't and hasn't been a U.S. RPHC and that as of disposition, interests in it aren't "U.S. real property interests" by reason of Sec. 897(c)(1)(B)—i.e., the affidavit now covers a "non-U.S. real property interest" exemption.

Other rules. The new law clarifies that no notice-giving or withholding duty is imposed on an agent of a foreign corporate transferor who doesn't have *actual knowledge* that a "non-U.S. real property interest" affidavit of a domestic corporation whose stock he transfers is false. The Committee Report notes, however, that such an agent is charged with knowledge of falsity of a false "nonforeign" affadavit furnished by his own principal. It also conforms the FIRPTA penalty provisions (Sec. 6652(g)) to '84 TRA rules, and it clarifies the filing and tax payment requirements for real property interests located in the Virgin Islands.

Act Sec. 1810(f) amends Secs. 897(i), 1445(b)(3), (d)(1), (e)(1), (3), (4) and (6), 6039C(d), and 6652(g). The law changes are effective as if included in the 1984 Tax Reform Act (generally for post-1984 dispositions) and as indicated above.

[¶1813]   **Transfers to Foreign Persons in Divisive Reorganizations and Distributions.** The new law makes Sec. 355 (and 356) stock (or related "boot") transfers by domestic corporations to foreign persons (whether or not corporate) give rise to recognized gain under Sec. 367(e) to the extent that regs provide.

Act Sec. 1810(g) amends Secs. 367(a)(1) and (e), 6501(c)(8), 7482(b), and repeals Sec. 367(f) providing a transitional rule, effective as if included in the 1984 Tax Reform Act (generally for post-1984 transfers or exchanges).

[¶1814]   **Other Foreign Provisions.** The new law also makes changes in the following areas affected by the foreign provisions of the '84 TRA.

Related person factoring income. Under the '84 TRA, income from factoring receivables of a U.S. obligor acquired directly or indirectly from a "related" U.S. person is generally currently taxable under controlled foreign corporation or foreign personal holding company rules. Receivables transferred after 3-1-84 are treated as "U.S. property." The income is treated as interest on a loan to the obligor. The new law does the following: First, it provides that the exclusion from "U.S. property" of post-1962 earnings and profits

(Sec. 956(b)(2)(H)) applies in case of acquisitions of related person factoring receivables. In addition, the new law exempts from current inclusion, income from factoring receivables whose acquirer and related-person-transferor are organized under the laws of the same foreign country and the related transferor has a substantial part of its assets used in its trade or business there. *Exception:* This rule doesn't apply if the transferor would have derived from a collection on the receivable any foreign base company income (without regard of the 10% exception) or income that's effectively connected with a U.S. trade or business. According to both Committee Reports, this treatment of factoring income also extends to income from analogous transaction-financing loans by CFCs to related parties. Finally, the new law provides that the factoring income treated as interest is subject to the foreign tax credit separate limitation *without regard* to the exception that applies to certain interest received from members of the same affiliated group.

Repeal of 30% withholding on interest paid to foreigners. Generally for portfolio interest on obligations issued after 7-18-84, the new law expressly narrows the definition of "portfolio interest" covered by the repeal to interest that would've been covered by the 30% tax but for the repeal. This is designed to confine the correlative denial to CFCs of the benefit of otherwise applicable Subpart F exceptions to such portfolio interest only. In addition, the exception from the repeal of the 30% tax that covers interest received by "10% shareholders" is broadened to include shareholdings derived constructively through attribution of stock owned by a foreign shareholder in the U.S. payor to a less-than-50%-owned foreign subsidiary. The new law also clarifies that the beneficial owner of a registered obligation can claim a refund of tax withheld on interest covered by the repeal (within the general limitation period for refund claims) if he files a statement after (and not necessarily before) interest payments are made.

Original issue discount. Effective for payments after 9-16-84 on obligations issued after 3-31-72, the rule that delays until time of payment the deduction for interest on an OID obligation held by a related foreign person, doesn't apply to the extent the OID is effectively connected with the lender's U.S. trade or business *unless* the OID income is either exempt from U.S. tax or subject to a lower treaty rate. The new law also provides that a payment of principal or interest on an OID obligation to a foreign investor is taxable income to the extent of previously untaxed OID accrued on the obligation, whether or not the OID accrued since the last interest payment. And it provides that on a sale, exchange, or retirement of an OID obligation, the foreign investor is taxed on hitherto untaxed

OID that accrued while he held it, even if that OID exceeds his gain on the obligation's disposition.

Foreign personal holding company rules. Generally for tax years that begin after 1983, the new law supplies a definition of "related person" for the "same country dividend and interest" exclusion from gross income and foreign personal holding company income in FPHC calculations. It imports the definition from the provision dealing with CFC foreign base company sales income (Sec. 954(d)(3)). The new law also clarifies that the "tracing" rule covering stock held through foreign entities applies to all foreign trusts and estates interposed between U.S. taxpayers and FPHCs.

Gain on indirect transfers of stock in a foreign corporation. Under the 1984 Tax Reform Act, a post-7-18-84 exchange by a U.S. corporation of its stock for stock of its 10%-or-more-owned (by voting stock) foreign corporation is generally recast as a distribution of the foreign corporation's stock by the U.S. corporation to its shareholder for purposes of Sec. 1248(a). That provision treats as ordinary income, gains by certain U.S. persons on dispositions of stock in a foreign corporation to the extent of the foreign corporation's allocable earnings and profits. The new law:

• Clarifies that such an indirect transfer is recast as either a stock redemption or liquidation distribution, whichever is appropriate. A liquidating distribution could be then treated as a nonrecognition distribution in complete liquidation of a subsidiary by a corporate shareholder (Sec. 332), and the U.S. corporation could qualify for the Sec. 1248(f)(1) exception from Sec. 1248(f)(2).

• Extends the period for electing retroactive application (to post-10-9-75 transactions) of the '84 TRA amendments, which provide that a CFC's accumulated earnings and profits that previously characterized a U.S. person's gain as ordinary income won't do so another time (i.e., prevented "double counting"). The election can now be made until one year from enactment of the new law (rather than within 180 days after enactment of the '84 TRA).

• As noted at ¶1875, amends Sec. 1248(g)(2) to limit this exception to a shareholder's gain characterized as dividend income under Sec. 356.

Stapled entities. Generally effective 7-18-84, the '84 TRA in effect treats as a U.S. corporation taxable on its worldwide income, a foreign corporation whose interests are "stapled" to the stock interests of a U.S. corporation. The new law excludes from the "stapled entity" rules a foreign corporation if it has established to the IRS that both it and the U.S. corporation to which it's stapled are foreign-owned (i.e., each of them is less-than 50% owned, by total stock vote or value either directly or indirectly by U.S. persons). The new law also authorizes regs to provide that any tax not paid by the foreign corporation will be collected from the U.S. corporation to which it's stapled or from the shareholders of the foreign corporation.

Insurance of related parties by CFCs. Generally effective for tax years of the CFC that begin after 7-18-84, the new law clarifies that the broader Sec. 864(d)(4) definition of "related person" is used for determining the amount of insurance or reinsurance service income that is foreign base company service income. It clarifies that a primary insured is a "related" person if it's a 10% U.S. shareholder or a person related to him.

Definition of resident alien. Generally for tax years that begin after 1984, the new law allows foreign teachers or trainees in the U.S. whose entire compensation was nontaxable under Sec. 872(b)(3) to qualify as "exempt individuals" for purposes of the "substantial presence" test to avoid becoming resident aliens, even if they were "exempt" as a teacher, trainee, or student for any part of four out of seven calendar years. They can't be treated as "exempt" for a calendar year, if they were exempt for any part of four (under prior law two) out of the six years that preceded it. And under the substantial presence test, days in which a professional athlete is present in the U.S. competing in certain charitable sports events aren't counted.

The new law also allows a "qualifying alien individual" who doesn't meet the "permanent residence" and "substantial presence" tests for resident alien treatment for the current year but who satisfies the "substantial presence" test for the following year, to elect tax treatment as a U.S. resident for part of the current calendar year. Under this first-year election, the individual (1) can't be a U.S. resident for the preceding calendar year; (2) must be present in the U.S. for at least 31 consecutive days in the current year; and (3) the individual must be present in the U.S. for at least 75% of the number of days in a "testing period" that starts with the first day of such a 31-day presence and ends with the last day of the current year.

For the 75% test, a total of up to 5 days of actual absence from the U.S. is disregarded, and days on which the individual is an "exempt individual" are not days of presence in the U.S. for both the 31-day and 75% test. The election results in the alien's treatment as a U.S. resident for the part of the current year that starts with the first day of the earliest presence period that meets both the 31-day and 75% tests. The election (revocable only with IRS consent) is made on the return for the current year, but not before the substantial presence test for the following year has been met.

Example: Alien (not a U.S. resident for the preceding year) vacations in the U.S. January 1—31 of the current year, then leaves and returns on October 15. He is considered absent for only 10 days from the U.S. during the remainder of current year, and satisfies the substantial presence test for next year. Result: He can elect to be treated as U.S. resident (e.g., to get joint filing, personal exemptions and itemized deduction) starting on October 15 of the current year (both the 31-day and 75% tests are satisfied for the period October 15—December 31 of the current year).

Act Sec. 1810(c) dealing with related person factoring income amends Secs. 864(d)(5)(A) and 956(b)(3)(A) and adds new Sec. 864(d)(7). Act Sec. 1810(d) dealing with the repeal of the 30% withholding tax amends Secs. 871(a)(1), (h)(2), (3)(C), 881(c)(2), 1441(c)(9) and 1442(a). Act Sec. 1810(e) dealing with OID deductions and income amends Secs. 163(e)(3), 871(a)(1)(C) and 881(a)(3). Act Sec. 1810(h) dealing with FPHC rules amends Secs. 551(f) and 552(c). Act Sec. 1810(i) dealing with gain on indirect transfers of a foreign corporation's stock amend Sec. 1248(i)(1)(B), and also Sec. 133(d)(3)(B) of the 1984 Tax Reform Act. Act Sec. 1810(j) dealing with stapled entities amends Sec. 269B(b) and adds new Sec. 269B(e). Act Sec. 1810(k) dealing with insurance of related parties by CFCs amends Sec. 954(e). Act Sec. 1810(l) dealing with the definition of resident aliens amends Sec. 7701(b). The law changes are effective as if included in the 1984 TRA and as indicated above.

[¶1815] Reporting, Deposits, and Penalties. There are a number of changes to the '84 TRA's compliance provisions. First, effective for mortgage interest payments received after 1984, cooperative housing corporations must report to tenant shareholders and the IRS the tenant's proportionate part of interest paid to the co-op. Second, the failure to supply a taxpayer identification number for obligations in existence on 12-31-84 won't be penalized under Sec. 6676 (rather than 6652) if it relates to mortgage interest reporting rules of amounts received before 1986. Third, a partnership need not make a return under Sec. 6050K (rather than under Sec. 6050K(c)) for post-1984 exchanges of partnership interests until it's notified of the exchange. Fourth, for payments received after 1984, failures to furnish substitute payment statements by brokers (Sec. 6045(d)) are included among penalized failures to file statements (Sec. 6678), and the penalty for intentional disregard to report them is 10% of the aggregate reportable amount. Finally, for tax years that begin after the enactment date, nominees who hold partnership interests for others must furnish the partnership with IRS-prescribed information (e.g., name, address) about the actual owners of the interests, and must be supplied with partnership return information that they will furnish to the actual interest owners as prescribed by regs to come. Similar rules govern trust and estate interests held by nominees.

The new law also supplies by cross reference a definition of "underpayment" in the provision penalizing valuation understatements of estate and gift taxes effective for returns filed after 1984. And it clarifies that the '84 TRA rules for post-7-31-84 deposits of $20,000 or more apply to any taxpayer required to deposit any tax under Sec. 6302(c) more than once a month.

Act Sec. 1811 amends Secs. 6031, 6050K(c), 6652(a)(3), 6678(a)(3) and 7502(e)(3), and amends 1984 Act Sec. 145(d), and adds Secs. 6050H(g) and 6660(f). The law changes are effective as if included in the 1984 Act and as indicated above.

[¶1816] Miscellaneous 1984 Reform Law Provisions. *The "tax benefit" rule.* For amounts recovered after 1983, the new law provides that the exclusion from gross income under the tax benefit rule is limited to amounts that didn't reduce income tax under Chapter 1 of the Code (Secs. 1—1399). This applies, e.g., if an individual who receives a state income tax refund, either had no taxable income in the prior year or was subject to the alternative minimum tax, or if credits reduced the tax to zero. In other cases, the exclusion is determined by comparing the refund with the amount by which itemized deductions exceeded the zero bracket amount (standard deduction), and including the lesser amount in current year's income.

Below-market loans. Generally for term loans made after, and demand loans outstanding after, 6-6-84, the new law grants authority for regs to treat a loan with an indefinite maturity as a demand loan (because of the impracticality of determining the present value of the payments due under it). "Demand loans" for determining the timing of deemed interest and compensation payments also include loans whose interest arrangement isn't transferable and which is contingent on the performance of future services. The new law provides for semiannual compounding in calculating interest on demand loans under Sec. 7872 and excepts from withholding deemed payments of compensation arising from below-market term loans. It clarifies that enactment of Sec. 7872 doesn't affect the definition of self-dealing with private foundations. Finally, the new law provides an exception from Sec. 7872 for obligations of the State of Israel if the obligation is payable in U.S. dollars and bears an annual interest rate of not less than 4%.

Transactions with 'related' persons. Generally for deductions and transactions in tax years beginning after 1983, the new law requires regs to apply the principles that match the timing of a payor's deduction and a payee's inclusion in income (Sec. 267(a)(2)) for payments made to payors who aren't U.S. persons. This could apply, for instance, to require a U.S. subsidiary to use the cash method for payments to its foreign parent that's not engaged in a U.S. trade or business; or to match a "related" payor's accounting methods for amounts accrued to a controlled foreign corporation, to that corporation's method for U.S. tax purposes; or to match accounting methods for accruals of payments to foreign persons in whose hands the payments aren't "effectively connected" income. The new law also extends the exception from the loss deferral rules for inventory transfers to or from a foreign corporation (Sec. 267(f)(3)(B)) to sales between a partnership and a foreign corporation "related" by a more-than-50% common ownership.

For sales or exchanges after 9-27-85 that involve a controlled partnership, the new law extends the loss disallowance rules and the treatment of gains as ordinary income (Sec. 707(b)(1)(A), (2)(A)) to transactions with a *constructive more-than-50% owner* of a partnership interest who isn't an actual partner. The rule is intended to replace the rule in Temp. Reg. Sec. 1.267(a)-2T(c), Questions 2 and 3.

The new law also provides that the deduction-and-income matching rules of Sec. 267(a)(2) apply between partnerships commonly owned through more-than-50% interests.

Distributions related to repeal of exemption of Freddie Mac. The new law expressly denies the dividends-received deduction for dividends paid by the Federal Home Loan Mortgage Corporation (Freddie Mac) out of E&P accumulated before 1-1-85, and repeals the prior law rule that treats Freddie Mac as having no accumulated profits as of 1-1-85. It clarifies that dividends paid by Freddie Mac can't produce more than one dividends-received deduction as to income (routed via and) received from a Federal Home Loan Bank. And it provides that a dividends received deduction for dividends paid by a Home Loan Bank is determined by reference to its retained earnings for financial purposes. It also allows a dividends received deduction for dividends received after 1984 directly from Freddie Mac by taxable corporate shareholders. The new law also provides that for all Code purposes the late-1984 preferred stock distribution by Freddie Mac to Federal Home Loan Banks, and the January 1985 distributions of that stock by these banks to their member institutions, are treated as money distributions equal to the stock's value when distributed by the Home Loan Banks followed by the institutions' payment of this money to Freddie Mac in return for its stock.

Listed property and luxury automobiles. The new law clarifies that the maximum weight of vehicles defined as "passenger automobile" (but not of trucks and vans within that definition)for the limitations on the investment credit and depreciation (Sec. 280F), as well as for the gas guzzler excise tax (Sec. 4064) is indicated in terms of their gross *unloaded* weight (i.e., without passengers or cargo). For the gas guzzler tax, the rule applies as of 1-1-80 with special rules for 1985 and 1986 station wagons. And for the gas guzzler tax, the term "manufacturer" doesn't include a "small manufacturer" who merely lengthens existing cars. The Treasury is to prescribe alternative rate schedules for small manufacturers.

The new law clarifies that both deductions for *rentals and other lease payments* (as well as other deductions or credits) by employees on listed property are conditioned on its use for the employer's convenience and as a condition of employment. It also provides that to be excepted from treatment as listed property, a computer must be owned or leased by the person operating the business establishment and used exclusively in the establishment. (This is designed to prevent credits or deductions for employee-owned computers used mostly in the office.)

The new law excludes from treatment as "listed property" property almost entirely used in transporting persons or goods for compensation or under hire.

The changes for listed property and luxury cars in general apply to property placed in service and leases entered into after 6-18-84.

Act Sec. 1812(a) dealing with the tax benefit rule amends Sec. 111(a) and (c), 381(c)(12), 1351(d)(2) and 1398(g)(3). Act Sec. 1812(b) dealing with below market loans amends Sec. 7872(f)(2), (5) and (9) and Sec. 4941(d)(2). Act Sec. 1812(b)(5) dealing with Israel Bonds doesn't amend the Code. Act Sec. 1812(c) amends Secs. 267(f)(3)(B), 707(b)(1)(A) and (2)(A) and adds Sec. 267(a)(3). It also provides a transitional rule for a specified situation (Act Sec. 1812(c)(5)). Act Sec. 1812(d) dealing with Freddie Mac distributions amends Sec. 246(a)(2) and 1984 Tax Reform Act Sec. 177(d)(4). Act Sec. 1812(e) amends Sec. 280F(d)(2)—(5) and 4064(b). The law changes are effective as if included in the 1984 Tax Reform Act and as indicated above.

Life Insurance

[¶1821] Corrections to Life Insurance Company Code Provisions. The new law contains several corrections to the life insurance company Code provisions, as amended by the '84 TRA.

Reserves. The new law provides that, in computing the increases or decreases of amounts discounted at interest under insurance and annuity contracts (Sec. 807(c)(3)), the amount taken into account for any such contract can't be less than the net surrender value of that contract.

The new law also provides that when a Treasury mortality and morbidity table is used for a type of contract (because there is no commissioner's standard table for such a contract) and the Treasury *changes* that table by regulation, the new table will be treated as if it were a new prevailing commissioner's standard table adopted by the 26th state as of a date specified by the Treasury. That date can be no earlier than the date the regulation is issued.

Excess interest. The new law amends the definition of "excess interest" under Sec. 808(d)(1) to make it clear that excess interest refers only to the *excess amounts*, and not to the *entire* amount in the nature of interest (including the amount determined at the prevailing state assumed interest rate).

Fresh-start adjustment and policyholder dividends. The '84 TRA changed the method by which life insurance companies figure their deduction for policyholder dividends—that is, such deductions are now figured on an accrual, rather than a reserve, basis. This change wasn't treated as an accounting method change. Thus, no income or loss was recognized as to existing policyholder dividend reserves, and life companies were given a "fresh start" in figuring policyholder dividend deductions.

The fresh start was intended to mitigate the detriment caused by the statutory accounting change. However, by changing its business practice (e.g., by guaranteeing policy dividends on termination, or by changing the payment date by making policy dividends available on declaration), a company can accelerate into the current year deductions that under its former business practice would have been deductible in the following year. This would, in part, put the company in the position it enjoyed under prior law.

To correct this problem, the new law reduces a company's policyholders dividend deduction by the amount that was accelerated because of a change in business practice. This reduction (which is made before any reduction for the ownership differential provision for mutual companies) is limited, on a cumulative basis, to the amount of the company's 1984 fresh-start adjustment. Both the amount of the accelerated deduction and the amount of the 1984 fresh-start adjustment are figured separately for each line of business. The 1984 fresh-start adjustment is the company's amount of policyholder dividend reserves as of 12-31-83, reduced by (1) dividends accrued before 1-1-84; and (2) previously nondeductible dividends under pre-1984 TRA Sec. 809(f).

The reduction for accelerated deductions doesn't apply to a mere change in the amount of policyholder dividends. Nor does it apply to dividends paid or accrued on policies issued after 12-31-83 unless the policy was issued in exchange for a substantially similar policy that was issued on or before 12-31-81. Further, it doesn't apply to policyholder dividends paid or accrued as to a group policy bought by an employer under an employee welfare benefit plan.

Equity base. The new law clarifies the term "equity base," which is a factor in determining a mutual life company's differential earnings amount. The new law specifically provides that no item will be taken into account more than once in determining the equity base. This ensures that items that are *specifically* included in the equity base aren't included a second time because they're *indirectly* included under another specifically included item.

50 largest stock companies. The new law modifies the statutory authority given to the Treasury to issue regulations that would exclude companies from the group of 50 largest stock companies. (The numerical average of the earnings rates of the 50 largest stock companies is a factor taken into account in figuring a mutual life company's differential earnings amount.) Under the new law, the Treasury must exclude from the group for any calendar year any company that has a negative equity base. It can also exclude by regulations any other company whose equity base is so small that its inclusion in the group would seriously distort the stock earnings rate; however, such companies can be excluded only to the extent their exclusion doesn't cause the *total* number of excluded companies to exceed two. Thus, if two or more companies must be excluded because they have negative equity bases, then no "distorting companies" can be excluded. The new law also provides that, in determining the base period stock earnings rate, the Treasury must exclude from the group any company that had a negative equity base at any time during 1981, 1982, or 1983.

The new law also makes it clear that only the 50 largest *domestic* stock life insurance companies are taken into account. Similarly, only *domestic* mutual life insurance companies are taken into account in determining the average mutual earnings rate.

Statement gain or loss from operations. The new law modifies the definition of "statement gain or loss from operations" under Sec. 809(g)(1). The term refers to net gain or loss from operations as set out in the annual statement, determined without regard to federal income taxes, with further adjustment for certain items. The new law makes it clear that statement gain or loss from operations must be adjusted by substituting (1) the amount of the *deduction* for policyholder dividends, unreduced by the differential earnings amount, for (2) the amount shown on the annual statement for policyholder dividends. Using the unreduced tax amount eliminates a circularity in the computation of the differential earnings amount.

Differential earnings rate and estimated tax. The new law provides that if, as to any estimated tax installment, the differential earnings rate for the second tax year preceding the year for which the installment is paid is *less* than the rate applicable to the tax year for which the installment is paid (see Sec. 809(c)(1)), then in applying estimated tax underpayment penalties to that installment, the amount of tax will be determined by using that lesser rate.

Also, the recomputation of a mutual life company's differential earnings amount for any tax year won't affect the company's liability for estimated tax payments for the tax year in which the recomputed amount is included in, or deducted from, income under Sec. 809(f).

Proration formulas. The new law makes several clarifying amendments to the computation of "company share" and "policyholder's share."

- In arriving at the company's share of net investment income, net investment income is reduced by *all* interest on amounts left on deposit with the company.

- "Required interest," an item taken into account in computing policy interest, includes not only interest on reserves determined at the prevailing state assumed rate, but also interest determined at another appropriate rate if the prevailing state assumed rate isn't used.

- The denominator of the "minifraction" used for computing gross investment income's proportionate share of policyholder dividends is redefined as (1) life insurance gross income, reduced by (2) the excess of the closing balance of Sec. 807(c) reserve items over the opening balance for the tax year. Also, in computing the denominator, life insurance gross income is determined by *including* tax-exempt interest, and by computing decreases in reserves without reducing the closing balance of the reserve items by the company's share of tax-exempt interest.

- "Net investment income" is redefined as (1) 90% of gross investment income *or* (2) for gross investment income attributable to assets held in segregated asset accounts under variable contracts, 95% of gross investment income.

- In computing net increases or decreases in reserves (Sec. 807(a) and (b)) as well as the company's share and policyholder's share, gross investment income and tax-exempt income do *not* include interest received as to a Section 133(b) ESOP loan. ESOP loan interest is also excluded from life insurance gross income in determining gross investment income's proportionate share of policyholder dividends.

Foreign life insurance companies. If additional income has been imputed to a foreign life insurance company doing business in the United States (because the surplus held in the United States is less than the required surplus), the imputed income is added to life insurance gross income *before* computing the special and small life insurance company deductions. The imputed income is treated as gross investment income.

PSA distributions. As a result of the '84 TRA, life insurance companies can no longer make additions to their pre-1984 policyholders surplus accounts. They must, however, maintain those PSAs and include in income any direct or indirect distributions to shareholders from their PSAs. The new law provides that a bona fide loan with arm's-length terms and conditions won't be considered a direct or indirect PSA distribution.

For loans made before 3-1-86 that don't contain arm's-length terms and conditions, the amount that will be treated as an indirect PSA distribution is limited to the foregone interest on the loan. This limitation applies unless the loan was renegotiated, extended, renewed, or revised after 2-28-86.

The new law also reinstates a pre-1984 TRA provision (Sec. 819(b)) that provides instructions for PSA distributions of foreign life companies doing business in the United States.

Deficiency reserves. The new law excludes deficiency reserves from the definition of "life insurance reserves" and "total reserves" for purposes of Sec. 816 (which defines "life insurance company") and Sec. 813(a)(4)(B) (which defines "surplus held in the United States" for foreign life companies doing business in the United States).

Nondiversified contracts. The new law clarifies the special rule for variable life insurance contracts based on investments in Treasury securities. To the extent that any segregated asset account with respect to a variable life insurance contract is invested in U.S. Treasury securities, the investments made by the account will be considered adequately diversified under Sec. 818(h)(1). (Under that Section, variable contracts based on segregated asset accounts aren't treated as annuity, endowment, or life insurance contracts when investments made by the account aren't adequately diversified.)

The new law also provides that if all the beneficial interests in a regulated investment company (RIC) or a trust are held by one or more (1) insurance companies (or affiliated companies) in their general account or in segregated asset accounts, or (2) fund managers (or affiliated companies) in the creation or management of the RIC or trust, then the assets of the RIC or trust will be taken into account in applying the diversification requirements. This change broadens the prior-law "look through" rules to allow the use of seed money, or the ownership of fund shares by an insurance company or fund manager, in operating the underlying investment fund.

Deferred compensation plans. Diversification requirements for segregated asset accounts underlying variable contracts don't apply to pension plan contracts— that include government plans. The new law makes it clear that government plans include eligible state deferred compensation plans under Section 457(b), as well as government plans under Section 414(d).

Dividends within affiliated group. The new law reinstates a special rule for life insurance companies filing or required to file consolidated returns. The rule was eliminated by the '84 TRA, and is reinstated with modifications reflecting the structural changes made by the life company provisions of the '84 TRA. Under the new special rule, for life companies filing or required to file consolidated returns, any determination under the life company provisions of Subchapter L as to dividends paid by one member of the affiliated group to another member will be made as if the group weren't filing a consolidated return.

Dividends from subsidiaries. A life company's deduction for dividends received from a subsidiary is generally determined by prorating the dividends between the company and the policyholders. Under prior law, 100% dividends (those that would be 100% deductible by the recipient under Sec. 243, 244, or 245(b)) weren't subject to proration between the company and policyholders, except to the extent they were paid out of tax-exempt interest or dividends that would not qualify as 100% dividends in the taxpayer's hands. This rule applied whether the payer was a life company or any other corporation.

The new law generally retains the prior law proration rules for 100% dividends paid by a corporation other than an insurance company— but it adds a special rule for 100% dividends paid to a life company by another life company out of E&P for tax years beginning after 12-31-83. If the payer company's share under Sec. 812 for that tax year exceeds the recipient's share for its tax year in which it receives or accrues the dividend, then the recipient's deduction for the 100% dividend is reduced. The amount of the reduction is computed by multiplying (1) the part of the dividend that is attributable to prorated amounts (tax-exempt interest and non-100% dividends) by (2) the percentage obtained by subtracting the recipient's share from the payer company's share. The part of the dividend that is attributable to prorated amounts is determined by treating any dividend by the payer company as coming first out of E&P for tax years beginning after 12-31-83, attributable to prorated amounts; and by determining the portion of E&P attributable to prorated amounts without any reduction for federal income taxes. The new law also states that similar rules will apply to 100% dividends paid by an insurance company that isn't a life insurance company.

High-surplus mutual rules. The new law contains a provision that doesn't amend the Code, but affects the five-year transitional rule for high-surplus mutual life companies under Sec. 809(i). Under the provision, for a mutual life company that was incorporated on 2-23-1888, and acquired a stock subsidiary during 1982, the amount of the company's equity base for purposes of the transitional rule is $175 million. This provision applies without regard to any other provision that would otherwise limit the company's equity base.

Variable contracts. The new law adds a provision that allows certain variable contracts with guarantees to be treated as variable contracts under Sec. 817(d). Obligations under the guarantee that exceed obligations under the contract without regard to the guarantee will be accounted for as part of the company's general account. Under a special effective date, this provision applies to contracts issued after 12-31-86, and to contracts issued before 1-1-87 if the contract was treated as a variable contract on the taxpayer's return.

Act Sec. 1821(a) amends Sec. 807(c), relating to reserves; Act Sec. 1821(b) amends Sec. 808(d)(1)(B), relating to excess interest; Act Sec. 1821(c) adds new Sec. 808(f), relating to fresh-start adjustment and policyholder dividends; Act Sec. 1821(d) amends Sec. 809(b)(2), relating to equity base; Act Sec. 1821(e) amends Sec. 809(d)(4)(C), relating to 50 largest stock companies; Act Sec. 1821(f) amends Sec. 809(g)(1), relating to statement gain or loss from operations; Act Sec. 1821(g) amends Sec. 809(c), relating to estimated tax payments; Act Sec. 1821(h) amends Sec. 809(f), relating to recomputation of differential earnings amount; Act Sec. 1821(i) amends Secs. 812(b), (c), and adds new Sec. 812(g), relating to proration formulas; Act Sec. 1821(j) amends Sec. 813(a)(1), relating to foreign life companies; Act Sec. 1821(k) amends Secs. 815(a), (f), relating to distributions from policyholders surplus account; Act Sec. 1821(l) adds new Sec. 816(h), relating to deficiency reserves; Act Sec. 1821(m) amends Sec. 817(h), relating to nondiversified contracts; Act Sec. 1821(n) amends Sec. 818(a)(6)(A), relating to deferred compensation plans; Act Sec. 1821(o) amends Sec. 818(e), relating to consolidated returns; Act Sec. 1821(p) amends Sec. 805(a)(4), relating to dividends from subsidiaries; Act Sec. 1821(q), relating to high-surplus mutuals, doesn't amend the Code; Act Sec. 1821(r) makes a clerical amendment to Sec. 809(f)(3); Act Sec. 1821(s) amends Sec. 807(d)(5)(C), relating to changes in Treasury tables; Act Sec. 1821(t), relating to variable contracts, amends Sec. 817(d); all effective as if included in the 1984 TRA and as shown above.

[¶1822] Life Company 'Fresh-Start' Rule. The new law provides several clarifications on the effect of the '84 TRA's "fresh-start" rule for life insurance reserves. The '84 TRA required life insurance companies to recompute their life insurance reserves. Under a provision of the '84 TRA that didn't amend the Code—the fresh-start rule—any change in accounting method or in the method of computing reserves that was required solely because of the provisions of the Act generally did not give rise to income or loss. However, the benefit of the fresh start was denied to (1) reserves transferred under a reinsurance agreement entered into after 9-27-83 and before 1-1-84, and (2) reserve strengthening reported for federal income tax purposes after 9-27-83 for a tax year ending before 1-1-84.

The new law makes the following clarifications:

• The change in a life company's reserves attributable to the fresh start will be taken into account in computing the company's E&P. The adjustment to E&P must be made for the company's first tax year beginning in 1984 (1985 in the case of two particular life insurance companies).

• As to reserves for which the fresh start is denied, the new law clarifies that the rule that allows a company to spread a change in the basis of computing reserves over 10 years will apply to the extent a 10-year spread would have been required under pre-'84 TRA law.

- To prevent abuse of the fresh-start provisions by use of reinsurance transactions *after* 1983 when the reinsurer is on a fiscal rather than a calendar year, the new law conforms the closing date (1-1-84 under the '84 TRA) to the date for revaluation of reserves. Thus, if a reinsurer's tax year is a fiscal year, "the first day of the first taxable year beginning after 1983" is substituted for "January 1, 1984."

- Under the '84 TRA, an election after 9-27-83, to revalue preliminary term reserves to net level reserves (former Section 818(c)) was generally not given effect. There was an exception to this rule that gave effect to a Section 818(c) election if more than 95% of the reserves computed under the election were attributable to risks under life insurance contracts issued by the taxpayer under an insurance plan first filed after 3-1-82 and before 9-28-83. However, the legislative history to the '84 TRA indicated that a post-9-27-83 Sec. 818(c) election would be treated as reserve strengthening for purposes of denying the benefits of the fresh-start rule. The new law clarifies that a Sec. 818(c) election made under the exception described above won't be treated as reserve strengthening for purposes of denying the fresh start. Also, if a corporation made a Sec. 818(c) election before 9-28-83, and was acquired in a Sec. 338 qualified stock purchase before 12-31-83, the fact that the corporation is treated as a *new* corporation won't render the Sec. 818(c) election nonapplicable to it. For such a corporation, the new law extends the time for making a Sec. 818(c) election as to its first tax year beginning in 1983 and ending after 9-28-83, and for making a Sec. 338 election as to the qualified stock purchase, to 60 days after the enactment date of the 1986 TRA. It also extends the statute of limitations as to either election if the election would not have been timely but for the extension.

- Under the '84 TRA, qualified life companies can elect not to recompute reserves for contracts issued before the first day of the first tax year beginning after 12-31-83. And if a company makes that election, and had tentative life insurance company taxable income (LICTI) of $3 million or less for its first tax year beginning after 12-31-83, it could make a second election to treat the reserve for any contract issued on or after the first day of that tax year (and before 1-1-89) as being equal to the statutory reserve for that contract (with an adjustment similar to the Menge formula under TEFRA). The new law makes the following changes: (1) When testing whether a company can make the second election, it must compute the $3 million tentative LICTI limitation by determining reserves as if the second election were in effect; (2) for a company making the second election, the reserve will be the *greater* of the adjusted statutory reserve or the net surrender value of the contract; and (3) the Menge adjustment is to be applied to the opening and closing reserves in computing net increases or decreases in life insurance reserves.

Act Sec. 1822 amends 1984 TRA Secs. 216(b)(1); (b)(3)(A), (c); (b)(4)(B); and (c)(2)(A), (B); and adds new Sec. 216(b)(4)(C) to the 1984 TRA; all effective as if included in the 1984 TRA and as shown above.

[¶1823] **Life Company Net Level Reserve Election.** Recognizing that, for practical reasons, *no company* would elect to use the special rule for companies using the net level reserve method for noncancellable accident and health insurance contracts ('84 TRA, Sec. 217(n)), the new law expands the coverage of the rule. Under the new law, a company can use the net level reserve method for tax purposes on any directly written noncancellable accident and health insurance contract—whether under existing or *new* plans of insurance. To qualify for treatment under this rule for any tax year, the company must have (1) used the net level reserve method to compute at least 99% of its statutory reserves for such contracts as of 12-31-82, and (2) received more than half of its total direct premiums for calendar year 1982 from directly written noncancellable accident and health insurance. In addition, after 12-31-83, the company will be treated as using the proper reserve method for directly written noncancellable accident and health contracts for a tax year if, through that tax year, the company has continuously used the net level reserve method for computing at least 99% of its tax and statutory reserves on such contracts. As to any contracts for which the company *doesn't* use the net level reserve method, the company must use the same method for tax reserves as it uses for statutory reserves.

Act Sec. 1823(a) amends 1984 TRA Sec. 217(n), relating to the net level reserve election, effective as if included in the 1984 TRA and as shown above.

[¶1824] **Insurance Company Estimated Tax Underpayments.** The '84 TRA contained a special rule providing relief from penalties for estimated tax underpayments caused by the insurance company provisions. The new law repeals that special rule in favor of a broader general relief provision of the new law. For corporations, the new provision (contained in Act Sec. 1879) provides generally that no penalties will be imposed for estimated tax underpayments for any period before March 16, 1985, to the extent that the underpayment was caused by the 1984 TRA.

Act Sec. 1824 repeals 1984 TRA Sec. 218.

[¶1825] **Tax Treatment of Universal Life and Other Investment-Oriented Policies.** Since 1982 (TEFRA), to qualify as life insurance, a policy had to meet requirements of applicable state and foreign law, plus either of two alternative tests: (1) the cash value accumulation test or (2) the guideline premium and cash corridor test.

In addition, since 1982, prior law further provided three general computational rules that restrict the actual provisions and benefits that can be offered in a life insurance contract. First, the net single premium (under the cash value accumulation test) or the guideline premium limitation for any contract assumes the death benefit never increases (it treats qualified additional benefits the same way). Second, the maturity date is no earlier than the insured's 95th birthday, and no later than the insured's 100th birthday. Third, the amount of any endowment benefit may not exceed the smallest death benefit payable at any time.

The new law clarifies the second computational rule: The maturity date may not be before age 95 or later than age 100. This conforms the second computational rule to the first and third.

The new law also adds an additional computational rule to apply the second computational rule and to determine the cash value on the maturity date under the third computational rule. The death benefits are deemed to be provided until the maturity date in the second computational rule. This, coupled with the second computational rule generally will disqualify contracts endowing at face value before age 95, but will allow pre age 95 endowment amounts of less than face value.

The additional computational rule doesn't apply to qualification determinations under the cash value corridor test.

Tax effect. Assuming earnings in excess of premiums at the end of 20 years on a $100,000 policy issued at age 35 amount to $53,260 and cash values are $80,000, the policyholder's income taxes—from the year his policy fails the tests until the end of year 20—will total $13,315 in the 25% bracket, $17,576 in the 33% bracket, $22,369 in the 42% bracket, and $26,630 in the 50% bracket.

Death benefits taxable, too. Only the $20,000 insurance at risk at age 55 ($100,000 minus $80,000) will qualify for the Sec. 101(a)(1) exclusion. Result: If the insured dies at age 55, a steep tax will hit the $80,000 included in the beneficiary's income.

Universal life withdrawals. Sec. 7702(f)(7)(B) states: "In the case of any change which reduces the future benefits under the contract, such change shall be treated as an exchange of the contract for another contract."

And Sec. 1035(a)-(1) states: "No gain or loss shall be recognized on the exchange of a contract of life insurance for another contract of life insurance. . ."

But Sec. 1031(b) says: "If an exchange would be within the provisions of section 1035(a). . .if it were not for the fact that the property received in exchange consists. . . also of. . .money, then the gain. . .shall be. . .the sum of such money and the fair market value of such. . .property."

Question. Do partial withdrawals from universal life policies trigger current income taxes to the extent the withdrawal plus the cash value of the new policy exceed the policyholder's investment in the original contract?

The '84 TRA authorized regulations in this withdrawal area, revising some of the adjustment rules prospectively, if necessary.

But the new law replaces Treasury's authority to prescribe regulations affecting withdrawals with these specific new rules:

Any withdrawals from a life insurance contract will be treated as "first paid out of income" only if the reduction in benefits occurs during 15 years after the issue date.

For the first five years, the maximum amount paid first out of income will depend on whether the contract meets (1) the cash value accumulation test or (2) the guideline premium/cash value corridor test.

Under (1), the required distribution is the excess of the cash value over the net single premium determined after the reduction.

Under (2), the required distribution is the greater of the excess of total premiums paid over the redetermined guideline premium limit or the excess of the cash value over the redetermined cash value corridor.

From the end of year 5 to the end of year 15, the maximum amount paid first out of income is the excess of the cash value before the distribution over the maximum cash value that wouldn't violate the cash value corridor after the reduction in benefits.

No interest deduction on policy loans. Many life underwriters characterize universal life insurance policies as annual premium contracts that qualify for interest deductions under the four-out-of-seven rule [Sec. 264(c)(1)].

But single premium policies include contracts where an amount is deposited with the insurer to pay a substantial number of future premiums [Sec. 264(a)(2) and Reg. §264-2]. The Committee Report—restating these Code and Reg. sections—points out that Sec. 264 never has allowed interest deductions on loans against universal life and other single premium policies. Such contracts are not eligible for the four-out-of-seven rule.

Contracts that don't qualify as life insurance contracts. Under the '84 TRA, a policyholder must include in income the excess of the contract's cash value increase and cost of insurance during the year over the year's net premium (premium minus dividend).

The new law uses the gross premium in computing income; it doesn't use the dividend to reduce the premium.

Contracts issued during 1984 that meet new requirements. Under the new law, any policy issued in 1984 that qualified under Sec. 7702 also will qualify under prior law Sec. 101(f) as extended through 1984.

Certain contracts issued after 9-30-84. The new law clarifies the '84 TRA's Sec. 7702 transition rule. The new law allows 3% rather than 4% as the minimum interest rate under the cash value accumulation test, without regard to any higher rate guaranteed initially.

Act Sec. 1825(a) amends the Sec. 7702(e)(1) computational rules that restrict the benefits under a life insurance contract; Act Sec. 1825(b) amends Sec. 7702(f)(7), that determines how universal life withdrawals are taxed; Act Sec. 1825(c) amends Sec. 7702(g) on treatment of contracts that don't qualify as life insurance contracts; Act Sec. 1825(d) and (e) and Sec. 221(d)(1) and (2)(C) clarify Sec. 7702.

[¶1826] **Deferred Annuity Withdrawals.** The '84 law imposed a 5% penalty on any distribution from a deferred annuity before age 59½, unless the policyholder was disabled, died, or received an annuity for life or a minimum period of at least five years. Premature withdrawals were taxed to the extent the cash value exceeded the investment in the contract.

Distribution at annuity holder's death. Under the '84 law, when an annuity holder died before the annuity starting date, the cash value had to (1) be distributed within five years after the date of death, or (2) used within one year of death to provide a life annuity or installments payable over a period not longer than the beneficiary's life expectancy. In addition, a spousal beneficiary could continue the contract under the same terms as the decedent.

If the annuity holder died on or after the annuity starting date, any remaining proceeds had to be distributed to the beneficiary at least as rapidly as the rate of distribution to the decedent.

The new law makes clear that these rules need not be met by annuity contracts provided under a qualified pension plan or an IRA. These annuities must satisfy the qualified plan or IRA distribution rules.

In addition, the new law clarifies the application of the required distribution rules when the contract holder is not an individual. Here, the primary annuitant is the holder of the contract. The "primary annuitant" is the person whose life primarily affects the payout's timing or amount; e.g., that person whose life measures the annuity starting date or the annuity benefits. The new law also clarifies the penalty exception for death benefits. The penalty doesn't apply to any benefit on or after an individual's death or, where the contract holder isn't an individual, on or after the primary annuitant's death.

If an individual owner transfers an annuity contract by gift or, if the holder is not an individual or if there is any change in the primary annuitant, the transfer or change is treated as the death of the holder. This implements the forced distribution rules adopted under the '84 TRA law (intended to terminate tax deferral allowed when annuity contracts no longer were required as a retirement vehicle for the contractholder who was enjoying the tax deferral on the income). Without the correction covering transfers of annuity contracts by gift, the required distribution rules adopted in the '84 law could be avoided easily by a transfer to a person much younger.

Otherwise, the rules would allow taxpayers to continue tax deferral beyond the life of an individual taxpayer. As with the required distribution rules, a distribution of the entire interest in the contract will not be required with respect to any Sec. 1041(a) transfer (relating to transfers of property between spouses or incident to divorce).

Premature withdrawal penalty. The new law increases to 10% the 5% penalty now imposed on premature distributions from an annuity. No penalty applies, however, if the policyholder is 59½, disabled, dies or receives the payout under an annuity for life or over a period of at least five years.

The new law (1) shows how to treat joint contractholders when one dies and (2) clarifies that the forced distribution requirements adopted in the '84 Act apply on the death of any contract holder. These provisions apply only to contracts issued six months after the new law's date of enactment.

Act Sec. 1826 amends Secs. 72(q), that levies the 15% penalty, and (p), that explains the required distribution rules, effective as if included in the '84 TRA and as shown above.

[¶1827] Group-Term Insurance. The '84 law provided that a retired employee's group-term life insurance may continue only on the same terms as an active employee. In effect, an employer no longer could pay the full cost of as much insurance as desired without any cost included in the retired employee's income. The law exempted employees retired on disability.

In addition, employer-paid premiums for any key employee under a discriminatory group-term plan—including the first $50,000—were included in the employee's income. And the amount couldn't be determined under Table I. Instead, the key employee's taxable income included the actual cost.

Effective Date: The rules applied to taxable years beginning after 12-31-83, but not to any plan in existence on 1-1-84. However, the exception applied only to individuals age 55 or more and either (1) retired on or before 1-1-84, or (2) employed during 1983 and —if the plan was discriminatory—retired before 1-1-87.

Under the new law, in a discriminatory plan, any key employee's cost is the greater of the actual group-term cost or the Table I cost. The '84 law's intent was to discourage the further use of discriminatory group-term plans. But this requirement would work only if the actual cost exceeded the Table I cost. The new law gives full effect to prior Congressional intent not to encourage discrimination (when actual cost may be less than Table I cost). Key employee is redefined to include any retired employee if he or she was a key employee at retirement. For applying the nondiscrimination requirements of the group-term life insurance provisions, the new law also clarifies that, to the extent provided in regulations, coverage and benefit tests may be applied separately to active and former employees.

The new law also makes a clerical correction to coordinate Sec. 83(e)(5), with Sec. 79. Sec. 83(e)(5) currently excepts the cost of group-term life insurance to which Sec. 79 applies from the application of Sec. 83 (governing the taxation of property transferred in connection with performance of services). The new law provides: Sec. 83 doesn't apply to group-term life insurance covered by Sec. 79. When an employee retires, the present value of any future group-term life insurance coverage that may become nonforfeitable on retirement will be taxed immediately to the employee upon retirement if the employee receives a permanent guarantee of life insurance coverage from the insurance company. But if the coverage is group-term life insurance within the meaning of Sec. 79, the cost of the coverage will be taxable annually to the retired employee.

Act Sec. 1827 amends Sec. 79, relating to separate treatment of former employees, cost to a key employee under a discriminatory plan, and Sec. 83(e), covering the immediate inclusion in a retiree's income of the present value of the lifetime coverage, effective for taxable years ending after the date of enactment.

[¶1828] Amendment Related to Certain Changes of Insurance Policies. The new law extends the tax-free policy-exchange rules to endowment contracts issued by nontaxable insurance companies.

Act Sec. 1828 amends Sec. 1035(b).

[¶1829] Waiver of Interest. The new law provides that no interest will be payable for any period before 7-19-84, on any underpayment of tax to the extent the underpayment was caused by the life insurance company provisions in Subtitle A of Title 11 of the '84 TRA.

Act Sec. 1829, effective as shown above.

[¶1830] **Modco Grandfather Provision Reaffirmed.** The 1982 Tax Equity and Fiscal Responsibility Act repealed Section 820, under which life insurance companies could elect to treat modified coinsurance as conventional coinsurance. TEFRA also grandfathered the federal income tax treatment of existing agreements for tax years before 1982. Thus, unless the IRS could prove fraud, the tax savings attributable to Modco agreements would be free from an IRS challenge for pre-1982 years.

In 1986, however, the IRS issued audit guidelines on when agents should raise pre-1982 Modco issues *even in the absence of fraud.* Under the guidelines, the IRS would take a close look at Modco agreements that were antedated to take effect before they were signed, and the rate at which investment income was transferred under Modco agreements.

The new law reaffirms TEFRA's grandfather rule. Thus, the IRS won't be able to challenge pre-1982 Modco agreements except for fraud.

Act Sec. 1830.

Private Foundations

[¶1831] **Reduction in Section 4940 Excise Tax.** The new law modifies the rules under which the excise tax on a private foundation's net investment income is reduced from 2% to 1%. The reduction is permitted if qualified distributions during the year equaled or exceeded the sum of the foundations assets for the year multiplied by the average percentage payout for the previous five years plus 1% of the foundation's net investment income for the year. In addition, the average percentage payout had to be at least 5% (3⅓% if a private operating foundation).

The new law replaces the average percentage payout requirement by providing that the rate reduction is available only if the foundation wasn't liable for tax for failure to make minimum expenditures for charitable purposes (under Sec. 4942) for any year during the base period.

Clerical amendments. The new law makes a clerical amendment expanding the application of the definition of "capital gain property." It also makes it clear that a game-of-chance exception to the definition of unrelated trade or business applies only to North Dakota.

Act Sec. 1831, defining capital gain property, amends Sec. 170(b)(1)(C)(iv); Act Sec. 1832, modifying the excise tax reduction, amends Sec. 4940(e)(2)(B); both effective as if included in the 1984 TRA (effective for taxable years beginning after 12-31-84). Act Sec. 1833, corrects a reference to second tier taxes, by amending Sec. 6214(c), effective as if included in the 1984 TRA. Act

Sec. 1834, dealing with games of chance, amends 1984 TRA Sec. 311(a)(3)(A), effective for games of chance conducted after 6-30-81.

Tax Simplification Provisions

[¶1841] Estimated Tax of Nonresident Aliens. The new law restores the pre-1984 TRA estimated tax provisions applying to nonresident aliens. These payments must be made in three (not four) installments, due June 15, September 15, and January 15. And 50% of the amount will be due with the first payment.

Act Sec. 1841, reinstating the nonresident alien estimated tax, redesignates Secs. 6654(j), (i), and (l), as (k), (l), and (m) and adds new (j), effective as if included in the 1984 TRA (tax years beginning after 12-31-84).

[¶1842] Property Transfers in Divorce. The new law makes the following changes to clear up some provisions from the '84 TRA. First, the Section 267 loss disallowance rules won't apply to any transfer incident to a divorce under Sec. 1041(a).

Second, a transferor must recognize gain under a transfer in trust, incident to divorce, to the extent that liabilities assumed by the trust exceed the transferor's basis, notwithstanding Sec. 1041.

Third, the transferor must recognize gain on the transfer of installment obligations to the trust.

Fourth, the Sec. 2516 property settlement gift tax exclusion applies to transfers of "ex-husbands" and "ex-wives" as well as "husbands" and "wives."

Act Sec. 1842(a), relating to loss transactions, adds new Sec. 267(g); Act Sec. 1842(b), relating to transfers in trust adds new Sec. 1041(e); Act Sec. 1842(c), relating to installment obligations, amends Sec. 453B; Act Sec. 1842(d), relating to property settlements, amends Sec. 7701(a)(17); all effective as if included in the 1984 TRA, for transfers after 7-18-84.

[¶1843] Alimony and Support. The new law makes it clear that payments under any decree won't be disqualified from treatment as alimony or separate maintenance solely because the decree doesn't specifically state that the payments will terminate at the payee's death.

The new law also makes it clear what events are considered a contingency for child support purposes by correcting a cross reference.

Six-year rule reduced to three. The new law revises the front-loading alimony rules by generally reducing the six-year rule to three years. If alimony payments in the first year exceed the average of annual payments in the second year (reduced by excess payments for that year) and the third year, by more than $15,000 the excess amounts are recaptured in the third year by requiring the payor to include the excess in income and allowing the payee a deduction for such excess payments. A similar rule operates the extent payments in the second year exceed payments in the third year by more than $15,000.

As under prior law, recapture isn't required (1) if either party dies; (2) if the payee remarries within certain time limits; (3) for certain temporary support payments; or (4) for certain fluctuations that aren't within the control of the payor.

Effective Date: The new three-year rule is effective for divorce or separation instruments executed after 12-31-86. A special rule allows pre-1987 instruments that are modified after 1986 to come within the new rules. The new law also reduces the recapture period to three years for instruments not covered by the changes (pre-1987 instruments).

Act Secs. 1843(a) and (d), correcting cross references, amends Sec. 71; Act Sec. 1843(b), relating to alimony contingencies, amends Sec. 71(b)(1)(D); Act Sec. 1843(c), reducing the six-year rules to three years, amends Sec. 71(f); all effective as included in the '84 TRA (for decrees and agreements executed after 12-31-84) and as shown above.

[¶1844] At-Risk Rules. The new law clarifies how the investment credit at-risk rules are affected by nonqualified nonrecourse financing. The new rules provide that any net increase in nonqualified financing will be treated as reducing the property's credit base (and thus the qualified investment) in the year the property was first placed in service. The same is true of any increase in the credit base.

A number of corrections clarify that the appropriate term, for investment credit at-risk purposes, is "credit base" and not "qualified investment." Another correction applies the Sec. 168(e)(4) definition of related person for at-risk purposes.

Act Sec. 1844, relating to the investment credit at-risk rules, amends Secs. 46(c)(8)(D)(v), (c)(9)(A), (c)(9)(C)(i), and 47(d)(1) and (d)(3)(e) and repeals Sec. 47(d)(3)(F), effective as if included in the 1984 TRA (property placed in service after 7-18-84).

[¶1845] Distilled Spirits. The '84 TRA provision allowing manufacturers of distilled spirits to "draw back" all but $1 of the distilled spirit tax if used for non-beverage products is effective for products manufactured or produced after October 31, 1984.

Act Sec. 1845 adds new TRA Sec. 456(d), as if included in the 1984 TRA.

[¶1846] Carryover and Carrybacks. A number of corrections are made in Sec. 39, which reflect the new numbering system that applies to credits.

Act Sec. 1847, correcting cross references, amend Sec. 39, effective as if included in the 1984 TRA (tax years beginning after 12-31-83).

〔¶1847〕 Minimum Tax. The new law restores the pre-'84 law principles relating to credit carryovers by taxpayers subject to the alternative minimum tax. So for purposes of determining credit carryovers and carrybacks to other years for the residential energy credit, certified mortgage interest credit, research credit, and general business credit, the amount of the limitations under Secs. 26, 30(g), or 38(c) will be the amount of *credit allowable* reduced but not below zero by the alternative minimum tax and certain other credits. The '84 TRA language had the three limitations reduced, rather than the allowable credit.

In addition, a conforming amendment provides that, for alternative minimum tax purposes, in determining foreign taxes paid in one year that may be treated as paid or accrued in another taxable year under Sec. 904(c), the Sec. 904(c) limitation will be equal to the credit allowable under Sec. 27(a) (the foreign tax credit) increased by the amount determined by the ratio under Section 55(c)(2)(C).

Clerical amendments. The new law also provides that the period for assessing a deficiency attributable to elections to have the alcohol fuels credit or targeted jobs credit not apply (or any revocation) is one year after the date of notification.

Act Sec. 1847(a), relating to minimum tax carrybacks and carryovers, amends Sec. 55(c)(3) and Sec. 55(c)(2)(E), effective for taxable years beginning after 12-31-83 (general credits) and 12-31-82 (foreign tax credits). Act Sec. 1847(b)(13), setting up a deficiency assessment period adds new Sec. 6501(n), effective as if included in the 1984 TRA. Act Sec. 1847(b) makes technical amendments to Secs. 30(b)(2)(D), 48(l), 86(f), 108(b)(2), 146(b)(2), 151(e)(5), 280(b), 415(c)(3)(C), 422(A)(c), 655(d), 6411, 6501, 6511 and 6999 and Sec. 1631(b) of the 1984 TRA.

〔¶1848〕 Conforming Corrections. The new law makes a number of corrections reflecting the repeal of the extra investment credit and individual retirement bonds.

Act Sec. 1848, getting rid of certain deadwood, repeals Sec. 46(f)(9) and amends Secs. 404(a)(8), 2039(e), 4973(b), and 6047 (which in some places is misdesignated 6704).

Employee Benefit Provisions

〔¶1851〕 Funded Welfare Benefit Plans. Under the '84 TRA, amounts otherwise allowable as a deduction for a contribution to a welfare benefit fund for any year can't exceed the qualified cost of the fund for the year. That cost is the sum of the fund's qualified direct cost and any addition to reserves for the year (qualified asset account), less the fund's after-tax income. Generally, a welfare benefit is any benefit, other than one under a qualified retirement plan, for which the employer deductions are usually postponed until taken into income by employees (or independent contractors) or vacation pay subject to certain elections. A "fund" is any tax-exempt social club, VEBA, supplemental unemployment benefit compensation trust (SUB), or group legal service plan; any trust, corporation or other organization not exempt from tax; and any such account held for any employer by a qualified third party.

The new law makes a number of changes and clarifications to the funded welfare benefit plans.

Definition of fund. The new law amends the definition of fund to exclude amounts held under an insurance contract described in Sec. 264(a)(1), certain qualified nonguaranteed contracts, and, according to the committee report, certain guaranteed renewal contracts.

An insurance policy described in Sec. 264(a)(1) is one on the life of an officer, employee, or person financially interested in the employer's trade or business and the employer is the direct or indirect beneficiary of the policy.

Also excluded are amounts held under certain "qualified nonguaranteed insurance contracts." That's a contract under which (1) there is no guarantee of renewal and, (2) other than insurance protection, the only payments to which the employees or employer are entitled are experience rated refunds or policy dividends that aren't guaranteed and that are determined by factors other than the amount of welfare benefits paid to (or on behalf of) the employees or their beneficiaries. As a result, if the amounts are subject to a significant current risk of economic loss that may be determined by factors other than employee payouts, the amount held by the insurance company won't be considered a fund.

An arrangement that satisfies these requirements, however, will qualify for treatment as a fund unless the amount of any experience-rated refund or policy dividend payable to an employer for a policy year is treated by the employer as received or accrued in the tax year in which the policy year ends.

According to the Senate Committee report, amounts held by an insurance company for a reasonable premium stabilization reserve for an employer are treated as a fund. Amounts released from such a reserve to buy current insurance coverage are to be treated as experience-related refunds or policy dividends.

Finally, the new law provides that any account defined as a fund under regs issued under Sec. 419(e)(3)(c) will be considered a fund no earlier than six months after the final regs are published. This rule doesn't apply to certain reserves for post-retirement benefits or arrangements with certain refund features.

One further exclusion. According to the House Committee report, a "fund" doesn't include amounts held by an insurance company subject to certain "guaranteed renewal contracts." Those are contracts under which the employer's right to renew is guaranteed, but the level of premiums is not.

Postretirement medical benefits and qualified plans. Under the '84 TRA, any amount allocated to a separate account for a key employee for postretirement medical benefits is treated as an annual addition to a defined contribution plan. The new law makes it clear that the amount so treated is not subject to the 25% of compensation limit applicable to annual additions for defined contribution limit.

WATCH THIS: The amount so contributed would be subject to the Sec. 415(c)(1)(A) dollar limits for annual additions.

Separate accounting for key employees. The '84 TRA, to provide an overall limit for preretirement deductions for post-retirement medical and life insurance benefits of key employees, required a separate accounting for contributions to provide certain postretirement benefits to an employee who is or ever was (after the '84 TRA) a key employee. The new law clarifies that the separate accounting doesn't apply until the first taxable year for which a reserve is computed under Sec. 419A(c)(2).

Discriminatory postretirement reserves. Under the new law, no reserve may be taken into account in determining an account limit, under Sec. 419(c)(2), for postretirement medical or life insurance benefits for covered employees, unless the plan meets the nondiscrimination requirements under Sec. 505(b) for those benefits. Those requirements must be met even if they don't apply in determining the tax-exempt status of the fund. A special exception to the ban against taking the reserve into account applies to collective bargaining agreements that Treasury finds were the subject of good faith bargaining.

The new law also provides that life insurance benefit won't be taken into account to the extent the aggregate amount of such benefits provided for an employee exceeds $50,000.

GRANDFATHER CLAUSES: Certain postretirement group insurance plans that failed the Sec. 505(b) nondiscrimination plans or the benefits of which exceed $50,000, that were grandfathered by the '84 TRA, continue to be taken into account for determining the reserve account limit.

Actuarial certification. As a general rule, unless there is an actuarial certification for benefits, the account limit for certain welfare benefit funds can't exceed special safe-harbor limits. The actuarial certification requirement now applies to post-retirement medical and life insurance benefits as well, unless a safe-harbor computation is used.

Aggregation rules. Under the new law, in computing the limits applicable to the reserves for disability benefits, SUBs, and severance pay benefits, and postretirement medical and life insurance benefits, all welfare benefit funds of a single employer are treated as a single fund. For all other purposes, the employer may elect to treat two or more welfare benefit plans as a single plan.

Adjustment to existing reserves. The '84 TRA provided that the account limit for any of the first four years to which the welfare benefit rules apply will be increased by an applicable percentage of the existing excess reserve. The '84 TRA didn't make it clear what "existing excess reserves" meant. The new law defines it as the excess (if any) of the amount of assets set aside at the close of the first taxable year ending after 7-18-84 to provide disability benefits, medical benefits, SUB or severance pay benefits, or life insurance benefits over the account limit (disregarding the adjustment) determined for the taxable year for which the increase is computed. This rule increasing the account limit applies only to a welfare benefit fund that, as of 7-18-84, had assets set aside to provide the previously mentioned benefits.

Unrelated business income. The '84 TRA set up a tax on unrelated business income of a social club, VEBA, SUB, or group legal services plan on the lesser of the fund's income or the amount by which assets in the fund exceed a specific limit on amounts set aside for exempt purposes. An employer must include in income an amount similar (deemed unrelated income) to that includable by a welfare benefit fund that's not tax exempt (subject to regs to limit double taxation).

The new law does the following:

- Clarifies that the tax on unrelated business income applies to 10-or-more employer plans.

- Clarifies that the account limit is determined as if the rules limiting deductions for employer contributions applied.

- Points out that the '84 TRA rule, which states that the amount that may be set aside for purposes of the unrelated business income tax won't apply to income from pre-existing reserve for post-retirement medical or life insurance benefits, applies only to assets set aside as of 7-18-84.

- Deletes the provision barring a "set aside" for assets used in providing certain benefits (generally facilities).

- Provides that if any amount included in the gross income of an employer as deemed unrelated income from a welfare benefit fund then the amount of the income tax imposed on that income is to be treated as an employer contribution as of the last day of the taxable year. As a result, the tax is deductible, subject to the deduction limits for fund contributions. Also, the tax on such income is to be treated as if it were imposed on the fund for purposes of determining the fund's after-tax income.

Disqualified benefit. The '84 TRA imposed a nondeductible excise tax on a welfare benefit fund that provides a disqualified benefit. The tax is 100% of the benefit.

The new law changes the definition of disqualified benefits. These benefits now include: (1) any post-retirement medical or life insurance benefit provided for a key employee for whom the employer was required to establish a separate account and the payment is not from the account; (2) any post-retirement medical or life insurance benefit provided to an individual in whose favor discrimination is prohibited unless the plan meets the nondiscrimination requirements under Sec. 505(b) with respect to the benefit, even if those requirements don't apply to such plans; and (3) any portion of the welfare benefit fund reverting to the employer.

As to the first definition, preretirement benefits that were disqualified under the '84 TRA won't be considered disqualified merely because they're not paid to a key employee from a separate account.

A benefit that comes within the second definition won't be disqualified if it is maintained under a recognized collective bargaining agreement and the benefit was the subject of good faith bargaining.

A payment that reverts to the benefit of an employer under the third definition won't be disqualified if attributable to a contribution for which no deduction is allowable in the current or proceeding taxable year. A reduction must be made to the amount treated as a carryover to the extent nondeducted contributions revert to the employer's benefit.

The first two definitions of disqualified benefit won't apply to post-retirement benefits charged against a pre-TRA of 1984 existing reserve for post-retirement medical or life insurance benefits.

Exemption for collectively bargained and pay-all welfare benefit fund. The new law permanently exempts collectively bargained welfare benefit funds from the account limits. That includes limits set up by any regs. So contributions are deductible and assets held by such funds are tax exempt.

Also exempted are certain VEBAs funded solely with employee contributions. The exemption is available if the plan has at least 50 employees and no employee is entitled to refund other than a refund based on the experience of the entire fund. As a result, there is an element of risk. However, according to the Conference report, a pay-all VEBA also won't lose the exemption merely because the refund may vary depending on the number of years the employee contributed to the fund.

Fully vested vacation benefits. The new law provides a transitional rule in the case of a fully vested vacation pay plan in which payments are required within one year after the accrual of vacation. If the taxpayer makes the Section 463 election for the first taxable year ending after the '84 TRA enactment date (7-18-84), then instead of establishing a suspense account, the election is treated as a change in accounting method and the adjustments required by the change will be taken into account under Sec. 481.

The time for making that election for the first taxable year ending after 7-18-84 is extended to six months after the new law's enactment date. However, the rule applies only if vacation pay is expected to be paid (or is in fact paid) within 12 months after the close of employer's year.

Other changes and corrections. The new law also does the following:

- Clarifies that the Sec. 404(a) deduction rules would disallow deductions for deferred compensation plans under any other provisions except Sec. 404(a)(5), not just Sections 162 and 212. These rules also apply to foreign deferred compensation under Sec. 404A and the welfare benefit fund provisions.

- Clarifies that the rules apply to plans for independent contractors.

- Extends the application of the higher account limits to all welfare benefit funds maintained under collective bargaining agreements, not just those established by such agreements.

- Clarifies that the Sec. 404(b) contribution rules apply not only to unfunded deferred benefits.

- Makes certain that all of Section 505(b) is used to determine discrimination.

- Gives a clearer definition of "collective bargaining agreement" for purposes of the discrimination requirements.

Effective Dates: The new law clarifies certain 1984 TRA effective dates. First, the tax on disqualified benefits applies to benefits provided after December 31, 1985. That tax doesn't apply to benefits charged against existing reserves for certain post-retirement benefits.

The '84 TRA changes relating to the unrelated business income tax apply to taxable years ending after December 31, 1985. Such changes are to be treated as a change in income tax rate for purposes of Section 15.

Act Sec. 1851(a)(8), clarifying the definition of fund, adds new Sec. 419(e)(4); Act Sec. 1851(a)(2)(A), dealing with annual additions, amends Sec. 419(d)(2); Act Sec. 1851(a)(2)(B), relating to separate accounts, amends Sec.

419A(d)(1); Act Sec. 1851(a)(3)(A), relating to post retirement reserves, amends Sec. 419A(e); Act Sec. 1851(a)(5), dealing with actuarial certification, amends Sec. 419(c)(5)(A); Act Sec. 1851(a)(6), dealing with the aggregation rules, amends Sec. 419(h)(1); Act Sec. 1851(a)(7), clarifying adjustments of existing reserves, amends Secs. 419A(f)(7)(C) and (D); Act Secs. 1851(a)(9) and (10), relating to the tax on unrelated business income, amends Secs. 419A(g) and 512(a)(3)(E); Act Sec. 1851(a)(11), relating to the tax on disqualified benefits, amends Sec. 4976(b); Act Secs. 1851(a)(12) and (14), amending the TRA effective dates, amends Sec. 511(e) of the 1984 TRA; Act Sec. 1851(a)(13), exempting certain VEBAs from the account limits, amends Sec. 419A(f)(5); Act Sec. 1851(b), relates to vacation pay plansand amends Sec. 404; Act Secs. 1851(a)(1), (a)(4), (b)(2), and (c) making technical corrections amend Sec. 419(g)(1), 419A(f)(5), 404(b) and 505(a) and (b); all effective as if included in the 1984 TRA and as shown above.

[¶1852] Pension Plan Provisions. Retirement plans don't escape correction. Here are the changes.

Distributions. The new law clarifies that distributions from individual retirement accounts and annuities must start no later than April 1 of the calendar year following the year in which the owner reaches 70½. Such distributions are also subject to the incidental death benefit rule (present value of payments projected to be made to the owner must be more than 50% of the present value of total payments to be made). In addition, distributions from a Sec. 403(b) annuity must begin no later than when the employee reaches age 70½, under rules that are similar to those that apply to IRAs.

The new law also defines a 5% owner for purposes of the required beginning date (that is, no later than April 1 following the year the 5% owner reaches age 70½). Such individual is a 5% owner if the individual was a 5% owner at any time during the plan year ending in the calendar year in which the individual attains age 70½ or the four preceding years. If the individual becomes a 5% owner in a year attaining age 70½, the required beginning date April 1 following that year.

The new law repeals the exception to the required distribution rules for amounts held by an ESOP (subject to the 84-month rule). In its place is an exception to the 84-month rule for required distributions.

The new law also makes it clear that a distribution required under the incidental death benefit rules is a required distribution for purposes of the required distribution rules.

Rollovers and required distributions. Amounts that must be distributed under the required distribution rules aren't eligible for rollover treatment. This rule applies only to the amount required to be distributed (not to any excess).

Distributions before age 59½. The additional income tax on distributions to 5% owners before age 59½ will apply to all distributions except those on account of death or disability. The tax won't apply to amounts attributable to contributions paid before 1-1-85. The new law defines a 5% owner, for purposes of the tax, as any individual who at any time during the five plan years before the plan year in which the distribution is made is a 5% owner.

Thus, the status at the time of distributions determines if the extra tax applies—not the status at the time of contribution.

Qualifying rollover distributions. In the rollover area, the following clarifications are made:

• Distributions of the entire balance to an employee's credit in a qualified plan may be eligible for rollover under the partial distribution rollover rules as long as the distribution isn't a qualified total distribution. If the total distribution is on account of plan termination or is eligible for lump-sum distribution treatment, the partial distribution rules don't apply.

• Accumulated deductible employee contributions aren't taken into account for purposes of calculating the balance to the credit of an employee under the partial distribution rules.

• A self-employed individual is treated as an employee for purposes of the taxation of distribution and the rollover rules.

• An employee's spouse who receives a distribution after the employee's death can make a rollover to an IRA but not another qualified plan.

Plans substantially made up of employee contributions. If substantially all contributions under a plan are employee contributions, then distributions will be considered to be from income until all income is distributed. Such a plan is defined by the new law as one in which 85% or more during a representative period are employee contributions. For the 85% test, deductible employee contributions are not taken into account.

The new law also provides that the Sec. 72(q) additional income tax on premature distribution from an annuity doesn't apply to distributions from a plan substantially all of the contributions of which are employee contributions.

Whether a contribution is an employee or employer contribution under such a plan will be computed under the rules of Sec. 72(f) and Section 72(m)(2). The same rules apply for determining an investment in an annuity contract for an annuitant under Section 72(e)(6).

The new law makes it clear that distribution of income from a nonexempt trust before the annuity starting date will be determined without regard to Sec. 72(e)(5) (relating to investments in pre-8-14-82 contracts) rather than Sec. 72(e)(1) (the general annuity exclusion rules).

Top-heavy plans. The new law amends the definition of key employee to exclude any officer or employee of an entity referred to in Sec. 414(d) (relating to government plans). As a result, certain accounting and nondiscrimination rules won't apply to such individuals. Also, government plans stay exempt fron the top-heavy rules.

The new law also makes it clear that cumulative accrued benefits of any employee who has not performed any services for an employer maintaining a plan during a period of five plan years ending on the determination date may be disregarded for purposes of determining whether the plan is top heavy. Previously, the "performing services" requirement had been "receiving compensation."

Employee death benefit exclusion. After repealing the employee death benefit exclusion, the '84 TRA created an estate tax exclusion under which the estate of a spouse of a plan participant doesn't have to include any community property interest in the surviving spouse-participant's interest in plan benefits. A similar rule applied for certain transfers for the gift tax. The new law repeals the exclusions for estates of decedents dying after the new law date of enactment (for estate tax purposes) and transfers after that date (for gift tax purposes). However, if the transfer is made in a community property state, it qualifies for the marital deduction.

The new law also repeals the gift tax exemption for the employee's exercise or nonexercise of an election under which an annuity would be paid to a beneficiary after the employee's death from a qualified plan, tax-deferred annuity, IRA, or military pension.

The new law modifies the grandfather rules for the repeal of the estate tax exclusion. There are two ways to qualify. First, the individual must have irrevocably elected a form of benefits and been in pay status on the effective date of the repeal. Second, under the new law, if an individual separated from service before 1-1-85 (for purposes of '84 TRA Section 525(b)(2)) or 1-1-83 (for purposes of TEFRA Section 245(c)), and otherwise meets the requirements of those sections, the individual's estate may qualify for the exclusion provided the individual elected a form of benefit before the effective date and didn't change the form of benefit before his or her death.

Affiliated service groups and leasing arrangements. The new law repeals the special authority to issue regulations to prevent abuses through the use of affiliated service groups and employee leasing arrangements (for avoiding employee benefit requirements) in favor of the general regulatory authority. The new law also reinstates certain definitions relating to affiliated service groups that were inadvertently repealed by the '84 TRA.

Sec. 401(k) deferral tests. The new law makes it clear that as long as a Sec. 401(k) cash-or-deferred arrangements meets either of the Sec. 401(k)(3) deferral percentage tests, it will be considered to pass the Sect. 401(a)(4) test (i.e., doesn't discriminate in favor of officers, shareholders, or the highly compensated).

The new law also provides for the aggregation of all contributions to Sec. 401(k) arrangements of a single employer. If an employee participates in more than one arrangement of an employer, all such arrangements are treated as one arrangement for purposes of the Sec. 401(k)(3) deferral tests.

Postretirement medical benefits. The new law conforms the treatment of postretirement medical benefits provided by a pension or annuity plan to those for welfare benefit plans. Any pension or annuity (previously "defined benefit") plan providing that benefit must maintain a separate account for each key employee (previously 5% owner) under Sec. 416(i). In addition, as with the postretirement medical benefit plan, the amount treated as an annual addition under the rules coordinating the benefit with the overall limit on qualified plan isn't subject to the 25% of compensation limit in Sec. 415(c)(1)(B). It will be subject to the dollar limit in Sec. 415(c)(1)(A).

Multiemployer employer plan withdrawal liability. The new law modifies the 9-26-80 effective date of the withdrawal liability of the Multi-Employer Pension Plan Amendments Act of 1980 for two employers who meet certain conditions. For one, the magic date is 1-16-82 while for the other it's 6-30-81.

Act Sec. 1852(a)(1), relating to IRA distributions, amends Secs. 408(a)(6) and (b)(3); Act Sec. 1852(a)(3), relating to Sec. 403(b) annuities, amends Sec. 403(b); Act Sec. 1852(a)(4)(A), clarifying the required beginning date, amends Sec. 401(a)(9)(C); Act Sec. 1852(a)(4)(B), relating to ESOPs, amends Sec. 409(d); Act Sec. 1852(a)(6), dealing with the incidental death benefit rules, adds new Sec. 401(a)(9)(G); Act Sec. 1852(a)(5), relating to required distributions and rollovers, amends Secs. 402(a)(5) and 403(a)(4)(B), (b)(8), and 4(d)(3); Act Sec. 1852(a)(2), relating to the tax on early distributions, amends Sec. 72(m)(5)(A); Act Secs. 1852(b)(1) and (2), relating to partial rollovers, amends Secs. 402(a)(5)(E) and (D); Act Sec. 1852(b)(3), relating to self-employees, adds new Sec. 402(g) and amends Sec. 402(e)(4); Act Sec. 402(a)(7), dealing with employees' spouses, amends Sec. 402(a)(7); Act Sec. 1852(c), relating to contributions to plans substantially made by employees, amends Secs. 72(e)(7)(B), (f), (m)(2) and (q)(2) and 402(b); Act Sec. 1852(d), relating to top heavy rules, amends Secs. 416(g)(4) and (i)(1)(A); Act Sec. 1852(e), relating to the estate and gift tax exclusion, repeals Sec. 406(e)(5), 407(e)(5), 2039(c) and 2517, and amends Sec. 525(b) of the 1984 TRA for estates of decedents dying after and transfers made after the date of enactment; Act Sec. 1852(f), relating to affiliated service groups, amends Sec. 526(d)(2) of the 1984 TRA; Act Sec. 1852(g), dealing with Sec. 401(k) plans, amends Sec. 401(k)(3); Act Sec. 1852(h), relating to post retirement medical benefits, amends Secs. 401(h) and 416(l); Secs. 1852(a)(7) and (b)(5)—(10), making clerical corrections amend Sec. 408(c)(1), 4974(a) and (b), 402(a)(5) and (6), 401(a), and 403(b)(8)(C) and 1984 TRA Sec. 522(e); Act Sec. 1852(i), modifying the withdrawal liability effective date, amends 1984 TRA Sec. 558; all effective as if included in the 1984 TRA and as shown above.

[¶1853] **Fringe Benefits.** Having added the fringe benefits provisions to the Code in 1984, Congress now makes a number of technical corrections.

Dependent child. The exclusions for no additional cost services and qualified employee discounts apply to the employee, his or her spouse, and dependent children (all collectively referred to as the employee). The new law defines dependent child to be a child (1) who is the dependent of the employee or (2) both of whose parents are dead and who hasn't attained age 25.

Employee discount. The new law conforms the definition of employee discount with that of no additional cost service by applying the exclusions where the price paid by the employee for goods or services provided by the employer for the use of the employee (plus spouse or dependent child) is less than the price for nonemployee customers.

Customer. The definition of customers generally includes only nonemployee customers. However, for purposes of determining gross profit percentages for the qualified employee discount exclusion, "customers" will also include employee customers.

Cafeteria plans. The new law changes the definition of permissible cafeteria plan benefits by calling them "qualified benefits" rather than "statutory nontaxable benefits." This makes it clear, according to the House Committee Report, that certain taxable benefits can be provided in the plan and don't lose their taxable status.

The new law contains two transitional rules for cafeteria plans. One applies to cafeteria plans in existence on 7-18-84 maintained under collective bargaining agreements. Those plans will be granted relief until the expiration of the last collective bargaining agreement under the plan. The second rule grants transition relief to a plan that suspended a type or amount of benefit after 2-10-84 and later reinstates the benefit.

Excise tax on fringe benefits. The '84 TRA created a 30% excise tax on certain excess benefits provided by companies with a number of lines of business, which elected to continue its pre-1984 policy. The new law makes it clear that at all times on and after 1-1-84 and before the close of the year in question, substantially all employees have to be entitled to employee discounts or services provided by the employee in one line of business for the election to remain in effect. Previously, the requirement only had to be met on 1-1-84.

Also, the new law provides that the tax only applies to employment within the U.S. In addition, there's an exception to the tax for an agricultural cooperative that's a member of a certain controlled group.

Predivestiture retired employees. The new law provides a transitional rule under which the fair market value of free telephone service provided to employees of the Bell system who retired before 1-1-84 is excluded from income.

Leased section of department store. For purposes of qualified employee discounts, a leased section of a department store is treated as part of the line of business of the store and employees of the leased section are treated as employees of the store if the leased section makes over-the-counter sales of property. The new law makes it clear that the exclusion applies to beautician services, provided there are substantial sales of beauty aids by such service in the ordinary course of business.

Working condition fringes. According to the House Committee Report, the rules for the product testing provision covering automobile testing (which were mentioned in the '84 TRA Committee Report, but not the act itself) are clarified. There must be limitations on the employee's personal use of the car. This requirement is met if there's a reasonable charge for that use.

The exception to the working condition fringe for auto salespeople also applies to auto sales managers and others who regularly perform either function. This clarification is contained in the Committee Reports.

De minimis fringe benefits. The *de minimis* fringe benefit exclusion applies to public transit passes and reimbursements, as long as the value of the total of such benefits is not more than $15 a month. This provision is contained only in the committee reports—not in the statute.

Qualified tuition reduction. A tuition reduction plan will be treated as meeting the nondiscriminatory fringe benefit requirements if it met the current requirements on the day eligibility closed and at all times thereafter, and such plan closed on 6-30-72, 6-30-74, or 12-31-75. Such plans can exclude employees covered by collectively bargained plans if the plan was a subject of good faith bargaining. Another exception applies for a particular student.

Act Sec. 1853(a)(1), defining dependent child amends Sec. 132(f)(2)(b)(ii); Act Sec. 1853(a)(2), defining employee discount, amends Sec. 132(c)(3)(A); Act Sec. 1853(a)(3), defining customer, amends Sec. 132(i); Act Sec. 1853(b)(1), converting statutory nontaxable benefits into qualified benefits, amends Secs. 125(c), (d), and (f); Act Sec. 1853(b)(2), creating a cafeteria plan transitional rule, amends Sec. 531(b)(D) of the 1984 TRA; Act Sec. 1853(b)(3), relating to suspend benefits, amends Sec. 531(b)(E), Act Sec. 1853(c), relating to the excess benefits excise tax, amends Secs. 4977(c) and adds new Sec. 4977(f); Act Sec. 1853(d), relating to retired A T &T employees, amends Sec. 559 of the 1984 TRA; Act Sec. 1853(e), relating to the definition of leased section of a department store; Act Sec. 1853(f), relates to tuition reductions, effective as if included in the 1984 TRA and as shown above.

[¶1854] **ESOPs and EWOCs.** A taxpayer may elect to defer the recognition of gain on the sale of certain qualified securities to an employee stock ownership plan or to an eligible worker-owned cooperative to the extent the corporation reinvests in qualified replacement property within a certain period of time. The new law clarifies the requirements for the sale.

Qualified securities. The new law provides that the nonrecognition provision applies only if the gain on the sale would have been long-term capital gain (i.e., held more than 6 months). Previously, the requirement had been that the stock be held more than one year.

Also, the new law clarifies that the executor of the individual who makes the sale can invest the proceeds in qualified replacement property if the individual dies before making or designating the investment.

30% test. Effective for sales after 7-18-84, the employee organization (ESOP or EWOC) must own, immediately after the sale, 30% of each class of stock (other than preferred stock described in Sec. 1504(a)(4)) or 30% of the total value of all stock (other than preferred stock described in Sec. 1504(a)(4)) of the corporation that issued the qualified securities. Ownership will be determined under the Sec. 318(a)(4) attribution rules (but only for sales after 5-6-86).

Prohibited allocations. The new law clarifies that for sales of securities after the date of enactment, the requirement that the ESOP or EWOC be maintained for the exclusive benefit of employees. Generally, no portion of the qualified securities (or assets attributable to the securities) for which a Sec. 1042 election has been made may be allocated, during the "non-allocation period" to (1) a taxpayer (i.e., seller) seeking nonrecognition treatment, (2) persons related to that taxpayer under Sec. 267(b) with certain exceptions for de minimis amounts, or (3) any person who owns (after applying the Sec. 318(a) attribution rules) more than 25% of any class of stock of the issuing corporation or any class of stock of certain related corporations. The "nonallocation period" is the 10-year period beginning with the later of the date of the sale of qualified securities or the date of the plan allocation attributable to final payment of acquisition indebtedness attributable to the sale.

If the plan doesn't meet the exclusive benefit requirement, the plan will be disqualified for those participants receiving prohibited allocations. Thus, the allocation will be included in that person's income. In addition, if there is a prohibited allocation, a 50% excise tax will be imposed on the amount involved in the prohibited allocation. The tax is to be paid by the employer maintaining an ESOP or by the EWOC involved. A special three-year statute of limitations applies to the excise tax.

NOTE: The same rules apply to allocations after a sale by an estate claiming the new 50% estate tax exclusion for qualified sales of employer securities (see ¶1173). The new rules don't apply to amounts provided to prohibited class members outside of the plan.

Qualified replacement property. Qualified replacement property is any security issued by a domestic corporation, other than the corporation that issued the securities involved in the nonrecognition transaction, that had no passive income exceeding 25% of gross receipts for the year preceding the year of the transaction. An operating corporation is one in which more than 50% of the assets are used in the active conduct of a trade or business. Financial institutions described in Secs. 581 or 593 and insurance companies described in subchapter L are operating corporations.

Special rules apply to controlling and controlled corporations to treat them as a single corporation. Also, securities will be treated as replacement property if it is a security within Sec. 165(g)(2) (other than securities issued by a governmental or political subdivision).

TRANSITIONAL RULE: An extended replacement period applies to sellers who acquired replacement property that's no longer qualified. Provided the acquisition was before 1-1-87, replacement can be made until then.

Eligible taxpayers. Generally, C corporations may not elect nonrecognition treatment for sales after March 28, 1985. However, such treatment is made available for sales made before July 1, 1985 if a binding contract was in effect on March 28, 1985 and at all times afterward.

Basis reduction. Generally, the basis of the replacement property is reduced by the nonrecognized gain. That reduction won't be taken into account for purposes of determining market discount under Sec. 1278(a)(2)(A)(ii).

Recapture on disposition. Effective for disposition of replacement property after the date of enactment, gain must be recognized on the property "disposed of" at the time of such disposition. The amount of gain that must be recognized will be the amount not recognized because of the election.

NOTE: If the taxpayer making the election owns stock representing control of the corporation that issued the replacement property and the corporation disposes of a substantial portion of its assets out of the ordinary course of business, the taxpayer will be treated as having disposed of the qualified replacement property.

Recapture won't apply: (1) to Sec. 368 reorganizations (unless the person making the election owns stock representing control on the acquiring or acquired corporation), (2) by reason of the electing person's death, (3) by gift, or (4) to any transaction subject to Sec. 1042(a).

Deductions for dividends on employer stock. The new law clarifies the general rule that permits an employer to deduct the dividends paid during the year for employer stock held by an ESOP but only to the extent they're actually paid out currently to participants or beneficiaries. Other changes are as follows:

- Although the deductible dividends are treated as distributions under the plan, they are fully taxable. They are not treated as distributions of net employee contributions. This rule doesn't apply to dividends paid before 1-1-86 if the taxpayer treated the distribution as a nontaxable return of capital in a return filed before the enactment date.

- The employer deduction for dividends paid on employer stock held by an ESOP is permitted only in the year in which the dividend is paid in cash to the participant or in the year in which the dividend is distributed by the plan to the beneficiary, effective only for dividends paid after the date of enactment. However, according to the conference report, a deduction is allowed for certain dividends, even if the stock isn't yet allocated to an account.

- Current distributions of dividends paid on employer stock allocated to a participant's account won't be treated as a disqualifying distribution under Sec. 401, 409, or 4975(e)(7).

- Treasury can disallow the dividend-paid deduction if the dividend constitutes, in substance, an avoidance of taxation.

- The corporation will be allowed the deduction whether the dividends are passed through to plan participants or to their beneficiaries.

- Dividends paid on employer stock held by an ESOP are treated as paid under a contract separate from the contract under which the stock is held. This rule doesn't apply to dividends paid before 1-1-86 if the employer deducted the dividends for the year they were paid to the ESOP and filed a return for that year before the date of enactment.

Interest earned on ESOP loans. Certain financial institutions may, under Sec. 133, exclude from gross income 50% of the interest received on loans to a corporation or ESOP to the extent the proceeds are used to acquire employer securities (within the definition of Sec. 409(l)). The new law makes it clear that for purposes of Sec. 291(e), which defines a financial institution preference item, the interest exclusion won't be treated as exempt from tax.

For purposes of the exclusion, in testing the adequacy of the stated interest rate for purposes of Section 483 (installment payments) and Sec. 1271 through 1275 (original issue discount), appropriate adjustments will be made to the applicable federal rate to take into account the partial interest exclusion.

Loans between a corporation and an ESOP won't be subject to the below- market interest rules if the interest rate is equal to the rate paid on a related securities acquisition loan to such corporation. Also, although a securities acquisition loan can't originate with a member of the controlled group, it can be held by such member. However, during the time it is held, the member won't qualify for the interest exclusion.

In addition, a loan to a corporation will be treated as a securities acquisition loan, even though the proceeds of such loans are lent to the corporate-sponsored ESOP, provided repayment is on terms substantially similar to the terms of the loan to the corporation. Repayment by the ESOP to the corporation can be on more rapid terms if plan allocations don't discriminate in favor of the highly compensated and the repayment period for the loan to the corporation doesn't exceed seven years.

ESOP's payment of estate tax. An executor of a decedent's estate will generally be relieved of estate tax liability to the extent the ESOP or EWOC is required to pay the liability on the employer securities transferred. To qualify, qualified employer securities must be acquired by the ESOP "from or on behalf of the decedent." The ESOP plan administrator or EWOC authorized officer must consent to the payment and the employer whose employees participate must guarantee payment. In addition, if the estate qualifies for the deferred payments of taxes under the installment method of Section 6166 for the interest in such securities and the executor elects to make such payments, the ESOP or EWOC may also so elect.

> **RELIEF LIMITED:** The new law makes it clear that, for estates of decedents dying after 9-27-85, only executors of those estates that qualify for the Section 6166 deferral may be relieved of the estate tax liability by the ESOP under this provision.

The new law also provides that the transfer of employer securities to an ESOP or EWOC won't be treated as a disposition or withdrawal that triggers acceleration of the remaining unpaid tax. After the transfer, the issue of whether the estate and the ESOP (or EWOC) remains eligible to make installment payments, will be treated separately. In addition, required distributions of securities (because of retirement after age 59½, death, disability, or separations from service of more than a year) won't be treated as a disposition or withdrawal requiring acceleration and won't be taken into account in determining if a later disposition will cause acceleration.

The new law also makes it clear that agreement by an EWOC can be made by an authorized officer. And whereas the employer must guarantee payment of estate tax for transfers to an ESOP, the EWOC must make the guarantee for transfers to it.

For purposes of these provisions, estate tax liability includes interest, penalty, additions to tax or any other amount relating to any tax imposed by Section 2001, as well as the tax itself.

Excise tax. There's a 10% excise tax on premature distributions of qualified securities acquired by an ESOP or EWOC under Sec. 1042. The employer (for an ESOP) or the EWOC is liable for the tax. The new law corrects a number of cross references to this effect. Also, any exchange of qualified securities because of a liquidation by the issuer into the EWOC is a transaction that meets the requirements of Section 332 (complete liquidation of subsidiaries), using a 100% rather than 80% ownership test, won't be treated as a disposition for purposes of the 10% excise tax.

Voting rights. The new law allows an ESOP or EWOC trustee, which by its by-laws require the interests of the plan to be governed by a one- vote per participant basis, to so vote the ESOPs interests in the corporation, effective on enactment. It also requires that the voting rights be passed through to participants on certain issues like merger, liquidation, dissolution and similar transactions. The pass-through provision applies to votes after 12-31-86 for stock acquired after 12-31-87.

Distributions. The new law also provides that an ESOP of a closely held business may distribute employer securities instead of cash, subject to the requirement that such securities may be resold to the employer. This permits a plan sponsored by a corporation whose stock is subject to ownership restrictions (only employees or qualified trusts) to distribute employer securities. Previously, the distribution could only be in cash.

Net unrealized appreciation. Under the new law, appreciation on ESOP held employer stock isn't realized until the stock is sold after a distribution. If there's a corporate acquisition, and employer securities are exchanged for cash or corporate securities, the basis of the securities received is stepped up to reflect the fair market value of the securities used to acquire the new ones.

Under the new law, if there's a straight stock-for-stock exchange, the ESOP carries over the basis of the old stock to the new. If there's a sale, and the proceeds are reinvested in new employer securities within 90 days (plus extensions), the plan will have the same basis as it had in the old stock. The new rule applies to transactions after 12-31-84, but for transactions before the enactment date, the reinvestment period ends the earlier of one year after the transaction or 180 days after enactment.

Act Secs. 1854(a)(1) and (4), redefining qualified securities, amends Secs. 1042(a) and (c)(1); Act Sec. 1854(a)(2), relating to the 30% test, amends Sec.

1042(b)(2) effective for sales after 7-18-84, with a 5-6-86 effective date for the Sec. 318(a) attribution rule; Act Sec. 1854(a)(3), (10), and (11)(A), relating to the exclusive benefit rules, amend Sec. 1042(b)(3) and 1042(e) and adds new Secs. 4979A, effective for sales after the date of enactment; Act Sec. 1854(a)(5), defining qualified replacement property, amends Sec. 1042(c)(4); Act Sec. 1854(a)(6), excluding C corporations, adds new Sec. 1042(c)(7) effective for sales after 3-28-85 with a binding contract exception; Act Sec. 1854(a)(7), relating to the basis reduction, amends Sec. 1042(e); Act Sec. 1854(a)(8), dealing with recapture, inserts a new Sec. 1042(e), by redesignating (e) as (f), effective for dispositions after the date of enactment; Act Sec. 1854(a)(9)(B) and (C), (10), (11), and (12) technically correct Secs. 1042(b)(4) and 1042(c)(5); Act Secs. 1854(b)(1) and (2), relating to the dividends paid deductions, amends Secs. 72(e)(5) and 404(k) for dividends paid after enactment; Act Sec. 1854(b)(3), relating to required distributions, amends Sec. 404(k)(3), Act Sec. 1854(b)(4), dealing with unreasonable compensation, amends Sec. 404(k); Act Sec. 1854(b)(5), defining recipient, amends Sec. 404(k)(2), Act Sec. 1854(c), relating to the partial interest exclusion, adds new Secs. 133(d), 291(e)(1)(iv) and 7872(f)(11) and amends Sec. 133(b); Act Sec. 1854(d), relating to estate tax liability, amends Sec. 2210(a), (c), (d) and (g); Act Sec. 1854(e), relating to the excise tax on premature distributions, amends Secs. 4978(a)(1), (b)(1), (c), (d)(1)(C), and (e)(2) and (3), and adds new Sec. 4978(d)(3); Act Sec. 1854(f)(1) relating to voting rights amends Sec. 409(e); Act Sec. 1854(f)(2), relating to net unrealized appreciation adds new Sec. 402(g) and amends Secs. 4975(e)(7) and 1042(b)(3)(B); Act Sec. 1854(f)(3), relating to stock distributions amends Sec. 409(h)(2); effective as if included in the 1984 TRA and as shown above.

[¶1855] **Miscellaneous Employee Benefit Provisions.** *Incentive stock options.* The new law clarifies that the fair market value of stock for ISOP purposes, will be determined without regard to lapse restrictions, effective as in the '84 TRA. However, the same rule, for purposes of the minimum tax, won't apply to options exercised before 1-1-85 if the option was granted under the plan adopted or corporate action taken before 5-15-84. A problem occurred because the effective date relating to ISOPs were cross-referenced incorrectly. The new law corrects the mistake.

Restricted stock. ERTA treated stock subject to Sec. 16(b) of the 1934 Securities Exchange Act as being subject to a substantial risk of forfeiture for six months after receipt. Unless the recipient elected to be taxed on receipt, the taxpayer had to treat as income the value of the stock at the expiration of the Sec. 16(b) period, less any amount paid. The new law permits certain particular individuals to elect to have those provisions apply retroactively to 1973 but limits any individual reduction in tax to $100,000.

Sec. 83(b) elections. The new law expands the group of employees who can make a Section 83(b) election to include in income the bargain element in a sale of restricted stock to an employee when the employee pays fair market value (i.e., there's no bargain element). Such employees can now make such election to include $-0- for all transfers relating to the performance of services on or before 11-18-82, not just those after 6-30-76. The election must be made on a return for any taxable year ending after 7-18-84 and beginning before the enactment date of the new law.

Act Sec. 1855(a), correcting the ISOP effective dates, amends Sec. 555(c) of the 1984 TRA effective as if included in that act. Act Sec. 1879(p), relates to restricted stock and ERTA Sec. 252, applying that section retroactively to 1973; Act Sec. 1854(c), relating to Sec. 83(b) elections, amends 1984 TRA Sec. 556(b), for transfers before 6-30-76.

Tax Exempt Bonds

[¶1861] **Mortgage Subsidy Bonds.** The new law makes a number of changes to the mortgage subsidy bond provisions of 1984 TRA. First, Treasury may grant extension of time for publishing or submitting annual policy statements that issuers of mortgage subsidy bonds are required to make. Those statements explain measures taken to comply with the objective of providing low income housing.

The new law also clarifies that veterans eligible for loans financed by qualified veterans' mortgage bonds must apply for financing by the later of 30 years leaving active service or January 31, 1985 (moved from January 1, 1985).

Finally, the new law provides that the annual policy statement requirement along with the information reporting the state certification requirements will be treated as met if the issuers in good faith tried to meet the requirements and the failure to so meet them is due to inadvertent error.

Act Sec. 1861(a), relating to policy statements, adds new Sec. 103A(o)(4); Act Sec. 1861(b), relating to veterans loans amends Sec. 103A(o)(4)(B); Act Sec. 1861(c), dealing with good faith efforts, amends Sec. 103A(c)(2); all effective as if included in the 1984 TRA.

[¶1862] **Mortgage Credit Certificates.** The new law provides that the requirements that apply to qualified mortgage subsidy bonds dealing with information reporting, state certification, and annual policy statements will also apply to mortgage credit certificate issuers. In addition the good faith effort rules that apply to mortgage subsidy bonds under Secs. 103A(c)(2)(B) and (C) will also apply to mortgage credit certificates. The new law also clarifies how the mortgage credit can be carried forward for three years. Finally, for purposes of figuring the credit, the credit is based on interest paid or accrued (as opposed to incurred).

Act Sec. 1862, relating to qualified mortgage credit certificates, amends Secs. 25(a)(1)(B), (c)(2)(A), and (e)(1)(B) and redesignates Sec. 6708 as 6709; effective as if included in the 1984 TRA.

[¶1863] **Advance Refunding of Certain Veterans' Bonds.**
The new law provides that certain issuers may advance refund up to
$300 million of qualified veterans' mortgage funds. The refunding
replaces the 1984 TRA provision allowing that agency to receive
cash flow loans not exceeding $300 million from the Federal Financ-
ing Bank. There's also a special carryforward of the amounts under
the unused "volume" cap. According to both Committee Reports, Oregon is the only state affected.

*Act Sec. 1863, relating to advance refunding, amends Sec. 613 of the 1984
TRA, effective on the date of enactment with an exception.*

[¶1864] **Private Activity Bonds Volume Limitations.** Generally, a state's annual private activity bond volume limitation may
only be used to finance facilities within the state. There are exceptions provided the state's share of the facility's use exceeds the
state's share of bonds issued to finance the facilities. Those exceptions are (1) eligible sewage and waste disposed facilities or facilities
for the local furnishing of electricity and gas; (2) certain water furnishing facilities, and (3) qualified hydroelectric generating facilities.

This provision is effective for bonds issued after the new law's
date of enactment. However, states may elect to apply the provision
to bonds issued on or before that date.

Allocation to nongovernmental units. Under the new law, a state
may allocate its private activity bond volume limitations to issuing
authorities that aren't governmental units as well as those that are.

Exempt activities. The determination of whether facilities form-
ing a part of an airport, dock, wharf, mass commuting facility, or
trade or convention center may be financed outside a state's volume
limitations is to be made on a property-by-property basis rather
than by reference to the entire facility. However, all property to be
financed under this exception must be owned by or on behalf of the
governmental unit.

Information reporting. The new law allows Treasury to require
reports on allocation of volume limitations.

Carryforward of unused bond authority. Under the new law, the
election to carryforward any unused volume limitation must be
made for specific projects. Identification of specific projects must be
more specific than the '84 TRA seemed to indicate (including the address of the project); in fact, the conference report considers identification to be of primary importance.

*Act Sec. 1864(a), relating to out-of-state facilities, adds new Sec. 103(n)(13),
for bonds issued after the new law's date of enactment with an election to
include previous issues; Act Sec. 1864(b), relating to in-state allocations,
amends Sec. 103(n)(6); Act Sec. 1864(c), relating to publicly owned facilities,*

amends Sec. 103(n)(7)(c)(i); Act Sec. 1864(d), dealing with information report-ing, adds new Sec. 103(l)(2)(f); Act Sec. 1864(c), related to the unused bond cap carryforward, amends Sec. 103(n)(1); all effective as if included in the 1984 TRA and as shown above.

[¶1865] **Federal Guarantees.** The new law conforms the rules for obligations issued to finance certain energy projects under fed-eral programs to the general rules denying tax-exempt status if there's a federal guarantee present. There's transitional relief for a convention center in Carbondale, Illinois, financed under a guaran-tee issued by the Farmer's Home Administration before July 1, 1984. There's also a transitional exception for four solid waste facili-ties for which it's anticipated that the federal government will pur-chase a more than insignificant amount of the output and expendi-tures were made before October 19, 1983. Those facilities are located in Annapolis and Aberdeen, Maryland, Portsmouth, Virginia and Charleston, South Carolina. Another exemption is created for a ther-mal transfer facility near Tullahoma, Tennessee.

Act Sec. 1865, relating to federal guarantees, amends Sec. 103(h)(5), effec-tive as if included in the '84 TRA.

[¶1866] **Limit on Small Issue Exception.** Under the new law, small issue industrial development bonds can (in some cases) be refunded (through other bonds) to reduce the interest rate on the borrowing, even though a beneficiary benefits from more than $40 million in total tax-exempt financing. Such IDBs can be refunded if (1) the maturity date of the refunding bond isn't later than that of the refunded bond; (2) the amount of the refunding bonds doesn't exceed the refunded bonds; (3) the interest rate on the refunding bond is less than the interest rate on the refunded bond; and (4) the proceeds of the refunding bonds are used to redeem the refunded bonds not later than 30 days after the date the refunding bonds are issued.

Act Sec. 1866, creates exceptions to the refunding prohibition of Section 623 of the 1984 TRA.

[¶1867] **Exception to Arbitrage Limitation.** The new law corrects a reference to a resource recovery project of Essex County, New Jersey contained in an exception to the arbitrage restrictions (i.e., limiting the investment of bond proceeds in bonds that aren't related to the purpose of the borrowing). It also expands a rule that applies to Muskogee, Oklahoma to include a limited exception from the IDB arbitrage rebate rules.

Act Sec. 1867 amends Sec. 624(c)(2) of the 1984 TRA, and extends an ex-ception to the arbitrage restrictions, as if included in that act.

[¶1868] Arbitrage Restrictions for Student Loan Bonds. The new law makes it clear that a series of refundings of student loan bonds are included in the exception from coverage of the regs treating student loan bonds as arbitrage bonds for purposes of the arbitrage restrictions.

Act Sec. 1868, relating to student loan bonds, amends Sec. 625(a)(3)(C) of the 1984 TRA as if included in that act.

[¶1869] Consumer Loan Bonds. The new law renames consumer loan bonds as private loan bonds. This makes it clear that all bonds for which 5% or more of the proceeds are used to finance loans to nonexempt persons, are subject to the consumer loan bond restrictions, which, in turn, are subject to exceptions for certain types of bonds.

The new law creates transitional exceptions for (1) Baltimore, Maryland; (2) an Illinois student loan program; (3) St. Johns River Power Park, Florida; (4) the White Pine Power Project, Nevada; and (5) the Eastern Maine Electric Cooperative, and according to both committee reports; (6) Mead-Phoenix Power Project.

The private loan bond restriction won't apply to tax-increment financing bonds issued before August 16, 1986, substantially all of the proceeds of which are used to finance (1) certain governmental improvements to real property; (2) acquisition of such property under eminent domain, preparing the property for new use, or transfer to a private developer; or (3) payments of reasonable relocation costs to the property's previous users. The activities must be under a redevelopment plan adopted before the bonds are issued. In addition, repayment of the issued must be secured by increases in property tax revenue from the property. The provision applies to bonds issued before 8-16-86.

Act Sec. 1869, relating to consumer loan bonds, amends Code Secs. 103(o) and Sec. 626(b)(2)(A) of the 1984 TRA effective as if included in that act and as shown above.

[¶1870] Limitation of Use for Land Acquisition. The 1984 TRA limited the issuance of bonds for use in acquiring land. The new law makes it clear, that an issue won't be tax exempt if 50% or more of the proceeds will be used to acquire land for an industrial park.

Act Sec. 1870, relating to land acquisiton amends Sec. 103(b)(16)(A), as if included in the 1984 TRA.

[¶1871] Non-Code Bonds. The new law makes it clear that tax-exempt bonds issued under provisions of the law other than the

Code, must be issued in registered form. Also, the consumer loan bond rules apply to those non-Code bonds.

The new law also conforms a limited exception permitting advance refunding of certain bonds for facilities issued before the 1984 TRA.

Act Sec. 1871(a), relating to non-Code bonds, amends Sec. 103(m)(1), effective for bonds issued after 3-28-85. Act Sec. 1871(b), making a conforming amendment, amends Sec. 103(b), effective as if included in the 1984 TRA.

[¶1872] Effective Date Clarification. The new law clarifies the provisions to which the effective dates of '34 TRA Sec. 631(c) applies (i.e., bonds issued after 12-31-83 with a 10-19-83 binding contract exception). They include, among others, the prohibition on federal guarantees, aggregate small issue IDBs, restrictions of financing certain facilities and aggregation of related facilities. Only those provisions are subject to the binding contract exception, which itself is clarified. The binding contract exception applies only to (1) activities for which construction began before 10-19-83 and was finished on or after that date or (2) property acquired on or after 10-19-83. The clarification to the binding contract exception applies to bonds issued after 3-28-85.

Health club facilities. The prohibition on financing health clubs applies to bonds issued after 4-12-84, subject to transitional rules.

Special exception. The new law creates an exception to the '84 TRA rules (especially the ban on federal guarantees) for a solid waste disposal facilitity in Huntsville, Alabama.

Act Sec. 1872, relating to effective dates amends Sec. 631 and repeals Sec. 632(a)(1) of the 1984 TRA, effective as shown above.

[¶1873] Exceptions. The new law makes it clear that items exempted from the rules under Section 632(a) of the '84 TRA are excepted from the arbitrage rules and the items exempted under Sec. 632(d) are exempt from the consumer (private) loan bond rules.

The new law excepts five hydroelectric generating facilities (Hastings, Minnesota, Warren County, New York, and Richmond, Placerville, and Los Banos, California) from the small-issue IDB rules.

Act Sec. 1873, creating exceptions to the private activity bond rules, amends Sec. 632 of the 1984 TRA, effective as if included in the act.

Miscellaneous Provisions

[¶1875] Corrections to the Technical Corrections. *Tax preferences of trusts and estates.* For purposes of the alternative minimum tax, itemized deductions as well as the preferences, themselves, must be apportioned between the estate or trust, on the one hand, and the beneficiaries on the other, according to regs.

Corporate provision. Under prior law, if a shareholder of a 50% owned corporation transfers stock of that corporation to another 50% owned corporation in exchange for property, the transaction was treated as a redemption of the shareholder's stock in the acquiring corporation. The transferred stock was considered to be transferred as a contribution to capital of the acquiring corporation. Its basis would be the transferor's basis plus any gain recognized.

The new law provides that the contribution to capital rule won't apply if the shareholder is treated as having exchanged its stock under Sec. 302(a). The corporation will be treated as buying the stock for purposes of Sec. 338. However, the tax treatment for the shareholder remains the same.

Pension provisions. The new law conforms the rules relating to qualified rollover distributions to the 10% additional income tax on early withdrawals from qualified plans by key-employees and 5% owners. Generally, distributions from a qualified trust or annuity made after the date of enactment to a 5% owner may not be rolled over into another qualified plan. Distributions after July 18, 1984, but on or before the date of enactment of the new law may not be rolled over if any part of the distribution is a benefit attributable to contributions made while the employee is a key employee in a top heavy plan.

5% owner defined. A 5% owner is any individual who is a 5% owner (under Section 416(i)) at any time during the five plan years preceding the year of distribution. If there's a qualified total distribution, a 5% owner must wait five years from the time of distribution to make a tax-free IRA to IRA rollover.

The new law also makes it clear that the '84 TRA's repeal of the rule relating to the return of excess contributions made on behalf of a self- employed, applies to contributions made in tax years after 12-13-83.

SEPs. In the area of simplified employee pensions, the new law conforms the limits on certain distributions of excess IRA contributions and the limits on employer contributions on behalf of certain officers, shareholders or owner employees to the Sec. 415(c)(1)(A) dollar limits on annual additions to qualified defined contribution plans ($30,000), effective as if included in TEFRA.

Keoghs. In the area of Keogh plans, the new law makes it clear the earned income of a self-employed is determined without regard to the deductions allowable for Keogh contributions, solely for the purpose of determining to the extent the contributions are ordinary and necessary.

The new law takes into account the fact that a self-employed individual's deductions for contributions aren't necessarily limited to the cost of his or her own benefits. As a result effective as if included in TEFRA, a self-employed can deduct his or her allocable share of Keogh contributions (for example, his or her partnership share if the business is a partnership).

Other pension provisions. The new law also takes into account that there may be a double deduction in determining compensation under Sec. 219(f)(1). Previously, the term "compensation" was earned income under Sec. 401(c)(2) reduced by the amount allowable as a deduction under Sec. 62(7). Since Sec. 401(c)(2) already took into account the deduction rules under Section 404, a double deduction may have been possible. The reference to Sec. 62(7) has been removed, effective as if included in TEFRA.

Under the new law, the rule precluding anticipated cost-of-living adjustments to the overall benefit limits applies to limit benefits payable as a single life annuity beginning at age 62—not just those paid in alternative forms, those beginning before age 62, and those beginning after age 65.

In the withholding area, the new law exempts from the pension withholding rules, amounts subject to withholding of tax on income paid to nonresident aliens by the person paying the amount on which would be so subject but for a tax treaty.

Finally, the new law points out that a disabled's compensation is determined under Sec. 415(c)(3)(C) for all defined contribution plans.

Partnerships. The new law extends the special three-year period of limitations for assessing income tax against partnerships to include assessments of any addition to tax or additional amount arising under subchapter A of Chapter 68.

In addition, under prior law, the general deficiency procedures generally don't apply to certain computational adjustments for any partnerships (which are subject to their own special rules). The new law creates exceptions for: (1) affected items that require partner level determinations or (2) items that are "nonpartnership" items (under Sec. 6231(e)(1)(B). The general procedure will be applied separately to each deficiency attributable to each item. Also, any notice or proceeding under the general rules won't preclude or be precluded by any other notice, proceeding, or determination dealing with the partner's tax liabilities. This coordinates the Tax Court deficiency rules for partner level determinations arising from a partnership proceeding with the deficiency procedures applying to the taxpayer from items unrelated to the partnership proceeding. As a result, a second deficiency notice is possible in certain instances.

Interest on carrybacks and refunds. For purposes of computing interest on refunds arising from net operating loss carrybacks when a tentative adjustment claim is filed, the refund is treated as filed on the date that the tentative adjustment claim is filed. The effective date of this '84 TRA provision is for applications filed after 7-18-84.

Nominee reporting. The new law requires a nominee holding an interest in a trust or an estate for another person to supply to the trust or estate, the name and address of such person along with any other information Treasury requires. The nominee in turn, must forward the information given to him or her by the estate or trust fiduciary to the person for whom the interest is held. *Result:* Information should be passed through more easily. Note that Treasury will provide the rules for transmitting the information.

Gain from dispositions of foreign corporate stock. Under Section 1248, gain on the sale or exchange of stock of foreign corporations will be treated as a dividend to the extent of earnings and profits if, among other things, the United States taxpayer owns 10% or more of the stock. The new law removes, from coverage of these rules, gain realized on exchanges to which Section 356 (receipt of additional consideration in an otherwise tax-free exchange) applies.

Act Sec. 1875(a), dealing with the minimum tax, amends Sec. 58(c); Act Sec. 1875(b), dealing with the capital contribution rule, amends Sec. 304(a)(1); Act Secs. 1875(c)(1), (2), and (8), amends Code Secs. 402(a)(5)(F)(ii) and 408(d)(3), and 1984 TRA Sec. 713(c), effective as shown above; Act Sec. 1875(c)(5), relating to returns of excess contributions, amends 1984 TRA Sec. 713(d)(1); Act Sec. 1875(c)(6), raising the SEP limit, amends Secs. 219(b)(2)(c) and 408(d)(5) for years beginning after 12-31-83; Act Sec. 1875(c)(7), dealing with the definition of earned income for Keogh plans, amends Secs. 404(a)(8)(C) and (D); Act Secs. 1875(c)(3) and (4), relating to the definitions of AGI and compensation, amend Secs. 62(7) and 219(f)(1), for years beginning after 12-31-83; Act Sec. 1875(c)(9), relating to annuity adjustments, amends Sec. 415(b)(2)(E)(iii); Act Sec. 1875(c)(10), relating to withholding, amends Sec. 3405(d)(1)(B), Act Sec. 1875(c)(11), relating to disability income, amends Sec. 415(c)(3); Act Sec. 1875(d)(1), relating to a statute of limitations adds Sec. 6229(g), effective for partnership years beginning after 9-3-82; Act Sec. 1875(d)(2), dealing with deficiency procedures, amends Secs. 6230, 6213 and 6503, for partnership years beginning after 9-3-82 (TEFRA's effective date); Act Sec. 1875(d)(3), dealing with carrybacks under Sec. 6611(f), effective for applications filed after 7-18-84; Act Sec. 1875(d)(4), misnumbered (3), relating to trust and estate passthroughs, amends Sec. 6034A, effective for taxable years of trusts and estates beginning after the enactment date. Act Sec. 1875(e), correcting a cross reference, amends Sec. 201(a) of the 1965 Land and Water Conservation Fund Act; Act Sec. 1875(f) corrects spelling; Act Sec. 1875(g), relating to exemptions to the foreign stock sales rules, amends Sec. 1248(g), effective for exchanges after 3-1-86.

[¶1876] **Foreign Sales Corporations.** The new law makes a number of changes to the FSC rules.

FSC income without administrative pricing rules. The new law provides that "effectively connected foreign trade income" that a FSC earns without using administrative pricing rules (Sec. 923(a)(2) nonexempt income), will be treated like other effectively connected foreign trade income. Taxes on that income won't be creditable, but distributions out of earnings and profits will qualify for a 100% dividends-received deduction (i.e., they will be subject to tax only at the FSC level).

FSC income under Sec. 1248. The new law changes the prior treatment under which FSC earnings and profits attributable to certain foreign trade income were excluded from ordinary income treatment under Sec. 1248 on disposition of foreign corporate stock. Under the new law, Sec. 923(a)(2) non-exempt income and certain foreign trade income, which would be taxable on a distribution, are subject to ordinary income treatment under Section 1248.

Preference cutbacks. The new law makes it clear that the Sec. 291 preference cutback for FSCs applies to the FSC and *not* the corporate shareholder. The exempt portion of foreign trade income is reduced from 32% to 30% for income determined without administrative pricing rules and from 16/23 to 15/23 for income determined with them. The portion of foreign trade income will be adjusted for shareholders for whom there are no preference cutbacks.

Also, the deemed distribution of 1/17 of a DISC's excess taxable income applies, as with the preference cutback factor, only to C corporations. And a special rule is provided to determine the method for computing such distribution attributable to boycott income.

Foreign trade income under Subpart F. The new law clarifies that there will be no taxation under Subpart F's anti-avoidance rules of income already taxed at the FSC level.

Dividends-received deduction. In addition to the old 100% dividends-received deduction for distributions from earnings and profits attributable to foreign trade income of a FSC, the new law adds an 85% deduction for dividends from earnings and profits attributable to qualified interest and carrying charges derived from a transaction resulting in foreign trade income. Gross income giving rise to earnings and profits from both foreign trade income and qualified interest and carrying charges won't be taken into account to calculate a dividends-received deduction under the general rules for the other income of the FSC.

Foreign tax credit limitation. The new law provides that distributions from a FSC (or former FSC) out of earnings and profits attributable to qualified interest and carrying charges, as well as foreign trade income, are subject to a separate foreign tax credit limitation from the other items listed in Section 904(d)(1).

The new law also provides that taxes paid or accrued by a foreign corporation to a foreign country or United States possession on income effectively connected with the conduct of a trade or business within the United States won't be taken into account for purposes of the deemed paid credit under Section 902. In addition, no accumulated profits attributable to such income will be taken into account for purposes of the credit. This provision prevents certain corporate U.S. shareholders from taking a double credit.

Exchange of information. Under the new law, a corporation can't continue to be an FSC if its country of incorporation ceases to qualify as a host country for FSCs. The new law also would grant host country status to certain countries entering information exchange agreements and tax treaties with the United States.

Finally, effective for periods after 1985, the principal bank account of an FSC (other than a small FSC), must be maintained in a U.S. possession or a country that qualifies as a host country for that entire taxable year.

Possessions taxation. Under the new law a U.S. possession can impose a tax on any FSC income attributable to the sale of property or the performance of services for ultimate use, consumption, or disposition within the possession. Also, a U.S. possession can exempt from tax any foreign trade income or interest, dividends, or carrying charge of a FSC. In addition, no provision of law may be construed as requiring any tax imposed by the U.S. on a FSC to be covered over (or otherwise transferred) to any U.S. possession. Finally, the rule exempting FSCs from the Sec. 934 limitation of reduction in income tax liability incurred to the Virgin Islands has been repealed.

Interest on DISC-related deferred liability. The new law makes it clear that an interest charge is imposed on the deferred income tax liability of a former DISC in the same way it's imposed on a DISC.

Exemption of accumulated DISC income. Generally, pre-1985 accumulated DISC income is exempt from tax by treating post-1984 distributions as previously taxed income for which there had been a deemed distribution. The new law provides that distributions in liquidation will be treated as "an actual distribution" of previously taxed income. Also, the earnings and profits of any corporation receiving a distribution that's treated as previously taxed income will be increased by the amount of the tax-free distribution.

Taxable year. The '84 TRA's provision requiring conformity of tax years between FSCs (and DISCs) and their shareholders is effective for taxable years beginning after 12-31-84.

Qualified DISC distributions. The new law, in the case of a distribution to a C corporation, would treat $16/17$ of a DISC distribution that's designed to meet the 95%-qualified-export-receipts test as coming from accumulated DISC income. The balance is treated as previously taxed income. That's because post-1984 law treats only $1/17$ of income as a deemed distribution and currently taxable.

Receipts from another FSC. An FSC will now be able to treat receipts received from another FSC that's a member of the same controlled group as foreign trading gross receipts if no FSC in the group uses the pricing rules of Sec. 925(a)(1) (the gross receipts methods of calculating income).

Former export trading corporation. Under the new law, corporations that had been export trade corporations but were not such for their most recent taxable year ending before 7-18-84, may qualify for the 1984 law's treatment of active export trade corporation. This treatment includes exempting certain income from U.S. tax.

To qualify, the former export trade corporation must be precluded by Sec. 971(a)(3)(B) from again electing such status or must elect, within six months after the new law's date of enactment, never to qualify for such status.

Accumulated DISC income of cooperatives. Amounts distributed from accumulated DISC income to a cooperative described in Sec. 1381 that are excluded from income won't be included in the gross income of the cooperative's members when distributed to them. In addition, the cooperative isn't allowed a deduction when distribution to the members occur.

Contracts and effective dates. The foreign management, foreign economic process, and administrative pricing prerequisites will be treated as met for (1) any lease of longer than three years that was entered before 1-1-85, (2) any contract under which the completed contract method of accounting, which was entered into before 1-1-85, and (3) any other type of contract that was entered into before 1-1-85, but only for the first three taxable years of the FSC ending after that date or as regs will prescribe.

Act Sec. 1876(a), relating to FSC non-exempt income, amends Secs. 927(d)(6) and 1248(d)(6); Act Sec. 1876(b), dealing with preference cutbacks, amends Sec. 212(a)(4); Act Sec. 1876(c), dealing with Subpart F, amends Secs. 951(e) and 952(b); Act Secs. 1876(d)(1) and (j), refining the dividends-received deduction, amend Sec. 245(c); Act Secs. 1876(d)(2) and (3), relating to the foreign tax credit, amend Secs. 904(d)(1)(D) and 906(b); Act Sec. 1876(e), dealing with exchange of information, amends Sec. 927(e)(3) and for periods after 3-28-85, Sec. 924(c)(2); Act Sec. 1876(f), coordinating FSCs with possessions taxation, amends Sec. 927(e)(5) and repeals 934(F), as added by 1984 TRA Sec. 801(d)(7)(F); Act Sec. 1876(g), clarifying the interest rules for deferred liability, adds Sec. 995(F)(7); Act Sec. 1876(h), dealing with the exemption for accumulated DISC income, amends Sec. 805(b)(2)(A) of the 1984 TRA; Act Sec. 1876(i), relating to taxable years, amends Sec. 805(a)(4), effective for taxable years beginning after 12-31-84; Act Sec. 1876(k), concerning DISC distribution to C corporations, amends Sec. 996(a)(2); Act Sec. 1876(l), dealing with controlled groups amends Sec. 924(F)(1); Act Sec. 1876(m) relates to certain former export trade corporations; Act Sec. 1876(n), dealing with distributions to cooperatives, amends 1984 TRA Sec. 805(b)(2); Act Sec. 1876(o), clarifying the binding contract exception, amends '84 TRA Sec. 805(a)(2); Act Sec. 1876(p), making clerical amendments, amends Secs. 995(f) and 901, and 1984 TRA

Secs. 802(c) and 805(a)(2)(A); all effective as if included in the 1984 TRA and as shown above.

[¶1877] Highway Revenue Provisions. The new law makes technical corrections to three areas of the highway revenue provisions. First, the new law makes it clear that the credit for gasoline and special fuels applies to, among others, amounts payable to the taxpayer under Sec. 6427 for any qualified diesel-powered highway vehicle bought, as well as for fuels used for nontaxable purposes or resold, during the taxable year, regardless of the noncommercial aviation special rules.

Second, the new law allows a full 15¢ a gallon refund (instead of 12¢) of excise tax on diesel fuel used in a school bus engaged in transporting students and school employees.

Third, the additional 6% excise tax on a later sale of a piggyback trailer originally sold after 7-17-84 and before 7-18-85, won't apply to any sale occurring more than six years after the original sale.

Act Sec. 1877(a), relating to the special fuels credit, amends Sec. 34(a)(3); Act Sec. 1877(b), dealing with the diesel tax refund, amends Sec. 6427(b)(2); Act Sec. 1877(c) phasing out the tax on piggyback trailers, amends Sec. 4051(d)(3); all effective as if included in the 1984 TRA.

[¶1878] Miscellaneous Revenue Provisions. *Capital gain holding period.* To conform the market discount bond rules to the capital gain holding period, these bonds don't include those with a maturity of six months or less.

Sport fishing tax. The new law adds fishing hook disgorgers to the list of items subject to the 10% sport fishing equipment tax.

Excise tax exemption for certain helicopter uses. The exemption from aviation excise taxes for helicopters engaged in qualified timber and hard mineral activities where no FAA facilities are used, has been expanded to fully cover such use for oil and gas activities.

The language of the '84 TRA had inadvertently extended the rules to only some oil and gas activities.

Estate tax credit. The new law clarifies an estate tax credit for two specific contributions of land to the Toiyabe National Forest.

Debt-financed realty of tax-exempt organizations. The 1984 TRA exempted certain debt-financed realty held by qualified exempt organizations from the unrelated business income tax. An organization will qualify for the exemption if the organization is in a partnership (with taxable entities) as long as each allocation to a qualified organization is a qualified allocation under Sec. 168(j)(6). The exemption also applies if each partner is a qualified organization.

The new law makes it clear that, for purposes of the all-qualified organization exemption, an organization won't be considered qualified if any of its income is unrelated business income. For purposes of the other exemption, Treasury may treat the allocation rule as met if it is convinced that there's no tax avoidance potential.

The new law also makes it clear that a qualified organization includes a Sec. 170(b)(1)(A)(ii) educational organization and its affiliated support organizations under Sec. 509(c)(3), as well as certain pension trusts.

Targeted jobs credit. The new law sorts out the problem of two Sec. 51(j)s by designating the successor employer section as Sec. 51(k) and the election out as Sec. 51(j).

Military housing rollover. The new law corrects a provision to the '84 TRA to conform to the committee report for that act. As a result, the extended nonrecognition period for rollover of gain of a personal residence by certain military personnel won't expire before the day that's one year after the last day the taxpayer is stationed outside the United States or is required to reside in government quarters at a remote base site in the United States. This period can't exceed eight years after the old residence's date of sale. The '84 TRA didn't contain the "one-year" period.

Deduction for demolition costs. The new law provides that the prohibition on deducting costs incurred in demolition applies only to demolitions beginning after 7-18-84 (other than to demolitions of certified historic structure). If a demolition is delayed until the completion of a replacement structure on the same site, the demolition will be treated as beginning when the construction began. There's a transitional rule for one bank headquarters building and one company's petroleum storage facilities.

Tribal governments treated as states. The new law corrects a cross reference in the section expanding the treatment of tribal governments as states.

Regulated investment companies. The new law provides that adequate records of shareholders need no longer be kept by a regulated investment company. These records were originally intended to assure that the company was not a personal holding company. Under pre-'84 TRA law, keeping adequate records was a requirement for RIC status.

However, the new law provides that the investment company taxable income of an RIC that doesn't keep these records will be taxed at the highest corporate tax rate under Section 11(b).

    KEEP RECORDS: Unless an RIC is also a PHC, the RIC will have to keep shareholder records to take advantage of the graduated rates in the lower tax brackets.

Act Sec. 1878(a), dealing with market discount, amends TRA Sec. 1001(b); Act Sec. 1878(b), relating to sport fishing, amends Sec. 4162(a)(6); Act Sec. 1878(c), dealing with helicopters, amends Secs. 4041(l)(1) and 4261(e)(1); Act

Sec. 1878(d), relating to gifts of land, amends 1984 TRA Section 1028(b); Act Sec. 1878(e), relating to UBI, amends Sec. 514(c)(9); Act Sec. 1878(f), dealing with the targeted jobs credit, amends Sec. 51(j); Act Sec. 1878(g), dealing with housing rollovers, amends Sec. 1034(h)(2); Act Sec. 1878(h), creating a transitional rule for demolition costs, amends 1984 TRA Sec. 1063(c), effective for demolition beginning after July 18, 1984, Act Sec. 1878(i), dealing with tribal governments, amends the 1984 TRA Sec. 1065(b); Act Sec. 1878(j), relating to RICs, amends Secs. 852(a) and (b)(1); all effective as if included in the 1984 TRA and as shown above.

⟦¶1879⟧ Miscellaneous Provisions. *Estimated tax penalty waiver.* The '84 TRA tightened the estimated tax rules. The rules were designed to increase liability from the beginning of 1984. The new law grants relief by allowing individuals until 4-15-85 and corporations until 3-15-85 to pay the full 1984 income tax liabilities without incurring any additions to tax because of underpayments to estimated tax, to the extent the underpayments were due to the changes.

Orphan drug credit. The term "clinical testing" for purposes of the orphan drug credit is, under the '84 TRA, defined with reference to the date an application is approved under the Federal Food, Drug, and Cosmetic Act. The new law expands the term by also defining it with reference, for drugs that are biological products, to the date on which a license for such drug is issued under Sec. 351 of the Public Health Services Act.

The new law redefines "rare disease or condition" as one that (1) affects less than 200,000 people in the United States or (2) affects more than 200,000 in the United States but for which there's no reasonable expectation that the cost of developing and making available in the United States a drug for such disease or condition will be recovered from sales of the drug in the United States.

The changes to the credit apply to amounts paid or incurred after December 31, 1982, in taxable years ending after that date.

Nonconventional source fuel credit. Under the new law, the sale of qualifying fuel to an unrelated person, by a corporation that files a consolidated return with the corporation producing the fuel, can qualify for the nonconventional source fuel credit. This provision is effective as if included in Sec. 231 of the 1980 Crude Oil Windfall Profit Tax Act—that is, taxable years ending after 1979.

Fringe benefit reports. The new law clarifies that the return filing and recordkeeping requirements of Sec. 6039D apply to qualified group legal services plans, cafeteria plans, and educational assistance plans.

Joint Committee report requirements. The new law repeals the requirement that the Joint Committee on Taxation submit an annual report to Congress on proposed refunds or credits in excess of $200,000, including names of the taxpayers and amounts involved.

Recovery period for real property. The new law makes it clear that the statutory recovery period with reference to Sec. 467(a) rental agreements is 19 years. The change is effective as if included in the Imputed Interest Act, generally for property placed in service after May 8, 1985, with binding contract exceptions.

Rural electric cooperatives. The new law clarifies that any organization that's tax exempt and that provides electric service on a cooperative basis can maintain a Sec. 401(k) cash-or-deferred arrangement. The same is true of a national association of such rural cooperatives. This provision is effective for plan years beginning after 12-31-84.

Newly discovered oil. Under the new law, newly discovered oil includes for windfall profit purposes, production from a property that didn't produce commercial quantities during 1978. For those purposes only, a property won't be treated as producing oil in commercial quantities during 1978, if during 1978, (1) the aggregate amount of oil produced didn't exceed 2,200 barrels (whether or not the oil was sold), and (2) no well on the property was in production for a total of more than 72 hours. According to the Conference report, a dual well is treated as two wells. This provision applies to oil removed after February 29, 1980.

Investment credit for Sec. 501(d) organizations. The new law provides that any business of Sec. 501(d) religious or apostolic associations, conducted for the common benefit of its members and the income of which is included in gross income, is to be treated as a Sec. 511 unrelated trade or business for purposes of the investment credit. As a result, provided certain requirements are met, the credit is passed through to its members pro rata, in the same manner as income is apportioned.

The used property and recapture provisions will apply at the organizational level (but the increase in tax from recapture will be passed through). In addition, no individual can claim a credit under this section if that person can claim a credit in his or her own right. The new provisions are effective for periods after 1978. A special rule extends the period for claiming refunds or credits by use of the section, for closed years, to one-year after the date of enactment.

Mutual savings bank. A stock association that's treated as a mutual savings bank for purposes of computing a bad debt deduction will now be treated as a mutual savings bank for purposes of the tax-exemption for mutual organizations insuring these banks. This provision is effective for taxable years ending after August 13, 1981 (as if included in ERTA).

Reorganization of investment companies. For purposes of determining if certain investment companies qualify for tax-free reorganization, the stock of a regulated investment company, real estate investment trust, or diversified investment company won't be treated as stock of a single issuer under the diversification requirements of Sec. 368(a)(2)(F)(ii). This provision is effective as if included in Sec. 2131 of the 1976 Tax Reform Act.

S corporation changes. For purposes of the qualified trust requirements, shares of a trust treated as separate trusts under Sec. 663(c) (the DNI rules) will be treated as separate trusts under the S corporation rules. Also, the S corporation's accumulated adjustments account (amounts available for distribution) won't be reduced because of federal taxes that arose while the corporation was a C corporation. Both provisions apply to taxable years beginning after 1982.

QTIP gift tax. The new law provides that effective for gifts after 1985, the QTIP gift tax election made under Sec. 2523(f) must be made under the gift tax return rules of Sec. 6075(b). Previously it had to be made by April 15 after the calendar year of transfer. In addition, a special rule allows a certain donor to file a late return.

Windfall profit tax exemption. Oil interests held by the Episcopal Royalty Company will be treated as "qualified charitable interests," for oil recovered after 2-29-80.

Refunds for medicinal alcohol. Medicinal alcohol produced in Puerto Rico and the Virgin Islands will qualify for refunds of the tax on distilled spirits paid when the alcohol is brought into the United States. The producers will be treated as U.S. persons. The refund is determined as if tax is paid at the rate prescribed in Section 7652(f). The new law applies to articles brought into the United States after the date of enactment, with a clarification for allowable payments to Puerto Rico and the Virgin Islands.

Self-insured workers compensation funds. The new law creates a moratorium on IRS collection activities beginning on the date of enactment and ending on 8-16-87 for certain self-insured workers compensation funds. The provision does the following:

• The time to file a Tax Court petition won't expire before 8-16-87 (if the time to file hadn't expired before 8-16-86).

• All pending and continuing audits are suspended until 8-16-87.

• The running of interest is suspended from 8-16-86 to 8-16-87.

• The collection of penalties is suspended until 8-16-87.

Alcohol, tobacco, and firearms tax returns. The new law provides that Treasury regs will set out the place for filing returns and other documents for alcohol, tobacco, and firearms. As a result, the Secretary has authority to assign all such returns to a particular IRS service center. This applies to all documents due on or after the first day of the first calendar month beginning more than 90 days after the date of enactment.

Stripped tax-exempt bonds. The new law applies the stripped bond rules to stripped tax-exempt bonds. For stripped bonds and coupons, the original issue discount (OID) under Section 1286(a) is equal to the amount of OID that produces a yield to maturity (based on the purchase price of the coupon or bond on the purchase date equal to the lower of the (10 coupon rate before separation of coupons or (2) the actual yield to maturity of the stripped bond or coupon.

The amount of OID is tax exempt, but it must be taken into account in determining adjusted basis. This provision applies to any purchase or sale of any stripped tax-exempt bond or stripped coupon after the date of enactment.

Disposition of subsidiary. One specific corporation is given permission to report the sale of stock in its subsidiary over a 15-year period.

Single Employer Pension Plan Amendments Act of 1986. The new law makes a number of technical corrections to the recently enacted Single Employee Pension Plan Act. The new law

- Clarifies the notice requirement for siginificant reduction in benefit accruals by defining the plans to which it applies (in ERISA Sec. 204(h)(2) misnumbered as Section 206(h)(2)).

- Applies the ERISA Sec. 4049 trust rules to certain terminated plans.

- Corrects the definition of "multiemployer plan."

The notice requirement applies only for plan amendments adopted on or after the date of enactment. The Sec. 4049 trust rules are effective 1-1-86. The correction of the multiemployer plan definition is effective on 4-7-86.

Act Sec. 1879(a) waives estimated tax penalties; Act Sec. 1879(b), dealing with the orphan drug credit, amends Secs. 28(b)(2)(A) and 28(d)(1), effective for amounts paid or incurred after 12-31-82; Act Sec. 1879(c), dealing with the nonconventional fuels credit, amends Sec. 29(d)(8), effective for taxable years ending after 12-31-79; Act Sec. 1879(d), relating to fringe benefits, amends Sec. 6039D(d); Act Sec. 1879(e), relating to the Joint Committee report, amends Sec. 6405; Act Sec. 1879(f), dealing with rental property agreements, amends Sec. 467(e)(3)(A), effective for property placed in service after 5-8-85, with binding contract exceptions; Act Sec. 1879(g), relating to rural electric cooperatives, amends Secs. 401(k)(1) and (2) and adds Sec. 401(k)(6), effective for plan years beginning after 12-31-84; Act Sec. 1879(h), defining newly discovered oil, amends Sec. 4991(e)(2), effective for oil removed after 2-29-80; Act Sec. 1879(j), extending the investment credit to Sec. 501(d) organizations, amends Sec. 48(r), effective for periods after 12-31-78; Act Sec.

*1879(k), relating to mutual-savings banks, amends Sec. 501(c)(14)(B), effective
to taxable years ending after 8-13-81; Act Sec. 1879(l), dealing with investment company reorganizations, amends Sec. 368(a)(2)(F)(ii), effective for transfers after 2-17-76; Act Sec. 1879(m), relating to S corporations, amends Secs.
1361(d)(3) and 1368(e)(1), effective for taxable years beginning after 12-31-82;
Act Sec. 1879(n), changing the QTIP gift tax filing requirements, amends Sec.
2523(f)(4)(A), effective for transfers made after 12-31-85; Act Sec. 1879(o)
treats a windfall profit tax exemption, effective for oil recovered after
2-29-80; Act Sec. 1579(i), relating to medicinal alcohol, adds new Sec. 7652(g),
effective for articles brought to the United States after the date of enactment;
Act Sec. 1879(q) suspends the operation of collection activities, effective
8-16-86 to 8-17-86; Act Sec. 1879(r) relating to alcohol, firearms, and tobacco
returns, amends Sec. 6091(b); Act Sec. 1879(s), dealing with stripped tax-
exempt bonds, amends Sec. 1286(d); Act Sec. 1879(f) permits a tax deferral on
the sale of a subsidiary; Act Sec. 1879(u), relating to the Single Employer
Pension Plan Amendments Act, amends ERISA Secs. 204(h) (misnumbered
Sec. 206(h)) and 4049(a), and repeals SEPPAA Sec. 11016(c)(1), effective as if
included in the act to which each section relates and as shown above.*

[¶1881] Effective Date. The new law provides that except as
otherwise stated in the technical corrections section, any provision is
treated as included in the provision of the '84 TRA (or other law) to
which it relates and, as such, is effective on the '84 TRA (or other
law) provision's effective date.

**[¶1882] Social Security Treatment for Church Employees
and Clergy.** *Application to members of religious faiths.* The Social
Security Act allows a church or qualifying church-controlled organization to make a one-time election to exclude from the definition of
"employment," for purposes of FICA taxes, services performed in the
employ of the church or organization. If an election is made to exclude services for FICA purposes, the employee is treated similarly
to a self-employed person as to those services. Thus, the employee is
liable for self-employment (SECA) taxes on remuneration for these
services. The amount of remuneration on which an employee of an
electing organization is liable for SECA tax is generally the same as
the amount that would have been subject to FICA tax absent an
election.

Also, under Sec. 1402(g), an exemption from SECA taxes is provided for self-employed members of a religious sect who are consci-
entiously opposed to public or private death, retirement, or medical
insurance (including social security). This exemption isn't available
to employees. It is granted only on application by the individual,
which must include evidence of the sect's tenants or teachings and
of the individual's adherence to them. To get an exemption, the individual must waive all social security benefits.

The new law makes clear that the exemption from SECA taxes for
members of certain religious faiths (Sec. 1402(g)) isn't available for
services as to which SECA tax is due as a result of an election under

the Social Security Act. Thus, if a member of a religious faith covered by that exception is an employee of a church, and that church elects to treat the employee as self-employed for FICA tax purposes, the employee can't also claim a Sec. 1402(g) exception from SECA taxes as to those services. This provision prevents the combination of an election under the Social Security Act, and a Sec. 1402(g) exception, from resulting in avoiding any employment taxes on the services performed for the electing organization. The provision doesn't affect the individual's ability to claim a Sec. 1402(g) exception as to other services not covered by an election.

Computing income subject to SECA tax. Under the Social Security Act, the remuneration on which the employee of an electing church or organization is liable for SECA tax generally is the same as the amount that would have been subject to FICA tax if that individual had continued to be treated as an employee. So trade or business expenses aren't subtracted in computing self-employment income (reimbursed business expenses aren't included in self-employment income, however), and the $400 threshold generally applicable to self-employment income doesn't apply. Similarly, a $100 (per employer) threshold for a tax year applies in determining whether remuneration for services covered by an election is subject to SECA tax. However, after 1989, these employees will be eligible for a deduction in computing SECA taxes for the product of net earnings from self-employment and one-half of the SECA rate.

The new law provides several changes to insure that church employee income will be determined, as far as possible, using FICA principles, and that the taxation of other self-employment income won't be affected by an election. Specifically, the bill specifies that the SECA tax base for services covered by an election is to be computed in a separate "basket" from the tax base for other self-employment income. Thus, church employee income isn't reduced by any deduction, while other income and deductions aren't affected by items attributable to church employee income. (This rule doesn't apply to the deduction for the product of all net self-employment earnings and one-half the SECA tax rate, beginning after 1989.) Also, the $100 threshold for taxing church employee income, and the $400 threshold applicable to other self-employment income, are separately applied under the bill (that is, church employee income doesn't count toward the general $400 threshold).

Effective Date: This provision is effective only for a remuneration paid or derived in tax years beginning on or after 1-1-86.

Voluntary revocation of election. Under the Social Security Act, a church must make an election to treat services performed for the church as subject to SECA (rather than FICA) taxes before its first quarterly employment tax return is due, or if later, 90 days after 7-18-84. Once made, the church can't revoke the election. However, the Treasury can permanently revoke an election if the electing church doesn't provide required information regarding its employees for a period of two years or more and, on the Treasury's request, fails to give previously unfurnished information for the period covered by the election. This rule could allow an electing church effectively to revoke its election by failing to provide the required information.

The new law allows a church to revoke an election under regulations the Treasury will prescribe. Treasury could still revoke an election for failure to provide required information. A church that revokes an election (or for which the election is revoked) can't make another election because the time for making such an election would have lapsed.

The regulations allowing a church or qualified church-controlled organization to revoke a Sec. 3121(w)(2) election will provide that any such revocation isn't to be effective before January 1, 1987, unless such electing church or organization had withheld and paid over all employment taxes due, as if such election had never been in effect, during the period from the stated effective date of the election being revoked through 12-31-86.

Act Sec. 1882, amending Sec. 211 of the Social Security Act, and Secs. 1402(g) and 3121(w)(2), takes effect on enactment, except that the provisions affecting computation of income subject to SECA taxes is effective after 1985.

〔¶1883〕 AFDC and Child Support Programs. *Disregarding income of stepparent.* The AFDC (aid to families with dependent children) plan requirement for treatment of a stepparent's earned income allows a monthly disregard of $75 (in recognition of work expenses). Currently, the Secretary can prescribe the disregard or a lesser amount for individuals not in full-time employment or not employed throughout the month.

The new law deletes the Secretary's authority for the disregard of a lesser amount in the case of earnings of a stepfather, since the Deficit Reduction Act deleted the comparable authority for the general income disregard provision of Sec. 402(a)(8) of the Act.

Family unit rule. The Social Security Act requires the inclusion in the AFDC family unit of all parents of the dependent child, and all siblings who are themselves dependent children.

The new law clarifies that the sibling who is deprived of parental support or care by reason of the employment of a parent (and meets the other criteria of a dependent child), as well as one who is deprived by reason of the death, absence, or incapacity of a parent, is to be included in the AFDC. No such distinction between these two categories was intended, and this provision will clarify that, in a state that provides AFDC on the basis of the unemployment of a parent, siblings who are dependent children for that reason must be included in the AFDC unit.

Income of a minor AFDC parent. The Social Security Act requires, that in determining the income of a minor parent (of an AFDC child) who is living with her own parents or legal guardian, the state agency must include the income of the parents or legal guardian. In deciding what age defines "minor" for this purpose, the Act refers to the upper age limit chosen by the state for establishing eligibility as an AFDC child.

The new law clarifies that for purposes of defining the age limit of a "minor" parent, the age is that selected by the state for purposes of defining a dependent child, without regard to whether the minor parent is attending school. It clarifies that only the age limit, and not the school attendance element, was intended to be relevant to the income computation. (This is meant to reduce any incentive on the part of the minor parent to drop out of school.) This provision applies to minor parents up to age 18.

Federal incentive payments in interstate support collections. To encourage states to enforce complicated interstate child support obligations which arise when the custodial parent and child(ren) live in one state and the noncustodial parent lives in another state, Congress provided that in interstate cases "support which is collected by one state on behalf of individuals residing in another state shall be treated as having been collected in full by each such state." As a result, in interstate collection efforts, both states are to be credited with the collection for the purposes of calculating the incentive payment.

The new law clarifies the intent of Congress that the incentive be credited to both the state *initiating* the collection and the state *making* the collection. It describes the initiating state as the state requesting the collection, rather than the state of residence of the individuals on whose behalf the collection is made. The change is necessary because the state of residence isn't always the same as the state initiating the collection request.

Exclusion from AFDC unit of siblings receiving foster care maintenance payments. Before the 1984 Deficit Reduction Act added the family unit rule in AFDC, a sibling of an AFDC child, residing in the AFDC household but receiving foster care maintenance payments, was excluded from the AFDC family.

The new law adds a new section to make clear that the sibling of an AFDC child receiving foster care maintenance payments isn't a member of the AFDC unit.

Act Sec. 1883(b)(1)(A), amending Sec. 402(a)(8) of the 1984 Deficit Reduction Act, is effective 10-1-84; Act Sec. 1883(b)(2)(A), amending Sec. 402(a)(38) of the Social Security Act, is effective 10-1-84; Act Sec. 1883(b)(2)(B), amending Sec. 402(a)(38) of the Social Security Act, is effective 10-1-84; Act Sec.

1883(b)(3), amending Sec. 402(a)(39) of the Social Security Act, is effective 10-1-84; Act Sec. 1883(b)(7), amending Sec. 458(d) of the Social Security Act, takes effect on the date of enactment; Act Sec. 1883(b)(9), is effective 10-1-84; Act Sec. 1883(a), making technical corrections to Secs. 202 and 210 of the Social Security Act, is effective, generally, on the date of enactment.

For those amendments with an effective date of 10-1-84 (Act Secs. 1883(1), (2), (3), (9)), no state is considered to have failed to comply with the Social Security Act or to have made overpayments or underpayments by reason of its compliance with these amendments for the period beginning 10-1-84 and ending on the day preceding the date of enactment.

[¶1884] **Federal Unemployment Tax Act.** *Partial limitation on the reduction of credit against unemployment tax.* States can borrow funds from the Federal Unemployment accounts to pay unemployment benefits. Depending on the month in which such a loan is advanced, a state has between 22 and 34 months to repay the loan. If the loan is not repaid in time, the FUTA tax credit for employers in the state is reduced by .3% for each year the loan is in arrears.

For states that take legislative steps to improve the solvency of their unemployment insurance systems, the FUTA credit reduction is limited to 0.1% a year for each year a state has a loan in arrears. This limitation on the FUTA credit reduction is effective for 1983, 1984, and 1985.

The new law clarifies that the limitation on the FUTA credit reduction in states meeting the solvency test expires at the end of calendar year 1985, not 1986 as the Code presently indicates.

Definition of 'agricultural worker.' Section 3306(O)(1)(A)(i) provides, that for purposes of the Federal Unemployment Tax Act, an individual who is a member of a crew furnished by a crew leader to perform agricultural labor for any other person shall be treated as an employee of such crew leader if such crew leader holds a valid certificate of registration under the 1963 Farm Labor Contractor Act. This act has been repealed and replaced with the 1983 Migrant and Seasonal Agricultural Workers Protection Act.

Thus, the new law strikes the reference to the 1963 Farm Labor Contractor Act and replaces it with a reference to the 1983 Migrant and Seasonal Agricultural Workers Protection Act.

Act Sec. 1884, amending Sec. 3302(f)(8) (relating to a partial limitation on the reduction of the credit against the unemployment tax), and Sec. 3306(o)(1-)(A) (relating to crew leaders who are registered or provide specialized agricultural labor), is effective on the date of enactment.

[¶1885] **Tariff Schedule Amendments.** *Telecommunications product classification corrections.* The 1984 Trade and Tariff Act revised the provisions of part 5 of schedule 6 of the Tariff Schedules applicable to telecommunications products to better reflect the state of current technology in such products.

The new law makes conforming changes to several headnotes in the Tariff Schedules which refer to the items in part 5 of schedule 6, which were changed by the 1984 Trade and Tariff Act. It also adds the appropriate column 2 rate of duty for new items 685.34, which was inadvertently omitted.

Other corrections. The new law makes corrections in the article descriptions of Tariff Schedule items 906.38, 907.38, 912.13, and in headnote 1 of part 4D of schedule 1 and headnote 1 of part 4C of schedule 3 (as amended by the 1984 Trade and Tariff Act), to correct spelling, utilize proper chemical nomenclature, correct Tariff Schedule references, and eliminate duplication.

Act Sec. 1885, amending Secs. 111, 112, 123, 124, 146, 182 of the 1984 Trade and Tariff Act and various provisions of the Tariff Schedules of the United States, is effective, generally, for articles entered, or withdrawn from, a warehouse for consumption on or after the date that is 15 days after the date of the new law's enactment.

[¶1886] Countervailing and Antidumping Duty Provisions. *Definition of "interested party."* Section 612(a)(3) of the 1984 Trade and Tariff Act amended section 711(9) of the 1930 Tariff Act to include industry-labor coalitions within the definition of "interested party" for purposes of countervailing duty or antidumping investigations.

The new law makes similar conforming changes in Secs. 702(b)(1) and 732(b)(1) of the 1930 Tariff Act to ensure that industry-labor coalitions will be considered proper petitioners under the countervailing duty and antidumping laws.

Imports under suspension agreements. Sec. 704(b) of the 1930 Tariff Act authorized suspending countervailing duty investigations if the foreign government or exporters accounting for substantially all imports of merchandise agreed to eliminate or offset the subsidy or to cease exports of subsidized merchandise within six months after the suspension.

The new law restores Sec. 704(d)(2) of the 1930 Tariff Act, which was inadvertently deleted. Sec. 704(d)(2) requires that a suspension agreement provide a means of ensuring that exports shall not surge during the six-month period of phase-in of measures to eliminate or offset subsidies.

Waiver of deposit of estimated antidumping duties. The 1930 Tariff Act authorizes the administering authority, for 90 days after publication of an antidumping order, to continue to permit entry of merchandise subject to the order under bond, instead of the deposit of estimated duties for individual importers, if it has reason to believe these importers have taken steps to eliminate or substantially reduce dumping margins. This provision covers all merchandise entered as of the date of the first affirmative antidumping determination, whether or not sold to an unrelated buyer that is necessary to compute price.

The new law amends the 1930 Tariff Act to change its scope to cover only entries entered and resold to unrelated buyers during the period between the first affirmative antidumping determination and the International Trade Commission's final affirmative determination. This amendment was inadvertently omitted from the 1984 Trade and Tariff Act.

Revocation of orders. A party seeking revocation of an antidumping order has the burden of persuasion as to whether there are changed circumstances sufficient to warrant revocation. The new law applies the same standard to revocations of countervailing duty orders as applies to antidumping orders. The amendment corrects an inadvertent omission from the 1984 Trade and Tariff Act, since there's no reason to distinguish between the two types of revocations.

Upstream subsidies. Sec. 771A(a) of the 1930 Tariff Act, as added by Sec. 613 of the 1984 Trade and Tariff Act, defines upstream subsidies in part in terms of the types of practices described under Sec. 771(5)(B)(i)(ii), or (iii) of the Tariff Act as domestic subsidies. The new law amends the 1930 Tariff Act to correct the unintended omission of Sec. 771(5)(B)(iv) from the list of domestic subsidy practices which may constitute an upstream subsidy.

Release of confidential information. The 1930 Tariff Act contains various provisions relating to the release of confidential information. As amended by Sec. 619 of the 1984 Trade and Tariff Act, it provides that the administering authority may release such information under an administrative protective order if it's accompanied by a statement of permission.

The new law amends the 1930 Tariff Act to substitute the terms "proprietary" for "confidential" throughout Sec. 777, a change that was omitted inadvertently from the 1984 Trade and Tariff Act. The provision also amends subsection (b)(1)(B)(i) to correct the inadvertent omission of the International Trade Commission as being permitted to release information, as well as the administering authority, consistent with the rest of the section.

Effective Dates: Sec. 626(b) of the 1984 Trade and Tariff Act made amendments in Secs. 602, 609, 611, 612, and 620 of that Act to Title VII of the 1930 Tariff Act applicable to investigations initiated on or after the date of enactment and the amendments made by section 623 were made applicable to civil actions pending or filed on or after the date of enactment.

The new law amends Sec. 626(b) so that the amendments in Secs. 602, 609, 611, 612, and 620 of the 1984 Trade and Tariff Act will apply to reviews of oustanding antidumping and countervailing duty orders, as well as to new investigations. These orders would involve merchandise entered, or withdrawn from warehouse, for consumption many years after the date of enactment. This amendment is consistent with the Congressional intent of these amendments to reduce the cost and increase of efficiency of proceedings.

The new law authorizes the administering authority to delay implementation of any of the amendments to Title VII as to investigations in progress on the date of enactment of the 1984 Trade and Tariff Act if it determines that immediate implementation would prevent compliance with an applicable statutory deadline. New questionnaires would have to be issued to seek information required by certain amendments that may not be obtainable on cases in progress within the statutory deadlines.

The law also clarifies that the amendments made by the 1984 Trade and Tariff Act to the 1930 Tariff Act concerning the rate of interest payable on overpayments and underpayments of antidumping and countervailing duties apply to merchandise unliquidated as of five days after date of enactment, that is, on or after 11-4-84, consistent with U.S. Customs Service practice.

Act Sec. 1886, amending Secs. 702(b)(1), 704, 732(b)(1), 751(b)(1), 771A(a), 777, 7369(c)(1) of Title IV of the 1930 Tariff Act and Secs. 611(a)(2)(B)(iii), 613, 619, 626(b) of the 1984 Trade and Tariff Act, is effective, generally, on that Act's enactment date (10/29/84); Act Secs. 1886(a)(1), (3), (5), (6), (9), (11), (12) making technical corrections to Title VII of the 1930 Tariff Act, is effective, generally, on the date of enactment.

[¶1887]   Amendments to the 1974 Trade Act. *Waiver authority under generalized system of preferences (GSP)*. The 1974 Trade Act limits Presidential authority to waive more restrictive GSP competitive need limits as to products from advanced beneficiary developing countries to no more than 15% of the total value of GSP duty-free imports during the preceding calendar year.

The new law clarifies that the 15% limit on the President's waiver authority applies to the aggregate value of all waivers granted in a given year on GSP imports from advanced beneficiary countries taken as a group, not to each country individually.

Transistors. To fully implement an agreement to reduce U.S. duties on transistors, the bill corrects a numbering error of a TSUS line item.

Act Sec. 1887, amending Sec. 504(c)(3)(D)(ii) of the 1974 Trade and Tariff Act, is effective, generally, on the date of enactment; Act Secs. 1887(a)(1)—(4), making technical corrections to various sections of the 1974 Trade Act, is effective on the date of enactment.

[¶1888]   Amendments to the 1930 Tariff Act. *Marking of pipes, tubes, and fittings.* The 1984 Trade and Tariff Act added a new subsection (c) to Sec. 403 of the 1930 Traiff Act, providing that no exceptions may be made to the marking requirements of section 304 for certain pipes and pipe fittings, and required these products to be marked with the country of origin by means of die stamping, cast-in-mold lettering, etching, or engraving.

The new law provides a limited exception to the marking requirement for articles which, due to their nature, may not be marked by one of the four prescribed methods because it's technically or commercially infeasable to do so. These articles may be marked by an equally permanent method of marking, such as paint stenciling, or in the case of a small diameter pipe, tube, or fitting, by tagging the containers or bundles. Those articles that Customs decides can be marked by die stamping, cast-in-mold lettering, etching or engraving without adversely affecting their structural integrity or significantly reducing their commercial utility would continue to be marked in this manner.

Tagging of containers or bundles may only be used for small diameter pipes, tubes, and fittings for which individual marking would be impractical or inconspicuous. If Customs determines that tagging is the only feasible method of marking imported goods so that the ultimate consumer will know the country of origin of the goods, such products must be bundled and tagged in accordance with applicable industry standards. The U.S. Customs Service must report back to the Ways and Means Committee within one year after enactment on how the provision is working.

Drawback to incidental operations. The 1984 Trade and Tariff Act amends the 1930 Tariff Act to permit substituting domestic fungible merchandise for imported merchandise under prescribed circumstances and still get the benefits of drawback when these products are exported. However, incidental operations which may be performed on imported merchandise under section 313(j)(4) without depriving them of drawback privileges may not be performed on such substituted domestic merchandise.

The new law changes this so that incidental operations may be performed on both domestic and imported merchandise so that the intent of the original provision (that is, allowing fungible domestic and imported merchandise to be mixed together and still be entitled to drawback) is accomplished.

Interested parties. Sec. 771(9) of the 1930 Tariff Act, as amended by section 612(a) of the 1984 Trade and Tariff Act, defines the term "interested party" for purposes of countervailing duty or antidumping proceedings to incude industry-labor coalitions. The term is also used in the provisions for judicial review of such proceedings under Title V of the 1930 Tariff Act.

The law amends the 1930 Tariff Act to conform the definition of the term interested party to the inclusion of industry-labor coalitions under Sec. 771(9) of the 1930 Tariff Act.

Customs provision. The bill deletes duplicative language created by the 1985 Continuing Resolution.

Act Sec. 1888, amending Secs. 304(c), 313(j), 514(a), 516(a)(2) of the 1930 Tariff Act and Secs. 202, 207 of the 1984 Trade and Tariff Act, is effective on the Act's enactment date; Act Secs. 1888(3), (6), making technical corrections to Secs. 339(c)(2)(A), 516A(a)(3) of the 1930 Tariff Act, is effective on the Act's enactment date.

[¶1889]   Amendments to the 1984 Trade and Tariff Act.

Chipper knife steel. The new law deletes unnecessary language added by the 1984 Trade and Tariff Act.

Watch glasses. The 1984 Trade and Tariff Act reduced the level of duty on watch glasses other than round to the same level as the duty applicable to round watch glasses. However, the Act doesn't provide for the third-year staged reduction on 1-1-87, for watch glasses other than round. The new law amends the Act to provide for the third-year reduction to 4.9% ad valorem tax for such watch glasses.

Act Sec. 1889, amending Secs. 126, 174(b) of the 1984 Trade and Tariff Act, is effective on the Act's enactment date; Act Secs. 1889(3)—(7), correcting various paragraphs in the 1984 Trade and Tariff Act, is effective on the Act's enactment date.

[¶1890]   Amendments to the Caribbean Basin Economic Recovery Act. The Caribbean Basin Economic Recovery Act (CBI) allows products of a beneficiary country to be processed in a bonded warehouse in Puerto Rico after being imported directly from such country and be eligible for duty-free treatment under the CBI on withdrawal from the warehouse if they meet the rule-of-origin requirements set out in Sec. 213(a)(1)(B).

The new law corrects a reference to a wrong Tariff Schedules item in Sec. 213(f)(5)(B) of the CBI and clarifies that products entering Puerto Rico directly from *any* CBI beneficiary country, not merely the country of manufacture, should qualify for entry under bond.

Act Sec. 1890, amending Sec. 213 of the Caribbean Basin Economic Recovery Act, is effective on the Act's enactment date.

[¶1891]   Customs Brokers. The new law makes corrections to conforming amendments made by the 1984 Trade and Tariff Act in Title 28 of the U.S. Code to cross-references in the 1930 Tariff Act relating to customs brokers. It also deletes an incorrect reference in Sec. 1581(g)(1) of Title 28.

Act Sec. 1891, amending Sec. 212 of the 1984 Trade and Tariff Act, is effective on the Act's enactment date.

【¶1892】 Articles Given Duty-Free Treatment Under the 1984 Trade and Tariff Act. Sections 112, 115, 118, 167, and 179 of the 1984 Trade and Tariff Act were made effective 15 days after enactment because the provisions providing for retroactive application of such provisions were inadvertently omitted from the Act.

The new law provides for the retroactive application of sections 112, 115, 118, 167, and 179 of the 1984 Trade and Tariff Act.

Act Sec. 1892, amending Secs. 112, 115, 118, 167, 179 of the 1984 Trade and Tariff Act, is retroactively effective to the date of enactment of such sections (10/29/84).

【¶1893】 Customs Users Fees.
Transit passenger fees. The new law clarifies that the exemption from the $5 fee applicable to passengers arriving on commercial aircraft and vessels also exempts passengers originating in the United States who transit only those locations to which the exemption applies before reentering the United States.

Foreign pre-clearance services. The new law precludes Customs from assessing overtime charges against airlines for pre-clearance of passengers in foreign locations when U.S. Customs officers undertake such pre-clearance.

Remittance fee regulations. The new law directs that regulations issued by the IRS to collect such fees should be consistent with the current regulations on collecting the airport departure tax.

Reinstating limit on charges for inspection services. The new law provides that overtime charges for inspectional or quarantine services (other than customs services) on Sundays or holidays be reimbursed as if they had been performed during a weekday. This is intended to reinstate the limit on weekend and holiday overtime charges for private aircraft and others not benefitting from the inspectional overtime account funded through the customs user fees.

Vessels, barges, bulk carriers, and ferries. A cap of $5,955 is placed on the fees charged for the arrival of any commercial vessel of more than 100 net tons in the United States. This cap on vessel fees is computed on the basis of 15 arrivals per year. The fee on commercial vessels applies to each arrival at a U.S. port regardless of whether these arrivals occur as a series of calls at U.S. ports on the same trip or on several trips.

A lower user fee of $100 on barges and bulk carriers arriving from Canada and Mexico is provided, as such vessels compete with trucks and rail cars arriving by land from Canada and Mexico, which are subject to much lower user fees. A cap of $1,500, also representing

15 arrivals, is placed on the annual total of the user fees that such barges and bulk carriers arriving from contiguous countries must pay.

Regardless of which fee may be applicable during the calendar year, no barge or bulk carrier is liable for more than the $5,955 annual cap applicable to vessels.

The new law exempts tugboats from the application of any vessel fees. This exemption is intended to prevent the Customs Service from applying the vessel user fee to a tugboat that provides propulsion to barges or merely accompanies vessels that are themselves subject to a user fee. This exception does not apply to tugboats that are not being used as tugboats at the time of arrival.

The new law contains a definition of "ferry" for the purposes of the exemption from the user fee applicable to commercial vessels of over 100 net tons. For purposes of this exemption, a ferry includes a vessel that transports passengers, vehicles, or railroad cars, or any combination thereof, for distances of 300 miles or less. While such a ferry is exempted from the fee, trucks or railroad cars carried by such a ferry would be subject to the applicable fee. For commercial vessels subject to the user fee that transport vehicles or rail cars, there is no fee assessed on the vehicles or rail cars.

Railroad cars. The fee would be changed to $7.50 for cars carrying merchandise, and no fee would be assessed on empty cars.

Customs broker fees. The new law clarifies that the annual fee for the issuance of a broker permit is to be prorated so that the applicable fee in 1986 would be one-half the annual fee, based on the 7-1-86 effective date of the fee. The Customs Service is required to provide 60 days notice of the due date for the fee, and is barred from revoking a delinquent broker's permit absent such notice.

Customs broker's freight forwarding. The new law clarifies Congressional intent as to the compensation of customs brokers for certain services. It provides licensed customs brokers, when performing ocean freight forwarder services on export shipments from the United States, with the benefits of the right of independent action as to the level of forwarder compensation in a shipping conference's freight tariff. Under current law, a conference may prohibit its members from taking independent action on forwarder compensation. The new law clarifies that a conference must allow its members to take independent action on compensation to the extent that compensation is or will be paid to a forwarder who is also a licensed customs broker under the 1930 Tariff Act.

The new law also benefits customs brokers when they act in the capacity of a licensed freight forwarder on shipments exported from the United States. Despite the requirement of current law that conferences not deny forwarders a reasonable percentage of the carrier's freight charges as compensation for the forwarder's service, some conferences are limiting forwarder's compensation to a percentage of some, but not all, of the rates and charges assessed against the cargo in their tariffs. The new law clarifies that when compensation is paid to a forwarder who is also a licensed customs broker, the compensation must be based on all the freight charges, including, but not limited to, surcharges, handling charges, service charges, terminal charges, supplements, currency adjustment factors, and any and all other charges required to be paid by the shipper or consignee under the tariff.

NOTE: The new law does not in any way modify or diminish the existing scope or protections of the 1984 Shipping Act as applied to ocean freight forwarders in general. Its purpose is to impose additional requirements on conferences or carrier groups in their concerted dealings with forwarders who are also licensed customs brokers.

Act Sec. 1893, amending Secs. 13031 (a), (b), (d), (e), (f) of the 1985 Consolidated Omnibus Budget Reconciliation Act and Sec. 53 of the 1970 Airport and Airway Development Act, is effective, generally, for services rendered after the date that is 15 days after the date of enactment. On written request, Act Sec. 1893(g)(2) permits the Secretary of the Treasury to refund excess fees paid due to this enactment for customs services provided after 7-6-86 and on or before the date that is 15 days after the date of enactment. If a customs broker's permit fee exceeds $62.50 for 1986, Act Sec. 1893(g)(3) permits the Secretary of the Treasury to refund the excess or, if requested by the customs broker, credit the excess to 1987. Act Sec. 1888(8), amending Sec. 641 of the 1930 Tariff Act (regarding compensation of ocean freight forwarders), is effective on enactment.

[¶1894] **Foreign Trade Zones.** The new law clarifies that the fifth provision in the Foreign Trade Zone Act allows domestic denatured alcohol to be used in the manufacture of other articles.

[¶1895] **Technical Corrections to the 1985 Consolidated Omnibus Budget Reconciliation Act.**

Medicare. The new law corrects the termination of the ACCESS demonstration program, currently 9-30-86, to 7-31-87. It also clarifies that the Director of OTA should initially provide for such terms for members of the Prospective Payment Assessment Commission so that no more than eight members' terms would expire in the same year.

It also makes the following clarifications: (1) corrects and clarifies the section regarding payments under the indirect medical education provision; (2) corrects and clarifies the section regarding payment under the disproportionate share provision; (3) clarifies that all hospitals that have a medicare provider agreement would have to abide by the emergency care requirements of COBRA and the requirements regarding participation in the CHAMPUS program; (4) allows skilled nursing facilities to make an election to be paid on a prospective payment basis on their costs reporting periods rather than on a federal fiscal-year basis; (5) clarifies that the medicare HI tax on state and local governments does not apply to certain campaign workers; (6) clarifies that a one-year transition period is provided for foreign medical graduates who have not passed the FMGEMS; (7) allows the Secretary to announce HMO/CMP rates by September 7 of each year rather than publish them; (8) clarifies the effective date of the provision regarding penalties for billing for assistants at surgery for certain cataract procedures; (9) allows temporary use of carrier prepayment screens as a substitute for preprocedure review; (10) clarifies that the termination date of the ACCESS demonstration project is 7-31-87; and (11) corrects citation, indentation, and other technical errors.

Continuing health care. The new law makes the following technical corrections to the continuing health care provisions of COBRA.

Notification requirement. The new law establishes a 60-day notification period for divorced or legally separated spouses of covered employees, or dependent children ceasing to be dependent children under the generally applicable requirements of the plan, to notify the plan administrator of a qualifying event entitling the spouse or dependent children to continuation health coverage.

Maximum period of continuation coverage. The new law clarifies that a qualfied beneficiary may have more than one qualifying event that entitles the beneficiary to continuation coverage, but in no event may the coverage period as to such events generally exceed a 36-month period. The second qualifying event must take place during the period of coverage of the first qualifying event to be eligible for a total of 36 months continuation coverage beginning from the first qualifying event.

Election of coverage. The new law clarifies that each qualified beneficiary is entitled to a separate election of continuation coverage. For example, if a covered employee does not elect continuation coverage, the spouse or dependent children are entitled to elect such coverage. Moreover, even if the employee elects certain coverage, the spouse or dependents may elect different coverage.

Failure to pay premiums. The new law provides that the grace period for failure to pay premiums is the longest of (1) 30 days; (2) the period the plan allows employees for failure to pay premiums; or (3) the period the insurance company allows the plan or the employer for failure to pay premiums.

Type of coverage. The new law provides that, for all purposes, qualified beneficiaries are to be treated under the plan in the same manner as similarly situated beneficiaries for whom a qualifying event has not taken place. For example, if the plan provides for an open enrollment period, then qualified beneficiaries are to be permitted to make elections during the open enrollment period in the same manner as active employees. Thus, an individual who is a qualified beneficiary by reason of being a spouse of a covered employee would have the same rights as active employees during an open enrollment period and would not be limited to the rights of spouses of covered employees.

"Health benefits" mean health benefit plans, including dental and vision care (within the meaning of Sec. 213). It is not intended that an employer could compel a qualified beneficiary to pay for non care benefits (such as dental and vision care) even if active employees are required to buy coverage for such benefits under the plan.

Act Sec. 1895, amending Secs. 9122(b), 9202(j), 9517(c)(2), and 9528(a) of the 1985 Consolidated Omnibus Budget Reconciliation Act, Secs. 602(2), 602(3), 605(2), 606(3), and 607 of ERISA, Secs. 2202(2) and 2206(3) of the Public Health Service Act, Secs. 1164(b)(4), 1837(i)(1), 1842(b)(4), 1842(h), 1842(k), 1866(a), 1867(e)(3), 1876(a)(1), 1886(d), 1886(g), 1886(h), 1888(d)(1), 1902(a)(10), 1902(a)(13), 1903(m)(2), 1905(a), and 1920(a) of the Social Security Act, and Code Secs. 162(k)(2), (6), (7), 3121(u)(2)(B)(i), is effective, generally, as if included in the 1985 Consolidated Omnibus Budget Reconciliation Act.

[¶1896] Extension of Time for Investment Farmers to File for Refunds. The new law provides that claims arising from the minimum tax amendment made by the 1985 Consolidated Omnibus Budget Reconciliation Act (relating to certain insolvent farmers allowed to reduce capital gains preference items for purposes of the individual minimum tax) may be made within one year after the enactment of the new law.

Act Sec. 1896, amending Sec. 13208 of the 1985 Consolidated Omnibus Budget Reconciliation Act, is effective on the Act's enactment.

[¶1897] Technical Corrections to the REA. The new law includes provisions which make technical corrections in the Retirement Equity Act of 1984, and clarify certain provisions of that act.

Break-in-service rules. Class year plans. A class-year plan is a profit-sharing, stock bonus, or money purchase plan which provides for separate vesting of benefits attributable to employer contributions for each plan year. Such benefits generally must be 100% vested as of the close of the fifth plan year of service following the plan year for which the contribution is made. Under the new law, such benefits cannot be forfeited unless, before becoming vested, the employee incurs five consecutive one-year break-in-service. A plan year of service is a plan year, on the last day of which the participant is performing services for the employer; break-in-service years are all other plan years.

Lump-sum distributions. To receive the favorable tax treatment accorded lump-sum distributions, a participant must receive a distribution of the entire balance to his credit in the plan within one taxable year. If a participant, who is partially vested in his accrued benefit, separates from service and receives a distribution of his or her vested interest before incurring five consecutive one-year breaks in service, the potential increase in vesting that might occur if he or she returned to employment might make the distribution ineligible for lump-sum treatment. The new law provides that the determination of whether a distribution made on account of separation from service qualifies as a lump-sum distribution, is made without regard to any increase in vesting that could occur if the participant is reemployed by the employer. If, however, the employee is reemployed and, as a result, his or her vested interest in benefits accrued before the break-in-service increases, the tax savings from treating the distribution as a lump-sum distribution are recaptured. If the tax savings are recaptured, the previous lump-sum distribution will not prevent the participant from treating a subsequent distribution as a lump-sum distribution.

Rollovers. The new law also provides that, for the purpose of determining whether a distribution on account of a separation from service is eligible for rollover treatment, the balance to the credit of the employee is determined without regard to any potential increase in vesting. If, however, the employee is reemployed and the vested percentage of benefits accrued before the separation from service increases, subsequent distributions generally will not be eligible for favorable tax treatment. Favorable tax treatment of subsequent distributions may be available if the rolled over distribution is made without the consent of the participant (e.g., a distribution of $3,500 or less).

Repayment of mandatory employee contributions. Under prior law, if a plan participant who was less than 50% vested in the accrued benefit derived from employer contributions withdrew any portion of mandatory employee contributions from the plan, the accrued benefit derived from employee contributions could be forfeited. However, the plan had to provide that the forfeited amounts would be restored if the employee repaid the amount of mandatory contributions withdrawn. Defined contribution plans could require that repayment be made before the employee incurred a one-year break-in-service.

The new law conforms the repayment period for mandatory contributions to the repayment period for accrued benefits after a separation from service, and eliminates the distinction between defined contribution and defined benefit plans. Now either type of plan may provide that repayment of mandatory contributions which have been withdrawn, or of accrued benefits which have been distributed, must be made no later than (1) in the case of a withdrawal or distribution on account of separation from service, the earlier of five years after the date of subsequent reemployment by the employer or the close of the fifth consecutive one-year break-in-service, and (2) in the case of any other withdrawal, five years after the date of withdrawal.

Maximum age requirements—SEPs. The new law conforms the maximum age which may be required as a condition of participation in a Simplified Employee Pension Plan to the REA requirements for other qualified plans. The maximum age is reduced from 25 to 21. This change is effective for plan years beginning after the date of enactment.

Joint and survivor annuities and preretirement survivor annuities. Under REA, it is unclear whether the qualified joint and survivor annuity (QJSA) provisions or the qualified preretirement survivor annuity (QPSA) provisions apply when (1) a participant retires, or attains the normal retirement age under the plan, but dies before the annuity starting date, and (2) a participant receives a disability benefit under a plan. The new law provides that the QJSA is payable if the participant does not die before the annuity starting date unless it has been waived. The QPSA is payable (unless waived) if the participant dies before the annuity starting date.

The annuity starting date is the first day of the first period for which an amount is payable as an annuity. If the benefit isn't payable as an annuity, the annuity starting date is the first day on which all events have occurred which entitle the participant to a benefit.

If a disability benefit is an auxiliary benefit, the commencement of disability benefits would not be an annuity starting date. If a participant who is receiving a disability benefit will, upon reaching the normal retirement age, receive a retirement benefit which satisfies the benefit accrual and vesting rules of Sec. 411, without taking the disability benefit into account, the disability benefit is auxiliary. In such a case, if the employee died before reaching the plan's normal retirement date, the employee's spouse would be entitled to the QPSA. If the employee dies after reaching the normal retirement age, the spouse would be entitled to the survivor portion of a QJSA.

The new law also clarifies that a plan which is exempt from the QJSA and QPSA requirements is not required to pay the participant's vested accrued benefit to the participant's spouse on the death of the participant unless the participant and spouse were married for at least one year on the date of the participant's death.

Transferee plan rules. Under REA, a plan not otherwise subject to the QJSA or QPSA rules will be subjected to those rules if it receives a direct transfer of assets in connection with a merger, spin-off, or conversion of a plan which is subject to the rules, or receives a direct transfer of assets from such a plan solely with respect to a participant. The new law clarifies that a transfer completed before 1-1-85 will not cause a plan not otherwise subject to the survivor annuity rules to be made subject to them. Further, under the new law, the survivor annuity rules, if applicable, will be limited to benefits attributable to the transferred assets, provided the plan accounts for the transferred assets and the allocable investment yield from those assets separately.

Amount of QPSA. REA provides that the amount of a QPSA must be no less than the amount which would be payable to the surviving spouse under a QJSA if (1) in the case of a participant who dies after attaining the earliest retirement age under the plan, the participant had retired on the day before his death with an immediate QJSA, and (2) in the case of a participant who dies on or before the earliest retirement age, the participant had separated from service on the date of death, survived until the earliest retirement age, and then retired with an immediate QJSA.

The new law clarifies that the QPSA payable to the spouse of a participant who separates from service prior to death, will be calculated by reference to the date of separation. Thus, no benefits accrue after the participant's separation from service.

If a participant's accrued benefit is attributable to both employee and employer contributions, the QPSA must be treated as attributable to employee contributions in the same ratio as the portion of the accrued benefit which is derived from employee contributions bears to the participant's total accrued benefit. The plan is not permitted to allocate the survivor annuity only to employee contributions. For the purposes of determining the amount of QPSA under a defined contribution plan subject to the survivor annuity requirements, the participant's vested account balance includes any portion attributable to employee contributions.

The earliest retirement age should be determined counting only the participant's actual years of service at separation from service or death. Therefore, if a participant dies or leaves employment before satisfying a service requirement for early retirement, the "earliest retirement age" will be the date the participant would have reached the normal retirement age under the plan.

Spousal consent requirements. Under the new law, a spouse's consent to the waiver of the QJSA or QPSA, must either name a non-spouse beneficiary to receive any death benefits which become payable, and the form of the death benefit, or acknowledge that the spouse voluntarily relinquishes the right to name the beneficiary and/or specify the form of payment. If the spouse's consent specifies the beneficiary or form of payment, a subsequent change in either will require a new spousal consent.

NOTE: This position varies from that of the IRS regs [Reg. Sec. 1.401(a)-11T, Q-A 25], which would require that *all* spousal consents specify the nonspouse beneficiary.

If a waiver of a survivor benefit is required, the consenting spouse must be given an opportunity to consent to the waiver only in favor of a specific beneficiary or form of payment. The plan may not restrict the spouse's ability to waive the survivor benefit by providing only a general consent under which the spouse relinquishes the right to designate a beneficiary or form of payment.

The new law clarifies that a spousal consent to a waiver of a survivor benefit is not a transfer for gift tax purposes.

Spousal consent is required for the accrued benefit of a participant to be used as security for loans from plans which are subject to the survivor annuity requirements. Unlike Reg. Sec. 1.417(e)-IT(d), which requires spousal consent to all loans from qualified plans, the new law does not require consent to a loan from a profit-sharing plan which is not a transferee plan with respect to the participant.

If a participant's accrued benefit is used as security for a loan and the participant's spouse consents, then upon default the plan may realize its security interest, even if at the time of default the participant is married to a different spouse. Similar rules apply if the participant is unmarried when the security agreement is made, and a default occurs later when the participant is married.

For the purpose of determining the amount of any survivor benefit, any security interest held by the plan because of an outstanding loan is taken into account, as is the value of amounts payable under any outstanding Qualified Domestic Relations Order (QDRO).

The notice requirements and election periods pertaining to spousal consent to waivers of survivor annuity benefits also apply to spousal consents to (1) waive survivor benefits under plans exempt from the QPSA and QJSA requirements; (2) pledge the participant's accrued benefits as security for a loan; (3) permit distributions after the annuity starting date; and (4) permit immediate distribution of amounts in excess of $3,500.

The provisions relating to spousal consents to changes in beneficiary designations and changes in benefit form apply to plan years beginning after the date of enactment.

The provision relating to notice and election periods for plans that are exempt from the survivors benefit requirements is effective on the date of enactment.

The provisions relating to spousal consents to pledge accrued benefits as security for loans apply to loans made after 8-18-85. However, any loan that is revised, extended, renewed, or renegotiated after 8-18-85, is treated as a new loan (and a new security pledge).

Notice requirement for persons hired after age 35. REA requires that plan participants be notified of their rights to decline the QPSA during the period beginning with the first day of the plan year in which the participant attains age 32 and ending with the last day of the plan year in which he or she attains age 35. Under the new law the notice period will not in any event end before the latest of (1) a reasonable time after the individual becomes a plan participant; (2) a reasonable time after survivor benefits cease to be subsidized; or (3) a reasonable time after the survivor benefit requirements become applicable with respect to a participant. If a participant separates from service prior to age 35, the plan must notify the participant, within a reasonable time after separation from service, of the participant's right to decline the QPSA.

Subsidized benefits. Under REA, a plan is not required to notify a participant of his or her right to waive the QJSA or QPSA if the plan fully subsidizes the cost of the benefits. Under the new law, the exception would not apply if a participant were permitted to waive the benefit or to designate a nonspouse beneficiary. Moreover, a benefit will not be considered to be fully subsidized if the costs are spread among all plan participants, or a group of plan participants, even if benefits of those to whom the costs are allocated are not affected by a waiver or failure to waive survivor benefits.

QDROs. Under REA, payments to an alternate payee, pursuant to a Qualified Domestic Relations Order, do not violate the prohibitions in ERISA and the Code against the assignment or alienation of benefits under the pension plan. The alternate payee is treated as a distributee of benefits for tax purposes. Moreover, net employee contributions are apportioned between the participant and the alternate payee. Under the new law the special tax treatment of payments under QDRO is applicable only if the alternate payee is the spouse or former spouse of the participant. Effective for payments after the date of enactment, if the alternate payee is other than a spouse or former spouse (e.g., a child), the payments are included in the participant's income, and all employee contributions (and other investment in the contract) recoverable by the participant under general basis-recovery rules.

When a plan administrator receives a domestic relations order, it must determine within an 18-month period whether the order is a "qualified" domestic relations order. The new law clarifies that the 18-month period begins on the date payments are due to commence under the order.

During the 18-month period, the plan administrator is to defer payment of the amounts subject to the domestic relations order until it determines whether the domestic relations order is qualified. The new law eliminates the prior law's requirement that the deferred amounts be held in an escrow account, and requires only that the deferred amounts be separately accounted for.

If a domestic relations order is determined not to be qualified, the plan administrator must pay the deferred amounts to the person entitled thereto as if there were no order. However, if the administrator is notified that the parties are attempting to cure the defects in the order, it is required to continue to defer the amounts until the end of the 18-month period.

Generally, a domestic relations order will not be qualified if it requires benefits to be paid in a form not permitted under the plan. However, if the form of benefit ceases to be permitted under the plan, as a result of a plan amendment or a change in the law, a QDRO will not lose its qualified status. If the plan is amended in a way which makes the form of benefit no longer permissible, the alternate payee will be entitled to continue receiving benefits in the form specified in the order, or to elect another form of benefit which will not affect the amount or form of benefit payable to the participant. If the form of benefit specified in the order becomes impermissible because of a change in the law, the plan must permit the alternate payee to select a form of payment permitted under the plan, which does not affect, in any way, the amount or form of benefit payable to the participant.

A QDRO can also require that benefits be paid to the alternate payee prior to the participants separation from service, provided the participant has attained the earliest retirement age. Earliest retirement age means, for this purpose, the earlier of: (1) the earliest date benefits are payable under the plan or (2) the later of the date the participant attains age 50 or the date on which the participant could obtain a distribution from the plan if the participant separated from service.

The present value of the benefits payable to an alternate payee is determined without regard to the value of the benefit payable to the participant. Likewise, the present value of the benefit payable to the participant is determined without regard to the present value of the benefit payable to the alternate payee.

The new law permits a spouse will be treated as a nonspouse to the extent provided in a QDRO. If a QDRO provides, for example, for the division of a participant's accrued benefits under a plan as part of a separation agreement, and also provides that the nonparticipant spouse is entitled to no other part of the accrued benefits, the usual survivor benefit provisions will not apply. A QDRO may also provide that a former spouse is to be treated as a surviving spouse for purposes of the survivor annuity provisions, in which case the participant's present spouse would not be treated as a surviving spouse.

The new law also clarifies that a plan which offers a joint and survivor annuity option cannot be required by a QDRO to make payments, prior or subsequent to the participant's separation from service, in the form of a QISA to the alternate payee and his or her subsequent spouse.

Death benefit—transitional rules. REA imposes certain survivor benefit provisions on plans with respect to participants who die before the plans are required to be amended to comply with the Act. During the transition period, the plan is required to pay survivor benefits to a surviving spouse notwithstanding possible contractual claims of other designated beneficiaries. The new law protects the plan against having to pay double death benefits by providing that the death benefit otherwise payable to such designated beneficiaries may be reduced by the present value of benefits required under REA to be paid to the survivor spouse. Moreover, the plan will be treated as satisfying the QJSA requirements if the survivor benefit was paid to the spouse in a nonannuity form.

Plan loans to owner-employees. The new law amends ERISA to remove the absolute ban on plan loans to owner-employees. However, it gives Treasury almost absolute discretion in setting up procedures for granting exemptions from the prohibition. For these purposes only, the term owner-employee includes the owner-employee (defined in Sec. 401(c)(3)), a member of his or her family (under Sec. 267(c)(4)), and certain 50% controlled corporations. Also included are S corporation shareholder-employees and IRA participants and beneficiaries.

The new law also permits Treasury to establish procedures to allow plans to (1) pay owner-employees compensation for personal services rendered to the plan and (2) buy or sell any property to the owner-employee.

The fact that the prohibition was repealed doesn't mean that loans will be permitted in the near future. That's because Treasury need not establish such procedures for granting exemptions if it finds that permitting such transactions

- isn't administratively feasible;
- isn't in the interests of the plan or its participants; and
- isn't protective of the rights of the participants and beneficiaries.

This provision applies only for transactions occurring after the date of enactment.

Special rules for distributions from ESOPs. The new law provides that distribution options under an ESOP may be modified in a nondiscriminatory manner without violating the Sec. 411(d)(6) prohibition against removing options. Moreover, the restrictions on mandatory distributions in excess of $3,500 are not applicable to deductible dividend distributions from ESOPs to participants or beneficiaries.

Additional technical corrections. The new law makes further technical amendments to REA, to clarify that the annuity starting date for nonannuity benefits is the date all events have occurred to entitle the participant to the benefits, to coordinate with federal garnishment restrictions, to clarify that QDRO provisions do not apply to plans not subject to assignment and alienation restrictions, to define when an accrued benefit worth more than $3,500 isn't considered forfeitable for minimum vesting purposes, and clarify when a plan administrator must provide notices of rollover treatment.

Act Sec. 1898(a) amends Code Secs. 402, 408, 411; ERISA Secs. 203(c), (d) clarifying class year vesting rules, lump sum payments to partially vested employees, rules relating to withdrawal of mandatory contributions, effective for plan years beginning after 12-31-84, except that class year vesting rules and the SEP maximum age requirement apply to plan years beginning after enactment date. Provisions do not apply to collectively bargained plans before expiration of latest collective bargaining agreement or 7-1-88, if earlier. Act Sec. 1898(b) amends Code Secs. 401(a), 417; ERISA Sec. 205, relating to joint and survivor annuities, spousal consents, notice requirements, generally effective for plan years beginning after 12-31-84. Requirement that spouse must consent to change in form of benefits is effective for plan years beginning after date of enactment. Provisions relating to spousal consent to loans apply to loans made, revised renewed, renegotiated, or extended after 8-18-85. Act Sec. 1898(c) amends Code Secs. 72, 401(m), 402(a), 414(p); ERISA Sec. 206(d) to clarify rules relating to Qualified Domestic Relations Orders, effective for plan years beginning after 12-31-84, except that provision taxing participants on payments received by a non-spouse alternate payee is applicable to payments made after date of enactment. Act. Sec. 1898(h) amends transitional rules under REA Section 303(c), to preclude double death benefits, effective 8-23-84, and amends Sec. 2503 to preclude a gift tax on certain waivers. Act Secs. 1898(d)-(g) amends Code Secs. 402(f), 411(a)(11), 411(d)(6); ERISA Secs. 203(e), 204(g); REA Sec. 302(b), relating to distributions from ESOPs, notice of rollover treatment, REA effective date for collectively bargained plans. Act Sec. 1898(i) amends ERISA Sec. 408(d), for plan loans, effective for transactions after the date of enactment. This section is generally effective for years beginning after 12-31-84. Provision permitting changes in ESOP distribution option applies to plan amendments after 7-30-84, with special rule for collectively bargained plans.

〔¶1898〕 Distribution of Child Support Collections.

The Social Security Act provides that when child support is collected on behalf of an AFDC child, amounts for current support exceeding the current AFDC payment (for which the State and Federal governments may reimburse themselves), are paid to the family up to the amount of monthly support required by the court order.

The new law changes the amount required by "court order" to "court or administrative order," to conform it with a parallel provision added by the 1984 Child Support Enforcement Amendments to use administrative processes for establishing support obligations.

Act Sec. 1899, amending Sec. 457(b)(3) of the Social Security Act, takes effect on the date of the '84 Child Support Enforcement Amendments enactment.

[The page following this is Page 1905.]

GLOSSARY

ACRS	Accelerated Cost Recovery System
ADR	Asset Depreciation Range
AFR	Applicable Federal Rate
AGI	Adjusted Gross Income
AII	Allocable Installment Indebtedness
AMT	Alternative Minimum Tax
CBA	Collective Bargaining Agreement
CBERA	Caribbean Basin Economic Recovery Act
CBI	Caribbean Basin Initiative
CFC	Controlled Foreign Corporation
CODA	Cash or Deferred Arrangement
COLA	Cost of Living Adjustment
CPI	Consumer Price Index
CRCO	Consolidated Return Change of Ownership
CSRS	Civil Service Retirement System
DB	Defined Benefit
DC	Defined Contribution
DISC	Domestic International Sales Corporation
E&P	Earnings and Profits
ERISA	Employee Retirement Income Security Act of 1974
ESOP	Employee Stock Ownership Plan
EWOC	Eligible Worker Owned Cooperatives
FBCI	Foreign Base Company Income
FERC	Federal Energy Regulatory Commission
FICA	Federal Insurance Contribution Act (Social Security)
FIFO	First-In, First-Out
FMV	Fair Market Value
FPHC	Foreign Personal Holding Company
FPHCI	Foreign Personal Holding Company Income
FSC	Foreign Sales Corporation
FTI	Foreign Trade Income
FUTA	Federal Unemployment Tax Act
GDBPR	Government Development Bank for Puerto Rico
GSL	Guaranteed Student Loan Bonds
GSOC	General Stock Ownership Corporation
IDB	Industrial Development Bonds
IDC	Intangible Drilling Cost
IRA	Individual Retirement Arrangement
ITC	Investment Tax Credit
LIFO	Last-In, Last-Out
LSD	Lump Sum Distribution
MCC	Mortgage Credit Certificate
MRB	Mortgage Revenue Bonds
NAIC	National Association of Insurance Commissioners

NOL	Net Operating Loss
NRA	Nonresident Alien
OASDI	Old Age, Survivor and Disability Insurance
OID	Original Issue Discount
PAL	Protection Against Loss
PBGC	Pension Benefit Guaranty Corporation
P&C	Property and Casualty
PFIC	Passive Foreign Investment Company
PHC	Personal Holding Company
PLUS	Parent Loans for Undergraduate Students
PRDB	Puerto Rico Development Bank
PSA	Policyholders Surplus Account
PSC	Personal Service Corporation
QDC	Qualified Direct Costs
QPA	Qualified Plan Awards
QPSII	Qualified Possession-Source Investment Income
QSA	Qualified Segregated Asset
QTIP	Qualified Terminal Interest Property
R&D	Research & Development

R&E	Research and Experimentation
REIT	Real Estate Investment Trust
REMP	Real Estate Mortgage Pool
RFC	Regulated Futures Contract
RIC	Regulated Investment Companies
SEC	Securities and Exchange Commission
SEP	Simplified Employee Pension
SLGS	State and Local Goverment Series
SRLY	Separate Return Limitation Year
TCA	Technical Corrections Act
T&E	Travel and Entertainment
TEFRA	Tax Equity and Fiscal Responsibility Act of 1982
TIN	Taxpayer Identification Number
UBI	Unrelated Business Income
VDEC	Voluntary Deductible Employee Contributions
VEBA	Voluntary Employee Beneficiary Association
WB	Welfare Benefit Plan
ZBA	Zero Bracket Amount

TABLE OF EFFECTIVE DATES

[¶2601]   This table contains the effective dates of the provisions of the Tax Reform Act of 1986 ('86 TRA) arranged by Act section number. It lists the subject matter of the Act provision and lists in brackets the main sections of the Internal Revenue Code (or other law) being amended. If a provision has more than one effective date, or if there are exceptions or transitional rules, the table usually lists the general effective date and refers you to the paragraph in the Explanation that gives the transitional and special rules.

Abbreviations. The table uses the following abbreviations: TYBA means tax years beginning after. TYEA means tax years ending after.

Act Sec.	Topic	Effective Date
2	Internal Revenue Code of 1954 ('54 Code) redesignated as Internal Revenue Code of 1986 ('86 Code).	Enactment date.
3	Act section references are to '86 Code unless otherwise provided; proration of rate changes limited to corporate rate reductions. [pertains to Sec. 15]	Enactment date.

TITLE I—INDIVIDUAL INCOME TAX PROVISIONS

Subtitle A—Rate Reductions; Increase in Standard Deduction and Personal Exemptions

101	Basic tax rate structure revised in two stages for individuals and estates and trusts. [Sec. 1; 15]	TYBA 12-31-86; inflation indexing of tax tables for calendar years after 1988.
102	Standard deduction replaces zero bracket amount; taxable income redefined. [Secs. 3; 63]	TYBA 12-31-86; inflation indexing of standard deduction for TYBA 12-31-89.
103	Deductions for personal exemptions revised. [Sec. 151]	TYBA 12-31-86; inflation adjustment for TYBA 12-31-89.
104	Technical amendments made to conform filing requirements and other provisions. [Secs. 21; 32; 108; 129; 152; 172; 402; 441; 443; 541; 613A; 667; 861; 862; 904; 1398; 2032A; 3402; 6012; 6013; 6014; 6212; 6504]	TYBA 12-31-86.

Subtitle B—Provisions Related to Tax Credits

111	Earned income credit increased; provision made for inflation indexing. [Sec. 32]	TYBA 12-31-86.
112	Political contributions credit repealed. [Sec. 24]	TYBA 12-31-86.

Subtitle C—Provisions Related to Exclusions

121	Limited exclusion for unemployment compensation benefits repealed. [Sec. 85]	Amounts received after 12-31-86 in TYEA such date.
122	Exclusion for charitable and employee achievement awards reduced. [Secs. 74; 102; 274]	Prizes and awards granted after 12-31-86.
123	Limits imposed on income exclusions for scholarships, fellowships, and tuition reductions. [Sec. 117]	TYBA 12-31-86, but applies only for scholarships and fellowships granted after 8-16-86, see ¶110.

Act Sec.	Topic	Effective Date
	Subtitle D—Provision Related to Deductions	
131	Two-earner married couple deduction repealed. [Sec. 221]	TYBA 12-31-86.
132	Nondeductible floor imposed on certain misc. itemized deductions; moving expenses allowed only as itemized deduction; treatment of employee business expenses revised. [Secs. 62; 67]	TYBA 12-31-86.
133	Nondeductible floor for medical expenses increased from 5 to 7.5% [Sec. 213]	TYBA 12-31-86.
134	State and local sales tax deduction repealed. [Sec. 164]	TYBA 12-31-86.
135	Adoption expense deduction repealed. [Sec. 222]	TYBA 12-31-86.
	Subtitle E—Miscellaneous Provisions	
141	Income averaging repealed. [Secs. 1301; 1302; 1303; 1304; 1305]	TYBA 12-31-86.
142	Limitations on deductions for meals, travel and entertainment expenses. [Secs. 162; 170; 274]	TYBA 12-31-86.
143	Presumption that activity is for profit for hobby loss rules made tougher; home office deduction rules tightened. [Secs. 183; 280A]	TYBA 12-31-86.
144	Housing allowances for ministers and military personnel cause no loss of deduction for home-mortgage interest and property taxes. [Sec. 265]	All taxable years beginning before, on, or after 12-31-86.
	TITLE II—PROVISIONS RELATING TO CAPITAL COST	
	Subtitle A—Depreciation Provisions	
201	Rules relating to Accelerated Cost Recovery System (ACRS) modified; alternative depreciation system added. [Secs. 168; 312(k); 7701]	Generally provisions apply to property placed in service after 12-31-86 for TYEA that date, unless subject to transitional rules. For property placed in service after 7-31-86 and 1-1-87, election may be made to have rules apply. For special rules see ¶209.
202	Limits on election to expense certain depreciable business assets increased. [Sec. 179]	Property placed in service after 12-31-86 in TYEA that date.
	Subtitle B—Repeal of Regular Investment Tax Credit	
211	Repeal of regular investment tax credit; rules for reduction in carried credits provided. [Sec. 49]	Generally applies to property placed in service after 12-31-85. For transitional rules and special effective dates, see ¶209.
212	Elective 15-year carryback of existing carryforwards of qualified steel companies. [Pertains to Secs. 38; 46]	Corporation's first TYBA 12-31-86.
213	Elective 15-year carryback of existing carryforwards of qualified farmers. [Pertains to Secs. 38; 46]	Farmer's first TYBA 12-31-86.
	Subtitle C—General Business Credit Reduction	
221	Reduction of general business credit to offset tax liability. [Sec. 38(c)(1)]	TYBA 12-31-85.

Act Sec.	Topic	Effective Date

Subtitle D—Research and Development Provisions

231	Qualified research tax credit provisions modified; credit for basic research expenses added. [Secs. 30; 38; 41]	TYBA 12-31-85 generally; Basic research credit applies to costs TYBA 12-31-86.
232	Credit for orphan drug testing extended. [Sec. 28(e)]	Enactment date; credit extended to 12-31-90.

Subtitle E—Changes in Certain Amortization Provisions

241	Rapid writeoff of trademark and trade name expenditures repealed. [Sec. 177]	Expenditures paid or incurred after 12-31-86 generally.
242	Amortization of railroad grading and tunnel bores repealed. [Sec. 185]	Expenditures paid or incurred after 12-31-86 generally.
243	Deduction allowed for certain bus or freight forwarding authorities. ['81 ERTA Sec. 266]	Applies retroactively to TYBA 11-18-82.
244	Expensing of costs for removing architectural barriers for the elderly and handicapped made permanent. [Sec. 190(d)]	Effective for TYBA 12-31-85.

Subtitle F—Provisions Relating to Real Estate

251	Investment credit for certain rehabilitation expenditures modified. [Secs. 46(b); 48(g), (q)]	Generally applies for property placed in service after 12-31-86. For special transitional rules on certain property placed in service by 1-1-94, see ¶217.
252	New credits for providing low-income housing added. [Secs. 38(b); 42]	Generally applies to property placed in service after 12-31-86 in TYEA that date, see ¶218.

Subtitle G—Merchant Marine Capital Construction Funds

261	Tax treatment of deposits to Merchant Marine capital construction fund coordinated with Merchant Marine Act provisions. [Sec. 26(b); 7518]	TYBA 12-31-86.

TITLE III—CAPITAL GAINS

Subtitle A—Individual Capital Gains

301	Exclusion for long-term capital gains of individuals repealed. [Sec. 1202]	TYBA 12-31-86.
302	Maximun 28-percent capital gains rate for taxpayers other than corporations. [Sec. 1(j)]	TYBA 12-31-86.

Subtitle B—Repeal of Corporate Capital Gains Treatment

311	Corporate capital gains treatment repealed. [Sec. 1201]	Generally TYBA 12-31-86. Transitional rules provided for years beginning in 1986 and ending in 1987. See ¶302 and 311.

Subtitle C—Incentive Stock Options

321	Requirement that incentive stock options are exercisable only in chronological order repealed. [Sec. 422A(b)(7)]	Options granted after 12-31-86.

Act Sec.	Topic	Effective Date
	Subtitle D—Straddles	
331	Year-end qualified covered call exception rule expanded [Sec. 1092(c)(4)(E)]	Positions established after 12-31-86.
	TITLE IV—AGRICULTURE, ENERGY, AND NATURAL RESOURCES	
	Subtitle A—Agriculture	
401	Expensing of soil and conservation expenditures limited. [Sec. 175(c)]	For amounts paid or incurred after 12-31-86 in TYEA that date.
402	Expenditures for clearing land are added to the land's basis. [Sec. 182]	For amounts paid or incurred after 12-31-85 in TYEA that date.
403	Gain on disposition of "converted wet lands" or "highly erodible cropland" is treated as ordinary income; loss is long-term capital loss. [Sec. 1257]	For dispositions first used for farming after 3-1-86 in TYEA that date.
404	Deductibility of certain prepaid farming expenses for cash-basis taxpayers limited. [Sec. 464]	For amounts paid or incurred after 3-1-86 in TYBA that date.
405	Rules created for treatment of discharge of qualified indebtedness of solvent farmers. [Secs. 108; 1017(b)]	Discharge of indebtedness occurring after 4-9-86 in TYEA that date.
406	Pre-'86 TRA capital gains treatment retained for dairy cattle under Milk Production Termination Program.	Gains on sale of cattle taken into account after 1-1-87 and before 9-1-87.
	Subtitle B—Treatment of Oil, Gas, Geothermal, and Hard Minerals	
411	Changes made in treatment of IDCs and mining exploration and development costs; special rules for IDC and mining exploration and development costs for foreign ventures. [Secs. 263(i); 291(b); 617(h)]	Generally apply for costs paid or incurred after 12-31-86 in TYEA that date; transitional rules for certain North Sea interests acquired on or before 12-31-85.
412	Repeal of percentage depletion deduction on oil, gas, and geothermal payments not based on production; reduction in percentage depletion deduction on coal and iron ore. [Secs. 291(a)(2); 613A(d)(5)]	Repeal provisions apply for payments received or accrued after 8-16-86 in TYEA that date; reduction applies to TYBA 12-31-86.
413	IDC recapture rules extended to mine exploration and development costs and percentage depletion. [Sec. 1254]	For dispositions of property placed in service after 12-31-86, unless acquired under a written contract entered into before 9-26-85 and binding at all times thereafter.
	Subtitle C—Other Provisions	
421(a)	Extension of business energy investment credit for solar, geothermal, ocean thermal and biomass property. [Sec. 46(b)(2)(A)]	For periods beginning after 12-31-85, within transition rules of Code Sec. 48(m). Biomass credit ends after 12-31-87; others end after 12-31-88.
421(b)	Application of certain '86 TRA investment credit transition rules to long-term alternative energy and hydroelectric projects. [Sec. 46(b)(2)(E)]	For periods beginning after 12-31-85, within transition rules of Code Sec. 48(m).
422(a)	Exemption from excise tax on special fuels for "neat" alcohol fuels reduced. [Sec. 4041(b)(2)(A)]	For sales and use after 12-31-86.

Act Sec.	Topic	Effective Date
422(b)	Extension of taxis' partial exemption from excise taxes on motor fuels. [Sec. 6427(e)]	From 10-1-85 through 9-30-88.
423	Restrictions on exemption from import duty for alcohol and mixtures used as fuel.	Generally for articles entered after 12-31-86, see ¶416.

TITLE V—TAX SHELTER LIMITATIONS; INTEREST LIMITATIONS

Subtitle A—Limitations on Tax Shelters

501	New rules limiting use of losses and credits from passive sources; special rules for taxpayers who are active participants in real estate activities and exemption for working interest in oil and gas. [Sec. 469]	TYBA 12-31-86, except as to carryovers from a tax year beginning before 1-1-87, see ¶507.
502	Losses from investment in qualified low-income housing not treated as loss from passive activity; transitional rules. [pertains to Sec. 469]	Generally property placed in service before 1-1-89, see ¶507.
503	At-risk limitations extended to real property; special rules for partnerships. [Sec. 465(b), (c)]	Losses incurred after 12-31-86 with respect to property placed in service after 12-31-86 and partnership S corp. and pass-through entity property placed in service on, before, or after 1-1-86, see ¶501.

Subtitle B—Interest Expense

511	Limitations on deduction for nonbusiness investment and personal interest. [Sec. 163(d), (h)]	TYBA 12-31-86.

TITLE VI—CORPORATE PROVISIONS

Subtitle A—Corporate Rate Reductions

601	Corporate tax rates reduced. [Sec. 11]	For tax years beginning on or after 7-1-87.

Subtitle B—Treatment of Stock and Stock Dividends

611	Reduction in dividends received deduction. [Sec. 243; 244; 246A; 805]	Dividends received or accrued after 12-31-86 in TYEA such date; amended limit on aggregate deduction applies to TYBA 12-31-86.
612	Partial dividend exclusion for individuals repealed. [Sec. 116]	TYBA 12-31-86.
613	Corp.'s stock redemption expenses made nondeductible. [Sec. 162(l)]	Amounts paid or incurred after 2-28-86 in TYEA that date.
614	Stock basis reduced for nontaxed portion of extraordinary dividends. [Sec. 1059]	Dividends declared after 7-18-86 in TYEA that date; dividends aren't aggregated with those declared before 7-18-86; rules on redemptions apply to dividends declared after enactment date in TYEA such date.

Subtitle C—Limitation on Net Operating Loss Carryforwards and Excess Credit Carryforwards

621	Limitations on net operating loss and other carryforwards; '76 TRA amendments repealed. [Secs. 382; 383; and '76 TRA Sec. 806(e)(f) and '84 TRA Sec. 59(b)]	Generally effective after 12-31-86; repeal of '76 TRA amendments take effect 1-1-86, see ¶614.

Act Sec.	Topic	Effective Date

Subtitle D—Recognition of Gain and Loss on Distributions of Property in Liquidation

631	Recognition of gain or loss on liquidating sale or distribution rules amended. [Secs. 311; 312(n); 332; 333;. 334; 336; 337; 338(h); 367; 453(h)]	Distributions and sales made after 7-31-86 unless complete liquidation before 1-1-87. For grandfathered liquidations and other transitional rules, see ¶619.
632	Rules on treatment of C corps. electing S corp. status amended. [Secs. 1363; 1374]	TYBA 12-31-86, but only in cases where 1st taxable year for which corp. is an S corp. is under an election made after 12-31-86. For special effective dates and transitional rules, see ¶619.
634	Treasury study of corporate provisions authorized.	Study due 1-1-88.

Subtitle E—Other Corporate Provisions

641	Allocating purchase price in certain asset sales. [Sec. 1060]	Acquisitions after 5-6-86 unless entered under a binding contract in effect on that date and at all times thereafter.
642	Definition of related party for certain sales amended. [Sec. 1239(b)(1)]	Generally sales after enactment date in TYEA that date, unless made after 8-14-86 under a contract in effect on that date and binding at all times thereafter.
643	Amortizable bond premium treated as interest. [Sec. 171]	Obligations acquired after enactment date in TYEA that date; certain taxpayers may revoke taxable bond elections made before that date.
644	Cooperative housing corp. provisions amended. [Sec. 216]	Generally TYBA 12-31-86. Treatment of amounts received to refinance indebtedness apply to taxable years beginning before 1-1-86; qualified refinancing related reserve applies to amounts paid or incurred, and property acquired, in TYBA 12-31-85.
645	Rules relating to personal holding company and foreign personal holding company income amended. [Sec. 543; 553]	Generally apply to royalties received on or after enactment date.
646	Election for certain entity to be treated as trust rather than corporation.	Generally enactment date.
647	Special income inclusion rule for disposition of a certain subsidiary's stock.	Dispositions included on consolidated returns for taxable year ending on or before 12-31-87.

Subtitle F—Regulated Investment Companies

651	Excise tax imposed on undistributed income of regulated investment companies. [Sec. 852; 4902]	Calendar years beginning after 12-31-86.
652	Treatment of business development companies revised. [Sec. 851]	TYBA 12-31-86.
653	Regulated investment company's treatment of hedging transactions revised. [Sec. 851]	TYBA enactment date.
654	Series funds treated as separate corps. [Sec. 851]	Generally TYBA enactment date; special rules applied for certain existing series funds. See ¶634.
655	Period for mailing notices to shareholders extended. [Secs. 852–855]	TYBA enactment date.

Act Sec.	Topic	Effective Date
656	Rules on protection of mutual funds receiving third-party summonses amended. [Sec. 7609(n)]	Summonses served after enactment date.
657	Certain distributions by regulated investment company to shareholder not treated as preferential dividends. [Sec. 562]	Distributions made after enactment date.

Subtitle G—Real Estate Investment Trusts

Act Sec.	Topic	Effective Date
661	REIT qualification requirements modified; closely held and E&P rules amended; accounting changes. [Sec. 856(a); 857(a); 859]	TYBA 12-31-86.
662	REIT asset and income requirements modified; treatment of certain wholly-owned subsidiaries, temporary investment of new equity capital, and Shared Appreciation Mortgages revised. [Sec. 856]	TYBA 12-31-86.
663	Amendments made to definitions of rents and interest; requirements for independent contractor modified. [Sec. 856(d), (f)]	Generally TYBA 12-31-86. Amendment for interest income won't apply to loans made pursuant to a binding commitment entered into before 5-28-76.
664	Exclusion of certain noncash income from REIT distribution requirements. [Sec. 857(a)(1), (e)]	TYBA 12-31-86.
665	REIT treatment of capital gains modified; coordination of NOL deduction with capital gains dividend payment; rules for mailing of annual dividend reports clarified. [Sec. 857(b)(3); 858(c)]	TYBA 12-31-86.
666	Rules on prohibited transactions of REITs modified. [Sec. 857(b)(6)(B), (C)]	TYBA 12-31-86.
667	REIT deficiency dividends exempted from Sec. 6697 penalty. [Sec. 860; 6697]	TYBA 12-31-86.
668	Excise tax imposed on undistributed income of REITs. [Sec. 4981]	Calendar years beginning after 12-31-86.

Subtitle H—Taxation of Interests in Entities Holding Real Estate Mortgages

Act Sec.	Topic	Effective Date
671	Creation of Real Estate Mortgage Investment Conduits, (REMICs); taxation of entity, interest holders and residual interests; definitions and other rules provided. [Secs. 860A—860G]	TYBA 12-31-86.
672	OID rules applied to interests in REMICs. [Sec. 1272]	Debt instruments issued after 12-31-86 in TYEA such date.
673	Definition of taxable mortgage pool modified to reflect creation of REMICs; special rule for coordination with wash-sale provisions made. [Sec. 7701(i)]	Generally 1-1-92. Provision won't apply to entities existing on 12-31-91 unless there is a substantial transfer to such entity. Wash-sale coordination applies to TYBA 12-31-86.
674	Compliance provisions amended to reflect creation of REMICs. [Sec. 6049]	TYBA 12-31-86.

Act Sec.	Topic	Effective Date

TITLE VII—ALTERNATIVE MINIMUM TAX

Act Sec.	Topic	Effective Date
701	Rules relating to the imposition of the alternative minimum tax on individuals and corporations, including adjustments to computations; corporate add-on minimum tax repealed. [Secs. 26; 28; 29; 38; 53; 55—59; 6154; 6425; 6655]	Generally provisions apply to TYBA 12-31-86. For other dates relating to adjustments and preference items, see ¶702—715.
702	Treasury directed to study E&P adjustments on alternative minimum tax on corporations.	Enactment date.

TITLE VIII—ACCOUNTING PROVISIONS

Subtitle A—General Provisions

Act Sec.	Topic	Effective Date
801	Use of cash method limited. [Sec. 448]	Generally TYBA 12-31-86. Election not to have provisions apply may be made for certain related party transactions entered into before 9-25-85; see ¶801.
802	Election provided for simplified dollar-value LIFO method for certain small businesses. [Sec. 474]	TYBA 12-31-86 except amendment doesn't apply to elections made prior to enactment date as long as they remain in effect.
803	Certain expenses must be included in inventory costs and capitalized. [Sec. 263A]	Costs incurred after 12-31-86 in TYBA that date. Rule for casualty losses applies to expenses incurred on or after enactment, see ¶805.
804	Method of accounting for long-term contracts modified. [Sec. 460]	Long-term contracts entered into after 2-28-86, see ¶806.
805	Reserve for bad debts of taxpayers other than financial institutions repealed. [Sec. 166(c), (f)]	TYBA 12-31-86, see ¶807.
806	Determinations of tax years of partnerships, S corps. and personal service corps. [Secs. 441, 706, 1378]	TYBA 12-31-86, see ¶808.

Subtitle B—Treatment of Installment Obligations

Act Sec.	Topic	Effective Date
811	Use of installment method limited by amount of allocable installment indebtedness. [Sec. 453C]	Generally applies to TYEA 12-31-86, for property dispositions after 2-28-86. For exceptions and special rules, see ¶803.
812	Installment method disallowed for revolving credit plans and certain sales of publicly traded property. [Sec. 453(j)]	Generally TYBA 12-31-86, see ¶803 & 804.

Subtitle C—Other Provisions

Act Sec.	Topic	Effective Date
821	Income of accrual taxpayer attributable to utility services must be included in year services are provided. [Sec. 451(f)]	TYBA 12-31-86.
822	Application of discharge of indebtedness rules to qualified business indebtedness repealed. [Sec. 108(a)]	Debt discharges after 12-31-86.
823	Qualified discount coupons deduction repealed. [Sec. 466]	TYBA 12-31-86.
824	Income exclusion for contributions received by regulated public utility in aid of construction repealed. [Sec. 118]	Amounts received after 12-31-86 in TYEA such date.

Act Sec.	Topic	Effective Date

TITLE IX—FINANCIAL INSTITUTIONS

Act Sec.	Topic	Effective Date
901	Limitations imposed on bad debt deduction for certain commercial banks and thrift institutions; definitions of institutions to which provisions apply. [Secs. 582; 585; 593]	TYBA 12-31-86
902	Disallowance of interest expense deduction for financial institutions on interest to buy or carry tax-exempt obligations acquired after 8-7-86. [Secs. 265; 291(e)(1)(B)]	Generally applies to interest incurred in TYEA 12-31-86. Limited disallowance for obligations acquired after 12-31-82 and before 8-8-86. For special transitional rules, see ¶902.
903	Spcial NOL carryback and carryforward rules for commercial banks and thrift institutions terminated; new rules on bad debt carryback and carryforward for commercial banks and NOL carryforward for thirfts added. [Sec. 172(b)]	Generally apply for losses incurred in TYBA 12-31-86. Bad debt carryback provision applies to TYBA 12-31-86 and before 1-1-94; NOL carryforward for thrifts applies to losses after 12-31-81 for TYBA that date and before 1-1-86.
904	Repeal of special reorganization rules for financially troubled thrift institutions. [Secs. 368(a)(3)(D); 597]	Generally to acquisitions occurring after 12-31-88; in TYEA that date; FSLIC provisions generally apply to transfers after 12-31-88 in TYEA that date, see ¶904.
905	Casualty loss deduction allowed for deposits in insolvent financial institutions; income inclusion deferral allowed for interest on certain frozen deposits. [Secs. 165(1); 451]	Generally TYBA 12-31-82. Provision on frozen deposits applies TYBA 12-31-82 and before 1-1-87, only if election made by taxpayer.

TITLE X—INSURANCE PRODUCTS AND COMPANIES

Subtitle A—Policyholder Issues

Act Sec.	Topic	Effective Date
1001	Interest exclusion on installment payments of life insurance proceeds repealed. [Sec. 101(d)]	Applies to amounts received with respect to deaths occurring after date of enactment in TYEA that date.
1002	Income exclusion for structured settlements limited to physical injury or sickness cases. [Sec. 130(c)]	Amendment applies to assignments entered into after 12-31-86 in TYEA that date.
1003	Deduction for interest on loans from certain life insurance contracts denied. [Sec. 264(a)(4)]	Applies to contracts purchased after 6-20-86 in TYEA that date.
1004	Personal casualty loss deduction denied when insurance claim isn't filed. [Sec. 165(h)(4)(E)]	Losses sustained in TYBA 12-31-86.

Subtitle B—Life Insurance Companies

Act Sec.	Topic	Effective Date
1011	Repeal of 20% special life insurance company deduction. [Sec. 806 and '84 TRA Sec. 217(k)]	TYBA 12-31-86, see ¶1011.
1012	Tax-exempt status of certain organizations providing commercial-type insurance repealed; tax treatment of Blue Cross/Blue Shield organizations explained; study of insurance premiums received by fraternal beneficiary associations directed. [Secs. 508(m); 833]	Generally TYBA 12-31-86. Treasury study directed by 1-1-88. See ¶1012.
1013	Operations loss deduction of insolvent insurance companies may offset distributions from policyholders surplus account. [pertains to Sec. 815(a)(2)]	Liquidations on or after 11-15-85 in TYEA that date.

Act Sec.	Topic	Effective Date

Subtitle C—Property and Casualty Insurance Companies

1021	Reduction of deduction for unearned premiums; 6-year ratable inclusion of 20% of unearned premiums as of end of most recent tax year beginning before 1-1-87. [Sec. 832(b)]	Generally TYBA 12-31-86. See ¶1021 for special rule.
1022	Deduction for losses incurred by property and casualty companies reduced by percentage of tax-exempt interest and deductible portion of dividends received. [Sec. 832(b)(5)]	Generally TYBA 12-31-86. For percentages and exceptions, see ¶1032.
1023	Unpaid losses and certain unpaid expenses relating to insurance contracts discounted. [Secs. 807(c); 832(b)(5), (b)(6); 846]	TYBA 12-31-86. For transitional and special rules, see ¶1022.
1024	Protection against loss account repealed; special treatment for small companies revised; provisions combined. [Secs. 501(c)(15); 821-826; 831; 834; 835]	TYBA 12-31-86. For transitional rule, see ¶1023 & 1024.
1025	Treasury study of tax treatment of mutual property and casualty companies authorized.	Due date of 1-1-89.

Subtitle D—Miscellaneous Provisions

1031	Treatment of contributions to physician's mutual protection and interindemnity associations. [Sec. 821(d)]	Payments made to and receipts of, and refunds by, eligible associations after enactment date in TYEA that date.

TITLE XI—PENSIONS AND DEFERRED COMPENSATION; EMPLOYEE BENEFITS; EMPLOYEE STOCK OWNERSHIP PLANS

Subtitle A—Pensions and Deferred Compensation

Part I—Limitations on Tax-Deferred Savings

Subpart A—Rules Applicable to IRAs

1101	Limitation on eligibility to make IRA contributions. [Sec. 219]	Contributions for TYBA 12-31-86.
1102	Rules for nondeductible contributions to IRAs. [Secs. 408(d), (o); 3405(d)(1)(b); 4973(b); 6693(c)]	Contributions and distributions for TYBA 12-31-86.
1103	Spousal deduction when spouse has minimal income. [Sec. 219(c)(1)]	Taxable years beginning before, on, or after 12-31-85.

Subpart B—Other Provisions

1105	Limits imposed on income exclusion for elective deferrals. [Secs. 402(g); 6051(a)]	Generally TYBA 12-31-86. For special rules see ¶1104 & 1105.
1106	Adjustments made for limits to contributions and benefits under qualified plans. [Secs. 401(a)(17); 402(e)(4)(N); 404(1); 415(b), (c), (d), (k); 416(d)]	Generally for years beginning after 12-31-86. For special rules, see ¶1106.
1107	Modification of rules on deferred compensation plans for State and local governments and tax-exempt organizations. [Sec. 457]	Generally TYBA 12-31-88. Provisions on transfer between plans and cash-outs apply to TYBA 12-31-86, see ¶1107.
1108	Rules for simplified employee plans (SEPs) modified. [Secs. 219(b); 402(h); 404(h); 408(k); 3121(a)(5); 3306(b)(5)]	TYBA 12-31-86.
1109	Deduction permitted for Section 501(c)(18) plans. [Secs. 219(b); 501(c)(18)]	TYBA 12-31-86.

Act Sec.	Topic	Effective Date
	Part II—Nondiscrimination Requirements	
	Subpart A—General Requirements	
1111	Nondiscrimination rules for integrated plans revised. [Sec. 401]	Generally for benefits attributable to plan years beginning after 12-31-88, see ¶1110.
1112	Minimum coverage requirements for qualified employee plans modified. [Secs. 401(a)(26; 410(b)]	Generally for plan years beginning after 12-31-88, see ¶1111.
1113	Minimum vesting standards for certain plans revised. [Sec. 411(a)]	Generally for plan years beginning after 12-31-88. For effective dates for collectively bargained plans, see ¶1113.
1114	Highly compensated employee redefined. [Sec. 414(q)]	Generally for TYBA 12-31-86; conforming amendments for employee benefits sections apply for TYBA 12-31-87; conforming sections for pension sections apply for TYBA 12-31-88.
1115	Special rules added for employers operating separate lines of business provided. [Sec. 414(r)]	Years beginning after 12-31-86.
	Subpart B—Other Provisions	
1116	Rules relating to requirements for CODAs amended; transitional rule provided for certain governmental and tax-exempt plans; special rules on qualified offset arrangements and on sale of assets. [Sec. 401(k)]	Generally apply to year beginning after 12-31-88. Non-discrimination rules generally apply to years beginning after 12-31-86. For special rules, see ¶1116.
1117	Nondiscrimination requirements test provided for employer matching contributions and employee contributions; excise tax imposed on certain excess contributions. [Secs. 401(m); 4979]	Plan years after 12-31-86. For dates on collectively bargained plans, see ¶1117.
1118	Benefits treated as accruing ratably when determining top-heaviness. [Sec. 416]	Plan years beginning after 12-31-86.
1119	Money purchase plans allowed to reallocate forfeitures under nondiscriminatory plans. [Sec. 401(a)(8)]	Plan years beginning after 12-31-85.
1120	Nondiscrimination requirements for tax-sheltered annuities provided. [Sec. 403(b)]	Years beginning after 12-31-88.
	Part III—Treatment of Distributions	
1121	Uniform minimum distribution rules added; excise tax added for failure to distribute. [Secs. 401(a)(9); 402(a)(5); 408(d)(3); 4974]	Generally applies to TYBA 12-31-88. Rule for transfers treated as rollover contributions applies to TYBA 12-31-86.

Act Sec.	Topic	Effective Date
1122	Rules on tax treatment of lump sum distributions revised; specific provisions include repeal of capital gains, employees' annuities, and frozen deposits. [Secs. 72(b), (d), (e); 402(e); 403(a)(2), (b), (c)]	Generally amounts distributed after 12-31-86 in TYBA that date. For special rules, see ¶1122.
1123	Additional tax imposed on early distributions from qualified retirement plans. [Secs. 72(m), (q), (t); 408(f)]	Generally applies to TYBA 12-31-86. For Sec. 403(b) annuities, applies to TYBA 12-31-88. See also ¶1123.
1124	Election added to treat certain lump sum distribution in 1987 as received in 1986.	Applies to separation from service in 1986 with distribution after 12-31-86 and before 3-16-87.

Part IV—Miscellaneous Provisions

Act Sec.	Topic	Effective Date
1131	Adjustments made to limitations on deductible contributions to certain plans; excise tax imposed on nondeductible contributions. [Secs. 404(a)(3)(A), (a)(7); 4972]	TYBA 12-31-86.
1132	Excise tax imposed for reversion of plan assets to employer. [Sec. 4980]	Generally reversions occurring after 12-31-85, except for plans terminating before 1-1-86. ESOP exception expires for plan terminations after 12-31-88.
1133	Excise tax added for excess distributions from qualified retirement plans. [Sec. 4981]	Distributions made, and decedents dying (for purposes of estate tax), after 12-31-86. Provision does not apply to distributions before 1-1-88 under terminations before 1-1-87.
1134	Tax treatment of loans to plan participants. [Sec. 72(p)]	Loans made, renewed, renegotiated, modified, or extended after 12-31-86.
1135	Deferred annuity contracts limited to natural persons. [Sec. 72(u)]	Contributions to annuity contracts after 2-28-86.
1136	Contributions to profit-sharing plans allowed when there are no profits. [Sec. 401(a)(26)]	Plan years beginning after 12-31-85.
1137	Requirement added that collective bargaining agreement be bona fide. [Sec. 7701(a)(46)]	Enactment date.
1138	Penalty added for overstatements of pension liabilities. [Sec. 6659A]	Overstatements made after enactment date.
1139	Increase in interest rate assumption used to calculate lump sum benefits. [Secs. 411(a); 417(e)(3)]	Distributions made after 12-31-84, except distributions made after that date and before 1-1-87 under regs issued under '84 REA. See ¶1139.
1140	Amendments to conform to new law; Treasury to issue model amendment; special rule for collectively bargained plans.	Generally plan years beginning after 1-1-89, see ¶1141.
1141	Issuance of final regs on nondiscrimination requirements, coverage and vesting, 401(k) plans, and excess distributions.	Before 2-1-88.
1142	Treasury to accept opinion letters with respect to master and prototype of 401(k) plans.	Not later than 5-1-87.
1143	Certain fishermen treated as self-employed individuals. [Sec. 401(c)]	TYBA 12-31-86.
1144	IRAs can acquire gold and silver coins; acquisition not treated as distribution. [Sec. 408(m)]	Acquisitions after 12-31-86.

Act Sec.	Topic	Effective Date
1145	Exemptions created from joint and survivor, and preretirement survivor, annuity requirements imposed under '84 REA.	Amendments apply with same effective dates as '84 REA provisions.
1146	Leased employee provisions modified. [Sec. 414(n), (o)]	Generally TYBA 12-31-83. Safe-harbor provision applies for services performed after 12-31-86.
1147	Federal Thrift Savings Fund treated as exempt trust. [Sec. 7701(j)]	Enactment date.

Subtitle B—Employee Benefit Provisions

Part I—Nondiscrimination Rules for Certain Statutory Employee Benefit Plans

1151	New nondiscrimination requirements for employee benefit plans and uniform definitions; amended rules applying to cafeteria plans. [Secs. 89; 125(b); 6039D; 6652]	Generally provisions apply to later of (a) 12-31-87 or (b) earlier of 3 months after issuance of regs or 12-31-88. For effective dates on church plans and cafeteria plan provisions, see ¶1151—1157.

Part II—Other Provisions

1161	Deduction of 25% of health insurance costs allowed self-employeds; Treasury to provide guidance in meeting requirements. [Sec. 162(m)]	TYBA 12-31-86, see also ¶1161.
1162	Extends income exclusion and cap for educational assistance programs; extends group legal services exclusion and adds transitional rule for legal services under cafeteria plans. [Secs. 120(e); 127(d)]	Educational assistance-provisions apply to TYBA 12-31-85; legal services to TYEA 12-31-85.
1163	Dependent care assistance exclusion limited to $5,000; clarification where child care facilities on the employer's premises. [Sec. 129]	TYBA 12-31-86.
1164	Exclusion created for qualified campus lodging for school employees. [Sec. 119(d)]	TYBA 12-31-85.
1165	Special accrued vacation pay provision limited. [Sec. 463(a)(1)]	TYBA 12-31-86.
1166	Full-time life insurance salespeople may be treated as employees for cafeteria plan purposes. [Sec. 7701(a)(20)]	TYBA 12-31-85.
1167	Due date for previously authorized Treasury study on standards for welfare benefit plans extended. ['84 TRA Sec. 560]	One year after enactment date of '86 TRA.
1168	Qualified military benefits excluded from income. [Sec. 134]	TYBA 12-31-86.

Subtitle C—Changes Relating to Employee Stock Ownership Plans

1171	Repeal of payroll based ESOP credit. [Sec. 41]	Compensation paid or accrued after 12-31-86 in TYEA that date, see ¶1172.
1172	Estate tax deduction for proceeds from sale of qualified securities to ESOPs or EWOCs. [Sec. 2057]	Sales after enactment date and before 1-1-92, for returns required to be filed after enactment date.

Act Sec.	Topic	Effective Date
1173	Tax treatment of dividends to ESOPs to repay securities acquisitions loans; interest exclusion provisions. [Secs. 404(k); 852(b)(5)]	Dividends paid in TYBA enactment date; loans used for acquisitions after enactment date, see ¶1174.
1174(a)	Distributions permitted on ESOP terminations. [Sec. 409(d)]	Plan terminations after 12-31-84.
1174(b), (c)	Distribution and payment requirements modified; put option provision added. [Sec. 409(h), (o)]	Distributions attributable to stock acquired after 12-31-86, see also ¶1177.
1174(d)	Nondiscrimination requirements for ESOP modified. [Sec. 415]	Years beginning after 12-31-86.
1175	Investment diversification requirement for ESOPs. [Sec. 401(a)(28)]	Stock acquired after 12-31-86.
1176	Special requirement provisions added relating to voting rights of newspapers with stock not publicly traded. [Sec. 401(a)(22)]	Effective 12-31-86; acquisitions of securities after 12-31-86.

TITLE XII—FOREIGN TAX PROVISIONS

Subtitle A—Foreign Tax Credit Modifications

Act Sec.	Topic	Effective Date
1201	Separate foreign tax credit limitations for certain types of income; special rules provided for treatment of "qualified loan" interest. [Sec. 904(d)]	TYBA 12-31-86. For special rules, see ¶1201.
1202	Deemed-paid credit determined on accumulated basis. [Secs. 902; 960(a)]	Distributions by foreign corporations from and inclusions attributable to E&P for TYBA 12-31-86.
1203	Treatment of separate limitation losses clarified. [Sec. 904(f)]	Losses incurred in TYBA 12-31-86.
1204	Taxes used to provide subsidies not allowed for foreign tax credit purpose. [Sec. 901(i)]	Foreign taxes paid or accrued in TYBA 12-31-86.
1205	Limitation on carryback of excess tax credit. [pertains to sec. 904]	Applies to carrybacks to years before 1987, see ¶1205.

Subtitle B—Source Rules

Act Sec.	Topic	Effective Date
1211	Determination of source for sales of personal property; Authorization of Treasury study of source rules. [Secs. 865]	Generally TYBA 12-31-86. For foreign persons other than CFCs, source rules apply to transactions entered into after 3-18-86. Study is due 9-30-87.
1212	Tax imposed on transportation income of NRAs and foreign corps.; special rules provided for certain leased property. [Secs. 861(e); 863; 872; 883; 887]	Generally applies to TYBA 12-31-86. Rules for leased property apply for property held on and leased before 1-1-86; U.S. Navy property held on and leased before 1-1-87, see ¶1213.
1213	Source rules created for space and certain ocean activities. [Sec. 863]	TYBA 12-31-86.
1214	Limitations on special treatment of 80-20 corps.; exceptions to provisions for certain interest. [Secs. 861; 871; 881; 1441]	Generally apply for payments made after 12-31-86. Grandfather rule applies to interest on obligations outstanding on 12-31-85, see ¶1212.
1215	Allocation of interest and other expenses to foreign source income. [Sec. 864]	Generally TYBA 12-31-86. For transitional rules for certain outstanding indebtedness and certain qualified corporations, see ¶1214.

Act Sec.	Topic	Effective Date
1216	Allocation of research and experimental expenditures. [Secs. 861(b); 862(b); 863(b)]	TYBA 8-1-86 and on or before 8-1-87.

Subtitle C—Taxation of Income Earned Through Foreign Corporations

Act Sec.	Topic	Effective Date
1221	Defines Subpart F income subject to current taxation. [Secs. 952; 953; 954]	Generally foreign corp. TYBA 12-31-86, see ¶1217.
1222	CFCs and FPHCs redefined to reflect stock value as well as voting power. [Secs. 552(a)(2); 957(a)]	Generally foreign corp. TYBA 12-31-86, see ¶1218.
1223	Subpart F de minimis rule amended. [Sec. 954(b)(3)]	Foreign corp. TYBA 12-31-86.
1224	Possessions corp. exemption from CFC status repealed. [Sec. 957(c)]	Generally foreign corp. TYBA 12-31-86. Transitional rule applies for corps. treated as CFCs under this provision, see ¶1220.
1225	Accumulated earnings tax and personal holding company tax calculations amended for effectively connected gains and losses. [Secs. 535(b)(9); 545(b)(7)]	Gains and losses realized on or after 3-1-86.
1226	Dividends received deduction provisions for dividends received from foreign corp. revised. [Sec. 245(a)]	Generally applies to distributions out of E&P for TYBA 12-31-86. E&P reduction applies after enactment date.
1227	Special rule for qualified Brazilian corp. as to certain dividends.	Dividends received after 12-31-86.
1228	Special rule for qualified corp. as to gain on disposition of investment in U.S. real property. [Sec. 897]	Enactment date.

Subtitle D—Special Tax Provisions for United States Persons

Act Sec.	Topic	Effective Date
1231	Modifications made to possessions tax credit. [Sec. 936]	Generally TYBA 12-31-86. For special rules, see ¶1223.
1232	Panama Canal Treaty doesn't exempt anyone from U.S. taxation; partial exclusion provided for certain employee allowances.	Generally to all taxable years beginning before, on, or after date of enactment; exclusion applies to TYBA 12-31-86. See also ¶1224.
1233	Foreign earned income exclusion reduced; Exclusion eliminated for individuals violating federal travel restrictions. [Sec. 911(b), (d)]	TYBA 12-31-86.
1234	Information required on application for resident status. Withholding election not available for certain foreign deferred payments. [Secs. 3405; 6039E]	Information provision applies to applications submitted after 12-31-87, or, if earlier, to those after effective date of regs (however not earlier than 1-1-87). Withholding provision applies to payments after 12-31-86.
1235	Treatment of certain passive foreign investment companies. [Secs. 1291; 1293—1297]	Foreign corp. TYBA 12-31-86.
1236	Interest on U.S. obligations received by certain Guam banks not taxed as effectively connected. [Sec. 882(e)]	TYBA 11-16-85.

Subtitle E—Treatment of Foreign Taxpayers

Act Sec.	Topic	Effective Date
1241	Branch profits tax added. [Sec. 884]	TYBA 12-31-86.

Act Sec.	Topic	Effective Date
1242	Certain deferred payments and income from property transactions treated as effectively connected. [Sec. 864(c)]	TYBA 12-31-86.
1243	Property received in tax-free exchanges by expatriates treated as U.S. income. [Sec. 877(c)]	To sales or exchanges of property received in exchanges after 9-25-85.
1244	Treasury study of competitiveness of U.S. reinsurance companies authorized.	Study due 1-1-88.
1245	Information required with respect to certain foreign-owned corporations. [Sec. 6038A].	TYBA 12-31-86.
1246	Withholding tax imposed on amounts paid by U.S. and foreign partnerships to foreign partners. [Sec. 1446]	Distributions after 12-31-87, or, if earlier, the later of the effective date of regs (however not before 1-1-87).
1247	Exemption provision revised for certain income of foreign governments and international organizations. [Sec. 892]	Amounts accrued or received on or after 7-1-86; no withholding obligation is imposed for amounts paid before enactment date.
1248	Limitation on cost of property imported from related persons. [Sec. 1059A]	Transactions entered into after 3-18-86.
1249	Limits imposed on reduction to income for certain losses of dual resident corps. [Sec. 1503(d)]	NOLs for TYBA 12-31-86.

Subtitle F—Foreign Currency Transactions

Act Sec.	Topic	Effective Date
1261	Rules on treatment of foreign currency transactions added. [Secs. 985—989; 1092(d)(7); 1256(e)]	TYBA 12-31-86. For special rules relating to E&P of foreign corps., see ¶1261.

Subtitle G—Tax Treatment of Possessions

Part I—Treatment of Guam, American Samoa, and the Northern Mariana Islands

Act Sec.	Topic	Effective Date
1271—1273	Tax treatment of Guam, American Samoa, and Northern Marianas amended. [Secs. 876; 881(b); 931; 957(c); 3401(a)(8)(D)]	TYBA 12-31-86, as long as specific agreements with possessions remain in effect.

Part II—Treatment of the Virgin Islands

Act Sec.	Topic	Effective Date
1274	Coordination of U.S. and Virgin Islands tax systems. [Sec. 932]	TYBA 12-31-86, as long as agreement remains in effect.
1275	Possessions tax credit allowed Virgin Islands corps. [Secs. 28(d)(3)(B); 48(a)(2)(B); 338(h)(6)(B); 864(d)(5)(B); 936(d); 7651]	Generally TYBA 12-31-86, see ¶1275.

Part III—Cover Over of Income Taxes

Act Sec.	Topic	Effective Date
1276	Coordination of U.S. and certain possession individual income taxes. [Sec. 7654]	TYBA 12-31-86.

TITLE XIII—TAX-EXEMPT BONDS

Subtitle A—Amendments of Internal Revenue Code of 1954

Act Sec.	Topic	Effective Date
1301	Rules on tax exemption of interest on state and local bonds reorganized and amended; arbitrage and output regulations, mortgage credit certificate program, and penalty for failure to file report on compliance with qualified residential rental project rules; state and local government series and guidelines on business use of property under management contracts	Generally bonds issued after 8-15-86 except mortgage credit certificate program provisons—increase in trade-in rate applies to nonissued bond amounts elected after 8-15-86, and conforming amendments apply to certificates issued after 8-15-86. For transitional rules see ¶1301.

Act Sec.	Topic	Effective Date
	modified; mortgage review bond program report repealed. [Secs. 25; 103; 141—150; 6652; and '84 TRA Sec. 611(d)(7)]	
1302	Treatment of qualified 501(c)(3) bonds clarified. [Sec. 103(c)]	Generally bonds issued after 8-15-86. For transitional rules, see ¶1305.
1303	General stock ownership corp. [GSOC] provisions repealed. [Sec. 1391—1397]	Enactment date

Subtitle B—Effective Dates and Transitional Rules

Act Sec.	Topic	Effective Date
1312—1318	Transitional rules on construction or binding agreements and certain government bonds issued after 8-15-86; refundings; volume caps and specific facilities; special rules overriding other provisions; provisions relating to certain established state programs; definitions relating to effective dates and transitional rules.	For transitional and special rule effective dates, see ¶1301—1303.

Subtitle A—Income Taxation of Trusts and Estates

TITLE XIV—TRUST AND ESTATES; UNEARNED INCOME OF CERTAIN MINOR CHILDREN; GIFT AND ESTATE TAXES; GENERATION-SKIPPING TRANSFER TAX

Act Sec.	Topic	Effective Date
1401	Grantor treated as holding spouse's power or interest. [Sec. 672]	Transfers in trust made after 3-1-86.
1402	Limits to reversionary interest rule exceptions. [Sec. 673]	Transfers in trust made after 3-1-86, except when made pursuant to certain property settlement agreements entered into on or before 3-1-86, see ¶1402.
1403	Taxable year of trusts to be calendar year, except for exempt and charitable trusts. [Sec. 645]	TYBA 12-31-86 but transition rule applies to trust beneficiaries required to include income under '86 TRA. See ¶1403.
1404	Trusts and certain estates to make estimated payments of income taxes. [Secs. 643(g); 6654(k)]	TYBA 12-31-86.

Subtitle B—Unearned Income of Certain Minor Children

Act Sec.	Topic	Effective Date
1411	Certain unearned income of minor children taxed as if parent's income. [Secs. 1; 6103(e)(1)(A)]	TYBA 12-31-86.

Subtitle C—Gift and Estate Taxes

Act Sec.	Topic	Effective Date
1421	Information necessary for valid special use valuation election. [pertains to Sec. 2032(A)]	Any decedent dying before 1-1-86, but not if, before enactment date, specified statute of limitations for returns has expired.
1422	Gift and estate tax deductions for certain conservation easement donations; special rules for irrevocable transfers of easements. [Secs. 2055; 2522]	Transfers and contributions made after 12-31-86.
1423	Special relief; decedent's property conveyance to charitable foundation treated as charitable contribution. [pertains to Sec. 2055]	Enactment date.

Act Sec.	Topic	Effective Date

Act Sec.	Topic	Effective Date
1532	Penalty for failure to register tax shelter increased. [Sec. 6707]	Shelters in which interests are first offered for sale after enactment date.
1533 ﹅	Penalty for failure to report tax shelter identification number increased to $250. [Sec. 6707]	Returns filed after enactment date.
1534	Penalty for failure to maintain list of shelter investors increased. [Sec. 6708]	Failures occurring or continuing after enactment date.
1535	Treatment of sham or fraudulent transactions clarified. [Sec. 6621]	Interest accruing after 12-31-84 (but not on underpayments relating to final court decision before enactment date).

Subtitle E—Estimated Tax Provisions

1541	Individual estimated tax payments test increased. [Sec. 6654]	TYBA 12-31-86.
1542	Estimated tax payments required for TEO's UBI tax and private foundation's investment income excise tax. [Sec. 6154].	TYBA 12-31-86.
1543	Waiver of 1986 estimated tax penalties. [pertains to Secs. 6654; 6655]	For individuals, periods before 4-15-87; for corporations, periods before 3-15-87.

Subtitle F—Provisions Regarding Judicial Proceedings

1551	Awards of reasonable costs and attorney's fees in tax cases modified and extended permanently. [Sec. 7430]	Generally amounts paid after 9-30-86 in proceedings commenced after 12-31-85, see ¶1551.
1552	Failure to exhaust administrative remedies is additional basis for imposition of discretionary penalty by Tax Court. Treasury and Tax Court will report to Congress every two years on Tax Court inventory. [Sec. 6673]	Proceedings started after enactment date; reports to begin for 1987.
1553	Registration fee is imposed on practitioners admitted to practice before Tax Court. [Sec. 7475]	1-1-87.
1554	Clarification that Tax Court has jurisdiction over penalty for failure to pay amount of tax shown on return. [Sec. 6214]	Actions or proceedings before Tax Court not final before enactment date.
1555	Tax Court has authority to require attendance of U.S. Marshals at any Tax Court session. [Sec. 7456]	Enactment date.
1556	Appointments, authority, and clarification of pay and travel rules for Special Trial Judges. [Sec. 7443A]	Enactment date (salary provision effective first day of first month beginning after enactment date).
1557	Tax Court judges permitted to practice law after retirement continue to receive retirement pay. [Secs. 7447; 7448]	Generally enactment date.
1558	Appeals from interlocutory orders of Tax Court. [Sec. 7842(a)(2)]	Tax Court orders entered after enactment date.
1559	Provisions on annuities for surviving spouses and dependent children of Tax Court judges amended. [Sec. 7448]	Generally amounts paid, services performed, and annuity starting dates after 11-1-86, see ¶1559.

Act Sec.	Topic	Effective Date
	Subtitle G—Tax Administration Provisions	
1561	Statute of limitations suspended third-party records not timely produced after service of summons.	Enactment date.
1562	Authority given to rescind notice of deficiency. [Sec. 6212(d)]	Deficiency notices issued on or after 1-1-86.
1563	Authority given IRS to abate interest on deficiencies or payments due to IRS error or delay. [Sec. 6404(e)]	Generally interest accruing on deficiencies or payment for TYBA 12-31-78; one-year extension to seek refund for certain otherwise barred claims.
1564	Interest compounding suspended when interest on deficiency suspended. [Sec. 6601(c)]	Interest accruing after 12-31-82; one-year extension to seek refund for certain otherwise barred claims.
1565	Exemption from levy provided for certain service-connected disability payments. [Sec. 6334(a)]	Amounts payable after 12-31-86.
1566	Value of personal property that may be seized and sold by IRS increased. [Sec. 7325]	Enactment date.
1567	Recordkeeping requirements imposed for automobile use by IRS special agents. [pertains to Secs. 132; 274]	1-1-85.
1568	Disclosure of returns and return information made to certain cities. [Sec. 6103(b)]	Enactment date.
1569	Application of relation-back rule to certain forfeitures under local authorities. [Sec. 6323(i)(3)]	Enactment date.
1570	Certain seized property released to owner if not declared sold at auction. [Sec. 6335(e)(1)]	Property seized after enactment date and property held by the U.S. that is seized on or before that date.
1571	Method of allocation of employee tips modified.	Payroll periods starting after 12-31-86.
1572	For discharge of lien provisions, sales include forfeitures of land sales contracts. [Sec. 7425(c)(4)]	Forfeitures after 30th day after enactment date.
	Subtitle H—Miscellaneous Provisions	
1572 [should probably read 1581]	Modification of withholding schedules; filing of new W-4 Forms; repeal of authority to permit employees to request decreases in withholding. [Sec. 3402]	Generally enactment date; special rule if employee doesn't furnish W-4 before 10-1-87.
1572 [should probably read 1582]	Treasury directed to prepare report on return-free system.	Six months after enactment date.
	TITLE XVI—EXEMPT AND NONPROFIT ORGANIZATIONS	
1601	Exemption from UBI tax for certain low cost article distributions and exchange and rentals of membership or donor lists. [Sec. 513(h)]	Distributions and exchanges after enactment date.
1602	Trade show activities' exclusion from UBI expanded. [Sec. 513(d)]	Activities in TYBA enactment date.

Act Sec.	Topic	Effective Date
1603	Exemption extended to certain companies holding title for tax-exempt organizations. [Sec. 501(c)(25)]	TYBA 12-31-86.
1604	Additional exception to Sec. 277 deduction limitation rule for organizations who gather and distribute news to members for publication. [Sec. 277]	TYBA enactment date.
1605	Tax-exempt status for organization transfering technology from qualified organizations to public.	Enactment date.
1606	Annual compensation rate used in defining certain governmental officials increased. [4946(c)(5)]	Compensation received after 12-31-85.
1607	Transitional rule for acquisition of indebtedness of a community college regarding certain land.	Enactment date.
1608	Right to stadium seating won't disqualify charitable contributions to certain school.	Amounts paid in taxable years beginning on or after 1-1-84.

TITLE XVII—MISCELLANEOUS PROVISIONS

Act Sec.	Topic	Effective Date
1701	Targeted jobs credit modified and extended for three years. [Sec. 51]	Individuals who begin work for employer after 12-31-85 but before 1-1-89.
1702	Election to collect tax on sales of diesel fuel at wholesale level rather than retail level. [Sec. 4041; 6652]	Effective for sales of fuel for use in highway vehicles after first calendar quarter beginning more than 60 days after enactment date.
1703	Gasoline excise tax shifted from producer to refiner, importer, or terminal operator; bond may be required; exempt purposes; special rule for filing gasohol credit; floor stock taxes imposed. [Sec. 4081—4083; 4101; 6421]	Gasoline removed after 12-31-87.
1704	Rules granting exemption from Social Security coverage clarified; application for revocation of election. [Sec. 1402]	Applications filed after 12-31-86; revocation provisions generally apply to service performed in taxable years ending on or after enactment date.
1705	Exception to FUTA taxes for employees of certain Indian tribes.	For services performed before, on, or after enactment date, but before 1-1-88.
1706	Certain technical service personnel treated as employees for withholding purposes. [Sec. 530 of '78 Revenue Act]	Remuneration paid and services rendered after 12-31-86.
1707	Exclusion for certain foster care payments. [Sec. 131]	TYBA 12-31-85.
1708	Reinstatement of tax breaks for spouses of Vietnam MIAs. [Secs. 2(a)(3)(B); 692(b); 6013(f)(1); 7508(b)]	TYBA 12-31-82.
1709	Native Alaskans exempted from tax for sale of reindeer and reindeer products during period of trust. [Sec. 8 of '37 Reindeer Industry Act.]	As if included in Sec. 8 of 9-1-37 Act.
1711	Adoption assistance program modified. [Sec. 473(a) of Social Security Act]	Expenditures made after 12-31-86.

Act Sec.	Topic	Effective Date

TITLE XVIII—TECHNICAL CORRECTIONS

Act Sec.	Topic	Effective Date
1800	Coordination of technical corrections to earlier Acts with law changes made by other Titles of '86 TRA.	Technical corrections are treated as enacted *immediately before* other provisions of '86 TRA.

Subtitle A—Amendments Related to the Tax Reform Act of 1984

Chapter 1—Amendments Related to Title 1 of the Act

Act Sec.	Topic	Effective Date
1801(a)	Election to postpone lease finance rules that never went into effect for most taxpayers. [Sec. 12(c)(1), '84 Tax Reform Act]	Pre-3-7-84 acquisitions, started construction or binding contracts.
1801(b)	Telephone excise tax extension omission corrected. [Sec. 4251]	Bills first rendered during 1985.
1801(c)	Electronic transfer of alcohol and tobacco taxes by controlled groups; floor stock tax on distilled spirits. [Secs. 5061; 5703; and '84 TRA Sec. 27(b)]	Electronic transfer provisions apply to taxes required to be paid on or after 9-30-84; floor stock tax applies to distilled spirits in foreign trade zone on 10-1-85.
1802	Clarification of tax-exempt entity leasing rules and of special effective date provisions. [Secs. 46(e)(4); 47(a)(9); 48(a)(5); 168(j); 7701(e)(4); and '84 TRA Sec. 31(g)]	Generally property placed in service after 5-23-83 in TYEA such date, subject to special effective date rules explained at ¶1804.
1803	Changes in treatment of debt instruments made; amendments include OID, market discount, imputed interest, and amortization of bond premium. [Secs. 163; 171; 483; 1271; 1273; 1276; 1278; 1281; 1282; 1283; and '84 TRA Sec. 44(b)]	Short-term nongovernment and government provisions apply generally for sales and exchanges after 1984. Specific rules apply to obligations acquired after 7-18-84 or 9-27-85, and post-5-6-86 exchanges. For additional special effective dates, see ¶1805.
1804(a)	Limitation on dividends received deduction clarified as to debt-financed portfolio stock of foreign corporations. [Sec. 246A(a)]	Generally applies to portfolio stock with holding periods starting after 7-18-84 in TYEA such date.
1804(b)	Holding period rule for dividends received deduction. Application of related party provisions to interest incurred to buy or carry tax-exempt obligations clarified. [Sec. 246(c) and '84 TRA Sec. 53(a)(3)]	Holding period provision applies to stock acquired after 3-1-86. Related person provisions apply as of 7-18-84; interest provisions apply generally to term loans made and demand loans outstanding after 7-18-84.
1804(c)	Loss on regulated investment stock held less than 6 months disallowed if exempt interest dividends received. [Sec. 852(b)]	Stock with holding periods starting after 3-28-85.
1804(d)	Dividends paid disallowance for liquidation distributions of holding or investment companies other than RICs. [Sec. 562(b)(1)]	Distributions after 9-27-85.
1804(e)	Affiliated group definitions revised. [Secs. 1504(a), (b); 332(b)(1); 337(c)(3); 338(d)]	Generally TYBA 12-31-84. Sec. 332(b)(1) change applies to complete liquidation plans adopted after 3-28-55. For other special rules, qualified stock purchases, corps. affiliated on 6-22-84, certain sell-downs and native corps, see ¶1806.
1804(f)	E&P adjustments on appreciated property distributions. [Sec. 312(b), (c), (n)]	Generally, distributions or redemptions in TYBA 9-30-84. See also ¶1806.
1804(g)	Amendments to treatment of transferor corporations in reorganizations. [Secs. 361; 368(a)(2)(G)(i)]	Reorganization plans adopted after enactment date of this Act.
1804(h)	Definition of control for "D" reorganizations clarified. [Sec. 368(a), (c)]	Generally applies to plans adopted after 7-18-84.

Act Sec.	Topic	Effective Date
1804(i)	Collapsible corporation ordinary income provision extends to short-term stock. [Sec. 341]	Sales, exchanges, and distributions after 9-27-85.
1804(j)	Revision of golden parachute provisions. [Sec. 280G]	Generally agreements made or amended after 6-14-84 in TYEA such date.
1804(k)	Reduction of preference benefits doesn't apply to S corporations. [pre-1984 version of Sec. 291(a)(4)]	TYBA 12-31-82.
1805(a)	Clarification on prorated cash method items. [Sec. 706(d)]	Periods after 3-31-84.
1805(b)	Certain transfers treated as disguised sales. [Sec. 707(a)]	Transfers after 3-31-84.
1805(c)	Limitation on gain recognized on distribution of partnership interest by corporation; limitation of sale or exchange treatment to distributions of partnership interests. [Secs. 386(d); 761(e)]	Distributions and sales after 3-31-84.
1805(d)	Property identification for like-kind exchanges allowed on day of exchange. [Sec. 1031(a)]	Generally applies to transfers after 3-31-84.
1806(a)	Estate's or trust's election to recognize gain applies to all distributions-in-kind during taxable year. [Sec. 643(e)(3)]	Distributions after 6-1-84 in TYEA such date.
1806(b)	Treatment of multiple trusts as one trust limited for pre-existing irrevocable trusts. ['84 TRA Sec. 82(b)]	Generally TYBA 3-1-84; for pre-existing irrevocable trusts, applies only to portions attributable to post-3-1-84 contributions to corpus.
1807	Various accounting changes and clarifications to rule for taxable year of deduction. [Secs. 461; 467; 468; 468A; 468B; and '84 TRA Sec. 91(g)]	Generally, amounts deductible after 7-18-84 as to TYEA such date, without regard to economic performance requirements. For special rules, see ¶1808.
1808	Tax straddle rules clarified. [Secs. 263; 1092; and '84 TRA Sec. 102]	Generally positions established after 7-18-84 in TYEA such date, subject to various exceptions and elections.
1809(a)	Clarification of depreciation rules for real property and low-income housing. [Secs. 57(a)(12); 168(b), (f); 312(k); and '84 TRA Sec. 111]	Generally applies to property placed in service after 3-15-84.
1809(b)	Rules on treatment of transferees of recovery property clarified. [Sec. 168(f)(10)]	Property placed in service after 12-31-85 in TYEA that date.
1809(c)	Applicability of Section 751 (unrealized receivables) to recapture provisions for installment sales. [Sec. 453(i)]	Generally dispositions made after 6-6-84.
1809(d)	Limitation on depreciation methods for films, videotapes, and sound recordings. [Sec. 167(c)]	Property placed in service after 3-28-85.
1809(e)	Definition of "new Sec. 38 property" clarified. [Sec. 48(b)]	Property placed in service after 4-11-84.
1810(a)	Recharacterizing foreign income as U.S. income; source rules; coordination with Treaty obligations. [Sec. 904(g)(9); '84 TRA Secs. 121(b); 125(b)(5)]	Recharacterizing foreign income: generally 3-28-85, and see ¶1811. Effect of Treaty obligations; Treaties entered after enactment date. Transitional rule relates to separate application of Sec. 904.

Act Sec.	Topic	Effective Date
1810(b)	Rules relating to separate limitation interest amended. [Sec. 904(d)]	Generally for distributions after 7-18-84. For changes regarding designated payor corporations that can give rise to dividends recharacterized as separate limitation interest income, see ¶1811.
1810(c)	Exception to related persons factoring income for persons doing business in same foreign country. [Secs. 864(d); 956(b)]	Receivables transferred after 3-1-84.
1810(d)	Portfolio interest definition amended for non-withholding provisions. [Secs. 871(a), (h); 881(c); 1441(c); 1442(a)]	Portfolio interest on obligations issued after 7-18-84.
1810(e)	Effectively connected OID of foreign related persons. [Secs. 163(e); 871(a); 881(a)]	Obligations issued after 6-9-84.
1810(f)	Rules provided for withholding on sales of U.S. real property by foreigners under FIRPTA. [Sec. 897(i); 1445(b), (d), (e); 6039C(d); 6652(g)].	Generally provisions apply to post-1984 dispositions. Provision on dispositions by partnerships, estates and trusts applies to disposition after 30 days after enactment date of '86 TRA.
1810(g)	Extent of gain recognition on transfers to foreign persons in divisive reorganizations. [Secs. 367(a), (e), (f); 6501(c); 7482(b)]	Generally, post-12-31-84 transfers or exchanges in TYEA that date.
1810(h)	Related party defined for foreign personal holding co.; tracing rule extended to foreign estates and trusts. [Secs. 551(f); 552(c)]	Regarding related party, taxable years of foreign corps. beginning after 3-15-84. Tracing rule extension applies to taxable years of foreign corps. beginning after 12-31-83, with 1-year extension in specified instances.
1810(i)	Gain on indirect transfers of stock of foreign corporations; retroactive election for certain transfers extended. [Sec. 1248(i) and '84 TRA Sec. 133(d)]	Generally transfers after 7-18-84. Retroactive one year after enactment of '86 TRA.
1810(j)	Collection of tax from stapled entities; limitation on application of stapled entity rules. [Sec. 269B(b), (e)]	Generally 7-18-84.
1810(k)	Amended definition of related parties for CFC insurance income provisions. [Sec. 954(e)]	Taxable years of CFCs beginning after 7-18-84.
1810(l)	Changes made in substantial presence test for resident alien status. [Sec. 7701]	Generally TYBA 12-31-84.
1811(a)	Special rule created for cooperative housing corporation's reporting of interest to shareholders. [Sec. 6050H(g)]	Mortgage interest payments received after 12-31-84.
1811(b)	Improvements made to nominee reporting of partnership interests; corrections made to provisions on exchange of partnership interests. [Secs. 6031; 6050K(c)]	Reporting provisions TYBA enactment date; Exchange provisions: 12-31-84.
1811(c)	Conforming amendment made for brokers' substitute payments statement and failure to file provisions. [Sec. 6678(a)]	Payments after 12-31-84.
1811(d)	Cross-reference made to estate and gift tax underpayment provisions for valuation understatements. [Sec. 6660]	Returns filed after 12-31-84.
1811(e)	Clarification of rule relating to federal tax deposits of $20,000 or more. [Sec. 7502(e)]	Deposits that must be made after 12-31-84.

Act Sec.	Topic	Effective Date
1812(a)	Application of tax benefit rule amended. [Sec. 111(a),(c); 381(c); 1315(d); 1398(g)]	Amounts recovered after 12-31-83 in TYEA that date.
1812(b)	Rules governing below-market loans modified. [Sec. 4941(d)(2); 7872(f)]	Generally term loans made and demand loans outstanding after 6-6-84.
1812(c)	Rules relating to transactions with certain related parties revised. [Sec. 178(b); 267(a); 707(b)]	Foreign persons provision applies generally to TYBA 12-31-83; partnership provision applies to sales or exchanges after 3-1-86.
1812(d)	Rules on Federal Home Loan Bank dividends "Freddie Macs" amended. [Sec. 246(a) and '84 TRA Sec. 177(d)]	Generally applies on or after 1-1-85.
1812(e)	Definitions in personal use property provisions clarified. [Sec. 280F(d)]	Generally apply to property placed in service and leases entered after 6-18-84 in TYEA that date.

Chapter 2—Amendments Related to Title II of the Act

Act Sec.	Topic	Effective Date
1821(a)—(s)	Amendments to rules for taxation of life insurance companies. [Secs. 805; 807—809; 812; 813; 815—818]	TYBA 12-31-83.
1821(t)	Variable contracts with guarantees. [Sec. 817(d)]	Contracts issued after 12-31-86 and contracts issued before 1-1-87 if treated as variable contract on taxpayer's return.
1822	Technical corrections to transitional rules for reserves of life insurance companies. ['84 TRA Sec. 216]	See explanation at ¶1822.
1823	Clarifications to special rule under the Act for companies using the net level reserve method for noncancellable accident and health insurance contracts. ['84 TRA Sec. 217(n)]	See explanation at ¶1823.
1824	Repeal of estimated tax underpayment relief provision. ['84 TRA Sec. 218]	Interest on underpayments of installments required to be paid before 7-18-84.
Sec.1825(a)	Computational rules related to definition of life insurance contract amended. [Sec. 7702(b)(2), (e)(1), (e)(2)]	Generally contracts issued after 12-31-84 in TYEA such date.
1825(b)	Adjustments to future benefits clarified. [Sec. 7702(f)(7)]	Generally contracts issued after 12-31-84 in TYEA such date.
1825(c)	Tax treatment of contracts that don't qualify clarified. [Sec. 7702(g)(1)(B)]	Generally contracts issued after 12-31-84 in TYEA such date.
1825(d)	Contracts issued during 1984 can qualify as flexible premium contracts by satisfying post-1984 requirements. ['84 TRA Sec. 221(b)]	Generally effective 1-1-84 for flexible premium contracts entered into before 1-1-85.
1825(e)	Initial excess interest guarantees disregarded in determining guaranteed rates for qualification as life insurance contract. ['84 TRA Sec. 221(d)(2)(C)]	Effective 1-1-84 for certain contracts issued before 10-1-84.
1826(a)	Qualified retirement plans exempted from distribution requirements as to deceased annuitants. [Sec. 72(s)]	Contracts issued after 1-18-85 in TYEA such date.
1826(b)	Special rules for transfers of annuity contracts or where holder isn't an individual. [Sec. 72(e), (s)]	Contracts issued after date which is 6 months after '86 TRA enactment date in TYEA such date.

Act Sec.	Topic	Effective Date
1826(c)	Exception for distribution after death clarified. [Sec. 72(q)(2)(B)]	Distributions made after date 6 months after '86 TRA enactment date.
1826(d)	Exception for annuities which are qualified funding assets amended. [Sec. 72(q)(2)(G)]	Contracts issued after 1-18-85 in TYEA such date.
1827(a)	Determination of cost in discriminatory group-term insurance plans. [Sec. 79(d)]	TYEA enactment date of '86 TRA.
1827(b)—(e)	Provisions on treatment of former employees clarified. [Secs. 79; 83; and '84 TRA Sec. 223(d)(2)]	See ¶1827.
1828	Amendment related to certain policy exchanges. [Sec. 1035(b)(1)]	Effective for taxable years ending before, on, or after '86 TRA enactment date.
1829	Waiver of interest on tax underpayments of life insurance companies caused by '84 TRA. provisions. [Pertains to Secs. 801—845]	Periods before 7-19-84.
1830	Reaffirmation of Modco grandfather rule. ['82 TEFRA Sec. 255(c)(2)]	Tax years beginning before 1-1-82.

Chapter 3—Amendments Related to Title III of the Act

1831	Scope of definition of contributed capital gain property clarified. [Sec. 170(b)(1)(C)]	TYEA 7-18-84.
1832	Rule disqualifying certain foundations from excise tax rate reduction. [Sec. 4940(e)]	TYBA 12-31-84.
1833	Technical correction. [Sec. 6214(c)]	Taxable events occurring after 12-31-84.
1834	Certain games of chance exempted from UBI rules. ['84 TRA Sec. 311(a)(3)]	Games of chance conducted after 6-30-81 in TYEA that date.

Chapter 4—Amendments Related to Title IV of the Act

1841	Special rules for estimated tax for NRAs. [Sec. 6654(j)]	TYBA 12-31-84.
1842	Transfers between spouses or incident to divorce. [Secs. 267(g); 453B(g); 1041(e)]	Generally transfers after 7-18-84 in TYEA that date.
1843	Recomputation regarding excess front-loading of alimony payments; 6-year rule reduced to 3. [Sec. 71]	New 3-year rule is effective for divorce or separation instruments executed after 12-31-86. For instruments executed before that time, see ¶1843.
1844	Recapture rule for investment credit at-risk rules clarified. [Secs. 46(c); 47(d)]	Generally property placed in service after 7-18-84 in TYEA that date.
1845	Effective date of distilled spirit drawback rule revised. ['84 TRA Sec. 452]	Products manufactured or produced after 10-31-84.
1846	Transitional rule as to carryforward clarified; as to carryback, amended. [Sec. 39(d)]	TYBA 12-31-83 and to carrybacks from such years.
1847	Provisions relating to minimum tax carryovers and to foreign tax credit clarified; clerical amendments added to reflect renumbering of credits. [Sec. 55(c)]	TYBA 12-31-83 and to carrybacks from such years.
1848	Deadwood eliminated as to retirement bonds and extra investment credit. [Secs. 46(f)(9); 401(c)(2); 2039(e); 4973(b); 6047]	Obligations issued after 12-31-83; and credit amounts after 12-31-83.

Act Sec.	Topic	Effective Date
	Chapter 5—Amendments Related to Section 216 of the Act	
1851(a)	Rules for contributions to welfare benefit plans clarified; UBI tax amended; new definition of disqualified benefit for excise tax purposes; special rules for collective bargaining agreements. [Secs. 419; 419A(f)(5); 512(a)(3); 4976(b)]	Generally, contributions paid or incurred, benefits provided, and UBI after 12-31-85 in TYEA that date.
1851(b)	Transitional rule for certain taxpayers with fully vested vacation plans. [Secs. 404(a); 463]	Election must be made within six months after '86 TRA enactment date.
1851(c)	Qualifications for VEBAs, SUBs, and group legal services plans. [Sec. 505]	Years beginning after 12-31-84.
1852(a)(1), (4)-(6)	Required distribution rules for pensions amended; required beginning date defined; no rollovers for required distribution rules. [Secs. 401; 402(a); 403; 4974]	Generally years beginning after 12-31-84.
1852(a)(2)	10% additional tax on distributions before age 59 1/2 extended to 5% owner. [Sec. 72(m)(5)]	Amounts attributable to contributions paid or benefits accrued after 12-31-84.
1852(a)(3)	Required distribution rules applied to Sec. 403(b) annuities. [Sec. 403(b)(10)]	Benefits accrued after 12-31-86 in TYEA that date.
1852(b)	Partial distribution rollover rules apply to some distributions of entire balance; rollover by surviving spouse of decedent's spouse's account limited to IRA. [Sec. 401(a); 402(a), (e), (g); 403(b); 405; and '84 TRA Sec. 522]	Distributions made after 7-18-84 in TYEA such date.
1852(c)	Distributions from plans where substantially all benefits are derived from employee contributions. [Secs. 72; 402]	Amounts received or loan made after 90 days after 7-18-84.
1852(d)(1)	Top heavy plan provisions disregard government plans. [Sec. 416(i)]	Plan years beginning after 12-31-83.
1852(d)(2)	Top heavy provisions disregard benefits of certain retired employees. [Sec. 416(g)]	Plan years beginning after 12-31-84.
1852(e)(1), (2)	Repeal of community property interest exception to estate and gift tax rules; repeals gift tax exclusion for election of beneficiary. [Secs. 406; 407; 2039; 2517]	Estates of decedents dying after and transfers after enactment date of '86 TRA.
1852(e)(3)	Estate tax exclusion grandfathered for certain benefit elections. [84 'TRA Sec. 525(b)]	For decedents dying after 12-31-84 who separated from service before 1-1-85 or before 1-1-83 with respect to '82 TEFRA Sec. 245(c).
1852(f)	Affiliated service group regulation authority. ['84 TRA Sec. 526(d)]	TYBA 12-31-83.
1852(g)	Sec. 401(k) of single employer to be aggregated; special nondiscrimination rules. [Sec. 401(k)(3)]	Plan years beginning after 12-31-84, generally.
1852(h)	Treatment of post-retirement medical benefits for key employees conformed to welfare benefit fund rules. [Sec. 401(h); 415(l); 416(l)]	Years beginning after 3-31-84.
1852(i)	Liability of 2 specific employers for withdrawals from multiemployer plans voided. ['74 ERISA Sec. 4402]	See ¶1852.

Act Sec.	Topic	Effective Date
1853(a)-(e)	Fringe benefit exclusion clarified; cafeteria plans clarified with transitional and special rules; additional excise tax clarified; special rules for telephone service organization and department store leased operations. [Secs. 125; 132; 4977; and '84 TRA Secs. 531; 559]	Generally 1-1-85, see ¶1853
1853(f)	Tuition reduction transitional rules. [pertains to Sec. 117(d) (3)]	Education furnished after 6-30-85 in TYEA such date.
1854	Rules on treatment of ESOPs amended; specific provisions relate to gains on sales of qualified securities, prohibited allocations, dividends on stock, employer deductions, treatment of loans, and estate and excise tax treatment. [Sec. 72(e); 133; 291; 402(g); 404(k); 409; 1042; 2210; 4975; 4978; 4979A; 6166]	Generally provisions apply to TYBA, or transactions entered into after, 7-18-84. For special effective dates for certain provisions, see ¶1854.
1855(a)	ISOP minimum tax transitional rule clarified. ['84 TRA Sec. 555]	Generally applies to modifications of options after 3-20-84.
1855(b)	Permits taxpayers receiving stock in exchange for performance of services to elect Sec. 83(b). [Sec. '84 TRA 556]	TYEA 7-18-84 and beginning before '86 TRA enactment date.

Chapter 6—Amendments Related to Title VI of the Act

Act Sec.	Topic	Effective Date
1861	Mortgage subsidy bond good faith requirements for annual policy statement clarified; veteran mortgage bond rules liberalized. [Secs. 25; 103A]	Reporting requirement applies to obligations issued after 12-31-84. Veterans must apply for mortgage loans by the later of 30 years after service or 1-31-85, effective after 7-18-84.
1862	Mortgage subsidy bond procedural rules apply to mortgage credit certificates (MCCs). [Secs. 25; 6708]	For interest paid or accrued after 12-31-84 on indebtedness incurred after that date.
1863	Advance refunding of certain veterans bonds allowed. [Sec. 613 of '84 TRA]	'86 TRA date of enactment; exception for loan made to Oregon under credit agreement entered 4-16-85.
1864(a)	Out-of-state exception to private activity limitation created for bonds in which state shares benefit.	Obligations issued after '85 TRA enactment date in TYEA that date. Issuers can elect to have the exception apply to any issue on or before '86 TRA enactment date.
1864(b)-(e)	Private activity bond information reporting, exempt activities, carryforwards. [Sec. 103(n)]	Obligations issued after 12-31-83, with an exception for certain action before 6-19-84.
1865	Exception against federally guaranteed loan treatment made for certain projects. ['84 TRA Sec. 622]	For requirements of individual projects, see ¶1865.
1866	Transitional rule provided for aggregate limit on small issue bond exception. ['84 TRA Sec. 623]	Obligations issued after 12-31-83.
1867	Amends reference to exceptions to arbitrage bond provisions for Essex County, New Jersey project and adds exception for Muskogee, Oklahoma project. ['84 TRA Sec. 624(c)]	Exception for N.J. applies to bond authorized on 11-10-83 and approved on 7-7-81 and 12-31-81. For Okla., grant approved on 5-5-81 and obligation issued before 1-1-86.
1868	Series of refundings of student loan bonds are exceptions to the arbitrage rules. ['84 TRA Sec. 625(a)]	Obligations issued after the earlier of the date the '65 Higher Education Act expires or the date such act is reauthorized after 7-18-84.

Act Sec.	Topic	Effective Date
1869	Renames consumer loan bonds as private loan bonds and creates exceptions. [Sec. 103(o) and '84 TRA Sec. 626(b)(2)(A)]	Obligations issued after 7-18-84. The denial of tax exemption won't apply to tax increment financing bonds issued before 8-16-86. Transitional rules apply to exceptions. See¶1869.
1870	Limitations on use of industrial development bonds (IDB) for land acquisitions. [Sec. 103(b)(16)]	Obligations issued after 12-31-83.
1871	Registered form and consumer loan bond rules apply to non-Code bonds. [Sec. 103(m)]	Obligations issued after 3-28-85 in TYEA such date.
1872	10-19-83 binding contract exception is extended to certain bonds issued after 3-28-85. ['84 TRA Sec. 631(c)]	7-18-84.
1873	Exception to private loan bond rules for certain electric generating facilities. ['84 TRA Sec. 632]	7-18-84.

Chapter 7—Miscellaneous Provisions

Act Sec.	Topic	Effective Date
1875(a)	Clarification of minimum tax apportionment between trust or estate beneficiary. [Sec. 58(c)]	Transfers occurring after 8-31-82 in TYEA that date.
1875(b)	Redemption of a controlling shareholder's interest. [Sec. 304(a)(1)]	Transfers occurring after 8-31-82 in TYEA that date.
1875(c)(1)-(2), (8)	10% additional income tax applied to withdrawals by 5% owner. [Secs. 402(a)(5)(F)(ii); 408(d)(3)]	Distributions after the enactment date; for those who aren't 5% owners, the provision applies to distributions after 12-31-83 and on or before the enactment date. The tax applies to key employees after 7-18-84 and on or before '86 TRA enactment date.
1875(c)(3)-(4)	Definitions of compensation and gross income clarified. [Secs. 62(7); 219]	Years beginning after 12-31-83.
1875(c)(5)	Repeal of rule relating to return of excess contributions to self-employed. ['84 TRA Sec. 713(d)(1)]	Contributions made in TYBA 12-31-83.
1875(c)(6)	SEP dollar limits conformed to defined contribution dollar limits. [Secs. 219(b)(2); 408(d)(5)]	Years beginning after 12-31-83.
1875(c)(7)	Defines earned income for Keogh plans. [Sec. 404(a)(8)]	TYBA 12-31-84.
1875(c)(9)	Rules prohibiting anticipated cost-of-living adjustments to benefits conformed. [Sec. 415(b)(2)(E)]	Years beginning after 1983.
1875(c)(10)	Exemption from pension withholding rules for certain nonresident aliens. [Sec. 3405(d)(1)(B)]	Distributions after 12-31-82.
1875(c)(11)	Definition of compensation for disabled. [Sec. 415(c)(3)]	Years beginning after 1983.
1875(d)	Time for computing interest on tentative carrybacks revised. Application of deficiency proceedings to computational adjustment. Reporting by nominees holding estate and trust interests. [Secs. 6629(g); 6230(o); 6034A]	Applications filed after 7-18-84. Partnership years ending after 9-3-82. Taxable years of estates and trusts beginning after enactment date of '86 TRA.
1875(e), (f)	Technical corrections.	7-18-84.

Act Sec.	Topic	Effective Date
1875(g)	Exception from the Section 1248 dividend rules. [Sec. 1248(g)]	Exchanges after 3-1-86. Transitional rule for treatment of certain exchanges. See ¶1875.
1876(a)-(e)(1), (f)-(h), (j)-(l), (n), (o)	Corrections and clarifications for FSCs and DISCs. [Secs. 245, 291; 901; 904; 906; 923; 924; 927; 934; 951; 952; 995-996; 1248; and '84 TRA Secs. 802 and 805]	Generally, transactions after 12-31-84 in TYEA such date. Special rules for certain contracts, see ¶1876.
1876(e)(2)	New principal bank account requirement for FSCs. [Sec. 924(c)(2)]	Periods after 3-28-85.
1876(i)	Taxable year of FSC and DISC must conform to that of majority shareholder. ['84 TRA Sec. 805(a)(4)]	TYBA 12-31-84.
1876(m)	Election of former export trade corporations to qualify for special treatment. ['84 TRA Sec. 805(b)]	Elections within six months after '86 TRA enactment date.
1876(o)	Treatment of existing contracts taken over by a FSC. ['84 TRA Sec. 805(a)(2)]	Certain leases and contracts entered into before 1-1-85, see ¶1876.
1876(p)	Clerical amendments.	See ¶1876.
1877(a)	Clarification and extension of gasoline and special fuels credit. [Sec. 34(a)(3)]	8-1-84.
1877(b)	Refund of excise tax on diesel fuel increased for school buses. [Sec. 6427(b)(2)]	8-1-84.
1877(c)	No tax on certain resales of piggyback trailers. [Sec. 4051(d)(3)]	Use or resale occurring more than 6 years after original sale.
1878(a)	Capital gain holding period conformed. ['84 TRA Sec. 1001(b)]	Property acquired after 6-22-84 and before 1-1-88.
1878(b)	Sport fishing tax extended. [Sec. 4162(a)(6)]	Generally, articles sold by the manufacturer, producer or importer after 9-30-84.
1878(c)	Exemption from aviation excise tax on helicopters extended to oil and gas activities. [Sec. 4041(l)(1)]	4-1-84 for fuel tax exemption; transportation beginning after 3-31-84 for amounts paid after that date.
1878(d)	Estate tax credit for gifts to the Toiyabe National Forest. ['84 TRA Sec. 1028]	Special rule for two estates.
1878(e)	Rules for debt-financed realty of tax-exempt organization extended and clarified. [Sec. 514(c)]	Indebtedness incurred after 7-18-84 with a transitional rule for partnerships.
1878(f)	Targeted jobs credit corrected. [Sec. 51(j) and '84 TRA Sec. 1041(k)(5)(B)]	Individuals beginning work after 7-18-84. Special rule for certain employer.
1878(g)	Rollover period for homes of military personnel extended by one year. [Sec. 1034(h)(2)]	Sale of old residences after 7-18-84.
1878(h)	Change of effective date for disallowance of demolition costs. ['84 TRA Sec. 1063(c)]	Demolitions (of other than a certified historic structure) beginning after 7-19-84 in TYEA 12-31-83. Special rules for demolitions beginning after replacement structure on same site is finished. For special rules for bank and petroleum company, see ¶1878.
1878(i)	Indian tribal government cross-reference corrected. ['84 TRA Sec. 1065(b)]	TYBA 12-31-84.

Act Sec.	Topic	Effective Date
1878(j)	Eliminates requirement that RIC keep adequate shareholder records; Higher tax imposed on RICs that don't keep such records. [Sec. 852]	TYBA 12-31-82, generally.
1879(a)	Relief from 1984 estimated tax underpayments caused by '84 TRA changes. [Secs. 6654; 6655]	1984 estimated tax underpayments; before 4-16-85 for individuals, 3-16-85 for corporations.
1879(b)	Orphan drug credit definitions of "clinical testing" and "rare disease or condition" modified. [Sec. 28]	Amounts paid or incurred after 12-31-82 in TYEA that date.
1879(c)	Nonconventional source fuel credit includes sales within affiliated group. [Sec. 29(d)]	Sales in TYEA 12-31-79.
1879(d)	Fringe benefit reporting requirements clarified. [Sec. 6039D(d)]	1-1-85.
1879(e)	Joint Committee Report to Congress on credits and refunds provision repealed. [Sec. 6405]	Effective as if originally part of '84 TRA.
1879(f)	Conform the 19-year real property recovery period to rental agreements. [Sec. 467(e)]	Property placed in service after 5-8-85, with binding contract exception.
1879(g)	Rural electric cooperatives qualify for Sec. 401(k) plans. [Sec. 401(k)]	Plan years beginning after 12-31-84.
1879(h)	New definition of newly discovered oil for WPT. [Sec. 4991(e)(2)]	Oil removed after 2-29-80.
1879(i)	Refunds extended to medicinal alcohol imported from Puerto Rico and the Virgin Islands. [Sec. 7652(g)]	Articles brought into the U.S. after enactment date. Clarification for payments to Puerto Rico or the Virgin Islands.
1879(j)	Investment credit allowed to certain Section 501(d) organization members. [Sec. 48(r)]	Periods after 12-31-78 in TYEA that date. Claim for refunds must be made within one year of enactment date.
1879(k)	Stock association treated as mutual savings bank for insurance purposes. [Sec. 501(c)(14)(B)]	TYEA 8-13-81.
1879(l)	Stock of REITs, RICs, or diversified investment companies isn't stock of single issuer for reorganization purposes. [Sec. 368(a)(2)(F)]	Exchanges after 2-17-76.
1879(m)(1)(A)	Shares are treated as separate qualified subch. S trusts. [Sec. 1361(d)(3)]	TYBA 12-31-82.
1879(m)(1)(B)	No adjustment to accumulated adjustments accounts for federal taxes paid while a C corporation. [Sec. 1368(e)(1)]	TYBA 12-31-82.
1879(n)	QTIP election filing requirements for gifts conformed to general gift tax return rules. [Sec. 2523(f)]	Transfers after 12-31-85. Special rate for October '84 transfers.
1879(o)	An exemption from the Windfall Profit Tax for a certain charitable interest. [pertains to Secs. 4991(b) 4994]	Oil recovered after 2-29-80.
1879(p)	Amendments to transfers of stock under '81 ERTA. ['81 ERTA Sec. 252].	Refunds, credits, and deficiencies barred by statute of limitations may be made within 6 months of '86 TRA enactment date.

Act Sec.	Topic	Effective Date
1879(q)(1),(3),(4)	Moratorium on collection activities against self-insured workers' compensation fund. Additional time to file Tax Court proceedings.	Period beinning on '86 TRA enactment date and ending on 8-16-87.
1879(q)(2)	Suspension of running of interest on underpayments of self-insured workers' compensation fund.	Period beginning on 8-16-86 and ending 8-16-87.
1879(r)	Separate treatment for filing of returns for alcohol, tobacco, and firearms taxes. [Sec. 6091 (b)(6)]	1st day of 1st calendar month beginning more than 90 days after '86 TRA enactment date.
1879(s)	Amendment made to rules on stripped tax-exempt bonds. [Sec. 1286(d)]	Purchases and sales of stripped obligations or coupons after '86 TRA enactment date.
1879(t)	Ratable income inclusion on disposition of certain specified subsidiary.	'86 TRA enactment date.
1879(u)	Amendments made with relation to Single-Employer Pension Plan Amendments Act. ['74 ERISA Secs. 206(h); 4049(a)]	Generally apply as if included in '86 Single-Employer Pension Plan Amendments Act; ERISA Sec. 206(h)(2) rule applies to plan amendments after '86 TRA enactment date.

Subtitle B—Related to Other Programs Affected by the Deficit Reduction Act of 1984

Chapter 1—Amendments Related to Social Security Act Programs

Act Sec.	Topic	Effective Date
1882(a)	Exception from social security taxes for members of certain religious faiths clarified. [Sec. 1402(g)]	'86 TRA enactment date.
1882(b)	Special rules for determining church employee income. [Sec. 1402(j)]	Remuneration paid or derived in TYBA 12-31-85.
1882(c)	Revocation of church election to treat services performed for the church as subject to SECA allowed. [Sec. 3121(w)]	'86 TRA enactment date.

Chapter 2—Amendments Related to Unemployment Compensation Program

Act Sec.	Topic	Effective Date
1883	Technical corrections regarding AFDC and child support programs.	See ¶1883.
1884	Limitation on FUTA credit reduction in states meeting solvancy test clarified; agricultural worker defined. [Secs. 3302(c), (f); 3306]	'86 TRA enactment date.

Chapter 3—Amendments Related to Trade and Tariff Programs

Act Sec.	Topic	Effective Date
1885—1894	Various amendments related to trade and tariff provisions.	See ¶1885—1894

Subtitle C—Miscellaneous

Chapter 1—Amendments Related to the Consolidated Omnibus Budget Reconciliation Act of 1985

Act Sec.	Topic	Effective Date
1895(b)(18)(A)	Definition of medicare Federal employment amended. [Sec. 3121(u)(2)(B)(ii) and '85 COBRA Sec. 13205(a)(1)]	Services performed after 3-31-86.
1895(d)(1)-(5), (7), (8)	Amendments relating to continuation of employer-based health insurance coverage. [Sec. 162(k)(2), (7) and '74 ERISA Sec. 602; 605; 607]	Effective as if included in enactment of '85 COBRA.
Sec. 1895(d)(6)	Notice requirement provisions amended. [Sec. 162(k)(6) and '74 ERISA Sec. 606]	Applies only to qualifying events occuring after '86 TRA enactment date.

Act Sec.	Topic	Effective Date
Sec. 1895(d)(9)	Aggregation rules for employer for '74 ERISA amended. ['74 ERISA Sec. 607 and pertaining to IRC Sec. 414]	Take effect same as '86 TRA Sec. 1151(e) and (i). See ¶1895.
1896	Gives insolvent farmers who are allowed to reduce capital gains preference items for individual minimum tax purposes one year from enactment to file claim for credit or refund. ['85 COBRA Sec. 13208]	Enactment date.
Sec. 1897	Clerical errors in amendments to coal tax corrected. [Sec. 4121(b)]	Sales after 3-31-86.

Chapter 2—Amendments Related to the Retirement Equity Act of 1984

Act Sec.	Topic	Effective Date
1898(a)(1)	Treatment of class-year plans under 5-year break and service rules clarified. [Sec. 411(d); '74 ERISA Sec. 203(c)]	Contributions made for plan years beginning after '86 TRA enactment date except for plan years not effected under '84 REA Sec. 302(b).
1898(a)(2)-(4)	Amendments to lump-sum treatment rules, rollovers, and withdrawal of mandatory contributions. [Secs. 402(a),(e); 411; and '74 ERISA Sec. 203(d)]	Effective as if originally included in '84 REA.
1898(a)(5)	Minimum age requirement for SEPs reduced to age 21. [Sec. 408(k)]	Plan years beginning after '86 TRA enactment date.
Sec. 1898(b)(1)-(3), (5), (7)-(14)	Clarification of qualified preretirement survivor annuity and transferee plan rules; coordination with qualified joint and survivor annuity, notice requirements, nonforfeitable accrued benefit definition of vested participant, subsidized plan rules, annuity starting date, and plan and survivor benefit application. [Secs. 401; 417; and '74 ERISA Sec. 205]	Effective as if originally included in '84 REA.
1898(b)(4)	Spousal consent required for plan assets to be used as security for a loan. [Sec. 417; '74 ERISA Sec. 205(c)]	Loans made after 8-18-85. Loans revised, extended, renewed, or renegotiated after 8-18-85 are treated as made after that date.
1898(b)(6)	Spouse must consent to certain changes in beneficiary designations. [Sec. 417(a)(2); '74 ERISA Sec. 205(c)(2)]	Plan years beginning after '86 TRA enactment date.
1898(c)	Clarification of rules relating to Qualified Domestic Relations Orders. [Secs. 72(m)(10), 401(m), 402(a), 414(p); '74 ERISA Sec. 206(d)]	Effective as if originally included in '84 REA except amendment relating to individuals other than spouses or former spouse applies to payments made after enactment date.
1898(d)-(h)	ESOP dividend distributions not subject to mandatory cash-out restrictions; rollover notice requirements clarified; ESOPs permitted to modify distribution options; effective date for certain collectively bargained plans extended; transitional rules double death benefits eliminated. [Secs. 402(f); 411(a), (d)(6) and '74 ERISA Secs. 203; 204(g) and '84 REA Secs. 302(b)(2); 303(c)]	Effective as if originally included in '84 REA.
1898(i)	Technical amendments to '74 ERISA. ['74 ERISA Sec. 408(d)]	Transactions after '86 TRA enactment date.

Chapter 3—Amendment Related to the Child Support Enforcement Amendments of 1984

Act Sec.	Topic	Effective Date
1898	Distribution of child support collections. [Sec. 457(b)(3) of the Social Security Act]	'86 TRA enactment date.

Act Sec.	Topic	Effective Date
	Chapter 4—Miscellaneous Amendments Correcting Errors of Spelling, Punctuation, Etc.	
1899	Miscellaneous correction of spelling, punctuation, etc. errors. [Various IRC secs.]	'86 TRA enactment date.

INDEX

_____ References are to Paragraph [¶] Numbers of the Explanation _____

— W —

Wage and tax statements, see Information returns; Returns

Waste disposal facilities, tax exempt bonds financing:
. hazardous waste ..1303
. sewage and solid waste ..1303
. volume cap ..1307

Water:
. conservation expenditures ..401
. facilities for furnishing, tax exempt bonds financing ..1303
. pollution control facilities, industrial development bonds financing ..1303
. transportation, luxury, deductibility ..122

Welfare benefit plans:
. funded, technical corrections ..1851
. nondiscrimination in ..1156
. studies of ..1166

Wetlands:
. "converted," disposition of ..403
. filling costs ..401

Wharves, tax exempt bonds financing ..1303
. volume cap ..1307

Widow/widower, see Surviving spouse

Wife, see Husband and wife

Windfall profit tax, technical correction ..1879

Withholding taxes:
. backup withholding, real estate transactions ..1521

Withholding taxes (continued):
. branch profits tax ..1251
. dividends and interest paid by 80-20 corporations ..1212
. foreign partners ..1284
. Form W-4, changes in ..1581
. interest paid to foreigners, technical correction ..1814
. IRS authority relating to decreases in withholding from wages ..1581
. pensions, similar payments delivered outside U.S. ..1285
. tables, changes in ..1581
. technical service personnel, status of, for withholding purposes ..1705
. U.S. real property dispositions, technical corrections ..1812

Work clothes expenses, itemized deduction ..128

Workers' compensation plan, self-insured, moratorium on enforcement procedures, technical correction ..1879

Working condition fringes, technical correction ..1853

— Z —

Zero bracket amount, replacement in 1987 with standard deduction ..101, 102